Inside the Clinton
White House

Inside the Clinton White House

An Oral History

RUSSELL L. RILEY

OXFORD
UNIVERSITY PRESS

OXFORD
UNIVERSITY PRESS

Oxford University Press is a department of the University of Oxford. It furthers
the University's objective of excellence in research, scholarship, and education
by publishing worldwide. Oxford is a registered trademark of Oxford University
Press in the UK and certain other countries.

Published in the United States of America by Oxford University Press
198 Madison Avenue, New York, NY 10016, United States of America.

Library of Congress Cataloging-in-Publication Data
Names: Riley, Russell L. (Russell Lynn), 1958–
Title: Inside the Clinton White House: an oral history / Russell L. Riley.
Description: New York, NY : Oxford University Press, 2016. | Series: Oxford
 oral history series
Identifiers: LCCN 2016010377 | ISBN 9780190605469 (hardback)
Subjects: LCSH: Clinton, Bill, 1946—Interviews. | United States—Politics and
government—1993-2001—Interviews. | Clinton, Bill, 1946—Friends and associates—
Interviews. | Presidents—United States—Interviews. | BISAC: HISTORY / United States /
20th Century. | HISTORY / United States / General. | POLITICAL SCIENCE / Government /
Executive Branch.
Classification: LCC E886 .R55 2016 | DDC 973.929092—dc23 LC record available at
http://lccn.loc.gov/2016010377

9 8 7 6 5 4 3 2 1
Printed by Edwards Brothers Malloy, United States of America

Contents

Preface

Just over a year after Bill Clinton left the presidency, a stream of his former White House aides and Cabinet officers began making quiet, unannounced visits to the University of Virginia to reflect privately into a tape recorder on what they had experienced. At an antebellum mansion named after William Faulkner, they sat around a table talking with scholars affiliated with the university's Miller Center, a nonpartisan research institute with a special focus on the presidency. Peering down at them from one nearby photograph was a group of their predecessors fresh from Gerald Ford's White House in April 1977, present at the center's very first oral history interview—including a surprisingly youthful Donald Rumsfeld and Dick Cheney.

In the intervening decades, the Miller Center's Presidential Oral History Program has conducted some seven hundred interviews, including major projects on Presidents Carter, Reagan, Bush the elder, and Bill Clinton.[1] The Clinton Project is the largest ever of these efforts, comprising 134 interviews collected over a ten-year span. Among those contributing interviews to this project were Secretaries of State Warren Christopher and Madeleine Albright, White House Chiefs of Staff Mack McLarty and Leon Panetta, Treasury Secretary Robert Rubin, and several key members of Congress and foreign leaders who served during Clinton's time. Although the majority of these interviews were recorded in Charlottesville, the job of collecting them also took the center's scholars to other places, including my own visits as project director to the residence of Nobel Peace Prize winner Kim Dae-jung in Seoul and to Vaclav Havel's modest but whimsical office in Prague.

In November 2014, the first set of these interviews was opened to the public on the Miller Center's website. This book is an effort to present in an accessible way a picture of the Clinton presidency drawn from those four hundred hours of oral histories, an unmediated look into the White House as described by those who were there. The chapters that follow include privileged, firsthand accounts of the

---

1. The center also has completed a major project on the life and career of Senator Edward M. Kennedy, which included nearly three hundred interviews. A project on George W. Bush follows the Clinton Project.

1992 presidential campaign, a major budget victory in 1993, a failed effort to reform the nation's health care system, a successful reform of national welfare policy, a recalibration of the nation's position in a post–Cold War world, a revolution in congressional leadership, scandal management, re-election, and more. They detail the inner workings of a presidency through success and failure, from the painful learning curve of the first term through the effort to survive impeachment in the second. And they provide candid portraiture of the rare political gifts, prodigious intellect, and expansive appetites of the man who was the nation's forty-second president.

What distinguishes this published collection of oral histories from most is that the reader has free access to the complete archive of opened interviews from which its contents are extracted. Indeed, this book serves as a gateway to further reading and research in that broader collection. Each of the interviews quoted in this book can be found at http://millercenter.org/president/clinton/oralhistory.

There are two unique contributions these interviews make to our understanding of the modern presidency in general and of Bill Clinton's presidency in particular. First, because oral history is not subject to the legal regimens that govern the release of official presidential papers, interviews can be opened for public use relatively quickly. To the casual observer this will not seem to be very significant. But today, for example, more than twenty years after George H. W. Bush left office, only about 25 percent of his White House's papers are available to the public. (The rest either have not gone through the glacially slow process of clearance by an understaffed archives administration or have been retained in secret for reasons such as national security or personal privacy.) The dilatory pace of this release deprives those who rely on documents alone as the bread of their existence. Conversely, oral histories provide original evidence about recent presidents while we wait out the protracted interval for the official papers to be opened. If it were necessary to suspend our consideration of Clinton's presidency until half or more of his records becomes available, we would have to delay any work until close to 2050.

Second, much that is historically important within every White House is never written down—meaning that the written documents, even when they are opened, will have significant deficiencies. To some extent this is a function of the pace and culture of the modern presidency, where so much key interaction takes place by word of mouth. Arthur M. Schlesinger, Jr., recognized this problem as early as 1967, when in an essay for *The Atlantic* he bemoaned what use of the telephone was doing to the presidential paper trails that historians had always relied on—and he praised oral history as an invaluable corrective.[2]

---

2. Schlesinger, "On the Writing of Contemporary History," *The Atlantic*, March 1967, available at http://www.theatlantic.com/magazine/toc/1967/03.

By the time Bill Clinton came to the White House a quarter century later, however, the paper-trail problem was catastrophically worse. The hostile investigative climate in Washington that began with the Vietnam War and Watergate, and was exacerbated by incriminating email traffic during the Iran-Contra affair of the Reagan years, made careful record-keeping in the White House a dangerous habit. The twin perils of leaks and subpoenas chilled virtually every form of serious internal writing by presidents and their aides, as Clinton's associates confirmed over and over.

National Security Advisor Sandy Berger explained, "I did not keep notes, nor did most of my colleagues. You recall that in the early days of the Clinton administration there was a flap about whether [Deputy Treasury Secretary] Roger Altman had tipped off the White House about something involving Resolution Trust. I don't even remember what the episode was. But Josh Steiner, who was a young—twentyish, thirtyish at most—staffer at the Treasury Department had a diary, and that diary got subpoenaed.[3] Young Mr. Steiner spent tens of thousands of dollars defending himself with respect to things that were in his diary. I think one of the unfortunate consequences of what has been described as the politics of personal destruction, which has crept into Washington to a large degree, is that you don't write things down. You don't take notes."

Press Secretary Joe Lockhart agreed. "I can tell you this. One challenge for historians on this president is, for instance, if they ever want to find a piece of paper I generated, don't bother looking. They don't exist. I didn't keep them. I didn't have a bank account that could support the legal fees that keeping paper would have [required]. My commitment to history is stronger than you might think, but it was not that strong."

And Deputy National Security Advisor James Steinberg told his interviewer: "I have literally no notes from my seven-plus years in government. I took no notes because every time anybody took notes, they ended up ... being subpoenaed. It wasn't worth it. It's a huge loss.... But we understood the Federal Records Act rules. I could make contemporaneous notes—if I threw them away at the end of the day. And I did. They were not federal records. Nothing was saved. There's literally nothing—nothing left behind and nothing taken away." Under such conditions, memory often remains the only evidence of what happened.

But these interviews also provide an opportunity for scholars to probe into areas for which there would normally be little written record under the best of circumstances. On a matter of great delicacy, White House counsel Bernard Nussbaum responded to questions about why he believed that rumors of an extramarital relationship between Hillary Clinton and Deputy Counsel Vince

---

3. Congressional investigators were interested in knowing whether the president had been given improper notice of a federal investigation into financial activities associated with the failed Whitewater land deal in Arkansas. Steiner's diary indicated contacts not otherwise recorded.

Foster, who committed suicide in 1993, were unfounded. The president's personal secretary, Betty Currie, spoke about her painful experience appearing before a federal grand jury in the Monica Lewinsky case—and repeated for history her assertions about her conversations with the president as the scandal was breaking in 1998. Several insiders on the Clinton economic team challenged Bob Woodward's account of the 1993 economic package, which held that the Clinton administration had forged a deal with Alan Greenspan, chairman of the Federal Reserve, for interest rate cuts in exchange for hitting a specific deficit-cutting target he had named.[4] And Peter Edelman, undersecretary of Health and Human Services, and pollster Stanley Greenberg offer fascinating comparisons between Clinton and Robert Kennedy and Clinton and British prime minister Tony Blair, respectively, observations that help promote greater understanding of Clinton's leadership style.

Finally, there is no better way than oral history to gather the hard-earned wisdom of experienced Washington professionals, or their considered judgments about the president and his times. Some object that the subjectivity inherent in this method renders it suspect. "These are spin-meisters spinning history," they will say. Schlesinger staunchly rejected this critique in *The Atlantic*, favorably quoting George Santayana: "It is not true that contemporaries misjudge a man. Competent contemporaries judge him ... much better than posterity, which is composed of critics no less egotistical, and obliged to rely exclusively on documents easily misinterpreted."[5]

To be sure, oral history does have its deficiencies—as do all forms of historical evidence.[6] Yet every effort was made in the conduct of these interviews to get an honest accounting. The respondents were usually questioned by teams of experts, who know whether certain answers pass the smell test—and can follow up to press for explanation when something sounds suspect. They asked hard questions, but respectfully so. These were not hostile interviews. All interviewers were cautioned not to bring partisan or ideological agendas into the interview room, as they impair good rapport, which is both an ethical imperative and in practice the best way to move discussions to productive candor. Our mission was to assist the interviewee in the process of creating as candid and accurate a set of reflections as is possible—in effect helping to bring forth the equivalent of a frank, spoken memoir, by a "competent contemporary."

---

4. See Woodward, *The Agenda: Inside the Clinton White House* (New York: Simon & Schuster, 1994), pp. 120–21, 139.

5. Schlesinger, "On the Writing of Contemporary History."

6. Memory is, for example, a delicate instrument and fades over time. Usually sequencing is the first thing to go—"I can't recall whether this was 1993 or 1994 ..."—meaning that oral history is usually unreliable as a way to establish a timeline. For elaboration on this broad topic, see "The Deficiencies of Oral History," in Russell L. Riley, "The White House as a Black Box: Oral History and the Problem of Evidence in Presidential Studies," *Political Studies* (Vol. 57, no. 1, March 2009), 187–206.

Respondents were always reminded before the recording device was turned on that the main audience for their recollections was not the small group of scholars at the table, but future generations, who will want to understand the presidency as they actually experienced it.

To aid this process, all interviews were conducted under a veil of strict confidentiality, and following standard oral history protocols. We were subsequently obligated by law and best practices to obtain written permission from each interviewee before we could release his or her words, a procedure we followed in this project as well as all others.[7] In addition, also following standard protocols, each interviewee was given the opportunity to make edits in his or her transcript before release. Normally such changes are made for editorial purposes only, but some respondents do exercise their right to edit matters of substance. If redactions are made, this is indicated on the transcript, normally down to the letter.

In sum, our experience has been that people have been remarkably frank in reporting on their successes and their failures—often admitting their own personal mistakes. They also were remarkably free in assessing the work of their colleagues—and the accomplishments, as well as the flaws and missed opportunities, of the president they served.

This book is based on roughly half of the oral histories recorded for the Clinton Project. Sometimes the price of honesty for the historical record is a prolonged interval until a given speaker feels comfortable opening his or her interview. That a significant number of Clinton interviews have not yet been released is hardly unusual. Several of those peering down from the Gerald Ford group portrait have not yet seen fit to open their words almost forty years later. Moreover, as we have learned from working on interview projects across party lines over the last fifteen years, dynasties are bad for business. There is an understandable inclination among those who have served a president to avoid publishing observations about the recent past that might be exploited for partisan advantage in the immediate future. Accordingly, the continuing viability of candidates named Bush and Clinton at the presidential level has created some challenges in moving interviews about the recent past presidency into the public domain. Still, as this book will show, there is much that is edifying in the reports of those who have already opened their accounts. Fortunately, as Joe Lockhart observed, their commitment to history is stronger than we might think.

The list of those deserving credit for making this book possible is extensive, because the project upon which it is based was a collective enterprise. The most important two groups are those people associated with the Clinton presidency who contributed their recollections in these oral histories, and those scholars who volunteered—unpaid—days of their time to help in the questioning. I am

---

7. See the standard procedures outlined in John A. Neuenschwander, *A Guide to Oral History and the Law*, 2nd ed. (Oxford: Oxford University Press, 2014).

pleased to include an appendix listing the full roster of participants for the interviews used in this book. I omit naming here those who have not yet released their oral histories only to avoid inconveniencing them with unwanted appeals from the curious. But my appreciation surely extends to the unnamed as well.

Special thanks go to the Clinton Library Foundation/Clinton Foundation, and its successive heads, Bruce Lindsey and Stephanie Streett, for endorsing the Clinton interview project and for providing the substantial sums to cover the transaction costs of doing these interviews (research, travel, recording, transcription, etc.). No interviewers or faculty received any Foundation funds, and the Miller Center maintained complete editorial control over the interviews, including the ultimate selection of respondents and the topics discussed. The funding model used in this project was the Center's standard arrangement, identical to that with the George H. W. Bush and George W. Bush Foundations. The Clinton Foundation was an ideal partner in this effort, providing timely support in the execution of the project and helping us secure the cooperation of busy Clinton alumni without ever intruding in any way on our academic freedom. That our efforts succeeded surely must in some measure be due ultimately to the support of President Clinton himself. Importantly, all involved understood from the outset that this archive would have value and credibility *only* if the integrity of the process was absolutely beyond reproach.

We were greatly aided in devising the contours of the project by a volunteer advisory board. Special thanks go to its membership, including eminent scholars and political practitioners: Taylor Branch, Charles V. Hamilton, Darlene Clark Hine, Jacquelyn Hall, David Levering Lewis, Bruce Lindsey, Sylvia Matthews Burwell, Richard E. Neustadt (deceased), and Skip Rutherford. This board was especially helpful in deciding who among the vast constellation of public figures meaningful for the Clinton years should be interviewed—including members of the political opposition. Far more of those were invited than would agree to participate.

Thanks also go to our project partners at the University of Arkansas–Fayetteville, whose efforts in recording interviews about Bill Clinton's pre-presidential years supplement our own work on the presidency. Leading that effort were Professors Jeannie Whayne, Randall Woods, and Andrew Dowdle.

At the Miller Center, many deserve credit for the project unfolding as it did. Former director Philip Zelikow planted the seeds for it as President Clinton was preparing to leave office, and my mentor, the late James Sterling Young, worked through the particulars to get the project started in 2001. Zelikow's successor, Governor Gerald Baliles, was instrumental in seeing the project to conclusion, and in helping to organize an event at the Clinton Library highlighting the release in 2014. The Center's Governing Council also merits thanks for agreeing to allocate nearly thirty years of paid faculty time to complete the project.

The successful execution of the Clinton interviews was in every way a team effort. Scheduling busy people to commit as many as three full days to a single oral history is no mean feat, but was a chore handled remarkably well by Katrina Kuhn and Beatriz Swerdlow. Jane Rafal Wilson has been a constant across all our oral history projects, and has handled deftly and with great professionalism the task of editing spoken words into readable written English. Her team of contract editors also deserves credit for their contributions. The quality of each of these interviews was lifted immeasurably because of the work of the Center's in-house research team, which prepared professional briefing books for each session. The contents of these books (absent material copyrighted by others) are available on the Center's website, including very valuable respondent-specific timelines. The name of each student-researcher responsible for the book appears there, properly credited. Special thanks, however, go to senior researchers who directed the book production process, including Jeff Chidester, Bryan Craig, and Rob Martin. Tracey Crehan and Keri Matthews also supplied key administrative support on the front and back ends of the project.

No project that runs this long, or was this complicated, can reach a successful conclusion without a network of reliable professional colleagues. Professors Stephen Knott, Paul Martin, Darby Morrisroe, Barbara Perry (all at the Miller Center), and Michael Nelson (at Rhodes College) worked hand-in-glove with me as the Clinton Project moved toward completion, each not only doing interviews but also offering advice and counsel on matters practical and intellectual. The interviews in this project constitute a significant addition to each of their scholarly legacies.

Special thanks also go to my editor at Oxford University Press, Nancy Toff, whose enthusiasm for the idea of this book moved it to the top of my agenda while other writing projects went unattended. Her advocacy for oral history plays a vital part in its survival as a valued intellectual form. And her fine editing hand much improved the published version of this text.

Finally, a personal word of gratitude to my family, who had to tolerate too often a husband and father away from home. There is no short way to Seoul, and there was no easy way to tell a spouse (Monique) that I would be returning to a favorite city (Prague)—alone. Joseph was two when this project began and a teenager when it ended, so for a good part of his formative years dad was spending a lot of time with White House counsels and secretaries of the treasury. Had they pitched for the Red Sox he might have been impressed. Cathryn was much younger—so easily bribed with candy from the airport. For all their tolerances of my time living vicariously inside the Clinton White House—which was usually riveting—I am a lucky man.

Editorial Note

Because spoken English differs from the written form, a great challenge in creating oral history transcripts is preserving the spontaneity of the verbal exchange while not allowing its informality to obscure what is being communicated. The main goal in transcription is, to the maximum extent possible, fidelity to the spoken word. Although the conversational tone of these interviews has been preserved throughout this book, far greater editorial liberties have been taken here to produce a clear, uncluttered, and reader-friendly compendium on the Clinton presidency. To this end, some of the longer exchanges in particular have been condensed, with the goal of highlighting the main contours of the speaker's points. As always, then, readers are strongly encouraged to consult the original transcripts for passages of interest, especially if there are questions about context or omissions.

In order to focus attention exclusively on the words of the respondents, questioners are identified in the text with a simple Q. Anyone interested in the identity of a specific questioner will again find that information in the original transcript, online.

Finally, this book is not intended to be a comprehensive treatment of the Clinton presidency. My method was less to seek out material in the archive about a predetermined set of key topics than to extract from the individual discussions what seemed to me to be especially illuminating or interesting, or both. In the section on foreign policy, for example, one could easily make the case that the Middle East was a more important area for Bill Clinton's presidency than Haiti. But the released interview holdings on Haiti were especially rich—including complementary narratives from both the Oval Office and the personal residence of the Haitian general being forcibly removed from power. The detailed nature of that material created the choice to focus on that issue rather than others. Further details on matters not covered thoroughly in this book may be found in the full text of the oral histories, which are online and searchable.

Part I

Beginnings

1

The Man Who Would Be President

Prelude to the White House

Many of those who worked in Bill Clinton's 1992 presidential campaign or went with him to Washington had been acquainted with him for a very long time, some all the way back to kindergarten. Their observations about the man who would become president of the United States document the development of his skills as a politician and track the emergence of his standing as a national figure.

Clinton's interest in American politics reaches at least as far back as his visit to Washington, in the summer of 1963, as an Arkansas senator for Boys Nation, where he famously had a handshake encounter with President John F. Kennedy. He studied international relations as an undergraduate at Georgetown and then as a Rhodes Scholar at Oxford.

After earning his law degree at Yale, he returned home to Arkansas. In 1974, he failed in his first attempt at elective office, an effort to unseat Republican incumbent congressman John Paul Hammerschmidt. Two years later, he successfully ran for attorney general of Arkansas, and in 1978 he was elected the nation's youngest governor. He became the youngest ex-governor only two years later, victim of a backlash against tax increases and a general perception that he was too liberal for the state. After a period of soul-searching and political recalibration, he returned to the governor's office in 1983 and was subsequently re-elected three times.

Clinton began to give serious consideration to a presidential race in the mid-1980s, almost declaring his candidacy in 1988. Shortly thereafter, he was invited to chair the Democratic Leadership Council (DLC), an organization created to help move the Democratic Party away from the political left after losses by large margins in the presidential elections of 1980, 1984, and 1988. The DLC subsequently provided Clinton a platform for partnering with other like-minded party leaders and for honing his policy ideas and speaking skills. These would be important developments as the 1992 presidential election cycle approached.

Susan Thomases, a New York political activist and longtime friend of Bill and Hillary Clinton: [Bill Clinton] told me at a very early stage that he wanted to be president of the United States. He knew it was hard, and he might not make it, but that was his objective. . . . I thought, *That's interesting. Poor boy from Little Rock, Arkansas, that's cool.* But very smart. I was very impressed first off with how smart he was. The thing about him that always amazed me was if you talked to him about something he hadn't heard of before, he would say, "Send me something to read on that." And then the next time you talked to him, he would know more about it than you did. . . . [Clinton] is the quickest study on any subject I've ever met. . . . He could have been good at anything he wanted to be good at.

Mike Espy, former congressman (D-MS) and the nation's first African-American secretary of agriculture: [Bill Clinton] . . . was raised around black people. . . . [His] his grandfather raised him, [and] lived in a mixed community, and there was a store. . . . I'm not sure if his grandfather owned it or the black guy owned it. [Bill] would go around the store a lot, and the store was frequented by black people. He became accustomed to the rhythms and the cadence in the conversation, and the moods of black people. As he grew up, it was an acculturation exercise, and he became comfortable. He began playing saxophone, began playing jazz, blues. . . . Black people understood that he knew them, that he felt comfortable around them.

David Kusnet, White House speechwriter (on Clinton's unusual upbringing): [Bill Clinton] is just such an eclectic personality. He is a Southern Baptist, who grew up, first in a small town (Hope, Arkansas) and then in a freewheeling city (Hot Springs, Arkansas). He went to a leading Catholic university (Georgetown University); he studied at Oxford as a Rhodes Scholar; and he went to Yale Law School. He worked on campaigns in Arkansas, in Connecticut, and in Texas, and then he went home to run for office in Arkansas.[1] He supported the civil rights movement, was active in the antiwar movement, and then became a leader of centrist Democrats, while retaining his links to the liberal community. . . . Someone from his background wouldn't [normally] have his life experience.

Strobe Talbott, deputy secretary of state and fellow Rhodes Scholar with Clinton at Oxford: The line I've used is Rhodes Scholars individually and collectively are not known for their modesty. So, if you had put to them the

---

1. Clinton worked on Senator J. William Fulbright's re-election efforts in Arkansas, the 1970 Senate campaign for Joe Duffy while at Yale Law School, and George McGovern's 1972 presidential campaign in Texas.

proposition that one member of this group would be president of the United States someday, there would have been willingness to accept that as a possibility.... But if you were to take a poll of them and say who in *this* group is going to be president of the United States, [Clinton] would have won hands down.... You just knew that Bill Clinton was going to be a politician and that he was going to probably be president. It was part of his charm that he didn't make a big deal of it. He didn't say, "I'm Bill Clinton, I'm running for president." You just knew it and you didn't resent it.... [That] was his destiny.

Sandy Berger, later White House national security advisor: I worked in the McGovern campaign from probably May or June of 1972 through the end. I traveled with McGovern after the convention, and that's how I met Bill Clinton. Bill Clinton was working in the McGovern campaign, running the state of Texas.... We went to San Antonio for a rally at the Alamo. Usually when the candidate lands, the local state coordinator comes up into the plane and says, "Down at the bottom you can see Mayor Jones and Governor Smith and Senator so-and-so and City Council. Here's the plan. We're going to motorcade over to the Alamo. You'll give a speech and we'll have this reception and lay out the territory." This guy bounded up the stairs. He had a white Colonel Sanders suit on. He cut quite a dashing figure. He shepherded us around that day. . . .

One of my first impressions of Clinton—it certainly doesn't come from the meeting at the Alamo, but sometime around then—is sitting in a bar, talking to him. He was Arkansas. Some of the other young people were *from* someplace, but they were not *of* someplace. They were from Illinois, Wisconsin, or California. Or they were from New York. But Clinton was grounded in Arkansas, and there was never any doubt in my mind that he was returning to Arkansas, from the very first time we had any kind of extended conversation.

So he went back to Arkansas, and as you know he ran for Congress and lost. He ran for attorney general and won. Then he ran for governor. He was the youngest governor ever elected in the United States at that point. He served one two-year term and lost. Youngest *former* governor, he used to kid. Then he won again, and won three more terms as governor. In the '80s he'd come to Washington quite frequently, either as part of the National Governors Association or he was working a lot on education at that point, various task forces. We'd see each other—three or four or five of us who were from that period—the McGovern campaign—would have dinner. He was always energetic, exuberant, and full of life and joy. If we went for an ice cream cone he would wind up in a conversation with the scooper for fifteen minutes about something.

Strobe Talbott: [He] used to come to Washington a lot [when he was Governor] . . . and he would often stay at our house. My kids were very small at the time . . . , but they used to call him the guy who eats all the ice cream. He'd raid the refrigerator and eat all the ice cream and then go to sleep on the couch, even though we had a bed for him.

Senator Dale Bumpers (D-AR): [In 1974, Clinton spoke] at the Democratic rally in Russellville, Arkansas, on the campus of Arkansas Tech.[2] I had never laid eyes on him, but I had heard quite a bit about him, about how brilliant and charismatic he was. He was handsome. He had a good speaking voice. He had everything that a politician needs. . . . [Any] politician who sees another politician with a lot of talent, speaking ability, intelligence . . . and so on can't help but worry about the future. On the way home, I said to one of my aides, "I hope I don't ever have to run against that guy." . . . He talked into the microphone but he looked that audience over all the time he was talking. He did everything precisely the way you're taught to do it if you ever go to a speaking school. It was beautiful.

Bernard Nussbaum, senior attorney for the House committee investigating Watergate, and later White House counsel: I was thirty-six, thirty-seven years old. I was one of the oldest people on this staff. . . . I had a car and I used to drive people home in the evening. I mean this was Washington in 1974. It was a dangerous place. I was this big, fancy law partner, a partner of my firm, and I had a very important job—I had to take all of these young staff members home. I had this huge, red Oldsmobile Toronado and I used to drive people home at night. [*laughter*] . . . We were all working around the clock on the Nixon impeachment inquiry. One of the people in the car I used to take home was Hillary Rodham.

One night, I dropped her off last. . . . As I dropped her off, she says to me, "You've got to come and meet my boyfriend tomorrow. He's coming in." I said, "Boyfriend, you have a boyfriend?" I didn't even know she had a boyfriend. She says, "Yes. . . . His name is Bill Clinton. I went to Yale with him, and he's from Arkansas." . . . I said, "Oh, great. What firm is he going to be with?" She said, "Actually, Bernie, he's going to run for office." I said, "Hillary, how old is he?" She says, "He's twenty-eight," or something like that. I said, "What's he running for, the state legislature?" "No, he's running for Congress this year." "He's running for Congress? He's twenty-eight years old." She said, "Yes, he's running for Congress in Arkansas this year."

I said, "Hillary, he should go to work first. He should get a job and get some experience." She said, "No, no, he's going to run for Congress and he's going to win. You'll see, Bernie. He's going to win, and then he's going to go on to be a U.S. senator or governor of Arkansas." I said, "*What?*" . . . I'm under this great strain with a lot of young people, and I had this woman in my car . . . telling me her boyfriend is going to run for Congress. He's going to be governor or senator

---

2. At this time Bumpers was governor of Arkansas, but running successfully for a U.S. Senate seat.

from Arkansas. And then, the *coup de grace:* "Bernie, he's going to be president of the United States."

At this point—this is a true story—from all the pressures, I crack up. I start screaming at her. "Hillary . . ., I'm working with a bunch of idiots! [*laughter*] They think their boyfriend is going to be president of the United States! These crazy people! What are you saying?" It was really these other pressures, obviously, that were affecting me. Normally, I would laugh if somebody said their boyfriend was going to be president of the United States. I was furious at her for telling me this, which is crazy. [*laughter*]

But you don't know Hillary. Hillary is a tough lady at twenty-six years old. I don't know if I should use the actual words, but I remember the actual words. She looks at me and says, "You don't know a goddamn thing you're talking about. You're a *blank*. You're a *blank*." She used a strong curse word that she uses. . . . "You're a—" God, she started *bawling* me out. I mean, she worked for me on the staff but she was reacting to this. She walks out and slams the door on me and she storms into the building.

The next morning, I was sort of sheepish about this. I walk in to see her and I apologize for screaming at her. And she apologizes for screaming back at me in a much more effective way than I screamed at her. She introduced me. Her boyfriend came in. He was a very nice guy. He was a handsome guy from Arkansas. I asked him. He said yes, he's going to run for office. I wasn't going to get into more fights with Hillary. And ultimately he does run. Bill Clinton did run for the Congress in 1974 and lost by four percentage points, which amazed me at the time. It was the Watergate year. At the end of the election, she goes off to Arkansas, contrary to my advice. . . . She goes off to Arkansas to live with him and then marry him.

And we stay in touch because we really were good friends. So she went to the Rose Law Firm. He runs the following year, 1976. I think he was attorney general. Hillary writes me a note that he's running for attorney general, would I contribute. You want to know how I became White House counsel? This is how. I contributed to races for attorney general in Arkansas. [*laughter*] Then he runs for governor at the age of thirty and he wins. . . . Then he runs again for governor and he loses. "Ah," I said. See? History will have proven me correct. . . . I was *right* in that car. He's now an ex-governor of Arkansas. What could be lower than an ex-governor of Arkansas? [*laughter*]

Mickey Kantor, chairman of the 1992 campaign (on Clinton's reaction to losing his re-election bid for governor in 1980): He had lost. First, he calls me and he wants to run for DNC [Democratic National Convention] chair, against Chuck [Charles] Manatt. Well, Chuck Manatt was my law partner.[3] I was chair

---

3. Charles Manatt was a prominent California-based attorney who chaired the Democratic National Committee from 1981 to 1985.

of Chuck's campaign for the DNC, which he won, and I said at that point, "Bill, why would you want to do such a thing? One, you can't win, but two, the worst thing is if you would win. You can't ever go back to Arkansas as a *national* Democrat." . . . He just needed something to do . . . [and] couldn't stand not to be part of the action. . . .

Second, Jerry Brown calls him: "Why don't you come be my chief of staff?" Jerry was still governor [of California] at the time before Jerry ran for the Senate in '82. How you could be Jerry's chief of staff and have any credibility left in Arkansas? Jerry Brown?[4] The DNC? Just stop and think about that. That's a true story, I couldn't make that up. And, of course, I disabused him of that notion, too. But he knew that, he didn't need to ask me the question. Anyone would have said, "Of course you shouldn't do that," given his career, where he was, who he was, what he wanted to do. Of course you wouldn't.

As the years passed, he became more and more focused on what he was, what he could be, and how he's going to get there, and much more resolute about not being taken off on all kinds of other things. . . . That's part of the maturation of Bill Clinton.

Joan Baggett, director of White House Political Affairs: He was governor of Arkansas and he was giving a speech to one of the DNC money groups and telling a story, one of his many about when he lost the race for governor [in 1980]. He ran into this guy when he was campaigning to get into the governor's seat again. Clinton said to this guy, "I'd really appreciate your vote," and the guy said, "Yes, I voted against you last time, but I'm going to vote for you this time." Clinton said, "Do you mind me asking why? . . . He goes, "Well, I voted against you because you raised"—I think it was the fee on the hunting license. And Clinton said, "Yes, I remember that. But why are you going to vote for me now?" He said, "I figure you're not stupid enough to do it again." [*laughter*] . . . I just remember thinking, *There's a guy that can tell a good story about himself.*

Kris Engskov, Clinton's personal aide in the White House: One night we were flying back from Little Rock and it was just me and him and we were sitting . . . there catty-cornered in the conference room in *Air Force One*. . . . We got into a conversation—it was a one-way conversation—about election results from 1980 . . . and then when he came back in '82 and won again, because he lost on the used-car tax [hike]. He went through, county by county, the number of votes he got in the '80 election. He knew every count. . . . I'm talking about a couple of *hours* we talked about election results in the '80 campaign. I walked away from

---

4. Jerry Brown had been nicknamed by Chicago journalist Mike Royko "Governor Moonbeam" because of his political and personal eccentricities.

that conversation thinking, *That really impacted him.* It did. He's written about it. The '80 campaign was a turning point for Clinton in how he approached everything he did.

Sandy Berger: I began to believe in the mid-'80s that this guy should run for president, and I started talking about him. . . . We were doing some preparatory work and were getting ready for setting up an exploratory committee in 1988. He actually set a date for a press conference to announce an exploratory committee. This must have been '87 or '88.

Some of us flew down to Little Rock. . . . Clinton and Hillary and Carl Wagner[5] and a couple of people were upstairs [in the mansion] conferring. They'd been up most of the night, I think. The rest of us were milling around downstairs waiting. He came downstairs and sat us all down around the dining room table in the big Governor's Mansion and said, "I've decided I'm not going to run." Chelsea was at that time about seven years old maybe, and he said, "I just don't think I could put Chelsea through a campaign. I don't want to neglect her, and we've decided this is not the right time."

I remember walking in the backyard with Mickey Kantor and looking into the kitchen as he told this to Chelsea. She jumped up and grabbed him around the neck and kissed him. She obviously didn't want him to do this. So there was a flirtation with running in 1988, but after '88 and [Michael] Dukakis's loss, I think there was not much doubt in his mind that he was going to run in 1992.

Alice Rivlin, economist and later Office of Management and Budget director: Peter Edelman,[6] whom I knew well, called me one day and said, "There's a really terribly bright, charismatic governor of Arkansas named Bill Clinton, and I think he's a potential presidential candidate, and I'm setting up some interviews for him to meet important policy people in Washington. Would you be willing to meet with him?" And I said, "Sure."

I'd never heard of Bill Clinton, but they had a hotel suite . . . somewhere up on Capitol Hill. I went over and spent about an hour with Clinton and was bowled over. I just thought he was terrific. He asked all the right questions. He was very personable, all the Clinton things. And I just thought, *Wow, this guy is really something terrific.* . . . I came away totally bowled over, and I called my friend Donna Shalala [then president of Hunter College], and I said, "I just met this really smart, charismatic governor of Arkansas. Do you think he's a presidential possibility?" And Donna says, "Well I know Bill Clinton . . . and

---

5. Carl Wagner was a longtime party activist with strong union ties, whom Clinton had come to know in the McGovern campaign.

6. Edelman was a Democratic political activist at the time teaching at Georgetown University Law School. He later held a sub-cabinet post in the Department of Health and Human Services under Clinton.

he's terrific, and everything you say is right, but he's never going to be president of the United States." And I said, "Why not?" She said, "He's got a woman problem."

Sandy Berger (on the seemingly endless 1988 nomination speech Clinton gave for Democratic nominee Michael Dukakis): I was not only at the convention; I have to admit that I actually worked on the speech.... There are two wildly different interpretations of what Clinton was expected to do. If you talk to the Dukakis people ... they say, "We wanted him to give a rip-roaring 'Dukakis is the greatest thing since sliced bread' speech." If you talk to Clinton, he says that Dukakis told him he wanted him to give a serious speech. He didn't want it to be a tub-thumper.... The truth, I'm sure, lies somewhere in between.

Clinton was writing the speech himself. He's a good writer. He's a somewhat prolix writer, if that's the right word.... He kept adding and I kept editing, and he kept adding. I'd take some stuff out and he would put some stuff back in. Now, I'm not wholly harmless here because my understanding was that the Dukakis people wanted a really serious speech about Michael Dukakis, which this was, if you actually read the speech. It just was totally inappropriate for its purpose, which was to get the crowd on their feet screaming, "Michael Dukakis, Michael Dukakis, Michael Dukakis!"

I went to the speech and I sat—I remember as if it was yesterday—in the mezzanine section, and I watched this unfold. It was like watching a car crash in slow motion. It was so painful. . . . At some point this thing got so unruly that they turned up the lights. Then they have people starting chants, "Dukakis!" It was one of the few times I must say where Clinton did not read the room. Clinton is marvelous at reading a room and understanding what's happening, adjusting and adapting, throwing away and discarding, and going in a different direction.

I think it's just so awesome to be standing there in front of this huge convention with lights blaring in your eyes so you really can't see what's going on, and I don't think he realized to the very end what a disaster it had been. It was so painful for me. My stomach was absolutely tied in knots. I couldn't even watch the end of it. I had to get up and start walking. It's a basketball arena in Atlanta with a concourse that goes all around. I made about two laps of the concourse and he was still talking. He finally said, "In conclusion—" and people cheered. I was standing there as he came up the ramp after the speech and he said, "That wasn't very good, was it?" I said, "No, Bill, that was not good."

He was a little annoyed that he thought there had been lack of coordination ... [but] he said, "I'm going into the press room." This is actually a story I used to tell a lot when I was trying to convince people in '91 and '92 about Bill Clinton. My instinct would have been to go immediately to my hotel room, get a large bottle of Jack Daniels, drink the entire thing, crawl into bed, and hide there for about three days. He went right into the press room and took it head-on. It was a pretty bloody session.

Frank Greer, media advisor (on the aftermath of the Dukakis nomination speech): Harry Thomason, a Hollywood producer who is a very good friend of Clinton's, helped him get on the talk show circuit and make fun of himself in a very self-effacing way.[7] I told him that was the smartest thing he could do.

William Galston, later deputy domestic policy advisor: The period between the mid-1980s and the formal declaration of Bill Clinton's candidacy in the fall of 1991 was one of the most fertile, fruitful periods for policy development in the twentieth-century history of the Democratic Party. I'm proud to have been a part of it.

Stanley Greenberg, pollster (on the roots of the DLC in the losses to Reagan, and his efforts to develop an approach for luring back to the party Reagan Democrats): [After] the Reagan landslide ... I was then asked ... by the [Michigan] State [Democratic] Party chair to do what became the Macomb County Studies, funded by the UAW [United Auto Workers], in which I then wrote about the Reagan Democrats.... They were very controversial because you couldn't really talk about race at that time among Democrats.... [Paul] Kirk,[8] who is party chair, says, "We're not going to have any more of this." You've got an emergence of Jesse Jackson and they don't want this.[9] I'm kind of *persona non grata* with the party. ...

But there are a number of groups that are interested in what I'm doing, who end up supporting it. One is the NEA [National Educational Association], and the other is the DLC. I develop a relationship with the DLC, which is important to the Clinton piece of it.... [Al] From brings me in, [and] ... through that period I'm in an ongoing discussion with them about the character of the party. The central part of my discussion is, "You can't have a majority Democratic Party without a working-class base, without a popular base. You can't carve out that part of it."

I was focused very much on the race issues and values in that discussion, somewhat on military security issues.... For the whole period that the DLC is emerging as the main intellectual and political force for changing the

---

7. Thomason arranged for Clinton to go on *The Tonight Show* with Johnny Carson.

8. Paul Kirk was a Massachusetts-based attorney who chaired the DNC from 1985 to 1989. He later filled Edward Kennedy's unexpired Senate seat for several months after Kennedy's death in 2009.

9. Jesse Jackson is a prominent civil rights activist who operated out of Chicago for most of his adult life. He mounted nationwide campaigns for the Democratic nomination in 1984 and 1988, doing especially well in Southern primaries with heavy concentrations of black voters.

Democratic Party, that's who I'm working for. I have this odd politics, because I come from the Left in my own thinking, but [the DLC-types] are comfortable with that because we have a similar kind of interest in trying to reach the same kind of [white] voters. . . .

I'm coming to this out of studying people who are at the time politically reviled, and making the case that they're making these decisions [about Democratic politics] on understandable grounds. . . . When I wrote about [Macomb County voters], even though I didn't suggest that Democrats cater to them on race issues, I didn't write about them as people who were "outs" because they were clearly racist and angry about what blacks were doing in their neighborhoods. They were also people who had families and were trying to live in safe communities and wanted the best for their kids. They were not precluded from my narrative because of their racial views. You know, coming out of the civil rights period, and particularly Detroit and that whole tense history there, just to say that these are people we're talking to was a very important change for Democrats.

Al From, head of the DLC: We start the DLC in 1985. My friend Bob Squier,[10] whom I've known forever . . . dubs us as the "Southern white boys' caucus." . . . The reality is the DLC was formed because there were a lot of people in our party who believed that their survival was in danger. . . . Essentially what I believed is that you had to reach out to the middle class. . . . So the reason I wanted to do Clinton as the chair of the DLC was I just thought he was such a great talent. He had a great reputation in the liberal part of the party, but . . . we had that same understanding of where liberalism had to go. So I thought he was a natural choice. [Former Virginia governor] Chuck Robb told me, "If he spends the next four years running for president on our stuff, all the better for it." Clinton was a big step for us because a lot of people, probably, in the DLC leadership thought he was too liberal for us.

Q: Based on?
From: His history with McGovern and all that. And he had the [liberal] reputation coming out of that first gubernatorial term. But I just thought he was—I'm probably the only person in America who believes he has this very deep-felt philosophy, that it has driven him, that it's very similar to mine—I just thought he was the right guy and that he would expand the DLC. I must say that when I went down there in 1989 [to convince him to become the DLC's chair], I told him that I thought he could be president someday and he'd make us both important, but I didn't really think it was going to be '92. . . .

---

10. Bob Squier (1934–2000) was a Democratic political consultant known for his image-making abilities and his work with Southern presidential candidates, including Al Gore.

What we spent all our time on was figuring out what we were going to say and checking the message, the philosophy of opportunity, responsibility, and community. The most important thing Bruce Reed [who was later his chief domestic policy advisor] ever did in his life, I always tell him, is that when we came out of the DLC Cleveland convention and I had to reprint the resolutions in Clinton's speech, the three words he chose to put on the cover were "opportunity," "responsibility," and "community." That reshaped progressive politics all over the world. . . .

We worked a long time on that [Cleveland] speech, and Bruce Reed in particular. I remember going over it, over and over again, in my office. Then the night before, since it was a nine-o'clock-in-the-morning speech, Clinton stayed up all night, because otherwise he couldn't deliver it—worked it and reworked it. We went in—I might not be exactly accurate on this, but I'm pretty close—we went into his suite about seven in the morning and went over it. One of the receptionists or something at the DLC had been there with him typing the speech. He reads this new draft and gives it to us, and we said it looked pretty good. Then he read it again and said, "I've got it." Wrote nine or ten words on a piece of paper, threw the draft away, and went out and gave the speech of his life.

Senator Charles Robb (D-VA), an early leader of the DLC: Bill Clinton was not a part of [the DLC] at [first]. . . . So we start recruiting, and the toughest member to recruit, bar none, was Bill Clinton. Bar none. . . . Bill at that point had real credibility with the national party, with the liberal intelligentsia as well as the good old boys, the Bubbas of the world. There weren't many people who had that.

Bruce Reed, a staff member of the DLC and later Clinton's domestic policy advisor: I was attracted to Gore and to [Joe] Biden[11] and eventually to Clinton because I saw them as the closest thing to a Bobby Kennedy of my time, somebody who could bring together working stiffs and the more liberal parts of the party. I wouldn't have liked the label "conservative." I can remember one of the first meetings I went to at the DLC while we were trying to figure out where to go. We came to the conclusion that we couldn't win this battle for the soul of the party if we tried to define it as a conservative vs. liberal or moderate vs. liberal fight. We had to make it a fight between new and old. . . .

The DLC was still in its early years, and had a mixed reception within the party because it was seen as primarily a white, Southern, conservative operation. In fact, the kinds of ideas that the DLC had begun to work with were more radical than that. But it was really Bill Clinton who transformed the DLC into a

---

11. Joe Biden served as U.S. senator from Delaware from 1973 to 2009, before being elected vice president with Barack Obama.

successful enterprise. Because he was the one who made it possible to get out of the traditional left/right box that seemed like a zero-sum game within the party. The Democrats had run campaigns that were perceived as somewhat too far to the left. But understandably, people didn't want to just change labels or shift their principles. Then Clinton came along, and he was neither fish nor fowl. He had some liberal passions, but conservative governing values. . . .

The first time I heard him speak was when he took over as chairman [of the DLC] in March of 1990. That was in a ballroom at the Fairmont Hotel in New Orleans. I knew right then that he would be president someday. It was a spellbinding experience. You could hear a pin drop in the room. People had never seen anything like it. He was the first Democrat I had ever come across who talked about values instead of programs. He absolutely captivated the audience and looked at the issues in a completely different way. . . . [He later] gave the speech of his life at the Cleveland [DLC] meeting, which was still one of the best political speeches I've ever seen anyone give. We'd written a few things for him, but Craig Smith, his chief of staff, had said, "Don't worry, he knows what he wants to say." I watched him that morning backstage at Cleveland prepare for the speech he was about to give. He wrote twenty words on the page. They were just reminders, "Opportunity, responsibility—" I can't remember what they all were.

Then he went out and gave a twenty-minute speech that was perfect pitch. . . . The response to that speech was so overwhelming I think we all knew that if Clinton decided to run and was able to put together a halfway decent organization, he would be a force to be reckoned with. . . . After he took over as chairman, Al From and Deb Smulyan—who was the deputy director of the DLC— and I went down to visit him in May at the Mansion in Little Rock. I will never forget that morning. We came from a breakfast meeting. We sat with him at the table in the Mansion. They brought out a tray of biscuits and breakfast for all four of us and Clinton ate everything. [*laughter*] Never saw anything like it.

Q: He ate all four servings?
Reed: It was for four people and then some. It was a phenomenal display.

William Galston, domestic policy advisor: I knew what the country was in for when I had a meeting with him at Logan Airport. There were four of us arrayed around a table about half this size . . . and four little packets of cookies. I don't think I need to tell the rest of this story. [*laughter*] I found out two things about Bill Clinton that day: how long his arms are and how big his appetite is.

Frank Greer (on Clinton's final re-election campaign for governor): [Right] before the '90 gubernatorial campaign, which was the only Clinton gubernatorial campaign I worked on, Clinton calls. I can remember the words as clear as if he were on the phone today. He said, "Frank, I'm in trouble. My numbers are dropping like a rock, they're tired of me. 'It's been ten years and taxes,' that's all

I hear on the campaign trail." He says, "I'm about to mess around and lose this governor's race and you wanted me to run for president. Hell, I won't be able to run for dog catcher if I lose this race, so you've got to get your ass down here and help me out." So I said, "Okay." And I went down. . . .

I brought in Stan Greenberg. Stan was a real pro, one of the smartest people in the Democratic Party, I thought, and a terrific researcher, terrific pollster. We went to places like Darnell, Arkansas, where they don't have a focus group facility, you have to sit in the Holiday Inn dining room or conference room with the participants. You're sitting in the corner watching this. But we did focus groups all over. Another funny thing is, Stan overslept the morning we were supposed to go to the Mansion in Little Rock to brief Clinton. We were searching for him and finally found him, but he was like two hours, three hours late. But they still developed a good relationship and Stan recovered. Clinton wasn't always on time for things himself, so he was very understanding. I was angry as hell. . . .

[Clinton] said, "You want me to run for president, you've got to get me re-elected governor." That was the whole idea. . . . He knew that Greenberg and I, if no one else in the country, were absolutely convinced that he was the one person who could win in '92, and knew he had to run. We talked about it . . . and he would always put it off, "I'll think about it, I'll think about it, I'll think about it." But we said, "The one thing you cannot do . . . is go out there and say unequivocally that you're not going to run for president." . . .

Sure enough, he went up somewhere in north Arkansas for one of these little candidate forums, a debate, and Gloria Cabe,[12] the campaign manager, called and said, "You're not going to believe what Bill Clinton just said." She had gone out into the hall or whatever. I said, "Oh, my God, what?" She said, "He just said that he was going to serve his four years and he wasn't going to—" He didn't say he wasn't going to run for president, but he did say he was going to basically serve his four years as governor. I was furious. I mean, I know how, in a debate, he could get boxed into that, but it was a big, big disappointment.

We actually spent a lot of time in the early days of the [presidential] campaign figuring out, with the people of Arkansas, how to let them urge him to run so that he wouldn't have to break a promise to the people of Arkansas, although the Republicans, and his enemies that have always been there, basically like to say he broke his promise to the people of Arkansas, and that's how he started his presidential campaign.

Stanley Greenberg (on Clinton's 1990 re-election bid for governor): I am a morning person and [Clinton] is a night person. I also have a philosophy on how I do focus groups. I believe the sooner you begin to draw conclusions, the

---

12. Gloria Cabe was a former member of the Arkansas House of Representatives who became one of Clinton's closest political advisors when he was governor.

sooner you close out information and learning. I try not to draw conclusions. I try to watch the groups that I can. I take some notes. I'll then read the transcript and begin to say what I think the main narrative is. I usually go through about three times before I decide, *All right, this is where it is.* I'm one of the people who do this, who get transcripts and still do, because I want to be able to go over and over it. . . .

So we do the focus groups. . . . The groups end at probably ten o'clock, and [Clinton] wants a preliminary report. Frank says, "He has to have a preliminary report." I go to the Governor's Mansion after the focus groups . . . late at night. It's got to be eleven-thirty, twelve o'clock at night. I go there, I sit down, and I start to do this, and then I say, "You know what? I can't do this." I'm mumbling. "I don't know, I haven't drawn conclusions. I'm not doing this." He says, "Okay, when do you want to do it?" And I said, "Well, how about early in the morning?" [Clinton] says, "Okay," which surprises everybody because he's not a morning person. I go back to my hotel. I have my notes, I have the written things that people have written, and I work into the night sorting this out, what I'm going to say, which is much sooner than I would do it in any case. And I sleep through the alarm.

I get a call from Bruce Lindsey,[13] "Where are you?" I show up, I don't know, an hour late, an hour-and-a-half late, for the meeting with the governor. I did my presentation. That I have any relationship with Bill Clinton is clearly testimony to his good nature. It's hard to imagine that this did not end the relationship but it didn't, maybe because of what I had to say. . . . I figured out a rationale [for the campaign] that centered around not going back. . . . "Turn the clock back" became the symbol, and [the message] was all around the idea of . . . not allowing the clock to be turned back on a modern Arkansas.

Frank Greer: In the midst of this campaign [1990] I get a call from the campaign manager, Gloria Cabe, who . . . says, "You're not going to believe this, but there is this crazy former state employee," . . . Larry Nichols. "He's going to hold a press conference at the state capitol and he's going to talk about how Bill Clinton has had affairs with five women. You've got to understand—" I mean, if you could imagine how bizarre all this was—"Larry Nichols was fired from the state government for making too many phone calls on his state phone to the Contras in Central America." This guy thought of himself as kind of a Special Forces [operative], *I'm going to help the Contras from rural Arkansas.* He was just weird. There's a whole culture around Arkansas of these kinds of people.

---

13. Bruce Lindsey was Clinton's former law partner and his most trusted personal advisor through the duration of his presidency. Although he held several formal positions in the White House, including director of personnel, Lindsey's relationship with Clinton far transcended those formal roles.

I swung into action and ... basically just said, "We've got to stop it. No legitimate press person should give this kind of thing credibility without any substantiation, without any second sources," and all of that. So we talked with everybody in the press and not one reporter reported it. ... I grew up in the politics where the press would not go with something unless they had substantiation and a second source. You can't just stand up and say, "You're an adulterer," and have people run with it. So we dodged that bullet in Arkansas.

Strobe Talbott: The [womanizing] issue had been out there either as buzz or louder than buzz for a very long time, and I had always been both upset by it and mystified by it. It didn't connect with my sense of the individual from having been a twenty-two- and twenty-three-year-old with him as young bachelors in Oxford, England, in the '60s for God's sake. This was not a monkish existence. There were plenty of my contemporaries who were, even by those standards, libertine. Bill Clinton just wasn't one of them.

Peter Edelman, longtime friend of the Clintons: We had two views [about Clinton].[14] One was that he was more liberal than his performance in Arkansas and that he would be different on the national stage, but we knew that even so he was more conservative than we are. But people who are as liberal as we are don't get elected president. ... He certainly sounded different in the drawing rooms of Cleveland Park[15] than what his record showed in Arkansas. ... We weren't in the category of people who said, "Oh, well, the way he sounds in Cleveland Park is the way he is." Much more complicated than that in our case. Having said that, we liked him very much. ... So all things considered, we thought [his candidacy would be] a very good idea.

David Kusnet: [Bill Clinton's] last salary before being president of the United States was $35,000 a year. His wife made decent money as a lawyer, but the Governor's Mansion in Arkansas would not be considered much of a home in northwest Washington. He shopped. [So] you didn't have to have a briefing with him; he knew how much groceries cost. He was in touch with everyday life. Before becoming president he was in touch with life as it is lived in this country. I think people recognized that in him. Reagan used to say that the American people know that he liked them. For all his many faults, I think the people knew that Bill Clinton liked them. They knew that he cared about them, and they knew that he understood how they lived.

---

14. Edelman was speaking about himself and his wife Marian Wright Edelman, a social and political activist who founded the Children's Defense Fund in 1973. She came to know Hillary Rodham Clinton, a fellow Yale Law School alumna, through their work for this organization.

15. Cleveland Park is a wealthy residential neighborhood in the District of Columbia, west of Rock Creek Park.

2

The Decision

Bill Clinton had aspired to run for the presidency since childhood, but the unanswered question for him was "When?" In the summer of 1987, he had assembled a large group of friends from across the country in Little Rock in anticipation of a campaign launch for the following year's election, only to inform them at the last minute that he had decided against running, for family reasons. When he sought another term as governor of Arkansas in 1990, however, he recast his team of political advisors so as to better position himself for a national campaign, although in an unguarded moment he undercut his prospects by pledging publicly to serve his full four-year term if re-elected.

Clinton's political calculus after securing re-election was further complicated by the unprecedented popularity of incumbent Republican George H. W. Bush, whose approval ratings soared above 90 percent in the aftermath of the successful liberation of Kuwait in the First Persian Gulf War. There were thus ample reasons to wonder whether Clinton, a still-young man in his mid-forties, would chose 1992 as the time to pursue his lifelong ambition.

Frank Greer, media advisor: After the [1990] governor's race . . . Clinton was still reluctant [to run for president]. . . . We began meeting in the winter [of 1990–1991], visiting down there [Little Rock] and then having regular conference calls. I think we started really getting serious about it in the spring. The interesting thing is, I would get reports from [Clinton advisor] Gloria Cabe that he was waffling, "I think he's heading in the wrong direction, you better get him back." It was always this kind of seesaw that spring and summer.

[At] the National Governors Association meeting in Seattle, . . . Bruce Lindsey, Stephanie [Solien],[1] and I, and some of his other key staff people, we literally sat on the bed in his hotel room . . . with Clinton eating something all the time—and just mapped out everything we needed to do.[2] My theory was, you don't force him to make a decision, because in '88 he had gotten up to that point and backed out. You say to him [instead], "We need to be putting in place the

---

1. Stephanie Solien was a Democratic political activist and became national political director of the 1992 Clinton campaign. She was married to Frank Greer.
2. The Seattle meeting of the National Governors Association occurred in mid-August 1991.

organization, the fundraising, the research, and the programmatic plans for the country, et cetera, so that *if* you decide to run, we've done everything necessary to make it possible."

There were two things that he was deeply concerned about. One, "I've never served in the military, we've just had a war. George Bush is a war hero. How are they going to elect somebody who has never served?" I cannot tell you how many times he wanted to go over this, over and over and over again. "I just don't think [the nomination] can happen, they're just not [ready]...." And I would say to him, "We're the same age, we both went through the era of Vietnam. There are millions of Americans out there who did not serve." At the time, his explanation was always, "I was willing to serve but I got passed over and didn't have to serve and my number was high." I said, "You're like millions of other Americans. If you have a good, strong foreign policy and a commitment to the military and you're willing to use American force, you can still be elected president."[3]

Secondly, he said, "I have now said to the people of Arkansas that I'm going to serve my four-year term as governor. What do I do? How do I get out of that? They're going to say, 'He broke his promise, you can't trust him.' It reinforces 'Slick Willie' and all of the negatives that people have, and it will be a disaster. If I don't have the support of my home state, then I'm not going to be successful running for president."

I fundamentally agreed with that, especially if you're running as a successful governor who has done a good job in your state. But Roy Spence, an advertising guy I had known in 1984, who worked as the lead advertising guy for [Walter] Mondale—Roy Spence lived in Texas [and] ... does the advertising for Wal-Mart. So Roy had an idea that I reinforced.... I said, "Why do you have to make this decision when you can ask the people of Arkansas what they would like? Why don't you go out and barnstorm?" It may have been Memorial Day. Roy's idea was to tour the state, just get out there, no press, don't make it a big deal, and talk to people. So Clinton did a whole [tour]—he did like fifteen or twenty events. What he did not know is that, with Gloria Cabe and Bruce Lindsey and everybody else, we had organized an awful lot of people all over Arkansas to come to his events and tell him he ought to run for president. He would call me and say, "It's just amazing! You were right and Roy was right, if you just go out and ask people, they want me to run for president."

Marcia Hale: I did most of Clinton's pre-election focus groups, which was fascinating. It ... helped that I had a bit of a Southern accent.... The gist of it was, Could he go ahead and run for president even though he had told the people in Arkansas that he wasn't going to? Stan and I did these focus

---

3. In retrospect, Clinton's concerns about this issue were heightened by the complexities of his draft history, of which Greer was at that time unaware.

groups and Bruce [Lindsey] came to most of them. It was funny because after we finished, Bruce said, "Well, Governor, we've figured out how you can do this. You just send Marcia around the state and she'll talk to voters twelve at a time and it will be okay." They were genuinely very supportive.... In all the ones we did—I think we did eight—it was, *If he can run, he should run. It's okay.*

Al From, head of the centrist DLC: I remember him saying, this was March of '91 ...,"Maybe we ought to just go in '92 because if we test our ideas, as long as we're respectable, we'll be much stronger for '96." Now, I'm sure he didn't think we were going to test the ideas in '92 and win in '96. I'm sure he thought we were going to win in '92.

Bruce Reed, of the DLC and later domestic policy advisor in the 1992 campaign: Clinton spent the summer [of 1991] mulling it over. Almost no practical work on the organizational front was done, because I think the people closest to him in Arkansas were genuinely unsure what he would decide to do. They'd been through this once before, in '87.... There were lots of reasons to hesitate. I don't know if *he* knew how good he was. No one from Arkansas had successfully run for president—or really come close. He had real doubts, as did some others. There were some people at the DLC who thought that he was such a fluid manager that he could never put a decent campaign together. He'd had half a dozen—or close to it—four or five chiefs of staff in Arkansas. No one really knew who was chief of staff most of the time. He just didn't put a premium on that sort of thing.

He was so much better than anybody else at politics that he felt like he could run the whole state himself. We'd asked him to raise money for us; he hadn't done anything. So there was serious doubt if he had the discipline to raise the kind of money necessary to be an effective candidate. Al From and I were so smitten with his talents that we didn't worry about that. We thought that the rest of the country would swoon for him the way we had. Our biggest worry was just that he would decide for some reason not to run. But in August he decided.

Mack McLarty, a longtime friend of Clinton and later White House chief of staff: Governor Clinton called me, as I recall, in August [of 1991]. It was a very hot afternoon that we visited, and the air conditioning in the Governor's Mansion ... was being refurbished. So Governor Clinton and Mrs. Clinton were living in the guest quarters, and Governor Clinton and I visited on the porch.... But he did discuss ... his thoughts about running for president.

He talked about how happy he was as governor, both in his professional life and his personal life. He was enormously proud of Chelsea [Clinton], who was becoming a young woman. I think she was in middle school.[4] He was very, very

---

4. Chelsea Clinton was born in 1980, so would have been eleven at the time.

pleased with that. He was very pleased and proud of Hillary's accomplishments, both in the legal profession and in public life as well. He talked about his satisfaction with seeing a lot of the programs he had worked on as governor over a ten-year period ... coming to fruition, particularly job creation, education, these types of things. Having said all that, it was clear to me that he did have that proverbial fire in his belly.

We did talk about some of the personal rigors of a national campaign and the criticism, and so forth, that inevitably happens in the primary process and beyond. We had a second visit, as I recall, two or three weeks later, where we discussed some of the same issues. He gave me some feedback from other people he was talking to including, of course, his wife, Hillary. That was the beginning of his crystallizing his decision to run.

Frank Greer: [Clinton] insisted, as we went down this path [toward deciding to run], that we have a big meeting of all of his old friends and advisors, which we had at the Sheraton on Capitol Hill by the Hyatt. . . . He had to have a day-and-a-half-long meeting, which our staff put together. . . . Thirty people. All of them basically kept coming to the conclusion that he should run, but they ... were concerned about the buzz, the question marks [about Clinton's personal life].

We left that meeting and came back to my office, which was over on Pennsylvania Avenue, and sat in my conference room. Greenberg was there, Mark Gearan,[5] and myself. And I just said, "You have got to deal with this in a proactive way." I had set up a breakfast meeting [for September 16] with the [Godfrey] Sperling group, which is kind of a political reporter insider group, it meets on a regular basis.[6] I said, "You need to go into that meeting with Hillary and you need to say, 'Things have not always been perfect in our lives but we're deeply committed to each other. So if the question is, *Are we perfect?* No, we're not. But if the question is, *Are we committed to our marriage?* The answer is yes. And we're also committed to the families of this country,' " that kind of thing.

We agonized about it. There was a lot of resistance, didn't want to admit to any problems, et cetera, but I said, "You've just got to clear the air." . . . [Bill] and Hillary went in that morning and it was a cathartic effect on the national press." . . . [We] had two reporters primed . . .—not in a manipulative way, but we said, "If you ask this question . . . you're going to get an answer." . . . [It] was the one

---

5. Mark Gearan had been executive director of the Democratic Governors Association from 1989 to 1992, and was involved in formal and informal ways in Clinton's presidential campaign, including as liaison between the Clinton and Gore networks after the 1992 party convention. He later held several positions in the Clinton White House, and he became director of the Peace Corps in 1995.

6. Godfrey Sperling wrote for the *Christian Science Monitor*. His *New York Times* obituary (September 12, 2013) indicates that he presided over 3,241 meals, most at the St. Regis Hotel in Washington.

action that laid that to rest, [at least] until Gennifer Flowers[7] in New Hampshire. But I think it was just the courage of both of them stepping up and dealing with it, and not pretending that the issue was not out there, but saying, "The real question is our commitment to one another, and the commitment that we have to America's families." I've always thought . . . that people in this country were a lot more concerned about their future than they were about Bill Clinton's past. That's why he made it through so much of this.

Stanley Greenberg, pollster: [We] had one [very early] meeting that was solely on this subject [womanizing], at which Hillary was present. It was an uncomfortable meeting, I can assure you. . . . I remember Hillary saying that, "Obviously, if I could say 'no' to this question, we would say 'no', and therefore, there is an issue." She spoke about this as much as he did. I don't remember the specific kind of things that were said, because it wasn't a meeting where he said, "Okay, there's these five relationships. Let's talk about those and what the exposure is." That wasn't the nature of the conversation. It was more a general characterization of the types of potential risks, but assurances that, given the people and given the long-term relationships, this was not going to be a major problem. And that they were able to handle it because their relationship was strong. They'd be able to respond to it in ways that would minimize the problems.

Susan Thomases, longtime Clinton friend and campaign scheduler: I told him if I found him having sex on the campaign, he was dead, that I was leaving and taking everybody with me. I said, "You're stupid enough to blow this whole presidential thing over your dick. And if that turns out to be true, buddy, I'm going home, and I'm taking people with me. If you don't have enough self-control to keep yourself straight, then it's just dumb." . . . It worked. During the campaign he was as straight as could be. He just was. They knew that I would land on his neck with both feet. Sometimes you have to be that blunt, and he gets it. That's not a long speech. It takes all of about thirty seconds.

David Kusnet, speechwriter: Nineteen ninety-two was a very unusual year politically. The first President [George H. W.] Bush started out that election cycle prohibitively ahead of any possible opponent, and as a result a lot of the punditry in the early drafts of history says that none of the first-tier Democrats ran for president that year because they didn't think they could win.

Maybe I'm a partisan, but I would argue that one first-tier Democrat *did* run and won, and his name was Bill Clinton. Of all the Democrats at that

---

7. Gennifer Flowers was an Arkansas lounge singer who claimed in the heat of the 1992 New Hampshire primary campaign that she and Governor Clinton had carried on a long extramarital affair.

time who were seen as credible presidents—Bill Bradley, Sam Nunn, Al Gore, Mario Cuomo, Lloyd Bentsen, and others[8]—the only one who did run was Bill Clinton. He was someone who had been preparing to run for president and to be president almost all of his life. He was someone who had given a great deal of thought, not just to what it took to be elected president, but to what he would do after becoming president.

There was something that the journalist and later Clinton staffer, Sidney Blumenthal, called "the conversation." There was quite a discussion during that period . . . of what it would take to elect a Democratic president and what a Democratic president should do after being elected. . . . The one thing that united the conversation was a sense that whatever we had done in 1984 and in 1988 clearly had not been working, and we had to do something different if we intended to win. As Bill Clinton used to say, the definition of insanity is doing the same thing over and over again and thinking if you keep on doing it you're going to get a different result. There was, I think, a consensus in the Democratic Party between '88 and '92 that whatever we did, if we wanted to get a different result from '84 and '88, it had to be different from what we did in '84 and '88.

---

8. Bill Bradley was U.S. senator from New Jersey (1979–1997). Sam Nunn served in the Senate from Georgia (1972–1997). Mario Cuomo was governor of New York (1983–1994). Lloyd Bentsen represented Texas in the Senate (1971–1993) before becoming President Clinton's first treasury secretary.

3

The Announcement and "Ideas Primary"

Bill Clinton made his formal announcement that he would run for the presidency in Little Rock on October 3, 1991. This speech was unquestionably the most important of his career to that point. It needed both to establish the basic terms of his campaign and to remove any lingering doubts about his speaking abilities raised by his thirty-three-minute introduction of Michael Dukakis at the 1988 Democratic National Convention. Shortly after proclaiming his intention to seek the presidency, Clinton deftly scheduled three major speeches at his alma mater, Georgetown University, each devoted to a major theme of the campaign. At a time when the incumbent President George H. W. Bush still seemed nearly invincible, Clinton laid the intellectual foundation for his challenge to Bush, winning what policy advisor Bruce Reed has called the "ideas primary."

Mickey Kantor, campaign chair: The campaign officially began on October 3, 1991. . . . He had an advantage that no other Democrat had. He had friends everywhere. He had governors who were devoted to him, who had worked with him in the governors' conference. He had a base out of Al From's organization, the DLC, which he headed before he ran. He had a clear idea, not only how to run, but what he wanted to accomplish, and he understood the Democratic nomination was not worth having unless he ran in the way he wanted to govern. Too many Democrats had run to the left during the '70s and '80s, tried to then shift their position in a general election, and they had turned out not to be successful. He was bound and determined not to do that.

And if you look back at both his speech in Little Rock on October 3 and the . . . speeches at Georgetown that fall, I believe you will agree with me that in the history of modern politics, in terms of winning presidential candidates, he was more consistent with what he had laid out and [what he did] throughout his presidency than almost anyone. Maybe Ronald Reagan was the only one who might have been more consistent than he. He truly understood what he wanted to do and what he wanted to accomplish, both politically and substantively, and how to marry those together.

Bruce Reed, speechwriter and campaign policy advisor: But first, we had to get him to actually say the words—that he was declaring for the presidency. He finally decided to focus on the speech the night before. We were working out of the Governor's Mansion. I think he read our draft and it wasn't right. It wasn't his yet. He decided to start from scratch in his own way. I vividly remember Hillary [Clinton] ... bringing us plates of food and shaking her head about how disorganized he was being. Chelsea was practicing ballet in the foyer of the Mansion.

I was well prepared. I had spent most of my time with Gore staying up all night working on speeches. We hadn't finished Gore's announcement speech until 3:30 in the morning the night before he was to give it in Carthage, Tennessee, in 1987. Clinton had the good sense of scheduling his speech midday so we could stay up all night and still get a little bit of sleep—in theory, at least. He went to bed—he was happy by about 2:30 or 3:00. But we still had a bunch of work to do to enter his changes. So Frank and Stan and I huddled around the computer until about 4:00.

William Galston, deputy White House domestic policy advisor: Writing speeches with or for Bill Clinton is not a linear process, and most of it tends to take place in the hours immediately before the speech ...: creative chaos. Writing a speech for Bill Clinton was a lot like writing a script for a Hollywood movie. Everybody was involved. You were doing it and doing it and doing it, and if you thought the speech was done but you weren't the person driving with him to the venue, you were wrong.

Frank Greer, media advisor: [We] literally stayed up all night, until three in the morning, four in the morning. I get over there at six o'clock the evening before, and he has just eviscerated this great speech that Bruce [Reed] and I had worked on. It was in tatters, and had no theme, and he was going back to this academic college thesis kind of stuff and talking about what he'd learned in Georgetown. I said, "This is not an announcement speech." So it was just a knock-down-drag-out—and Greenberg was there, too. We're all just tearing our hair out. So finally we bring it back around, and Clinton finally makes it his own, and we finally get it. It's three in the morning. The event is that same morning.

We walked out and I said, "This is it, this is the speech, right?" "No, no, no. I think we ought to practice it again in the morning. You get up here at seven o'clock." ... I said, "You can't change it. We'll practice it, I'll be here at seven o'clock, but you can't change it." I went from there back to the Capitol Hotel, the old hotel, and I found out what room John King from the Associated Press [was in]—John King, now at CNN [Cable News Network]—I took the speech and I stuck it under his door. I said, "This is the speech, John, and you've got it." He's still a dear friend to this day because he had the exclusive that night so he could put it on the wire the next morning.

I get back up to the Mansion and Clinton has, of course, torn it apart again. I said, "You can't do this because I've already given it to John King." [*screams*] "You what??!!" [*laughter*] I said, "It was the only way to get you to quit rewriting it." So that was the speech. He made a few changes in nuance, but he basically stuck to it. As far as the world is concerned, that's what they read on the wire. So that was how we finally had to shake it loose. . . .

"New Covenant" was first mentioned in the announcement speech. I will be very honest with you, I was uneasy about it. I thought it sounded almost too evangelical. I'll tell you where it came from. It came from Al From, who is Jewish, who had the idea that the covenant was an agreement between God and his people. For all those reasons, I was saying, "This is a little over the top." Clinton agonized about it and we went back and forth and everything, and I finally backed off. It's interesting, the three watchwords for the campaign became "responsibility," "opportunity," and "community." But it had started as "responsibility," "opportunity," and "new covenant." We finally got to the point—although I had kind of warmed up to the whole new covenant thing—but eventually, a new sense of community emerged from the concept—we owe you opportunity, you have to take responsibility, and we need to build a new sense of community. That's how it all originated and evolved.

Stanley Greenberg, pollster: None of the other announcement speeches stood out like Clinton's. And you quickly rolled into the [Georgetown] New Covenant speeches, which was an amazing thing to do. The New Covenant speeches, the idea that what you do in your campaign is to give very high level speeches about the future of the country, to deal with military and security issues, and economic policy, and philosophy—nobody else was doing it. It was something that From had raised coming out of the announcement. He had raised this as something we should do. We constituted a group out of my office where we worked through the speeches. . . . The dominant themes in his announcement speech in October [of 1991] that become the dominant themes in the New Covenant addresses [delivered that fall at Georgetown University] are his. They're not derived from any kind of [public opinion] research process. There is interaction: "What do you think of these ideas?" But there's no research commissioned. It's coming out of an intellectual process for Bill Clinton over the year. . . . *He* had a vision.

Bruce Reed: At first [speechwriting for Clinton] was very hard, like trying to capture a wild horse. He was capable of speaking so well that he was impatient that we couldn't keep up. I can remember one speech, early on, a Georgetown speech—one of the first speeches we had to do. . . . I was scribbling as fast as I could to try to keep up. He dictated something for the New Covenant speech, the first Georgetown speech in October. He said something that made all our jaws drop, it was so good. I wrote it down as best I could, but I missed a few phrases. And he was disdainful of what amateurs we were. To this day, I still can't quite reconstruct what it was that he actually said.

In the [1988] Gore campaign, we had given a series of speeches—three policy speeches, starting at Georgetown—as a way to distinguish him.... We decided to repeat that exercise with Clinton, and set up the Georgetown speeches. As soon as the announcement was over, I came back to Washington and started work on that. We decided to give a social policy speech, an economic policy speech, and a foreign policy speech, in the reverse order of what Gore had done, because Clinton knew the most about the first and the least about the last. I was still working out of the DLC because there was no campaign to join yet.

The first New Covenant speech was my favorite because it distilled his philosophy in the most refreshing way. To go back to his announcement speech— in the key paragraph of that speech, he announced his intention. He said that "government has a responsibility to provide more opportunity, and people have a responsibility to make the most of it." It was the first time he'd ever said it quite that way. Those were his words. I've always thought that his biggest intellectual, philosophical contribution to the Democratic Party was to restore the link between those two concepts. Almost everything that he did that mattered combined more opportunity and more responsibility.... Republicans had successfully suggested that Democrats had lost touch with those values. A lot of Democrats had forgotten about them, too.

By the time we turned out the three Georgetown speeches, Clinton was the toast of the chattering classes. He'd won the ideas primary, won the thinking man's nod.

4

Staffing the Campaign

Leading up to the announcement of his candidacy in October 1991, Bill Clinton had devoted vastly more time to thinking about the rationale for his campaign than about the team of people who might make his election possible. Indeed, nearing the eve of the announcement, Clinton almost pulled the plug on the campaign because he had not yet designated somebody to chair it. Moreover, among those who knew Clinton well, there was some concern that he might not be able to assemble the top-flight team of professionals necessary to wage a successful nationwide effort. This skepticism was based partly on Clinton's scant fundraising experience—something essential for supporting a big professional operation—and partly on his casual leadership style as governor of Arkansas, where he relied on a handful of close personal aides to tend to a small state's business.

Yet Clinton succeeded in bringing to Little Rock an accomplished group of campaign professionals who would use the success of 1992 as a springboard into the White House and beyond. Their teamwork was celebrated in D. A. Pennebaker's 1993 documentary The War Room, *which helped make stars of James Carville and George Stephanopoulos. Not everyone on Clinton's campaign team agreed, however, that the film was a good idea.*

Sandy Berger, foreign policy advisor: Clinton called [just before launching his bid] and said, "I can't announce next week, I don't have a campaign manager." I said, "No one cares who your campaign manager is." He said, "This does not seem like a serious campaign if I can't say who my campaign manager is." . . . There was [also] a big debate whether this campaign was going to be run out of Washington or out of Little Rock. The vote was about 100 to 2; 100 for Washington, 2 for Little Rock. The two were Bill and Hillary Clinton.

Al From, head of the DLC: I still remember, on announcement day, October 3, 1991, being [in Little Rock], and after Clinton gave his speech . . . we had a drink back there inside the Old State House, and he said to a few of us, "You'd better go over to [Bruce] Lindsey's office and put together a campaign because I just announced for president of the United States, and I don't have anybody on board."

Eli Segal, campaign chief of staff: In October of '91, when he announced his candidacy with a lot of hoopla at the state capitol in Arkansas, it drove Bill Clinton crazy that he had announced his campaign and didn't have a campaign manager.... I finally agreed that what I would do would be to go not to Little Rock [to lead the campaign] but to Washington, and interview 50, 100, 150, whatever number of people it made sense to interview in order to put together a crackerjack team. That was something that appealed to everybody because while [Stanley] Greenberg and [Frank] Greer and [Al] From were fighting for what their own roles were going to be in it, . . there was no glue person, kind of what my role was historically in this thing, to bring the pieces together.

So I went to Washington, interestingly to the law offices of Susan Thomases.... I hired one person who happened to be my son's college roommate to assist me with résumés, telephone calls, meetings—and over a very short period of time, I'd define it as a week or two, I hired everyone from David Wilhelm to Dee Dee Myers to, more or less, Rahm Emanuel to Richard Mintz, who became the campaign manager for Hillary Clinton, to Stephanie Solien, who became the political director, and I think one or two more. Clinton said to [George] Stephanopoulos, "You're hired. However, until you meet with Eli Segal, you're not hired." Clear instruction to me. Clear instruction to George. I met George, whom I had never met before, and I could tell this was a real talent. I spent a maximum of a half-hour with him and said, "Okay, you've got the job."[1]

Susan Thomases, scheduler: His decision to run his campaign out of Arkansas was the smartest thing he ever did. Being in Washington would have been disastrous. We would have had people hanging all over us all the time. Making the people who wanted to be around us come out to Arkansas and deal with Little Rock, a place where he was beloved, was much nicer. It was smart.

Bruce Reed, speechwriter and policy advisor: We had a talented campaign. It was a small operation.... Because we didn't think Clinton was going to be able to raise that much money, we didn't hire a lot of people. It was in Little Rock, so that dramatically narrowed the number of people who were willing to sign on.... Little Rock, though I resisted going there, saved the Clinton campaign for a couple of reasons.

---

1. David Wilhelm was an Illinois-based political operative who focused on day-to-day operations and helped develop electoral college strategy for the 1992 campaign. Dee Dee Myers was a California-based communications specialist who handled the press. Rahm Emanuel, also from Illinois, steered fundraising. (He later had a prominent political career of his own, in Congress and as mayor of Chicago.) Richard Mintz had been a media advisor for several organizations before becoming staff director for Hillary Rodham Clinton's campaign efforts. George Stephanopoulos had worked for Congressman Richard Gephardt (D-MO) before becoming the presidential campaign's communications director.

First, it was truly an outside-Washington campaign. There was no way we could think like Washington insiders, when we were eatin' at Doe's,[2] and walkin' the streets of Little Rock. It was so far away from the Beltway that we had a perspective closer to what the voters had. That was immensely helpful. Second, we spent, as a result, a whole lot less time talking to people inside the Beltway and being influenced by the ups and downs. . . . [And] it wasn't just that their advice would have been bad, although it might well have been. It was that the mood swings of Washington are devastating. I don't think the Clinton campaign could have psychologically survived the Gennifer Flowers and draft stories if it had been based in Washington. My wife stopped going out over those two months because everybody in Washington had given up on Bill Clinton and she was tired of hearing about it from them.

Madeleine Albright, foreign policy advisor: Getting to Little Rock from Washington is like going to outer space.

Sandy Berger: I became Bill Clinton's senior foreign policy advisor in late '91 after he had declared and decided he was going to give three speeches at Georgetown, the trifecta. One was on the economy and economic policy, one on the opportunity, responsibility, the "third way" theme, and the third was on foreign policy. I was the only person on the conference call with any foreign policy experience.

The bar was not extremely high in 1991 to become senior foreign policy advisor to Bill Clinton, who wasn't even a blip on anybody's chart. I spent a great deal of time working on that speech. That's when I reached out to Tony Lake, my former boss at the State Department. . . . Clearly by '91 [Clinton] is running, and there are several meetings that take place in Washington. . . . One of the things that impressed me so much was when we got to the policy part of the program . . ., Clinton would handle that part. This is not a candidate who was fed his policy framework. He knew what he wanted to say and he would lead the discussion of what the policy direction would be. He was weaker in foreign policy obviously than he was in domestic policy, but knowledgeable.

Tony Lake, foreign policy advisor: This would have been early fall '91, early autumn. [Clinton and I] spoke for about three minutes on arms control. Then when he was asking me where I was from, I started talking about my neighbors in western Massachusetts who were having a hard time of it economically and he got very passionate about their plight; I was passionate about their plight.[3]

---

2. Doe's Eat Place is a small-town Little Rock establishment that became famous in 1992 as a campaign hangout.
3. Lake lived on, and worked, his own farm at the time.

STAFFING THE CAMPAIGN | 31

Completely without apology I will say that I decided . . . [to] work for Governor Clinton's election for a while because of his position on domestic issues. . . . [He] asked me to then stay on into the spring. This sounds frivolous now, but my thought was, "Okay, I'll go on doing this until the beginning of baseball season," because I figured he'd probably be out of the campaign by then.

Senator Harris Wofford (D-PA): The morning after my victory, . . . within twenty-four hours or so Clinton was on the phone to me saying, "Tell me about this fellow [James] Carville.[4] Should I consider him to be campaign manager for me? What do you say?"

I said, "He's wild and he's brilliant and he's tough. It was a good gamble for me, and it would probably be a good gamble for you." . . . So for better or worse . . . we gave Carville to the public scene. They're a very good team, especially when they're together. Paul Begala is as sharp, but has a softer edge.[5] No, that isn't the right word. He's more collegial. Carville is dominating, and he expects you to be strong enough to push him back if you don't like it. Paul Begala is easier-going, and so they balance each other; they're a very good team. It's easier to like Paul almost all the time. James can get carried away with his conviction about something. He's learned that to get something clear with the public or even talking to anyone, you have to [*spoken emphatically*] overstate it and dramatize it as much as you can. Not only the way he talks, which I was imitating, but the thrust of his language. When you're riding high with him, it's exciting. When you're trying to get another thought in edgewise, it's a little harder.

Roy Neel, longtime aide to Al Gore: Mickey [Kantor] was the titular campaign chairman. The campaign manager was David Wilhelm. The chief of staff was Eli Segal. James was just sort of a consultant to the campaign. George was communications director. But the titles didn't really reflect the roles so much.

Up until the convention, it had been not a rag-tag operation, but a volatile operation. . . . Nobody in that room had ever won a presidential campaign. No one in that room had ever worked in the White House, and they were hungry. They were ardent Democrats. They all had some policy and communications experience and they all desperately wanted to win this election and they were tireless. So it wasn't so much a well-oiled machine as much as it was a kind of a constantly chugging-along machine. James was not a manager. It was just sort of free-floating . . . like a house party on speed that never stopped.

---

4. Wofford won a November 1991 special election to complete the unexpired term of Senator John Heinz (R-PA), who had been killed in an airplane crash. James Carville was then little known outside Democratic campaign circles, but successes working for Georgia Governor Zell Miller and Wofford drew him to Clinton's attention.

5. Paul Begala was Carville's partner—and by most accounts his balance wheel.

Frank Greer, media advisor: Everything in this campaign, message-wise, strategy-wise, policy-wise was set before James and Paul got involved. We never wavered, and it had nothing to do with James. James created the mythology and the persona that he was the person responsible, and it just wasn't the case. James played a good coordinating role in the general election, but this is not a campaign or strategy that James Carville put together. This was a Bill Clinton campaign and he put it together. If there's anything that's unfortunate about what happened as a result of all this, it's the lasting mythology, because there was a lot of self-promoting going on, that this was not Bill Clinton, but was rather the smart people who came from Harris Wofford's campaign or whatever, and that is just not the case. I say to my core, that is not the case. This is Bill Clinton, Bill Clinton mapping it out, Bill Clinton understanding it, et cetera.

Bruce Reed: The good thing about [the campaign] was that there were divisions, but there weren't quite factions. People didn't line up predictably. There were people who were more traditional Democrats, who were in the political department. Frank Greer's wife, Stephanie Solien, her job was to talk to Democratic constituents. So she, naturally, didn't want to offend them. Susan Thomases, who was the scheduler, had her own views about where the party ought to go. We had a bunch of consultants: Greenberg, Greer, Mandy Grunwald,[6] Paul Begala, who at that point were still sorting out their pecking order and didn't always agree. It was just chaotic. There wasn't anybody in charge. So almost every decision was kind of a jump ball. As I said, it wasn't organized factions, the way we'd later have in the White House, where people would scheme with one another. I think [Clinton] kind of liked it that way. He knew he was his own best strategist; he liked being able to make the decisions. So he didn't worry too much about the fact that his advisors couldn't agree.... Clinton was his own best strategist. Organization didn't matter a whole heck of a lot to him.

Marcia Hale, public opinion advisor: Carville brings an energy level that is fabulous for a campaign, and he's a great strategic thinker. You almost have to have somebody decode him for you, but he's a great strategic thinker. They all had such distinct personalities that it made them a great team. James is who he is. Paul has many qualities but he's also a great writer and he understands people. He was traveling with Clinton and he could help talk Clinton through things. It was really quite remarkable. I have great respect for Paul.

Rahm, who had worked with me at the DCCC in a previous cycle, was phenomenal at raising money and has more energy than anybody except for James perhaps. Maybe they're tied. Because Rahm was so good at raising money, there

---

6. Mandy Grunwald was a New York–based media specialist who became the 1992 campaign's director of advertising.

was always money when difficulties like the draft and Gennifer Flowers came along. Had Clinton run out of money at particular times, the campaign would not have succeeded. Rahm not only has the energy and the organization to be able to do that, but also he became close friends with the fundraisers and really inspired them to do more. And he'd criticize them if they didn't, but in a positive way. The same thing happened in the last election.[7]

George is, as you know, thoughtful, brilliant, steady. I think Clinton really relied on him through a lot of these sequences. It was really just a great team of very different personalities. Clinton feeds off all those different types of personalities. He likes that. So it worked, better than any campaign I've ever been involved in.

David Kusnet, speechwriter: His campaign was sort of—I wouldn't say unwieldy, because it worked very well, but rather wieldy if there is such a word—a wieldy coalition of the DLC and the economic populists. If you'd asked us in 1990 and 1991 what we were, James Carville, Paul Begala, Stan Greenberg, Frank Greer, David Wilhelm, and I would have said that we were economic populists. With economic populists at that time, whatever your views on social issues would be—and I think all the people I mentioned were social liberals—you couldn't really say that you were an absolutist social liberal because that would overshadow the economic populism. So even though there were tensions, there was some commonality between the economic populists and the DLC people then. With sides, there were elements of a "communitarian" philosophy. If you're an economic populist, it is more than just bashing irresponsible people in positions of power and privilege. It was more than just wanting a whole bunch of economic benefits for people who needed some help. You have to have some idea of some common communities and common society that is going to hold people on top to some standard of responsibility and is going to offer some kind of help for people in need. . . .

The Clinton campaign was consciously not hierarchical. What is remembered about the war room is the war metaphor and the quick response. But the other thing about it was that it was, I think, intended to be egalitarian and information sharing. That was the original point of it, that you would have one person from every function there. It was like Michael Bloomberg's bullpen in City Hall in New York City.[8] There were no walls. You could hear what everyone

---

7. Hale is evidently referring here to Emanuel's role in raising money as head of the Democratic Congressional Campaign Committee in the 2006 election cycle. The Democrats regained control of Congress that year in part because of Emanuel's fundraising prowess.

8. Michael Bloomberg was mayor of New York from 2002 to 2013. He was known for working in a "bullpen," a large open space populated by a warren of cubicles, including his own.

was saying and doing. It was the high-status place to be. That's where Carville was, that's where Stephanopoulos was.

You would have a meeting there every morning, I forget when, but relatively early in the morning, and then every evening. Everyone and anyone could go to the meeting and was encouraged to do so. I don't think there were any offices with doors, never a closed-door meeting at the headquarters, although there were private meetings at the Governor's Mansion and other places away from the headquarters.... And, because we were in the South in the summer, no one wore a tie. Carville wore blue jeans and tee shirts and whatnot. [If] you see the movie of the war room, no one is wearing a tie. There's nothing corporate about the place.

Nancy Soderberg, foreign policy advisor: The same two hundred people run these campaigns, so all your friends call you up and say, "You have to come work!" George Stephanopoulos ... and I worked on the Hill: he was in the House, I was in the Senate. He called me. I, of course, had heard of Clinton. I wasn't particularly dying to go back to work on a third failed presidential campaign. [George H. W.] Bush was at 90 percent in the polls. I didn't want to do it. He kept saying, "We need somebody who has done foreign policy before; you'll be perfect. The campaign headquarters will be in D.C. Come on, come on." So I finally went and talked to [my boss, Senator Edward] Kennedy about it because I figured he'd hear that they approached me.

He said, "You should do it." I said, "Why?" ... He said, "Because he's going to win." I looked at him as if to say, "There's no way. What are you talking about? You're such a romantic." He said, "Yes, I may be a romantic, but he's going to win." ... He said Clinton was going to move the party to the center, that Bush's polls were inflated. Clinton was much more conservative than I was. He'd just sent a lobotomized black guy to the death chamber.[9] I believe women when they talk about affairs; they don't make that stuff up. I didn't see how he could win, given all those problems. But I thought, *Well, it will lead to something.* So I made all these demands on George: I want housing, I want to travel, I want this. He called me on a cell phone from a cab in Los Angeles, and said, "Will you take it?" I said yes. He said, "By the way, the campaign is in Little Rock." *Click.* That's how I got to Little Rock.

Eli Segal (on filming *The War Room*): I was completely opposed to it.... First, when I got there the decision to do the movie had already been made. I always believed that it would become the Carville-Stephanopoulos movie. It would

---

9. Clinton returned home to Arkansas from the campaign trail in January 1992 to preside over the execution by lethal injection of Ricky Ray Rector. Rector was convicted of shooting and killing two people, including a police officer, before turning the gun on himself, resulting in the brain procedure Soderberg refers to.

come out after the election. It would not do the one thing we were all in Little Rock to do together, which was win an election for Bill Clinton. And while I am today very friendly with James Carville, I have a little difference of opinions with George. I saw no reason to be elevating the star appeal of these two fellows, to be taking away one minute, much less probably hundreds and my guess is thousands of minutes of valuable campaign time … [on] that film. So I just thought it was a huge waste of campaign resources.

Frank Greer: Then there was the big push to allow [D. A.] Pennebaker and the documentary film crew in, and I was totally opposed to that. You will not see me in that film at all, I think. And the funny thing is, I've never seen the film. I think doing that is so destructive to a campaign. To begin with, it makes the process and the people involved in the process more important than the candidate, and they should not be. In thirty years of working on this side of campaigns, I've always tried to play a fairly—not an invisible role, but certainly not making myself more important than the candidate. Two, it creates a dynamic within the campaign where people are playing for the camera, the reporter, the promotion of it all, as opposed to what is best for the campaign.... It's a question of whether the campaign is about self-promotion for people or about winning for the citizens you're trying to represent, and I think it's a heck of a lot more important to work for the people and the candidate who is going to represent the people, instead of making yourself important. The film … was all about self-promotion and it was not about promoting Bill Clinton. I think it was a culture that did not serve the president well all the way through [the White House years].

5

Vertigo

The New Hampshire Primary

The Clinton team decided to skip the normal first stop in the Democratic campaign season, the Iowa caucuses, because native son Senator Tom Harkin was also seeking the nomination and was certain to win his own state. Next up was the New Hampshire primary. Clinton believed he would do very well there because the state's economy was deeply mired in recession, making New Hampshire voters receptive to his message. Senator Paul Tsongas, from neighboring Massachusetts, was also running for the nomination, so Clinton's success did not depend on winning New Hampshire outright—he merely needed to place better than the rest of the field in the contest against an opponent with strong local ties. Yet the very viability of the Clinton campaign came into question just weeks before voters in New Hampshire would go to the polls—setting into motion some of the most dramatic scenes in the annals of American campaign history.

Stories of Bill Clinton's alleged womanizing had long followed him in Arkansas, and by some accounts contributed to his decision to skip the 1988 presidential campaign. On January 23, 1992, a tabloid newspaper, The Star, ran a story publicizing claims by an Arkansas woman, Gennifer Flowers, that she and Clinton had had a long-running affair. She soon thereafter produced taped telephone conversations with Clinton seemingly supporting her claims. The Clinton team was rocked by these allegations, which produced an unprecedented damage-control effort, including a joint appearance by Bill and Hillary on the television program 60 Minutes just before the Super Bowl.

Their efforts appeared to have stabilized the campaign, when a second blow hit them less than two weeks later. A Wall Street Journal story, relying on sources in Arkansas, reported that Clinton had manipulated the draft system to avoid military service in the Vietnam War, contrary to his long-standing claims that he had made himself available to serve but had benefited from a high draft lottery number. That second charge sent the campaign into what campaign pollster Stanley Greenberg called a "meltdown."

New Hampshire voters, however, weighed these allegations against what they themselves saw of Clinton—and of Hillary—and saved the campaign by giving him a strong second-place showing behind Tsongas. Clinton declared himself "the Comeback Kid" and left New Hampshire, almost inexplicably, with a boost of momentum.

Frank Greer, media advisor: Here's one of my observations about Democratic Party politics—and this may stand Hillary in good stead, too—the thing that helped Bill Clinton become president is that he didn't have to run in Iowa. Whenever Democrats do, they generally have a hard time winning the general election, even if they win the primary, like John Kerry did.[1] The nature of Iowa politics, the nature of caucuses and grassroots and the policy positions you have to take, makes it harder to stay in the center. So, if you look back, historically, the only one who came out of there with a boost was Jimmy Carter.[2] . . . Because Harkin was running, we made no effort in Iowa and we could say, "We're not going to run in Iowa because he's the favorite son and of course they're going to win." So we could go to a state that actually had a vote, where you could actually persuade people to vote for you. [Primaries are] a very different thing, having worked in both.

In New Hampshire, we were bringing up the rear, there's no doubt about it. We had developed a different kind of spot that basically had Clinton to camera for sixty seconds. Most people thought that was pretty unusual. He offered a[n economic] plan and said that we wanted people to be involved in the campaign, we wanted them to take a look at the plan, we wanted them to have a copy of the plan. And we offered that on the air. . . . [People] really responded in this age of cynicism and alienation. They said, "Great, here's a guy who knows what he wants to do for the country, and he wants us to know. He actually will offer us a copy of his plan." . . . It made a big difference. . . . We went on the air, I believe, the second or third week of January. . . . We ran that ad for seven days and we went from 13 percent to 35 percent in seven days, in a crowded field, with Tsongas as next-door neighbor. We literally held on to that all the way through, until Gennifer Flowers.

Al From, DLC: This was January of '92. The *New York Times* publisher's office is on the eleventh floor. I get off the elevator, and Arthur [Sulzberger] is there to meet me saying, "You've got to call your office. They've got an emergency." So I call and it's Elaine Kamarck,[3] and she's reading me the *Star* story on Gennifer Flowers. So here I am with Arthur Sulzberger, the publisher of the *New York Times*, and Jack Rosenthal, who was the editor of the editorial page, just a wonderful guy, one of my favorite people of all time. Rosenthal and I, for years, had had this unspoken wager where he said the Democratic Party would never

---

1. John Kerry, Democratic senator from Massachusetts (1985–2013), earned the party's presidential nomination in 2004, but was defeated by President George W. Bush. He later served as secretary of state under President Barack Obama.

2. Carter's boost during the 1976 campaign came because he was until that moment largely a political unknown on the national stage.

3. Elaine Kamarck was a centrist political activist deeply involved in developing the New Democrat movement. She later worked on the reinventing government initiative in the Clinton White House.

have another Bobby Kennedy who could put together working-class whites and blacks, and I said we would.

So I spent some time with Arthur. We go down to Jack's office, and they're telling me how brilliant I am because we have this candidate who is able to do all these things that I said we were going to be able to do and they never would have believed it. And I'm sitting there thinking, *In twenty-four hours, forty-eight hours, they're not going to think he's quite so good.*

Frank Greer: Then Gennifer Flowers hits.... There were two things that happened. I was at a fundraiser in Boston and George Stephanopoulos comes up to me and says—I think he was there, he may have been on the phone—he said, "We've got a real problem with this story from Arkansas and the *Star* is going to run with it." I said, "The *Star*?" I literally didn't know what the *Star* was. He said, "It's a tabloid." I said, "What are we worried about?" He said, "I think somebody else is going to pick up on it." In other words, I was saying, "We have already dealt with this, we were able, in Arkansas—" and that was probably a mistake on my part, to say to the legitimate media, "There's no substantiation for this, there's no corroboration for this, you can't run with this story, there's nothing to it." . . .

So . . . this story hit and . . . [then] Gennifer does her press conference where she has a tape, but still, we were holding up in the numbers. It proves my point that people were more concerned about what he offered for the future than what he had done in the past. There was this forgiving nature. So I went back to my basic position, which had worked so well at the Sperling breakfast, which was, take it head-on, don't get into the details, people don't want to know that much about your personal life, but they do want you and your wife to reassure them about your marriage and your commitment to one another, and that's it. Then go on and talk about what you want to do for the country.

There was dissent on that issue. But we decided—and I was very in favor of this—take it on in the biggest forum you can, don't try to deal with it piecemeal in a lot of small forums. Originally it was going to be Ted Koppel[4] and we were talking with various folks about that. Then it was going to be *Good Morning America* or the *Today* show. This broke on Thursday, and this is all vague memory, but it was a major decision—how do we deal with it? Then George says, "Well, we've got an offer for *60 Minutes*." A lot of people said, "Oh, God, you don't want to do *60 Minutes*," and it was airing right before the Super Bowl. I said, "Perfect. Take it, accept it."

We went and did focus groups in Manchester, New Hampshire, on Friday night. This also shows you the value of Greenberg's research approach. Let's go research this.

Marcia Hale, public opinion advisor: I remember distinctly being in New York on some other business and getting a phone call from Stan and Stan asking

---

4. Ted Koppel hosted *Nightline*, the prominent late-night news program of ABC television.

me if I can catch a plane to New Hampshire and do a focus group.... We did a series of focus groups about Gennifer Flowers. They were probably the most open-ended of any focus groups I've been in. By that I mean that if you do a focus group, you have a strong script you're supposed to follow. In this [case], I had more freedom to let the conversations go where they were going.... [But] it was one of the toughest ones I've ever done, not so much that talking to the voters was difficult, but I had James and Paul and Mandy [Grunwald] and Bruce and Stan, Bob Boorstin,[5] and, God knows, Stephanopoulos—there were about twelve people who were sitting behind the screen and second-guessing every question I asked.... In the most general terms, they were just basically trying to figure out what real people thought of [the Flowers allegations], as opposed to this incredible cyclone of press that was stirring everything up. They were trying to figure out, "Can we survive this, and if we survive it, how do we talk about it?"

Stanley Greenberg, pollster: We did hold focus groups and we did test things that he'd been saying. I think we tested some phrases, some parts of it, to see his credibility and reactions to it.... I reported on the results. To be honest, the fact is that we did research we never want to talk about, and never have talked about. I reported on how people were reacting. The bottom line was that people were still very open, that they were still making a judgment, hadn't closed down, weren't about to break away from us. They were quite willing to listen to [the Clintons], which was the main thing you wanted to know.... Having some confidence that what you're doing will get heard and not be viewed cynically gave some confidence to the piece.

There's a dynamic throughout this whole thing, throughout his presidency, but particularly during the Gennifer Flowers [episode] there was a dynamic with the media. The public doesn't like the media and when there's this horde of media going after somebody, the public can become sympathetic.... Part of the dynamic was, "Gennifer Flowers is not a reputable critic or source of information. This couple is under pressure. The press is trying to heat up the story." And so the press were part of this. We were mainly testing the exchanges between them and the press, since we were about to have a press exchange....

In the [focus] groups, we listened to people and had them talk about Clinton. What they took away from it was that he didn't lean back on his heels; he kind of leaned into them and he was comfortable. He didn't look like someone who was on the run, who was defensive. He was comfortable with himself under pressure. They were making a judgment about his character in different kinds of ways. There was, certainly, absolute resistance to the invasion of privacy, to this kind of scandal stuff.

---

5. Bob Boorstin was a Democratic political activist and former reporter for the *New York Times*, valued in the campaign for his policy and writing skills.

Part of the reason why [the numbers] didn't drop was that . . . there was some kind of blockage to allowing themselves to make a judgment based on Gennifer Flowers. They looked at him and they were judging him on, "How does he look? Does he look like a guilty guy?" But also, they were judging him as a guy. "How does he handle pressure?" He's a pretty self-confident guy under pressure. He has strengths that may be admirable leadership qualities. They came away positive. . . . Hillary was [also] a very important part of affirming for people that he could be trusted. We understood that they had to do this together. And that was true from the beginning. It was true in that earliest meeting I talked about. It was true at the Sperling breakfast. And it was true in the 60 Minutes appearance. He couldn't do this without her. There was no point at which he could go forward without her affirmation. . . . What's happening with people is they're reading the two of them and making a judgment.

[The] reaction to [the 60 Minutes appearance] was it was fine. This was the Super Bowl. The day of the Super Bowl, I went to Connecticut with my family to see the game. I didn't stay and watch it with [the Clintons]. People kind of dispersed. . . . 60 Minutes gives a closure to it.

Frank Greer: So, we made it through Gennifer Flowers, and I'm thinking, *We made it*. Then the draft letter hits.[6]

Stanley Greenberg: Then we have the draft story. . . . The *Wall Street Journal* story—the press treats this differently because it's a legitimate source. This is a legitimate story. It's not a sex scandal . . . [so] people thought it to be a real issue. It became apparent, either because it was different in character or because it came on top of the other story, that it was like, *enough*. It's just too much trouble for one person. And the focus groups were a problem. Unlike Gennifer Flowers where we were watching people react and they were drawing positive conclusions, that wasn't happening on this story . . ., because it's on top of the previous story. It was not about a sex scandal; it's about whether he served his country.

[Clinton] was not feeling well. He went back to Arkansas, which was a mistake. We should have stayed and campaigned right through. Unlike the Gennifer

6. The "draft letter" was sent by a young Bill Clinton in December 1969 to Colonel Eugene Holmes, head of the Reserve Officer Training Corps program (ROTC) at the University of Arkansas, thanking Holmes for "saving me from the draft." Until that letter was leaked to the press during the campaign by his critics, Clinton had always claimed that his lack of service in Vietnam had been the product of pure luck—a high draft number. In reality Clinton had received a military induction notice, but was able to avoid reporting by securing a privileged spot in the Arkansas Law School ROTC, although he was then attending Oxford. Clinton subsequently asked to be moved back into the draft as the lottery was being reinstated (and the call-ups for service diminished), drawing a high number (311). In the letter, Clinton also offered a detailed explanation of his opposition to the war and described his own conflicted feelings about the military service.

Flowers story, this one did not have him in the middle of it, responding. I also think he was a little less certain on how to respond. So he goes to Arkansas. He has a cold and goes to Arkansas. We have our survey in the field. I go to Connecticut. James and George are with them at the [Governor's] Mansion. I remember I get the results at my house in Connecticut. I remember which room I was in on the second floor, getting the results. It was disastrous.... [The] polling numbers had crashed. I called George. He was with them. They were in the room. He asked what it was and I said, "Meltdown." ... I mean, I forget how many we dropped. I can't remember the number, but we dropped something like twelve points. It was a gigantic drop after a period of great stability. I think he paused, and then I gave the basic numbers. It was a very short conversation. And they decided what to do. I'm pretty sure this was Sunday night that I got the results.

The next day I flew back to New Hampshire. They flew up and I believe that's when they were given the letter ... he wrote to his draft board when they arrived in New Hampshire. Then we were immediately gathered in the war room in the hotel on how to handle the letter. This has been reported on. James [Carville] is actually the one who took the lead on this, that this [letter] is our friend. Actually, to be honest, when I read the letter I said, "This is one impressive letter for a kid to write." I read this letter and I said, "This is one impressive letter. This is not as problematic—there's something revealed here that is very interesting." As we kept talking it through, we increasingly came to the view that we have to treat this letter as a plus rather than a problem.

That's when he decided—we went on *Nightline*, in which they read the whole letter and then he did the whole show, which was—again, we were risk-taking. That's when we went to the town meetings format after that. Then it was just energy. It was just pure energy and intensity and fighting back, and we began to see our numbers coming back in the primary. I still have in my head that we won the primary even though we came in second. But we treated it as—coming in second was miraculous. As we talk about it it's hard to believe that we came in second after all that.

Frank Greer: On the draft letter ... if you look at the thoughtfulness with which he had written this, I thought it showed a window into someone whom I would like to be president....This was a Clinton who, if you read the letter, was very thoughtful. This time we went on Koppel. I thought Clinton did a very good job of explaining: this was a young man, this was heartfelt, this is what we were going through at that period of time. I actually thought we were going to be okay.

The problem was, the feeding frenzy continued. If you've ever been on a campaign trail where you're two weeks out from the primary, every reporter in the world is in New Hampshire, and every reporter thinks they've got to do this story, and they're screaming at you, and you literally can't move from the hotel to an event without these mobs of people. It was just out of control. Feeding frenzy beyond any feeding frenzy I've ever seen, and I've been around politics a long time.

So *What do we do, what do we do, what do we do?* So I said—and it was kind of a crazy idea, but this also comes from listening to focus groups—I said, "The people of New Hampshire are more concerned about their future than they are about Bill Clinton's past. We should hold town meetings—" it was the beginning of the town meetings, by the way—"and we should buy time on the local television station in New Hampshire." I think we bought two or three blocks of time. "We should have an independent research firm recruit undecided voters"—not decided voters, but undecided voters—"put them in the audience and let them talk to Bill Clinton." . . . In the first thirty minutes on our program that we produced, not one person asked about Gennifer Flowers. Not one person asked about the draft. This is in the midst of the feeding frenzy. So all of a sudden you're saying to the press and everybody else, "Hey, the voters may be concerned about something else." This was true all the way through Clinton's career. The press were totally consumed with Clinton's problems, and the people were not.

In the second town hall, . . . guess how many questions we got about Gennifer Flowers and the draft? One. Someone asked, in a very respectful way, "Given that you did not serve in the military, do you still believe you would be an effective commander-in-chief," Not, "You were a draft-dodger," or, "Why did you lie to your draft board?" All of a sudden, I think even the national press corps said, "We may be a little carried away on this."

Stanley Greenberg: [Clinton] campaigned with great intensity. There was just this tremendous momentum to the campaign schedule. None of the other candidates were able to emerge. First of all, they were blanketed out. They could do their advertising, but there was so much free media centered on Clinton that they, ironically, got buried. He was getting covered in a way that the others weren't, and he just campaigned non-stop into the night. The rallies had tremendous energy. I think people rallied to his stamina, to his comeback, to his intensity, and believed that he had strength, and special leadership qualities.

[We] all thought we were dead. None of us thought we could win. I still describe it as a win. Now, we knew in the last few days that the numbers were coming back, that we had a very good chance of coming in second. We then knew that it was quite possible we were going to have a strong result. . . . We had to finish a credible second to go on. We had basically two scenarios, disaster and—"Comeback Kid" was the name of the scenario that we wrote out. . . . "Comeback Kid" was the name of the scenario. Then, when Begala did the speech, "Comeback Kid" became the key phrase. The name of the scenario that we worked through was called the Comeback Kid scenario—to announce early.[7] Under this scenario we wouldn't wait for results. As soon as we had anything, we'd go out, because we wanted to be out there before anybody else so we could

---

7. In the "victory" speech Clinton delivered the night of the New Hampshire primary (he finished second), he thanked the state's voters for making him the "Comeback Kid."

characterize the results. Creating the sense of a victory, all that energy, was a decision that we made. . . . We decided earlier in the planning for that night that we would go out, that we would make sure we were out there first, to characterize this and to create the sense that we won the primary. And I still think we won.

Bruce Reed, campaign speechwriter and domestic policy advisor: There is one story that has always struck me as indicative of why Clinton survived. . . . The campaign was in complete panic. He was scheduled that next day to do an event [in New Hampshire] on putting forth a proposal we called "Lifeline," to enable people whose houses were being foreclosed on because of the recession to hang onto their houses until they got their jobs back and things turned around. We'd worked on it with a friend of Clinton's who was a banker up there. It was something the people of New Hampshire were really interested in.

All the consultants were in despair and trying to figure out what to do. Clinton had just been told that his political future was probably over. His reaction was to pull me aside and ask me a whole bunch of questions and make some suggestions on what we should do to refine our proposal that he was going to announce the next morning on this Lifeline. The consultants had a totally different view on what he's got to do. After the meeting was over, Begala, Stephanopoulos, and I went back to headquarters and wrote a new speech—that I think Carville had asked for—that was all this political language about, "No matter what happens, I'm gonna fight like hell." It was just a classic politician speech. We all thought it was the thing to do.

He went to New Hampshire . . . and did this event and stood in the snow, all alone on the front yard of this home and gave this tinny, "I'm gonna fight like Hell" speech. The press thought he was toast. They smelled fear. Our [local] campaign people in New Hampshire were devastated and said, "What are you doing? Everybody up here wanted to hear about what you're going to do to help them keep their homes. They can't believe that you talked about all this other stuff." And sure enough, Clinton, after weathering those couple of days, went back to talking about what it was that New Hampshire wanted to talk about, not what the national press wanted to talk about. The people in New Hampshire, at the end of the day, didn't really care about Vietnam or Gennifer Flowers. They were willing to take his word for it, that those weren't big deals. That's when he said, "The hits I've taken are nothing compared to the hits that you've taken." He made it about them, not about him. They loved that about him.

Congressman Mike Espy (D-MS): They did such a good job [under pressure in New Hampshire], I think people began to say, "This guy is a good crisis manager; his wife is extremely bright; she's on his side. They thought it out, and he survived it. If he survives this, it may get worse, but we've seen his political skills, and he could survive that." I think people began to say, "This guy's serious," and they began to trickle on in.

6

Competitors, Issues, and Style

After the New Hampshire primary, Clinton and his team began to build a solid lead in successive weeks over a stable of opponents, none of whom showed Clinton's ability to sustain support from state to state. Clinton undoubtedly benefited from the fact that some of the Democratic Party's strongest contenders—including Dick Gephardt, Bill Bradley, and Mario Cuomo—had decided not to risk a challenge to George Bush that year. But the presence in the race of independent gadfly Ross Perot—a wealthy Texas businessman with a folksy style and a populist commitment to budget discipline—added an unpredictable dimension.

As the campaign proceeded, Clinton and his staff charted a course on policy issues largely drawing on his experience as governor and his inclinations as a moderate New Democrat. The campaign's priorities were enumerated simply on a whiteboard in the Little Rock headquarters: "The economy, stupid; Change vs. more of the same; Don't forget health care." And during the process Clinton revealed an exceptional capacity for campaigning. Even Bill Clinton's political opponents—Democrats and Republicans alike—marveled at his skill as a political animal: his prodigious memory for people, places, and events; his ability to work a room, connecting with voters one-on-one; his effortless speaking style; his strategic sense; and his tireless enthusiasm for politics.

Lawrence Stein, later White House congressional liaison: Dick Gephardt[1] had been priming himself for [the presidency] ever since he got to Washington. When he chose not to run [in 1992 because President Bush was seen as invincible], that was as clear a reflection of the conventional wisdom as you're going to get. I can't fault his analysis.

Sandy Berger, foreign policy advisor: Mario Cuomo was really the 800-pound gorilla. Everybody wanted Mario to run. Mario had given that electrifying

---

1. Congressman Richard Gephardt (D-MO) served in the U.S. House of Representatives from 1977 to 2005, including multiple terms as majority leader and minority leader.

keynote speech at the '84 convention that had not been exceeded by the keynote speech at the '88 convention. We were all thrilled—I was thrilled—when Cuomo said he was not going to run. Clinton was disappointed because he was absolutely convinced that he would have beaten Cuomo in the primaries—you establish your credentials by knocking off Goliath. He would have been the giant-killer, and at that point he would have the nomination. He wasn't afraid of Cuomo coming in. He wanted Cuomo to come in. He thought he could beat Cuomo. The rest of us of course were relieved because we thought Cuomo would be a very attractive candidate.

Frank Greer, media advisor (on Mario Cuomo): Of course, we had the chutzpah to say, "Bring him on, we're hoping he runs because we'll be the giant-killer and that will be the best thing that ever happened to this campaign. That will put us on the map." But when [Cuomo declined to run] Greenberg and I just said, "Thank God! That would have been awful!"

Stanley Greenberg, pollster: [With Senator Robert] Kerrey[2] there was a lot of worry. He was the [candidate] who had the biography, an interesting guy, outsider kind of style, and he owned health care as an issue. Health care was a consuming issue in '92, and there was great worry that he would ride health care right into the White House. I'd say we worried more about Kerrey than anybody else. . . . We were consumed with getting [a policy] out on health care.

Chris Jennings, health care advisor: What happened really is that Bob Kerrey, during the campaign, was making health care his number one issue. He was lobbing significant criticism against Bill Clinton for not having an explicit proposal. . . . The then-governor was quite frustrated. . . . So a few quick calls were made and frankly I think it was Bruce Reed and me just doing something very quickly. It was sort of a pseudo-competition, play-or-pay model, but it had all the right rhetoric. It wasn't designed to have a lot of specifics, but it was designed to get through New Hampshire, which I think it succeeded in doing.

The governor, as a general matter, was trying to find a new way to address health care, just like all presidential candidates want to do. There were a lot of people who were saying, "Well, this is the easy way you can go about talking about health care, managed competition," and then they overlaid on top of that, "within a budget." It was unclear what that meant, but it basically sounded pretty good. . . .Then the policy evolved over time. I think both James Carville and Paul Begala and some of his advisors always stressed, "Don't get too specific. Focus on the broader themes of health care," because all of us who have

---

2. Robert Kerrey was a U.S. senator representing Nebraska from 1989 to 2001. He was also a decorated war veteran, losing part of a leg while serving in Vietnam, a fact that no doubt concerned Clinton's team as a point of comparison.

dealt with health care know the details do matter and that details can hurt and are hard to defend occasionally.... But there was never a belief that we could say anything other than universal coverage, because Bob Kerrey was for universal coverage.

Frank Greer (on why Senator Robert Kerrey's campaign unexpectedly floundered): You really want me to tell you? He had terrible television spots. He assumed, because of the war record and everything else, that he would be, on the résumé, popular, and he never went out and worked for it, never worked very hard. They did a hockey player ad, on a deserted ice rink, where he's talking about trade—which was not the key issue in New Hampshire, trust me. [*laughter*] At the end of the spot he turns away from the camera, meaning you, the voter, and walks away. Beautiful. I'm saying, "That is the biggest turn-off I've ever seen in my life."

Stanley Greenberg: It bothered Clinton a lot that college-educated voters were voting for [candidate Paul] Tsongas,[3] and that editorial writers ... were endorsing Tsongas, because Clinton thought he was, in fact, the more thoughtful candidate in the race. Tsongas bothered him a lot.

Frank Greer: There are two things that I will confess drove [Clinton] crazy [during the primaries]. One, that Tsongas was considered to be more honest about public policy issues and better on telling the truth about Social Security and other challenges that we faced. The other thing is ... the sixty-second spot we did ... that said, "Middle-class taxpayers [will] get a break, and those who make over $250,000 pay more." Well, all of Clinton's wealthy, intellectual friends in New York, and maybe the farmer crowd, I don't know, they were furious with him that he said that he was going to tax the rich. He always gave me hell that we had done that.... [Here] is one of the great struggles with Clinton. He always wanted to win every demographic group, not just the ones we needed to win to win, but he wanted to win *every* demographic group. Therefore he couldn't stand the fact that he wasn't doing as well as Tsongas among college-educated, graduate-school-educated, higher-income people. And he said, "It's because of that damn tax proposal you stuck in there, Greer. If we hadn't done that, we would have had [them]."

Eileen Baumgartner, staff director of the House Budget Committee: [The] '92 presidential race was defined by Ross Perot. He educated the American public on the budget.... In 1992 Ross Perot ... gave the American public ownership of the budget process in a way they hadn't had before.

---

3. Paul Tsongas represented Massachusetts in the U.S. Senate from 1979 to 1985.

Roger Altman, economic policy advisor: I knew a lot about Perot, having been heavily involved in Wall Street for many years.[4] I thought Perot was a flake, I think Perot is a flake, so I didn't take him terribly seriously. Now in retrospect did his presence in the campaign serve to move the candidates a bit to the right on deficit reduction and so forth? I think it did.... I think Clinton was better served by virtue of Perot's presence in the campaign than without it. I just never took him seriously as a candidate. Is he going to become president? No. Would I have considered moving to Switzerland if he did become president? Yes.

Bruce Reed, domestic policy advisor: Perot reinforced [Clinton's] own instincts. He didn't want to get beat to the reform punch by Perot, so he kept pushing us to read Perot's work, come up with our own ideas in the same vein. So I think it had a significant kind of gravitational impact on the race, and also underscored how open the country was to dramatic change.

Alan Blinder, economic policy advisor: The [Clinton] campaign did not really run on deficit reduction to speak of. The perceived political wisdom at the time was that doing so was political poison. After all, deficit reduction is about cutting somebody's program or raising somebody's taxes. You don't have to have studied political science a lot to know that that's probably not a winning formula, and Clinton was very much aware of that. It was the Perot thing, I think, that changed that.

Congressman Mike Espy (D-MS): I think Jesse [Jackson] was used to being the emissary for validation for white politicians in the black community. He would be called on to endorse these white candidates who sought and needed votes in the black community, and Bill didn't need that. He could go himself. He was very comfortable already; even if he didn't know them, he would soon know them through his demeanor and his conversation. Maybe Jesse resented that a little bit, because he wasn't needed as much as he had been needed heretofore.

Frank Greer: Once we were in a satellite interview—we did a lot of satellite interviews—and the microphone was still open, I'm not sure if the camera was still on. Somebody, which shouldn't have happened, walked up to Clinton and said, "The word is that Jesse is going to endorse Tom Harkin today." Clinton exploded. Clinton does have a temper. He said something like, "He's a traitor, he stabbed us in the back, you can't trust—" I don't even remember the exact words, all of which ended up on tape or ended up being broadcast. If we had wanted Jesse to stay neutral, I was thinking, this is going to completely blow the whole thing apart and he probably will announce he's going to run, much less support

4. Altman was a New York investment banker with a long history of fundraising for Democratic political candidates.

Harkin. But we were able to overcome it, we soothed the waters and said it was a natural reaction. The sad thing about it, that outburst probably wasn't called for because I don't think Jesse was actually planning to endorse Tom Harkin. But it's one of those dangerous things where you just don't want to tell a candidate some bad news in front of other people, and it was an emotional reaction on Clinton's part. . . . I think Bill called and apologized and I think Jesse accepted it. . . . [But] I'll tell you the truth, it was truly amazing, when Clinton was having his problems in the White House, Jesse was one of his religious counselors. I guess they had a friendly relationship. I never thought they were that close politically.

Stanley Greenberg (on Clinton's decision to change his standard answer during the campaign about whether he had used marijuana): I forget what show he was on. It was during the New York primary. It was one of the morning shows, I think Sunday. George [Stephanopoulos] and I were with him. George and I are in the green room watching the show, and he gives his answer about not inhaling.[5] George and I know immediately that this is a disaster, and he comes off the stage and he immediately says, "What do you think? There's no problem. There's no problem, there's no problem."

He was convinced that this was [not a problem], but it was not an answer that he had given in any discussion prior to [that one]. He clearly had built this up in his head—at some point he was going to say it. He had never run it by us, or anybody that I know of. He said it and he thought it was great. I mean, it was also true. I think it's true. I think he didn't inhale. He thought it would be reassuring to people, and it was not. But he didn't get it that it wasn't.

Sandy Berger: [Clinton] positioned himself during the campaign in the center on the military budget issue. A big issue in the campaign in '92 was how much to cut the military budget. We forget, in '89 the Berlin Wall collapses, and it's the end of the Cold War. George H. W. Bush starts cutting the military. The precipitous drop in military spending begins in '89. We're talking about the peace dividend and how we were going to spend the peace dividend. So '89, '90, '91, and the debate in '92 was between [Bob Kerrey], who said, 50 percent further cut in the budget, and Clinton, who was much more cautious. . . . So he was to the right of the other candidates on defense, although it was in the context of everyone, including President Bush, saying, "With the end of the Cold War, we ought to be able to save a considerable amount of money from the military."

In 1992 foreign policy was not uppermost in people's minds. What was uppermost in people's minds was an economy that was either in recession or just

---

5. Clinton's answer was: "When I was in England, I experimented with marijuana a time or two, and didn't like it. I didn't inhale and I didn't try it again."

coming out of recession, depending on whose view you adopt. People were hurting economically, so obviously the economic issue, "It's the economy, stupid," was [James] Carville's very clear message. Keep focused on the message. But to James's chagrin, from time to time we were able to have Clinton speak [on foreign affairs]. . . . [Again] our goal was that we were not going to lose any votes because of foreign policy. We're going to demonstrate that he's not afraid of it. He's going to go right at Bush on it. He's going to be more energetic and more creative than Bush on it. I think that we succeeded in that strategy.

Nancy Soderberg, foreign policy advisor: The hardest thing about running a campaign on foreign policy is keeping all the people who want to be helpful and want to be national security advisor out of the room so you can actually get some work done.

Tony Lake, foreign policy advisor: I suspect that Clinton said more than Bush did on foreign policy. . . . [Indeed Bush] made a terrible mistake, I think, in refusing to talk more about foreign policy. Whereas if he had been all over us, he could have killed us.

Mickey Kantor, campaign chair: Bill Clinton in the campaign was somewhat different than Bill Clinton as president or as governor, certainly as president the first couple of years. Bill Clinton in the campaign is very disciplined. He is a well-trained politician. He understands that when you're running for office, you can't get in the way of a campaign making decisions and moving ahead. He also is the best campaign manager I ever met, and I've met a few of them in my life. His ideas are usually very, very good. Not always, but usually, as opposed to many candidates who are good candidates but just have a lot of ideas that should be junked on first reading.

Susan Thomases, scheduler (on Bill Clinton's skills as a campaigner): He was amazing. . . . He touches people, physically. Have you ever seen his hands? You have to meet him and shake his hands. He's a person who touches people. First of all, he's so tall. I think people don't realize how tall he is until they see him in person. . . . He's a very tall man, and in politics that does make a difference. And he has these incredibly beautiful hands, not just physically beautiful, but they're big hands, and he touches people. If you watch him, he sort of scoops people up with his hands and includes them—he has a way of including people. When he's talking to you, you know that he's paying attention to you and he hears you. He has the most incredible memory. So every person he sees, if he's ever seen them before, he remembers something about them, and they cannot believe that he remembered it. He has this incredible personal touch because of his great way of focusing on whoever he's speaking to—and this incredibly memory of having met someone. I know a lot of politicians, and they don't all have that skill.

David Kusnet, speechwriter: Clinton was different from the other presidential nominees I had worked for. I had met [Walter] Mondale and [Michael] Dukakis and they were both somewhat forbidding figures. . . . [But Clinton] can treat you like his best friend in the world when he's first met you. Everything about him, the body language. He just beckons. Everything about him is just to draw you in.

There is a funny, an arcane reference, but I remember reading something that Norman Mailer[6] wrote about when he met President [John F.] Kennedy. . . . *Barbary Shore* was a novel that Mailer wrote that he was very proud of but never got anywhere. It was not well reviewed, didn't sell any copies. Everyone knew Mailer from *The Naked and the Dead*. Mailer wrote that he had assumed that because *The Naked and the Dead* was what everyone associated him with—it was about the war in the Pacific and Kennedy had served in the war in the Pacific—he was certain that Kennedy would pretend to have read and loved *The Naked and the Dead*. Instead Kennedy engages him in a conversation about *Barbary Shore*. Mailer writes that he just fell in love with Kennedy then, because here Kennedy liked his favorite book and Kennedy clearly had actually read something that he wrote. But Mailer has enough self-knowledge to write that politicians should understand that if they ever meet an author, compliment them on something obscure, because that's what will really flatter them. I'd only written one book at that time, so Clinton couldn't comment on another book, but he engaged me in some obscure part of *Speaking American*.[7] It wasn't the main point, but it was about unions. So he understood that that mattered to me and also that that would prove to me that he had really read it, he hadn't just read the first few pages—he started discussing with me something in the middle of the book. So that won me over. I could tell he had really read my book.

Tony Lake: [The] people I admire, the way Abraham Lincoln is my hero and Winston Churchill is not, are those who bring a heartfelt passion to the issues but then an essential skepticism and moderation as they apply their minds to the issues. Because I think when you move from ideals to ideology you get in trouble. That was certainly the great lesson of Vietnam. If you don't have the ideals and the passion, then you're simply a technician. But if you have only the ideals and the passion, you're a danger to humanity because you go off on ideological crusades. Clinton had struck me as very much balanced like that. . . . I think that appealed to me in how he approached things.

---

6. Norman Mailer (1923–2007) was an American writer known for his novels, counterculture journalism, and leftist political activism.

7. Kusnet, *Speaking American: How the Democrats Can Win in the Nineties* (New York: Thunder's Mouth Press, 1992). In this book Kusnet offered prescriptions Clinton would find appealing, including encouragement to use strong language on crime and foreign policy and to frame arguments to win middle-class voters.

7

The Manhattan Project and the Veep

The Bill Clinton who secured the Democratic nomination for president in the spring of 1992 was, in the words of one political advisor, "damaged goods." Although the Clinton campaign had survived both scandal and a bruising primary process, the accumulated battles had left Clinton in a weakened condition; at one point he was running third in national voter surveys behind President Bush and independent candidate Ross Perot. The Democratic Party itself was ambivalent about Clinton, surely in part because of concerns about his electability, but also because he had challenged so many party orthodoxies that some Democrats could reasonably wonder whether he was truly one of their own. Further, Clinton's pollsters had picked up worrisome signals that the public had developed solidly constructed images of the candidate as a spoiled child of privilege, which, left unchanged, would make it almost impossible for him to gain traction with voters in the general election. Small wonder that the nominee-to-be would be in a foul mood.

Facing these realities, several of the campaign's top advisors sequestered themselves to work on what they called the Manhattan Project, an effort to reset the electorate's image of Bill Clinton leading up to the Democratic National Convention in July. Added to this was the decision to announce the choice of Al Gore as Clinton's running mate—yet another unorthodox move. But the combination of these two factors reversed Clinton's momentum—and his attitude—moving into the convention in New York City.

Bernard Nussbaum, later White House counsel: I went around with Bill Clinton during the New York primary. . . . Those were interesting days, actually, that political time. Here this man was on his way to getting the nomination. He and Hillary were going to accomplish this enormous feat, but everybody with the Clinton campaign was super-depressed. It was incredible. April, May, and June of 1992—June, that's when he was running third in the polls. Everybody was enormously depressed. "What can we do? A Democrat is going to run third in the election. Not even second."

Stanley Greenberg, pollster: [Clinton] was in a funk . . . coming out of the primaries. . . . [Part] of the [general election] plan was to play off of various traditional Democratic support groups, to counter-schedule and talk to the groups about things that would not be popular. NAFTA [North American Free Trade Agreement] came up in this period, but [the plan] was to go speak to the unions and say tough things to them on trade, and go to Jesse Jackson's Rainbow Coalition and be tough there.[1]

[Paul] Begala was pushing it very hard, and Clinton was pushing back, partly because of the risk, partly because he was uncomfortable with the whole ... counter-scheduling part of this.... On the Jesse Jackson one, we had to have a vigil that lasted at least forty-eight hours of having somebody with him at all times to make sure he didn't ... call Jesse Jackson and apologize, ... because he wanted to. It really was a vigil. George called and said, "We have problems here. He's going to call." ... I'm not making this up. We really did have a tag team making sure that someone was there to make sure he didn't call Jesse Jackson.... We were a month before the convention, in third place. I think we were like 23 percent. There is a threshold on your public [funds] match, federal match. I think you had to have 25 percent threshold or something, so it was a worry that we were below the threshold and we could lose our federal match. People were talking about not going to the convention. In retrospect it all looks great, but at the time, it was ugly.

David Kusnet, speechwriter (on a radio talk-show caller who phoned in before the Democratic National Convention): She [said] something like, "I'm a Democrat. I know that Clinton is going to get nominated. I want to be for him. Give me some reason why I should be for him." I tried to give some reasons and wasn't terribly convincing. She said, "I'm sorry, but the only things I know about him are he dodged the draft, he slept with some cocktail waitress, and he electrocuted somebody." ... Clinton was winning a lot of primaries, but he wasn't held in terribly high esteem.

Bruce Reed, domestic policy advisor: There was considerable debate taking place in June ... about whether we should be aiming for a majority or a plurality [in the general election]. There were advocates of what we called the "34 percent solution." I don't think Greenberg was alone in this, but I think that was his first instinct, that if it was going to be a three-way race, he felt that our best shot was to make sure that our 34 percent showed up. I think that influenced his views on who would be the right vice-presidential pick.... Thankfully, Clinton dismissed the 34 percent solution out of hand. He felt that that was a

---

1. NAFTA, which Clinton supported, was troublesome for Democrats because of fears by unions that open borders would create channels for cheap labor to flood the U.S. marketplace. Clinton spoke in June to a Rainbow Coalition conference, and he used the opportunity to criticize publicly the musical performer Sister Souljah, whom Jackson had defended, for asserting after an episode of racial unrest, "[If] black people kill black people every day, why not have a week and kill white people?" Clinton's willingness to confront Jackson's group directly on this helped him to establish his independence with centrist voters, but partially alienated one of the party's core constituencies.

false choice. There was nothing about what he was saying to the swing voters that was going to alienate the 34 percent.

Stanley Greenberg: James [Carville] and I went to [campaign chairman] Mickey Kantor. I remember meeting with him in his room and we proposed a project called the Manhattan Project. We called it that because we thought we were dealing with that scale of a problem, actually, not because we had this conversation in Manhattan. It was because we thought we were dealing with nuclear issues. We were locking up the primaries, but [the candidate was] badly damaged . . . and going to go into a tough general election damaged goods. What we proposed was that we . . . divide the campaign. "There is nothing now more important than to figure out how to reemerge from the primary process with character, firmed by the convention." We took myself, Frank Greer, James [Carville]—I'm trying to think who else was part of the project. Mandy [Grunwald] was doing the media. . . . We [all] pulled out of the campaign to focus on this question. I was back based in Washington, and in charge of that. I had an open-ended research budget to go figure this out.

The most important part of it was . . . an exercise that I hadn't done before, because we were beginning from scratch, in which we took twenty-five items on a sheet of paper, just facts about his life. We would pass that out in the [focus] group and have people talk, circle things that stood out, and what it said about him. What came out of it was humble origins and biography. The humble origins was [crucial]—everything played back [from that]. People . . . create a narrative [about politics] that follows from things they know. The story [they already knew] was marijuana, Oxford, Yale, draft. So the assumption was *privileged kid*—not just that these things were happening, but that he was a privileged kid. That impacted the totality of the image. [But] when you get that he comes from humble origins and ends up going to Oxford and [then] going back to the state as governor, and working on education, there's a narrative about biography that allowed people to completely rethink him.

Frank Greer, media advisor: We found in Stan's focus groups that people thought he was born with a silver spoon in his mouth, he went to all these Ivy League schools, he went to Oxford, he wasn't one of them. They had forgotten that he came from Arkansas, his father died before he was born, and that he grew up poor. So we had to reintroduce him in that regard. . . . And it worked.

Stanley Greenberg: We were into using everything, and during the Manhattan Project we did dial meters,[2] which was the first time I'd used them, to look at

---

2. A dial meter is an opinion research tool in which the members of the test group are given dials that register numbers, 1 to 100, and are asked to turn the meter up or down depending on whether they like or dislike what they are seeing and hearing. This method allows researchers to get a continuous measure of how much the audience is buying or rejecting the arguments being made in a political ad or a debate.

ways to—we were up to try to solve this problem in any way we could find. Also, it is a very effective tool for convincing candidates that they should do something or not do something, because they watch this picture, they're carrying on, and then the line [*makes sound of blowing up*] is going down [*laughing*]. So it's good for that purpose.

The first time we tested it Hillary was in the visual. We were in his motel room in West Virginia and we were—I think George [Stephanopoulos] was on the floor, and James, and myself—I can't remember who else was there.... We were looking for all kinds of things to get a sense of how people were reacting. Hillary's picture comes on and the line goes [*sound of bomb falling*]. The line goes down. We're all sitting there waiting for [Clinton] to say something. And he says, "You know, they just hated the way she was doing her hair then." [*laughter*] And we all kept a straight face, and moved on.

Bruce Reed (on the prospect of adding Senator Al Gore to the ticket as running mate): Since I'd worked for both of them [Gore and Clinton], I'd started telling friends and reporters that spring that I thought they would be a very interesting match because they had complementary interests and strengths. That, in fact, Gore was strong in almost all the areas where Clinton needed help—and vice versa. The big question was whether they could actually get along. They'd been natural rivals. They were presidential wannabes who had almost run against each other four years earlier. They had eyed each other ... about running in '92. Both young, competitive, from the same part of the country, which defied the convention of ticket-balancing.

Gore made the short list because he did have a lot of strengths that Clinton needed. I pleaded with the vetting committee that actually they'd be a good fit, that Gore was a Southern gentleman and a good soldier, and that they'd get along. When they met, they got along famously—much better than they'd expected. Roy Neel, who was Gore's chief of staff at the time, famously referred to them as two guys who had gone to college together but hadn't known each other in college, and met at their twenty-fifth reunion and decided to drive across the country with their wives—which is what happened. They went on the [post-convention] bus tours and became friends.

Frank Greer: We were filming for the convention film, and I was in Hope, Arkansas, standing with Clinton in the train station that says "Hope" on it.... [He] said, "What do you think about [the possibility of] Gore?" I made a twenty-minute argument against Gore. [*laughter*] ... "You're too close regionally, you need more geographic diversity on the ticket," all the things that turned out to be the assets. Age, "You're about the same age, you need somebody older, with more experience, who has more gravitas." Clinton said, "I really think it would work." I said, "Okay." Thank God he followed his own instincts.

Mickey Kantor, campaign chair: Clinton and I would discuss the idea of starting early, after the New York primary, putting the process together for selecting a vice president.... [We] had a list of sixty Democrats from all kinds of backgrounds who might be considered, including some people who would be quite unusual. We talked it through, we narrowed it down to, I think, about twenty-five, I can't remember now. We did an initial run and built a book of background on the twenty-five. Narrowed it down to about ten in another meeting. Narrowed it down to three.

He met with [these] three in Washington and other places, in secret.... [We] talked by phone two or three times at night with Hillary and the president and I think Bruce Lindsey must have been there. I don't know if George was there or not and that's when he said Al Gore was his choice and he called Gore in Carthage [Tennessee]. I've got to say that although [Warren] Christopher[3] and his team did the background work and we discussed it all, this was really [Clinton's] decision. Decisions like this are so personal to a president or presidential candidate that you don't—He knew where he wanted to go and he believed, more important in the age of the primacy of television, in the information age, that regional lines had been blurred and that all this balancing of tickets really didn't make any difference at all.... He was impressed by Gore's intellect, by his experience, by his commitments, by their similar views and by Gore's discipline and ability to work hard, focus. He also thought, and this was his thought, that two guys like them—new, fresh, young, vigorous—would be such a contrast to George Bush and Dan Quayle that it would make a huge difference.

If you'd asked me at the time I'd say, good choice, solid choice, I'm not sure it would make a lot of difference. It made a lot difference. I would have been wrong about that. If you remember the *Time* or *Newsweek* cover, the two of them walking out of the Governor's Mansion together, I mean, you could see it happen in the polls, as soon as they covered it. The American people took a preexisting notion, that George Bush wasn't connected, to the notion these two young guys were—that they were good-looking and vigorous, vital and vibrant, and this was exactly what the country needed.

Roy Neel, Gore chief of staff: [Before 1992] Al and Clinton had virtually no relationship. They knew each other from a distance, they were kind of would-be rivals or potential rivals at some point, but they had a kind of healthy respect for each other. They were not friendly and didn't have much of a relationship.... Then, of course, the summer of '91 [Gore] opted out of the [presidential] race. He decided that he wasn't going to run.... But sometime in May [1992], could

---

3. Christopher, a Los Angeles–based lawyer, was charged by Clinton with helping to locate and screen a feasible list of vice-presidential candidates. He later became Clinton's first secretary of state.

have been early June ..., Warren Christopher called Al and related to him that Clinton wanted Al to allow himself to be considered. Now what that means is, rather than say, "Would you consider running," it is allowing yourself to be considered. Because coming with that is a very intrusive process of vetting and review.

So Gore agreed that he would do so and ... that jump-started a process all through the late spring and early summer in which the Clinton campaign had a team of vetters poring over all of Gore's background.... It was my job to find those records, talk to Gore and others and get all the information they needed, and then go over it with them to make sure it was what they needed. This is everything from a high school transcript to bank records, all of your financial records, tax returns for as long as you're in public life. Just about every imaginable thing that was on record about you. At the same time they were looking at public records, news clips and that sort of thing.... And interviewing people, to ask them what they know about Gore, would there be any reason for him not to be on the ticket. Very extensive. Ten times more ambitious than a typical FBI background check. They were following up every conceivable rumor. I mean, suffice it to say that there was probably no one with a more blemish-free record, both public and private record, than Al Gore. He was certainly Dudley Do-Right, in fact to the point where some of their investigators just didn't believe it. It wasn't possible. But it held up.

[Once] that started, I believed, and a number of us believed, that while it was improbable that he would be chosen for all the obvious political reasons, or conventional political reasons, that it was a good idea. Clinton was still pretty far behind in the polls to Bush at the time but had come on a bit. The economy was still weakening and Clinton was getting his sea legs at that point. He had hit a stride.... What really made it look possible was the meeting that the two of them had in Washington in that process.... [They] had an extraordinary meeting. They were supposed to meet for an hour at the Capitol Hilton one night, starting at 10 o'clock, and they talked until one or two in the morning. Al came back from that meeting thinking that they had hit it off and that he thought that probably Clinton would choose him. ...

Q: Was there any anxiety within the Gore networks that joining the ticket was a risky thing to do?
Neel: Before he responded to Christopher as to whether he wanted to be considered, there was a good deal of debate. There were those who thought this would be suicidal, that Clinton was going to go down and take whatever vice-presidential nominee he had with him. This was at a time, right up until almost the convention, certainly up until the time he chose Gore, Clinton was not beloved within the Democratic Party, much less the electorate. You still had people just weeping because Mario Cuomo hadn't come into the race.

Clinton was not a choice that many Democrats were excited about. I mean, they were resigned to it. So there was a feeling that this would not be good for Al. Conventional wisdom was that the vice presidency itself—even if you win, what good is the vice presidency? No one other than George Bush had risen to the presidency in a hundred years or something like that. Still, it wasn't the best path to the presidency and clearly Al Gore wanted to be president and expected to run again some day.

He had a different perspective, in part because I think he instinctively knew that the vice presidency didn't have to be a dead end or just a guy waiting for something to happen to the president. . . . Al believed that Clinton had a vision for how he would govern with Al Gore that was very attractive to Al Gore. That he would be not an equal partner, but he would be a major player and not relegated to funerals and obscure commissions and miscellaneous things like that and raising money.

Q: Was there a research operation by the Gore people on Clinton? I mean, there's all of this stuff out there.
Neel: You don't grill the nominee and his people. You're in a subordinate position at that point. They had a very candid conversation for those three hours that night on what the problems would be in a campaign, what problems the two of them would have, how it would be perceived and so on and so forth. . . . Al may have talked to some people about these things. But he didn't have another conversation with Clinton and I didn't have any conversations with any Clinton people along those lines.

Neel (on the choice to invite Gore onto the ticket): Nobody was getting anything real, but Al just had a sense. It all came from that meeting they had in Washington. . . . The Gore farm sits up on a hill probably about a quarter of a mile down a road to the main road. At the bottom of the hill on the main road were dozens of TV trucks. At some point we decided to leave and go over to Al's parents' house, which was kind of across the road and across the river. This was really cool—they were all paying attention to everything we were doing.

At one point we have binoculars looking at the reporters and seeing that they had binoculars looking at us, because they had nothing better to do. They were sent out there by the networks and whatever, in case it was Gore. I'm sure the same thing was in place with these other candidates, with these other potential running mates. So it went on, late into the evening, and I think around 10:30 or so, the call came. Al went into the bedroom with Tipper and then they were talking for a while so it seemed like that was probably what it was going to be. But with Clinton you didn't know. I mean, he could have talked for a while and then said, "It's going to be [Lloyd] Bentsen" or someone, and then chatted for another ten minutes. But we didn't know. Al came out and said, "He asked me to join the ticket."

Al From, head of the DLC: I'll never forget when [Clinton] picked Gore. He called me and said, "The message is going to be 'the changing of the guard.'"

Bruce Reed: [What] really turned the campaign around was the decision to pick Gore as the vice president.

8

The Democratic National Convention and the Bus Tour

The positive results of the Manhattan Project and the addition of Al Gore to the ticket created a favorable dynamic for the Democratic National Convention, which ran from July 13 to 16, 1992. Prominently displayed at the convention was a short film on Clinton's life, The Man from Hope, *which was an effort to reshape the popular image of Clinton's biography in ways that would make voters more receptive to him as a candidate. The acceptance addresses by both the nominee and his running mate were well received, but what added a genuine sense of elation was the unexpected announcement by Ross Perot during the course of the convention that he was dropping his bid for the presidency. That left Clinton in a head-to-head contest with George H. W. Bush, a very different dynamic than had existed before.*

The Clinton team also devised an innovative way to kick off its general election efforts, taking advantage of what typically is downtime in coverage after the convention. Bill and Hillary Clinton were joined on buses by Al and Tipper Gore, making a pilgrimage through the heartland of America to see and be seen by the American voters.

William Galston, domestic policy advisor: Ron Brown,[1] bless his heart— although his heart was elsewhere, his heart of hearts—decided that the '92 convention was going to be a Clinton-Gore convention, period, full stop. And if you weren't with the program, you weren't on the program. So there weren't a lot of loose ends in 1992. It was orchestrated very efficiently and tightly.

Al From, head of the DLC: [It] was not surprising that [the convention platform] was the New Covenant—opportunity, responsibility, and community—and the

---

1. Ron Brown (1941–1996) was chair of the Democratic National Committee (1989–1993). An African American, he had helped to lead Jesse Jackson's 1988 campaign, and was generally considered to be to the left of Clinton politically. He later served as secretary of commerce under Clinton, and was killed in a plane crash while on a trade mission in southern Europe.

Third Way and all this stuff. [That] was an important thing for us, I think, because what had happened traditionally is the presidential candidates had given away the platform as the consolation prize to the losers. My thought about that was that if you couldn't run on your own platform, you're going to have a hell of a time running for president. I think there's a connection between not being able to run on your own platform and losing. I thought it was a pretty important deal.

Madeleine Albright, foreign policy advisor: At the '92 convention I was cochair of the platform committee that time with Bill Richardson.[2] We'd been in Santa Fe for [platform] meetings. Already there seemed to be something I was quite uncomfortable with, which [was Al From] from the DLC—[who] had worked for [Edmund] Muskie,[3] too [when I was there]. We had known each other for a very long time. There was a little bit of competition between the Center for National Policy[4] and the DLC. But I also found that all of a sudden the platform was going kind of antilabor to me. Some of the discussions that we had in Santa Fe, the DLC line, was a little too centrist for where I was [on domestic issues].

David Kusnet, speechwriter (on the development of the nomination acceptance address): I think something like two or three weeks at most before the convention we had a meeting in the Governor's Mansion in Little Rock. My recollection is a lot of Clinton meetings were sort of a floating thing. People came in, people came out. He dressed informally. Half of it is just banter. But obviously Bill Clinton is there, Hillary Clinton is there part of the time, Paul Begala, me, Carville may be drifting in and out. I think that might have been it, but for all I know I may be leaving out someone who played a major role and made a major contribution or something.

He [Clinton] starts talking about the acceptance speech. A lot of it is sort of banter about we have to have some joke about his nominating speech of Dukakis. We went through all kinds of jokes. "It wasn't my finest hour; it wasn't even my finest hour and a half." "The real reason I ran was so I could get to finish that speech I was giving four years ago." Just all kinds. "I would do anything to audition for the Johnny Carson show." It was every possible joke you could tell about his nominating speech.

---

2. Bill Richardson was a New Mexico politician who served in the U.S. House of Representatives from 1983 to 1997. Under Clinton, he was U.S. ambassador to the United Nations (1997–1998) and secretary of energy (1998–2001).

3. Edmund Muskie (1914–1996) was a U.S. senator representing Maine from 1959 to 1980. He served as secretary of state under Jimmy Carter in 1980–1981.

4. The Center for National Policy is a Washington-based think tank focused primarily on national security issues.

Then he went through what he liked about his stump speech [and] what he had to do differently.... Part of the strategic doctrine of the Clinton campaign at that time was that he was saying things that people agreed with, but the people didn't trust him both because of the character issues that had been raised against him and the widespread but inaccurate view that he came from a privileged background and hadn't been tested by tough times. There were some basic doubts about him as a person that he had to overcome. It wasn't so much the personal life at that time, but this misconception of him, that he was young, callow, untested, and overprivileged, and that the perceived slickness followed from that and that you had to do something to get people to see him differently so that they would listen to him.

A lot of what was done then—*The Man from Hope* video at the convention, the biographical stuff—was to overcome that. I was thinking on the plane, and then put it in longhand, how we could do that in the acceptance speech. I've always had the idea that a speech like that has to have an emotional rhythm to it. The structure is similar to a lot of sermons, where you start out on something of a high note, then you bring people down, and then you bring them up to a higher level than they started out on. There is something emotionally and perhaps spiritually cleansing and uplifting about the process of bringing people down from a kind of false happiness to understand the grim realities, to bring them up to a higher level. I was thinking, *How could Clinton do that?* . . .

I would . . . begin with just the basic case for a change, which was not a difficult one to make: unemployment, the economic crisis, the sense of drift after the victory in the Gulf War, the sense that if President Bush had a job to do he had already done it. Just make the easy case for him. Then people would naturally think he's going to keep going at the same emotional pitch—that would get a convention audience rocking and rolling. But instead, he would bring them down. What I did was just have him repeat something that actually happened to him in the New York primary. He would say, "I told this to an audience in the Lower East Side of Manhattan." The audience for the convention speech would expect Clinton to say, "And they said, 'Yes, we've got to change.' But in fact what really happened was a man got up and said, 'Well, you're just a politician. Why should I believe a word you're saying?' " So all of a sudden he would get the audience for the convention speech to wake up and listen carefully. This section of the convention speech would not be what the audience, in the convention hall and, more importantly, the national television audience, would expect a supposedly slick politician like Bill Clinton to be saying.

Then, after telling the story of the voter who asked why he should believe a word he's saying, Clinton would tell his personal story, which was very different from the privileged upbringing that many voters thought he had. Clinton introduced this section with these words—which also made it from the first draft on my legal pad on the plane to the spoken version—something like, "Let me tell you as clearly as I can who I am, what I believe, and what I want to do as president."

Then you get a whole bunch of stuff that isn't applause lines. At the end it comes back to being something emotional. But it goes through an emotional low point, a section of the speech that is both somewhat personal, philosophical, and has no applause lines. Then it gets back up again.

[Clinton's] way of editing a speech then and throughout my work with him was not to edit it, but to rehearse it, editing while rehearsing. He would get up at an improvised podium in the room where he was rehearsing/editing the speech and either read from the latest draft or extemporize. We'd have tape recorders and notepads. He would edit while speaking. His schedule would describe our meetings with the ambiguous title of "speech preparation." But the man didn't need to rehearse, it was editing by speaking. There was a lot of that. There was also just sending it around to all kinds of people inside and outside the campaign. So Bruce Reed and the DLC contingent had some input into it and a lot went in about the New Covenant, which was the formulation that Clinton had developed early in the campaign for linking opportunity and responsibility—a big part of the DLC approach. Sandy Berger and the foreign policy people had some input and we had a bit about foreign policy. Rodney Slater[5] and other longtime friends from Arkansas would have an input into it.

There was Roy Spence, a media consultant from Texas. . . . The great thing he contributed was that we had to incorporate *The Man from Hope* into the speech. "I still believe in a place called Hope" is probably the most quoted line from his acceptance speech. The line was especially effective because Clinton delivered his convention speech right after *The Man from Hope* film was shown. Together, the film and the speech showed and told the American people who Bill Clinton really is—someone who has overcome adversity in his own life and who understands hardworking Americans.

If a speech is "written by committee," it usually isn't that good. But I think this speech benefited by having so many people have input into it. It's not an elegant speech, but I think it served the purpose perfectly of telling Clinton's story, presenting his point of view, and making the critique of Bush. And the proof of its effectiveness is that it helped to take him from running third behind Bush and Perot before the convention to running first from after the convention through Election Day.

Frank Greer, media advisor: Of the convention, I mean, it was truly astounding that [Ross Perot would drop out] then. And our numbers just zoomed, just went up. From that point forward . . . our numbers were at 45-plus and they stayed. Greenberg will tell you, they were solid as a rock. Ross Perot got back in before

---

5. Rodney Slater held several appointed and political positions in Arkansas under Governor Clinton, and was subsequently secretary of transportation under President Clinton, the second African American to hold that position (1997–2001).

the first debate, but still we held that lead. . . . We had a really good message out of the convention. . . . [By] the end of the convention, I thought it was inevitable that we were going to win.

Leon Panetta, later White House chief of staff: I don't think I really thought [Clinton's election] was possible until he got on the bus with Gore and they began those bus trips and you began to see the public's reaction. When that happens, you know there's something magic in the air.

Mickey Kantor, campaign chair: Many people on the campaign fought this trip, saying you can't put two Southern guys on a bus, they're going to look like hayseeds. Mort Engleberg and Bev [Lindsey][6] to their credit stayed on my back, day after day, saying, *This will work, this will be great.* Frankly, they were such pains in the rear, I said, "Enough is enough, let's just do it." I've got to say, I did not see the power of this. People who say they saw the power of this are just not telling the truth, they're just not telling the truth.

Susan Thomases, scheduler: Gore started out by saying that he didn't want to do the bus trip. I said, "I don't care if you end up hating the bus trip. All I want you to do is leave the convention. We're going to start with the bus trip, and if you want to leave after stop number three, after we get to Pennsylvania, you can leave. It's a message we want to send about his accessibility and the kind of candidate he'll be, and I think it should be fun. You should end up liking it." And he did. He ended up loving it, but he would never own up to that.

Frank Greer: The bus trip became a phenomenon. I called the office and I talked to George [Stephanopoulos] and Eli [Segal], and I said, "We've got to film this." It was the best footage I ever had—I met the bus with my team and crew in Kentucky and went on with them through Illinois. We got to one place in southern Illinois. It was at night, because we were late—and we were always late because it was the Bill Clinton campaign. We were probably an hour-and-a-half late—and there were ten thousand people on this square, in a town that probably didn't have more than three thousand people. And we were filming. We had a cherry-picker, just because I wanted to get the whole sense of the crowd. All through the heartland you had all these people sitting out on the roadside in their folding chairs holding up signs for Clinton and Gore. It was phenomenal. It was really a turning point emotionally.

---

6. Mort Engleberg was a Hollywood movie producer who also did volunteer advance work for the 1992 Clinton campaign. He had played a similar role in the Mondale and Dukakis presidential campaigns. His film credits included *Smokey and the Bandit.* Bev Lindsey was Bruce Lindsey's wife, and worked for Governor Clinton and was an advisor in the 1992 campaign.

Bruce Reed, domestic policy advisor: [The bus tour] was an amazing experience. I deeply regretted that I didn't buy a video camera in New York City to film the whole thing. . . . We had a rough patch in the first half hour because we got through the tunnel into New Jersey and realized one of the people on our bus—there were five or six buses—was actually a stowaway. I think they were homeless and just climbed on the bus. We'd been talking to the person. We just thought it was a new campaign staffer. [*laughter*] So we had to pull over and the police had to come and take this person away. Delayed the bus tour for a little bit. Our first thought was, *This is going to be a very long trip.* . . .

It was a great chance for [the Clintons and Gores] to get to know each other, because no matter how you slice it, there was still a lot of time between stops. We'd go for fourteen and sixteen hours. A good half of that was road time, so they got to know each other and their wives got to know each other. Clinton really hit it off with Tipper, and Gore hit it off with Hillary. At every stop, all four of them would speak. They were having the time of their lives.

As I said, these bus trips were unbelievably exhausting. But Clinton was the opposite of everyone else. He was energized by the experience. He fed off the crowds. The more people he saw, the stronger he got and the more energized he got. At one point . . . we pulled into Erie, Pennsylvania, at 3:30 in the morning. There was a crowd of a few thousand waiting for us. Everybody on the trip was just dying to go to sleep. But there was a rope line, and Clinton decided to work the rope line, which had all of us groaning. The reason I remember it is that instead of just shaking hands, he was actually talking to the people he met. A young man asked him what was his plan to pay for college. Clinton gave a seven-minute answer at 3:30 in the morning to one voter in Pennsylvania, and would have gone on longer if the kid hadn't looked like he wanted to go to sleep. [*laughter*] . . . He loved the game, and was sorry every night when he had to go to bed.

9

The General Election Campaign—Clinton vs. George H. W. Bush

Those involved in the Clinton campaign indicate that they seldom feared, after the two political conventions in July, that they would not be successful. In part this was because their candidate was well positioned politically to reap the harvest of their past efforts, and partly because, by their thinking, their Republican opposition did not run an astute campaign. There was, as always, the opportunity for something unexpected to develop, which Ross Perot's return to the race confirmed. But the campaign avoided any serious errors, and Clinton's solid performance in the high-stakes presidential debates left the Bush campaign few opportunities to gain ground as Election Day approached.

Stanley Greenberg, pollster: Between the conventions, we did what was called the Teeter Project. Bob Teeter was the pollster for Bush. We did a whole research exercise, almost like a Manhattan Project, on "How do we lose?" In other words, let's role-play.... We play their campaign. We did our research on Clinton. We created ads for them against us and developed the response ads to those ads.

I think we would have won no matter what, but the key piece to this is not so much bio, it's about record.... When we tested attacks on his character we found that they weren't effective. However, we found that if you attacked his Arkansas record as being a bad record—raising taxes, failed governor—that that was much more effective. More importantly, the sequence was critical. Given how much people had heard and how sick they were of this [other] stuff, if you started with Arkansas and then went back to draft and character at the end, that could be effective. We developed response ads to that. [The Bush campaign] did the opposite, a fundamental mistake.

Al From, head of the DLC: [A] critical juncture, for me anyway, was right after the convention when Bush accused Clinton of raising taxes in Arkansas 128 times. The campaign responded by saying, *No, it was only 65*, or whatever the hell it was. So I called Clinton. . . . I said to them that the campaign—in the effort to not repeat the mistakes of the Dukakis campaign—had learned only part of the lesson. The lesson they should have learned was that you can't let your opponent set the context of the debate. What they learned was that you've got to answer your opponent. That was probably right, but not always right. . . . So I said, "Next time he says you raised taxes in Arkansas 128 times, you respond this way: 'I don't know what he's talking about. I'm for capital punishment; I'm for ending welfare as we know it; I'm for asking kids who get college scholarships to serve their country; I'm a different kind of Democrat.'"

Sandy Berger, foreign policy advisor: You hope in a campaign to not make too many promises that you have to swallow when you're president. . . . The one that really surprised me was gays in the military. . . . He made this commitment that he would allow gays in the military in New York, and it always made me very nervous, not on the merits but on the politics. . . .

Q: Was this then not a case where the position had been fully vetted and a conscious decision taken? Was it a case where the candidate got ahead of the staff?
Berger: First of all, Clinton never exists in a box where there are four people and those four people are the people who brief him and the decision gets made in that little box. He is on the phone with people, he's talking with people. He's forming his opinions. He sees you and talks to you and he asks you what you think, or you say to him, "Really it's outrageous that other armies, the Israeli army has allowed homosexuals and we don't." He formulates his opinion from not just the people who are formally tasked with that, but from his own larger contacts. I don't know where this came from. This hadn't been something discussed before in my presence.

Q. Were there, conversely, areas that you look back on where you feel you did an especially good job of being proactive?
Berger: There are a couple of them. I think on Bosnia, Clinton was heavily influenced by Gore, who was very hawkish about the fact that we needed to be more interventionist with respect to Bosnia. . . . I was [also] very pleased that we'd beat them to the punch on Russia. . . . It was Clinton who outlined how there could be a new U.S.–Russia relationship and aid to Russia. We were at that point trying to save this new Russian democracy, which was still very much under siege from the left and the right. I think those are two areas where we outflanked Bush.

David Kusnet, speechwriter: There was also a speech about NAFTA, which I think ended up being written by Clinton himself. I was against NAFTA. Most people on the campaign had very defined views for or against NAFTA, like that county in West Virginia with the song, "There are no neutrals here."[1] I think the only person in the whole campaign who had a nuanced view of NAFTA was Bill Clinton himself. I think everyone else—pretty much the populists were against it, the DLC people were for it, the corporate people were for it. He was for it but understood all the arguments against it. There were no neutrals, but the candidate took a complex view. There was just no one who could have written a NAFTA speech for Bill Clinton but Bill Clinton.

Sandy Berger: I can't remember what was the action forcing the event, but we basically had to come to grips with where [Clinton] was going to be on NAFTA. We had a meeting in Rosslyn, Virginia. All the political people were there, Carville and Begala and Stephanopoulos and the vice president was there and there probably were twenty people in the room.

All the political people said, "If you come out for NAFTA you're going to lose the election because you will give Perot, . . . [who] sounded like he was coming back in the race, . . . precisely what he wants, which is the wedge issue between you and Democrats." Around that table, the only people who were contrary to that were Gore and myself and ultimately Stan Greenberg, very interestingly and prob- ably decisively. . . . Greenberg said to Clinton, "I think the polling on this shows this being a negative by X, but I think it would be so contrary to your worldview and the way people understand you're talking about the global economy, that the disconnect between your position on NAFTA and your larger position would cause a separate issue of credibility, and therefore I think you should be for it."

I think Clinton had, and still does to this day, an understanding of global- ization that is more sophisticated than most, and I don't know that there ever was, in his mind, too much doubt. I think that he believes—and he was able to articulate this much better in the second term than in the first term—that there is a struggle between the forces of integration and the forces of disintegration. Trade, he believes, is a force of integration and liberalization. It would have been a really discordant note for him to suddenly say, *But not NAFTA*. So the vote was probably fourteen to four for him coming out against, but he did anyhow. I think that was one of the braver things he did in the campaign.

Roy Neel, Gore chief of staff: We knew in the campaign, the '92 campaign, that Gore's book *Earth in the Balance*[2] would be controversial and would give some ammunition to the Republicans that would take a lot of what he said and try to scare the business community, auto workers, as well as all kinds of folks, with either what he said or how they would characterize what he said. So we scoured

---

1. The song is an old miners anthem entitled "Which Side Are You On?"
2. Al Gore, *Earth in the Balance: Ecology and the Human Spirit* (Boston: Houghton Mifflin, 1992). This book was Gore's effort to grapple with environmental issues and their deeper moral and political implications.

the book. We asked a guy that we knew, a friend of our campaign that was involved on the periphery of our campaign, a guy by the name of Jonathan Sallet, to organize a team of smart people to take that book and break it down and to annotate and highlight everything in that book that could be used against Gore in the '92 vice-presidential campaign.

Well, Jonathan did a great job with this. In fact, it was so good, he put these things together in terms of challenges: here are the worst things that can be said about *Earth in the Balance*, and enumerated them.... He then took the list, or the collection, and faxed it back to the ten guys who were supposed to look at this one more time before it came to us in Little Rock and on the plane. One of the guys who was supposed to get the fax, his fax number was 224-7682. Someone in Jonathan's office, or Jonathan, mistakenly faxed it to 224-7683. In other words, miss-hit one digit. Who does that fax belong to but Richard Armey, at that time Republican congressman from Texas. Well Armey's staff, they pull this off the fax and it says, "From Jonathan Sallet, Gore campaign." They think it's a hoax. They don't believe it, that they've been set up somehow. Why is this being faxed to them? They don't believe it. But they give it to a *Wall Street Journal* reporter, who then doubles back and follows up and does the research and finds out in fact what it was.

The *Wall Street Journal* reporter on the campaign confronts [Press Secretary] Marla [Romash], who is on the plane with Gore. Marla freaks out, calls me, "What happened?" Calls Jonathan, we sort of figure out what happened. Then Gore finally says, "What is going on here?" I mean, he knows there's some crisis brewing and Marla has to tell him. He doesn't call Jonathan, he calls me. And for twenty minutes gives me hell. I mean, I don't need to repeat it all; it's still emblazoned on my mind. At that point I think, *God, we've blown the whole campaign.* Because the *Wall Street Journal* then uses it to ridicule the book, the campaign, everybody. It just makes everybody look absolutely idiotic and totally incompetent.

It was clearly the low point in the campaign. I can't remember when it happened. It was probably late September or something like that. I thought we had just by our sheer stupidity blown this campaign somehow.... Of course it blew over very quickly and was not really much of an issue, but it seemed to be a catastrophic event at the time, all because of a misdialing of a fax number one digit.

Nancy Soderberg, foreign policy advisor: It's crazy on a campaign plane, because FAA [Federal Aviation Administration] rules go out the window. People are sliding down the aisles on trays as you take off. I forget what they called it—skiing or something. They're playing cards, running around. Nobody wears their seat belts. You get to feel the crowds.

I can still remember the moment I felt Bill Clinton might actually win. It was in mid-August. We were on the back roads, the really back roads of Texas. It was about 120 degrees out. We were, of course, late—like four hours late. These people had been out there for hours waiting for us. They had signs, "Give us four minutes, and we'll give you four years." Whole families were out there. Then we'd go to these rallies, and increasingly they were—I'd been to a lot of campaign events, but this was just different. All of a sudden, we could feel that these people saw in Clinton somebody different. That's when I finally said, "Uh-oh, he might actually win this." You could just feel it. It never stopped.

Bruce Reed, domestic policy advisor (on the presidential debates): We had a big team of people that prepped him for the various debates. Debating was not his strong suit. In the primaries, he was good on his feet and knew his arguments cold. But in the primaries, he had lost his temper a few times. He came close to punching Jerry Brown in the New York debate when Brown attacked Hillary for being on the Wal-Mart board, something like that. Anyway, he did not blow away the field in the primary debates, so he wanted to practice quite a bit. . . . It was a pretty disciplined exercise. He watched some tapes of himself, which was not something he ordinarily did. He had an unusually good sense of how others perceived him. . . . It was just methodical. There were no great surprises, no epiphanies, just grinding it out. That's the way that he was in all the debate preparation I ever saw him in. He was always terrible the first time and he knew it. . . . It was just disciplined practice for him, and he got better each time.

Sandy Berger (on preparation for the presidential debates): It was one of the most fun things. . . . Fun in retrospect; it probably wasn't so much fun going through it. There were three debates in '92. In each case we found a location that was remote—in upstate New York, in Kansas City, and one other location. The debate team went up there and we basically would spend three days blocked out from everything else. The candidate might go out at 9 o'clock in the morning and do a little photo op event someplace and then come back by 10 o'clock. But it was totally focused on the debate.

Clinton was a good debater and very confident. Our first job was to shake his confidence. In '92, Bob Barnett served as Bush [in the campaign's practice debates]. This is Bob's avocation. He's a very well known, prominent, Washington lawyer. He represents half the world. But he keeps books on each potential candidate during the four years because he's done this now several times. So it's not just that he goes away for the weekend and does this LexisNexis. He's been thinking about this, how is he going to be George Bush and how is he going to attack Bill Clinton or Bob Kerrey or Michael Dukakis or whoever the candidate was.

The first job was to get Clinton to really focus. . . . The afternoon of the first day we said we'd take a little break and come down here at 7 o'clock and do a ninety-minute debate. We'll just do a run through debate without any preparation. Clinton was very confident. He went to his room and came down at 7 o'clock. Bob ate his lunch. He had thought about everything that Clinton was going to say. He destroyed it. He had every attack line against Clinton, which Clinton really hadn't thought through. You play how you practice. Clinton really came away from that first evening, in my judgment, somewhat sobered that he could be beaten in a debate by George Bush. Suddenly he got very focused.

Stanley Greenberg: Clinton was not that great a debater. You know, we think—I mean, if you reflect back to the primaries, we were not winning the debates. He was not that strong in the debates. He was much better as someone giving a speech, but he was not that strong in debates. We did not emerge and win in the primaries because of the debates. If you take the first debate, it was Perot who clearly won the first debate. We won the second because of the town hall format. And then the third debate was mixed. But it was not obvious that he was the strongest person on the field there in debating. Debating is a difficult thing. The skills you develop as a governor, or skills you develop as a public speaker, are just not necessarily [the same as a good debater's].

Mickey Kantor, campaign chair: The first debate, if you remember, Ross Perot stole the show. Ross, interesting personality, he didn't do a walk-through like everybody else did. He didn't have a lot of staff. This is the God's honest truth. It's about thirty minutes before the debate and Clinton is being made up by a makeup person, and a few of us are sitting there, talking to him. [*knock knock*] "Clinton in there?" [*laughter*] It's Ross Perot, and I go to the door and I say, "Ross, you know he's getting made up." He says, "Mickey, could I talk to you?" "Sure." He said, "How do I walk in here?" Absolute God's honest truth.

I said, "Well, Ross, haven't they told you?" He said, "No, no one's told me anything." So I walked him through it, told him how he walked in, what he did. He absolutely was walking as loose as he appeared to be. This to him was just another show, just another thing. I think that President Bush and then-Governor Clinton were probably too uptight, too tense, this was so important to them. . . .

Well, we realized after the first debate that Perot was a factor, number one. Number two, our key was going to be the people's debate, which was the second debate in Richmond. Went to Williamsburg to prepare and he then did an amazing job, which he was prepared to do, including walking up to that woman after Bush couldn't answer the question and answering the Bush's question in a way that just was the metaphor for the entire campaign. And then of course the picture of Bush in the back, looking at his watch. That was the end of that campaign for all intents and purposes.

Congressman Mike Espy (D-MS): I remember [the debate] where he stood up from the table and began to approach the black woman who had asked a question. I said, "That's the guy I know." This guy was taking control. You have

President Bush looking at his watch. *He* [Clinton] is empathizing with the questioner. He's getting close to her, but respecting her zone of privacy.

Black people's zone of privacy is very important; you can't break it. He knows that. So many white politicians I've seen think the closer they get the more serious they are, and it's not true. It's actually the opposite. It's respect; it's a sign of respect when you don't break the zone of privacy. I don't think very many white politicians know that. You have to get close enough to be sincere, but far enough away to demonstrate your respect. He understands that.

Mickey Kantor: When he walked up to the woman, we were sitting in the green room—Stephanopoulos, Carville, myself—we were all up and cheering. We knew as soon as he started toward it, this was it, he was prepared for it, he knew what he wanted to do. We insisted on the remote mikes. Harry Thomason and Heidi,[3] my wife, insisted, because they knew if Clinton could move around, indicate his comfort with people, it so contrasted with Perot and Bush that it would make a difference. And they were absolutely right.

Frank Greer, media advisor: In Williamsburg for the town hall debate, we not only mapped out the set for the debate but we had chairs that were just the right height for Clinton that we practiced on. Then we heard that they were trying to find high stools, for the debate. I called up and I said, "You know, we've got some. If you'd like to use them, we'll let you use them." So Clinton had the benefit of having a chair exactly the right height for him and Bush did not. We heard that they needed them and we sent them in. It was the chair that Clinton had been practicing on in Williamsburg. It was terrific. So that was one of the reasons Clinton was so comfortable and Bush was not. . . . It's one of those little footnotes in history where you end up with a godsend.

Roy Neel: There was a little issue when during the vice-presidential debate, there were some in the Clinton camp who believed that Gore was not aggressive enough in defending Clinton's character. I was told later by Clinton, who [*sic*] I have no reason to doubt, he had no reason to say this to me, that that was not his view. He was never the least bit concerned that Al didn't go out of his way. He said, "It would have looked contrived and false to do that and programmed." He thought Al did fine. But some of Clinton's people thought Al was not aggressive enough in defending or being an advocate for Clinton's character as [Vice President Dan] Quayle was trying to go after.

Quayle was trying to turn the debate into a Quayle-Clinton debate, which looked a little weird too. Still, it stung a little because we had been trying, and certainly Gore was, to bend over backwards being soldiers for Clinton. We

---

3. Heidi Schulman was a broadcast journalist who had been an NBC News correspondent.

wouldn't have been there if it hadn't been for Clinton. We looked at the debate afterwards and we could understand why they thought that. It may have been Hillary who had this idea and that kind of spun out. It sort of makes sense that that might have been the case. . . .

We believe, the Gore crowd believe, that we were central to Clinton's pulling ahead in the polls and winning. I know it is a fairly egocentric analysis. We were convinced that Clinton would not have won without Gore. Many of the ideas in that campaign were at least advanced and made even stronger by Gore's contribution. The bus trips—they were going to end the bus trip after the convention and that was going to be it. Gore convinced Clinton to keep doing the bus trips all around the country, much against the advice of Clinton's staff.

Eli Segal, campaign chief of staff: The reason I knew the campaign was over . . . this must have been in August—each day I got a phone call, direct and indirect, from a prominent Republican leader, announcing that they wanted me to know that they were going to make a six-figure gift, which was still legal at the time, to the Democratic National Committee. The call was always from somebody to let it be known to whomever was the highest-up person in the Clinton campaign that the campaign was over. . . . One a day, it was like clockwork.

Sandy Berger: I remember watching [Clinton] Sunday before Tuesday of the election. He was on the phone with Stan Greenberg, our pollster. Stan was going through the overnight polling data. I saw Clinton exhale [in relief]. What happened was [Ross] Perot got back in the race [earlier], and it became a three-way race. Perot was gaining some ground on NAFTA and driving a wedge between us and Democrats on NAFTA, and for a while we were falling. It [finally] stabilized and started going back up again.

[On election night] I remember Clinton coming out on the stage, finally, after the crowd had built to thousands, and he looked different. There's something about stepping into a role. I don't know whether that's in the eyes of the beholder or whether that's in the actions of the principal, or if that's some combination of both. He seemed to stand up straighter, to be grander. Again, that may simply be, *My God, I'm now looking at the next president.* Or it may be his own sense that, *My God, I am now the president and I have to stand before the American people as the president-elect,* or some combination thereof.

Frank Greer: I was astounded [that the Republicans] ran such a bad campaign. I mean, I think we ran a pretty good campaign, and we made a lot of the right decisions, and we had a terrific candidate. Clinton was great as a candidate; Gore was a good candidate. What we really benefited from was the disarray of the other side. I never thought they had a strategy, didn't seem like they could make decisions quickly. They never had a consistent negative attack line on us. They never raised the issue of foreign policy. . . . They never really got on the offense. It was a campaign in some disarray. . . . I think we were blessed not to have [Roger] Ailes and company and Lee Atwater back in there.[4] It would have been a much, much tougher campaign.

Bruce Reed: There was a myth that emerged in the '80s, and to some extent in the '90s, that handlers were the most important thing, that they make [successful] campaigns. My view is somewhat different. I think there are good strategists and bad strategists, good handlers and bad handlers. But the job of a campaign is to execute the strategy of the candidate. Our campaign was—not in the primaries, not in the general—not anywhere near as good as the mythology around it. We had capable people, but the reason it was a successful campaign is that it didn't make mistakes and we didn't screw up. And we had a candidate who knew what he wanted to do as president, knew what he wanted to say, had his finger on the pulse and had a bond with the electorate that allowed him to hit perfect pitch.

Stanley Greenberg: We wouldn't have been in this election, we'd have been gone, if not for Hillary Clinton. Hillary Clinton was a strength. She's also a strong figure—a strong figure in her own right, a strong figure in the campaign, [and] a strong figure with the governor. . . . And she was what she was, so you don't sit there wondering, *Should we do something differently with her?*

---

4. Roger Ailes is chairman and chief executive officer of Fox News, and served as a media advisor for Presidents Nixon, Reagan, and George H. W. Bush. Lee Atwater (1951-1991) was a political consultant who directed the first President Bush's successful 1988 campaign. Both were known for their sharp elbows and unapologetic practice of political hardball. Atwater died of brain cancer in 1991, and his absence is often cited by Republicans and Democrats alike as a major factor in Bush's poor reelection showing.

10

The View from the Other Side

Not surprisingly, those working in 1992 to re-elect Republican incumbent George H. W. Bush recall that campaign differently than their successful Democratic opposition. Most members of the Bush team express grudging admiration for Clinton's political skill, but bewilderment that his personal foibles did not sink his candidacy. Many also reflect on the difficult fundamentals Bush confronted in trying to win a fourth consecutive term for the Republicans.[1]

John Sununu, Republican White House chief of staff: Let me just tell you. In June of '91, or May of '91, I convened a political meeting in the White House. The last thing we did is everybody went around the table and said whom they thought was going to get the nomination on the Democratic side and everybody was saying Cuomo, and I said Clinton. And they said, "Who is Clinton?" And I said, "If Cuomo runs in the primary against Bill Clinton, Bill Clinton will eat his lunch." . . . [Anyway], we had three or four meetings, I kept sticking to my Clinton predictions and they kept sticking with their Cuomo. That's how out of touch they were with the real threat that was there. None of them ever thought that Clinton would be a real threat. Remember, they were thrilled that [Clinton] was getting the nomination when he finally got it.

William Barr, attorney general: My own view was that the president [Bush] probably felt that when push comes to shove, he couldn't imagine that the American people would elect someone like Bill Clinton, a draft dodger, a huckster. That the American people would elect someone like that as president of the United States? I don't think he believed that could happen. Over me? Who has a record of service to the country, and the handling of Desert Storm [liberating Kuwait] and so forth? So I think he had a hard time coming to the realization

---

1. The interviews quoted in this chapter were undertaken as part of the George H. W. Bush Oral History Project, which can be found on the website of the Miller Center at http://millercenter.org/president/bush/oralhistory.

that it was potentially there. This is may be my own projection; I never heard him say anything about this. But it was certainly my own attitude: *Well, if the American people are going to do that, then let 'em do it. If that's what the American people ... want, I'm not going to debase myself. I've performed. I've done what I'm going to do. And if you want somebody else, be my guest if that's what it comes to.*

Dan Quayle, vice president: I think in his heart of hearts [President Bush] just viewed Clinton as so inferior that somehow, by golly, he was going to pull this thing out. He didn't really believe the polls. But he didn't realize what was going on, ... which was how disloyal that campaign staff really was. I mean, they were more interested in what their jobs were going to be after the election than they were in getting him re-elected.

One of my friends drove by the Democratic headquarters, or the Clinton headquarters, in Washington at six o'clock and there were just tons of cars there, people inside working. He went by the Bush headquarters and nobody was there. It was shut down, everybody gone. No problem. Nothing to do. This guy called me up and said, "You guys are in real trouble."

John Sununu: Bill Clinton may not have known, automatically, that economic carping was the route to victory, but he came to it pretty quickly. . . . If that [issue] hadn't worked, he would have jumped on environmental dissatisfaction or too much money for the war effort. He would have tested fifteen messages and he would have had the ear to pick up on what the right message was. You know, these things don't happen by some brilliant *a priori* analysis. There is an experiment in politics and Bill is a great experimenter. And he will experiment maybe first on three people in the White House or three people in the state house, and then he'll go down and have breakfast at Wendy's or at Honey Dip Donut, or whatever it is, and he'll try it there. Give the guy credit, he's a master, and he would have done that. President Bush trusted other people to do it.

Richard Thornburgh, attorney general: Clinton ran a good campaign. He had the same rogues that had run the campaign against me.[2] I knew what they were up to and they succeeded in keeping the president off-guard. Shouldn't have won, but they were masterful in the way that they ran their effort. And Clinton is—nobody will deny—is a superior politician. Just as good as they come. In his ability to reach out to voters and connect with them. . . .

I'll go back to my uneasy feeling at the time of the end of the Gulf War. If only the president had had the horses to frame a domestic policy, a six-point, eight-point, ten-point, twelve-point, whatever, domestic policy that he'd laid out just

---

2. The "rogues" were James Carville and Paul Begala, who ran Harris Wofford's successful campaign against Thornburgh in 1991.

after the celebration of the Gulf War victory in that speech to Congress. It's not hard to come up with what those points would have been. It doesn't matter whether or not they passed the Congress, because he faced a bigger majority of the opposition in the Congress than any president in recent history. It wasn't going to pass, but it would give him a Trumanesque-type finger to point at a do-nothing Congress.[3]

James A. Baker III, secretary of state: I'll tell you why we lost in '92.... And I'd like you to argue with this, if you will, because I'd like to know if you think there was any other. We lost, number one, because we'd been there for twelve years, and change is the only constant in politics. If you can't show that you're an agent for change, you start out way behind. And the press were tired of us. Washington was tired of us. We'd been there in power for twelve years.

Secondly, we had Ross Perot taking two out of every three votes from us, and there's no doubt about that. Don't believe that baloney that he puts out that he didn't take from us any more than he took from the Democrats. He took, our polling showed it consistently, two out of every three [votes from Bush]. He got 19 percent; we got 38 percent. Take two-thirds of 19 percent, and we got 51 percent.

But another major reason, which was our fault—those [first] two were not our fault—well, and I didn't mention the economy, which was not really our fault either, I don't think. So we have four reasons. So three of them were not really our fault. I would argue that the economy was not our fault, that it was the fault of the savings-and-loan debacle which put us into a one-year recession. The fourth reason *was* our fault, and that is we did not go up to Capitol Hill in January of '92 when George Bush was enjoying a 90 percent approval rating, and propose a domestic economic program around which we could build a campaign. Call it Domestic Storm, OK? I've taken care of Saddam Hussein and Desert Storm. I'm going to turn my attention now to the domestic problems facing this country. ... We didn't have [a program]. And that's our fault.

James Pinkerton, deputy assistant to the president for policy planning: I always say the three reasons Bush lost in '92 were: one, end of the Cold War, just took away the national security rationale.... The second thing was [reneging on] the tax pledge.... But the third thing is, the dry rot. And I wouldn't call it exhaustion, I would call it dry rot. I would say that ... if you're in power, you play your best cards, you play your kings and your aces first, and then you play your eights and nines and then you play your twos and threes. And we were down to twos and threes. [By 1992] we lacked the capacity to identify ... new fresh ideas that would put juice back.

---

3. Harry Truman successfully ran for re-election, in a difficult political environment in 1948, by attacking a "Do-nothing Republican Congress" for thwarting his legislative agenda.

Sig Rogich, media advisor: On the Gulf War and foreign visits, I'll tell you something we did. We arranged for film crews to film every aspect of our trips without any fanfare. In Moscow, in the Ukraine, in Czechoslovakia, in Turkey, in South America, on our visits to Venezuela, to Uruguay, to Argentina, Mexico, Japan, Australia, Korea, all that footage was assembled, all the pictures of the president actively working with world leaders, and we didn't use any of it. We didn't produce one foreign policy commercial. . . . Why? Because the polls didn't reflect that [the American people were interested in foreign policy].

David Demarest, White House communications director: [Pollster Robert] Teeter is the campaign manager of the '92 [Bush] campaign and he's complaining that the speechwriters aren't producing ringing speeches. [White House chief of staff Samuel K.] Skinner is now reflecting that to me. It's like every speech that we do, [President Bush] didn't get enough applause, he didn't get enough adulation. There wasn't a standing ovation or whatever. I was getting really tired of it.

We did a speech to the Southern Republican leadership group. I wrote it myself because I was tired of them hitting my speechwriters. The speech got, I don't know, twenty-seven applause lines and I got this, "Yes, it was okay." *What do you guys want?* So we agreed that Teeter would meet with my speechwriters. In June we finally got this on the schedule, June of '92. Teeter comes in. He starts talking to us about this message architecture and he passes out—which I still have, actually—he passes out a sheet of paper that has a pyramid of boxes with domestic policy, foreign policy, and so forth, and it all rolls up to a box called theme.

He is explaining all the different boxes, and we're navigating this thing as it gets up to theme, and when it gets to theme he says, "That's where we need your help." All of us just about dropped our jaws. He then got called out to a meeting and left us there and never came back. We were so angry, because the *campaign has no theme* and all the while we had been castigated for not articulating the theme.

Chase Untermeyer, White House personnel director: Lee [Atwater] died in 1991. I contend that had he lived that he would have been of immense help to President Bush in figuring out what to do about the three gents who bedeviled George Bush in 1992, namely Pat Buchanan,[4] Ross Perot, and Bill Clinton. Each of those came from an element of American political society Lee Atwater knew very well, certainly knew far better than George Bush and the rest of us. I have

---

4. Pat Buchanan was a Republican publicist and conservative journalist who challenged President Bush for his party's nomination in 1992. He drew 38 percent of the primary vote in New Hampshire, indicating significant Republican discontent with the incumbent at the outset of the campaign.

no idea what counterstrategies Lee would have recommended, but he would have had [them].

David Demarest: [When] Clinton was asked about the national debt by an African–American woman [in the town hall debate], she said, "How has the national debt affected you personally?" What she meant to say was, "How bad is the economy?" Bush . . . was so much of a literalist, he kept trying to figure out what it was she was getting at, and then he didn't give a very good answer. Then Clinton walks right up to her and he talks about all the people that he knows personally in Arkansas who lost their jobs and their factories and he's talking to her like she's the only person in the universe. It was just such a contrast. It was great. He was incredibly compelling.

Clinton also had gone to that site before, and he had talked to his media people. He knew where the camera shoots were and he knew when they'd be doing an over-the-shoulder cut. He was into that sort of stuff. Bush hated that. He no more would have done that than fly to the moon.

James Pinkerton: This campaign is full of twenty-one-year-olds, the '92 campaign now, who didn't get a good break out of this. When I was twenty-one I got to work in the Reagan campaign and no thanks to me whatsoever, Reagan had a big victory and I got to be in the White House and all this cool stuff. So I sort of felt bad for these kids. . . . The Bush campaign headquarters was across the street from the *Washington Post* . . . and there is a place around the corner, the Post Pub. So I said, "Look, anybody who wants to talk about the campaign and what happened"—this was like Wednesday night after the election, we'd lost.

I just got up [at the Pub] and said "Listen, you know, all of you tried hard and that kind of stuff. The fact that Bush, the incumbent president with a 90 percent approval rating, managed to lose to a draft-dodging, pot-smoking, womanizing, whatever, says something about—." [A] *Washington Post* business reporter . . . show[ed] up at this meeting. . . . [The] next morning in the paper there I am saying, "George Bush lost to a draft-dodging, womanizing sleazeball." So I managed to take down both Bush and Clinton in the same sentence.

11

The Transition
to Governing

*Having secured the White House for the Democratic Party for the first time in twelve
years, Bill Clinton was confronted with one of the most daunting—if recurring—
challenges in American politics: setting up a government to be fully operational in
an interval of less than three months, relying on people who are exhausted from the
marathon of a presidential election. Cognizant of the magnitude of this challenge,
Clinton had, even before the election, quietly dispatched a small group of advisors
to begin working on the transition. But among those laboring in the campaign there
was considerable anxiety over why others were making decisions about what a Clinton
administration would look like while they, the campaign staff, were actually on the
front lines. Clinton responded to those anxieties by effectively ignoring the work of the
planning group once the election was won. The subsequent in-fighting over positions
and influence led James Carville to observe that "a campaign is about screwing your
enemies, and a transition is about screwing your friends."*[1]

*During the formal transition period the president busied himself finding a Cabinet
that "looked like America" and hosting an economic summit in Little Rock. But
errors made during this interval created headwinds for the president once he got to
Washington. Perhaps foremost among these was a decision to defer selection of his
White House staff until very late in the transition, leading to enduring confusion
about how the team would work. These interviews show that, contrary to the conventional perception, Clinton approached his longtime friend Mack McLarty almost immediately after the election to ask him to be White House chief of staff, but McLarty's
reluctance to accept the top job—described in his own oral history—had the effect of
putting everything else on hold, with lingering consequences.*

Roy Neel, Gore chief of staff: [The presidential transition] is an almost unique
management challenge in American society.... I can't think of anything close

---

1. A slightly earthier version of this widely circulated quote appears in Hunter S. Thompson,
Better than Sex: Confessions of a Political Junkie (New York: Random House, 1994), 183.

to this, where you have to sort of create a new business overnight and make it successful from day one. You don't have a glide path. You're under the gun. Everything you do is noticed and it has great consequences. There's no management challenge even close to this in American society in my limited observation.

Chris Jennings, health policy advisor: I guess I should say that if anybody ever has the opportunity to do a transition, you should just not do it. [*laughter*] It is the absolute worst experience in anyone's life. I was under the illusion that we were working twenty-four hours a day to develop policy, but I think most people in the transition were just trying to position themselves for subsequent jobs in the Clinton administration. It was a lot of hard work, and in many ways it was much ado about nothing.

Bernard Nussbaum, White House counsel: To envision what it was like, imagine entering your law firm one day in November and being told that by mid-January, everybody would be gone. Every partner, every associate, every paralegal, every secretary, every messenger, every meaningful file, would be gone. But you had to see to it that the firm would [remain] fully operational, that it would be prepared to hear crises on a daily basis, with an entirely new team of professionals and staff.... The cases are there, the telephone is ringing all the time, there's crisis after crisis, and you have to deal with that.

Bruce Reed, deputy domestic policy advisor:[2] I imagine that most campaign workers feel the same anxiety the moment that their candidate wins, in realizing that now you have to share this thing that you helped build with everybody else: with a whole party full of people who either weren't helpful, were actively unhelpful, didn't root for your guy, or opposed what you were trying to do. And now they were in as good a position to get an influential role in the administration as you were, even though you'd given up your life for a couple of years and you actually believed in the guy you just elected. It's difficult and important for a White House to figure out how to integrate the rest of the world that it's going to have to live with and make sure that people from the campaign are in a position to fight for the promises that they helped make.

* * *

2. This excerpt is taken from Bruce Reed's commentary at a group oral history session of domestic policy advisors convened in June 2009, representing every administration from Nixon to George W. Bush. A published version of that event appears in Michael Nelson and Russell L. Riley, eds., *Governing at Home: The White House and Domestic Policymaking* (Lawrence: University Press of Kansas, 2011), 61.

Q: Maybe we could talk a bit about the formal transition period after the election, in particular what your roles and responsibilities were? You said the next day it's a different universe.

Roy Neel: Well, yes, it was. In one respect it's a warm glow because you've won. Now you're going to take office, you're now going to get to do what you've been wanting to do for two years. But almost overnight problems arose.

There was an internal coup.... After the convention, Mickey Kantor came to Little Rock as chairman, ostensibly to bring some order to the campaign.... The Clintons asked him to come.... On the face of it, it was a pretty good idea but it didn't really work.... One of Mickey's responsibilities from the Clintons was to set up a transition operation. The Clintons had been told that you have to start doing this before the election. Traditionally, or at least going back to [Richard] Neustadt[3] with [John F.] Kennedy, you started doing some of this planning even before the election. Usually the candidates don't like to do that. They're loath to do it for reasons of superstition—

Q: Tempting the gods?

Neel: Yes, superstition or whatever. And you don't want to take resources away from the campaign and you don't want to create anxiety within the campaign staff that some group is deciding your future, which office you're going to sit in, whatever.... Anyway, they set up an office in Little Rock to begin pre-election campaign planning. They came to Washington and did some meetings. They were doing the boilerplate stuff, the stuff you have to do. Collecting information, finding what the laws are, all this stuff that anybody responsibly doing pre-election campaign planning would have to do. Interviewing various people and so on. Stopping short of names, of anything that would be radioactive.

Well, the problem was that the senior campaign staff was never made comfortable with that.... Mickey had an operation going that they knew nothing about. While they were trying to get Bill Clinton elected, Mickey Kantor was running an operation to decide who was going to do what after the election. Well, that wasn't what was happening. Mickey didn't handle the internal politics of that very well at all. There were ways that it could have been done better. But Mickey could appear abrasive. Mickey and I got along great; I got along great with everybody because I was not a threat to anyone. Everybody knew what my role was, I was going to be the vice president's chief of staff after the election if he won. There were no issues there, so it was easy for me. I can see why

---

3. Richard E. Neustadt (1919–2003), a Harvard political scientist, was the preeminent student of the presidency of his generation. He authored the influential book *Presidential Power*, which went through multiple editions. Neustadt had a special interest in transitions and provided guidance to President Kennedy on his transition in 1960–1961.

the Clinton people were nervous about it, but I was also very sympathetic with Mickey.

What they decided to do was keep it totally away from the campaign and have no interaction so there wouldn't be a distraction. Instead what it did, it created anxiety because people in the campaign wanted to go to work for Bill Clinton in the White House, in the administration.

* * *

Q: Can you talk a little bit about this [transition] planning group that you headed up in advance of the election?

Mickey Kantor: You mean during September, October, the transition.... If I'd have been more thoughtful I would have understood just how threatening that was to people and probably been more careful about it. We'd all agreed there would need to be some group preparing for a presidency. It would be irresponsible not to assume you're going to win and therefore be prepared. The transition period is all too short. The demands of a transition are large and, of course, we did not have a government behind us [at that time] to do a successful transition. ...

Q: How did you get that job?

Kantor: Well I didn't head it, I was chair of the campaign and it was suggested by Clinton and Hillary and others we put something together. I've got to say, I should have paid more attention to it. I paid less attention to it than I should have.... Today, there's a personal reason of course that I'm upset with what I didn't do, but more important I'm upset I didn't pay much attention because the Clinton transition was not exactly a triumph. Most have written that and I think they're right in their analysis.

There had been one incident, about two or three weeks out [from Election Day], where Warren Christopher and Vernon Jordan[4] came to me and said that I should be [White House] chief of staff. They said, "We're going to talk to Clinton, do you care?" I said, "Look, that's up to you, but I don't know if this is the time or the place." Well, they did. Clearly, I should have recognized from his lack of response to it—like all politicians, if they don't say "yes," the answer is really no, even though they'll never say "no" to anyone—I should have recognized something was wrong. Not that I did or didn't want to be chief of staff, I should have realized that I was somehow controversial within the ranks of the campaign.

The campaign ended. Clearly, something was wrong. He told me the next morning I wouldn't be heading the [formal] transition, he'd have me on the

---

4. Vernon Jordan was a businessman and civil rights activist, formerly president of the National Urban League. Clinton asked him to work with Warren Christopher and others on the formal part of his transition.

transition board, et cetera, would I do that? Of course you say "yes," but I was disappointed and concerned, not about the chief of staff as much that, clearly, there were real problems. The issue of the economic conference came up very quickly because Vernon Jordan went on *Meet the Press* and said we were going to have one. We had not made a decision to do or not do so, but we were committed publicly, and Bill Clinton would never contradict Vernon. And so he asked me to run it. I made the decision to do so, but my wife thought she'd come back to LA, we had a good run, it was interesting, but I wasn't going to be part of the administration, so why do this? . . . The conference turned out to be a terrific success because of [Clinton], not anything I did. I think it is fair to say he mesmerized the press and the country during that period.

Eli Segal, campaign chief of staff: [Mickey Kantor] was assigned to do the transition stuff by me. The reason was to get him out of the mainstream of the campaign. It was . . . an elegant mechanism for giving him face and no role. That was it. No matter what you hear from anybody, that was Bill Clinton and Eli Segal, and no one else.

Roy Neel: The morning after the election in Little Rock, a large group of us gathered at the [Governor's] Mansion. The Gores, the Clintons, myself. I don't know who else from the Gore operation, probably no one else other than me. Then probably a dozen Clinton campaign staffers. . . . All gathered to start the transition process.

Mickey came in, maybe by himself, maybe with a few of his people, and laid out this plan for the transition. It had the ring to some people as being a foregone conclusion. That what he expected was for the president-elect to rubber-stamp this and say, "Okay Mickey, you're going to be the transition director, put this in place." Or, "Let's take comments and then get started." Didn't happen. The fix was in at that point, or the long knives were out, I should say, to use a different metaphor for Mickey and his operation. So they listened to Mickey lay out his plan and dismissed him. Said, "Okay, thanks, we'll get back to you." Mickey went away from that meeting I think not having a clue what was going on. He presumed that he would be running the transition, I suppose. They had their plan, it was a reasonable one. Well, within twenty-four hours Mickey was history. Mickey would not run the transition; the transition would be run by Vernon Jordan and Warren Christopher, and they would set up an operation. Mark Gearan would go to Washington with Alexis Herman and Dick Riley and set up the transition headquarters.[5] The Clintons would stay in Little Rock and do their work out of there.

---

5. Alexis Herman is a Democratic political activist who served in the Clinton White House and then as the first African-American secretary of labor (1997–2001). Richard Riley had been governor of South Carolina (1979–1987), active in the New Democrat movement, and then served as secretary of education under Clinton for the duration of his presidency.

But Mickey just disappeared. He basically, like something happening in the Gulag, was just disappeared. Nobody saw Mickey after that for a while. The same with Eli Segal, who was marginalized and was out. I remember a party the next night, the night after the election that was supposed to be a kind of barbecue, country music thing, good time. And I've never seen so many unhappy people.

Q: The night after the election?
Neel: It was either the night after the election or two nights, but it was probably the night after the election. I saw Eli and he was just ashen. He had been basically told he wasn't going to be involved or included; he wasn't going to have a role in this transition. . . .

I had to get started right away putting together the vice-presidential operation. At the same time, Gore and Clinton had agreed that Gore would be involved in the day-to-day decision-making process on the Cabinet out of Little Rock. The Cabinet and the top sub-Cabinet positions would be done in Little Rock at the Governor's Mansion, in deliberations with Christopher and Vernon. There would be a small group around a table in Little Rock doing this work every day. Christopher would come in and brief the group. It was basically Clinton and Christopher and Vernon usually at all the meetings, and Gore and sometimes Hillary, and I was included with Gore. Clinton was very gracious to me and said, "You should stay." So I'm at a table, about like this, smaller than this, with these guys and I'm thinking, like Stockdale,[6] *Why am I here? At any moment some Secret Service guy is going to tap me on the shoulder and say, "You're not supposed to be here."* But it was really intoxicating.

They used Gore very well. We were the only two around that table other than Christopher who had ever worked in Washington, in government. Christopher, within twenty-four hours he had the briefing books. We sat down and—I don't think that very afternoon, but the next day—they got their marching orders. You had Clinton and Gore and Hillary to a certain extent, and Christopher and Vernon sometimes, basically talking about their philosophy about how they wanted to govern and then looking at a plan.

Christopher would present a plan, then we were going to look at every department and we're going to talk about the mission of these departments. Then, how do you want to govern, how do you want to proceed? They would arrive at a process where Christopher would bring in a notebook about the agency and with a list of maybe ten potential candidates for that Cabinet

---

6. Admiral James Stockdale was selected by Ross Perot as his vice-presidential running mate in 1992, and he introduced himself at that year's vice-presidential debate in Atlanta by asking (rhetorically), "Who am I? Why am I here?" His self-deprecating moment created a lasting impression of someone in over his head.

position and they would debate them around the table. They would take some off, add some on, and then try to whittle the list down and send Christopher back to vet the ones that they had chosen. Maybe four or five for each Cabinet position.

Q: This was everything exclusive of the White House staff?
Neel: Exactly. The White House staff was not to be discussed. . . . Bruce [Lindsey] basically [told] me, "We're not going to touch the White House. We're not going to do anything about that." I think the intention was probably good, or the motive was good, that you don't want to create anxiety that people are organizing the White House behind your back if you're on the campaign staff, but it was a mistake. Somebody should have pushed back and said, "No, we've got to keep doing this work. We've got to be ready." So the work on the White House organization was largely suspended. Mickey's operation out of Little Rock, to my understanding, stopped looking at the White House. So the day after the election, you know, it was just like this monster in the corner. No one was looking at the White House and doing anything about the White House.

Now, it got out pretty quickly that Susan Thomases had a yardstick and was over at the West Wing and the Old Executive Office Building measuring offices and deciding who is going to sit where. Well, you couldn't have had a worse person to be alleged to be organizing anything for anyone, because that pissed off everybody, including the Gore people. Because the rumor then that came back was that Susan had decided that Gore wouldn't have the traditional vice president's office in the West Wing; that that would go to Hillary. That Gore would have his office over in the Old Executive Office Building. At this point you should be thinking about big things, important things, but people can devolve into the worst sentiments. Little human insecurities. Anyway, all these things were happening and that was creating havoc.

[We] had made the promise that the Cabinet would all be selected by Christmas, which was a mistake. So we had a deadline. He had made certain promises about diversity in the Cabinet, which was a mistake. It was going to be a diverse Cabinet but we set ourselves up. So the last four Cabinet selections were made at the eleventh hour under a bit of stress, and were probably not the best selections. They weren't given the kind of deliberations they might have been otherwise.

The process up to that point, the six weeks leading up to that, there was a fairly thorough process and very professionally done by Christopher and his team. Meanwhile, Mickey Kantor had been relegated to organize the economic summit, because Clinton, I'm sure, felt sorry for him, having sent him to Siberia. Mickey to his credit did a bang-up job with that and got himself back into not only good graces but a position of stature and became the trade representative. So he was tough enough to be able to do that.

Virtually no White House [staff] planning seemed to be done until fairly late in the process.... It was an absolute disaster. We all met in Little Rock at the Mansion to announce the senior White House staff, the day before we headed to Charlottesville to start the final roll into Washington for the inauguration. So there would have been thirty-five people in that picture—the assistants to the president and perhaps some of the deputy assistants to the president. I looked around that room. There was a riser and there were probably four steps and we were all up there like a high school graduation photo. I didn't know half the people in the room. Actually, I probably knew more than most because a lot of them were out of Washington, but I asked somebody who had been with the Clinton campaign who was there, "Do you know all these people?" She said, "I don't have a clue; I have no idea." It was a nightmare. ...

Q: *You commented earlier that you wish some of the energy that had gone into planning the inaugural parties had been diverted to more important things?*
Neel: Clinton himself has said this.... He was very candid about that and he had been told a thousand times and certainly had known himself that he made a big mistake waiting too long to organize the White House. And it was very apparent.... [We] had a lot of people who were miscast. They were good people but they were in the wrong jobs. If they wanted to serve in government they should have been somewhere else, either somewhere else in the White House or out in one of the agencies. We had too many people that were having to do on-the-job training. The problem with on-the-job training is they didn't have anybody managing their work who knew what they were doing either and no serious team-building.

We were getting by because people were smart and they were totally dedicated to Clinton and Gore and were committed to making it work. But the analogy I would use is putting on your running shoes in the middle of a hundred-yard sprint in the Olympics. It was madness, in a way.

Q: *At the time, did you take any of this as evidence of something essential in Bill Clinton's operating style? Or did you think this is just a function of lack of experience at this level?*
Neel: You could dismiss 30 percent of it to the fact that we had been out of office for twelve years, the Democrats, and most of the people coming into the White House were going to be newcomers to White House involvement or management or employment or whatever. The rest of it was a very obvious indication of the lack of discipline coming from the president-elect himself. Either he was getting confused, disorganized advice, or he was letting too many people get to him, basically immobilizing the process. That was pretty obvious and it was scary.

Q: And you were picking this up, during the course of your transition?
Neel: You picked it up before the campaign ended. The storm clouds in this were looming well before that, when Mickey came to Little Rock and for the first time you began to see the tension between the senior staff people. This foretold problems in setting up the White House, unless Bill Clinton was very decisive in naming a chief of staff who was clearly going to be in charge, *à la* James Baker for Reagan. And he didn't do that. . . .

Q: What's your explanation for this, in your gut?
Neel: I think it's at the root of Clinton's personality. The very thing that makes him the most seductive political personality in my lifetime, and the very reason I'm devoted to him and like him so much, was the very reason that he seemed to be incapable of organizing a White House effectively early on. It was painful to him to say no to people who had been with him a long time, whom he was loyal to, but who had no business working in senior White House jobs.

Mickey Kantor: [One] of the great failings of Bill Clinton is, when faced with the task of choosing someone for something, he does not want to make a decision. For [three] reasons: one, he'll think of fifty other people who might want it or be qualified for it. He knows too many people and therefore his head is like a Rolodex, he starts going through it. Second, he doesn't want to make a decision. Third, he recognizes that for every person you choose, then twenty other people believe they should have it and be mad at you, and the one you chose probably thinks they deserved it [anyway].[7] You get no credit whatsoever, none. And it drives him crazy. I've seen him do it time and time—he just pushes those files away, he doesn't want to do it.

Mack McLarty, White House chief of staff: [That] evening [after the election returns came in], just the two of us [visited], and had an exchange that you would expect. I said that I was enormously proud of him, and he had run a superb campaign, and it was a wonderful thing for our state and so forth, and he said he appreciated that, and we talked a bit more. Then he said, "I want to talk to you about serving in the administration." I said, "I'm surprised by that. You know I've got my responsibilities with Arkla and our family responsibilities with Franklin."[8] He said, "I know that." And I said, "What are you thinking?" He said, "I'd like you to consider serving as my chief of staff."

---

7. Kantor's assertion echoes a lament sounded centuries before (in various phrasings) usually credited to Thomas Jefferson: "Every appointment made means one ingrate and a hundred enemies."

8. McLarty was chairman and chief executive officer of Arkla, an Arkansas natural gas company. Franklin, his younger son, was then completing high school in Little Rock.

And I was surprised. I would have been less surprised had he said, perhaps, secretary of commerce or secretary of energy. I would still have been somewhat surprised because of the reasons I mentioned. And I said, "I'm greatly honored by that, I'm touched by it. Give me a little bit of your reasoning." It was pretty straightforward. He said, "Mack, when I get there, I'm going to need somebody that I fully trust, that I can communicate with, that understands me, that has the kind of relationship that can tell me if we're wrong, or I'm wrong, but will do it in the right way and will do it discreetly." It was kind of the sounding board. "I need a somber second opinion just to be sure I'm looking at the multitude of issues and decisions coming in in a correct manner, someone who will have the ability—not the courage, but the ability—to say that in a strong, direct way."

He said, "I ran as a New Democrat. I think it's important we continue that philosophy. You've been as involved in that effort in many ways as I have. I like the idea of a businessperson as opposed to a political person, and you know I like to get ideas from a lot of people. We ran an inclusive campaign, and I need someone who will be an honest broker and will give me these best points of view so that we can make decisions and go forward. For all of those reasons, and more, I want you to do this." And I said, "That's, an overly generous Mark Twain kind of an exaggeration here, but you know, I take my wonderful mother's advice and take compliments and run. Let me talk to Donna and give this some serious, thoughtful and, indeed, prayerful reflection, and we'll continue our discussion."

Then in a very creative manner he said, "Let's do this: Why don't you help me with the transition on the Cabinet selection?" which obviously was a very flattering offer. I said, "I can do that. I would be honored to do that, but only in a limited way because I have other responsibilities." He said, "This will be a good way for us to start this process and see if it evolves in a way that you're comfortable with and I'm comfortable with."[9]

Warren Christopher, transition director: Well, let me tell you first why I think it's important that the chief of staff be selected first. We have a unique system in our country, in which there is no continuing staff in the White House on a policy level. The president comes in and the offices are all vacant, the desks are clean, so the White House has to be staffed from the ground up. The time between election and inauguration, which was shortened for good reasons, doesn't give the president and the chief of staff very much time to organize the White House and to get things running, so I think the president ought to choose the chief of staff as soon as possible, to start filling those offices and

---

9. McLarty's description of this encounter is a critical piece of evidence about the transition period, because it helps to explain why Clinton was otherwise so late in getting around to staffing his White House: He was waiting to get this leading piece settled first.

getting some papers on the desk so he can get his administration under way when January 20 comes. So every day that the chief of staff of the White House is not named is a big loss.

Now, contrast that with the departments. The State Department, for example, is a continuing bureaucracy of not only size but talent. Any secretary of state is going to rely very heavily on the Foreign Service and is going to find most of the offices filled and most of the desks heavy with paper except for the seventh floor. So I think the lead time is so much more easily managed in the departments than it is in the White House.

There was a good deal of discussion at that time as to whether there should be any one chief of staff or whether he should try to operate on a kind of a roundtable system, like Franklin Roosevelt apparently did in an earlier day, or whether he should identify a chief of staff. That was fairly briskly resolved, I think, that there should be one. But then he had a great deal of difficulty coming to a decision and I think there was—at least as I viewed it from the outside in many conversations about it—some tension between wanting somebody who he knew well and was comfortable with on the one hand, and on the other hand somebody who had a lot of Washington experience and who could bring to it not so much personal familiarity with him as familiarity with the issues and personalities in Washington.

There was, in addition to that, the problem that when he made the decision for chief of staff he was making probably one person reasonably happy and also reasonably miserable, and several people unhappy for not having been chosen, or not having their nominee chosen.

Senator Dale Bumpers (D-AR): [Mack McLarty] is as fine as any man I've ever known in my life. . . . Mack came to see me and told me Bill was considering making him chief of staff, which indeed he later did. I tried to talk Mack out of taking it. I told him it was a killer. Everything that goes wrong, which it does several times a day, the chief of staff gets full responsibility. The president doesn't, you do. I don't know what happened to Mack. He didn't last very long in the job. It may have been a personal choice on his part, I don't know. All I know is that the White House just eats people up and spits them out. If you survive it for any length of time at all you're a genius.

Peter Knight, Gore aide: When I went over to [the transition office to] work in presidential personnel . . ., we had a rainbow of people who had to be deputies. . . . [People] who came and said, *I think I should be at the EPA [Environmental Protection Agency], I'd like to be assistant administrator.* I'd say, "Do you know how many people would work for you?" They'd say, "Well, I worked in scheduling in the campaign." [*laughter*] I'd say, "Do you know that you'll have 1,500 people working for you, career people, scientists, Ph.D.s, lawyers?" They'd say, "Oh, I didn't know that." . . . And you won't be able to fire [them], right . . .?

But ... you're hand-holding all the people who were there and thought that they should get these exalted positions.

Frankly, people like Rahm [Emanuel] and George [Stephanopoulos] initially overstepped what they should have been doing, and many other people did as well.[10] But there was a lot of inexperience.

Q: "Overstep" meaning they were out of their league initially?
Knight: Yes. Not that they weren't important to what the president was doing, and that isn't to diminish it, but didn't have the formal experience to—I mean, it takes a while to figure out that it is actually not a good idea to be in a job above your weight. You should be good at what you do rather than be struggling. Most of the time at the beginning of an administration there's just such a rush to get the biggest title and the biggest everything that you could possibly get. It's always a mistake.

* * *

Q: Did you, Tony Lake, and Sandy Berger have issues you wanted to deal with first?
Nancy Soderberg, foreign policy advisor: Sure, we had a whole plan; it went up in smoke. We had a whole transition plan. For the historians out there, all of this is in the Clinton Library, the transition memos, everything else. We had a "first hundred days" plan. I don't remember exactly what it was, but it was trying to move the peace process along in Bosnia, move the peace process along in Haiti, trying to come up with a plan to hand the UN peacekeeping operation in Somalia over to the UN. Probably some arms control issues, I don't remember. We had a whole agenda that we would have gone in with. Then reality hits, and none of it works, and it all blows up in your face. It's very hard to put into place a plan that's on paper.

James Woolsey, director of central intelligence: Now, how did I get the job? In late '91, shortly before Governor Clinton declared he was running for the presidency—I don't remember what month, but in the fall of '91—there was a dinner party at Pamela Harriman's house,[11] and Sandy [Samuel] Berger asked me to come to meet Governor Clinton. There were probably fifteen people at

---

10. Initially, Emanuel was assistant to the president and director of political affairs; Stephanopoulos assistant to the president and director of communications. Assistant to the president is the highest level staff appointment in the White House.

11. Pamela Harriman (1920–1997) was a Democratic Party political activist, fundraiser, and socialite—once married to Winston Churchill's son, then later to Averell Harriman, a Democratic politician and former governor of New York. President Clinton named her U.S. ambassador to France in 1993.

the dinner party. It was a pleasant evening. I don't recall much else about it, except being impressed by him. I certainly was, yes.

I joined a group of other so-called Scoop [Henry] Jackson[12] Democrats who took out a small ad during the campaign and endorsed then-governor Clinton. We were favorably disposed toward what he had been saying on a number of defense and foreign policy issues and thought he was going to be, from our point of view, a good candidate on those grounds. I contributed about $250 to the campaign, and the campaign asked me and Lee Hamilton on Labor Day of '92 to fly down to Little Rock and spend several hours meeting with the governor talking about all the things that were going on in former Yugoslavia, and also what opportunities there might be for arms control. I had a background of having been involved in a number of the arms control negotiations. We did that. That was it.

Then the governor was elected president. I had nothing, other than what I've described, to do with the campaign. A month-and-a-half after the election ... I get a call at home from Warren Christopher.... He said, "Jim, do you suppose you could come to Little Rock and talk to the president-elect about the CIA job?" I honestly thought he meant talk to the president-elect about who should have the CIA job. So I said, "Well, Chris, I'm on the way to California for Christmas with my family. Is it okay if I come after New Year's, or does it really need to be between Christmas and New Year's?" He paused for a second. He said, "Actually, you ought to come today." Obviously something was up. I said, "You really need me today?" He said, "Yes, if you could come to Little Rock, I'd appreciate it." "All right." I sent the family to California, and flew to Little Rock. I was met by a staffer. She said, "We'll check you into the so-and-so hotel. The president-elect wants to talk to you but he can't see you until 11:30 tonight because he's got a big fundraising dinner." ... I go to the hotel, they send a car, drive me a few blocks over to the Governor's Mansion about 11:30. I sit around for about an hour. I think Madeleine Albright was coming in after me, but I was there until about 12:30.

The president-elect and I met. That's the only time I ever saw him alone. It was for about an hour. We talked almost not at all about the CIA. I'm five years older than he, and I grew up in northeastern Oklahoma, Tulsa, and he grew up in northwestern Arkansas, in Hot Springs. We talked about Oklahoma and Arkansas football. We talked about where it was good to fish in the Ozarks. We talked about a lot of things. At one point he said something along the lines of, "Do you think the CIA director ought to give policy advice?" I said, "No, I really don't. People would think he was distorting intelligence in order to support the

---

12. Henry "Scoop" Jackson (1912–1983) served in the U.S. Senate from the state of Washington from 1953 to 1983, and was known as a vigorously anti-communist Democrat, tough on foreign policy issues.

policy. I think that if anybody in that job wants to give you policy advice they ought to do it very briefly, and one-on-one in some fashion, and not as part of the policy process." He said, "I agree with that." As I recall, that was about all that was said about the CIA. I went back to the hotel.

The next morning, I got a call from another staffer and she said, "We need for you to have a conflict-of-interest meeting. Would you walk down the street three blocks to the Rose Law Firm and ask for Webb Hubbell?" So I did. I met Webb Hubbell for the first time.[13] He had a folder on me. He asked me who my clients were—I was practicing law—and what my investments were. I told him. He said, "I don't think any of that causes any problem, do you?" I said, "No, I don't have any problems, not one."

I went back to the hotel. It was late morning. I got a call just before noon from a staffer and she said, ... "The press conference is at 12:30. We'll pick you up at 12:00." I said, "Could I speak to Warren Christopher?" She said, "Well, he's in a meeting and really can't be disturbed." I said, "I'd appreciate it if you'd disturb him. This is important." She said, "All right." Chris came to the phone. He said, "Jim, what is it?" I said, "Chris, by any chance, does the president-elect want me to be director of central intelligence?" He said, "Yes, sure. That's what he wants." I said, "Chris, he never said so. He never made an offer and I never answered." I'll never forget. He said, "Look, just come on over to the press conference we'll get it sorted out." I said, "Chris, I think I'd like to know before I come to the press conference." He said, "Okay, just a minute." He went away. He came back. He said, "Well, I just stuck my head in his office and asked if that's what he wanted and he said, 'Yes, sure.'"

By now it was about noon. I said, "Well, okay I guess, yes." They picked me up. We went to the Governor's Mansion. I walked into the living room of the Governor's Mansion and there was the president-elect and Mrs. [Hillary] Clinton. There's vice president–elect [Albert] Gore and Tipper [Gore]. There's Les Aspin.[14] There's Madeleine Albright, who is going to be the UN [United Nations] ambassador. There's Warren Christopher, of course, Tony Lake, and Sandy Berger, and the incoming deputy secretary of state.... Everybody said, "Jim, hi. Glad to have you with us." I said, "Yes, glad, sure." I sit down. Oh, and Dee Dee Myers and George Stephanopoulos. What they were doing, which I had come in the middle of, was gaming the press conference. I learned later that this was a frequent subject of meetings: "Suppose they ask this?" "Suppose they ask that?"

---

13. Webster Hubbell was an Arkansas lawyer who worked in the Rose Law Firm with Hillary Rodham Clinton. He joined the administration as associate attorney general in 1993, resigning the following year because of legal questions over his billing records before leaving Arkansas.

14. Les Aspin (1938–1995) served in the U.S. House of Representatives from Wisconsin from 1971 to 1993. He was President Clinton's first secretary of defense (1993–1994).

One of them said, "Well, suppose they say, 'Isn't this just a bunch of [Jimmy] Carter administration retreads?'" Since we *were* Carter administration retreads, there was this silence. I figured they probably ought to know what Woolsey is like, so I said, "Governor, you could say that Woolsey served in the [Ronald] Reagan and [George H. W.] Bush administrations and maybe that counteracts the fact that I served in the Carter administration." Clinton laughed, and Dee Dee said, "Admiral, I didn't know you served in the Bush and Reagan administrations." By now it is 12:25 and the press conference is 12:30. I said, "Dee Dee, I'm not an admiral. I never got above captain in the army." She said, "Whoops, we'd better change the press release." ... So that's pretty much the whole story of my becoming director of central intelligence.

Donna Shalala, secretary of health and human services: I had a few calls from friends in New York saying, "You're clearly on Clinton's short list." ... So I went back down [to Little Rock] and Christopher apologized. I said, "Give me a hint, Chris, what's he going to talk to me about?" I got in to talk to Clinton and again it was this vague conversation. Then he apologized to me. He said, "I really wanted you to be HHS secretary and I was going to bring it up with you [earlier] but Joycelyn Elders[15] thought she was going to be HHS secretary. So I had to make her surgeon general."

I said, "Mr. President, there's not a vacancy there." He said, "What do you mean there's not a vacancy?" I said, "Because the surgeon general of the United States has a term." He said, "How come none of my staff told me that?" So he called in Christopher and said, "Donna says the surgeon general has a term." Christopher looked surprised. Left, came back, and said, "Yes, the surgeon general has a term and there's a sitting surgeon general."

So Clinton turned to me and said, "Well, when you're HHS secretary that's the first thing you have to deal with because you've got to get that person out of that job." It was that casual, that disorganized, that casual. So Clinton said, "They're drafting the press release now." I said, "They're doing *what*?" He said, "They're drafting the press release, we're going to announce this right away." I hadn't called my mother, let alone the chairman of the board of Wisconsin or anyone else. That should have been a signal to me about how disorganized the Clinton White House was going to be, but I wasn't going to turn down HHS.

Henry Cisneros, secretary of housing and urban development: I was named secretary of HUD in early December, and Bill Richardson was slated to go to Interior and then ran into opposition. I think that's been documented, so I'm

---

15. Dr. Joycelyn Elders was a physician and public health professional who once served as the director of the Arkansas Department of Health. She was appointed surgeon general in September 1993 and served there for just over one year, resigning in controversy over a series of public remarks about such topics as drug use and sex education.

not telling stories out of school. He would have been the second Latino in the Cabinet. They needed to slot in Bruce Babbitt at the last second.[16] Literally, this is like the 22nd or 23rd of December, and the president had promised to have his Cabinet finished by Christmas. So Richardson is out, Babbitt is in. That opens a hole where Babbitt was going to be, which was the Trade office. So now that makes sense for Mickey Kantor who, when the musical chairs had stopped was left out, and he was a major player. So that's taken care of. But there is no second Hispanic, which the president had hoped to do.

So Gore called me and said, "We like Federico Peña[17] for this, but while he has served in the transition oversight group for transportation, he never envisioned doing it.... Can you get him?" ... So we found him in Albuquerque and he said, "Oh, my God, absolutely not, I cannot do this. I promised my wife I wouldn't do it. I told my business partners. They just had a board meeting and they made me pledge I wouldn't do this because they've got investments in this company and the company goes kaput without me." I said, "The president wants you to do it, the vice president, [too]. You've got to think about this." He said, "We're at the airport. We're boarding for our plane to Brownsville." I said, "Okay, I'm going to stay here in Nashville and I'm going to call you when you get to Brownsville. We're going to talk about this some more. Meantime, you need to call your partners and tell them the world is changing."

So while he was flying to Brownsville from Albuquerque, I stayed on the phone and I started calling friends in Texas to line up an airplane to pick him up and bring him to Little Rock by 8 o'clock the next morning. It's now getting on toward 11 o'clock or midnight in Nashville where I am and he has arrived in Brownsville. Sometime around midnight I said, "Federico, you don't have a choice, you have to do this." He said, "I can't. My partners wouldn't understand." I said, "Get on the phone and call your partners and tell them the world has just shifted, you're going to do this."

He said, "All right, I'll call you back." So he did. I told Gore, "I think it's done, call him, settle it." Gore called. They got it done. We had Tony Sanchez from Laredo National Bank have a plane en route that night, so it would be on hand to fly him to Little Rock for the announcement the next morning. So that's how Federico [got named to the Cabinet].

Charlene Barshefsky, deputy U.S. trade representative: Mickey [Kantor] had called. We subsequently chatted. He said, "I'd like you to be my deputy." I said

---

16. Bruce Babbitt was governor of Arizona from 1978 to 1987. He was Clinton's Interior secretary for the duration of his presidency.

17. Federico Peña was the first Hispanic mayor of Denver (1983–1991) and advised the Clinton campaign on transportation issues. He served as Transportation secretary from 1993 to 1997, and then spent a year as Energy secretary.

no. And he said, "Don't say no. Think about it." ... But ten days passed and I was still undecided. What then happened is a true story, on my life. Ed [Edward B. Cohen] and I were commuting down Connecticut Avenue on the morning of the tenth day, and I said to my husband, "I am just in equipoise. I honestly can't decide. I need a sign." A little white car in the next lane passed us. I could see his license plate, and it said "G-O-4-I-T." I said to my husband, "That's it. That's the sign." I got to the office, called Mickey and accepted.

Richard Riley, transition advisor: I remember when we were working on the transition and I would come in [to see Clinton] with [presentations on] six or seven positions. We'd have all the books and they would have them. They'd already gone through all the résumés and we would narrow it down to three or four people for a slot. We'd get over there in the afternoon at the Governor's Mansion. One time he came and we had lots of heavy stuff to do and knew it was going to take us a long time. He said, "Dick, I know you've got a lot on your mind and we've got lots to do. I've tried to read through some of these things, but Chelsea—it's going to be a big change for her. We're having family time with her. I simply have to finish that." I [then] sat there from about 8:00 until midnight. I didn't know what to do. I started thinking, *Has he gone to sleep or what?* I mean I got tired of reading those damn résumés. I had just about memorized them all.

Finally he came [back] down. He said, "I apologize. It was a family time. We had to work through some things for Chelsea. I feel much better about it now. Let's go to work." We worked until three or four in the morning. Of course, that takes me out for two days and he's fresh as a daisy at 6:00.

That's a hard life. He is a very caring father and husband. The American public gets one version of all that but when you're around him and you see him you really get another version of it.

Al From, head of the DLC: On the list of leaders of the transition he had liaisons for everybody but the Jew. Sarah Ehrman[18] ... comes up to us and she's really upset because, "There's this liaison and that liaison, but there's no Jewish liaison." Berger looks at her and he said, "Let's see, Mickey Kantor, Eli Segal, Bob Reich, Sandy Berger, Al From, Judy Feder—this transition is one-third Orthodox, one-third Conservative, and one-third Reform."[19] [*laughter*]

---

18. Sarah Ehrman was a longtime friend of the Clintons from the George McGovern campaign. Hillary Rodham lived with her in Washington when she worked on the House Watergate committee, and she evidently attempted to talk Hillary out of marrying Bill at the point she was moving to Arkansas to join him there.

19. Robert Reich was a longtime friend of Bill Clinton, first getting to know him on the ship across the Atlantic when they both went to Oxford as Rhodes Scholars. He would become

Sandy Berger, foreign policy advisor: President Clinton made a commitment during the campaign. We tend to focus on the statements he made that he did not comply with, but he said he was going to cut the White House staff by 25 percent. That was a statement based upon a memo he received that said that [George H. W.] Bush had increased the White House staff by 60 percent. That was wrong. Bush had actually cut the White House staff. The author of that memo—I have my strong suspicions who the author of that memo was. He has obviously kept his head down. It's almost like Deep Throat. [But] the president refused to budge from that commitment. We went to him on several different occasions and said, "Mr. President, this is a big government. You asked it to do a lot of things; we can't do all these things. People are already working twenty hours a day."

He said, "If we can't run this government with X number of people in the White House, we ought to be sent home." It reflected his more populist instinct. So we had two constraints on our staff. One was the budget, the other was the 25 percent cut.

William Galston, domestic policy advisor: The White House was young people with campaign experience and then some old Clinton friends, and not a lot in between. If you added up all the years of White House experience of all the people in the Clinton White House, I don't think you would have gotten to a hundred. I'm not sure you would have gotten to fifty. As a matter of fact, it's not clear to me you would have gotten to twenty-five. If you'd been in the White House before, you were extremely unlikely to be there then. Go figure.

Warren Christopher: The assembling of the economic team is an unappreciated aspect of the transition period. A great deal of time was spent on it and I think that the team that he assembled was really quite extraordinary in its depth and competence. Having persuaded Lloyd Bentsen to become secretary of the treasury was an important step in the president obtaining credibility. Having persuaded Bob Rubin to become first head of the National Economic Council meant the president had somebody who Lloyd Bentsen was prepared to work with in the White House who could be right next to him constantly. And then having persuaded Alice Rivlin, who was passed over for being head of OMB but then to become deputy head and then to serve so well in subsequent positions, and having persuaded Laura Tyson[20] to come in, he had a first-rate economic

---

Clinton's first secretary of labor. Judy Feder was a health policy expert on Capitol Hill, health care director for the transition team, and then served in a high-ranking position with Secretary Donna Shalala in the Department of Health and Human Services.

20. Laura Tyson is an economist who became the first chair of Clinton's Council of Economic Advisors.

team that served him very well and enabled him to make what I think was the crucial decision of the first year and that was to deal with the deficit.

That was important not just domestically, but it was very important internationally. It's hard to overestimate the degree of credibility the president gained internationally by taking steps to balance the budget, and I think he owed that to both his own determination but the presence of Lloyd Bentsen and Bob Rubin and Leon Panetta steeled him to make that very difficult decision and changed the whole course of the administration, I think, and put it on a much sounder track. I hope historians will pay more attention to that series of choices and that decision in the first year.

Alice Rivlin, economic advisor (on the Little Rock economic summit): It was a chance for the president to show he cared about the economy and the vice president cared about the economy. It was very Clinton-Gore. I thought it came off magnificently because the president is so good at interacting with people of different points of view. He's in his element when he's orchestrating that kind of thing, publicly or privately. Though I'd been skeptical at the beginning, I thought it was a huge success.

Roger Altman, economic advisor (on the summit): Well, that was, in retrospect, "the Bill Clinton Show," and he demonstrated—it was, I think, very clever in retrospect—he demonstrated his phenomenal grasp of policy issues, just through sitting there for many hours a day. The thing was televised, nonstop. I think it was over two days. Every imaginable issue arose and Clinton hit all those balls out of the park and it gave the American public a chance to see how astonishingly smart and deep this guy was. So I think it was quite smart to be done then. I'm not sure that was what they originally intended, I suppose it was, but I wasn't involved in the planning of the summit, I just went to it and had a role on one of the panels and sat around for a couple of days, really.

Chris Jennings: "My God, a Democratic president has won." Everyone in Washington, every Democrat was so excited. People desperately wanted to work in the Clinton administration. They said, "Oh, this is historic, this is going to be great. We have a Democratic Congress, we have a Democratic administration." People were kicking themselves to find any way they could to get in the Clinton administration. . . . This is where health care is going to happen. This is the transition team, we have to get in.

I was working my tail off—and we had just bought a house and I just had a kid and my wife was never seeing me. This all culminated in this big transition paper, report of options, which I have someplace buried, in which my job was basically to do the political evaluation and scene. But this group went down to Little Rock to present it. . . . I wasn't invited to come and I was sort of devastated, but in retrospect it couldn't have been better. . . . [These] were the

Washington-insider health care teams, going down to meet with the president-elect, and they were all so excited. The president received a presentation of these numbers that really didn't look very appealing, they looked painful. "You mean we can't find a way to save money when I expand coverage to everyone?" It was not very well received. Behind the scenes, Ira Magaziner[21] had been suggesting that they were being way, way too conservative with the level of savings that could be achieved. There was a lot more savings in the system, and he was basically saying there's an easier way to go . . . and here's a guy they know and they trust.

The president didn't know these Washington people and they were bringing bad news. [Then] these guys came back from Little Rock all depressed because they thought, *He hates us. It was a terrible meeting. We'll never be liked again, we'll never be part of this administration.* . . . I'm saying that the health care team thought they were viewed as the bearers of more bad news. First of all, the president was [already] upset because he knew the economy was bad when he got elected, but then the new CBO [Congressional Budget Office] numbers came out about how bad the deficits were. He thinks, *They were hiding from me how bad this was going to be, and now I have to revamp what I can do. I can't do my middle-income income tax cuts, and I can't do so many other things I want to do.* And all these budget people are saying basically, "Do the tough medicine stuff." And you know, politicians are willing to do tough medicine, but they want to have something to go with it. They weren't giving him many options that were very positive. Then you throw this health care team coming in saying, "Well, it's not as good as you thought it was going to be, I'm sorry." So the guy is saying, "I'm in the middle of my transition, I've got to pick my people. The deficit's worse, and health care numbers are worse. What have I got myself into?"

Nancy Soderberg: It's quite an extraordinary story when you think about it. To me, it demonstrated that the Bush administration didn't quite grasp the fact that they were leaving office in three months. They essentially agreed to send 25,000 troops to Somalia with no consultation with the next president of the United States. I found out about it from Clinton's press person, Steve Rabinowitz. He was out jogging Thanksgiving morning and called me. He said, "What's going on in Somalia?"

I was trying to take the day off. I said, "I don't know." So I started calling around. I called the White House and got Brent Scowcroft.[22] I said, "What's

---

21. Ira Magaziner was a management consultant with long ties to the Clintons and a history of reform efforts in the northeastern United States. He was designated the chief staff person to work with Hillary Rodham Clinton on reforming the American health care system.

22. Brent Scowcroft was national security advisor to President George H. W. Bush. Troops were in fact being deployed to Somalia on a humanitarian mission to secure food delivery lines in hopes of avoiding a broader famine.

going on in Somalia?" "Oh, nothing, we haven't decided anything. Happy Thanksgiving." I said, "You're in the office on Thanksgiving? That's a bad sign." Then I started calling some friends of mine in the press. They said, "No, they decided to send 25,000 troops." They gave me the whole story: they'd been up to the UN, gotten it done. I called Scowcroft back. I said, "You can either tell me what's going on, or I'm going to have to tell the press that you've sent 25,000 troops to Somalia without consulting with the next president of the United States. And I don't think that's in either of our interests." He finally said okay.

In his defense, it wasn't final, final, final, but it was pretty final, and they hadn't talked to us about it. We came up with some way to finesse the issue of when we had been briefed. Scowcroft sent a whole team down to brief us on it. It was very clear to us right away that there was no way these guys were going to be out by January 20. Scowcroft said, "Don't worry; they'll be out before you get here."

That was so naïve. We eventually realized that we were going to have to have a whole plan here. I was furious that they would do that without consulting us first, but we decided it wasn't in anybody's interest to have that out in the press. It never got out in the press, actually; I was surprised.

David Kusnet, speechwriter: Stephanopoulos called me at home and said, "Start thinking about the inaugural [address]. . . . The terrible news was that Father [Timothy] Healy[23] had died of a heart attack in Newark Airport where he was getting ready to board a flight to go on vacation for the Christmas–New Year's season. He had had a cassette, maybe a tape recorder with a cassette in his jacket pocket. A stenographer transcribed what was on his cassette—it was a memo to Bill Clinton about the inaugural speech. It was riffing off the metaphor of "forcing the spring." Gardeners could force the spring trying to get plants to . . . bloom before their natural time.

His memo included these phrasings—I'm reciting them from memory— which would be included in the inaugural address: "We meet in the depths of winter but through the words we speak"—he said it better—"and what we show the world, we force the spring." And then [Father Healy in his memo] he introduced this metaphor, "Pentecostal fire in the dark time of year." Easter and Christmas were the metaphors. The cover note from Stephanopoulos said something like, "See if you can do something with this." Clearly Clinton in his own mind was doing something with this also. So I did a first draft, which I faxed to Stephanopoulos in Little Rock with the understanding that Clinton would see it, but it was addressed to Stephanopoulos, not to Clinton. Even if

---

23. Timothy Healy (1923–1992) was a Jesuit priest who had served as president of Georgetown University. In that capacity he had developed a friendship with alumnus Bill Clinton.

we meant something for Clinton, a lot of us were much more comfortable addressing something to someone other than the next president. It was this kind of awe, not so much about the man but about the office. In addition to making some use of the Father Healy metaphor, forcing the spring, my first draft had the paragraph that leads up to the line, "There is nothing wrong with America that cannot be cured by what is right with America." . . .

The night before the inaugural, there was a marathon rehearsal/rewriting session. The basic structure of the inaugural address remained remarkably constant, just as with the acceptance speech at the convention. . . . [There's] a famous Mario Cuomo line, "You campaign in poetry, you govern in prose." In a sense the inaugural was your last exercise in poetry before the prose comes. But this inaugural is more, whatever its merits as poetry. It actually is a foreshadowing of what his administration would be about, especially the first few years. There you have, "We earn our livelihood in America today in peaceful competition with people all across the earth—" That really is the case for his public investment program—investing in American workers and communities so we can compete in the global economy, the "putting people first" [agenda].

That's thesis. Then you begin to get into antithesis, which was the need to pay down the debts. This became the conflict about the economic plan in the first year and became a theme throughout. Bill Clinton believed you had to do all kinds of public investments in people's skills and also in infrastructure. He also became persuaded by a different faction in the administration—Bentsen, [Robert] Rubin—that you had to pay down the debts and that paying down the debts would lead to an economic expansion because interest rates would go down. You find that here— . . . "We must do what no generation has had to do before. We must invest more in our own people . . . and at the same time cut our massive debt." So that sentence and that paragraph really are a foreshadowing of the great economic debate in the first year and throughout his administration of public investment versus debt reduction. . . .

[The] first drafts that we did had nothing specifically about the rest of the world, except the discussion of the imperatives of the global economy. I remember sitting with Nancy Soderberg—at that time she was the conduit for Tony Lake and Sandy Berger, the foreign policy people. At one point she said, almost, "I don't care what you say but there have to be some number of words about foreign policy." I don't remember what her quote was, forty words, fifty words, one paragraph. We have it, I think, on the paragraph that begins, "While America rebuilds at home we will not shrink from the challenges—" This I guess is our Kennedy rhetoric "—nor fail to seize the opportunities of this new world. Together, our friends and allies, we will work to shape change, lest it engulf us. When our vital interests are challenged, or the will and conscience of the international community is defied, we will act with peaceful diplomacy whenever possible and force when necessary." And so on. I think Tony Lake, who was a very elegant writer, probably wrote most of it and I may have put in a transition at the beginning and the end so it would not stick out too much from the rest of the speech.

Senator Alan Simpson (R-WY): Imagine, on inauguration day, [Senate Minority Leader Robert] Dole was up on the front platform, with the 200,000 plus out front; and out the back, I, as assistant leader of "the other faith," and Ann [Simpson] were taking George and Barbara [Bush] down the east Capitol steps to their chopper waiting there. Ann and I brought George and Barbara down those back steps and Hillary [Clinton] and Bill got out of the big black limo to go up the steps. In just a few minutes, he would be president of the United States. Fascinating little foursome we were—a trip I shall never forget.

So down the stairs with George and Barbara and we gave them a big hug and a kiss; off they went. Here came Clinton and Hillary walking up the back steps. I said, "Congratulations." He said, "Senator Simpson, I know all about you." I said, "What do you know?" He said, "[Senator Dale] Bumpers [of Arkansas] told me all about you." I said, "What did he say?" He said, "You'd tell me a lot of funny stories and then you'd stick it up my ass." [*laughing*] Hillary put her hand out and said, "Bill, stop it." ... A little more banter took place. I said, "I'll tear Bumpers's leg off when I see him" and all that chatter that goes with a couple of old pols. Then he went out there to sit there on the front platform and he was soon the president of the United States.

Betty Currie, personal secretary: After the ball and after the inauguration, we went to work the next day. It was pure chaos because they had a security system, not as tight as it is now but still a security system, and none of us had anything except they had our names. I got there and said, "Betty Currie." They found something and they gave me a pass. I went inside and I said, "Where do I go?" They said, "Go to the West Wing, which is over there." I got to the West Wing, and I said, "Betty Currie. Where do I go?" They had a list and they showed me where to go. I went into this room and I said, "Oh, it's a rose garden." There were two dozen fresh roses right there. I said, "Hmm, this is probably not right." So I kept my coat on and sat down and waited for someone to tell me where to go. I think it may have been Nancy [Hernreich] who finally came in said this was it. Wow! ... Being a retired government worker, the first thing I asked for was my job description. They didn't have that.

Part II

Domestic and Economic Policy

12

Out of the Gate
Deciding What to Do First

During the course of Bill Clinton's 1992 presidential campaign, his staff published Putting People First, *a detailed compendium of their plans for what President Clinton would do once elected. That book did not, however, include any indication of which of the hundreds of pages of campaign promises would be the new administration's highest priorities. Clinton had pledged on the campaign trail that he would "focus like a laser-beam on the economy," so there was a general sense that economic policymaking would be the first order of business. Even there, it was unclear, given the recent news of increased budget deficits, how Clinton would approach the economy. And during the course of the campaign, Clinton had pledged to do something on behalf of gays in the military, a commitment he reiterated just before assuming office in January. If, as President John F. Kennedy said, "to govern is to choose," Clinton had important choices to make right out of the box.[1] Senior advisors once uniformly committed to a common goal of getting Bill Clinton elected quickly found themselves in competition for the new president's time and commitment as they themselves grappled with these priorities.*

William Galston, deputy domestic policy advisor: There was an atmosphere of real optimism [at the beginning of this presidency]. There's a bigger story here having to do with the rise of the new American meritocracy and the distinctive sort of consciousness that it generated. I do think that there was a real sense that if you're smarter than anyone else and harder working than anyone else, there's nothing you can't do. And, God knows, Bill and Hillary Clinton met both of those standards and then some. I think they learned better. They may be an irresistible force, but they met an immovable object. I don't think it crossed their minds that they could fail, I really don't.

---

1. Kennedy, "Special Message to the Senate on the Nuclear Test Ban Treaty," August 8, 1963.

Stanley Greenberg, pollster: Our assumption throughout [this early period] is that the economic plan was number one.... He had a budget that had to be done. It wasn't discussable. So you knew you were doing the economic plan. But there were parallel meetings on health care in which there was the question of having the health care plan be part of the budget resolution. That was the First Lady's strong preference.

William Galston: I think ... a fundamental agenda decision had been made really early. The lead had to be the economic plan—that is, the macroeconomic and fiscal plan. The situation of the country, the logic of the campaign, made that mandatory. So the question was not what was going to come first. The question was what was going to come next. And that's where the struggle set in. You really had a sort of a triangular struggle at that point. For the rest of 1993, the issue was what the next phase of the economic plan—particularly the international dimension, NAFTA and GATT [General Agreement on Tariffs and Trade]—was going to be. Is it going to be health care, or is it going to be welfare? ... You could write a history of the twelve months from the late winter of '93 to the late winter of '94 around that triangular struggle and you wouldn't miss much.

Mickey Kantor, secretary of commerce: One thing that's never been reported, or not enough—there was an argument from the very first at Camp David, when he gathered the whole Cabinet at the first part of the administration, about do you go for health care and stimulus package first, or do you go for welfare reform and political reform first? There were some of us in the room, not many, who believed welfare reform, political reform. If you got political reform, you'd take the guts out of the ability of the special interests including the pharmaceutical companies, insurance companies to gut health care, on one hand. And you would also appeal to the Ross Perot voters with both, you'd continue to build your power as you tried to get health care approved.

Everybody knew that would be the toughest thing to do. If you went for a stimulus package and health care first and some other things, you'd just look like a typical liberal Democrat. Some of that also was a result of the flap over gays in the military and there were many worried that he had already positioned himself in the eyes of the public.[2] You need the public to move forward on these issues.

---

2. Clinton had pledged in the campaign to end discrimination against gay servicemen and women, a commitment he reiterated shortly before taking office. That promise brought swift and vocal opposition from conservatives on Capitol Hill and in the Pentagon. Clinton's efforts to navigate through those shoals in the first year led to the compromise policy of "Don't ask, don't tell," which left virtually everyone involved less than satisfied. The political capital invested in that issue was thus unavailable for others that had been more central to Clinton's election bid.

So as a result, the first six months we did come out with a stimulus package, as you recall.... [What] we didn't know is he had already committed to [Democrats] Tom Foley, George Mitchell, and Dick Gephardt, at a dinner in Little Rock, that he would not go for welfare reform because they didn't want him to do so.[3]

Stanley Greenberg: We did polling right after the election and also in December that was oriented toward the agenda going forward. It never occurred to us that gays in the military was going to be first. We didn't poll on it. This issue got blown up. I went back to Little Rock during the transition and tried to address the question there and was told that it was unavoidable, that they had to address the question. I couldn't understand why they couldn't put it off for six months.... [Based] on the public polls, the public was really evenly split on the issue. They just couldn't understand why that's what you're doing first after the election you had. So I was strongly, strongly opposed. Our poll numbers [consequently] crashed.

Lawrence Stein, Democratic aide, U.S. Senate: I don't know how the gays in the military thing evolved.... I've always wondered how he walked into that one. Before he even got to town, he walked into it! While it's not very consequential in a lot of ways, it determined a lot of what went on during the first three months. I can't look at them and say they were incompetent and that happened. I don't believe that. I think a lot of these things happened because of a multiplicity of forces over which no one can really exercise adequate control. So I don't think ... you go to their competence as a dispositive factor. ...

There was a lot of irritation [within the party] that he started off with gays in the military. A lot of people were infuriated by that. The most immediate debacle thereafter was stimulus. That was both a legislative and a public relations disaster.... Then you had his budget. We won legislatively, and lost in terms of public perception.... In fact, it was a capital-depleting exercise.... All of us had to use every bit of our capital to get the votes on the tax bill. So there was enormous frustration with him in Democratic circles, I'd say, as early as six months into his presidency.

* * *

Q: The decision was taken to begin with the budget as the first major item, and then there were several other important matters that could have been next in the queue—the next major item on the agenda. How was that settled?
Roy Neel, deputy White House chief of staff: This was a big internal struggle at the time and it began even before we finished the work on the budget

3. Tom Foley (1929–2013), from Washington State, was Speaker of the House (1989–1995). George Mitchell represented Maine in the U.S. Senate (1980–1995) and was Senate majority leader (1989–1995).

and the economic plan. NAFTA was coming into the pipeline, work was being done already and Clinton had already committed to it. The problem was there was both an ideological divide within the White House about whether to do NAFTA, and the congressional leadership was adamantly opposed to it, Gephardt in particular. I think George [Stephanopoulos] was opposed to it and there were just a number of people in the White House who thought we would lose all of our ground that we'd gained in the budget by going after NAFTA.

Complicating it further was that the health care reform group was itching to go. There was a strong contingent determined that Hillary would take a symbolic role in the White House in the health care reform, which obviously grew into something more. There were those who thought we should move to welfare reform, in other words, build on one victory with another victory, as one more triangulation effort and also something that Clinton believed in.

The problem was several-fold. One, you couldn't predict the outcome of any of these items, any of these agendas. They weren't necessarily uphill, but NAFTA was unclear. Certainly welfare reform was going to challenge our liberal base and health care reform was a complete unknown at that point. This came at a time when my work was focused largely on the schedule because of this train wreck. I decided that this would probably end up being my major contribution to my time in the White House, to somehow organize these agendas so that they wouldn't completely immobilize, or even worse, bring down the White House with a series of failures.

Everyone who had an agenda was trying to use the president's goodwill and his commitment to that agenda as a justification for pushing that agenda over all others. There were divided camps. There were clearly distinct groups that thought it ought to go this way or that way. Not only which item should come up next, but who should be running each agenda item. And everybody was just talking. You'd get a group of people to the president and he'd say, "Yes, I think that's right." Then to the next group he'd say, "That makes sense." They would all come out thinking that they had the president's blessing.

[It] occurred to me one day, I remembered something I had done with Gore early in our Senate days, or right after the '88 election. We were rebuilding our operation. I came up with a very crude technique to get everybody on the same song sheet on Gore's priorities. It was very simple. I simply took a whole bunch of large foam boards and created charts, calendars—January, February, March, so on—and then with different color codings, different agenda items and the amount of time that would have to be devoted. You could come up with a project, say, "How many days are we going to have to devote to this?" Thirty days. "How are we going to pace them?" So you take little colored pieces of paper and put them in there. Very quickly, everybody would be in the room and they'd say, "It's not going to work. You can't front-load ten projects, each of which require thirty days of work and get them done in two months." Then you could work this through and pace things and stage things better.

[Clinton] came in and he said, "What have you got, Roy?" And I said, "What we've got here is the fall schedule. We have to plan this. Everybody thinks that they know what you want. We've got everybody here now and this is the time to figure out what you really want to do and realistically allocate the time." It was probably my only serious successful contribution to the White House.

Q: How many people were in the room, Roy?
Neel: There were probably 15–18 people in the room. . . . A couple of consultants. James [Carville] may have been there, [Paul] Begala may have been there. Stan Greenberg, maybe. Gore certainly, and a couple of other people. We've got all these things, these lines, each date has a box that runs all across a six-month period for health care. All these different agenda items. I said, "There it is. The only totally limited resource we have is your time, the vice president's time and the First Lady's time. Let's go through each one of these things and figure out how much time is going to be devoted to each of these things." And it worked. Somehow, after about five or six hours, they came to the conclusion that they had to do NAFTA. . . . People groused, some thought it was the wrong thing to do, but everybody was on the same song sheet. They plotted after that, then, that health care would come next.

Q: You went ahead and made that decision at that point?
Neel: Yes. Gore was pushing his "reinventing government" initiative, which was already under way. He was determined to get the president's time devoted to that and we programmed that. The decision was made to simply put welfare off. Many believed, and I agree with them, that it was a mistake to put health care before welfare reform. But it's easy in hindsight because no one knew quite then how ambitious and undoable their agenda would be.

William Galston: If you take the health care cassette of the first two years and shove the welfare cassette in and leave everything else the same, the history of the Clinton administration is totally different. If Bill Clinton had gone to the country in the fall of 1994 saying, "It was tough, but we did it. We said in the campaign we were going to end welfare as we know it, and we have broken with fifty years of policy tradition and set this country on a fundamentally different course," it would have made all the difference in the world. . . . But once the decision was made, there was nothing to be done about it. The president had shoved all the chips onto the table, and he couldn't take them back.

Warren Christopher, secretary of state: There's no doubt that in the early months he did emphasize domestic issues, as he very well should have. As I said earlier, I regarded one of the most important foreign policy issues was getting our domestic house in order. When I took my first trip around the world to various capitals, I was being besieged in one capital after another: "Are you going to get your economic house in order?" . . . So I embraced the president's idea of spending maybe a predominant amount of his time on domestic affairs.

13

The 1993 Budget and the Stimulus Package

Having pledged during the 1992 campaign to restore America's economic vitality, Bill Clinton began his presidency committed to adopting economic policies to make good on that commitment. That job had become unexpectedly difficult during the transition period because of the news that the federal budget deficit was in even worse shape than the Clinton team had understood. The new president, convinced by his economic advisors that deficit reduction was the key to achieving a robust recovery, accordingly found himself having to scale back spending dramatically on the investments he had promised. The White House did attempt to preserve a relatively modest spending package to boost the economy back to full speed, but the stimulus bill met with a painful defeat. Soon thereafter the budget bill passed, by the slimmest of margins—with no Republican support in either house. Notwithstanding dire predictions by the opposition, the 1993 budget plan contributed to a decade of economic expansion.

Alan Blinder, Council of Economic Advisors: Candidate Bill Clinton did not really run on reducing the budget deficit in any strong way. That was not a major part of his campaign. It was all about investments and things like that, most of which never got done.

David Kusnet, speechwriter: [Fiscal] conservatism had not been part of [Clinton's] appeal [during the campaign]. A certain measure of fiscal responsibility was implicit, but it wasn't his selling-point.... [Deficit] reduction ... was Paul Tsongas's issue in the primaries and that was Perot's issue in the general election. Deficit reduction as an end in itself, or as a touchstone of economic policy, had not been, as I understood it, central to the Clinton campaign. The title of our campaign document was *Putting People First*. It wasn't *Getting America's Fiscal House in Order*.

Mack McLarty, White House chief of staff: I'll never forget it. Bob Rubin called me ... probably early to mid-December.... [He] sounded like a Houston Space

Center announcement. "Mack, we have a problem." And the problem was the deficit had been forecast at one level, and it was actually $60 to $80 billion higher than that once we evaluated where the real deficit was. And all of a sudden, all of these assumptions which had been relatively valid ... in the campaign were suddenly not workable. And so it meant you were either going to have to raise more taxes or make deeper spending cuts, and it was a serious issue.

Leon Panetta, OMB director: I think the first thing [after the election] is that Bob Reich comes by the office [on Capitol Hill] ... and it's that Robert Redford scene, "What the hell are we supposed to do now?"[1] ... Bob Reich was more interested, obviously, in how to develop funding for the [president's] priorities.... But he ... was [instead] developing the gut awareness that .. [to] get to where [the president] wants to go .. he had to walk through the deficit fire.

* * *

Q: When did the fight start, if fight is the right word, between those who wanted to make the "People First" investment agenda the Clinton agenda at the start, as opposed to those who were more concerned about deficit reduction and so on?
Stanley Greenberg, pollster: It was fairly early in the transition. There was some evidence just simply on who was selected. Particularly Leon Panetta had a long history on the [deficit] issue. You actually didn't know where [Robert] Rubin was. I didn't really know Rubin very well. He had not been very involved in the campaign.... [So] I wasn't sure on the economic side. None of the big economic people were part of the policy group that dealt with major speeches or debates [during the campaign]. They came in during the transition. In early January we had the meeting with Gene Sperling[2] and George [Stephanopoulos] in Little Rock in which he [Rubin] laid out the implications of the budget decisions made. That was the first time the scale of it was apparent.

We knew there were issues. I wrote a memo right afterwards, not highlighting the conflict, just noting priorities. I was actually more worried that welfare reform was going to get lost.... [Within] a few days of the election ... I wrote, "The closest thing we have to 'Read my lips' is on welfare reform and that ought to be part of the thinking."[3] What was animating me afterwards was not the

---

1. Redford starred as the title character in the 1972 political drama *The Candidate*. He concluded a successful, raucous campaign for the U.S. Senate with the film's final lines, "What do we do now?"

2. Gene Sperling had been a policy advisor during the 1992 campaign and became deputy director (1993–1996) and then director (1996–2001) of the National Economic Council.

3. As a presidential candidate in 1988, Vice President George H. W. Bush punctuated his opposition to tax increases by famously asserting in his Republican convention acceptance address, "Read my lips—no new taxes!"

deficit. I didn't think that was where the battle was. I thought the battle would be on the cultural issues that would get pushed back. . . .

The biggest issue that we pressed was not losing track of the investment agenda. In January I spoke on the Hill to the leadership, the message group, the various retreats of the House and Senate after Congress came back, in the lead-up to the inauguration. When I look at my presentation notes, it's very much focused on—it's almost as if I'm trying to create pressure myself for my position. I said, "[Clinton's] absolutely committed to this." Now, I don't know at the time that he is absolutely committed to it. I'm questioning whether he is. But I lay this out that this was in his gut and that if you go back through his entire history, this is what it is rooted in. This is how he wants to govern.

If I look at the amount of time devoted in my notes to various subjects, the main topic was the budget, the priority on investment, the economic plan with investment as a major part of it. There was a real disjunction—I now know things I didn't know at the time, even though we were briefed in early January on the budget and what it would mean. One, we didn't know whether it would stick with him. We'd been through this before where you go through a long process and you don't know where it's actually going to come out. But he actually committed to parameters on the budget, coming out of the early January meetings, which basically precluded the investment agenda. It was no longer possible.

[If] you . . . dropped out the investment agenda, we at best had about 40 percent support for the economic plan. We're talking about going to Congress with an economic plan with 40 percent support in the country. How do you get the Congress to move with you if you're going to them [with that]? . . . [During] the election, he was never focused very much on deficit reduction. We never advertised on deficit reduction. It was not his passion.

Roger Altman, deputy treasury secretary: [Much] has been made of the dueling camps [within the Clinton network], the deficit hawks versus the populists. . . I think as a general matter the perception, which has become the accepted wisdom, of those dueling camps is much overstated. There were not pitched battles. There was not a war going on. Mostly because Clinton put everyone in a room, for endless hours, to the point where most people wanted to drop and everybody was sitting there around the table. It wasn't a process where people were maneuvering furiously to see who could get the last word in to the president or something. Everybody was sitting in a room for the endless hours that have been so widely written about, which was quite a chaotic, disorganized process and not particularly presidential process. But everybody felt such a part of it because they were sitting right there. The two camps were right there sitting in front of the president for six hours at a time.

So there was not a war of the type that has so often been written about, just not true. Were there different views? Sure. But was it a battle? No. I've seen Washington battles and that wasn't one of them.

Robert Rubin, National Economic Council director: [During] the campaign, the so-called twin deficits, the fiscal deficit and the deficit in public investments, [were] all fit together into one program that eventually wound up in that little booklet *Putting People First*. During the campaign, at least, they put together a bit of a budget. It was an attempt—it wasn't a rigorous budgetary process, but it was something of an attempt to put it together in a complex way. As you know, when they got all finished with it, they had room for a vigorous public investment program, a middle-class tax cut, and deficit reduction.

Now, they weren't governing, and it's fair to say that some of the assumptions in that were a little bit permissive, but fundamentally, that was a framework that worked. It was only after the election, when [Richard] Darman[4] put out that last set of projections—I remember that very well, that last set of projections—and greatly increased their projections looking forward of the deficits, that we had to go to President, or President-elect, actually, Clinton, and say we have to reconfigure this thing because the configuration you have is based on numbers that no longer are applicable. That's when ... he had to give up his middle-class tax cut and he had to scale back his spending.

Q: There were some accounts after this period that Alan Greenspan[5] had played a part in helping move the president-elect in the right direction.
Rubin: I'm going to tell you what my account is and that is what actually happened. [*laughs*] There may be various other accounts. Yes, sometime during the transition Greenspan came down and met with Clinton.... Greenspan was a very constructive force in that sense, but all the discussions we had with President Clinton were framed in terms of what effect is this going to have on the bond market. Then we talked about the Fed, but it was the bond market that drives the economy and affects interest rates, too. That was really at issue here.

Bob Woodward, when he wrote his book[6]—He's a very good journalist, but he said that Greenspan and Clinton had made a deal. I was at NEC [National Economic Council]. I was certainly totally unaware of it. Nobody else on the economic team knew anything about it. I asked both Greenspan and Clinton whether that was so and both of them said no, so I didn't put that in my book. [*laughs*]

There was a memo of some kind. I don't remember now precisely what it was, and ... Bentsen had written something on there about Greenspan. Woodward may have inferred from that—... Bentsen I couldn't ask, unfortunately. As you

---

4. Richard Darman (1943–2008) was the outgoing director of the Office of Management and Budget under President George H. W. Bush.

5. Alan Greenspan was the chairman of the Federal Reserve of the United States from 1987 to 2006.

6. Woodward, *The Agenda: Inside the Clinton White House* (New York: Simon & Schuster, 1994).

know, he's not well. . . . But I can't conceive that we would have had all those discussions, first during the transition, then in the Roosevelt Room, about what to do, how much deficit reduction to have, how the budget should be framed, if in fact what was sitting there was a deal that had already been made. There's no question that it did not occur. . . . I think there's zero chance this could have happened without my knowing about it, but even beyond that, I did ask Bill Clinton and Greenspan; they're pretty good witnesses.

Roger Altman (on the key factors leading to President Clinton's initial economic decision to concentrate on the deficit): [*First*], it begins I think with the economic and fiscal circumstances that the administration faced: the recession of '91 and early or mid-'92, . . . [and] the evolution of the deficit estimates during that period. When we took office and took a hard look at the deficit estimates, they were considerably worse than we had thought. . . . If I'm not mistaken, we were looking at a $350 billion deficit, up from about $260 or something that we had been generally using during the campaign.

The *second* point is the nature of the key individuals chosen. It should have been, I suppose, more evident at the time, but such things never are. That by choosing Panetta, and Bentsen, and Rubin, he chose economic conservatives. . . . So, looking back on it, the nature and the history of those three men had a lot to do with the eventual outcome. Also, strong figures, not weak figures.

So, *third*, economic policy was number one. This had been the thrust of the campaign, so expectations were very high that Clinton would come forward with a real economic program, a comprehensive program, and from the moment that all these folks were chosen the question was, What is that program going to be?

Fourth, I recall that the economic forecasts for '93 were not very heartening. It's fashionable for conservatives to say that the recovery had already begun on George H. W. Bush's watch and that if we just stood aside, the same results would have occurred, but those weren't the economic forecasts we were looking at at the time, nor do I believe that school of thought to be accurate, but that's another matter.

So there are the four main elements. Also *fifth*, to some degree, Alan Greenspan weighed in, and a view developed that if we tightened fiscal policy, there would be the opportunity to loosen monetary policy. He didn't say so, but supposedly he never does. The notion, by the way, in Bob Woodward's book, *The Agenda*, that Greenspan was hovering over the proceedings like an angel of death is completely fictitious. Greenspan's name hardly came up during these discussions. So I attribute that to just the fact that Woodward talked a lot to Greenspan, but that may be just an incorrect take on it. But there was the sense, based on conversations—I think you could go back and say that there were some discussions between Bentsen and Greenspan, Rubin and Greenspan, Clinton and Greenspan, although the sum total of those conversations probably took an hour. But, in any event, there was some sense that if we would tighten fiscal policy, there was the opportunity to loosen monetary policy.

[The] next point I want to make is, there was a fateful meeting ... in Little Rock, up at the transition, with the economic team, lasted many hours, very organized meeting in the sense that it had a set of presentations and then a broad discussion. . . . I think the critical revelation that day was the notion—initially I believe put forth by Alan Blinder, that a certain amount of deficit reduction ought to translate into a certain level of interest rate response, which in turn should be more stimulative—should inject more stimulus into the economy than anything that we could do on the fiscal side. That notion took hold at that meeting ... in December. . . . The entire economic team flew on a chartered plane down to Little Rock. We met for six or seven hours in the Governor's Mansion there. That was the day the earth moved and Clinton's view changed.

Bob Rubin talked with great credibility about the bond market responding, and James Carville was so amusing for so long afterwards saying he wanted to come back in his next life and be the bond market because everybody paid such fealty to it. But, in any event, the presentations were very effective and that was, I think, the most important single day in the evolution of that original policy. . . . Clinton deserves tremendous credit. He saw the opportunity, he seized it, went against the grain, and, let's face it, presided over a period of unprecedented prosperity and balanced the budget for the first time in approximately fifty years.

* * *

Q: Could you talk about how the ideas in the campaign got shaped into a program during the transition?

Alan Blinder: That's a long question, we ought to take it in pieces. But the two big answers to that question are Ross Perot ... and the reality of number crunching. Taking Perot first, I think it was Perot and other people—like Rubin and others talking to [Clinton] in the transition period—that really convinced President-elect Clinton that he had to elevate deficit reduction to, if not number one on his priority list, at least close to number one—which had not been the case in the campaign. The second is the reality of number crunching. That is, now you had to go beyond *Putting People First*—a sort of rump budget that had about twelve lines—to a real budget with real numbers that would pass muster with the technicians at ... OMB. And at the Treasury, for the tax estimating. They wouldn't just give you any number you wanted. They had models, and they gave you their true best estimates.

So we then had to put together a program that would add up. . . . After you do all that . . ., you meet the U.S. Congress. Then you really learn the meaning of "The President proposes and the Congress disposes." That's where the BTU tax turned into nothing, and the investments turned into nothing, and the stimulus was obliterated, and so on.[7] . . .

---

7. During the course of the first year's economic debates, the president considered initiating an energy tax based on the British thermal unit (BTU) as a standard of measurement, to apply

Q: But the important thing about the transition period is there ultimately appears to be a crystallized effort to do something about deficit reduction that didn't clearly exist during the campaign period.
Blinder: Absolutely.

Q: And for those of us who were on the outside, the great puzzle is how you get from point A to point B.
Blinder: Now some people point to a meeting at Blair House.[8] I was not there, so you'll have to hear about this from someone else. Some people point to that as the sort of magic moment, in the transition, in December, when a number of people talked to Clinton about the deficit problem.... So I don't really know where the magic moment was. But what I do know is by the time we had the first full-scale briefing for the president-elect in Little Rock and, if memory serves, that was the 7th of January, he was already persuaded that the big deal was going to be deficit reduction.[9]

Q: You think by that meeting he'd already decided that.
Blinder: Definitely. The only questions were—because after all this was root canal politics—whose ox are you going to gore, how much, how, and what's plan B? He was smart enough to know. I'm the one who warned him ... that if things go wrong, what you'll probably have is a recession about the size of the one that George Bush experienced. He had a strong reaction to that. I mean, he was aware that there were hazards here, that if we didn't get the bond market rally, if we didn't get cooperation from the Fed [Federal Reserve Board]—and the Fed, remember, is very independent and Alan Greenspan was not known to be a Democrat—if that didn't happen, there was a hazard that you raise taxes and cut spending and the economy is not that strong anyway, and you wind up with a recession.

So I felt it was our obligation to tell him. There were a number of people in the economic team who really weren't eager to give this message to Clinton because they just wanted to make sure we reduced the deficit, and it was, "I don't want him to hear this." But I thought that was very irresponsible. He got elected president, not us, and he needed to hear this. So he did hear it. So that was the third thing that was on his mind, "What's plan B? How do we get out of this if

---

across various forms of energy. Both it and the administration's stimulus spending package—which included public investments Clinton had emphasized as a candidate in 1992—failed.

8. Blair House is across Pennsylvania Avenue from the White House and is usually placed at the disposal of the incoming administration to assist in the transition to power. It is also called the President's Guest House.

9. Other memories differ, including the account President Clinton provides in his memoir, *My Life*, which indicates (458–461) that he decided on this course of action based on the presentations made by Blinder and others on January 7.

this causes a mess?" We never had to go into any depth or think seriously about plan B because things went well instead of badly. But that was the reason for having a stimulus piece in the plan. The notion, which I don't think was economically naïve but was politically naïve, was that we could sell a package that said: because we're promising so much long-run deficit reduction, we're going to spend a little money up front to make sure the economy moves forward, not backward.

I think, to this day, that made economic sense. But it obviously didn't make political sense. And even more germane to the demise of that program was the way it was concocted.... The stimulus package was described in the original, it probably ran ten pages—all little things—$100 million there, $200 million there, $300 million there. It had no coherence and invited ridicule and accusations that it was pork and so on. I was very unhappy as an economist with what we put forward—not that we put forward a stimulus package, not of its rough size, but of the way it was composed, of a hundred little pieces.

[In the end,] I think it is to his tremendous credit that [Clinton] sized this up and decided to take the risk because he thought it was good policy. You know, a lot of bad things have been said about Bill Clinton over the years, but I really believe he decided to take this calculated risk because he thought it was good for the country. And, incidentally, if it proved to be good for the country, that would help him get re-elected in '96. But that's the way you want a president to think. You do something that's good, four years later the good chickens come home to roost and you get re-elected, and you don't worry so much about four weeks later. To my mind, that's the way you want your president to think, and I think that's the way he was thinking about it then.

The politicals around the table were moaning and groaning and saying, "You promised this, you can't do this, they'll hate you in Macomb County, Michigan, if you do this. They'll hate you in Iowa if you do this."[10] . . .

Q: Do you find Bob Woodward's account accurate insofar as your own personal recollections?
Blinder: The parts that were about the economic team's meetings, I thought were very, very accurate. The only part that I questioned Woodward on, and he then later showed me the proof—he's a good reporter—was the notion that the $140 billion number, which is that fourth-year deficit annual target that we settled on, came from Alan Greenspan. I never heard that in any of our meetings, never ever. But one day it was kind of anointed. I remember one White House

---

10. This reference would seem to be a swipe at the political advisors in general and Stanley Greenberg in particular, whose past work included controversial studies of Macomb County, Michigan.

meeting we came in and we were all around the table, and somehow it had been decided that 140 was the number. And Laura [Tyson] and I looked at each other, *Where did that come from?* And it was never attributed to Alan Greenspan in any of those meetings that I attended. So I said this to Woodward. I said, "I think you've greatly exaggerated the role of Alan Greenspan, I never saw anything like that." He then showed me documents at a subsequent meeting with him.... They were copies of handouts at the meetings with the handwriting of some of the participants saying something to the effect of "Greenspan says 140."

Q: That's very interesting because I was curious about exactly that point.
Blinder: I called him on it, and he showed me convincing evidence. But part of the deal when he showed me, is I can't reveal what he showed me.[11] But the point is, it was very subtle, and I'm glad to hear others have the same recollection. It was just never around the table that "this is the Greenspan number and Greenspan says if you don't hit 140, it will be considered a mouse." There was never any discussion like that in my presence. And I was there at all these big meetings....[There] was a subtle inference that that number would get Greenspan's blessing, and Greenspan's blessing would be awfully nice to have.

Leon Panetta: Well, understand that I think the reason the president wanted to move that stimulus package is because I think he really thought it was insurance against the economic reaction that the deficit-reduction economic plan would produce. And if he could jump-start and turn around the economy with the stimulus package as we were going into this larger economic plan, it made him feel like there was a better chance of having the economy turn around sooner rather than later.

[Robert] Reich and others were pushing it as well, that it's important to move it. I think there was a group of us who were also saying, "Look, we thought the economy was [already] beginning to turn around." ... Politically, do you need to do it, but ... it will take effect too late and it's going to cost a lot of money. So, having said all that, it goes back to the president's thinking. The president having analyzed this get-tough substance of what you have to do in an economic plan, the politics of it, the stimulus gave him that chemistry where he thought, *Aha, if I can do this, then perhaps I can have the best of both worlds*, which is to get the economy turned around and yet do what's right in terms of the deficit.

---

11. The probable source, as Robert Rubin hinted in his interview, was Treasury Secretary Lloyd Bentsen, who is elsewhere cited on multiple occasions by Woodward as a source in his book. Bentsen was too infirm at the end of the administration to contribute an oral history himself.

Roger Altman (on the failed stimulus package): We still joke about that today. That was not a high point of the Clinton presidency.... Clinton of course had committed to that during the campaign and it made fiscal sense in the sense of there being so much economic slack. But what actually turned out to happen was that each Cabinet officer ... came up with a list of favorite initiatives they wanted. Ultimately they were in effect combined into one big wish list, and that wish list went forward.... The Republicans quite shrewdly picked out some that didn't make sense and off the bat marshaled a very focused attack on it. Clinton was offered a compromise by Senators [John] Breaux and [David] Boren.[12] "You can have half of it," or something to that effect. He should have taken it. [Treasury Secretary Lloyd] Bentsen advised him to take it. Clinton made an error, didn't take it. Then it went down to defeat.

Q: Is this a case where the political people were encouraging him to hold his ground?
Altman: Yes, that was bad advice. You don't want to start your presidency off with a legislative defeat. The first vote on one of Clinton's issues was a defeat, which presaged a lot of the weakness that then afflicted him during 1993.

Charles Brain, senior aide to House Ways and Means Chair Dan Rostenkowski: [We] thought that [the stimulus package] was a strategic error, completely blew it. The Democrats coming in, the first thing you do is increase spending. Wrong.

Mack McLarty: Let me just assure you, the first hundred days ... [we] spent countless hours in that Roosevelt Room, going over the economic plan, line by line.... President Clinton knew that budget. He wanted to have his imprint on it, he wanted to discuss—not every issue—but he wanted to be sure it reflected his priorities.... President Clinton ... would go down these lines, and he would identify with something he understood, like airport subsidies for a rural airport, like here in Charlottesville. It's a big number. He would say, "Now, Mack, that would just be like Jonesboro." And I never will forget, Lloyd Bentsen would look like, "Where is Jonesboro? What are you talking about?" It was [Clinton's] way of saying, "I want to be sure I understand this, the decision we're making here, and what impact it's having. And are we going to get a return on this dollar? And is it really needed?" That's what he was saying.

Alice Rivlin, deputy OMB director: One of the things that struck me very much at the time was how much [Clinton] knew, in enormous detail, about programs that affected states, and particularly that affected a small, poor, agricultural

---

12. Southern conservative John Breaux (D-LA) served from 1987 to 2005, and David Boren (D-OK) from 1979 to 1994.

state like Arkansas. If we were talking about food stamps or Medicaid or some kinds of fairly esoteric agricultural programs that I didn't know much about, he knew all about it. So we'd go down these lists and talk about, "Can we cut this, can we cut that?" That conversation would be political, but not in the Begala sense. It was the politicians in the economic team—I thought at the time, *We're playing at parliamentary government here.* We've got a secretary of the treasury who has been a senator. We have a budget director who has been a congressman, and even on the periphery we had some others like Les Aspin and Mike Espy. We're trying to figure out, like we were the British Cabinet, how we pull this off in the Parliament. And the president was very much part of that discussion.

It was absolutely exhausting. The meetings usually convened late in the afternoon and went on through the early evening. Then the president usually had to go to some event. My main memory is being very hungry, because they would go through the dinner hour. Every once in a while the president would get hungry, and then he would call for something to be brought in. It was usually fruit and cookies. These things would be put on the table, and it was like a bunch of kids—Cabinet officers. We were all starving. We would be grabbing for the cookies, and they would disappear very, very fast. And the meeting would go on. That was my main preoccupation in the first few months of the administration.

Let me give you one more anecdote, to come back to the budget. We put together a document for the February 17 speech. . . . That was where I first really came to grips with the disconnect between the economic team and a lot of the White House staff. . . . [They] called a meeting in the White House, in some basement room. I went over to respond to questions, and I looked around the room, and I thought, *These people look really angry. What's going on here? What have I done? Why are they so mad?* And I thought, *Well, I guess they're mad because they've been the spokespeople, they've been running this campaign, and this is the first time they're not.* It was extremely hostile. They all just dumped all over this document. They didn't like it. What they really didn't like was the policy. They didn't like the deficit reduction, and they didn't like the fact that their programs that they'd been out there campaigning for weren't in it.

But they also didn't like the transfer of power: *We've been running this show and now all of a sudden these older folks we don't even know think they're running the government.* So we had that session, which I came away from sort of shaken. . . . That was the first moment that I really realized how angry they all were. It was tense. In retrospect, I don't know whether I could have handled it better. It was strange.

Q: They thought you were hijacking their president.
Rivlin: Absolutely. . . .

Q: In Bob Woodward's book, he says that there was some communication between the White House and Greenspan about how much deficit reduction was necessary to get interest rates down. Was there any kind of an arrangement?
Rivlin: There was no arrangement. If you know Alan Greenspan, you know that he wasn't going to make a deal with anybody.

Roger Altman: The vote [on Clinton's 1993 economic package] was really the most dramatic moment I ever experienced in six-and-a-half years of government service. . . . The House voted first, and on the day of the House vote we didn't think we had the votes, or at least we thought the odds were too high that we would lose. The most frantic imaginable effort was going on during the five or six hours preceding that vote. Whatever was going on on the deck of the *Titanic* was comparable, but it was absolutely frantic and incredibly dramatic and tense.

I spent the last couple of hours of that period in the Oval Office with the president and that was quite unforgettable too because the president was hugely animated, to some extent discouraged, to some extent angry, and there were moments when I was the only one in there with him. He knew that if we lost this vote it was a severe blow. So he was frantically calling members of Congress as various requests came in for him to do so. The number of possible votes at that stage had dwindled down to a tiny number, votes that were undecided.

I recall speaking about twenty minutes before the vote to [Congresswoman] Marjorie Margolies-Mezvinsky,[13] with whom I had developed a friendship, and it became evident to me that she was very reluctant but willing to vote for the bill. I put the president on the phone with her and of course, she cast the decisive vote. . . . It turned out to be the equivalent of walking the plank. The president said to me at one moment when we were alone, and with great heat, he said to me, "Roger, you see, there's no constituency at all for Wall Street economics," which is how he viewed his plan, that he'd sold himself to Wall Street and you see there's no constituency for that because we're about to lose.

Anyway, then Secretary Bentsen and I repaired to the little study off the White House, the two of us, just to watch the actual vote. When the voting began, we did not know if we were going to win. We just didn't know, and that's pretty amazing, the biggest piece of legislation, the voting has actually begun. We didn't know if we were going to win. Bentsen, of course, didn't know the House as well as he knew the Senate, so it wasn't unusual that he himself wouldn't know in the House. We sat there, the two of us, watching it on television, mostly in silence. Then Marjorie made her famous walk to the well, with the Republicans serenading her, "Bye, Bye Marjorie." But if there's a more dramatic moment that one can

---

13. Margolies (divorced from Congressman Edward Mezvinsky in 2007) later became Chelsea Clinton's mother-in-law, when Chelsea married Marc Mezvinsky in 2010.

have in government service, at least if you're working in some sort of economic capacity, I can't think of it.

Then of course, the Senate voted the next day and we only had forty-nine votes that we knew about and Senator Bob Kerrey was the undecided vote, the only one left. [All] Republicans had announced their opposition, forty-nine Democrats had announced their support, and Bob Kerrey was strolling around, going to the movies, which is what he was doing. During the day two or three people from the administration spoke to Kerrey—Mack McLarty and Leon Panetta spoke to Kerrey. Then the president spoke to Kerrey. They had a very unsuccessful discussion, which resulted in name calling and cursing. But then Senator [Daniel Patrick] Moynihan[14] spoke to Kerrey late in the day and I thought that was, if not decisive, very influential. He and Kerrey had a very close relationship. Then about an hour before the vote, that's it, we knew that Kerrey would vote for us and then of course Gore could break the tie.

I think history will probably record that as the most important achievement of President Clinton's overall presidency, not the vote itself of course, but the ultimate effects of it. It was absolutely breathtaking, profoundly dramatic and unforgettable, absolutely unforgettable.

Congresswoman Marjorie Margolies (D-PA): When I walked in that night they [the Republicans] were high-fiving. I was so mad. I was watching the vote. Democrats were behind me and they were saying they were going to change their votes. I said, "What, are you crazy? We're not going to get anything done for five months if this [loses]. Are you guys nuts?" There was such a spineless-ness there. . . . I said to [a couple of my aides], "I think we've got to vote for it," and both of them said, "You're crazy. They can find somebody else." I said, "I hope they can, but I'm getting the feeling that it might be awfully close." I used a couple of inappropriate invectives. "We're talking about people who want to stay here." So that was it. . . . I think what nature does is it protects you from remembering very bad accidents and voting at 218. It was just like a very bad, head-on collision for me, . . . absolutely one of the most unpleasant days of my life.

George Mitchell (D-ME), Senate majority leader: Every single . . . Republican voted against it and almost all of them said that if Clinton's budget passed, interest rates would go up, unemployment would go up, the economy would tank, job creation would go down, inflation would rise. In other words, what they said is all the bad things would go up and all the good things would go down. And of course as we all know, the opposite happened. All the good things went up and all the bad things went down. They were 100 percent wrong.

---

14. At the time, Daniel Patrick Moynihan (1927–2003) was a Democratic senator from New York (1977–2001).

Roger Altman: One of the many stunning things about [that vote] is the fact that none of those Republicans paid a price of any kind for that.... Phil Gramm,[15] I'll never forget, predicted that it would usher in a new depression—I mean depression, not recession. He voted against it, we had a boom, he never paid a dime's worth of price for that.

* * *

Q: In February '94 the interest rates started going up. And in some accounts, you get a picture of a president who is highly aggravated. Can you tell us about that?
Alan Blinder: Oh, yes, he had a very simple attitude. Now remember, you can go back and link this to the Little Rock briefings, where I had told him that he was betting his presidency on either the Fed being cooperative with interest rates or the bond market rallying. We had the bond market rally, so we had this tremendous success brewing.

Everything is going really swimmingly well by February 1994. And one day, Bill Clinton gets, to him, blindsided—although in fact the move was well telegraphed by [Alan] Greenspan. But Clinton's not a Fed watcher. He's got other things on his mind. He gets blindsided by Greenspan raising interest rates. "Why did he do that? Everything's working out great." He couldn't understand it. He was totally enraged, and a bunch of us went in to him probably more than once to try to explain what the Fed was doing. We said, "It isn't so bad, it isn't going to kill the recovery. There's a reason, interest rates were abnormally low. They couldn't stay that low," and we sort of calmed him down.

Then that got repeated with the next interest rate hike. Every time Greenspan raised interest rates, Clinton raged inside the White House. But to his everlasting credit, this just shows how smart he was, this was all private. He never made a peep publicly that he was angry at the Fed, or in any way hinted that he was trying to jawbone the Fed. And he didn't, to my knowledge, ever pick up the phone and scream at Alan Greenspan. If that ever happened, I didn't know about it. And I think I probably would have known about it. He was smart enough to take the advice he was getting from all of us—from Rubin, from me, from everybody—that a president who picks a fight with the Fed is likely to lose.

Alice Rivlin (on the extraordinary economic growth of the Clinton years): I'll give you my standard answer to this, which is that I think there were multiple causes for the boom of the '90s. The technology was just at the right moment, apparently, for a real surge in productivity in the mid-'90s. Now, that has a lot to do with the revolution in computing and telecommunications, but the mystery is, why did it occur in the mid-'90s? This was an ongoing technological

15. Phil Gramm represented Texas as a Republican in the U.S. Senate from 1985 to 2002.

revolution. We'd had computers and telecommunications evolving quite rapidly for about twenty years, and no apparent effect on productivity until the mid-'90s. There isn't really a very good explanation of that except that it does take a while for technology to affect production.

The economic historians who've looked at the impact of railroads or the electric motor, the steam engine find that it takes a while before the use of the technology catches up with what is possible. You actually rearrange the way things are done to take advantage of new technology. So I think the timing was just right. By the mid-'90s we were able to take advantage of the potential of information technology for increasing productivity, and the economy just took off. The increase in the rate of productivity increases is what is really significant there.

But I think policy helped, and it was three kinds of policy. One was the fiscal policy. We finally got the budget deficit coming down and very low interest rates, or interest rates coming down, and by the end of the decade, very low. The effort to get the budget deficit down—the main thing was getting it coming down rather than going up. At the beginning of the decade, all the forecasts had it going up, and more and more upward pressure on interest rates would have occurred if the turn hadn't come. Whether it was important to get it to balance, who knows? But that the direction was down, and that it was taking pressure off the bond markets and releasing more capital for investment, is certainly significant.

The Federal Reserve helped, I think, considerably. Monetary policy worked out well in this period. The Fed slowed the economy down in '94, when they thought there was some danger of inflation, and then reversed in '95. And by the time I got to the Fed in '96, we were beginning to realize that productivity was going up, that inflation was not an imminent danger. We didn't do the kind of interest rate increases that you might have thought when the economy was growing that rapidly. So I think the fiscal policy and the monetary policy really were the right ones. . . .

But then I think there's another set of things that were enabling conditions. We'd had a long series of policies that deregulated the economy in various dimensions, increased its competitiveness—trade, culminating with NAFTA, and deregulation of airlines, and a lot of other things, trucking. And then, even going back to the '80s, the restructuring of American industry in the '80s under the threat of Japanese competition and the high dollar, which was very punishing at that point, and really decimated the Rust Belt. They had to restructure in a major way.

But all of that had already happened, and so it all came together in the '90s: the technology, the good policy, the readiness of American industry to take advantage of it. Also a new business ethos, much more competitive and aggressive—It had become normal to re-engineer your company and try to be more efficient. That was kind of revolutionary stuff in the late '80s. By the '90s, it was what business people did. So I think that all of that came together, and it's very hard to sort it out. I don't think anybody will.

Henry Cisneros, secretary of housing and urban development: [The] deficit reduction strategy ... was the greatest success of the Clinton administration. That is to say, it created the conditions in which all of the other successes of the Clinton administration could go forward. The longest expansion in American history, record job formation, record business formation, declines in poverty rates, lowest minority poverty rate since statistics were compiled in the 1960s, actual reduction in the gaps in distribution and income, highest home ownership rate in American history. Social indicators improving, including educational dropout rates, teenage pregnancies. All of that based on general prosperity, which was a result of the deficit reduction strategy.

14

NAFTA

One of the ways that Bill Clinton established himself in 1992 as a different kind of Democrat was by embracing a free trade agenda at odds with his party's forceful labor constituency. The most concrete manifestation of this stance was Clinton's endorsement of the North American Free Trade Agreement (NAFTA), which was negotiated by his Republican predecessors and intended to reduce trade barriers between the United States and Canada and Mexico. Congress would have to vote in favor of NAFTA relatively quickly in the new administration, as the clock was ticking on the agreed-to time frame for its enactment. Democratic majorities in both chambers made those prospects slim, however, unless the president invested substantial political capital in its enactment. This he did—despite significant distress within even his own administration. Some labor-oriented members of the White House staff, when asked how they could go along with Clinton in what they saw as a betrayal of the party's interests, took to replying, "NAFTA? Because we hafta."

Charlene Barshefsky, deputy U.S. trade representative: Trade policy, despite the occasional fits and starts, has been on a reasonably consistent trajectory since Franklin Roosevelt. Every administration since—six Republican, six Democrat—has pursued a more open trade path, a freer trade path. Jerry Ford made the best comment on this. He once said that when he and John Kennedy were in the Congress, neither had a perfect record on trade. But when each became president, they became free traders. That is the picture you see at 10,000 feet when you're president of the United States—the importance of trade as an engine of growth, alliance-building, and an adjunct to peace and stability.

Mickey Kantor, U.S. trade representative: [Clinton] is not a free trader in the classic sense at all. People—observers, authors, reporters—get it wrong. He's an open trader, he believes in open markets, he believes in a rules-based system. But he also believes in order to move forward you've got to convince the American people of two things that we didn't do historically: one, trade was in our interest to build our own standard of living, and that two, he wouldn't give away our markets. That we believed in reciprocity of trade.

If you read his statements over the administration, you will see they come up time and time again. He also believed, third, that trade had become an integral part of foreign policy, that economic policy and foreign policy had become almost synonymous, that your connection to other nations in a globalized world that was interdependent was much through trade and you could use trade, both as a carrot and a stick, as you tried to move forward. And he also saw that economic issues couldn't be successful, domestically, economically, unless he built real connections to and opened markets outside the U.S. . . . People forget that in Arkansas where it is chickens or trucks, rice or other things, they're a fairly big export state. He had both been the beneficiary of it, and frustrated by inability to crack open markets in Japan and in other areas. He had traveled, not extensively but a fair amount, as governor of Arkansas. This was not a typical small-state governor.

Al From, head of the DLC: In September 1991, we had a meeting of the so-called Clinton exploratory committee. He was thinking of running. It was a day-and-a-half meeting of all these people from around the country who were giving him their advice, and a lot of it was to back off on NAFTA. At the end of it, Clinton listened and listened, and he finally just said, "If you want me to be a protectionist and an isolationist, get another candidate because I won't do it." I think that was a very important part of his presidency.

David Kusnet, speechwriter: I actually have some points to make about NAFTA that I don't think others who you have interviewed would be familiar with. During the campaign, Clinton had a very nuanced position on NAFTA that he was not really able to put—even assuming that the will had been there—was not able to put into practice as president because it would have involved all kinds of domestic public investments that economic conditions and the course he chose [emphasizing deficit-cutting over public investments] did not allow him to pursue. But I remember when he gave a speech that he gave before the California AFL-CIO [American Federation of Labor-Congress of Industrial Organizations] during the primary in that state in 1992. By that time, Clinton's only opponent was Jerry Brown [at that time, the former governor of California], who was against NAFTA. Brown was being seen as an eccentric, underfunded, so that Clinton, even in Brown's home state, had a very strong chance of winning, as he did.

Clinton gave an entirely extemporaneous, and I think uncovered and perhaps closed-meeting speech to the AFL-CIO in California about NAFTA. I had a friend who did trade issues for the AFL-CIO—they had a transcript, and she showed it to me after I joined the Clinton campaign. My friend was very impressed with it as was Richard Rothstein, who was a journalist. Rothstein has been a union organizer in the clothing and textile industry, which had been hit very hard by imports. But he was still very impressed with Clinton's approach to trade in general and NAFTA in particular. Now he is best known as an education expert. He was, as with me, someone who came from a union background. I remember that my friend at the AFL-CIO and Richard Rothstein, when I went to work for Clinton, both reached out to me and said, "You've just got to find out what he said in California and have him say that about NAFTA."

What he said—and this is very Clintonian, very complex—was, at least in my view not a way to fool people but a way to explore complex issues. He began with his usual rap in '92. "The American people, working Americans, are taking it on the chin." There were stagnant wages, rising unemployment, the whole litany. Then he asked the key questions: "Why is this happening? And what can we do about it? Part of it is globalization, but the world economy is being more global, we can't stop globalization, we can only adapt to it. A large part of it is our failure to adapt properly. West Germany, other countries are in the same global economy that we are in, but they provide better for their people and their workers without taking it on the chin the way ours are. I know that Americans, especially here in California, in Texas, are concerned about trade with a low-wage economy like Mexico." Then he gave a whole litany of abuses that were already happening to workers on both sides of the border, even without NAFTA.

He had a whole litany of what was happening on the border, the *maquiladoras* [assembly plants in free-trade zones in Mexico, where U.S. companies would ship work to take advantage of low wages and lax enforcement of labor standards], the jobs fleeing to Mexico and so on. Then he said, in effect, "But I have a secret for you. This is all happening now *before* NAFTA has gone into effect. You and I can argue about whether NAFTA will have a positive effect or a negative effect, but here's one thing I can tell you. Everything that you are afraid of happening with NAFTA is already happening. That's God's honest truth." That got people thinking. Because they knew the Bush approach to NAFTA was: it's going to be this great thing, trade is great, everything's great. Clinton was showing that he was not only in touch with reality, but maybe even a little more in touch with reality than some opponents of NAFTA, because he knew the problems that people were afraid that NAFTA would cause were already happening.

Then he says, "If we do NAFTA wrong, things will get worse." He didn't remember that by '93. [*laughter*] "But if we do NAFTA right, things will not get better, but maybe we'll be able to do the things that really matter." Then he goes into his domestic program, which included job training and retraining for workers displaced by trade, and public investments in infrastructure and technology to provide jobs for unemployed workers. That was the structure of his speech at the California AFL-CIO. While I tried to include these points in the draft for his NAFTA speech, in hindsight I should have said, "You should give that speech [the California AFL-CIO speech, minus what was specific to that audience] as your NAFTA speech." . . . Essentially he had a lot of the assumptions of the anti-NAFTA people and the conclusions of the pro-NAFTA people and you really couldn't find any human being on earth except him who saw it that way.

Roger Altman, deputy treasury secretary: I think one misunderstood aspect of his embracing NAFTA was—at that point [late summer of 1993] he was being widely criticized for lacking in principle, lacking in conviction, a weathervane all over the place politically. I think part of him saw an embrace of NAFTA as an opportunity to reestablish that he was a person of conviction, that he wasn't just in the pocket of the old traditional Democratic constituencies, wasn't just a tax-raiser and spender. I think he saw the political opportunity presented by that in addition to the basic merits of NAFTA. In retrospect, I think those are the two main reasons he embraced it. But it wasn't clear that he was going to do so until not long before he did.

Mack McLarty, White House chief of staff: I asked the president three times if he was sure he wanted to go forward with NAFTA. I knew that's what I thought was the right decision, but there were different points of view in the White House. I recall riding in one evening from Andrews [Air Force Base] with him in the car, and I said, "Mr. President, now we're getting ready to make this decision before the August break to announce we're going forward on NAFTA. Are you certain that's the decision you want to close on?" He looked at me, one of the few times he was slightly terse—not rude—and said, "Well, Mack, I told you this twice." And I said, "Yes, sir, I understand that, but I want to be sure, because not everybody feels this is the right sequence of legislation." He said, "I'm well aware of that. We need to go forward, or we're going to lose it." I said, "I understand that, Mr. President. I just want to be sure we got our signals straight."

William Galston, deputy domestic policy advisor: I think there was a reasonably clean decision made not to shelve NAFTA during this period.... [The clock running for enactment] was one of the arguments in favor of not shelving it. On the other hand, lots of people were saying, "Mr. President, if health care goes down, your presidency may as well. Aren't you taking risks that maybe you don't have to take?" So it was recognized that this was a fairly consequential decision. But the president, to his great credit—knowing that he didn't command anything like consensus, and perhaps not even a majority within his own party, and knowing that this would foul the political waters inside the party—really thought that it was important to send a signal to the country and the world that he meant it when he said a more open regime and international trade were in the long-term interest of the United States. This is why in the end-game he took the unusual step of mobilizing several past presidents and bringing them to the White House. That was a sign of how important he thought the issue was to the national interest. He lobbied ardently for it.

Alice Rivlin, deputy OMB director: [It] was the late summer of '93. Leon [Panetta] was in California, so I was the acting budget director. There was a meeting at the White House, which I really thought was, again, a very good decision process. The president brought in everybody—I don't remember if it was the full Cabinet, but it was everybody who was involved in NAFTA. He listened to the pro argument, which was Warren Christopher and probably Mickey Kantor. Certainly I remember Warren Christopher being very strong on the pro-NAFTA side and why it was so important.

Then the other side was held up by some of the political folks, and that might have been Howard Paster.[1] It was giving the union arguments against it and why this was not good for the American working folks. There was a lot of back and forth. I don't know whether this was a Bob Rubin–structured meeting, but it ran like a Bob Rubin–structured meeting.

I think the president had already made the decision, but he wanted to give everybody their day in court. He listened to the pro arguments and the con arguments, and then he made a decision right there. Now, he'd probably already made it, but he explained his decision right there, that this was something he had promised to do in the campaign that he thought was the right thing to do. It might be politically costly, but he thought that he had no choice but to go ahead with it. And I thought, *Wow, that's right.* I agree with that, and I'm glad he's got the courage to do it. Then we all fanned out and sold NAFTA. I got to do the steelworkers in Boston—no, machinists, I think it was. But I remember that one was a hard sell.

Mickey Kantor: [He] wavered in June, in July of '93. . . . If you ask me what was in his head—he works on so many levels, he may have been thinking he would have to back off ultimately with a Democratic Congress and the animosity towards NAFTA. Because what would you say to your USTR [trade representative]? Even to me, as close as I was to him, he wouldn't have said it to me even if he thought it. I don't know if he thought it or not.

We got to June and July. He had agreed with Bob Rubin we had to go for the tax rise and what I'd call fiscally responsible economic package. It was in the Congress and we needed every Democrat we could find, and we wanted to introduce health care. NAFTA ran against both. At least, on the surface you look and say, "Wait a minute, NAFTA is counter to our strategy, as an administration, because we lose Democrats. We can't afford to lose Democrats. How are we going to do this?"

We had one big meeting in the White House. . . . Maybe I shouldn't be doing this but I will say it, it's clear. I said, "Look, if in fact we can't get the stimulus package done and get health care introduced—" which was so important to the administration—"NAFTA will go bye-bye because all I have to do is be so tough on the environmental side agreements with Mexico and Canada [that they] will

---

1. Howard Paster (1944–2011) was President Clinton's first congressional liaison. He had previously lobbied for the United Automobile Workers union.

never agree. We'll look good to Democrats, we can hold our votes." I said, "I don't believe that is in the best interests of the country, in terms of trade and so on. I could argue this is a political decision that has to be made." And we talked it through and never said, "No, we can't do that. It wouldn't be responsible to do that." We actually had a discussion about that, there were maybe fifteen people in the room.

We were in terrible trouble when we started in terms of votes. Terrible trouble. And the president, through sheer force of personality and brilliance of presentation day after day, brought Democrats and Republicans down to that White House and convinced them they had to do this. We did some horse trading. We opened the candy store, we gave away everything we could find in order to make this pass.

Roger Altman: In the last forty-eight or seventy-two hours, because that vote was also a cliffhanger, ... there were deals being cut like crazy, deals on tomatoes, deals on Florida citrus. Everything imaginable.... There were so many exceptions and carve-outs and so forth from the final bill that you couldn't count them. Mexican trucking, citrus, tomatoes, I'm not joking. There were probably twenty-five major separate deals negotiated to win the passage.

Roy Neel, deputy chief of staff: Ross Perot represented a major roadblock for us in passing NAFTA. He had a big foghorn. He tapped into a small but deep and passionate opposition to a free trade agreement like this and he couldn't be ignored. When the invitation came forth from Larry King[2] to have Perot on, King's people figured it out, "Let's get someone to come on from the White House." It was easy to determine that the president shouldn't do it, that was not a presidential activity. The obvious suspects were Bentsen or any number of people. But Al [Gore] figured out that it was a big enough deal, and he had a lot of self-confidence that he could do this.

He also saw Perot as being vulnerable. It would be easy, if it was handled deftly, for Perot to look like a nut. You wouldn't have to go at him hard personally, but just that he was so volatile that he would rattle and the gloves would just come off if he were challenged in a certain way. Gore very quickly volunteered to do it. There were a number of people on Clinton's staff who strongly opposed it for a variety of reasons. None of those people could be found the next day.

---

2. Larry King hosted longtime interview programs on the radio and television, and was especially important in providing Ross Perot a platform to promote his candidacy for President in 1992. When King hosted a debate on NAFTA between Perot and the vice president in 1993, Gore was widely judged to have beaten back Perot and his arguments, creating favorable momentum for the agreement.

William Galston: The two most significant economic decisions he made in '93 ... were both agenda-driven and not poll-driven. [There] is no way that he polled his way to a Bob Rubin economic plan, ... [and] you didn't have to take more than a week of Democratic Politics 101 to know what a free trade agenda was going to do to the party when the country perceptually was still mired in a fairly prolonged recession.... So I have to give Clinton a lot of credit for those two decisions, which were very important decisions for the country for the remainder of the decade, because he paid a huge political price for them.

15

Health Care

Health care reform was the centerpiece of domestic policy in the Clinton presidency, in retrospect less because it was an issue upon which Clinton based his campaign for the White House than because of how he decided to feature it once he took office. First, at the very outset of his presidency he signaled to the world his personal commitment to the reform effort by designating Hillary Rodham Clinton to direct it. Second, once he had dispatched the two inherited items on the agenda that could not wait—the economic package and NAFTA—he moved health care reform to the head of the line of administration priorities. He made an extraordinary address to a joint session of Congress in September 1993 to proclaim his commitment to fixing a broken system. But the initiative died a painful death, victim both to self-inflicted wounds and to an opposition highly motivated by reasons of politics and policy to deny Clinton what would have been an epochal victory.

William Galston, deputy domestic policy advisor: I'm sure if you interviewed the former president … he would tell you that the decision to lead domestic policy with an issue that collapsed catastrophically and ignominiously dealt a blow to the momentum of the Clinton presidency from which it never recovered. From the collapse of the health care plan to the last day of his presidency he was on the defensive.

Stanley Greenberg, pollster: If you're taking a signature issue that helped bring [Clinton] down at the outset of his presidency, it's the failure on health care. But the design of his health care [plan] came out of his [own] intellectual work and thinking through what policy made the most sense. We never polled and said, "All right, what should be the form of this health care proposal?" It came out of a *policy* process, not out of a *polling* process. . . . He holed himself up in a hotel room [before the New Hampshire primary] writing it while we were waiting, like we were waiting for the Pope, for the smoke to change.

* * *

Q: *How much were you thinking about, or were other economists thinking about, prior U.S. health reform efforts as you put together the Clinton reforms?*

David Cutler, health care economics advisor: Very much so. Yes, it had been grappled with and the experience from [Franklin Delano] Roosevelt through [Harry S.] Truman and [John F.] Kennedy and [Jimmy] Carter and the [Ronald] Reagan years actually was there. [Everyone] thought that this time was different, when of course it wasn't. Also, the priorities in the government were different in that there was the enormous budget deficit, and there was a sense that the economy wasn't moving. So there was less focus on this broad vision and more focus on how health care could contribute to the other goals.

In fact, the health care economists ... were always much more skeptical about whether any reform effort would succeed because they knew more about the history of failed reforms. The general economists were less aware of that. In government, you tend to get folks who are worried a lot about the budget, so they were worried about health care and its impact on the economy—for firms and so on.... [So] there was some internal tension about how much of the focus was on health care as a problem today because of its cost, and how much was a focus on health care as a long-standing social concern that we have to address in the context of making it a better society.

[There] was a fateful meeting on health care [during the transition] in Little Rock.... It would be January 8th or 9th. It's with the president. The First Lady is there. She sat in the back of the room, quiet. I don't think she said anything. He had maybe decided at that point she was going to lead the health care task force.... That was not announced to anybody. Ira Magaziner was there, and I don't think he said a thing either.... The presentations were done by the health care transition team.... Bob Rubin came for that because the links between health care and the economic stuff were clear at that point.... If I remember right, the meeting did not go very well. The cost estimates were higher than the president had been expecting. He was very concerned about why the costs had gone up.... Yes, it was very clear at that meeting that he wasn't very happy.

Donna Shalala, secretary of health and human services: It's a famous meeting because they all went down [to Little Rock] and the president talked about how he was going to run the health care reform process with his own staff, basically with Ira [Magaziner], and I think everybody had a heart attack because it was so contrary to the way that anyone with Washington experience [would do it]. I'm told that when they got back on the plane, Bob Rubin had three scotches, one after another. ...

There was no way I could turf fight over that.... It was screwy, but when the president and the First Lady decide they want to do something first on, unless it's illegal you support it.

* * *

Q: *Did you have any independent sense about the advisability of putting Mrs. Clinton in charge of this reform?*
Robert Rubin, National Economic Council director: Yes, I did. He had asked me during the transition what I thought about it. I said I thought it was a terrific idea. I didn't know Hillary very well at the time, but she struck me as being smart. The little bit I'd seen of her I liked her. She was very sensible, but I didn't know her that well. I thought it was a terrific idea. In retrospect, it obviously wasn't, but I didn't know enough to know. Two years later I would have given, I think, very different advice.

Charles Brain, congressional aide: I remember that [Dan Rostenkowski][1] told Hillary Clinton, "Your husband has done you no favors by putting you in charge of this health care package, reform." It was really going to be tough stuff.

William Galston: To be direct—the way the leadership of that effort was constituted did not invite a lot of vocal dissent. If you really wanted to screw up things with the First Lady (and arguably with the president as well), expressing doubts about the health care process or its product was a damn good way to go about it.

* * *

Q: *I'm wondering about the value of placing Hillary in a very front-line position on something that central to the administration, especially if the president is inclined to take attacks on her very personally, as any husband would.*
Mickey Kantor, secretary of commerce: Two or three things, and I think they both would say the same thing. One, he did take it personally when she was attacked, whether it was the campaign or otherwise, and it made his reaction to it sometimes not as effective as it should be. I mean, you can get mad for purpose in politics, but you shouldn't get mad just because you're mad. You should try to figure out why.

Two, as has been said, you can't fire your wife. And as two people, forget that they're married and a couple, forget all the other stuff that surrounded their marriage and so on, they worked together better than any two people

---

1. Dan Rostenkowski (1928–2010) represented the Chicago area in the U.S. House from 1959 to 1995. At this time he was chairman of the House Ways and Means Committee.

you can imagine. They're very close. I'm talking about on substantive matters and talking it through and going back and forth at each other. But Hillary had the bit in her teeth, as she should have, and he was right there with her and he was going to support her and he was off on fifty other issues and on health care too.

And third, even if he had thought she was on the wrong road, what was he going to say? How was he going to bring it back? And so, in retrospect, of course it was a mistake. It's easy now to say that. Looking forward it wasn't so easy. Anyone in the administration you would have picked, she probably was the brightest, knew him the best, understood the subject. I mean she's the most— have you ever heard her speak? Full sentences, full paragraphs, organized, never needs a note. Unbelievable talent. She's a terrific lawyer. So he thought this was the best possible person, and looking forward she probably was. We didn't, he didn't, others didn't think, unfortunately, about what would happen if things go wrong, how do we pull it back.

And also, people are very reluctant, almost everyone, with few exceptions to say to him, to say to her, "This is wrong. You're really—" Because both would turn on the person who said it. He has great facility as a politician, usually you can say almost anything to him about anything and he will listen. There are other politicians you can't, you'll never be invited back if you disagree with them. You can disagree with him. When it comes to Hillary, you can't. It is the one thing you can't do.

Chris Jennings, health care advisor: Well, I am aware that they talked it through with Hillary. They knew it was going to be a risk. I don't think they had time to fully calculate how risky it really was, though. They were basically transferring a successful experience of using her and her abilities to navigate difficult policy issues and present something to him and help him promote it. That approach had already proven to be successful in Arkansas on education, so that wasn't so unusual. But I think they had little idea the degree to which it would be different in Washington and on the national stage.

Q: What you seem to be saying is that Ira Magaziner and Hillary Clinton and Bill Clinton basically decided on this task force idea with Hillary Clinton at the head of it. They would seem to be so savvy about some political things and this seemed a blind spot. Or am I misunderstanding it?

Jennings: People were very impressed with her, so I don't think at the time it was viewed as a negative thing at all. It was viewed as a surprising thing, but a non-negative thing. . . . I think in fairness it was more of an illustration of the importance of the issue to the president, I think, on Capitol Hill and elsewhere. "Well gee, he's willing to put her out there and put their capital on the line. He must really care about this issue." It wasn't viewed at the time as, "This is a real stupid idea." Soon thereafter, members of Congress were saying, "You have put her in an awful position, you know. She'll be blamed for anything that goes wrong, and if it fails it will be a disaster." So when people thought about it for a little while it got more negative. But I think the initial reaction was, "Wow, okay, how do I get close to her?" I mean, that's really kind of how it happened in Washington.

You may recall, when she testified at the five hearings, there was nothing but praise, nothing. Now Dick Armey went after her pretty negatively and she jumped right back down his throat. Basically it was viewed in Washington as, "She can handle herself. She knows my interests and she cares."

Senator Harris Wofford (D-PA): Remember that the health care plan was introduced by Hillary to the Congress in extraordinary all-day (maybe day-and-a-half) sessions of the Senate and the House. She and Ira Magaziner (and maybe somebody else) presented it and then for hours answered questions. I was sitting in the midst of Republican senators, who were dazzled by it. They said, "She's really got it." The plan was supported by 70 percent of the people in the first months of polling, and Clinton's popularity was way up.

* * *

Q: What did Hillary Clinton tell you she needed you for? What was that conversation about?
Chris Jennings: Well, she said, "I don't know the Hill, I don't know the members. I don't know the process. I need you to help me, explain. I need to know each of the members' backgrounds, each of their priorities. I need to understand the politics of the Hill as it relates to the policy." However, although I did a lot of policy work in the Senate, I wasn't hired to be the policy person—that was, of course, Ira Magaziner and others. But I was really there primarily to help prepare her for the hundreds of congressional meetings and to prep her for committee hearing testimony.... [It's] incredible. She had over four hundred meetings with members of Congress.... So this whole perception of her not listening or not talking to people, not consulting with Republicans or Democrats, is just completely, absolutely untrue—though some members of Congress would now say that meetings do not make it actual "consulting."

She had a meeting almost every day. So I would draft memos and try to get it to her at a reasonable hour at night, nine or ten, something like that, every night. She would read about each subsequent meeting, what the members' backgrounds were, what their priorities were. The dynamics, if there were to be multiple members in a room, et cetera.... Then we would take her car up to the Hill. I was in every single meeting with her. On the way up, if she hadn't read the whole memo or she had a question, we would talk about that. Then we would have the meetings. We usually would have more than one meeting every time she went up there, so we would go from meeting to meeting to meeting. Then we would come back and do a little of a debriefing. That was my role, that was my work. She would ask me, "What did the members really think?" She would ask me things like, "I'm picking up some negative things about Ira, what do you think? Are there ways we can do this better?" And, "What about this policy, what do you think?" So there was definitely feedback I was giving and a relationship I was building with her on a policy process and personal level. I came to know her as one of the most intelligent and disciplined people I have ever met. I also had the opportunity to see her light side, her dry sense of humor. She really connected well with people and she used her staff to their fullest potential.

Q: *Can you tell us, because you were a witness to these things, a little bit about her operating style with the members?*
Jennings: [These] meetings had the feeling of history. In some ways, it couldn't but help to feel that way when you have the House legislative titans in the room—Dan Rostenkowski or John Dingell[2] along with Mrs. Roosevelt's heir apparent, Hillary Clinton. Here's an anecdote for you.

We went into John Dingell's office. He has around him all of his trophies of all the deer and moose he's shot. He's a lifelong NRA [National Rifle Association] member. Hillary Clinton has just been quoted as saying, "Frankly I think we should have some sort of tax on ammunition," because there are all these people in hospitals who are being shot up and it's costing us huge amounts of money, et cetera. She was briefed, I told her, and she still had the gumption to say, "John, I think this is something worth considering. We should think about doing this." And he said, "Actually, Mrs. Clinton, I really think that's not a very good idea."

What was interesting about the exchange and the subsequent conversation I had with John Dingell about it was that he respected that she would bring up any issue directly to him, whether it was controversial or not, whether it would please him or not. He liked her spunk and her smarts. And he liked that she so idolized and deferred to him. It almost became like a father-daughter type thing. He and Rostenkowski loved her, just loved her. They hated Ira, didn't respect or understand him. But they viewed her as someone whom they wanted to help succeed. Those two members really did want to have health reform secured. To this day I think the whole indictment of Rostenkowski was a huge blow to the process.[3]

Just as I think another big mistake we made—although I'm not sure we had any viable option—was [having] Finance Committee Chairman Bentsen . . . become treasury secretary. If we had Senator Bentsen on the Finance Committee, we might not have the exact bill we proposed, but we'd have a bill.

---

2. John Dingell served Michigan as a Democrat in the U.S. House of Representatives from 1955 to 2015.
3. Rostenkowski was indicted on May 30, 1994, for a series of offenses related to exploiting his office for personal gain. When he stepped down from his leadership positions in Congress, a void was created that complicated the White House's ability to enact its legislative agenda. Rostenkowski subsequently lost his seat in the 1994 midterms. After a plea-bargained mail fraud conviction, he was pardoned by President Clinton in 2000.

Senator Moynihan couldn't deliver. Not only that, he hated the Clintons.[4] Or his staff tried to create barriers between the Clintons and him.

In terms of how each meeting would go, you'd go into a meeting and she would say something personal, generally, about something unrelated to health care. Something they had done or a joint experience, or something about a spouse, or whatever. It would start off with something that was designed to make people at ease with one another. Then she would be very deferential to them, saying, "I'm not the expert here. I want to hear from you," and would not just listen, but would take notes, which they liked. Then there would be a real exchange and it would be basically concluded by, "I'll do whatever is necessary to do, Mrs. Clinton. I really want this to succeed." I mean, it was always a very positive scene.

There were meetings that were less serene, but there was never any type of shouting or anything. I think it's a little bit of how she is, but also the office and the prestige and the decorum and all the rest that goes along with it. I do believe there was never that air of formal relationship or hesitancy to critique when Ira Magaziner was alone in a meeting.

Peter Edelman, health and human services assistant secretary: It was not just that Hillary was going to be the lead person, but the decision-making was going to be controlled from the White House, by Hillary and Ira Magaziner and other people who were on the White House staff. That's something I do know about. It was a continuing frustration for HHS from the very beginning. Whether or not they thought that Donna [Shalala] would be more pliable because she and Hillary had a relationship, Donna was continually irritated about that. Not on an ego level. It was because she and her staff felt, from a very early stage, that the White House was headed in a disastrous direction. She was constantly going to the White House and saying to Hillary this or that about content and being rebuffed. It was a very difficult period for all of those people. . . .

Q: Do you remember being surprised by the president naming the First Lady to head the task force?
Edelman: I wasn't troubled about that because I did not foresee all that it meant. I was troubled about Ira Magaziner, and maybe those are inseparable points.

Q: Why were you troubled by Ira?
Edelman: Because I had an impression of Ira Magaziner. He knew very little about health care. . . . But just because Ira is a very smart guy, the Clintons

---

4. Moynihan strongly disagreed with the Clintons' decision to move health care reform ahead of welfare reform, calling the president's rhetorical support for the latter "boob bait for Bubbas." Moynihan worried that Clinton intended to placate Southern conservatives with words instead of action. Clinton of course did sign a welfare reform bill late in his first term.

thought they could put him in charge of this incredibly complicated subject and he would be able to do what needed to be done. I was very skeptical of that, as were many people. I didn't make that up. I was buttressed in that view by the view of many people.

Q: Why do you suppose they did it?
Edelman: Ira was their pal. There's a combination of things here. The president and Hillary at the beginning, in my judgment, had an exaggerated view of their own combined capacity. It probably was a view that the two of them added together to a whole that was greater than the sum of the parts, that in their synergism they were even more powerful than each individually. So [they say] . . . "We'll all figure it out together, Ira will help us." As opposed to saying, "If I'm going to be in charge of this I need to have at my side the greatest expert in the United States of America to be my policy aide on it." I think it stems from an underlying view that they didn't really need any help, that the two of them could take any problem and solve it.

Roger Altman, deputy treasury secretary: Ira Magaziner himself, whom I had known for some time, was a gigantic intellect. I mean, wow, but an odd personality. So Ira was, to some degree, as you've read thousands of times, off in the corner doing this whole plan. Most of the people who'd been involved in the economic plan or NAFTA for example, weren't part of that. They weren't really involved in the doing of the plan. They'd review it and you'd go to a meeting where you received a nine-hundred-page memo, three quarters of which you didn't understand. The president was in a tough spot because he was hearing from a lot of people that the effort was too ambitious, but on the other hand, Mrs. Clinton was in charge of it. In a curious way he'd compromised his own position. . . . [It's] one thing to say to your secretary of state, at this time Warren Christopher or to Madeleine Albright, it's another thing to say to your wife, "I don't like it."

* * *

Q: Tell us about Magaziner and his operating style.
David Cutler: I think he was brought in to do it because, as a management consultant, he would bring a different perspective on the issue. . . . He's not somebody who knew much about health care. Although, he's very bright, so he learned a lot. . . . [If] you go back to what a lot of the driving issues were—there was a lot of waste, the system works poorly, we can do better—a lot of those sound like what you hire a management consultant for. So there was a sense that rather than the old-guard policy that had failed, it was that we ought to get this new way of thinking and really think of this as, "I want fresh ideas and bright ideas." So that's where he came in. Throughout, he didn't have a lot of sympathy for any of the old-line folks. . . . Those were people who had had their chance, they failed. "I don't want to hear about how hard it is."

Alan Blinder, Council of Economic Advisors: Ira is a very smart fellow who's totally frustrating to deal with. Whatever you argue, he argues back. He's a smart person, not a dummy by any means. But if there's a simple way and a complex way to do it, he always wants the complex way. I think that's the easiest way to describe Ira. So dealing with him was really very frustrating. Not personally, we never had any personality problems with him. He's not bombastic or nasty or anything like that, perfectly pleasant to deal with, nods his head, tells you why you're wrong.

Willis "Bill" Gradison, former member of Congress (R-OH) and president of the Health Insurance Association of America:[5] Ira just unfortunately had a political tin ear. Also, in fairness to him, because he's a very bright fellow, his plan, in my professional opinion—what everyone thinks about it—it was a little bit like a very fine Swiss watch. If somebody has a delicate mechanism with a lot of moving parts, and they've got to work well together to achieve the objective, it doesn't really help to have somebody come along and say, "I'd like to change the main spring," or "I'd like to do this or that," because it throws the whole thing off.

* * *

Q: There was an effort early on to imbed health care within the budget reconciliation process?
Chris Jennings: Yes, that's very important.... Senator [George] Mitchell concluded early on that the only way to pass this through the Senate, in his mind, was to do it in the reconciliation process. He felt that the Republicans, notwithstanding any talk to the contrary, were not going to support it. We didn't have sixty votes and the only way to do it was to protect it through the fifty-vote reconciliation process.[6] That was a heavy lift, because you're going to be throwing health care and deficit reduction into one large package. The economic team in our White House really didn't want it in. They thought it would undermine their ability to pass their number one priority—deficit reduction.

[At] that point in time, the health team was trying to protect Medicare savings for reinvestment in insurance coverage expansion—not deficit reduction. But we all know, there were definitely little camps. There was the Leon [Panetta] and Bob Rubin camp, who were the advocates of deficit reduction, deficit reduction, deficit reduction. The health team worried that we would lose momentum and took

---

5. Gradison's remarks quoted in this chapter are drawn from an interview recorded for the Miller Center's Edward M. Kennedy Oral History Project.

6. The budget reconciliation process is structured to facilitate the otherwise extremely complicated job of passing an annual budget—by limiting the opportunities for challengers to modify or to stop a bill. The reconciliation bill cannot be filibustered and passes with fifty-one votes (or a simple majority)—whereas under normal conditions a bill needs effectively sixty votes in the Senate to avoid filibuster.

Senator Mitchell seriously when he said, "You can't have too many hard votes in the Congress. You've got to put this health reform package into the budget." He didn't think he'd get health care outside of that context, and so he pushed really hard. The senators who stood in the way were Senator [Robert] Byrd[7] and Senator Moynihan. Senator Moynihan was rarely helpful in this process, ever. We all love him for many other things, but not for his role in health care.

I think there was outreach to Senator Byrd. I even think there was a presidential outreach to Senator Byrd.... But it didn't turn him at all. That is the pivot point because then all the focus turned to limiting the reconciliation bill to primarily budget issues—not as a vehicle for health reform. Health care, then, became largely just a funding source for deficit reduction. Basically all we were left with was protecting some of the savings from Medicare that we wanted to use for health care. So it was a fight between the health care team and the economic team about how much savings would come from Medicare for deficit reduction and how much would be left over for health care. Our instructions were, other than that internal quiet fight, to just shut up about health care until the fall.... So basically we were supposed to go into hibernation, which largely we did in the summer months.... Many people feel that the length of time that we tried to prolong the debate around health care really undermined the ability to pass it anyway, because it is so hard to sustain interest and presidential investment in an issue for so long.

Senator Edward M. Kennedy (D-MA):[8] They had very able, gifted, talented people, very knowledgeable, and they were going to get it and get it right, and get the best people to try and get that right and do it in a timely way. But the time slipped. It became disjointed, it became uncoordinated, and there were a number of other factors that interceded and became important, and moved and shifted the calendar back on it, and that caused an unraveling of the whole process. And as the process deteriorated, the groups that were focused in opposition became stronger and stronger, and their ability to influence became greater, and they had very considerable success.

We missed the opportunity, at a key time in this development, to move this whole process into what we would call the budget resolution, which would have permitted us to expedite the process, and you would have had the legislation in March instead of in October. Senator [Robert] Byrd refused to do it. It would have been massaging the budget process, certainly, to get it to have

---

7. Robert Byrd (1917–2010) was a Democratic member of the U.S. Senate representing West Virginia from 1959 to 2010. Byrd was known as a fierce defender of the prerogatives of the upper chamber, and accordingly policed the use of special provisions such as the reconciliation process vigorously.

8. Kennedy's remarks are taken from an interview recorded as part of the Miller Center's Edward M. Kennedy Project.

an inclusive kind of program, such a massive program, but its implications in terms of the budget are massive. We're talking about a health care system now of $2 trillion, so its implications in terms of the budget are massive.

But we were unable to get that done, and once we were unable to get that done, which was a major setback, we had mistake after mistake. Although, I have to give it to [Hillary] Clinton—She mastered the details of this, appeared before our committee and other committees, answered all the questions, and they were complicated and difficult questions. She understood it and she was an effective spokesperson for it.

Alan Blinder: The claim that was coming from Ira Magaziner, who was at a few of these [early budget] meetings but then dropped out of the process to do health care, was that he could deliver a health care plan that would actually save budgetary dollars ... [right] away, within the four-year budget framework that we were working on. Unanimously, the economic team greeted that claim with Bronx cheers: "What are you smoking?" Ira kept wanting to filter into the budget numbers some saving from health care. And, unanimously, the economic team said, "That's ridiculous. If we're going to have any credibility at all, you're going to blow it completely away." The question was how much more money health care was going to cost, not how much it was going to save.

Anyway, the idea was to bundle the health care reform into reconciliation, on the grounds that you needed only fifty-one votes and that might be the only way they could get the health care bill through the Congress. So ... Hillary or a representative or Ira would sometimes come to these budget meetings with the argument that "Never mind that this will be a way to make it easier to reduce the deficit because we'll show savings from health care, but for this very operational, political reason we need to bundle the health care reform into the budget and have one humongous bill that can't be filibustered."

As one, to a man and woman, the economic team went nuts over that idea, for a variety of reasons. But the simplest of which, and the most compelling to me, was there was no way in hell we were going to have a health care plan ready by the middle of February. So what are you telling us to do? Somehow we're also going to throw together a health care plan by the middle of February and submit the whole thing as a piece of legislation? It was completely ridiculous. But it took a while, and some table pounding, for that to go away. And of course, politically they had a point, they had a big point. Getting fifty-one votes instead of sixty votes is a very big difference. But the fact that there wasn't any health care plan to put in the budget at the time of the budget seemed to be an overwhelming consideration.

Roger Altman, deputy treasury secretary: The process was really quite intense and they were taking on a task that was utterly immense, a much bigger one really than the economic program, and came forth with a plan that was revolutionary, but whose revolutionariness doomed it.

Alice Rivlin, deputy OMB director: Ira had this whole scheme of how he was going to put the health plan together. He was very much out of the consultant world—a decision-making professional. He had this very complex schedule for all of these groups. They were going to meet, and they were going to put together plans. And this was all separate from this supposed task force that we were on. It was supposed to be feeding into it. It was a very large, complex structure, and these groups were to meet and come up with ideas.

Then there were periodic what he called "tollgates," at which, supposedly, decisions would be made, and then there would be more task groups, and then more tollgates.[9] This was all laid out in some kind of a document, which was quite amazing. I brought it home and showed it to my husband, who's a management professor, and he laughed. He said, "This isn't going to work, this is going to be a disaster." And he was right. It was over-organized, overcomplex, over-pressured, and somewhat mysterious from the point of view of the economic team.

Meanwhile, we were working on the budget. One of the questions was how the budget and the health plan were supposed to fit together. Ira had the notion that the health plan could be budget neutral. You could cover all of these new people, and there would be enough savings from more efficiency in the public programs, in Medicare and Medicaid, from the lower health costs to expand the coverage. A lot of us were skeptical of that.

Q: One of the criticisms that is sometimes levied against having Mrs. Clinton in this position is that it had the effect of intimidating—that may be too strong a word—but of intimidating opposition.
Rivlin: I wasn't intimidated by Hillary. I think we were all intimidated by Ira. Hillary was usually perfectly willing to talk about anything. Ira was very set on what he wanted to do, and I found that relationship difficult. . . . What I mainly remember was just watching it unravel and thinking, *We never should have gone down this road.* Until the very last minute, just before the '94 election, I think we still thought something could be done, that there would be a compromise and something might be enacted. George Mitchell was trying to salvage things. There were a few other stalwarts in the Congress who were trying to work it out. But, in the end, it just fizzled, basically.

---

9. Ira Magaziner's policymaking operation comprised scores of task forces. The broad work of these task forces was occasionally funneled through "tollgates," where their costs were tallied and the results reconciled with larger budget and policy goals.

Alan Blinder: The general process, I think, though it sounds paradoxical, was very welcoming of criticism and suggestions—and then ignoring them. That was the overall gestalt of the thing. We were very much encouraged to make our suggestions, but they didn't seem to have any effect.

* * *

Q: Your sense of the way the operation was being directed was that they weren't listening?

Peter Edelman: Fundamentally that they weren't listening on the health care, maybe on some details, but you remember the tollgates and the five hundred task force things. . . . Those people were being used and they were ignored as well. . . . They would announce themselves as, "We're working group number 72, and we're in charge of this little piece of thing here and that's why we're asking your advice." Another day I went to working group number 28. It was an amazing agglomeration of people from all over the country who were ecstatic about being asked to participate. What they all came up with was almost totally ignored in the stuff Ira came up with. So it wasn't just HHS that was ignored, although HHS is at least a focused, organized, coordinated place that will pull itself together and present you with one picture. These however many working groups, how in the world would you possibly synthesize everything they came up with?

It was a bogus process, actually an irrelevant part of the process. . . . It wasn't meaningful [consultation] at all. All the way, Ira is sitting there with, I don't know what help he got, but certainly talking to the First Lady and some others, there were a few junior people who were on the White House staff on health care. But it was basically centralized there.

Q: Did the people at HHS get to the point that they washed their hands of the effort?

Edelman: No, kept trying. I remember one time Donna [Shalala] came back and said to me, "I told Hillary that this thing is just headed for disaster, and she told me I was just jealous that I wasn't in charge and that was why I was complaining." It was very discouraging, but they kept trying. . . . I think at the time I could have given you a B+ quality explanation of [the bill]. We were saying to each other at the time that there were just a handful of people who really understood it completely. Maybe two handfuls.

* * *

Q: Were you involved in tollgates? All of them, some of them, how were you integrated into that process?

Chris Jennings: [The] whole tollgate process was Ira's process, a policy development process, that he thought would be a nontraditional way to get the best expertise around the country to address a broad array of issues. As it happened,

he felt, not only would you get the best expertise, but you would also get investment from those communities.

In a nonpolitical environment it probably could work. The problem with the
task force and the tollgates was the number of participants. Worse yet, you can
imagine that if you are any health care policy person or political person of any
salt and you didn't make the cut, it didn't help, because you're just mad. Those
on the outside were very open to the secrecy charge because, "After all, if I'm not
part of it, it must be a joke or a plot." Now, nothing that really came out of it
was a secret since it was on the front page of the paper every day. There was no
secret process here except the way that we handled it. . . . [So] we got the worst of
both worlds. We had the perception of secrecy without the reality of it. . . . By the
way, on top of this . . . you can imagine the security of getting all those people
in the building every day. You have to clear people every single day, and through
one foul up or another, countless VIPs who were trying to help out were locked
out. . . . Each morning, I was ready to jump out the window . . . just trying to help
get people in the building.

I want to say one more thing about the tollgate, one positive, one negative. There probably wasn't any place, at any time in world history, where
there were as many creative, smart people doing health care policy work together. And there was a lot of extraordinary work done, very thoughtful work.
People took their job seriously. They worked around the clock. They should
be credited for making a commitment to trying to do something. I've never
seen a group of people who were really—with all the complaints—people
committed to making the most of an historic opportunity to do something
right and good.

The downside of it, beyond the political downside, was that because you
had so many different tollgates and so many different issues, by definition,
they thought of every issue under the sun to address as you're thinking through
health policy, which is understandable, but neither realistic nor relevant. Too
many people forgot that they were drafting a proposal, not a law. As a consequence, too many details got integrated into a big document—things that probably should have been addressed in the legislative process or in the implementation process or subsequent to it.

David Cutler: I remember a couple of times we'd have meetings with the president, and people would come in and debate different sorts of issues. Invariably
the results of those meetings were leaked, and they would get shut off. So you'd
have one meeting out of a scheduled four. It would show up in the next day's
Washington Post, and so the other three would be canceled. I think what ultimately happened was most of the decisions were made probably by Ira and Mrs.
Clinton and the president, somewhere where nobody saw it. . . . I don't know
what Ira's view was, what Mrs. Clinton's view was in terms of that product—but
I don't think anybody I know of felt a great deal of pride in that product.

Alan Blinder: Everything got leaked. So much so that it was as if Robert Pear, who was covering it for the *New York Times*, was sitting in these meetings. That had a very negative effect on the process. First of all, the meetings got smaller. That wasn't so bad because they were probably too big anyway. But much more important than that, they went paperless. This is a very complicated issue, lots of numbers are flying around of all sizes, and things that aren't numerical. But because of the leaks they went paperless in the following sense. They started working like this. Ira would walk in, and his aides would start passing around paper. So first of all, no paper circulated before the meeting so you might know what you were going to talk about, think about these numbers, or something before. Attendance was by invitation only. We were invited, fortunately, so it would generally be Laura [Tyson] and me or maybe just me.

Ira would start talking, and the paper is getting passed around as he's talking. We'd go over these things, there'd be objections to the numbers, discussions of this or that policy. At the end of the meeting, the paper is all taken away. You can't bring it back, you can't think about it again, you can't read the parts that you couldn't read because you were trying to pay attention to the conversation. It went on like that for a long time. This is a very bad way to do things, and it is a real cost of leaks that I think is underappreciated. So eventually the famous, or I guess I should say these days infamous, 1,341-page, if I have all the digits right, Clinton health care plan is published in, when was it? August or September of '93?

I want to remind you, the first thought was this was going to be in the budget reconciliation bill in February. Then the Magaziner plan was we were going to do this in a hundred days. I'm thinking, *A hundred days, you're crazy.* So finally it came out on September 22nd, . . . around then, 1,341 pages long.[10]

David Cutler: The more congressionally oriented folks—particularly in the Treasury Department who had worked with Bentsen—always thought that we should put out a white paper instead of legislation. There were a number of discussions about "Are you sure we shouldn't do a white paper rather than legislation?" At some point the decision was reached, "No, we have to put out actual legislation." . . . I think it was to impress upon Congress and people the seriousness with which the issue was treated. Here's the president putting forward his plan. Here it was. You could work with it.

Chris Jennings: [Something that is] not well known is that when . . . we went up to listen to the members [we] were told repeatedly that they wanted to have—and this was even by the chairmen of the committees of jurisdiction—detailed legislation. They didn't want to have general specs or principles, they wanted to

---

10. The more commonly reported length was 1,342 pages.

have detailed policy. They wanted to get the scoring of the policy expedited, and they felt that the specific policy parameters and details were necessary. . . .

Q: Who had asked for it?
Jennings: It was a number of Democratic members who asked us to send up detailed policy. People always criticized us for releasing "this 1,300-page bill." "Why would you do such a silly thing?" It was because the congressional committees of jurisdiction, and because the scorekeepers from the Congressional Budget Office, demanded to have that detail to expedite the "scoring" process. All of us knew that time and political capital was limited, particularly since we deferred the unveiling until after we had resolution on the budget, crime, and trade [bills]. . . . In the end, though, the irony about this one issue was that the detailed policy was a perceived *response* to the Hill—not a rejection of congressional advice. . . . The staff wanted details too. Having said this, some of the members and the staff now say they never asked for so much detail. All I can say is my notes and the memories of Mrs. Clinton and I conflict with such statements.

Leon Panetta, OMB director: I can remember spending a lot of time in the task force saying, "You've got to have a simple way to explain things, and it's not just to the American people, but to a member of Congress. If you take more than two sentences to explain what's in a piece of legislation, chances are you're going to lose them. So you have to be able to explain what you're doing in the simplest of terms, and then you've got at least half a shot." I kept saying, "This thing is like a Rubik's cube in the sense that no matter how you talk it through you become so immersed in the detail of it that you can't say, 'What does this mean for the average citizen on the street in terms of what the impact is going to be?'"

I think Magaziner felt in the end, because this plan had been devised and would only work the way he had designed it, you couldn't compromise on these pieces. Otherwise, the thing would fall apart. And Hillary, who was very smart and was one of the few people who knew what Magaziner was talking about, thought the approach made the best sense in terms of health care policy. That obviously influenced the president. I think the decision was to go ahead and move this piece. The president went up, gave a speech on it. At the time, just like any speech by the president, you feel like it creates some impetus behind an issue. But what happened, as you know, is that ultimately the health care industry came together, put together $350 million on an ad package that tore the health care plan apart because it took its complexity and converted it into a thirty-second sound bite that was pretty effective as to what the problems with it were. And there was no real response to that.

David Cutler: I remember thinking at the time that no one had ever boiled the plan down to cocktail party size. You meet someone at a cocktail party, and they say, "So, tell me about the health plan." You have to be able, in three sentences or so, to say what it does in a way that makes sense to someone. I don't think we ever had that. Even if you look at when the president gave his speech in September [1993], he said there were six principles—not three, not one, not two, but six. Nobody will remember six principles. So a lot of the subsequent, "It's too complex," I think one could have seen coming. This wasn't a simple thing.

Pollster Stanley Greenberg: I can't remember when it was, but . . . Ira asked to brief [Mandy Grunwald and me] on the plan so that we could begin to think about communication and think about how to make the case for it. It took two days. It really did—two days. We were in awe because it was really incredibly interesting and fascinating. It was really creative and very innovative. But it took two days to explain it. We should have known at that moment that this was a problem. . . .

Q: There was relatively little in the way of public opinion research that informed it?
Greenberg: There's no [opinion] research that had formed the creation of the plan.

Bill Gradison: One other thing I should mention about the Clinton health plan is this was very unusual what we were doing. We [the opposition] were doing national polling on a day-by-day basis. That's almost never done, except in a presidential race or a tight Senate race. We were actually doing that and charting support for the Clinton health plan before it was presented, and it was very interesting what happened. I don't pretend to say that we were responsible. I'm just reporting what we observed. The numbers kept going up steadily, and the peak was reached just a few days after the president's speech, which in my personal opinion was one of the best political speeches I've ever heard. I'd put it up there with some of FDR's [Franklin Delano Roosevelt]. Then it just started to go down. It didn't plummet, it just started steadily down. It was the darnedest line you've ever seen. We stopped polling after a while because it was expensive and the trend was so evident. I don't know what happened out there. My hunch is that the fact that it took so long to get it out there made it possible for folks like us to get better organized in opposition to it, but it also, I think, made it possible for the people in the media, particularly the press, to do a little more comprehensive job of reporting it.

* * *

Q: Tell us a bit about health care. What did that look like from the Hill?
Lawrence Stein, congressional aide: Phew.

John Hilley, congressional aide (continuing from Stein): Well . . . they had not learned the lesson that you can go down to the Old Executive Office Building and plan away with five hundred experts all you want, but at the end of the day you better have a legislative strategy for getting this done, and that better include Republicans.... What was stunning to me was that he would appoint his wife ... to take on the most difficult legislative issue of probably the last three decades, health care reform. Why would you walk into that with a holistic approach as opposed to piecemeal, where clearly rifle shots would have worked—which was ultimately what we turned to that actually did work. Why would you walk into that? Ted Kennedy—an accomplished legislator—spent twenty years trying to do this and got nowhere. To think that you could come in from on high and propose this, in an election year, against a hardened Republican opposition was just beyond naïve to me.

Roger Altman: Bentsen had told me from the first moment this thing was going nowhere. He told me that at the very beginning. "I know the Congress and the Congress isn't going to buy it."

Bill Gradison: [The] chairman of the Health Insurance Association of America at the time was a fellow named Dave Hurd. Down-the-line Democrat, strong supporter of the Clintons, and he ran, in Des Moines, Iowa, the Principal, which is big, big, big: health, life, annuity, pensions. And he couldn't get in to talk to them about it. Granted, I couldn't either. In fact at one point, Danny [Rostenkowski] basically said to me, "I really think if you and the First Lady could sit down, you probably could work some of these things out." I said, "I'd love to." He said, "Well, here's what I'd like you to do. I'd like you to stop your ads and let me go and talk to them." I said, "I'll be glad to stop the ads. A tender of good faith—we'll stop." I said, "We're probably going to have to eat some money too, because we prepay, and you have to pay unless they can sell the time to somebody else." Danny Rostenkowski goes in there and says, "All he's asking for is a meeting." And they turned down a meeting with us.

Patrick Griffin, White House congressional liaison: There'd been no legislative activity [on health care] that first year of the administration. It had all been Mrs. Clinton, Ira, and whomever they were meeting in these meetings. Maybe one or two, less than a handful of members of Congress were somewhat involved, but not a lot.... We're now [early 1994] presenting this seven-hundred-page bill that no member of Congress had seen, to then have it passed by the end of the year, with twenty-seven committees needing to sign off. Anybody who'd been in Washington for a while would say this is an absurd notion on its face. [But] if you did seriously challenge it, then you were just an old insider, either shilling for the Hill or you were just not getting it.... [Hillary] would say, "Pat, you know we rely on you to keep the right tone." And it's not like, "Mrs.

Clinton, *but*—" It's like, "*Yes*, Mrs. Clinton. I'll keep the tone up." She knew the challenge but she believed strategically that the way to do it was, *No doubt, no doubt*. It would be an insult to suggest that she didn't understand. Some of the folks around her who were part of this huge team of health care folks. . . . Ira in particular—Ira didn't. . . . I love him, but he didn't have a clue as to what it was going to take to implement this legislation. . . .

Q: When was the first point you knew you were going to lose?
Griffin: I [actually] had a good [feeling] that we would get a health care bill. I figured at some point people would come to realize that we'd probably have to make a lot more changes than we were making. But I didn't know what they were. I just had an instinct. I thought we had a chance to get that bill. However, I'd say by March [1994], feeling the intransigence inside the White House, [and] seeing how [Daniel Patrick] Moynihan was not cooperating on process, it began to seriously trouble me. . . .

Q: If the White House had been willing to be a little more flexible, do you think you would have come out with something?
Griffin: Oh, there's no question. . . . [But] when the process appeared to be collapsing, we are telling Mrs. Clinton and the president that we are dying. However, the congressional leaders, who are saying the same thing to us, are telling them (the Clintons) in meetings we were having in the Map Room at night, that the legislation can still pass. . . . Mrs. Clinton angrily turns to me and . . . asks why are they telling us something else entirely different. It was a very surreal situation. After a while we just said, "This is bullshit. This is all I can tell you."

Q: This is just an inability to confront the president with the realities directly?
Griffin: No, it wasn't an inability to confront the president. It was an inability to confront Mrs. Clinton and indicate that it would die in July, when we had a few more months yet. They wanted to keep up the appearance of the good fight. In fact, I can remember that caused a lot of tension inside. Mrs. Clinton did not want to hear it and I don't blame her. But they were telling us one thing and her another, and it wasn't only just the leaders. It was everybody else in the Congress.

Senator Harris Wofford (D-PA): Clinton's popularity in six months had gone from 70 percent down to 38 percent or something like that, and the health care plan had gone down to 40-some percent. . . . It was in that context that the health care plan began to look very touch-and-go. We were beginning to be pessimistic about what could emerge—not that we were committed to her plan getting through as it was, but even getting any good, significant leap forward or big first step.

So we had that dinner to consider how to help get that first step. Then Pat Moynihan said, "Harris, this isn't the time for us to try to come up with a joint plan.... Come spring, there will come a time for a compromise, and you can count on me and we can count on Bob Dole. Bob is a patriot and he wants to make progress on health care for everybody. We will come up with a plan, and the sailing will be good." That was the end of that effort. Come spring, several times I said to Pat, "Don't you think the time has come?" Finally, rather bleakly, he said, "Harris, the time has passed. Bob tells me that they've tasted blood in the Republican caucus, and they're going to drive a stake into this plan. He said he couldn't get his caucus even to support his health care bill if we agreed that the Dole bill should pass."

Senator George Mitchell (D-ME): I may be off a little bit on my dates, but in November of '93, the president finally sent up a bill that Dick Gephardt and I introduced, Dick in the House and I in the Senate. This had been a product of a great deal of effort led by Mrs. Clinton and Ira Magaziner. A very complicated and what I would call a coalition of interests in support of reform was put together. Although not much noticed, I think it was December, probably just before Christmas, a Republican bill was introduced. John Chafee[11] was the principal architect, but he had about twenty Republican senators, including Bob Dole, on the bill. Chafee and I had a number of discussions over this period of time, the winter of '93–'94, about how we might be able to put together a reasonable package.

I genuinely felt that there was a reasonable chance that we could put together a pretty decent bill based upon a compromise between the bill that we had put in on behalf of the president and the bill that Chafee had put in in December. It was for that reason, I think it was in April [1994], when Clinton offered to nominate me for the Supreme Court, I declined.[12] I said to him, "I really think we have a chance at this." He was anxious to get some action on the health care bill. We agreed that I would stay put and try to push this. I had just announced in March that I was not going to seek re-election. So I said, "I'd just feel wonderful if in my last year we could pass comprehensive health care reform, so I want to stay and get that done."

Over the next few months, however, the prospects dimmed for a variety of reasons, which I'll get into. First, the interests against [reform] organized

---

11. John Chafee (1922–1999) represented Rhode Island in the U.S. Senate from 1976 to 1999. He was generally deemed to be a Republican moderate.

12. Associate Justice Harry Blackmun (1908–1999) announced his resignation in March. Clinton ultimately nominated Ruth Bader Ginsburg for the seat.

and conducted a skillful campaign of advertising outside [Washington]—the famous Harry and Louise insurance company ads.[13] And inside [Washington], with the Republicans working to undermine it, which they did with a considerable amount of success. You could see the support outside and within the Senate gradually declining, to the point where when the Finance Committee got to the bill, I think it was in July, I joked to Chafee, who was a very good friend of mine, "I'm going to offer your bill as an amendment and force the Republicans [to vote]." "Oh, gee, don't do that," he said. "That will be really embarrassing to do that." The Republicans, including those who had co-sponsored his bill, had moved away from it. As we moved toward the center, they moved further away. We never were able to narrow the gap. Although both sides were moving, they were just moving in the same direction and therefore not closing the gap.

It's hard to conceive of a set of tactics that would have produced the desired result.... It might have been better to send up a bill of general principles on health care rather than a detailed legislative proposal. I doubt the result would have been any different, but one never knows.... I had no problem with the process. I had a problem with the product—too big, too complicated, too difficult. That was the problem.

Peter Edelman: Bill Kristol comes out at some point and he says publicly, writes an op-ed or something, this must be early '94. He says, "Republicans, we could beat this thing."[14] Everybody laughed at him. Everybody said, "You're out of your mind, they've got so much momentum on this thing." Then Harry and Louise—you know the way media stuff is, it's insidious. It's out there and it's having an effect. You're cracking and you don't know you're cracking until one day you just break.... I would come home at night and my wife would say to me, "When are you people going to answer Harry and Louise?"

Senator Nancy Kassebaum (R-KS):[15] I always said that what killed [health care reform] was the Harry and Louise ads. I never will forget, I was out in Kansas and I was sitting with mother, who wasn't well at the time, and I saw that on TV and I thought, *I cannot believe that. That is really going to be a troublemaker.* Because I related.

---

13. These televised ads, sponsored by the Health Insurance Association of America, featured an eponymous everyday couple voicing worries about how they would manage under the Clinton system. Harry and Louise mortally wounded an already struggling effort.

14. On December 2, 1993, William Kristol, a conservative political activist and formerly an aide to Vice President Dan Quayle, had circulated a memorandum to Republican leaders nationwide urging them not only to oppose the Clinton health care plan, but to resist any temptation to compromise. Passage of any bill would empower Democrats who otherwise were vulnerable at the polls the following November.

15. Kassebaum's remarks are taken from her interview for the Miller Center's Edward M. Kennedy Oral History Project.

Ben Goddard, advertising consultant, creator of the Harry and Louise ads:
We thought the Harry and Louise concept was going to work. But we were quite
honestly surprised at how well it worked once we produced the first spot. I think
part of that was the chemistry of the actors.... I didn't have time to go back to
L.A. [Los Angeles] and do the whole casting process, so I called a casting agent
that I trusted and asked them to put together tapes of pairs of actors. I literally
sat in a hotel room here in D.C. and just by process of elimination actually got
down to Harry fairly quickly, because I knew I wanted an everyman who wasn't
too smart, not intimidating, could be just a very likeable guy.

It took longer to choose the Louise character. I finally came down to a choice
between two, Louise Caire Clark and another lady whose name I've forgotten
who was a very attractive redhead. I was single at the time, always had a fondness
for redheads. But decided that given the audience we were trying to reach, Louise
looked more like a real person. So I cast the actors from three thousand miles
away without ever meeting them. Over the course of the campaign Louise and
I became romantically involved and wound up getting married after the campaign. So the in-house family joke is I always could have picked the redhead. ...

Once we put it on the air, the response was amazing. We also didn't know if we
were going to do one or three or how many spots. The response was so powerful
that we immediately went into production with a second spot.... Then shortly
after the second one appeared, the First Lady went on the attack and started talking about "that woman." Bill Clinton, the president, made some slightly humorous reference in which he said, "I can't remember the name, Thelma and Louise,
whoever it is, you know, those people." ... This was something we were not
prepared for, but the Clintons have always had a "no attack goes unanswered"
approach toward politics. Their response really gave life to our campaign. The
fact was, you couldn't cover them talking about it without playing a clip from the
spot. So all of a sudden it wasn't just the 30 percent of the public that we reached
through our initial buy, but 60 or 70 percent of the public thought they'd seen a
Harry and Louise commercial because it was being covered on the evening news.

There was an overture from HIAA [Health Insurance Association of America]
essentially saying, I don't know if it was three or four substantive changes, *If you
would remove those from the proposal, we'll put Harry and Louise on the air in support
of your plan.* Again it was rejected by the White House. They made several big
mistakes and that was another one, because initially our objective was not to
defeat the Clinton proposal, it was simply to modify it. In part that was because
we didn't believe we could defeat it, hence the reform proposals that HIAA laid
out and the focus saying we support health care reform, but we need to fix this
piece. So there was a deal to be made, particularly in '94.

Patrick Griffin: Well, I think [health care reform] was one of the truly most vi-
sionary things that they were trying to do. Mrs. Clinton and the president were
really not following polls. They really were trying to get ahead of something and

I thought it was very courageous in that regard. It helped focus a debate that continues, obviously.

Chris Jennings: When I talk about [health care reform], and, more importantly, the president talks about these things, I think he feels that we did not fully understand the discomfort and distrust that the public at large had about government in '93 and '94. He thinks we didn't fully understand the impact of twelve years of Republicans in office, basically criticizing everything government does, questioning its ability to respond in a positive way to public needs. In fact, though, the president's message in the campaign was not just health care reform, it was welfare reform too. That was a big issue.

I think he now believes it is conceivable that health care would have been better to wait two years and do welfare early, for two reasons. One, we'd probably have a better welfare bill, but two, it would have enhanced the public's confidence that he and the Democrats got it, that there are some things that government is overdoing. There was a sense that government was providing too much dependency as opposed to empowerment. This whole dependency-empowerment issue he felt needed to be addressed. In the absence of being addressed, we were more vulnerable to (inaccurate) criticism that this was another government takeover, like welfare. So he feels that if we did welfare first, we might have had the enhanced public confidence to do other things.

Stanley Greenberg: [The bill] was vulnerable because of its design to be attacked that it was big government.... [It] was complex, [but] it was not a big-government program. It was complex because of maintaining all of the private sector [components] and the fact that you had a standard package [of benefits] that you needed to oversee. But it would have been attacked as a big-government takeover of health care, whatever its content. I think it could have withstood that.... We could have been more sensitive on the issue of big government, more alert to that critique.

David Cutler: [In] the aftermath of the Health Security Act, and some during it, there were always those who suggested that had there been an attempt to work out that middle-ground deal, something could have happened. And if it happened early enough, it would have been signed into law. For the record, if there was a deal, no one would have been happier than someone like me. I am what I would consider a radical incrementalist. If something can get done, one should get it done.

Having thought it through as I have over the years, I am not at all convinced that the politics or the environment would have supported such a deal. In fact ... I don't believe that there would have been Democratic support for the president to move to a more "centrist" position before it was clear it was necessary and before the relatively few number of Republicans who originally wanted a compromise altered their position or became so small in number that it didn't matter any way. In other words, I think it is far from a certainty that a grand deal was possible. It doesn't change anything that I said, I just want to say that I would have been very happy if we did it and it worked, but I just don't think it would have.

One of the things about the later years of the Clinton administration is that it had a lot of success when it took on bite-sized pieces.... [We] got an enormous amount done, with the one exception being that ... the major thing didn't happen. But the CHIP expansion was a very big deal, and the Kennedy–Kassebaum and the HIPAA [Health Insurance Portability and Accountability Act], and a lot of the patient safety.[16] It really did enormous amounts by focusing in and saying, "Okay, this is something that's digestible."

* * *

Q: *In '93 and '94, was getting to a consensus a doable proposition if you'd done it the right way?*
Donna Shalala: Yes, I thought so. I thought if we left people who had health insurance alone and worried about those who didn't or were underinsured, there was a chance. I also would have done it differently. I would have done it the way we did welfare reform. We put out forty waivers the first couple of years.[17] We learned a lot out there. I would use the states as the laboratories.... I thought we were going to start down that road. The problem is, the president wanted to do the whole thing all at once, as opposed to doing the experiments. I came from Wisconsin and New York. I believed in the states as the great places to experiment with social and health policy. So I would have used the waiver process. I thought we were skillful enough and knowledgeable enough about state government to do that.

Frank Greer, media advisor: Harold Ickes[18]—this may have been after the '94 midterm elections—calls and says, "You've got to come over and you've got to talk to the president. We're going to have four or five people in, he just wants to talk about what he should do and what went wrong." So I go to this dinner in the small dining room upstairs at the White House. Clinton is saying, "I just don't understand, we ran on health care and we tried to do the right thing.

16. CHIP (Children's Health Insurance Program], passed in 1997, provides matching federal funds to states to pay for health insurance for children otherwise ineligible for Medicaid. The [Edward] Kennedy–[Nancy] Kassebaum Bill created the Health Insurance Portability and Accountability Act of 1996, which provides coverage for workers who lose or change their jobs—and also advanced the use of electronic medical records in the United States.

17. Those waivers exempted states from certain federal constraints in the interest of fostering experimentation with otherwise unavailable alternatives.

18. Harold Ickes is a New York political operative who joined the Clinton White House as deputy chief of staff in December 1993.

I know there are a lot of interest groups that we're up against and"—I turned to him and I said, "Mr. President, how many spots do you think you ran on health care in the general election?" He said, "I don't know, four or five. We ran a lot on health care." I said, "Zero. You didn't get elected on health care. You didn't run one spot on health care. You ran on welfare reform and you might have been better off if you'd started with that. You ran on cops on the street and you did put that up and you got that passed and that became popular. You ran on economic opportunity and you got your budget passed. But you didn't run on health care."[19]

And the reason was, we did a lot of health care spots and we never could find a message that worked. People are too uneasy that if you change the health care system and if you expand coverage, but you don't guarantee their quality, [their care will suffer]. People are full of anxiety about whether this was a good idea or bad idea. People get very nervous about health care and if you have not run a campaign on it, if you haven't gone out and spent three or four years talking about how we can reform it, it comes out of the blue, and [then] you're an easy target.... But it was astounding to me that everybody around this White House thought that we ran on health care. We didn't.

---

19. The website "The Living Room Candidate," which preserves campaign commercials from every presidential election since 1952, confirms Greer's assertion. Health care did get an occasional passing mention in those general election spots, but there was no one ad devoted to the issue. See http://www.livingroomcandidate.org/commercials/1992.

16

Welfare Reform

Reform of the American welfare system had been a signature concern of Bill Clinton since he was governor of Arkansas. It also became one of his defining issues as he sought to establish a national reputation as a new kind of Democrat, pledging to "end welfare as we know it." The critical question for the White House in 1993 was how to prioritize this issue among the many requiring presidential attention and energy. Ultimately it was decided internally that the health care reform effort would come first, a decision that many within the administration would later regret. When the Democrats subsequently suffered a catastrophic defeat in the 1994 midterm elections, losing both chambers of Congress (including a so-called permanent Democratic House majority) to the Republicans, welfare reform looked to be one of the few issues upon which the two parties might find common ground. The path to successful reform was, however, a tortuous one, and in the end some of Clinton's closest advisors vigorously objected to his signing a bill they believed was too harsh on vulnerable Americans.

Al From, head of the DLC: I think welfare reform was the most important idea of the '92 campaign because, to me, the main message of the campaign was, you vote for this guy, you're voting for somebody who is different from the Democrats you've been voting against.... Ending welfare was one of the great successes of the administration.

Stanley Greenberg, pollster: I did poll on the priority of going ahead with welfare reform, but it was never on what should be in welfare reform.

Q: Was the public eager to move forward on welfare?
Greenberg: Yes, higher than almost anything on our list. I think it was the highest.

Bruce Reed, deputy domestic policy advisor: Bill Clinton's interest in welfare reform goes back much further than my own involvement. He'd been doing it as governor from just about his first term, I believe. It was one of the issues where he began to make a national name for himself.... When he was going around the country for the DLC giving his stump speech, one of the most surprising things he said that caught audiences' attention was that we should ask people on welfare to work and make sure they had the chance to do so, which caught a lot of Democrats by surprise.... As he would later say, he probably spent more time in welfare offices than anyone else who'd ever sought the presidency, so he was able to speak about the issue in a way that shared the frustrations of welfare recipients and voters alike.

The story that he told more often than any other about welfare was one that he told again at the signing of the welfare bill in 1996, of a woman from Arkansas who had testified at an NGA [National Governors Association] field hearing. He said that when he asked her what was the best thing about being off welfare she said, "When someone asks my son, 'What does your mama do for a living?', he can give an answer."

As it turned out, welfare reform and health reform met the same fate in the first month of the administration, when the economic team put together the five-year economic plan. They came to the conclusion that both health care and welfare reform would have to pay for themselves, that they wouldn't put the money aside in the budgetary framework that they were proposing to Congress in the reconciliation package.

Their theory was that health care wasn't far enough along to put a price tag on it, and welfare reform had a rough price tag but the rest of the details hadn't been worked out yet. They reasoned that this was a priority that Republicans shared so it would be easier to get Republicans to spend money on it. Now that turned out to be a colossal misinterpretation, because [although] the Republicans agreed on the importance of welfare reform, the last thing they wanted to do was spend money on it.

The first good news day that we had [as president] was when I got Clinton to give a welfare speech at the NGA where he basically repeated his campaign speech and said, "I'm serious, I'm going to end welfare as we know it, work with me." So it was big news that Clinton was going to keep a campaign promise.... Our real problem was that it quickly became apparent to us, [however], that nobody in Congress—nobody on the Democratic side, none of the Democratic leaders— wanted us to do a welfare bill. [Thomas] Foley and [Richard] Gephardt in particular pleaded with Clinton not to send one, [saying] that it would divide the party.

Anyway, nothing happened in that Congress.... We lost the [1994 midterm] elections badly, and when the dust had settled from the November elections, we realized that welfare reform was one of the few agenda items we had in common with the new Republican majority. They had spelled out a welfare reform proposal in their Contract [with America][1] which had nastier budgetary

---

1. The Contract with America was a set of policy commitments and institutional reforms that congressional Republicans pledged to make their governing program if elected to the majority in 1994. Scholars have differed over the extent to which the Contract itself was a factor in the outcome of the midterm elections, which resulted in Republican control of the House of Representatives for the first time in forty years.

offsets than our bill, but it was conceptually similar.... [And] there was no Democratic congressional leadership to tell us not to do it anymore.... In the first part of '95, the Republicans made an about-face and decided since they now controlled the majority of the governorships, that instead of being for the existing welfare structure, with a work requirement for everybody, which is what the Contract said, they should be for a block grant and turn the whole problem over to the states. That was a problem for us, because most Democrats were even more against that idea than they were against the work requirements, because they didn't trust the states. They hadn't trusted the states since the civil rights movement, and it brought out all their worst fears. . . .

[Congressman Newt] Gingrich[2] rolled the Contract through in the first hundred days, but welfare reform was the last thing because it was the hardest one for them to reach agreement [on].... The welfare battle [then] moved to the Senate and was in the hands of Bob Dole, the Senate majority leader, and to our happy surprise he encountered an enormous amount of difficulty reconciling the divisions within his party.... [In] September we had the Senate debate. We beat back, we stripped out, most of the conservative mandates. We beat them on [excluding] unwed mothers and on mandatory no additional benefits for additional children and a host of other conservative amendments. We added more money for child care. We got all the things that we had hoped for, and then some.

The Senate debate was winding to a close in late September [1995] . . ., so we decided to do a radio address endorsing the Senate bill. Despite some consternation at HHS, the president did that. Then the Senate passed it by something like 87 to 10, overwhelmingly bipartisan, but it wasn't a perfect bill. So we endorsed the Senate bill but said we'd like to see further improvements in conference. So we had a terrible House bill, we had a Senate bill that was good, and we were hoping to get a compromise that was better than the Senate bill, which didn't make much sense to people. We weren't quite sure how we were going to do it, but we thought that we would be in a much stronger position to advocate for the changes we wanted if we were actually for something.

So things were going swimmingly. We were on track to get a bipartisan bill, and then the budget showdown heated up and subsumed the entire welfare reform debate.[3] Congress decided to have a reconciliation debate that encompassed the entire federal budget and folded everything else in there. So we were no longer in a position where we were able to have a bipartisan debate, build a

---

2. Newt Gingrich was a representative from Georgia from 1979 to 1999 and was a primary author of the Contract with America. As a result of the 1994 midterm elections, he became Speaker of the House, a position he held until 1999.

3. Congressional Republicans sought more drastic cuts in the federal budget than Clinton would accept, leading to two dramatic shutdowns of the nation's government late in 1995 into early 1996.

bipartisan coalition [on welfare], because both sides retreated to their respective camps on the budget battle. They passed a budget bill that we opposed that was unacceptable on a thousand different fronts, [so] we shut down the government. The president vetoed the reconciliation bill. Then Leon Panetta was on one of the Sunday shows, was asked about welfare, and said that the welfare bill was so bad that the president would have vetoed it on its own, which we never debated, but the Republicans thought, *What a great idea.* So they passed the welfare bill again, separately, the same portion of the reconciliation bill that we just vetoed, and just for fun sent it down to the president and made him veto it again.

Q: So the two vetoes that we typically hear about, the first one was in the budget reconciliation.
Reed: Right. He vetoed the same thing twice, once as part of the reconciliation, once as a stand-alone bill. It was entirely a political response to the Sunday show appearance. I don't think it ever would have occurred to them to do that if Leon hadn't brought it up.... When President Clinton vetoed that second bill, he was grumpy about it and I was grumpy about it. We talked about it. I went in to brief him in the Oval to do it. We talked about how if anybody had been willing to sit down with us for a minute we could have worked out an acceptable compromise in no time.

Q: Grumpy because it's a missed opportunity?
Reed: Yes, we were grumpy that the historic chance to pass welfare reform might be slipping away from us, not because we had fundamental disagreements about welfare reform, but because of everything else. And I'm sure he was grumpy because the larger budget negotiations weren't going well either. But our congressional people assured us that we'd get another chance; there was still plenty of time left on the clock.

By this point Dole was wrapping up the [1996 presidential] nomination, so the Republicans put their heads together again to make sure that welfare reform would only come to us in an unacceptable manner [to force another veto], and they decided their next poison pill would be to link health care and welfare in an unacceptable way by giving us a welfare reform block grant linked to a Medicaid block grant. The Republican governors wanted block grants for everything, and one of the major issues in the government shutdown was over block-granting Medicaid, which Clinton was violently opposed to because his view was that the welfare program was already in essence a block grant because every state could set benefit levels at whatever amount it wanted.

We continued to do executive order after executive order to build political pressure on the Congress. Eventually in June of '96, House Republicans panicked, and the class that had been elected in the '94 elections realized that they were in danger of facing the electorate without having enacted a single item from the Contract into law, and that they couldn't afford to go 0 for the 104th

Congress, so a group of about seventy-five House Republicans wrote Gingrich a letter saying, "We want welfare reform to become law. Please drop the Medicaid poison pill. Let's send President Clinton a welfare bill and force the question."

That broke the logjam. The House passed the bill in July, the Senate did as well. They had a conference. The bills were in most respects even better than where we'd been a year earlier. We'd gotten more money for child care, more money for work. Then they conference them and the last remaining poison pill was deep cuts in benefits for illegal immigrants, and they conferenced. This was in late July '96, and they finally came out with a conference report—I think July 30th or something like that.

In any event, once it became apparent welfare reform was going to come back the president's way, he began to agonize over it.... [He] had to decide where he was going to come down on it because the Democrats didn't want to vote on the bill without knowing whether the president was for it or against it. Nobody wanted to be on the wrong side of the president. So we scheduled a meeting ... with the president the morning of the vote, and we didn't know how it was going to come out.... [We] met with him in the Cabinet Room with about half the Cabinet there and several White House advisors. It was supposed to be his day off so he showed up relaxed, in a golf shirt, about an hour late.

Q: No pollsters or party people or personal friends?
Reed: No, just key White House staff and most of the domestic Cabinet: Shalala, [Bob] Rubin, Cisneros, [Mickey] Kantor, [Bob] Reich—Panetta was chief of staff by then—Don Baer[4], Rahm Emanuel, [George] Stephanopoulos, [Harold] Ickes, a guy named Ken Apfel, who was the PAD [program associate director] at OMB for these issues, the vice president, and a couple of others.

It was probably the most remarkable meeting I took part in during the Clinton years because everybody recognized what a hard decision it was for the president and how momentous a decision it would be, so no one wanted to overstate their case, which was unusual. We had a remarkably civilized, respectful debate on an issue where everybody felt very strongly but no one wanted to put their thumb on the scale. The meeting started off with Ken Apfel laying out what the conference committee had agreed to and the plusses, and on the list of improvements we wanted, what ones we had gotten and what ones we hadn't, then Shalala made the case against the bill, and then the president opened it up for advisors to speak their minds. We went around the table. Most of the Cabinet was against it, with the exception of Mickey Kantor.

We probably spent half an hour listening to people's arguments against it, and then the president turned to me and said, "So Bruce, what's the case for the bill?" I told him that the welfare reform elements of the bill were better than we

---

4. Don Baer was a leading speechwriter and communications specialist in the White House.

could have hoped for, that it had more money for work, more money for child care, and we'd gotten every improvement we'd asked for, so that as a welfare reform bill it was a real achievement. He agreed that it was a good welfare bill wrapped in a "sack of shit," I think was his phrase. I said that the child support enforcement provisions alone were worth enacting the bill and that the dire consequences the opponents of the bill predicted really wouldn't happen because the cuts in benefits for illegal immigrants were too onerous and would never stand up over time. Congress would have to come back and fix them. Most important, we'd made a promise to the American people that we were going to end welfare as we know it and we'd be hard-pressed to go to them and explain why this bill didn't do that. We shouldn't assume that we'd ever get another chance, that the history of the issue was that it wouldn't come our way again and that we owed it to the country to keep our promise.

The president agreed that this might be his only chance. He said he didn't think a Democratic Congress would have given him a welfare bill he could sign. Harold Ickes had argued against the bill, so I told him the story of about how Roosevelt had faced this same dilemma when he created the WPA [Works Progress Administration], that [Harry] Hopkins had wanted to make sure that the dole was based on work and that another Harold Ickes [his father] had argued the opposite. Of course he wanted to know how that turned out, so I told him that Hopkins had won. The discussion continued from there for a while longer. A few other people chimed in on my side ... [including] Don Baer [and] John Hilley, who was the legislative affairs director.

Rahm said, "Do what you think is right." There's no question that Rahm was for it, but it was probably the best evidence that nobody was putting their thumb on the scale when Rahm, who *never* restrained himself, held himself back. The vice president turned to me a couple of times and whispered a couple of times—I was sitting next to him—asking me questions, and during the course of the meeting asked a number of helpful, leading questions that made me think he was in favor of the bill.

Q: But you didn't know where he was coming out on the bill.
Reed: I didn't know where the president was coming out, I didn't know for sure where the vice president was coming out, and they gave no indication whatsoever at the meeting. I think the president didn't want to decide at that meeting. The meeting broke up finally.... [The president] went into the Oval Office and then Panetta came to get me because the president had another question about a memo Shalala had given him. I went into the Oval Office to talk to him, to rebut yet another criticism, and we ended up having the meeting all over again with the president, vice president, Panetta, John Hilley, and me.

Q: What's different this time?

The president's sitting at his desk. We're standing around him. He was asking questions, but in essence, Panetta made the case against the bill, I made the case for it. The president agonized, the president desperately tried to get the vice president to help break the tie, and the vice president tried mightily to avoid making the decision, to avoid tipping the balance, but eventually said he thought that the cuts in benefits to immigrants would have a harsh impact on them and that the president had a responsibility to look out for groups of people who couldn't speak up for themselves. But on balance, the welfare system was so broken and had to be fixed, and this was our chance to do it, and the benefit of the welfare reform outweighed the cuts in immigrant benefits we didn't like. The president agonized some more.

We spent about half an hour in there with him. Finally he looked up from his desk and said, "Let's do it, I'll sign it," and told me to write the statement. . . . The president changed into a suit, reviewed the statement, went to the press room, and announced that he would sign the bill. . . .

He said that he'd never been so proud of his administration as he was of the way they conducted themselves in that meeting. I felt the same way, that it was an honest debate where people were respectful of each other's differences. We waited for him in the anteroom next to the press room and he came out and he said, "Sometimes you never know how right something is until you do it." As he was answering questions, he got more and more convinced that he was doing the right thing.

Peter Edelman: [When] I get to [be assistant secretary for planning and evaluation at HHS], it's just coincident with the time when Wendell [Primus] has worked up the memorandum that says enacting the Republican version [of welfare reform] ending the entitlement and having fixed time limits is going to drive a million kids into poverty.[5] Essentially coincident with my arrival, Donna is taking that and personally handing it to Clinton in the White House and saying, "This is what is going to happen if you come out"—as he had not yet—"if you come out and say that you'll take a bill that ends the entitlement and creates an arbitrary time limit, this will be the result. Don't send that signal to Congress that you're willing to sign a bill that does it." Last-ditch effort. He sends that message. In mid-September 1995, he informally sends word to Congress that he would sign a bill with those features.

My wife [Marian Wright Edelman] writes him an open letter in the *Washington Post*, an op-ed in the *Washington Post* that says, "Mr. President, please don't sign

---

5. Wendell Primus was deputy assistant secretary for human services policy at HHS. He joined Edelman and others in resigning from his sub-Cabinet post to protest the welfare reform act.

a bill that does those two things," and she quotes the Old Testament, the New Testament, Reinhold Niebuhr, Rabbi [Abraham] Heschel, Martin Luther King, Moses, and Jesus. It was an amazing thing to do—an open letter to the president saying, "Don't sign a bill like that." That's the context. Nobody in HHS thought it was a bad thing for her to write that letter, nobody! At least nobody who said anything out loud. So that puts Mary Jo [Bane], Wendell, me, Rich Tarplin, Harriet Rabb, and a few others in a regular meeting to say what have we done this week and what are we going to do next week to keep a bill that does that from ever getting to the president's desk.[6] That's our job.

Q: Is HHS working the Hill at some level apart from the White House—
Edelman: Yes.

Q: So you're sort of freelancing—
Edelman: Freelancing, yes. At one point Donna has me talk to Senator Moynihan on the phone, but mostly I wasn't out front on it.... Marian and I had a long, very uneasy relationship with him. At one point he attacked Donna for having been involved with the Children's Defense Fund that had "opposed the Family Support Act."[7] It's more complicated than that. But there was a long history that goes all the way back to when he was in the Nixon White House.... [Moynihan] was against having a national food stamp program because he thought it disturbed the beauty of the Family Assistance Plan. He didn't think that there should be a bifurcation in income assistance. Somebody was with him in the White House watching television with him. I don't remember who it was who happened to be there. Marian was speaking to that conference and he said something to the effect, but I think this is an exact quote, "There's that nigger woman who's married to that rich Jewish asshole." And it got back to us. So he had not been somebody we thought well of for a very long time. I'm not rich, which was our little joke about it. ...

Q: I want to go back to this question about the freelancing work because this is fascinating—HHS is taking a very different position from the president on—
Edelman: The main argument we made to them was, "You ought to take a look at the fiscal implications of this and see if your state is going to be better off or worse off. Maybe somebody ought to start a little discussion about the

---

6. These were all senior officials at HHS. Mary Jo Bane was an assistant secretary who also resigned in protest over the welfare reform act as signed by Clinton.

7. The Family Support Act of 1988 was a Moynihan initiative designed to restructure the welfare system to emphasize family support and work among welfare recipients.

distribution—start a food fight about how the money gets split among the states." I think that's the main thing we were saying. ...

Q: *Did you take heart—the first veto occurs in December of '95 and it's embedded in the budget reconciliation.*
Edelman: A little bit, but ... the governors come to town in early February, and the president—this is after he's had the two vetoes—calls a bunch of them upstairs after dinner and says, "I'd really like you folks to get more active on the welfare thing and get me a bill I can sign." They say to him, "That's fine, Mr. President, but what we really want is for you to support block-granting Medicaid." He says, "Yes, okay, that's possible."

The word comes back to us out of the White House ... [and our reaction is], "My God, he's talking about block-granting Medicaid." So somebody said, "That won't last." It turns out within a week he backs down from that and it's nursing homes, and the middle-class people for whom Medicaid pays for their nursing homes, the doctors, the hospitals, everybody comes down on the White House about that. So he backs away from it.

The governors then work with the House people to draft a combined Medicaid and welfare bill. But the point is that the House people don't want the president to get credit for signing a welfare bill. So the House Republicans cheerfully couple the Medicaid with the welfare in one bill because that's just insurance that it won't go anywhere. It sits there like that through the spring, and we're thinking, *Oh, maybe it's going okay here.* Then you get in June, the 104th [Congress] freshmen and sophomore members write this letter to Gingrich in which they say, "You've got to decouple the Medicaid and the welfare [provisions] because we've got to send him a bill that he can sign. *We* can't get re-elected if we don't show that we've done something." They really hadn't done very much.

Gingrich agrees to that.... [Essentially] Clinton is saying to the House, "Go ahead and stay Republican and I'll keep on being president. It's a deal." ...

Q: *Incumbent protection?*
Edelman: So they can say, we the Republican Congress passed this welfare thing and he happened to sign it, and he says, "I signed it." So he gets re-elected, they get re-elected. That's the proposition. ...

Q: *Is there ever a time when you feel as if you're truly going to beat this thing?*
Edelman: This all happens very fast. They write the letter, Gingrich starts to move the bill. The White House is clearly cooperating with it. Clinton goes on a West Coast political swing, and somebody asks him a question about the welfare bill. He says, and it's on the front page of the *New York Times,* "You can put

wings on a pig but you can't make it an eagle." We took that to mean that he had decided the bill was not perfectable.

In any case all of the groups, the unions, the children's, the women's, the minority groups, the faith-based, and so on, were mobilizing to put pressure on him. I think when they read that in the paper they all breathed a sigh of relief and let up. Then a couple of weeks later he has this climactic meeting on July 30th or 31st in the White House and "hears out all the arguments" of the various people. Everybody there, except for Vice President Gore and Bruce Reed and Mickey Kantor and Rahm Emanuel, wants him to veto the bill. That includes Harold Ickes, George Stephanopoulos, Leon Panetta, Secretary Rubin, Secretary Cisneros, Shalala, and I think Reich was there. [The president then agrees to sign it.]

[It] takes me about forty-eight hours for it to sink in. I start going to meetings where they're starting to talk about implementing it, and I realize this is making me very uncomfortable, even a little ill. I notice that Mary Jo Bane is having the same reaction. Wendell leaves right away. So I found myself saying to Donna, "I can't do this." . . . We didn't leave until, I think, September 11th because Donna asked us to wait until she could get successors, even on an acting basis, cleared by the White House. . . . So we agreed we would have no press conference, no appearances on any morning or news show. We would simply each put out a little statement to our staff and if that leaked so be it.

The president sends me a sort of a form letter, thanks me for my service, and then the rest of it is a rehash of a press release. I think it was probably signed by machine, I'm not sure. Hillary sent a handwritten note that said she understood that differences arose among friends and she hoped we would be able to find our way back together.

Q: One of the things the president did when he signed the bill was to say he thought it was a flawed bill on a couple of dimensions and that he would attempt to fix those flaws.
Edelman: That was a misleading statement. What he meant was the provisions about immigration, about legal immigrants. He also was quoted in the *New Yorker* as saying it was a decent welfare bill wrapped in a sack of shit. It's the same point. He's gotten credit for fixing those provisions. That's not even true. What they fixed is, anybody who was in this country prior to August 26, 1996, now can have SSI [Supplemental Security Income] but anybody who comes to this country afterwards still can't get SSI. He didn't fix that. There's been a fix on food stamps that's a little more successful or more encompassing. . . . There has been nothing done to the basic welfare provisions, zero.

Donna Shalala, secretary of health and human services: Everybody thinks that the department was opposed to welfare reform. We weren't at all. We just thought that the bill was a mess, with a lot of immigration stuff we didn't want.

Clinton finally decided that politically he couldn't veto it again, even though all of us had recommended he veto it. Because we were improving it every time he was vetoing it. The Republicans were giving in after each veto.

Q: Were there signals from the Hill that they would go another round?
Shalala: Yes, absolutely. But Clinton always cut his deals a little earlier than I would have cut the deals and it was his right. . . .[But] it was straight politics. Clinton talked me into staying the second term by saying, "I know I messed up on welfare, we've got to straighten it out, so you've got to stay so we can get a lot of that anti-immigration stuff out of it," which we did. . . . Henry [Cisneros] and I decided we weren't going to resign over welfare reform because we were going to make it right one way or another. . . .

Q: So if somebody wants to understand Clinton and welfare reform, you've got to look at what happens in the second term as well as the first—
Shalala: Exactly, and you've got to look at the implementation. The implementation, the power is in implementation. The visibility is in the policymaking, but the power is in implementation.

William Galston, deputy domestic policy advisor: I think he won the '96 election the day he signed the third version of the welfare bill. I don't think there's any doubt about the outcome of that. . . .

Q: Had he not signed the third version of the welfare reform, you think he would have lost the election?
Galston: I believe that. I believe that the most important promise he made to the American people, the one they remembered, was that he would end the single most unpopular symbol of the social policy of the old Democratic Party, the one that Republican presidents and candidates had used to beat up on the Democratic Party ever since the civil rights movement. There was not going to be a fourth version of the welfare bill. He would either sign the third version or live with his veto. I think the Republicans would have crammed it up every orifice in his body.

Roger Altman, deputy treasury secretary: [If] you survey the fifty most senior people who ever served in the Clinton administration, about twenty-five of them will say welfare reform was a great triumph for the president, about twenty-five of them will say he just caved. I'm in the first camp, it was a great triumph, but I'm not sure that history will accord him that.

17

A Domestic Reform President

Bill Clinton's rise to the presidency in 1992 came mainly because of his devotion to domestic policy. His predecessor had deployed the powers of the presidency vigorously in foreign affairs, including a celebrated liberation of Kuwait, but George H. W. Bush refused thereafter to mount a "domestic Desert Storm." Clinton understood the nation's yearning at the end of the Cold War to have a president fully focused on problems at home. He thus came into office committed to addressing a broad slate of domestic policy issues.

One of Clinton's signature initiatives was national service, a quintessential post–Cold War idea. AmeriCorps gave to young people the option of government-funded community service jobs in addition to the traditional alternative of military service. The concept of paid volunteers was, however, considered an oxymoron by many members of Congress, who also questioned the need for a new government program at a time of fiscal constraint. To get the enabling legislation enacted, then, Clinton and his team had to rely heavily on the president's considerable powers of persuasion, and on old-fashioned retail politics.

Senator Harris Wofford (D-PA): [My] experience with [Clinton] on two issues that were crucial to me—national service and civil rights ...—is that those were two deeply rooted things he ... does believe in, strongly. In the first year after he was elected, he said about national service, "AmeriCorps is the transcendent idea of my administration." Now, that isn't the way his priorities went in terms of his time or other things, any more than the Peace Corps was a priority with President Kennedy. In fact, I think Clinton believed in the two points more than Kennedy did—more than he did in civil rights, certainly when he began, and more than he maybe ever did on the Peace Corps.... [From] the time I first talked to him about them to this day, [my experience] tells me that they are deeply rooted, important political ideas [for Clinton].

Al From, head of the DLC: In '88–'89, actually a little before that, Clinton was down at a DLC conference in Williamsburg and heard a discussion of national service. He came up that night and said, "Jeez, what a good idea. I can just see kids taking a year off to work with people in the Mississippi Delta, and earn a year of college scholarship." So that became a staple of the campaign.

Eli Segal, AmeriCorps director: [There] were two Democrats who were reluctant to support what Bill Clinton was beginning to call AmeriCorps. It hadn't officially been named yet. One was Bob Kerrey, who I think ultimately may not have voted for the legislation, and the second was Bob Byrd, who was just opposed to one more spending package.

I went to see Jay Rockefeller, a fellow senator from West Virginia. . . . I walked into Rockefeller's room, in which I'd never been, and said, "Jay, we need Bob Byrd's vote." He said, "He's very hard to get." I said, "But I'm told you can do it," my usual line. Then we started chitchatting about things. I looked around his room and I could see that baseball was a very important part of his life. I said, "Jay, I'll tell you what I'm going to do. I'm going to let you off the hook easy. You ask me any baseball trivia question you want, whatever. If I get it right, you've got to ask [Byrd]. If I get it wrong, you're off the hook."

This is where my memory fades a little because this is twelve years ago. I think his first question was, "Who was the organist at Ebbets Field?" I said, "Everyone knows that was Gladys Gooding." He had a chuckle about it and then he said, "Everyone knows that in [1951] the Giants effectively won the pennant by getting Eddie Stanky and Al Dark from the [Boston] Braves, but no one knows whom the Braves got in return. If you can tell me who the Braves got from the Giants, you win." Who could remember a piece of trivia like this? This is a trade that had happened probably—let's see, this was 1993 and that event happened in 1948 or '49. Without hesitating a second, I said, "Everyone knows it was Willard Marshall and Sid Gordon." [*laughter*] It blew him away. It created a friendship, although I don't think he remembers that that's where our friendship comes from as well as I do. I was right and he delivered Bobby Byrd. Now whether that was a direct one-on-one I'll never know, but it was Rockefeller doing what he said he was going to do, and my using the last bit of skill I had. I knew baseball and politics pretty well.

Peter Edelman, assistant health and human services secretary: Eli [Segal] was perfectly suited for [heading AmeriCorps]. He didn't know anything in particular about the subject, but he's an entrepreneur, he's a start-up guy. That's exactly what he's good at. It was perfect casting.

Senator Harris Wofford: In his campaign Clinton was talking about large-scale national service where people could have an option of serving a year and getting, in Clinton's original thinking, $10,000 a year to go to college. But it got reduced to $5,000. The military said, "We, the military veterans, will block you if you offer more money than the GI Bill now gives." It's more varied, so it's hard to prove exactly. But $4,750 was a little bit under the $5,000 they estimated. So we settled on that as the award.

Eli Segal: It was shortly after the 1994 revolution. The Republicans were in full assault on everything related to the Clinton agenda, one of which was AmeriCorps. I'll never forget the moment when Newt Gingrich said to Bill Clinton, "AmeriCorps, that's history. It's out of here." Now Bill Clinton, who frequently is accused of being spineless, responded to this direct challenge to AmeriCorps by first, making me an honorary member of the Cabinet the night of the State of the Union in '95, and second, putting four young AmeriCorps members, the first year of the program, into the balcony with the First Lady, all wearing their AmeriCorps outfits. That was his response to Newt Gingrich, a bold commitment to the continuation of the program.... From that point until '98 we always knew that AmeriCorps was safe, that no matter what appropriations bills were sent up to the House, it wasn't going to be eliminated. And he was true to his word.

* * *

Although Bill Clinton ran for president as a New Democrat, some of his core policy commitments were deeply rooted in traditional Democratic soil. Nowhere was this more so than on civil rights. African Americans subsequently became one of Clinton's most reliably supportive constituencies. And when an issue presented itself with a compelling civil rights dimension, Clinton was typically sympathetic to the rights of the aggrieved.[1] This impulse led him to step into the controversy over gays in the military just as his presidency was being launched, at considerable political cost.

Judge Abner Mikva, White House counsel : If there's one issue that the president really cares about, it's diversity—particularly racial diversity—but all diversity. If you asked me the one issue that President Clinton, as deep as possible, thought was necessary ..., it would be diversity. He really cared—probably more than any president before or since—including Illinois' native son.[2] ... [If] there was a single issue on which he would go down with the ship, it would be race relations.

Mickey Kantor, secretary of commerce: Clinton was never more comfortable, more connected, or more involved than on issues that involved the black community or campaigning with African Americans. I'll tell you a story, this is the best example I can give about this, about him:

---

1. Critics of Clinton would object to this characterization—and can cite in their defense Clinton's 1992 campaign troubles with Jesse Jackson, the terms of the 1994 crime bill, some provisions of the 1996 welfare reform bill, and the Defense of Marriage Act the president signed.

2. The reference here is to Abraham Lincoln, whose political life was rooted in Illinois, although he was born in Kentucky.

In '96 he wanted to have a small transition team. Leon Panetta, Erskine Bowles, and I are standing there and he says, "The three of you, we should get Vernon [Jordan], Vernon will be the fourth." And then he looks and says, "You know, God, we ought to have somebody from the black community on this." True story, and we all broke out laughing and suddenly he realized what he had said. Well clearly, he is quite remarkable when it comes to that, and [the affection] is reciprocated, of course, in the black community.

Leon Panetta, White House chief of staff (on an internal White House review of affirmative action in 1995, which resulted in Clinton's appeal to "Mend it, don't end it"[3]): We went through a debate on civil rights, and it was very interesting because [Dick] Morris had basically polled civil rights in a way—to be frank, I never trusted Morris's poll because I always thought he polled pursuant to what he thought should be done, and you can shape those polls. Get back the answer you want. Well, that was my suspicion. I have no proof on that but there are probably a lot of other people who believe that was true.

So he did civil rights, and he produced a poll that said the public would not support affirmative action. It created a real problem in the sense that a group of us went and said, "Wait a minute, Mr. President. Civil rights, affirmative action is what you've been all about, it's the commitment you've made." There was this debate about what the president should say about affirmative action. Whether we ought to obviously come out against quotas, but be for affirmative action or whether we ought to, say, move away from affirmative action and just talk about how we ought to be a colorblind society, that sort of thing.

It was one of the first times that I thought, the president has now gotten his feedback from Morris about what he thinks the politics is and he's facing this, "Wait a minute, this is what I'm about, this is what I believe in." ... Blacks always had a special relationship with the president and they trusted him. Suddenly, it was, how is this thing going to come out? The president ultimately said, "Look, I cannot back off affirmative action." He had a speech set up at I think the National Archives Building, where he gave a speech on what the administration's position was going to be on civil rights, and it was well received. Actually, it was interesting to watch Morris. Because when Morris knew that the president made the decision, suddenly Morris's poll started showing how you could basically do some of the [things he earlier said you could not]. [*laughter*] That was Morris's way of dealing with things.

Bruce Reed, deputy domestic policy advisor (on Clinton's commitment to support gay members of the military):[4] [We] had "Don't ask, don't tell," right

---

3. Bill Clinton, "Address on Affirmative Action," July 19, 1995.
4. Reed's comments in Nelson and Riley, eds., *Governing at Home*, 65.

out of the box in the Clinton administration. I traveled with Bill Clinton for the better part of two years and I don't think I'd ever even heard that promise made. It was there in *Putting People First* somewhere, and he had in fact made it, but it was not one that had been emphasized. No one had thought through how you were actually going to convince the Joint Chiefs of Staff to go along with this. That was one where there just wasn't any way to get it done, and he had folded his hand. It was an example—You have to be careful in making your campaign promises you don't promise things that you have no possibility of delivering. Or if you make those kinds of promises, you have to level with people that it is going to be extremely difficult and you may not be able to do it. The hardest thing for a candidate to decide—one of the most important decisions is where they're going to accept reality and where they're going to try to transform it.

Sandy Berger, deputy national security advisor: [We] had this nice plan in place to kick the can down the road a little bit, not to avoid it but just give ourselves some time to work the military and get by. The Republicans really discovered this issue after the election. They realized it was a delicious issue for making mischief. Senator [Robert] Dole introduced S1 as I recall, which was a bill to prohibit gays in the military.

This was [all] very sudden. This was not a big issue in the campaign, as I said. Suddenly, out of the box, this becomes a defining issue. I think there was not enough time to have a serious discussion within the military about the pros and cons. I suspect, had we maintained the initiative on this and set up a commission including [Senator] Sam Nunn (D-GA) and others on how to implement this policy, there would have been six months or nine months in which you would have had an opportunity to find out where the support was.

William Perry, defense secretary: [The] president wanted to make good on his pledge to remove the restriction on gays in the military—evidently not being aware of the fact that he didn't really have that authority, that the Congress is the one that decides that. So he thought he could do it like [Harry] Truman had done it on integrating the services, which was by decree, but it doesn't work that way. Congress rose up in rebellion and was busy passing new legislation that would enshrine in legislation the ban on gays in the military. So every action has a reaction. In this case his action to try to do what he thought was the right thing to do on the campaign pledge led to a reaction in the Congress, which as I look back on it, no doubt they would have been successful in doing what they said they were going to do.

Now, this is where Les Aspin comes in. Les, of course, a former Congressman, a perfect person to mediate this problem, Clinton thought. And Aspin thought so as well. Aspin then got the job of mediating the problem, which was basically serving as an intermediary between the Congress on the one hand, which was dead set on passing this very restrictive legislation—and with the military on their side, I might say—and the White House that wanted to make good on the president's pledge. For the next, it must have been six months, that consumed everything. That sucked up all the air. Everything we did was somehow revolving around that problem. Les spent hours and hours each week in meetings with the military, with his staff, and with the Congress trying to work out a solution. He finally came up with a solution. It was a haywire solution, but it worked, in a sense.

It worked in the sense that it allowed the president to say he was doing something on his pledge, and it got the Congress to agree not to pass the restrictive legislation. And it was the infamous "Don't ask, don't tell" policy, which he crafted together after the six months or so with the help of Jamie Gorelick,[5] who was his very able counsel. Her job was to be a good counsel, which was to try to help her boss come up with something. That's what they came up with. The military was not happy with it, but was willing to accept it. The Congress was not happy with it, but was willing to accept it. The president was not happy with it, but was willing to accept it. The gay community was certainly not happy with it. But it ended, I said six months, almost close to a year—at least nine months ... of this acrimonious debate that ... solidified the view that the Clinton administration was hostile to, and didn't understand, the U.S. military.

Bernard Nussbaum, White House counsel: The thing blew up. I was sorry it blew up. I didn't want it to blow up. We needed to deal with this issue, but this is what you should do? [Clinton] was afraid. You should sign an order ordering gays to be permitted to be in the military by executive order just like [Harry] Truman did with [integrating] blacks. If Congress wants to override it, let Congress override it. You were true to what you said in your principles.

* * *

No issue had been more important to Bill Clinton as governor of Arkansas than education. Indeed it was on education policy that Clinton rose to prominence as a national figure, coming to the attention of Washington policymakers for his bipartisan leadership in the South. Although federal policy on education had usually been a backwater of White House activity, Clinton remained a leading figure on education reform during his presidency.

William Galston, deputy domestic policy advisor: People in the summer and fall of 1994 were desperate for good news. I wrote the president a memo saying, "While nobody was looking, we moved nine pieces of education legislation through the Congress of the United States, and you, right now, are one of the

---

5. Jamie Gorelick was at that time general counsel of the Department of Defense, and would later serve as deputy attorney general in the Clinton administration.

most significant education reform presidents in the history of the Republic." He started talking about that. But nobody in the White House other than me and a handful of others who were working on it knew that until I sent him that memo.

Richard Riley, education secretary: The Democrats were very dubious about [national standards] at first. In the end they were the strongest supporters of it. I talked about it all over the country, and Bill Clinton did, to big black audiences. I would get up and say, "You know, when we got to Washington, there was substandard testing for disadvantaged kids, largely minority kids. We did away with that. Challenging testing the same for Title I children as with all other children. Standards are standards. There's no such thing as a watered-down standard for poor minority kids." They would scream and holler. I mean they loved it. They didn't like the substandard testing, basically math and reading, that their children were having.

Clinton was always happy when we were on education, in the Cabinet or wherever. . . . I remember, I was introducing him at a big teachers' meeting in the East Room, all the Teachers of the Year, whatever it was. Anyway, it was jammed full of people. I said something about what teachers meant to him. He got up there and, unbeknownst to his speechwriters or anybody else, proceeded to name every teacher he had and how they had impressed him and taught him something special. It went through kindergarten, first grade—. . . The teachers' mouths would drop open. That guy really liked his teachers. He named every single one.

* * *

Bill Clinton did not come to the presidency with a demonstrated record of achievement on either labor or environmental issues. Arkansas had no influential union presence, and chickens are a key—and dirty—industry in the state. Yet both of these Democratic constituency groups had some reason to applaud Clinton for efforts on their behalf during his eight years as president.

Judge Abner Mikva: At one point Bob Reich, the secretary of labor, a good friend of the president's and one of the real good people in the Cabinet, had gone to see the president to try to get him to support an increase in the minimum wage. The president, especially when he was with his friends, couldn't say no, but an old friend could really tell that it hadn't grabbed the president. The president had never been that big on labor issues, and at that point we didn't have the majorities in either the House or the Senate, and the idea of raising the minimum wage sounded very far-fetched. But Bob kept saying, Mr. President, you really have to do something about it. Labor just feels like we're ignoring them, and they elected him. So he said, "Yes, I'll certainly think about it, Bob. Thanks for coming in."

[Bob] walked out; he knew he had gotten nowhere. Then he remembered that Al Gore was going down to Florida the next day to address the executive board of the AFL-CIO. Bob Reich was—notwithstanding never having worked inside government before—an insider's insider. He came in to Al and said, "You know, Al, I was just talking to the president about the minimum wage. You really ought to think about it. When you go down there tomorrow, it would be a good idea to tell them we're working on it, give them something to talk about."

So Saturday morning, there's Al Gore down in Florida telling the AFL-CIO executive council that the administration is going to back an increase in the minimum wage. Of course, it's all over the Sunday papers. Monday morning, Bob Rubin is furious, just furious. We agreed, we were not—the economy can't stand it. It's a terrible thing to do. You're not going to pass it anyway. All you're going to do is rattle the markets. It's just the craziest thing I ever—"You go tell him, Leon, he can't do that. He's got to pull the rug [from under Gore]." We all figured out what had happened. Clinton hadn't done it.

Rubin said, "You go tell him that he has to pull the rug out, this is crazy, we can't make policy this way." Leon said, "Okay, but before I do, can I get a show of hands? How many people think we ought to pull Gore back on this?" Everybody [at the senior staff meeting] raised his hand except Ickes and me; we were the two who thought that, for whatever reason, we were doing what we should be doing. So Leon, good faithful chief of staff, goes out. He's with the president about five minutes, ten minutes. Meanwhile, Rubin is lecturing us on the minimum wage and how the markets behave.

Leon came back with a smile on his face. He said, "Remember that wonderful Lincoln story about when Lincoln polled his Cabinet?" Most of us remembered; he told it anyway. Lincoln polled the Cabinet. It was 7–1 to do something, and he was the one who said no. He said, "Well, I just told the president what the vote was, it was 7–2, and now it's 7–3. You lose."[6]

Frank Greer, media advisor: He turns into the greatest environmental president since Teddy Roosevelt, and preserves more of the West—the Grand Staircase-Escalante, for example—than anybody else. Those of us who knew him, including my wife, were pleased that he became this great environmental president, because he did not have a sterling environmental record as governor and he did not have a good relationship with environmentalists.

* * *

One of the most controversial domestic policy initiatives of Bill Clinton's presidency was the 1994 crime bill. Although it helped to put 100,000 new police officers on the street, the inclusion of an assault weapon ban, over vigorous objections by congressional Democrats, contributed to the party's loss of both houses of Congress in 1994. And in subsequent years, the measure has been criticized for contributing to an explosion in

---

6. Clinton signed into law a ninety-cent increase in the minimum wage in August 1996.

inmate populations, because of such features as the bill's three-strikes-and-you're-out
provision imprisoning repeat offenders.

Patrick Griffin, White House congressional liaison: One of the first things that
[Clinton] took on when he got [to Washington] was this crime bill. There had
been crime bills floating around in the Democratic Congress for twelve years,
five bills that had never become law. Part of repositioning Democrats was to be
tough on crime and to be for the death penalty. We had twenty-eight new death
penalties in our proposed bill. It was not a high moment in criminal justice
policy.

The black caucus uniformly was against it. The Hispanic caucus was against
it. It was tough. How do we pass a crime bill with our constituency so stridently
against it? Clinton, remember, in the middle of his election campaign went
back and pulled the [switch to electrocute] some guy. That was one dynamic.
The other was Clinton insisted that we put the assault weapon ban in it. That
was a very big dynamic. There's one little story here that had a big impression
on me. We were out at a Senate retreat, he and I, and Mrs. Clinton were there,
as was Stephanopoulos. At the retreat he gives a speech. I'm sitting off the stage
and [Dianne] Feinstein[7] raises this question, "Where is the assault weapon ban
in the Senate?" This woman is a senator on the Judiciary Committee asking the
president of the United States. Up until this point I thought we were kind of
slow-walking the assault weapon ban, given the politics of it. I thought that was
a good idea—we'd react on the issue if we had to.

He turns to me and he says, "Griffin, where is it?" I said, "It's in the Senate
Committee waiting for mark-up." He knew she was trying to gin him up. I didn't
realize it at the moment. I just thought it was a stupid question, so I didn't think
anything of it. The next morning we're on *Marine One* going back to the White
House. We're playing hearts or something, and all of a sudden he puts the cards
down and says, "Why didn't you brief me as to where this was?" I said, "Mr.
President, it would be a ridiculous thing to brief you where all the legislation is.
It would never occur to me that you would need to know the status of all of our
proposed legislation when talking to senators who were responsible for the disposition of the legislation." I asked, "Why would you feel you needed to know?"

"What do you mean, 'Why do I need to know?'".... He's yelling back at me
how irresponsible of me to suggest that he wouldn't be terribly interested in
such an important piece of legislation like the assault ban. I said, "I thought
we were just kind of slow walking this provision," which I was sure we were.
He responded, appearing shocked and offended by saying "What? How dare
you think that I—that is so wrong!" He went into this righteous rage at me. I'm

---

7. Dianne Feinstein was mayor of San Francisco from 1978 to 1988. She began serving as a
Democratic senator from California in 1992.

looking at him. *Did I make this up? Is this a unilateral decision that I had made here with Mack [McLarty]?* He said, "We're going to move on every piece of legislation that makes sense—" I said, "Mr. President, I think this is going to be very difficult." His response was, "How dare you think that there is any other option. What would people think of me if I did not follow through on the assault weapon ban?" "I'm sorry, Mr. President. I really got that wrong."

So I come back, and I tell Leon. He said that I had not come up with this notion on my own. No one stepped in to correct the president. There was no need to go back into it with him now, because we're going to move ahead on the assault weapon ban. It was a disaster from day one. I go and tell Speaker Foley, who would wind up losing his seat in the upcoming election due to this issue.... [Speaker] Foley, Gephardt, and [David] Bonior[8] all said, "You are all crazy. We want to see the president." I responded stating, "Do you think I would be promoting this if I wasn't being told to do so?"

We brought them into the Oval Office. It was the three of them, myself, Leon [Panetta]—I don't know who else was there. Maybe George [Stephanopoulos] was there—the president and the vice president. The vice president was all, "We're going for it." These three guys said, "We're ready to help you on the crime bill, but Mr. President, don't push the assault weapon ban." The president said, "I'm absolutely going to promote it." I can't remember exactly the dynamic. I think we had to wind up doing it as an amendment. They said, "We're not going to bring up the crime bill that has the assault weapon ban in it. You're going to have to [amend] it on the floor. We're not going to have anything to do with it." In that meeting they asked him three times—Foley with the big old kind of hound dog [look], "Please, Mr. President, don't push the assault weapon ban." Just shaking his head. And Bonior and Gephardt. Gephardt, who said, "I'm for it, but this is going to be devastating to our troops. Please don't do it." They deliberately went at it three times and the president just says, "We're going for it."

They said, "Fine. We're not going to help you at all. If you're going to pass this crime bill, or this ban, we'll have nothing to do with it." They told us that we would have to set up our own whip operation. We were accustomed to using the leadership. "You're on your own," they said. The president says, "I understand that. We're going to take care of it." And he looks at Leon and me.

From that day forward we then get the crime bill scheduled. We now have no cooperation from the Democratic leadership. They give Leon and me a room to work out of to set up our own whip operation. We then work with some of the Democrats who are sympathetic. We know we can't pass it only with Democrats so we figure we've got thirty to forty Republicans. We need forty or forty-five.

---

8. David Bonior, a Democrat, represented a Michigan district in the U.S. House of Representatives from 1977 to 2003. He was House majority whip at the time of this incident.

We go to [Robert] Michel,[9] who's the head of the [House] Republicans at the time, and he says, "I don't know if I can help you. Why don't you talk to [Newt] Gingrich?" Newt was already moving in on Michel. So we go to Newt and he says, "I don't want any part of this crap. But I'll see if I can authorize somebody to work with you guys." Leon and I are setting up shop up in one of Gephardt's suite rooms, and Newt sends to us [Republican Michael] Castle[10] from Delaware as being the point person to work with Republicans on this, because Newt knew he had guys who would be supportive.

Leon and I set up our operation. We go through, member by member, trying to convince, basically the Democratic black caucus to vote for this bill. Almost every one of these members had never voted for a death penalty before—same thing with the Hispanic caucus. Then we're having a separate conversation with the Republicans. Basically, it became one of the real vintage stories of [this presidency]. The deals were not necessarily made on the substance of the issue. The candy store was open.

Q: Would you care to elaborate?
Griffin: Not entirely, but it was a very transactional kind of setup. Eventually, we got enough to get the crime bill through. The crime bill came to the floor without the assault ban. The intent was to have [Democrat Charles] Schumer[11] offer the ban as an amendment—I'd been dragging my feet about going up to the Hill that day. The vote was going to be very close and I guess I didn't want to be publicly associated with it. My staff pleaded with me to go. "You're crazy. You've got to be there." I said, "This just stinks. This is not going to work."

Eventually, they made me come down. I remember standing up with this big knot in my stomach, and we're voting on the assault weapon ban and we win by one vote. I just had all my fingers crossed [hoping] that we were going to lose. Everybody's delighted [in the White House]. There's cheering. It was a big operation. Rahm Emanuel had put together this external outreach operation working with cops and other external supporters. He did a brilliant thing with that.

I come back and I'm just sick to my stomach. Everybody's cheering, pictures are being taken, we're in the Rose Garden, high fives everywhere. I said, "Mr. President, there's going to be trouble on this." . . . Then it went to the Senate. Dole is now getting traction for stopping everything he can on the president's agenda. We're in August or July. It's now moved over to the Senate and we're having this leadership meeting to prepare for floor consideration. Foley comes over with the leadership. We're in Mitchell's office. I'll never forget—it was a night of storms, lightning just

9. Robert Michel served in Congress from Illinois from 1957 to 1995. He was House minority leader from 1981 to 1995.

10. Michael Castle represented Delaware in the U.S. House of Representatives from 1993 to 2011. Castle had previously been governor of Delaware.

11. At that time, Charles Schumer was representing a New York congressional district in the U.S. House of Representatives (1981–1999). He subsequently served in the U.S. Senate.

crashing. You can just hear Foley's mind racing, saying, "We're still not aligned with the gods on this thing," or some clever comment.... [We] made some concession [in the Senate] and, boom, we got the bill done and went to conference [and finally passed]. That was a whole other trauma, a story in itself. The rest is history. We lost fifty-three seats in the rural areas, particularly in the South.

Q: You think that was a key element?
Griffin: Absolutely. Yes. I'd say, for forty of those seats, yes. For Chairman [Jack] Brooks to lose his seat?[12] Foley? These guys had been safe forever. And they voted against all this stuff but they were still targeted politically because their president was for the ban.

* * *

Unexpected developments happen on the watch of every president. Such was the siege by federal law enforcement officials of a residential compound near Waco, Texas, beginning in February 1993. This incident arose from legal proceedings against a religious sect, the Branch Davidians, and their leader, David Koresh. Evidence indicated weapons violations and potential abuse of young people in the cloistered compound. Agents from the Alcohol, Tobacco and Firearms Division of the Treasury Department attempted to raid the compound, but met with armed resistance. Several people were killed. The FBI subsequently initiated the siege. Eventually a second raid was attempted on April 19. Over seventy occupants, including Koresh, were killed by gunshots or burned to death in structural fires.

Bernard Nussbaum: Janet Reno came in and the siege of Waco was going on. We were new in the administration. I met with Reno. My advice to Reno was ... let's look to the professionals. I think I said, "Consult with the FBI. They're the professional people who have been conducting the siege. It's your decision as to what we do or not do at any particular time, but if I were you, I would consult with them and really look to them for advice and guidance with respect to this thing. They've been on the firing line there. They know more what's happening. And I have confidence that they'll give you disinterested advice."

I don't feel the same way now about the FBI or the Secret Service or anything that I did then. I really came in with a high opinion of them at the time; my opinion is now somewhat less. Don't overstate it. It's a little bit like the Bay of Pigs, relying on the CIA.[13] This advice that I'm giving now, it's logical and sensible, but somehow I'm sorry about it in retrospect. ...

---

12. Jack Brooks (1922–2012) served in the U.S. House of Representatives from Texas for forty-two years (1953–1995). At the time of the crime bill he was chair of the House Judiciary Committee.

13. John Kennedy felt it necessary, as a very new president, to rely heavily on CIA expertise to inform his decision to approve the Bay of Pigs operation. He found his faith in them misplaced.

Then the president—there was a lot of publicity about Waco. This is prior to the attack, and the president spoke to me about it and said, "What do we do about Waco?" I said, "I met with the attorney general, I talked to the attorney general, and I told her she should look to the professionals and make a decision as to what to do. We should stay out of it." He said, "No, I know a lot about this stuff, Bernie, I was governor of Arkansas and there were prison riots and all that sort of stuff." I may, in retrospect, also have given him bad advice about this thing, although I thought the advice was good at the time. I said, "No, Mr. President, you really should stay out of this. The attorney general is handling it. She has the FBI to consult with and various things. You really shouldn't do it."

He said, "I want to have some input into this." I said, "Mr. President, you're the president of the United States, you're not the governor of the United States. It was a good line. That's what I came up with at the time. But the advice, when I think of it now—he basically did what I said. "Okay," he said, "the one thing I want you to do is before she does anything, she should consult with Colin Powell, the chief of staff of the armed forces. Tell the attorney general that before anything is done in Waco, she should consult with the military, specifically with Colin Powell, to see that whatever they would do, if they go in or they don't go in, makes sense." I said, "That's a good idea, Mr. President. I'll do that."

I called the attorney general and told her, "Before you do anything, talk to the FBI like I said, but my suggestion is you call Colin Powell," and that's what they did. Colin Powell is the most Teflon person in the world. None of this came up. Before they went into Waco, Powell or some of his people reviewed the plans and said they basically made sense.

We were involved. We didn't know when they were going to go in or if they were going to go in, because I kept the president out of it. I gave her the advice of relying on the FBI, which she then did. They came and told her there were children inside. I then went on a trip with the vice president to Poland. He spoke on the anniversary of the Warsaw ghetto and I was invited to go with him.[14] I flew on *Air Force Two*. We got to Warsaw. It was night, we got off, we were in cars, taken to our hotels, and changed clothes to go hear this great speech. I walk into the hotel and I turn on the TV, they're just starting the international news and there's Waco burning on the TV set. I'm in Poland, and Waco is burning.

I call the office. I don't know if I talked to [Vince] Foster or somebody else. "What's going on?" They said, "What's going on is what you see on TV. What's going on is they broke in and fire started and a lot of people are dead. But we're handling it. We and George Stephanopoulos." And then they kept the president from making a statement for twenty-four hours, which was also a mistake. I wasn't

---

14. Gore was in Poland on April 19, 1993, which was the day David Koresh was killed.

involved in that because I was in Poland at the time. I don't know what position I would have taken. Maybe I would have taken the same position they took. I was trying to keep him out of it too. The whole thing was a mistake. You couldn't really keep him out of it. He shouldn't have been kept out of it. I'm sort of sorry—I gave the advice I thought was right. Maybe it's still sort of right. You can always second-guess yourself. . . .

Of course Reno then saved herself. She went on TV. She took responsibility, she went on *Nightline*. She made the decision. She didn't blame the FBI. The reason she made the decision was this. She's sad with what happened, but she was the one—and she became a heroine because she took responsibility and didn't run away and didn't hide or anything like that. And Clinton, both by virtue of what happened, and also by virtue of not really speaking out at that time, coming out forcefully, having been kept by the White House, sort of following the line that I created, although I don't know if they were deliberately doing that, ended up being hurt by Waco. It was a great tragedy. . . .

Q: Did they feel that the attorney general managed the fallout from this well or was there a kind of internal jealousy that she—?
Nussbaum: . . . There was no jealousy of Reno. They were pleased. They were a little upset that the president was taking this hit and really it wasn't his fault. But that's what happens when you're president. It wasn't his fault. He didn't make the decision to go in; he didn't make the decision to stay out. He was kept out of it by me and maybe by other people also. But we were happy that Reno was strengthened.

* * *

One of the major domestic accomplishments Bill Clinton had hoped to achieve, but did not, was reform of the major entitlement systems in America, most prominently Social Security.

Senator Alan Simpson (R-WY): I remember one White House session in which he said, "I can pledge this early on, we're going to do something with Social Security and the entitlements." God, it was a beautiful talk, in the Cabinet Room, around the table. "What about you, Al? What are you thinking?" I said, "Look, you don't have a prayer as long as you can't muzzle the goddamned AARP [American Association of Retired Persons] and the Committee to Preserve Social Security and Medicare, and others. Those hysterical monsters will cremate any kind of reform you're doing, so you'd better get them in here first. If you can get them in here—and they may not come, but get them in—and you'll find out what you're facing." He said, "I'll do that."

He did and then he found out where the crematorium was erected. These bastards are the most selfish of people. They don't care about their grandchildren.

Their legislative agenda is that thick, two inches. It's all about more money for seniors—no means testing, no affluence testing. Monsters.

Al From: Clinton was such an extraordinary political leader that if he had taken on something like entitlement reform, I think we could have actually gotten it done. But that opportunity was taken away [by the impeachment controversy]. There are probably other things we could have done in the last couple of years.

PART III

Foreign Policy

18

A New Foreign Policy
for a New World Order

Bill Clinton was the first president to assume the office after the collapse of the Berlin Wall—indeed after the end of the Cold War. This was not a mere coincidence. Clinton's predecessor in the Oval Office, George H. W. Bush, was a quintessential Cold War president—with a long and distinguished résumé on matters of foreign and defense policy and intelligence. However, that experience and skill set seemed suddenly obsolescent in 1992, when a small-state governor with meager foreign policy credentials could mount a successful national campaign around the proposition, "It's the economy, stupid."

However much, in the new post–Cold War environment, Americans wished their leaders to turn their attention inward, and to benefit from the so-called peace dividend, the world did not go away. Indeed the "new world order" that President Bush had announced at the Cold War's end created vexing new problems for America's foreign policy establishment, both doctrinally and practically. What was the role of the world's sole superpower in this new era? And what kinds of new challenges came with this role?

Madeleine Albright, secretary of state: I think in the Clinton administration we really did have a sense that we were working for the first real post–Cold War president, and that there were so many more issues that needed to be integrated into what we thought of as national security. There really was a sense that you had to look at foreign assistance from a different perspective. There were many more countries that you had to deal with on the basis of their own importance rather than how they played in some sort of a competition with the Soviet Union, much more emphasis on economics and on trade and the difficulty of integrating the international economic portfolios.

Tony Lake, national security advisor: Right from the start, . . . [Bill Clinton] understood something that none of us foreign policy nerds did, and that was what later became called globalization. We just didn't fully understand. I'd been trained [to think] . . . you've got national security on the one hand, you have domestic security on the other. And I was not alone, this was true of all of us.

[But] because he had been a governor, and because he had brought a lot of trade into Arkansas . . . he was seeing the connections between the economics and the politics, and between the domestic and the foreign, and was less limited to the boxes that we were all living in. . . . [He's] the quickest study I've ever seen, more than Henry Kissinger, more than anybody I've ever worked with.

Nancy Soderberg, deputy national security advisor: In effect, what happened with foreign policy is that there was no rulebook after the Cold War. Clinton had the right instincts, but you get to the White House, and all these people say, "You can't do it because it's always been done this way." Bosnia was a perfect [example]. There are all these EU [European Union] and UN [United Nations] envoys running around, lots of busy work, little progress. It makes you think you're actually going to get to the big picture. It took us two and a half years to figure out that's not going to work. You have to let the current system wear itself out.

You can't come in and just change everything as a new president. So you just go along with it for a while. It took us two and a half years, essentially, to figure out the new rules of the post–Cold War era. Nobody gave us a book when we came in. The old way clearly wasn't working. The world had fundamentally changed. The way you do business has to change, but how you do it took a while. . . . [Trying] to rewrite the rules for the twenty-first century is a messy process, and it's not clear where you're going or how it's going to work out. Everybody has to learn a new system and a new way of speaking about it. They're looking for a new doctrine of containment to put everything into a neat box, and you can't do it. We tried to do it. We tried to come up with one phrase after another. . . . How were we going to explain what we were doing? We tried to come up with it. . . .

Q: Was there ever a point at which you thought you had figured out what the post–Cold War paradigm was?
Soderberg: No. I would say after about two and a half years after the Cold War we got the mix of force and diplomacy right: you need to use force, not to fight a communist empire, but rather to back up negotiations in limited places. That was the new piece of it. The old use of force was still very prevalent. You have to contain Saddam Hussein. You might have to go to war here and there. But for the most part, there wasn't any existential threat to the United States. Therefore you had a debate: if it's not an existential threat, why is it worth our lives, our soldiers' lives, our kids' lives? Then you realize that limited use of force can contain some of these problems before they become—not necessarily existential threats, but big ones. Then we'd ultimately have to deal with a bigger mess.

Sandy Berger, deputy national security advisor: Tony Lake's enlargement speech was an effort to create a new construct, containment vs.

enlargement.[1] Unfortunately it was probably a bad choice of words, because it became kind of phallic in its interpretation by the press.... It turned out that enlargement was not a construct that was sufficient for people. What to me was more compelling was that we were now living in a global world. We were a global power and we had responsibilities, economic and political, and security responsibilities around the world.

Tony Lake: It's not that Clinton couldn't [conceptualize], because he certainly had the mind to and even the instinct to. But it just didn't happen. And I would wish in retrospect—I hadn't thought of this before—that rather than saying, "Democracy, that's nice, give the speech," and then occasionally mentioning it, he'd said, "Wait a minute, ... let's talk about it." ... And [then] work it through for half a day. I should have been pressing him then, saying, "So what do you mean by—" because there was no such word as "globalization" as I can recall then. "What is it, what's this idea here that I can see lighting up when you're talking freedom, democracy whatever, what the world is?" ... Sandy did some good speeches for him on that, I think, towards the end. But that ... is hardly a clarion call. GLOBALIZATION. You know, "To the barricades my friends, follow me into the era of globalization."

James Woolsey, director of central intelligence: The first two years of the Clinton administration were really kind of halcyon days of American power in the world. We sort of bestrode the world like a Colossus in the early '90s.... The question before the president often during these two years was, "Are we going to go help them?" Not, "Whom do we need to defeat? Who is challenging us?" But, "Are we going to keep helping the Somalis? Are we going to help the Rwandans? Are we going to help the Bosnians?" Maybe next month. Maybe not this month. "Who are we going to help?"

Tony Lake: I don't like to admit this, but on Haiti and Bosnia especially, I was mostly pushed by reactions to the people dying and sort of squishy soft, liberal, Wilsonian emotion, and then finding clear-headed Kissingerian strato-policy reasons for why we had to do this. And you know, most officials are human beings so it is always a mix of the two. If you try to sell humanitarian interventions or involvement on strictly emotional appeals and humanitarian appeals, you're going to lose, while there are lives at stake. Now, I would sometimes take it to an extent that Clinton would disagree. When we were writing speeches on Haiti, for example, explaining the intervention, I would keep making the strategic argument for the speech and Clinton would say, "No, they're cutting people's

---

1. Lake delivered his address, an attempt to provide thematic unity to Clinton's foreign policy, at the Johns Hopkins School of Advanced International Studies in Washington, on September 21, 1993.

faces. We can make an emotional appeal here," and he was right, it did work. . . . But it is two different audiences.

Stanley Greenberg, pollster: I had a position of not polling on foreign policy issues. I recommended that because the president was being criticized as being poll-driven and being political. Given no military background and experience on foreign policy questions, the perception that he was doing polling on foreign policy issues might subject him to criticism. So we didn't poll on foreign policy issues.

Madeleine Albright: So . . . we were out of the Cold War. There were real questions about the size of the defense budget. There were issues about how to get some control over the deficit. There was the fact that "it's the economy, stupid." There was the weird relationship with the military over the gay issue. There was Colin Powell, who was viewed as the hero of the Western world. There were all these new issues on the table, plus twelve years of a Republican presidency. So there were a lot of different things going on, and some of them had to do with the larger issues about the role of the United States. My sense always was that Clinton was somebody who saw a large role for the United States in a kind of principled way, but when it came to trying to figure out what the steps were, he knew, we all began to realize—the difference frankly between being an academic and being a policymaker is you all of a sudden have to put your money where your mouth is.

Sandy Berger: We inherited Haiti, Somalia, and Bosnia. We had a lot of things we wanted to do—NATO enlargement, opening to China, global economic integration. But we were pretty overwhelmed in the first two years with the inherited agenda. . . . President Clinton generally was inductive rather than deductive in the way he approached a decision. That is, he started with the facts and built to the conclusion, rather than starting with the conclusion and going to the facts. . . . [More] often than not, he would listen and collect the viewpoints. Sometimes I would be the surrogate—every day I'd be the surrogate for at least the second order of decisions, saying, "We've got to decide X." Secretary [William] Cohen[2] thinks A for the following reasons, Secretary Albright thinks B for the following reasons. I would usually offer my opinion. But my guiding principle was if Cohen and Albright were standing behind me, listening to me present their viewpoint to the president, would they think that I had done a fair job with their viewpoint? I think they did, and I think we had that trust.

---

2. William Cohen was Clinton's third secretary of defense, serving from 1997 to 2001. A moderate Republican, Cohen had represented Maine in the U.S. Senate from 1979 to 1997.

You can't have meetings with the president every day with the whole team. The national security advisor is often the surrogate, presenting the points of view, offering his own point of view. The president would listen to all that. He'd often call the person against whose advice he was going. In other words, if Cohen was for A and Albright was for B, and he was inclined to go with A, he'd call Albright. He'd want to hear more from her why she thought A was a lousy option. He'd also call other people.

This was the most eclectic president we've had in many, many years. He didn't stay inside the box. He might see somebody in Martha's Vineyard at a reception or someone at a fundraiser, or simply pick up the phone and call Colin Powell. He used to call Colin frequently and say, "Colin, what do you think of this?" particularly when it involved issues of use of force. He would not necessarily stay within the box of his advisors. He would reach out beyond that. . . . Clinton would reach a conclusion and then he would subject that conclusion to the counterargument. In other words, if he said, "Okay, we're going to send forces to Haiti," he'd want to know all the reasons why that was a mistake and be very confident in his mind that he had reasonably good answers to all those reasons before he went forward. . . . He'd be the most devastating counter-questioner that you could possibly imagine. "That's ridiculous. That makes no sense because A, B, C, D, and E." So as I was preparing for those sessions, I not only prepared the answer, I prepared the answer to his question about my answer. When he felt that he was secure was when he felt comfortable in responding to the negatives of his proposition.

* * *

Q. The conventional story was that you and Chris [Warren Christopher] were hired to keep foreign policy issues away from the president so he could focus on the economy. Could you talk about that?

Tony Lake: [chuckling] Well, I've never said this to anybody and it sounds self-serving and I don't mean it to be, but Sandy once, as we came out of a meeting in the Oval Office, referred to me as the "president for foreign policy." This would have been in the first or second year. Which is a wild overstatement, but I think he was saying it in frustration. . . . That's on the one hand. On the other hand the cliché that the president wasn't interested in foreign policy or spending time on it is simply flat-out wrong. There was a constant battle with the schedulers and political folks, who believed that foreign policy was a threat to the president's political future.

[They] were always fighting to not let foreign policy intrude on his "real" work. I think it was probably towards the beginning of '94, the scheduling people, in order to make their point, did a computer run on how much time the president had spent on meetings with foreign leaders, phone calls with foreign leaders. Then they compared it with the first year, year and a half or whatever it was, of the foreign policy presidents—Bush 41's first year, year and a half in office—and damned if it wasn't identical.

Warren Christopher, secretary of state: [Clinton] seemed to have insights about the politics of countries that were just amazing. I read about secretaries of state who wanted to keep the president out of their matters so that he didn't mess it up. Well, I never felt that way about Clinton. I always was anxious to get him into any matter because I knew that he would add an extra 15 or 20 percent to whatever the bureaucracy and I would provide for him. So I just think it's a canard that he wasn't interested in foreign affairs. . . . Clinton's interest in foreign matters goes back to his days as a student at Oxford and his travels in Europe. It is certainly true that his twelve years as governor of Arkansas meant that he dealt in the context of his day-to-day life with domestic issues, and few presidents will ever come into office with more knowledge about domestic matters than Clinton. But the nature of the man is that there is nothing that goes on that doesn't interest him, and whenever he is confronted with a new area, suddenly he becomes very interested in it and reads about it and assembles his information in a way that is not sort of IBM orderliness, but nevertheless I found he took an interest in every foreign policy issue that came up.

Tony Lake: There are two kinds of issues here [at the White House]. You've got the urgent issues, the immediate issues, which are the crises that have to be resolved, and they're at the top of the inbox. When we came in they were Bosnia, Somalia, Haiti, issues like that. Crises that we goddamn inherited. And we inherited a situation in which there were troops in Somalia and no mission and no timetable, whatever people have said. In Bosnia, where there was a war going on, people were dying and there was no policy except, "This isn't our problem." Haiti, where there were increasing flows of refugees and no solution to the problem, and all with a lot of publicity.

When we left, and we may have done them wrong, but they were not crises anymore. And there weren't any new crises, after the first four years, that I'm aware of, that the second Clinton administration was dealing with. And by God, I'm certainly proud of that. More important, while those are the immediate issues that go to the top and they were the ones the president simply wanted to get rid of, there are also the important issues, which are the structural changes, like NATO enlargement or like free trade agreements, arms control issues, or whatever. And we made a pretty good start on a lot of those as well.

Al From, head of the DLC: One of the raps against Clinton was that our politics was just expedient. We were doing this for political reasons, and we didn't care about anything. I've always believed that the international meetings and the Third Way discussions made the argument that there was more to it than that. There's a real governing philosophy that guided countries all over the world.[3] One of the things that doesn't get as much attention that was critical, and it was an enormous accomplishment, an historic accomplishment, was the way he helped modernize center-left politics all over the world. The Third Way discussions were integral to that. It was really important. When we started, there were very few center-left governments, and I think at one point there were thirteen or fifteen European countries with center-left governments.

---

3. The most prominent of these was Tony Blair in the United Kingdom.

19

Haiti

If Bill Clinton harbored hopes that he would be free as president to set aside foreign af-
fairs to concentrate on the nation's economic and domestic problems, those aspirations
were dashed within weeks of his election. Bad news from Haiti, Somalia, and Bosnia
quickly found its way from the front pages of the nation's newspapers onto Clinton's
governing agenda, testing him and his newly assembled team of foreign policy advisors.

Political turmoil on the small Caribbean island nation of Haiti had boiled over in
1992, creating a dilemma for then-President George H. W. Bush. Refugees began trying
to escape to Florida by sea, leading Bush to order the Coast Guard to intercept them and
return them to their homeland. As a presidential candidate Clinton was critical of Bush's
decision. Accordingly, after Clinton defeated Bush in November, Haitians began prepar-
ing to rush into the United States by whatever means they could craft, in anticipation of
a change in the Bush policy. Clinton thus found it necessary to reverse course.

In so doing, however, the president committed to finding a political solution for
Haiti that would ameliorate the conditions at the root of the refugee crisis. The im-
mediate source of the problem was a military coup, led by Lieutenant General Raoul
Cedras, which removed the first popularly elected president in the nation's history,
Jean-Bertrand Aristide, in 1991. The new administration's goal, then, was to restore
Aristide to power. When diplomatic attempts to accomplish this failed, Clinton turned
to the use of military force. Aristide was returned to Haiti on October 15, 1994.

Sandy Berger, deputy national security advisor: Haiti, you need to go back
to the campaign. In 1991 Aristide is elected democratically, ousted from office,
exiled in Washington. President Bush says something to the functional equivalent of, "This will not stand." People start flooding out of Haiti on rickety boats,
a third of them capsizing at sea. President Bush instituted a policy of return.
He intercepted the boats and took the people back to Haiti. That seemed to be,
from candidate Clinton's perspective, a very difficult moral position, to send
these people back to face retaliation whether they were political exiles or not. So
he said during the campaign that he would no longer return people to Haiti if
they chose to come to the United States.

The foreign policy team at this point is very small. It's [Tony] Lake and Berger
and maybe one or two others. It was not a well-considered decision. Were there

political elements to it? There are a lot of Haitians in New York. I wouldn't rule out the possibility of some politics—just as in Cuba—we all recognize politics plays a role in Cuba policy. I'm sure it played some role in that Haiti statement. But Clinton also had moral qualms about the policy. In any case, during the transition the CIA came to me with photographs of people taking down their roofs in Haiti, building boats. They predicted there would be more than 150,000 boats on the water on January 21, 1993 [the day after Clinton assumed the presidency], headed for Florida, and that in the course of that tens of thousands of people would die. People literally were taking the roofs off their houses to build boats because President-elect Clinton had said he was not going to stop them.

I remember going down to Little Rock for this briefing. It was a sort of breathtaking briefing, literally. It took your breath away, the prospect of 300,000 Haitians heading to the United States, or 250,000 Haitians heading to the United States on January 20th. I remember Vice President Gore saying rather drolly, "Well, this is a worthy problem." Clearly that's not something we could permit to happen.

So basically we reversed field, but we didn't reverse field in a vacuum. The president said, "We're going to restore democracy to Haiti. We obviously cannot let these people make this trip. We can't see 30 to 40,000 people capsize. I'll basically backtrack on my commitment, but only on the condition that we, number one, substantially step up in Haiti the processing of political exiles, so that you can distinguish between those who are asserting political reasons for their departure and those who were simply economic exiles." Number two was that we'd have a plan for Aristide's return. That was a priority.

So he gets elected. He reverses field on the interdictions, took a lot of criticism from the Black Caucus and elsewhere for that. But it was always in his mind connected with restoring Aristide—he used to say, "If we can't restore democracy to this little island 100 miles off our coast, what kind of a great power are we?" I remember a meeting we had on a Saturday. It took place in the Roosevelt Room. We had spent time trying to think about how to do this, and he listened to this and erupted. "This is the same bullshit I heard in the campaign! There's nothing new in this plan. You guys have to do better than this. This is just bullshit." It was a bracing moment. He was actually speaking to me at the time.

After several weeks we came up with the Governors Island [New York] agreement. The Governors Island agreement had a timeline with a set of steps leading ultimately to the restoration of Aristide as president and Cedras leaving— [Michel-Joseph] François[1] and Cedras, the two military leaders. The famous incident with the . . . *Harlan County* is what's [usually] misunderstood.[2]

---

1. François was a colonel in the Haitian army in league with Cedras in removing Aristide and maintaining Cedras's rule through coercion, violence, and political repression.

2. The fact that the *Harlan County* was turned away from port by riotous Haitians was widely interpreted as a sign of American military weakness, which Berger contests here.

As part of this process, one step was that we were going to send Seabees to Haiti. Not troops, but basically Navy Civilian Corps of Engineer types who would be doing some good works and would be insinuating themselves a bit inside the FADH [Force Armée d'Haiti], the Haitian military. The *Harlan County* was not going down to knock down the door; the *Harlan County* was going down to send a bunch of military construction workers. Cedras and François sent their thugs to the port—blocked the port so that the boat could not get in, and we had a meeting about what should we do. This was right after Somalia. There was obviously a great deal of sensitivity about looking weak.

I remember one of the political guys at the meeting said, "You can't have the *Harlan County* going around in circles in the harbor; you've got to get it out of there." We made, I think, a fundamental mistake, which was to withdraw the *Harlan County*, because three days later we decided to impose an economic embargo on Haiti and to send six frigates to patrol, essentially to seal Haiti. Had we thought about it and sent the six frigates and imposed the embargo first, the *Harlan County* could have disappeared and no one would have ever noticed it. It would have just gone. But the withdrawal of the *Harlan County* became a kind of an emotional symbol of America's weakness, when it actually was the result of us being too rushed in terms of making a decision, not taking our time, not thinking through the consequences.

Tony Lake, national security advisor: By August and September, as the thugs kept cutting more and more people, and as it got worse and worse in Haiti, it became more and more evident that we would have to [go in militarily]. As I recall, the political people were opposed. The vice president would go back and forth a little on it. But by the end of the summer, the president decided, "We've got to do it." This was just months before the [midterm] election and I think it was the turning point for him. In retrospect it seems laughable that we would be concerned about a military operation against Haiti. And you could well say, "If you can't whomp Haiti, who the hell in the world can you whomp?" But I remember going over aerial photography of what looked like a serious camp with heavy armaments, which when I visited Haiti later were all rusted. But you couldn't tell that and it looked as if we were going to have to really take them down. The president said, "Yes, we're going to do it."

Sandy Berger: Then President [Jimmy] Carter called and said he was going to Haiti and taking Colin Powell and Sam Nunn with him. It was sort of a self-appointed delegation [to resolve the impasse]. He didn't realize that we had a military plan, and Sunday at 4 o'clock those planes were leaving from North Carolina and heading with troops to Haiti. We said to President Carter, "Okay, you go down there, but you've got to be out by 12 o'clock on Sunday."

Warren Christopher, secretary of state: President Carter has a particular ability to deal with rogues, political leaders who the rest of the world regards as unacceptable. I think he feels like he can understand them. So he went down and developed a relationship with Cedras and became a spokesman in a way for him.... [There] was a moment of tension [with the White House]. But I think it arises from the very natural problems when a former president as strong-willed as President Carter is wants to be active in the foreign affairs field.

Sandy Berger: We were in the Oval Office on Sunday. It was one of the tensest days of the administration. We knew at 4 o'clock the troops were leaving Fort Bragg [North Carolina]. I think there were about 25,000 troops and they were prepared for a forcible entry. I mean, the FADH was not exactly the Russian Army, but nonetheless, they had enough to have caused problems for us getting in, and then once we got in.

Carter called about 11:30 and he said, "I'm making progress." The president said, "Twelve o'clock, Mr. President, you've got to be out of there." Or "Jimmy"— I don't remember what he called him. Twelve o'clock the phone doesn't ring. Twelve-thirty the phone doesn't ring. One o'clock the phone rings; it's Carter. "I've got good news, Mr. President. They've agreed to leave." And the president said, "By when? They had already agreed to leave in the Governors Island agreement." Carter said, "I don't have a date, but they've agreed to leave. I think this is solved, and I feel very good about this. You should be proud of the fact—blah, blah, blah." The president said, "I'll call you back in ten minutes."

We caucused, Christopher, Tony, Clinton, and myself, in the room, and probably two or three others. We all agreed that simply getting another commitment from François and Cedras that they were going to leave without a date certain was meaningless.

William Perry, secretary of defense: I went over to the president and said, "Mr. President, Sir, please call President Carter and tell him to get the hell out of there. They're going to have paratroopers landing on their heads in about another two hours." So the president understood the wisdom of that recommendation and said, "Sure, I'll do that." So he called up Carter. And Carter is nothing if not stubborn. He said, "I understand your concern, President Clinton, but we're really very close to an agreement here, and I want to bring this to a head." I said, "Tell him—" he's talking over an open line; I didn't want to say too much, but—"Tell him that time is very short, and they're in danger staying there much longer." The president said that as well as he could say that, but Carter wasn't hearing that. He was just determined that they were going to get it resolved. I was beside myself. I said, "Mr. President, should I call off the operation?" He said no. "Can you get Carter out of there?" He said, "Well, yes, I'll get him out of there." But he didn't.

So to telescope the story, our forces took off from Fort Bragg. Carter, Nunn, Powell were still talking with General Cedras in his office when the forces took off. I was pleading with the president to get them out of there because I could just imagine a situation in which those three would be held as hostage down there—ex-president, Senator Nunn, ex-chairman of the staff—God almighty. So I was very concerned. While I'm usually very respectful and speak when I'm spoken to, to the president this time, I was not. I kept pushing myself forward. "Mr. President, get them out of there. Get them out of there, please, right away."

Well, at that stage, we learned later, our three were talking with General Cedras when another Haitian general came rushing into the room very excitedly and said, "General, the paratroopers have just taken off from Fort Bragg," which was true. They had. So he had, apparently, somebody watching the airfield. According to Colin Powell, within ten minutes of that point, Cedras had come to an agreement. That's not the way I would have chosen to conduct the meeting, but that's the way it happened. And it all worked out.

Then, finally, we got the agreement, and the president said to me, "Bill, can you call off the invasion?" I said, "I hope so." Then we were frantically getting in touch with all of the airplanes. You know, they're in the air, halfway to Haiti. Happily we were able to communicate to all of them, got them all turned around, and got them back. Usually in a deal like that, there's always somebody who doesn't get the word. We did get through to all of them, got them all turned back.... So all of that ended with a happy ending, but it was probably one of the most harrowing experiences of my life, having gone through that. That's not an embellished story. That's just the way it happened.

General Hugh Shelton, commander of the invasion joint task force: [We] sail into the claw of Port-au-Prince, about fifty miles off land, and it's about this time that Carter and Nunn and Colin are down there negotiating.... I have the Navy Seals already loaded in their boats, engines running. They need to be released in about the next thirty minutes in order to keep the [invasion] matrix going. Then I get a phone call of a sudden from Shali [chair of the Joint Chiefs John Shalikashvili]; I think I have about ten minutes to go. He says, "Okay, they have a deal. Turn it around. I'll tell you what your mission is in just a minute."

I turn to [my chief of staff] Frank Akers and say, "Put the word out." We had a code word for that. "Put the word out and make everybody acknowledge receipt." They do. Then Shali tells me, "Okay, you still have to go in tomorrow, but go in in a spirit of coordination and cooperation." I said, "What does that mean in military terms?" He said, "Coordination and cooperation. Get a hold of [Raoul] Cedras when you get in there, set the rules, and just do what you have to."

I turned to Frank ... and said, "Well, Frank, it's been a great career. I'm now the bag man. When this thing goes south on us, they have me to blame, and I accept that. That's what I signed up for. But I've been handed ten pounds of shit in a five-pound bag" (if you'll pardon my French).... I really thought that was the end of my career. I never anticipated I'd be able to pull this thing off and have it as relatively bloodless as it turned out to be. The next day I landed.... I [went] directly to Cedras's office [to] establish the ground rules. "Here's ... the way it's going to work. I'm here in a spirit of cooperation and coordination, and the way it works, General Cedras, is I will coordinate with you as long as you cooperate. You basically are going to do what I tell you, and if you don't, this will become a hostile environment very quickly, and your people are going to die in mass numbers. Do you understand?' ... [He] did.... There's no smiling with the guy. I wanted him to know I was 100 percent business. We sat across the table from one another. He had all of his thugs, all of his assistants, lined up beside him there.... There was a moment of a very stern stare between the two of us. He had just heard what I said, and he reached down—he took very meticulous notes, and he had very fine hand-printing—and he started writing. He looked back up at me and said, "Okay."

I warned him at the time, "I have well-trained and well-armed troops here, and we're anticipating you're going to get the word out." He said okay. I said, "Whether or not you carry it out will be evident from the manners I observe from your troops. I'm anticipating that this word will get out to them very quickly." He said, "It will."

A few days later the big day came. President Aristide arrived.... My job then was to get Cedras to agree to leave.... He said, "I can't go. My wife, Yanick, will kill me." We knew Yanick ruled him with an iron fist. I said, "You have to leave, so start making plans. The deal is you can go to any country you want." He said, "I'm not leaving." I said, "Is there anyone who can hear anything we're saying?" He said no. I knew he understood English, and he could understand what I was saying. I asked my translator to step outside and close the door. So now it's just the two of us, and I know that creates a sense of anxiety on his part.

I said, "General Cedras, you have to understand something. We had the change of command ... set up for the day after tomorrow. I'm providing protection for you. As you know, I'll keep any harm from coming to you until after you leave this job. But the minute you leave this job, you're no longer under my protection. You're going to be fair game. Now I have to tell you, there are elements of my government who think you should have been assassinated on day one; you shouldn't be here. You're going to be a dead man within two days of the time we change command if you're still on this island. You're going to be dead, you understand that?"

He looked at me and said, "I cannot leave." I said, "Then it's been nice knowing you. When I pass the flag, that's the end." "I understand." I left. Two o'clock in the morning, my guys came running in. I was trying to sleep. They ran in and said, "General Cedras is on the line, says he needed to speak to you." ... I was on the *Mt. Whitney*. He said, "In regard to our conversation today, I will leave. I would like to go to—" and he named the country. I've forgotten. I think it was Venezuela.

I said, "Okay, I'll make arrangements for that. We'll do it the same day. We have an airplane here. We'll fly you out with your family and any family members you want to carry to Venezuela. I just need to know how many, and we'll make arrangements." He said, "Okay. I need to be compensated for my house and my boats." I said, "We'll compensate you for the house and the boats. I'll get the money figure, and I'll get back to you in the morning." I called [Ambassador] Swing[3] and said, "Wake them up in Washington; we have a deal here."

Sandy Berger: Sometimes history is enormously banal. I'll never forget getting home one night about 11:30, the phone ringing and the situation room saying Ambassador [William] Swing, who was the ambassador that we sent to Haiti, was calling from the basement of Cedras's house and the issue was whether we were going to confiscate his house or whether we would pay the fair market-value rent. I thought, *My God, here I am, deputy national security advisor. I've got the ambassador to Haiti in the basement of this dictator's house and we're negotiating a rental agreement.* My wife's a real estate agent. I woke her up and said, "What are you supposed to do in this situation?" We wound up, I think, actually taking over the house.

General Hugh Shelton: I called General Cedras back and said, "Here's what they'll give you for your house. Here's what they'll give you for your boats. We have only one country that says it will take you, and it's Panama." He said, "Panama's okay, I'll go to Panama. But that's not enough money for my house. I need more money; I need an extra $5,000."

I said, "Okay, I'll go back to the State Department. But right now, here's what you'll get." I went back to the State Department, and they said, "No, we have to keep him there." In the meanwhile they brought the plane in. The plane was costing them $10,000 ... to sit there. We now have Cedras agreeing to leave, and he's given me a list of about twenty-seven "family members" who want to go with him. The State Department has agreed to fly them to Panama, but he refuses to get on the plane until we pay more for the house.

I finally went back and called Swing. He said, "They won't give any more." I said, "Listen, Bill, go back to the State Department and tell them they're paying $10,000 a day for the airplane. Give him $5,000, and let's get him out of here. It's one-half day's worth of airplane." They finally agreed to do it. Cedras agreed

---

3. William Lacy Swing, a career diplomat with a distinguished record of postings, was the U.S. ambassador to Haiti at the time.

to leave. We changed command that afternoon, and under the cover of darkness, as we had prearranged with him, we had a convoy go to the plane to load him up and get him out of there. They flew to Panama. The next day Aristide arrived.

Tony Lake: [Jean-Bertrand] Aristide ... [long] thought that we would sell him out. I didn't completely understand how strong his view was that we might sell him out, because after all, we were trustworthy, in my view. Bill Gray,[4] who was our special envoy for a while on Haiti, asked me at one point to look at ... the Episcopalian cathedral in Port-au-Prince. One of the wonderful Haitian murals over on the left as you're facing the altar is a mural of the Last Supper and there are Jesus and all the disciples and they're all black, except for one. Yes, Judas is white. And [so] we had sold them out often enough in the past century that Aristide was not easily going to be convinced by all this.

James Woolsey, director of central intelligence: I think I can say here—I don't know whether the Agency will want to have this in [the transcript] or not—Aristide is really bipolar and was very much on medication. You could see it if you ever talked to him. If he was on the good side of things, he is as friendly and articulate and smart as people get. If he is on the dark side, he's perfectly happy to be ranting at a torchlight rally, and putting tires around people's necks and pouring gasoline into them and lighting it—necklacing them.

The White House really wanted, and a number of supporters on the Hill really wanted, Aristide to be the Thomas Jefferson of Haiti. They really wanted to see him go back, to have everything work out, and they generally had the view that people who said that he was not capable of being a Thomas Jefferson of Haiti were probably in the pocket ... of the Tonton-Macoutes and the hardliners in the military.[5]

Strobe Talbott, deputy secretary of state: I think Haiti was an important episode [because] ... a president who was not naturally inclined to hard power became convinced fairly early on that it was going to require hard power to restore democracy.... Clinton is a conciliator, that's his thing. It's the Rodney King[6] doctrine and he's very good at it.... But, to his immense credit, when it came to needing to pull the trigger, he would pull the trigger.

---

4. William Gray (1941–2013) was an African-American political figure who served Pennsylvania in Congress from 1979 to 1991, including time as House majority whip.

5. The Tonton-Macoutes was a rural-based paramilitary force in Haiti created by François "Papa Doc" Duvalier, President for Life, to maintain his rule through force and terror.

6. Rodney King (1965–2012) was a Los Angeles taxi driver who became nationally known in 1991 when he was stopped after a high-speed chase and brutally beaten by local law enforcement officers, all caught on film. Major rioting broke out after the police officers were later acquitted—leading King to plead for peace on television (and this is Talbott's reference): "Can we all get along?"

Alice Rivlin, director of the OMB: [We] were talking about what international things OMB was involved in. I do remember one was the invasion of Haiti, where we had to figure out how to fund this invasion. Part of the problem was that it was the end of the fiscal year, and there was no extra money in the military budget. So we were trying to borrow—. . . [and] it was a significant difficulty. . . . Whatever high military officer I was talking to, I said, "Please don't have another war at the end of the fiscal year. Try to have them in October."

20

Africa

Probably the most unexpected foreign policy problem Bill Clinton found himself inherit-
ing was a military intervention in Somalia, which seems to have developed practically
overnight during the transition period. A rapidly unfolding catastrophe in that African
country—the product of famine compounded by clan warfare and the absence of any
functioning government—led President George H. W. Bush to send American troops
into the region to secure delivery lines for food in order to avoid mass starvation. At the
time, Bush was widely lauded for the decision to deploy the U.S. military on a purely
humanitarian mission. One historian proclaimed it "the most remarkable action ever
taken by a lame-duck president."[1] Bush's post-election approval ratings soared.

Conditions on the ground in Somalia complicated the mission, however. Having
identified Somalian warlord Mohammed Farah Aidid as the main culprit in the chaos,
U.S. and United Nations troops came to believe that stopping Aidid was a necessary
predicate for establishing security there. This made them an active party in the local war.
In October 1993, Aidid's partisans shot down two Black Hawk helicopters, resulting
in the deaths of eighteen American soldiers and subsequent desecration of their bodies.
Quickly thereafter President Clinton stopped combat operations and then removed the
U.S. forces, drawing withering criticism from Congress and the American public.

Only six months later, Africa suffered a second disaster, this one of monumen-
tal proportions. Over a period of roughly three months, beginning in April 1994, as
many as one million Rwandans were killed in a mass genocide there, the product of
tribal strife between Hutus and Tutsis. This time there was no American intervention.
Virtually every member of Clinton's foreign policy team voices anguish over what might
have been done in a post-Somalia political environment that foreclosed any reasonable
chance of intervention. Somalia left the Clinton foreign policy team scarred. Rwanda
left them with nightmares.

Sandy Berger, deputy national security advisor: I got a phone call from
Brent [Scowcroft] one day [during the transition]. We were all watching these

1. Leo Ribuffo, quoted in "Historic Humanitarian Effort May Bolster Bush Legacy,"
St. Petersburg [Fla] *Times*, December 5, 1992, p. 8A.

pictures on television of starving people in Somalia and the roving bands that were preventing the food from being transported inland to the starving people of Somalia. Brent called up, whatever D-day was on Somalia, maybe three days before, and he said, "I just wanted to let you know that we're going to send troops into Somalia to open up those supply lines. But it's not something you've got to worry about because they'll be gone by Inauguration Day." I think that's very revealing and important because what it suggests is that there really wasn't much thought given to things that we now know are extraordinarily important to peacekeeping: mission, exit strategy, achievability, public support. I think they saw a bunch of thugs that were harassing people at the docks.

[We] did clear the ports. The only problem was there was no government, so the moment we left, those same thugs would be back again and we were caught in Somalia by the failure—in my judgment—to think about a political strategy for Somalia, not just a humanitarian strategy.

Q: So is it safe to assume that President-elect Clinton had not been briefed on Somalia before this decision was made by the Bush administration?
Berger: Yes. I probably told [Clinton] what Brent had said to me, but there certainly had been no briefing, and the first briefing he got was as we got closer to Inauguration Day and it became clear that they weren't going anywhere and that we had this problem called Somalia. I took Admiral [David] Jeremiah, who was the vice-chairman of the Joint Chiefs of Staff, and his team and we went down to Little Rock. We spent a good afternoon with both the president-elect and the vice president–elect. He went through what was happening in Somalia.[2] This was a surprise.

Admiral David Jeremiah, vice chair of the Joint Chiefs of Staff:[3] I went down and briefed [the president] in Little Rock right after the election on Somalia and what was going on and what we intended to do so that he was not surprised. . . .

Q: You didn't get pushback or hostility from them about the intervention?
Jeremiah: "Thank you very much for the briefing," which is really all he could say. I believe they never really were engaged until . . . after the Black Hawk Down.[4] They expected to kind of muddle through. They had way too much faith in the UN, and that was across the board. The new White House staff was way

---

2. This briefing, with Admiral David Jeremiah (1934–2013), took place in Little Rock on December 4, 1992, the same day that President Bush 41 announced the deployment of troops in a national address.

3. Jeremiah's interview was recorded for the George H. W. Bush Oral History Project. He began his service, with Colin Powell as chair, in that administration.

4. This event was memorialized in 2002 by a Ridley Scott and Jerry Bruckheimer film by the same name.

over-enthusiastic about what they could expect out of the UN. They thought we would all get together and "kumbaya," and that wasn't going to happen at all.

Sandy Berger: What happened once we got in [Somalia]? We inherited this situation in which we had no government. We had these factions headed by [Mohamad Farah] Aidid and others fighting with each other. We turned the operation over to the UN. . . . Twenty-four Pakistanis had previously been killed by Aidid. Kofi Annan said we can't let them get away with it, and the mission gets shifted to get Aidid.[5]

We began, I think in June, July, and August, to realize that this was a flawed policy. In a country like Somalia, getting Aidid is like getting [Osama] bin Laden. We haven't got bin Laden yet.[6] We were running around chasing Aidid where we should be trying to put together some kind of political steering group that would take some responsibility for governing in Somalia. . . . As I look back, this is one regret that I do have: I don't think we pushed it hard enough and urgently enough on Kofi. He was the head of peacekeeping at that point.

Nancy Soderberg, deputy national security advisor: [The] mistake most people who've looked at this, myself included, made is that we didn't have a political process to go along with the military strategy for going after Aidid. . . . So we came in and had a strategy of handing the operation over to the UN, but not trying to solve the underlying conflict in Somalia. . . . But at the time [Colin] Powell was also running this show, saying, "We have this under control, we're doing it." You just assume they know what they're doing. You don't realize that in fact you always have to have a sanity check on these kinds of operations and say, "Let's review it," and ask the tough questions. We just didn't.

Q: You refer to Somalia as Clinton's Bay of Pigs, right?
Soderberg: Yes. . . . If you look at the big picture here, he should have been a lot more involved in what was going on there at the time. The reason he wasn't is the military was saying they had it under control.[7] Again, this is Powell. They weren't saying they needed any decisions. The interagency process all agreed

---

5. The Pakistani troops were part of a UN force in Somalia. Although Kofi Annan would later rise to lead the UN, at this time he was head of peacekeeping for the UN.

6. Osama bin Laden was killed by U.S. special forces in Pakistan on May 2, 2011, almost ten years after the September 11 attacks—and six years after Sandy Berger spoke these words.

7. The scholarly consensus about John F. Kennedy's failure with the Bay of Pigs invasion, undertaken to unseat Fidel Castro in April 1961, was that a young and inexperienced president allowed the CIA to undertake a fundamentally unsound plan because he did not have the confidence and awareness necessary at that stage to challenge the experts on their own ground. That changed by the time Kennedy had to manage the Cuban Missile Crisis eighteen months later, which he did successfully.

that we were on track to hand over and get out. With everything else going on, if there's interagency agreement on something, what's the point of a meeting?

William Perry, deputy secretary of defense: [My] observation is that it was [Defense Secretary] Les [Aspin] and Colin Powell who were making the decisions about what to do [in Somalia], informing the White House, which hadn't quite stumbled on the fact that this might become a big issue. Then when it blew up, Colin somehow became magically uninvolved with it, and it all focused on Les having made all these bad decisions.

Now, the big decision, for which Les got most of the criticism, was the request from Somalia to send reinforcements over before they conducted this mission, which Les "turned down." I don't know the full details on that, but I do know at the time the request came in he was on vacation, and he was answering—I mean, it was a phone call to him while he was on vacation. I would be doubtful that he really gave it serious consideration. Second, I believe it's also true that Colin and/or his military were advising that it wasn't necessary. But again, that never came out. It ended up being Les's decision, probably with, if not the recommendation, at least the assent of his senior military. And it was certainly done without much thought, because it was a phone call while he was on vacation. It didn't have the attention it should have had. That was a big decision, and that was the one he was most criticized for. So it became a debacle.

Sandy Berger: [There's] a lot of fault to go around in Somalia. Number one, the policy types like me, the policymakers like me, did not act more forcefully on our conviction that we were headed in the wrong direction. I also think there's some fault that lies with the military for not really owning the troops that we had on the ground. Then there's fault on the part of Congress, because of Congress's reaction to October 5th—probably one of the worst single days of my eight years in the White House. We all gather in the White House watching that picture time and time again.

Admiral David Jeremiah: Black Hawk Down, eighteen soldiers killed, dragged through the street. That was my first day on the job as acting chairman. I spent the worst week in my life daily in the White House doing foreign policy 101 in the Roosevelt Room with the newbies in the administration. People would come in and offer advice from time to time who knew nothing and then they'd go on about their business and check in on us every three or four days. Now we were at the stage where the Congress was banging on us to get out at the same time they were banging on us to put tanks in to protect people who were deployed on the ground so that they could evacuate. We were not about to put the tanks in there, then you've got to have infantry to be with the tanks so you're creating more targets. You want less targets and yadda, yadda, yadda. So this went on and on.

Madeleine Albright, U.S. ambassador to the United Nations: There's no way to overemphasize the horror of Somalia. It made people wonder why we were doing this and why were Americans dying in some place that nobody had heard of.... [Once] the helicopters went down ... people thought, *I thought we were feeding kids. This isn't what was supposed to happen.* There was just this general questioning about what were we doing there.

Tony Lake, national security advisor: The clichés about what happened here in Washington are wrong. The cliché is that we [in the White House] thought, *Oh, my God, Americans have died, we've got to get the hell out of here,* and turned tail and ran. In fact, there was a firestorm on the Hill about this. I can remember a vehement argument in the Oval Office with the political people, who were saying, "Get out, get out, get out, this is a loser." I remember arguing, "Big mistake if we do because you're going to put a bullseye on every American around the world if you simply get out."

Sandy Berger: There was a volcanic eruption from the Congress. It's Sunday, so the eruption didn't erupt until Monday. Aspin and Christopher were summoned to a joint session of Congress on Tuesday. Chris very adroitly let Aspin take the lead, and Aspin got massacred by his former colleagues, who demanded that we withdraw immediately. We had a meeting in the White House of probably forty members of the leadership of the Congress, all the committee chairs and the leadership. It took place in the Roosevelt Room, so it was a larger than normal meeting. One after another of the senators stood up and said, "We want those troops out now."

The president pleaded with them to not precipitously withdraw the forces. If we could not withdraw the forces in an orderly way, we would look like we cut and ran because we lost some troops in Mogadishu. It was one of the tensest meetings we had in the eight years.

I remember Senator [Robert] Byrd in particular, his voice quivering, talking about how we had to get our troops home tomorrow. "We are going to act. When the Congress reconvenes, we're going to cut off the money for any continuation of American presence there." We managed to negotiate, I believe, a ninety-day phase-out period, which at least allowed us to do this in some sort of orderly fashion.... We obviously needed to change our Somalia policy, but precipitously withdrawing in the wake of a military debacle sent the wrong message to adversaries of the United States. When you read the bin Laden screeds [later] ... he talks about Somalia. He talks about America as a paper tiger. These things have consequences.

James Woolsey, director of central intelligence: I believe it's the case that we had not had a National Security Council [NSC] meeting on Somalia, as of Black Hawk Down. We had had, of course, Principals' meetings, which Tony Lake chaired, but no meeting with the president and the full NSC, at least I don't recall one. The record would indicate. In any case, a few days after Black Hawk Down—a terrible situation with one American still in custody, and others had been dragged through the streets dead—we have an NSC meeting called on Somalia.

I'm told they need a five-minute or so summing-up for the situation and intelligence assessment, so I spend the day before the meeting talking to my Somali experts and talking to my station chief on the secure phone and getting my five minutes ready. We're also told that the meeting is too sensitive for the secretary of state or secretary of defense or chairman of Joint Chiefs or me to bring any support people. So I show up in the Cabinet room, and there, in addition to the president and vice president and the four of us—the secretaries of state, defense, chairman, and me—are about three NSC staffers—Tony Lake and Sandy Berger of course, but also another one or two other NSC staffers. And then there are about eight or ten White House staffers. This meeting is too sensitive for us to have one additional CIA expert or State Department expert, but eight or ten White House staffers, including not just the chief of staff and so forth, but Dee Dee Myers, George Stephanopoulos, Dave Gergen[8]—people who are there for public relations and communications issues. Also there is Bob Oakley, the former ambassador, retired, to Somalia, among other places.... He was just a retired individual at the time, but he was invited into the meeting.... He's an outsider who has been invited in.

We have explained to us, I forget exactly by whom, probably Tony [Lake], that (a) we're going to skip the intelligence briefing; and (b) it has been decided that they're going to send Bob Oakley over to set up a coalition government in Somalia. Now I believe he also may have had responsibility for negotiating a release of the one American who was still in custody but the main discussion was about the work on getting a coalition government together.

After that announcement, as I recall, we moved immediately to Dee Dee and George going back and forth across the table, talking about who was going to background the *Washington Post*, who was going to background the *New York Times*, who was going to be on the Sunday talk shows, to deal with the issue of the coalition government. This went on for fifteen or twenty minutes and then finally I raised my hand, was called on, and I said, "Mr. President, I've got several experts at the Agency who know this country pretty well because we were there in some numbers in the Cold War. I think if any of them were here, they'd say what I'm going to say, which is that this country has been engaged in clan warfare for a long time. It's going to be engaged in clan warfare for a long time in the future, and the chance of any coalition government

---

8. David Gergen was a senior Republican communications expert who was brought into the White House by the president in mid-1993 to help him get better control over the operations of the White House and its strategic communications.

between [Mohammed Farah] Aidid and Ali Mahdi [Muhammed] and Omar [Hagi Masalah] and [Ahmed Omar] Jess—these bandits—holding together is essentially zero." There's a long silence and it's a little bit like being at a football game and having a commercial timeout. The team doesn't have anything to do, so they kind of look up at the lights.

We're all kind of sitting around the table in the Cabinet Room looking up at the lights, and after a sort of embarrassingly long time, Dave Gergen, who is supposedly there for public relations functions, but an able and sensible guy, says, "Well look, if what Jim just said is true, none of this that we're talking about makes any sense." Then there was another pause and another commercial timeout, and everybody looks up at the lights for a while longer. Then finally, without anything intervening, Dee Dee and George go back to discussing who is going to background the *Post*, who's going to background the *Times*, who's going on the Sunday talk shows.

Nobody frowned at me; nobody came over afterwards and said, "You know, Jim, you were out of line," or anything like that. I had just sort of irrelevantly introduced substance into the PR [public relations] meeting. It was as if I had said, "Mr. President, I'd like everybody here to know that last Saturday I was up in Pennsylvania and I had two of my sons with me and by matching a mayfly hatch we were able to take ten nice rainbows out of a pool before nine o'clock in the morning. I'm going back this Saturday and if anybody would like to join me, I'd be glad to have you." People would have thought, *Well, it's odd that Jim is discussing fly fishing in the middle of this NSC meeting, but Jim is odd. Thanks for that, Jim.* Like I said, nobody got upset. It was just clearly not the purpose of the meeting.

Admiral David Jeremiah: I don't recall exactly the date and time, but Clinton called me in.... I went over to the Oval Office, went into the infamous little room.... The study.[9] We had a one-on-one conversation. He said, "What do we do? How do we get out of this?" At the risk of being parochial [as a Navy guy], "I have a carrier battle group in the North Arabian Sea, I have a Marine amphibious group in the eastern Mediterranean, and a Marine amphibious ready group in the South China Sea and we can get them there, the carrier first and the others next in a little over a week." I told all this to President Clinton and he told me to make it so. We did. So we got out.

Tony Lake: I did offer my resignation to the president after Somalia. It was kind of pro forma. One does. Frankly, if I thought he was going to accept it I would

---

9. The study is the president's private office. Jeremiah's phrasing here refers to the fact that this is where several encounters between the president and Monica Lewinsky were to have occurred.

have thought about it. . . . I can go into this, and this is really sad, because I love Les Aspin—but the president decided that he did have to make a change in Defense. I wasn't much involved in those discussions. . . . I remember going to one of the last meetings on the subject, then stupidly saying that I would tell Les because I was a friend and I thought that was the right thing to do. . . . The president should have said, "No, I'll do it," but they seldom do. I always did. I fired a bunch of folks and I'm afraid I got rather good at it. They don't piss on you as much later if you do it yourself, among other things. Anyway, so I met with Les in my office and I said, "Les, I have very bad news." And he immediately looked upset and said, "Tony, you're not leaving, are you?" And I felt like throwing up. Then I told him. . . .

Then the—and now we're going to get into really painful subjects—then the cliché is that because of Somalia we did PDD 25 [Presidential Decision Directive[10]], establishing the rules about peacekeeping, and then decided not to intervene militarily in Rwanda, even though there was a genocide, because we were so scared by Somalia.

There's some, but only some, truth to that, at least for me. It was clear we needed a PDD 25. We needed PDD 25 not so we could circumscribe peacekeeping operations and not do them anymore, which is what some of my fellow peacekeepers now believe, but because if we were to do a peacekeeping mission, (a) it had to make sense on the merits, and (b) politically it was going to be necessary to be able to show that this was serious and that we'd asked the right questions. . . . Anyway, the point is, unless you ask the questions and work through the answers, then you're not going to be professional about it and you won't have a political basis for doing peacekeeping in the future.

So we did do PDD 25 and the impetus was Somalia because we hadn't asked the questions [about the intervention there] properly. When those questions were asked about Rwanda, a lot of them came up zeros. . . . So there was no easy answer.

Warren Christopher, secretary of state (about Rwanda): A little picture of what was going on in America at that time. We were deep in the Haiti crisis and we were being pressured constantly to take some action in Haiti, pressured by ourselves and by external events. We were, as always, engaged in the Middle East. We were just coming out of the problems elsewhere in the world, especially in Bosnia, which was a very serious overhang from the prior administration. As far as Rwanda itself, we had evacuated our embassy: Ambassador [David] Rawson,

---

10. Presidential decision directives are executive orders typically drafted by the National Security Council to formalize and structure national security policy and decision-making. Such directives have been issued under varied nomenclature, including National Security Decision Directives (NSDDs) under President Reagan and Presidential Policy Directives (PPDs) under President Obama.

a very brave young ambassador, led his staff out of Rwanda overland, much to our relief. Shortly after April [1994], we'd had a task force operating in the State Department for weeks on end, and we were tremendously relieved to get all of our people out.

We were quite heavily reliant on both the French and the Belgians, thinking that those who had been there for a long time knew that issue best. It turned out that reliance was, as so often happened with our reliance on the Europeans, misplaced. The information that flowed in indicated that there was very intense fighting, but it was hard for us to picture who the fighting was between. Was it between the Hutus and the Tutsis or was it between various elements of the Hutus? And so it was far from clear to us.

Looking back, I think what I would want to convey is a sense as to how confused and confusing the situation was. The clarity that now comes from people saying, "If we'd sent in 5,000 troops we could have saved X hundred thousand people," was just a non-concept at that time as far as I was concerned.... Chip Bohlen[11] had a comment that there is hindsight and then there is hind myopia, and hind myopia occurs when people looking back on a situation fail to realize how complicated and confusing it was at the time. And I think Rwanda, not departing from the regret that I have that we didn't do more, nevertheless, it's a classic case of hind myopia and whether we could have done anything, even if we had been very prescient and tried.

James Steinberg, director of policy planning at the State Department: I've given enormous thought to this. Anybody who was involved has given thought to it. Obviously it was an extraordinary human tragedy of a magnitude that there are no words for. Even the brilliant graphic, journalistic, and film depictions don't begin to do justice to what we recognize was the horror of the genocide. There are lots of different aspects of this question. Could we have known that when the plane was shot down that the violence was going to explode?[12] We probably underestimated it from an intelligence point of view, but I don't think we generally underestimated the volatility of the region.

We had been more focused, to be honest, on Burundi, because in some respects the situation seemed slightly more stable in Rwanda and *quite* fragile in

---

11. Charles E. "Chip" Bohlen (1904–1974) was a noted American diplomat who served as U.S. ambassador to the Soviet Union from 1953 to 1957 and ambassador to France from 1962 to 1968.

12. On April 6, 1994, an airplane carrying Rwandan president Juvenal Habyarimana and Burundian president Cyprien Ntaryamira was shot from the sky on its approach to the airport in Kigali, Rwanda. Responsibility for the attack remains disputed. The resulting confusion and anger from this dual assassination sparked brutal violence between Hutus and Tutsis who had theretofore been living together in a fragile peace.

Burundi.[13] If people were going to guess in the late fall, early winter of '93 which of the two countries was more likely to have a genocide, I think we would have bet on Burundi. But there's no question that people understood how fragile and bad it was.

I don't think it was a massive intelligence failure in the sense that nobody knew or could have guessed. Probably, on that scale, yes, nobody could have guessed. I think most people find it hard to imagine that anybody could perpetrate horror of that type. But I think there was a clear sense in INR[14] when the plane was shot down that this was a very dangerous situation. People were very focused on the Great Lakes area as a place where an intense ethnic violence, even beyond the scale of the Balkans, was possible.[15] So . . . I think people were paying attention.

Then it becomes the policy question. There is an enormous amount that has been written about it in retrospect. I'm probably one of the few people left in the administration who understands why we did what we did. It's easy for people to say to others after the fact, "If you had put in a few people"—But the reality was that in the immediate aftermath, when the violence broke out, we saw the slaughter of the Belgian peacekeepers who were there.[16] It was an intensely violent situation in which there was absolutely no reason to believe that an insertion of a small force would have cauterized this, that the genocidairs would be intimidated by it. Not only was it not just their being there and saying, "We have to stop because they're there," but there was a serious risk that any UN force, other than a massive one, would have also been subject to great violence. They were afraid. So there wasn't an option of a small intervention force that would magically prevent it somehow.

Tony Lake: [In] part because of Somalia, and in part because Rwanda is a long, long way away and logistics are difficult—the sad fact is the possibility of an American intervention never came up. It was so far beyond anybody's imagining. We were, I know from a memo, trying to figure out how we could get sufficient resources, just money from the Congress to do anything, much less send in American troops. I met constantly with NGOs [nongovernmental organizations] during this period, they never suggested it. As they agree, I've talked to them since.

Now, we, on Rwanda, did a number of things wrong. Should have raised it, should have looked at it, should have gone back to our intelligence people,

---

13. Burundi is situated on the southern border of Rwanda.
14. INR is the Bureau of Intelligence and Research within the State Department.
15. The African Great Lakes include Tanganyika and Victoria. The region encompasses both Rwanda and Burundi.
16. Ten Belgian soldiers posted to Rwanda by the United Nations were captured, subjected to torture, and killed.

saying, "Tell me more." There was a meeting in the early stages of it, when I went over to the Pentagon to the Tank,[17] to talk about what we would do about the Americans who were caught in Rwanda, which was our first responsibility. Not our last, but our first. And I've always been interested in Africa and I knew that Rwanda and Burundi were the places that the OAU [Organization of African Unity] maybe could do something for the first time seriously. And I remember at this meeting, towards the end of it, as we were thinking, *Do we listen to the ambassador and let him lead a convoy out,* which he did and was right, or *Do we send troops into Bujumbura, Burundi, and if we have to, do a NEO* [Noncombatant Evacuation Operation], *and get them out....* A NEO, which is ... a hostile insertion to go in and get Americans out of a hostage situation. If you're ever in trouble abroad, yell, "NEO!" and see what happens. The 101st will arrive and save you.

So towards the end of this meeting I said, "What is this about? Who is fighting whom over what? What's going on?" The DIA [Defense Intelligence Agency] folks there couldn't tell me. That's how well we were on top of what was going on in Rwanda. I should have said, "Wait a minute, people are dying, tell me more," and didn't. I should have said, "We need to think about an American intervention here," and I didn't. But there was no meeting at which we thought, *Should we go in or not?* and decided not to.... I do remember at some point saying to, I think it was Susan Rice,[18] who was working in multilateral affairs at the time, "I think the best solution is for the patriotic front"—the RPA [Rwandese Patriotic Army]—"just to win." Because the UN is never going to be, based on Bosnia, assertive enough to get it done, which turned out to be true.

But anyway, when it was over, then I personally ran the Goma operations, getting water in, et cetera.[19] I'm very good at guilt, but I wasn't doing it out of guilt. It was just because there was a need there and I was interested. It wasn't until later, especially after I'd visited a churchyard there that fall and saw a couple of hundred bodies including pregnant women who had been raped and killed and everything, that I began to say to myself, *There should have been more things that we could do somehow.* It just didn't seem possible. So it is not a case of Somalia so scarring us that we couldn't do what evidently was the right thing. It was worse in a way— ... the questions didn't even arise. But again, I would assert, it included the Congress, the executive branch, the NGOs, the press, everybody. Go look and see. . . .

---

17. The "Tank" is the nickname given to the conference room used by the Joint Chiefs of Staff.

18. Susan Rice, an African-American diplomat and foreign policy expert, was at the time director of international organizations and peacekeeping for the National Security Council. She later became U. S. ambassador to the United Nations and then national security advisor for President Barack Obama.

19. Goma is a lakeside city in the Democratic Republic of the Congo, which sits on Rwanda's northern border.

Q: It is your retrospective judgment that the United States could have done something significant that would significantly inhibit genocide?

Lake: Yes. Sure, absolutely. We do have the 101st Airborne. It was within our capacity to do Rwanda. It would have been a lot harder than Haiti. There probably would have been a mess.... I can't even say that it was a political no-go and that we concluded that we can't get this done politically. It was just inconceivable to anybody, including the NGOs, anybody, that we would do what subsequently now, I wish I at least had raised in a quixotic way, maybe just for the sake of my own conscience.

William Perry: [The experience with Somalia] absolutely foreclosed the possibility of sending any troops.... I can say for a fact that there was no serious consideration at that time of sending American troops to Rwanda.... There would have been an explosion in Congress ..., I'm quite confident. President Clinton has said in retrospect, now out of office, that one of his great regrets of the presidency was not taking some action to try to stop the Rwanda massacre. But I can tell you there was no consideration.

Q: So there was virtually no pressure from any corner of the administration to do something?

Perry: On the contrary, had anybody proposed it to them, they would have been summarily dismissed as smoking dope or something.

* * *

Q: You were at the UN when Clinton went to Rwanda and made the apology.[20] Did he do the right thing?

Nancy Soderberg: Yes, I think so, although it's not an apology.... He never says, "I'm sorry." ... What he says is we should have done more to save these lives. There are certainly lots of things we could have done to save more lives more quickly than we did, and I think the fact that we didn't do more bears on all of our consciences and will to the day we die. It's just so horrible.

I remember going to Rwanda a couple of years after that, and it was just awful. We were there in '95, a little less than a year, about six months later. The bodies were still there, all hacked to death, the little children still with their clothes on lying in a church where they thought they would seek refuge. It's just awful to see it. That's on your conscience for the rest of your life. But when I look at it realistically, if this were to happen again, what would happen differently?

I think the difference now is the UN has learned never to send in a small force. You always put in a big force so they can move quickly. If people are in your care, you'll save them—so at least the 25,000 that were there. I can't bring

---

20. Clinton delivered this speech on March 25, 1998, at the Kigali airport.

myself to watch *Hotel Rwanda*.[21] I have it at home, and still I can't bring myself to watch it because I feel so bad.

Strobe Talbott, deputy secretary of state: I guess I'd make three points.... One is that the Pentagon, generally speaking, and certainly under Bill Perry and John Shalikashvili, deserves huge credit for having made the transition from the Cold War to the post–Cold War, from dealing with the Soviet threat to dealing with the new agenda issues.

It's in the context of that admiration that I would say with respect to Rwanda that the Pentagon was real clear that they didn't want anything to do with intervention in Africa in general and that part of Africa in particular. That was partly because we were less than a year ... away from the Mogadishu debacle and Mogadishu—within twenty-four hours, Mogadishu had become not a place-name, but sort of like Srebrenica[22] it had become a code word for terrible stuff and particularly humiliating and murderous defeat of American soldiers. There was that.

And not unrelated to that, there was in the other part of the world where we were dealing with genocide, i.e., Europe, southeastern Europe, in particular the Balkans, there was a kind of network of nesting, overlapping institutions—local, regional, trans-regional, even global institutions—whose resources and energies could be brought to bear on the problem, which is to say OSCE [Organization for Security and Cooperation in Europe], Council of Europe, and of course NATO and its attendant organizations. There was nothing like that in Africa.... [Maybe] the single most important, most strategic objective of the Clinton foreign policy, and the most important achievement of the Clinton foreign policy ... was help[ing] put in place an architecture appropriate to the post–Cold War world. And the part of the world most deficient with regard to structures was Africa. So there was really very little to get your hands on.

Now you add to that a point that Samantha [Power][23] and others make, and that is that Africa tends to be treated in a lot of American thinking as beyond the furthest imaginable perimeter of American vital interests, and you have a situation that is just unfortunately a setup of what happened. Chris [Warren Christopher] makes the point about the difficulty we had knowing either what

21. *Hotel Rwanda* was a 2004 film starring Don Cheadle memorializing one man's efforts to save victims from the slaughter.

22. In 1993, the United Nations declared the town of Srebrenica a safe haven, providing refuge for Bosniak Muslims against their Serbian attackers. Dutch soldiers assigned to protect the enclave were ultimately overwhelmed—resulting in the massacre of over 8,000 people in July 1995.

23. Samantha Power was at the time a journalist who had written a widely acclaimed study of the Rwanda case in *A Problem from Hell: America and the Age of Genocide* (New York: Basic Books, 2002). She won the Pulitzer Prize for nonfiction in 2003, and was later named U.S. ambassador to the United Nations by President Obama.

was happening or what was likely to happen. He sent me out to Africa, including a brief stop in Bujumbura in November of that year with George Moose (assistant secretary of state for African affairs), and I've got to tell you, I had the benefit of an on-the-scene look at the situation and I sure didn't grasp it at the time. I just plain didn't. . . .

And there are two ironies here that I guess President Clinton and the rest of us have to live with. One is that I don't think there has ever been a president who was more committed to the notion . . . not to see Africa as the ends of the earth, but to see Africa as part of a community that we're part of, and bringing Africa in. And second, a president who used his presidency to do something about genocide. He deployed NATO to stop genocide. And yet there it is, Rwanda. What can anybody say?

21

The Balkans

Although there were several surprises in the realm of foreign affairs that Bill Clinton had to confront immediately after he became president, Bosnia was not one of them. It was clear throughout 1992 that the disintegration of the Balkan countries, in all its complexity, would be awaiting the new president. Indeed this issue was in some ways the centerpiece of his criticism of his predecessor, whose secretary of state and close personal friend James A. Baker III had famously declared, "We don't have a dog in that fight." Bill Clinton believed otherwise—although he met with resistance among those at the Pentagon who were charged with planning and executing a war strategy.

A simple declaration that the United States had a stake in the matter, however, did not mean that Clinton and his team had a solution to the problem. He dispatched his secretary of state, Warren Christopher, to Europe early on to consult with allies there on developing an approach, a trip that produced no answers—and indeed a counterproductive image of an administration still uncertain of itself. Although the tension between American and European approaches to the problem continued, events on the ground ultimately produced a forceful response. The Serbian massacre of Muslims at Srebrenica in 1995, followed by marketplace shellings killing large numbers of civilians in Sarajevo, led to agreement among the allies to initiate an air campaign against the offending Serbs—which brought the warring parties to a negotiated settlement at Dayton, Ohio.

When renewed violence flared in the region—in Kosovo—in Clinton's second term, he acted more quickly and directly. A NATO air campaign was mounted beginning in March 1999. When the Serbs did not immediately concede, Clinton's foreign policy team began to prepare for what all involved greatly feared—a ground invasion in southeast Europe. Under continued NATO bombing, Slobodan Milosevic, at the time president of Serbia and of the Federal Republic of Yugoslavia, decided to accept the dictated terms of peace and the presence of NATO peacekeeping troops in Kosovo.

Judge Abner Mikva, White House counsel: We'd had a minor success in Haiti, and I saw [the president] that night and congratulated him. I said, "Now all you have left is Bosnia." He said, "That won't happen in my lifetime."

Madeleine Albright, U.S. ambassador to the United Nations: My initial reaction on Bosnia—this was before I was in office. I saw pictures out of Bosnia of people being loaded onto trucks and driven to concentration camps. It looked like some pictures out of World War II. I couldn't believe that this was happening at that particular time.

[During] the campaign I really had a sense that . . . one of the things we were going to do was be proactive on Bosnia. What happened then was that other issues [intruded]. I don't know all the aspects of this, but clearly the gays in the military issue had a big effect on how Clinton dealt with the military. Some of the questions that had come up over his draft status in Vietnam played a role. The military, until now, has not particularly liked Democrats. So there was some tension in that regard. There also was a huge economic agenda, and obviously the campaign had been about "the economy stupid." There were a lot of things that happened. [So] I felt that there was not enough happening on Bosnia. . . . I went to the Principals meetings and it did not seem to me that we were where we should have been. I have to admit that at that stage I hadn't learned to argue in a way that didn't strike Tony [Lake] as being "emotional," which is the best way to put a woman down. I remember one time I said something like, "Gentleman, history is going to judge us very badly if we don't do something."

Our main problem, in addition to everything else, was Colin Powell. I say this with a lot of regret, because Colin and I are very good friends. . . . Colin was the grownup. Here he was; he'd done it before. There is something about arriving in a meeting with medals from here to here and having just won the Gulf War and having been national security advisor and chairman of the Joint Chiefs. . . . So the thing that would happen on a regular basis would be that Tony or Les Aspin would say, "We need a plan from the Joint Chiefs about under what circumstances we could use the military." On a regular basis Colin would come in and do a presentation. He is a brilliant briefer, and the Pentagon is really good at pictures and charts and 3-D things. Colin had a little red pointer and he'd go through this and say, "We can take that hill and we can do that and we can do this. You know we have the best military in the world, but it's going to take 500,000 men and $500 billion and 50 years. What are you going to say to Sergeant Slepchok's mother when he dies from having stepped on a land mine?" So he'd lead you up the hill of possibilities and then drop you off the other side, and you'd end up with no options.

Nancy Soderberg, deputy national security advisor: Colin Powell was a hero, . . . the ultimate honorable American patriot, . . . but he wasn't a constructive player on the whole Bosnia issue. . . . He saw Bosnia as another Vietnam, and he was going to stop it. . . . He wouldn't creatively think about it and [he] effectively tied Clinton's hands, because you can't get this done if you don't have a Joint Chiefs of Staff chairman who will come up with options for you.

There was a sea change when Shalikashvili came in.[1] I don't think Shalikashvili has ever gotten the credit he deserves for what he did. He was the unsung hero of

---

1. General John Shalikashvili took over from Colin Powell as chairman of the Joint Chiefs of Staff in October 1993.

the first term. He was an incredible, thoughtful, interesting, brilliant man who came up with options. Being Polish, he understood the value of getting involved in the Bosnia war and why it mattered. Powell never understood why it mattered. Shali did. He would say, "Okay, let me go back and get you options." He wasn't making the decisions for the president; he was coming up with options that could then be seriously debated and decided.

Warren Christopher, secretary of state: I made a trip to Europe in May of 1993 in which we had a proposal for the Europeans, which was summarized in shorthand as "lift and strike." Lift the arms embargo so we could arm the Bosnians, and if somebody tried to take advantage of the lifting to take action before the Bosnians could be armed, we would use air power. I consulted with the Europeans on that and was told that they were either strongly against it or just against it. That was about the range of opinion. Now, that was a trip that widely had been criticized and perhaps with some justification. The trip was haunted by the fact that the day I took off ... the Vance-Owen people announced an agreement under which there would be elections permitted and the problem could somehow be resolved and the Serbs would agree to resolve it.[2] We never had much confidence in that proposed agreement, but nevertheless, wherever I went in Europe they would say, "Well, we're against your idea ..., we're on the verge of an agreement in Bosnia." ...

So I came back and reported to the president and the vice president, on a Saturday morning meeting that I shall not soon forget, that the reaction in Europe was negative and the only way that it could be turned around was for the president to announce he was going to do it and say basically, "Get on board and follow me." [But] there had been a sea change in the atmosphere in Washington from the time I'd left, to the time that I returned. In the course of one week attitudes had shifted. The people who in the "Sit" [Situation] Room had favored the lift-and-strike course did not speak up. I assumed that meant that the president had sent a different signal by that point.

Tony Lake, national security advisor: [Every] time I walked in for the [president's] morning brief, I had the big *B* for Bosnia written on my forehead and he was going to have to go to the dentist ... and deal with this damn issue, which was a nightmare. And it was a nightmare because we cared about it.

Okay, here's the dilemma. Remember the rhetoric of the time, on all sides. These are real dilemmas for everybody. Dilemma for the Europeans was that,

---

2. The Vance-Owen Plan, a diplomatic attempt to resolve the Bosnian conflict, was named for its chief negotiators Cyrus Vance (former U.S. secretary of state) and British diplomat Lord David Owen, working respectively for the United Nations and the European Community. The core of the plan was a detailed partition of Bosnia. It quickly proved impractical because of fluid conditions on the ground, rendering their line-drawing moot.

on the one hand, I think that many of them, just about all of them, did want to resolve this problem. It was not that they were callous, indifferent, Old World wimps. But they did have troops on the ground, in UNPROFOR [United Nations Protection Force], which was doing good humanitarian work and who were taking risks and should be honored for it, to get supplies to people in villages, et cetera. But they were acting under rules of engagement that were insane and that in effect made them hostages—in fact, later literally hostages from time to time—to the Serbs and the Bosnian Serbs.

So when we would say to them, "Let's do X, Y, or Z, lift and strike" or what- ever, they would say to themselves, "We can't do this because if our soldiers get killed as a result of that, we are in big trouble domestically, at home. And in any case, we don't want to put our soldiers at that risk." So they would come back to us with the debating point . . . of "Okay, put *your* troops on the ground," because they knew damn well that the hawkest of the hawks, Robert Dole, any of them, never were saying put one American boot on the ground in Bosnia absent an agreement, right?

William Perry, secretary of defense: Ninety-four was a frustrating year in Bosnia because atrocities continued to happen there. The UN forces were in- capable of dealing with them, and we couldn't get the Europeans to do any- thing about that, and the Republicans mostly—not just Republicans, but mostly Republicans—were pushing for arming the Bosnians. They wanted a cheap way out of the problem. They didn't want to send our forces. They wanted to lift the embargo. I was intellectually convinced that that would be disastrous.

They had on their side [former British prime minister] Margaret Thatcher, who was . . . still an eloquent spokeswoman. I remember at Aspen, [Colorado], the summer of '94, we were both on the same platform. She got up and made this stirring speech. She ended up talking about Bosnia and quoting back to World War II where [Franklin D.] Roosevelt had asked what the United States could do to help in the war. [Winston] Churchill said, "Send us the arms, and we will finish the job." So Margaret quoted that to great applause, that that is what we should be doing with the Bosnians—send them the arms, and they would finish the job.

Then my turn to speak, I got up. I said, "Well, we sent England the arms, and it took another ten million American troops, though, to really finish the job. That will be the problem in Bosnia as well. We'll send them arms. That won't finish the job. It will just create more bloodshed. We'll ultimately have to go in to finish the job as we did in World War II." . . . What [finally] broke the impasse was that the Bosnian Serbs, you might say in poker terminology, overplayed their hand. When they committed this atrocity at Srebrenica, they finally galva- nized the Europeans, who had to do something. At the turning point meeting, we decided we were going to take meaningful military action that was going to start off with very substantial NATO bombing attacks on the Bosnian Serbs, and we would keep that up until they agreed to sit down to what became the Dayton meeting to work out terms by which we would send NATO ground forces in there. So that was the meeting where we agreed to do that. Then we looked forward not to so-called pinprick raids, but to really a very substantial raid that was directed at the Bosnian Serbs' military ground forces. They were quite meaningful, quite effective. That led then to the decision of the Serbs, which influenced the Bosnian Serbs, to agree to see if we could get some sort of resolution to the problem. That led to the Dayton Agreement.[3]

Tony Lake: [There's] one point [I've seen] ... on Bosnia, which suggests, I believe, that I presented to President Clinton a plan for allowing the Iranians to send weapons into Bosnia, which I think came in the *Los Angeles Times* years later or something. You suggested I use the word, that is utter bullshit. My memory is good enough to be sure that I didn't do that. I think I'd remember it if I encouraged the Iranians to send arms anywhere.

Judge Abner Mikva: Congress had passed an [arms] embargo. Our ambassador over there [in Croatia] was [Peter] Galbraith, John Kenneth's son, a lovely man.[4] He was accused ... by the CIA operative in the embassy of countermanding the embargo and allowing weapons to go through when he was ambassador.... I remember we met with the ambassador, whom I was very impressed with. He said, "Before I went over, I went to the State Department and said, 'What are my instructions on the embargo and on these other items?' I was told specifically, 'You have no instructions.' So I did what I thought that meant: I did nothing. "Did I know that there were arms slipping through? Yes. But I don't know what 'no instructions' means if it doesn't mean that I just do nothing."

James Woolsey, director of central intelligence: [My] station chief in Croatia had the ambassador approach him and say, "Would you help me look the other way as these arms come through?" The station chief calls me right away, because while a CIA officer overseas has a lot of flexibility with respect to whom he can recruit to get information, once somebody says, "Will you try to influence policy? ... that becomes a covert action. So they needed a formal finding for that.... When I then raise this with State or with the NSC, they say, "Oh, we don't need to get into that," or words to that effect.

---

3. The Dayton Agreement, negotiated at Wright-Patterson Air Force base near Dayton, Ohio, brought an end to hostilities in the Bosnian War. It was signed on December 14, 1995.

4. John Kenneth Galbraith (1908–2006) was a prominent liberal economist at Harvard who served in a variety of policymaking and diplomatic positions for Democratic presidents from Franklin Roosevelt to Lyndon Johnson. Before serving as ambassador to Croatia, Peter Galbraith had worked as a staff expert with the Senate Foreign Relations Committee.

William Perry: In my last week before we actually had to [deploy] force in [Bosnia], I had a lonely one-on-one session with the president on a Saturday morning in the Oval Office. I listed for him all the things that could go wrong and what we had done to try to prepare for that contingency—insurgency operations springing up after we got there, terrorists attacking our bases and our troops, troops being killed on patrols, roadside bombs.... [As] I laid all these out to the president, I told him, "We're going to do this, that, and the other thing, and I think these will all be successful. I think we'll deal with these problems adequately, but maybe not. If this goes badly and we actually have hundreds of American casualties and you're doing this in the face of the opposition from Congress, Mr. President, this will be the end of your presidency. You're out of here."

He said, "I know that, but it's the right thing to do. I want to do it." Now, he might have just convinced himself that that was the right thing to say, but my own view is that he actually deeply believed that. He had been seized with the atrocities that had been happening for several years in Bosnia and saw this as an opportunity to stop the killing—which, in fact, it did—and that we had a responsibility, and that we were the only country that could find the leadership to make that happen and we ought to do it. He was willing to risk his presidency on doing it.

James Steinberg, director of policy planning, State Department: Well, the Balkans were the decisive moment.... I think that the credibility of the United States and NATO were reestablished by this effective intervention. It was late but it happened, and it succeeded.... I think it was critical for establishing the credibility of the United States and NATO as effective actors in dealing with these new post–Cold War challenges. That was enormously important.

* * *

The main Balkans problem confronting the Clinton administration in the first term was Bosnia. The main problem in the second was Kosovo.

Sandy Berger, deputy national security advisor: When you are committing American troops into harm's way, it's an awesome responsibility, and you want to be right. You know some of them are not going to come home. That's what separates those who have sat in the chair and those who have sat across the table from the president. I think the president in the beginning had a tendency to second-guess himself until we actually got to the point where we were moving, and then he would be fine.

I compare Haiti—where up to the end I was getting phone calls from the president saying, "What makes you think that when we drop these soldiers in Haiti that they're not going to be ambushed?" Those kinds of questions had already been resolved—to Kosovo where the president said, "We're going to stop this from happening. We're going to do what it takes. We're going to convince NATO." [British prime minister] Tony Blair is given a lot of the credit for Kosovo, but Blair did not convince Clinton. They were basically together in their determination to stop this from happening. He was solid as a rock. We had a seventy-eight-day bombing campaign in Kosovo, which nobody except Bill Clinton, Sandy Berger, Madeleine Albright, Bill Cohen, and our spouses believed would work.

When [Serbian leader Slobodan] Milosevic started moving against the Kosovars, having gone through Bosnia and having taken us two years to actually get NATO to go along with using military force, we were not about to see this happen again in Kosovo. We tried to negotiate Milosevic to back down, but he didn't. President Clinton and the rest of us agreed that we had to use military force to stop the Serbs from their intent, which was to ethnically cleanse Kosovo and drive a million Kosovars out of this part of Serbia.

We decided on an air campaign for a reason. This is important because many people think the only reason we did an air campaign was because we didn't want to have casualties. I believe that from the air we had a thousand-to-one advantage on Milosevic. Once we got into those mountains of Yugoslavia where the Germans had been savaged—we were on the ground—our advantage was no longer a thousand-to-one. Maybe it was two-to-one. It would have been a daunting prospect to go over the Albanian Alps and send a land force into Belgrade. . . . So the decision to use an air campaign was a strategic decision. The theory was that we would bomb military and command and control targets and then gradually we would select targets that were closer to the regime—some of Milosevic's cronies, their factories. We actually had quite good intelligence during Kosovo. We could see Milosevic under more and more pressure. We could see his wife under more and more pressure.

So track one was military, track two was political. Let me say one other thing. NATO had been created in the late 1940s and never really used except in Serbia for a brief period of time. This was the first war that NATO had fought. It was like building this great fire engine and never taking it out of the garage. When we finally took it out of the garage, it was kind of creaky and it didn't make decisions instantly. You had to go back to capitals for sensitive bombing targets in the beginning.

I think that many people, including some people in this administration, walked away from that lesson saying alliances are cumbersome ways to conduct war. We should do coalitions of the willing—where we lead, they follow. I believe just the opposite. I believe that we won in Kosovo because Milosevic discovered that he could not divide the nineteen democracies of NATO. To me the key day was the summit that we had in April [1999] during the bombing campaign and the nineteen leaders, including the three new leaders, came together. They looked each other in the eye and said, "We will not lose. Whatever it takes, we will get Milosevic to withdraw from Kosovo, we'll have a NATO-led peacekeeping force, and the Kosovars will come back."

Vaclav Havel, Czech Republic president: I remember when we had a summit of the NATO alliance with the new members in it. That was a session very close and confidential where only the heads of state were present. There was a deliberation about the [air] campaign, about the attack on the regime of [Slobodan] Milosevic, and [Clinton] had a very exhausting speech but it was by heart, he didn't read it. He knew everything that was going on in Bosnia-Herzegovina. He knew it much better than all these other heads of state who were present there.

Sandy Berger: The key to the political settlement was getting Russia on [our] side so that Milosevic did not feel that he had Russia to rely on, that Russia would save him. So we started a second track, which Strobe Talbott really led—the vice president was quite involved in this—to get Viktor Chernomyrdin, who was the prime minister of Russia at the time, to agree to our conditions for surrender. The Russians had a really hard time with the notion of a NATO-led force because they were not part of NATO. We finally got Chernomyrdin working with President [Martti] Ahtisaari of Finland, representing NATO, to agree that it would be a NATO-led force and we'd figure out some way in which Russia could attach itself to this force.

This is in many ways the most dramatic period for me in the White House. We're in day 70 of the bombing. We're under enormous criticism from [Senator] John McCain [R-AZ] and others saying we should be on the ground, we should have a land force there, we made a huge mistake by thinking we could do this from the air. I'm reading the intelligence, which says that Milosevic is beginning to crack up here a little bit. You can see the pressure he's under. This is going to work.

You've got Strobe over here working with Chernomyrdin and Ahtisaari getting them so they can go to Belgrade and deliver the same message. We wanted Ahtisaari saying, "Mr. Milosevic, the conditions are all Serb forces out, Kosovars returned, NATO-led force." We wanted Milosevic to turn to Chernomyrdin and Chernomyrdin to say, "I agree." So that effort is going on over on this track, the bombing effort is going on over in this track.

It was taking a long time and we were facing the possibility of heading into winter, and winter comes fairly early in Kosovo. It comes in September and October. We had the prospect of 200,000–300,000 Kosovars up in the mountains unable to survive. So we had to begin to think about the ground option. I remember calling Wes Clark[5] saying, "What's the lead-time you need?" We had always operated under the assumption that we needed a sixty-day lead-time from when we said, "Wes, we want to go in on the ground" to the time that

---

5. General Wesley Clark was at that time Supreme Allied Commander Europe (SACEUR), heading NATO forces in the Kosovo war.

he could get in on the ground. I called Wes and Wes said, "We've done some reexamination and it's a little bit harder than we thought because some of the tunnels are smaller than our M1 tanks, so we'd have to blast our way through some of the tunnels to get there, and there are other logistical problems." So it was a ninety-day lead-time. Suddenly we're at the end of May, beginning of June, July, August, September. You're getting pretty close to the time where you have to say, "Wes, get a ground force ready." The one thing we decided was we had to win. We couldn't lose. I remember one night—this is maybe the most dramatic night for me in the White House. . . . I sat in my office and I wrote in longhand a memo to the president saying, "Here's the decision you're going to have to make, now, in the next week or two. When sixty days went to ninety, July became June." I said, "Number one, we can let the Kosovars starve. Number two, we can stand down. Number three, we're going to go in there with a ground force of several hundred thousand troops and go in and take Belgrade." I wrote this thing through the night. It was the bleakest memo, because all three of these options were absolutely horrible.

The phone rang at about 5:00 in the morning. I don't know whether it was Strobe or somebody calling for Strobe saying Milosevic had met with Ahtisaari and Chernomyrdin and it had gone just exactly the way we'd planned. Ahtisaari said, "Mr. Milosevic, these are the conditions." He turned to Chernomyrdin. Chernomyrdin said, "I agree." Milosevic said, "I'll call a meeting of my Parliament in the morning," as if he had a functioning Parliament, and he put up the white flag. But we came very close to a ground invasion of Kosovo. . . . It would have been a bloody mess if we had gone in on the ground.

Just to make the larger point here, the conclusion I draw from Kosovo is that alliances work. It was the unity of the alliance that got Milosevic to back down.

Madeleine Albright: We were afraid that winter was going to start setting in. There were tons of refugees. We would have to do all kinds of things for tents and camps for the winter. I said, "We have got to begin to think about ground troops, because we have to put a stop to this." The military said, "But it's not a permissive environment." . . . Then Tony Blair came for a meeting. He had been arguing for ground troops. He actually persuaded the president—we had a meeting in the residence. There were too many people around. Tony Blair says, "I really need to go use the facilities." The president said, "Let me show you where they are." They never came back. [*laughter*] It was a great way to get out of talking with all of us. Tony Blair was arguing the same thing I was. . . . So they began to do some of the planning for ground troops, and then Milosevic capitulated. . . . When you have the military and the secretary of defense telling you this is a lousy idea and you have this woman secretary of state on the other side, I think [the president] questioned it. I think there was no question he wanted to be assured that this was the right thing to do.

General Hugh Shelton, chair of the Joint Chiefs of Staff: [Clinton] looked at me and said, "Hugh, if you were king for a day, what would you do at this point in this war?" I knew where he was coming from; we'd been at it for forty-five days, and on the surface, to the American people, it didn't look like the end was in sight. I had warned the president early on that an air campaign alone cannot guarantee victory. The only thing that could give us a victory for sure was if we decided to invade.... I looked at the president and said, "Mr. President ... I would not change a thing. We're starting to see, through intel, cracks and fissures in his armor over there. I really believe, with your help in getting [Jacques] Chirac's[6] approval on this, if anything is going to turn him around and make him surrender, this is what will do it. If this doesn't work, we'll have to have another session here, and I'll have to reassess. But right now, I would stay the course; I wouldn't change a thing you're doing." He smiled and said, "Good, okay." I left.

Two days later, I was in my office in the Pentagon and got a frantic call. I think it was my intel guy, J-2. He said, "Mr. Chairman, we're picking up on the intel net now that the Serbs have just surrendered."

Joseph Lockhart, press secretary: Those seventy days [of the Kosovo air campaign] gave me more insight into the president and his growth as president than any other time. It also gave me further insight into the deteriorating media in the country. The decision was made to launch this effort and to do it using air power alone, not using ground troops. There was a lot of criticism of that, of the president being afraid of body bags. The reality from my perspective, in all these discussions, was that it was something the president believed. But for sixty-seven, sixty-eight days there was unmerciful criticism from all sides of the president's strategy, and what I saw was a completely different president than the one I'd read about in the beginning and even the one I'd seen starting in 1996—someone who was patient and certain of his own decisions.... [At] various times there were various groups in the room saying to the president, "We're not sure about this. We may need to look at something else." The president was very stoic. He was the one person who reassured the team that this plan made sense and we were going to stick with it. "I don't care what they say about me. What could be worse than what they said about me last year? We're going to stick with it."

Sandy Berger: [Clinton] knew from the beginning that after Bosnia we were not going to watch a million Kosovars being expelled from Kosovo by the Serbs so that the last act of the twentieth century would be an act of ethnic cleansing. He knew that.

---

6. Jacques Chirac was president of the French Republic (1995–2007).

Madeleine Albright: I was just in Kosovo last summer [2005]. Now it's a pretty precarious story again. The saddest part is now the Serbian Orthodox churches are surrounded with barbed wire and are run-down. Some little girl started singing some song that I didn't understand a word of, but I knew she was singing about the fact that she wanted to cut the throats of the Serbs. So the bottom line is that nothing ever is totally done.... Foreign policy is a management process as much as anything, and you can't take your eye off the ball.

22

Northern Ireland

One of the great success stories of the Clinton presidency was the achievement of a peace agreement to stop decades of violence in Northern Ireland. Clinton's first hired foreign policy aide, Nancy Soderberg, claims that Clinton had been considering a U.S. role in mediating that conflict as far back as his time as a student at Oxford. During the 1992 campaign, he announced a willingness to give Sinn Féin leader Gerry Adams, who was long rumored to be a member of the Irish Republican Army, a visa to travel to the United States, a pledge that won favor among Irish American voters but outraged the British. That pledge was conveniently moved to the back burner during the early years of the Clinton presidency.

But Clinton's foreign policy team, especially Soderberg, began to hear over time from their sources inside Ireland that the time might indeed be ripe for peace. Clinton eventually was convinced that Adams was serious about bringing an end to the conflict, and thus he did issue a visa for Adams's travel into the country. Clinton himself made highly celebrated trips to Ireland, and dispatched a special envoy, former senator George Mitchell, to broker an agreement. The Good Friday accords bringing an end to the Irish "Troubles" were signed on April 10, 1998.

Sandy Berger, deputy national security advisor: Nancy Soderberg, who was our first paid foreign policy staff person [on the 1992 campaign], had worked for Senator [Edward M.] Kennedy and had been very close to the Northern Ireland issue for many years. She became convinced that [Gerry] Adams was genuinely committed to moving away from violence towards peace, but he was not strong enough within the greater IRA [Irish Republican Army] community, so to speak. His politics were not strong enough for him to be able to sustain that position. So the view had always been that he had to renounce violence and then he'd get a visa. The argument that we [on the National Security Council staff] made to President Clinton was, if we give him the visa he will come here and be able to go back with the stature to deliver the commitment.

That was a gutsy thing for Clinton to do. The State Department actually hated it with a passion. The State Department is very much Anglophile. The FBI [Federal Bureau of Investigation] hated it. They thought we were giving aid and comfort to terrorists. It was a calculated political decision based on the advice that he was getting from us as well as his own instinct that Adams—if we could take that risk, we could credential Adams enough to go back and renounce violence.

Nancy Soderberg, deputy national security advisor: The one [campaign stance] I didn't agree with was his Irish position, and Clinton actually got this wrong in his book. He gave me credit for writing the positions in April of '92. I corrected it, too, and I don't know why they didn't get the correction in. They sent me that part as it was being rushed to press and I corrected it, but they didn't get it in. I had nothing to do with it and would have opposed it had I been in the inner circle at that time. . . . Tony and Sandy and I see eye-to-eye on the world, with the exception of the Irish peace process issue, where I thought [Clinton] had gone too far in calling for an envoy and the visa. . . . But actually in the end he was right and I was wrong.

Clinton instinctively wanted to get [an agreement] done from day one. He wanted to get involved, see where we could [help]. But I wouldn't underestimate electoral politics. He wouldn't have done it had it been wrong from a foreign policy perspective. I literally never saw Clinton make a foreign policy decision for anything but policy reasons. But in this case, you get the added benefit of all the electoral votes. It's not just Massachusetts; it's all the Catholics around the world. There are 40 million in America, and a lot of them are in the swing states of the Midwest. There are a lot of Irish in this country.

Q: How do you get to the point of believing that there's a real possibility the IRA is getting ready to make a shift?
Soderberg: A couple of things. One, there's a split in Irish-America between the pro-IRA crowd and the peaceful crowd who supported John Hume, the SDLP [Social Democratic and Labour Party in Northern Ireland] leader, the peaceful party. I was definitely in that second camp and wouldn't have anything to do with the IRA crowd. . . . We didn't talk to these guys. I didn't have any sense of it, and I didn't have a lot of time or energy for it. I had no intention of spending a whole lot of time on Ireland when I went to the White House. But it just kept coming back, and it ended up on my desk because I had worked for Kennedy and actually knew the players and the issues. Essentially, the career people had no flexible views on it. It was all, "No, no, no, don't do it. Our relationship with Britain is too important; it will upset them."

I started thinking, *At least I'll look into it.* In the fall, I kept talking to John Hume and a few other people on the Hill. . . . Jean Kennedy Smith [the senator's sister] was now the ambassador, and I knew her through Kennedy. . . . John Hume had been having secret contacts with Gerry Adams for almost a decade. It started in '86. He had kept Kennedy's office informed of those. So he kept me informed of what was going on. He knew what Adams had better than almost anybody outside the inner IRA circle. He would say: "Look at this—" I said, "Nah, I don't think so." Then I had lunch with John Hume in the White House, and he . . . said, "I think you should start looking at it. I think there's something here." That got my attention.

On the Hill, Kennedy was for it. He was never for it before. This was all John Hume going to his friends on the Hill saying, "Now I think it's time." . . . [It] was a huge leap for Kennedy. This is a man who has lost two brothers to violence, and who always stayed very far away from the violent side of it. So for him to endorse this was a huge personal leap. The fact that he did it got my attention as well. I had grown up in that environment.

Then I started looking into it, and I pushed the FBI and the Justice Department and the State Department for an analysis of what was going on. I told them, "Look, this is what I'm hearing." It just came back so harsh: *No, no, no*—no nuances. We could tell something was happening. It's how we missed the fall of the Soviet Union. It's always been this way; they don't listen to what's happening in the grass roots. And I did. I had all these friends in the grass roots, and I could just feel it. It was obvious to me that there was something going on, and the fact that the U.S. government couldn't see it just made me more determined to do it. I ended up just doing it myself, with Tony [Lake's] strong support.

Senator Edward M. Kennedy (D-MA) (on the decision to allow Sinn Féin leader Gerry Adams to enter the United States):[1] So you had the British Embassy and the State Department against it. The FBI [Federal Bureau of Investigation] had a dossier on Adams and his terrorist connections, and it influenced the Justice Department. By January 25 [1994], our office was being advised by Nancy Soderberg, who was at the [Clinton] NSC, that the White House was leaning against the visa and we'd have to weigh in politically and not just substantively on this, and that's what we did.

We had a lot of other people who were talking to people in the White House. . . . Then on the 25th of January, the president called me to thank me for what I said about his State of the Union speech, and I spoke to him directly about this issue, and asked if I could come down and see him and he said fine. It was interesting with Clinton. I could get him on the phone easier than I can get my wife, Vicki. I mean, you call him and he calls you back in five minutes. You want to go down to see him, he's glad to see you. He's very accessible and available. . . .

---

1. Kennedy's remarks are drawn from one of his twenty-nine interviews conducted as a part of the Miller Center's Edward M. Kennedy Oral History Project.

Q: What was your reading of him during the meeting and when you brought it up in the conversation the day before?

Kennedy: This was a close case. There are a lot of cases that are 51 to 49, but you have to make a judgment, you have to go to one side or the other. So you make your judgment and then you're a hundred percent on that side. This was, I thought, by the time where my own thinking was at 90 to 10. I didn't even think it was close. . . . You don't often get political decisions that come down your way at the White House that are this compelling, I don't think. [But] I had been with President Clinton where I thought I had him convinced and it still didn't go, it didn't work.

Q: You didn't get that feeling on the visa issue?

Kennedy: No. I didn't know whether it was going [to work]. I thought he was convinced, but I didn't know what the other factors were going to be that would try and sink it.

Q: What was your sense of what resonated with him particularly?

Kennedy: One, the chance for peace, and two, the politics. He could understand both. Those were the two things, the chance for peace—you'd make a difference in terms of getting the chance for peace and be unique in that sense—the first president who reached this. And the politics of it—the fact that all Irish-Americans would appreciate that he had tried for peace. If he didn't, they'd all know he didn't. He could understand that.

Q: Was anything said about the internal politics on the Irish side?

Kennedy: Well, I think the argument came up about whether, if he gave [the visa] now, this would skew Sinn Féin to be willing to move towards a ceasefire and advantage those forces that wanted to move ahead. That was a good argument and it's a very powerful argument, but I never thought that it had quite the resonance that these other arguments had. It was a very good and important one for people who were deeply steeped in this conflict and understood the tensions and the antagonisms and the reluctance and the resistance going back over the history of surrendering their weapons and all the rest. It goes back a long way. There's a culture and a history on that thing that is dramatic. For people who understood all of that—I mean, he's multidimensional obviously, so he probably had some read on it.

Even after leaving there, I thought the meeting had gone well but we had this other action, that the State Department played its card about the interview. They were going to do an interview [with Adams], a pre-visa interview, to hand him the question about, "We know that you'll state publicly [and] personally renounce violence, and will work to that end." Sinn Féin and IRA [will] come in to end the conflict and support the joint declaration. The great challenge obviously with that statement is that it sounds reasonable to any ordinary person—Who wants to have a guest with a terrorist record who will not renounce the terrorism? But obviously it was totally unrealistic to expect Adams to do [it]. So there was a lot of back-channeling about what he was going to say and what the question was going to be.... We heard after the meeting at the White House that he was going to get the visa, and then we heard these questions, ... [so] we had a feeling that it might be getting away from us.

Q: *The questioning put it back in the court of the State Department.*
Kennedy: They were strongly against it and they were smart enough to know what questions to have [the consulate] ask that [he] can't answer. That's the direction that they were going in.

Q: *It boiled down to the issue of whether he would use the word "renounce," or say that he "would renounce," or something like that.*
Kennedy: All of us had a sense that this had been a very dicey road for Adams. He deserves a lot of credit for his personal courage over the whole process. I'm not sure that either Clinton or any of us were certain—once you see the word "renounce" and you see the alternatives side by side, you can understand it, but it's a little tough to get. The way I saw it is now they're over there in Belfast quizzing him, asking him questions they ask everybody about renouncing force or violence. They don't know whether we can let him in unless he does. We didn't see the language part. This is the way it comes at you. Then we understand they were trying to get a veto on this issue and I think by this time the White House was probably trying to get this thing cooking again. We've got the powers-that-be talking to him and getting mutually acceptable language that can be worked on through.

There's the old story about the Irishman who kept failing the immigration test and he only failed it by one, and he never got the answer to this one question: "Do you favor overthrow of the United States by force or violence?" The first year he said "force," and so he lost. The next year he said "violence," and he lost. Then finally the third year he said, "Neither. Which one do you want to overthrow them by?" Adams believed he had said what he needed to say to justify the visa.

Then early the next day, the 28th, I talked to [my sister, Ambassador] Jean [Kennedy Smith]. The consul general of Belfast had just interviewed him for an hour and a half and heard his statement, and he reported to the department that Adams had not changed his position. Even though the general was cordial to Adams, when Adams was leaving he told him, "In my opinion, there's no way you'll get the visa." I made a joke with Jean that if that was the decision, she'd have to resign, and she said, "No, I'm having too much fun." Later that morning, I called Tony Lake and said I thought this had gotten out of hand.

Q: *You really poured it on on that one, didn't you?*

Kennedy: Yes. It seemed that if they were not going to give him the visa, they should let us know and give it to us straight. To sharp shoot this thing and fly-speck it and sink it in that way was, I thought, devious, you know, [was] an un-becoming and unacceptable way of dealing with it. I had indicated to Lake that the word is going to get out fast about what decision the president has made on it, and the Irish are going to be worked up about it. I said that I was going to offer an amendment on the State Department authorization bill, which was on the Senate floor, saying that the visa should be granted and that I thought we had the votes to prevail, because we already had everybody lined up—well, an awful lot in line, in terms of the Senate. I'm convinced we would have gotten whistled through the House.

The next day, January 29, we found out that three grenades had been discovered in San Diego, each with a note urging a visa for Adams. Since this was going to get out, the White House wanted Adams to do some things before the visa could be issued—denounce the bombings, condemn the attacks on innocent civilians, and condemn the recent bombings in Oxford Street in London.

Q: *So it becomes condemning instead of renouncing.*

Kennedy: Yes. Adams agreed that if asked by the press, he would condemn the incidents and say they were the work of elements who seek to sabotage the efforts to support the peace process.... I never got the end of that story.

Q: *The intelligence on the grenades was that nothing like this ever happened. This is very uncharacteristic.*

Kennedy: It never added up, and then the next day they gave Adams the visa. Seven months later the IRA declared a full ceasefire and the long negotiations for the Good Friday Agreement began.

Trina Vargo, foreign policy advisor to Senator Edward M. Kennedy (D-MA):[2]
Clinton deserves the credit as it was his decision to make in the end. But Clinton had to be persuaded. We had to work on Clinton, despite the fact that he had promised [a visa] when he was running and then he denied it once or twice.... Clinton needed the cover of Kennedy. If Ted Kennedy wasn't for that visa, it was not going to happen. I think most people involved would agree with that. Clinton wasn't an expert with history in the issue. He knew a little bit about Northern Ireland. He cared about it in the campaign the way politicians do, but he wasn't knee-deep in it. It's the kind of thing that if you didn't know it really well, you wouldn't want to trust your own gut on it, just trust Gerry Adams on it.

---

2. Vargo's remarks are drawn from her interview for the Miller Center's Edward M. Kennedy Oral History Project.

You always had members of Congress who were for it, but they were just known to be supportive of the IRA. For Clinton to do it, he really had to have Ted Kennedy bless it, because if it all went south he could at least say, "Ted Kennedy thought it was okay." But Clinton definitely was the only person who could make the decision and he deserves full credit for taking it on.

* * *

Q: *You did make the first trip to Northern Ireland with Clinton?*[3]
Nancy Soderberg: Yes.... It was a real high on every level. The crowds grew during the day and you could feel it.... They couldn't believe that the president of the United States was taking time out of his busy work to come and see them. You could see that they thought, *Wow! This is really cool.* They were so appreciative.

Then he had stuck his neck out on the visa for Adams—for the first time in their lives, they could see a better life. Northern Ireland is dirt poor. The people live in tiny little houses and don't have jobs. The unemployment rate is huge. All of a sudden they thought, *Maybe my life is about to get better because the president of the United States is here.* And, in fact, it has gotten better because he did it. The highlight was the night in the square when he lit the Christmas tree. More people came out than we expected, hundreds of thousands. They were all happy and couldn't believe this man had brought them a chance for a better life. At that point, the people were so much farther ahead than the politicians. The politicians still weren't even talking to each other. The fact that the people came out and said, "Yes, this is where we want to go" forced the politicians to think a little bit differently. It was so carefully planned. Every step Clinton took, and every hand he shook, was carefully choreographed. We were up until 3:00 or 4:00 in the morning.

Adams wanted a public handshake, but we didn't. Finally we ended up orchestrating that Adams would just happen to be at a shop we were just happening to stop by. He came out and shook his hand. [*laughter*] It worked beautifully. I was petrified something was going to happen. It worked out brilliantly.

Q: *Something politically or something about security?*
Soderberg: No, I wasn't worried about the security. That's not what the IRA does. They're not going to blow up Bill Clinton. He's their biggest savior. There was a possibility that some hateful person from the other side could do something, but the minute we got there we realized the whole crowd was so excited about it. Protestant or Catholic, they still love America.

Once there was a real decision [to issue Adams a visa], the White House guys got into it. George [Stephanopoulos], the vice president got into it. The Cabinet

---

3. Clinton went to Belfast at the end of November 1995.

got into it, screamingly, saying, "Don't you dare!" Clinton always knew he was going to do it. It was more, "Find me a way to do it respectably." . . . Louis Freeh [the FBI director] was apoplectic. [Attorney General] Janet Reno was apoplectic. . . . Louis Freeh was anti-terrorism, and Janet Reno the same thing. "You can't do this; it will send a message to our anti-terrorist allies." Warren Christopher was saying that it would ruin our relationship with Britain; they'd stop cooperating with us on Bosnia and Iraq.

I said, "No, they're not. They're not doing that as a favor to us. It's in their interest to cooperate on those two issues." As far as the terrorism message goes, I wasn't worried about Adams coming here and blowing up anything. I thought, actually, in the long run, if he came here and the president of the United States stuck his neck out for him, and he didn't deliver a ceasefire, it would enable us to go to the Irish-Americans and say, "See? This guy's a fraud. Quit sending him money," and undermine him further. It was that kind of win-win logic that convinced Clinton to do it.

[The British] never in a million years thought we were going to actually give a visa to Gerry Adams, and they made it clear that this was a big issue for them. . . . The morning that Clinton was deciding to do it, he got a long letter from Rod Lyne, the national security advisor for [Prime Minister John] Major, about all the women and children the IRA had killed. He was asking, "How could you do this?" There was something about the Christmas spirit. I don't remember whether Major called Clinton beforehand, but I don't think he did; I think it was all through his national security advisor. Then when we did it, it leaked that afternoon—in fact, it leaked before we had time to tell them we had done it. . . . The whole British Empire shook, really; they just couldn't believe that we'd done it.

I ran into Major on a plane—probably in 1998, 1999, maybe a little bit later. . . . I wrote him a little note saying, "I think you did a great job on the Irish question." He called me up, and we had tea. He said, "You're right, you did the right thing." Most of the British involved at the time and the State Department people have since come to me and said, "You did the right thing." They recognize that now.

Tony Lake, national security advisor: I talked to most of the leaders in the Northern Ireland parties once every week or two. I was very careful not just to talk to Gerry Adams, who is an engaging fellow, but to David Trimble, even Ian Paisley, all of them, so that there was equal time.[4] And the British and the Irish. We sometimes got, especially with the British—with my friends, and they were

---

4. David Trimble was a British politician from Northern Ireland who led the Ulster Unionist Party. Along with John Hume he was awarded the Nobel Peace Prize in 1998 for helping to negotiate an end to the Troubles. Ian Paisley (1926–2014) was a hardline Northern Ireland loyalist who opposed the Good Friday Agreement.

friends, who were my opposite numbers—into very difficult conversations, because it was a very emotional issue for them.

It amused me because one thing we would do is before they would meet, the Brits and Sinn Féin, which they would do occasionally, we would talk to each of them. Making no promises, but knowing what each of them was going to say, saying, "Well I'll bet this might work if you said this," and "I'll bet that might work if you said that." So we'd have a pretty good fix on what the meeting would be like and we'd think that this is going to lead to a real breakthrough on issues like decommissioning.[5] Then they'd get into the room and take one look at each other, and the talking points would go out the window, and fur would be flying, and they couldn't get past hundreds of years of history and the "curse of [Oliver] Cromwell."[6]

I remember one conversation with one or the other, I can't remember if it was on the Irish side or the English side, when we were then talking about Bosnia. This guy, who had just had another blowup, said, "Why can't they (the Bosnians) get along? What's the matter with these people?" And then I'd think about my own feelings about Dallas Cowboy fans. You know, we're all prisoners of history. So we kept working it.

Sandy Berger: I think the Belfast visit was really important. There were probably 300,000 people who came out to hear [Clinton] in Belfast. The people who wanted peace, who wanted thirty years of the Troubles to end. They didn't know that they were not alone. Suddenly they were together, standing in the square ... [saying], "My God, it's not just me who wants this over; it's also my neighbor and my neighbor's neighbor and my schoolteacher." That was an electrifying experience because what the president did was empower the people of Northern Ireland to take this into their own hands.... That really launched the process.... Northern Ireland—there's a reason why it's the land of magic. These characters—David Trimble, Gerry Adams, and John Hume—they're all characters out of a novel. It's impossible not to get enthralled by their stubbornness and intransigence, their eloquence, their hope, and their despair.

Tony Lake: You know, most decisions are 51–49 and I'm still not sure whether [they are] right or wrong. This, we were right, dammit. I mean, just look at the results. They were wrong. But they probably still don't believe it, and British intelligence certainly doesn't believe that and went after me personally a few times in ways that I didn't particularly appreciate when I would catch them at it.

---

5. Decommissioning was the process of taking weapons out of circulation by the IRA.

6. Oliver Cromwell (1599–1658) came to Ireland with an anti-Catholic military force in 1649 intent on spreading English control. His harsh tactics—resulting in mass casualties (some speculate in the hundreds of thousands), deportations, starvation, and confiscation of land—left bitter memories that survive to this day among the Irish.

One of their leaders came over to meet with me and I think she wanted simply to see this devil firsthand or something. And it's so funny because I really was fairly balanced, my father was English, I'm an Anglophile. So I pressed her very gently: "Can I see the evidence that Gerry Adams is still involved in terrorism or whatever it was?" And it was pathetic. I mean, either she didn't have it or wouldn't show it. The British ambassador, who was a friend, I looked over at one point and ... he rolled his eyes in embarrassment. But they were just very locked in on it and that became a reality for Major because if he went too far, then they would get him and then he was in trouble politically.

Niall O'Dowd, journalist for the *Irish Times* and a key back-channel between the Irish and the Americans:[7] I think the fact that Clinton was a [political] outsider helped a lot, that he wasn't a creature of the establishment. I noticed that about him subsequently. He would say things and people would miss what he was saying, but I would take him very seriously because he was a guy who didn't necessarily recognize accepted wisdom. I think that was deeply important on the issue of Northern Ireland. He just wasn't snowed under by the FBI or whoever, coming to him saying, "These people are terrorists, they could blow up something." He had his own sense of being an outsider and saw what the chess move could be for Sinn Féin and how it could work out for himself, as well.

In that sense, he was the purest politician next to Kennedy I'd ever met, because he was capable of that kind of thought. We would never have had a hope with George Bush, either of them, to have that independence from the bureaucracy, because it's so much easier to say no to any of these things. I think getting someone to say yes is a tough deal.

Richard Riley, secretary of education: Clinton was such a hero in Ireland for what he did in Northern Ireland. . . . You go to Ireland and tell them you work for Bill Clinton, and the cab driver will hardly let you pay. They loved Bill Clinton over there, and still do.

---

7. O'Dowd's remarks are taken from his interview for the Miller Center's Edward M. Kennedy Oral History Project.

23

Bill Clinton and the World

Bill Clinton was elected to the presidency based largely on his commitment to refocusing the federal government on the economy, but he ultimately found himself devoting a major portion of his time to foreign policy—as all presidents do. Indeed the span of Clinton's international portfolio was truly global, from Mexico on the nation's southern border to Korea and China on the opposite side of the world. The president found himself by public necessity tending to problems that originated from Swiss banks to Afghan caves. But by the middle of his second term, foreign policy came to have a special appeal to Clinton, as the Republican Congress continued to oppose his domestic initiatives, and as the Lewinsky scandal undermined his standing at home. The president's constitutional prerogatives in the conduct of foreign policy gave Clinton incentives to invest his energies there, where he could act with greater freedom—and perhaps with better odds for success.

Although Clinton inherited a post–Cold War world, he did not have the luxury when he came into office of ignoring events in Moscow and Eastern Europe. Indeed, one of the first issues that occupied his time was the potential expansion of NATO, to provide an umbrella of protection to those nations newly freed from the Soviet orbit. The potential for that extended alliance created severe problems with Russia, which itself was teetering between freedom and revanchism.

Strobe Talbott, deputy secretary of state: The consistent intensity of Clinton's interest in and involvement in [the former Soviet Union] was stunning and it went back to the transition.... Even though Clinton was in the process of putting together a government, presiding over the economic summit in Little Rock and all that kind of thing, he was fascinated by what was going on in Russia, which was a lot. He was getting regular intelligence briefings in Little Rock and was calling me up at all times of day or night, particularly night, unfortunately for me, to ask about what was up with [Boris] Yeltsin.[1] When I saw him on New

---

1. Boris Yeltsin (1931–2007) was the president of Russia, although in the immediate aftermath of the Cold War his political position was seldom stable.

Year's at the Renaissance Weekend it was all he wanted to talk about.[2] And it wasn't just idle curiosity. It was: *What do we do about this?*

General John Shalikashvili, chair of the Joint Chiefs of Staff: We [the foreign policy establishment] had never thought about what would happen if the Cold War ended. Clearly the big issue was how do we integrate the states of the former Soviet Union into the [Atlantic] alliance. You cannot make them members of NATO [North Atlantic Treaty Organization], because then you take on the responsibility of coming to their defense. So it occurred to us that what we ought to do is develop a different participation than Article VI, which gives every NATO member a guarantee that we would come to their defense. So we needed to develop a new set of rules for NATO. . . .

So we came up with the term "Partnership for Peace." . . . It was really mostly for Russia, because we had to figure out a way to make them part of us without taking on the burden of defending them. I had thought for a long time that we would have peace in Europe if we ever convinced Russia that they must not think of defense against us, the West. The best way to do that is to embrace them as forcefully as possible so they would have no reason to think of their defense against us, but think of their defense in partnership with us. . . . Henry Kissinger once told me, "Shali, you're nuts; can't be done." I said, "Mr. Secretary, it can be and it will be done."

James Steinberg, director of policy planning, State Department: In some ways the centerpiece of the first administration—and, I think, one of the greatest achievements—was the evolution of NATO and NATO's enlargement. It was a signature feature of what Christopher came to do. It occupied a lot of his time. . . . There was always the option that NATO could wither away. The Cold War was over. It was created against the Soviet Union. So . . . the adaptation of NATO was critical to answering the question, How does the United States stay in harness with our European allies and stay involved on that stage?

Tony Lake, national security advisor: I remember one meeting with my Russian counterpart. It wasn't a meeting. It was a reception in Moscow at the time of an anniversary of the end of World War II. He'd had something to drink. I'd had something to drink. We had been talking about the twenty-five million Russians who had died in World War II, and he said, "You know, we made that sacrifice in World War II and we're prepared to make that sacrifice now against NATO enlargement." I remember thinking, *This is really good vodka.* [*laughter*]

What I used to argue strongly within the American government, and then with the Russians, was that, "It's going to happen. The timetable may not be sure,

---

2. The Renaissance Weekend, developed by South Carolinians Philip and Linda Lader (he was later deputy White House chief of staff for Clinton and then ambassador to the Court of St. James's), was a retreat for invited guests over a long New Year's weekend, featuring casual off-the-record panels on current topics.

but it's going to happen. And if you, the Russian reformers, make this a big issue politically, then it's going to undercut you at home, and you don't want to look weak by having made an issue of something that you can't control." I thought that was more honest than to pretend to them that it was open, because then you do make it a serious issue in our relations with the Russians.... I knew that in the end the president was for it ... because he, himself, was the one who coined the phrase, "a peaceful, undivided, and democratic Europe." He said in a speech, which we hadn't put into the text, that this was the first time that there was the possibility of a peaceful and undivided and democratic Europe in all of history. I remember saying, "Huh?" Thinking back on it, I guess it was true.

Vaclav Havel, Czech Republic president: I'm sure if it wasn't for the United States of America we wouldn't be members of NATO. The USA was the driving force for our membership.

Warren Christopher, secretary of state: I wanted to say that I think the historical record ought to give Clinton a lot of credit for NATO expansion. It would not have happened without him, and it would not have happened nearly as rapidly without his pushing for it. It's hard to remember how strongly aligned the intellectual forces on the eastern seaboard were in opposition to the expansion of NATO, starting with [George] Kennan,[3] but down through the newspapers in the East. They all thought that NATO could not be expanded without disrupting the U.S.-Russian relationship, and they thought that was the higher value. Clinton would not be deterred. His goal, as I said earlier, was the unification of Europe and he thought that moving to the center of Europe with NATO was essential and that did not need to cause an eruption in Russia.

Now I think we can thank Clinton's relations with Yeltsin, which were bought at such high cost in terms of time and disruptiveness, [for making] possible the expansion of NATO.... So I think in broad strokes, Clinton's role in expanding NATO and giving it a new mission, or a new sense of mission, preventing it from decaying, is something that ought to go down in the record for his historical achievements.

During the 1992 campaign, one of Clinton's most aggressive attacks on the foreign policies of his predecessor had been about China. Clinton argued that President Bush and his foreign policy team had been far too lenient on Beijing's leadership for the fatal crackdown on protesters in Tiananmen Square in 1989.[4] Clinton's campaign rhetoric

---

3. George Kennan (1904–2005) was an eminent American diplomat, who is usually credited with being one of the primary authors of the policy of containment of the Soviet Union.

4. Tiananmen Square is a vast central plaza in Beijing that saw pro-democracy rallies form in 1989. The protests were forcibly put down by the Chinese government, resulting in

suggested that he would be much tougher—with results. After he came into office, how-
ever, he found that China was a more intractable problem than he had anticipated, and
he ultimately adopted much the same posture of active engagement with the Chinese
that he had earlier criticized.

Sandy Berger, national security advisor: Clinton often says that there are some problems for which time is your friend and there are some problems for which time is your enemy. Northern Ireland, I believe, is a problem for which time is your friend, because basically, even though the politicians are still hurling insults, people are not hurling Molotov cocktails. There is prosperity in Northern Ireland. I don't think the people of Northern Ireland want to go back to the bad old days.... The Middle East is just the opposite. Because of Rabin's death, the process that was building hope suddenly became one of despair.[5] Life was not improving for the Palestinians, and security was not improving for the Israelis, so the two sides were pulling apart.

In Taiwan and China, time is our friend. If we can keep the status quo between China and Taiwan for another twenty years, they will be so entangled with one another that war will be impossible. There's already $40 billion of Taiwanese investment on the mainland; imagine what that's going to look like ten years from now. But in the meantime, you've got irrational politicians who want to seek independence or use force. This is a very emotional issue. I believe it's possible for there to be a conflict between China and Taiwan. But I think every year you buy, it's going to get easier, because the facts on the ground are going to work in your favor.

William Perry, secretary of defense: We were very slow off the mark with China. We spent a year trying to get the president to back off his campaign China-bashing rhetoric, to see that we needed to engage them. That was a view that I held, that Shali held, that Christopher held. But the president had dug himself in pretty deeply on the campaign. We had to persuade him that that was wrong, and it took a while to do that.

Tony Lake: An important part of the '92 campaign, in showing that we were for democracy and against dictatorships, was going after China. This was in the wake of Tiananmen Square. The Bush administration was completely isolated, at least initially, on its policy with overwhelming majorities in the Congress

---

an unknown number of casualties. The Bush administration's response was widely criticized as weak, leading to a debate in the 1992 campaign about the proper response to Chinese behavior.

5. Yitzhak Rabin (1922–1995) was the prime minister of Israel during the early years of the Clinton presidency, until he was assassinated by an extremist opposed to Rabin's efforts to negotiate with the Palestinians. Rabin's willingness to advance that process gave Clinton hope that he might be able to broker a peace settlement. His death was a deep loss for Clinton.

opposing their policy. And we believed what we were saying. We did get a little over-the-top sometimes in talking about "the butchers of Beijing," a phrase that I didn't write but certainly approved, and we did think that we could apply pressure on the Chinese in a way that would force them, in their own calculations of their own interest, to make some concessions on human rights issues. And we were wrong.

It became clear after a year that [the China policy] wasn't working. We weren't getting anywhere in particular. So then we tried something different, which was that Bob Rubin and I ... met with a Chinese representative at the Nixon funeral[6] very secretly to suggest to him that we needed to, in our mutual interest, work out some kind of deal and that we should send our representative over ... [to] try to work out a deal. And the bottom line was that the Chinese weren't dealing.... So we thought of a new approach. You had to renew [most favored nation trading status] once a year, in June.[7] We tried a new approach and it was a—I almost said "pathetic," but it wasn't, because we sold it actually—an approach which ... was to say that we will support MFN again, but we're going to do other practical things, such as getting American businesses to push harder on promoting human rights through their activities, and we're going to go after military industries ... et cetera.

I remember, to my regret, a meeting with some of the Chinese human rights activists here in the United States. And actually convincing them ... that this was a better policy than what we were trying before. I'm not saying that the other policy worked, because it wasn't. So they applauded it and that helped with the reporters. I do remember afterwards thinking, *My God I hope this works*, because I agree with these people and their approach.

Charlene Barshefsky, U.S. trade representative: The president became very frustrated and said, "You know, I've been hearing from some of you individually about this issue and I just don't think we have our act together. So I've been doing a lot of reading by myself. Think about a country like Cuba or Haiti where you try and go in and foster human rights, even by aggressive acts. How successful have we been? [Then] think about China, its size, its history. This is a completely nonsensical policy. It will produce no effect. If we can't change Cuba, if we can't change Haiti even with substantial intervention, we will certainly not change China through this policy." He said, "If we can't change these small countries, and these countries are pinpricks on a map"—I'll never forget that—*pinpricks on a map*—"this is the way we're going to change China? No. The

---

6. Richard Nixon's funeral was held on April 27, 1994.

7. "Most favored nation" [MFN] status provides trade advantages to the designated partner. Clinton continued the Bush policy of extending MFN status when the time for renewal came in 1993, but said that further continuations would depend on improvements in human rights in China. In May 1994 he decoupled those policies.

way you change China is you engage with them, you bring them into the tent, and you help mold them to the extent you can. The way you change China is to give their people enough opportunity and enough exposure to the outside world that they begin to see there's another way."

* * *

In 1994, the Mexican economy suddenly faced an abyss, with a looming collapse of the peso. Because of the grave nature of the problem and its implications for the United States, Clinton received assurances from the congressional leadership that the House and Senate would back the necessary steps to forestall disaster. Those legislative leaders quickly found that they had spoken prematurely, as they could not, in fact, persuade their members to go along. In the face of congressional opposition, then, Clinton's economic team crafted a set of risky financial supports the president could provide on his own authority to prevent Mexico's collapse. It worked. This intervention is often cited by Clinton insiders as one of the administration's finest hours.

Sandy Berger: We saved Mexico. I'll tell that story very quickly. Mexico was in serious financial trouble. We begin to watch it very carefully. It almost goes off the brink and the president calls down to the White House the leaders—Gingrich, Dole, [Richard] Gephardt, and [Tom] Daschle, or [George] Mitchell maybe at that point, and he says, "We're going to have to guarantee some substantial loans to Mexico or Mexico could crater, and if Mexico craters it will have a devastating effect on America. We'll have thousands of immigrants coming across the border. Our economies are very much intertwined." All four of them said, "Absolutely, Mr. President." But the problem was we didn't really have clear legal authority to use the money that was in an account for the IMF [International Monetary Fund] to stabilize currencies for loan guarantee.

So we sought from the Congress authority to use that fund to guarantee some loans to Mexico. A week went by, and two weeks went by, and three weeks went by, and finally the leaders said, "We can't deliver. We've tried to sell this, Mr. President, and we can't get twenty votes." So it's against that background that I'm sitting in my office about 8 o'clock one night and Bob Rubin comes in with Larry Summers[8] and says something to the effect that Mexico has forty-eight hours to live. It's about ready to collapse. Meanwhile there had been a [presidential] transition from [Carlos] Salinas to [Ernesto] Zedillo. Zedillo walked into this new office, hadn't even uncrated his boxes, and he's hit by this economic tsunami.

So we went down to [Chief of Staff] Leon Panetta's office and went through this with Leon, and Leon said, "Let's go see the president." We went into the Oval

---

8. Lawrence Summers is an eminent American economist, at this time undersecretary of the treasury for international affairs. He later became secretary of the treasury (1999–2001)—and then was named president of Harvard University.

Office and Bob and Larry laid this out quite concisely, and no one was offering the other point of view. I very often found myself in the role of the spinach server with President Clinton. Because I was relatively confident in my relationship with him, I felt I was able to say things that were the hard truths. I said, "You have to understand, Mr. President, I agree with Bob's and Larry's position here, but this is $20 billion that you're putting on the table. That's a lot of housing that you don't build in Detroit. They're saying there's a 60/40 chance it gets paid back. That means there's a 40 percent chance it doesn't. There aren't a hundred votes in the House and twenty-five votes in the Senate that will support you, and if you piss this $20 billion down a rat hole, you're going to be in trouble."

He listened to all that and said, "We have no other choice." End of meeting. This is the absolute opposite of the protracted meeting, debate, everything, for hours and hours. He said, "We have no other choice, do we?" All of us said, "No." And he said, "Do it." We wound up using somewhat questionable—it never was taken to court—legal authority to use this monetary fund to guarantee the loans, but the Mexicans wound up repaying the loans with interest. We actually made money on this deal in the end, although that was not the purpose.

It's a terribly important story about understanding Bill Clinton and those people who think that he's simply a political animal and that everything was a calculation and triangulation and was the personification of how you find the middle. He knew there was virtually no upside to doing this. No one was going to give him any credit if Mexico did not collapse. There was substantial downside. Imagine, $20 billion, with a Republican Congress— . . . that's a pretty big amount of money to throw down a rat hole. But he understood intellectually that we could not let Mexico fail. He was saying, "We'll deal with the political consequences if we have to."

Summers and Rubin were a great team and they figured out how to do it. Bob got the Mexicans to collateralize the loan with revenue from Mexican oil, so that was some protection. But there was still a lot of risk, and this was Clinton at his best. I left that meeting and thought to myself, *I'm really proud to work for this guy.*

Many Americans have forgotten that the first terrorist attack on the World Trade Center did not occur on September 11, 2001, but on February 26, 1993—barely more than a month after Bill Clinton's inauguration. Thereafter terrorism remained a problem on the president's agenda, although Clinton's worries tended to be focused more on overseas attacks rather than domestic targets. Still, Osama bin Laden was a known threat within the Clinton White House, and, even before 9/11, the focus of executive branch efforts to capture or kill him as a national security menace to the United States.

Nancy Soderberg, deputy national security advisor: One of the things I don't think Clinton has ever gotten full credit for—even though it has been written about extensively—is how much he did on the anti-terrorism front and how much he really did prevent and tee it up. You can drive yourself crazy thinking about whether you could have prevented 9/11. But clearly Clinton understood the terrorism threat and did a lot about it. He tried to set up a system that would prevent future attacks. It escalated a little bit with the Oklahoma City bombing and Timothy McVeigh. Even though it wasn't a foreign terrorist attack, it showed just how vulnerable everybody was. If a Timothy McVeigh can do that once, what could terrorists do around the country if they wanted to?

Tony Lake: I used to say at Principals meetings, "We can't prevent this." I remember saying this more than once, "We can't prevent it, but when it happens in the future, we ought to look back on this period and say we did all we could." Because that's all we can do. I remember at a meeting saying on this specific issue to the FBI and CIA people, "Do you have all the money you need?" And I remember this vividly because it was the only time I can recall I ever heard bureaucrats say, "Yes, we don't need any more money." But we should have spent more capital on reorganizing the government in ways to deal with [terrorism], . . . and should have spent even more time on trying to organize something.

Osama bin Laden. As I said, he was the only one that had an acronym.[9] It was at one of our Principals Committee meetings that we established a special cell to start tracking him. At the time, up through when I was there, through '96 and in early '97, which is before we knew of the formation of al-Qaeda, and before the attacks on the embassies [in Kenya and Tanzania],[10] which were in '98 I believe, we knew him as a financier of terrorism more than as a leader of terrorism, if you see what I mean. But it was serious enough so that we were trying to get on his case.

Not to be defensive about it at all, but let me be defensive here for a minute. There are two allegations from that period about this. One is . . . that the Sudanese kept trying to turn over documents to us that we refused because we didn't like the Sudanese. Let me use the word "bullshit" twice in one day. There is no evidence for this. I think this is Sudanese intelligence putting this out, post-9/11, as a way of showing that they're anti-terrorist. And it just doesn't make sense. We had repeated visitors to Khartoum. They could have turned them over. Our ambassador there, Tim Carney,[11] who is making these allegations, and who they knew was sympathetic, was our ambassador to the Sudan, they could have given them to Tim Carney and they never did. And there is no evidence that they

---

9. At the time he was routinely referred to as UBL (based on an alternative spelling of his first name, Usama).

10. On August 7, 1998, the U. S. embassies in Dar es Salaam, Tanzania, and Nairobi, Kenya were bombed by terrorists associated with Egyptian Islamic Jihad. Osama bin Laden helped to plan the attacks—which killed over two hundred people—subsequently landing him on the Federal Burea of Investigation's Top Ten Most Wanted list.

11. Tim Carney was a career Foreign Service officer with postings as ambassador to Haiti and Sudan. A January 2002 story in *Vanity Fair* magazine contains the allegations Lake refutes here.

approached the FBI and the FBI was told by the State Department, don't talk to these lowlifes. So, that's crazy.

The other one ... was that when the Sudanese came to us and said, "Okay, we'll get rid of Osama bin Laden, expel him," which we had been pushing them to do, to disrupt him, that they asked us to take him in. Now again, I don't have a clear memory of this. The argument now is that if that had happened, he never would have gone to Afghanistan and no 9/11. Here I'm being defensive, but that's what you do when there's an offensive charge.

In retrospect the problem was this. First of all, we did try to get the Saudis to take him. We didn't press it real hard because they were never going to take him, as was clear. We had other things we were trying to get them to do in the wake of Khobar.[12] But they would be in an impossible position, I assume this was their reason. If they killed him all hell breaks loose and if they don't kill him all hell breaks loose. And I don't remember what our reasoning was about his coming to the United States, but I'm quite sure that it would be the following:

If you bring him here and don't tell anybody, then we've got a constitutional problem, if we just hold him in the slammer and nobody ever knows. You can't do that, really. Or you could bring him here and put him on trial and since we didn't have the goods on him, we lose. That's unattractive. Or we could bring him here, as I say in response to this question, give him a tourist visa and have him visit Disneyland, which is unattractive also. So what do you do? This is before the Taliban took over in Afghanistan, so not being prescient, we didn't know what was going to happen if he went to Afghanistan and we were delighted. We did say don't send him to Somalia because we were worried about his links to Aidid and Somalia. We had no idea that Afghanistan would be such a bad place to send him and, of course, had we known, we would have resisted that but we didn't.

General Hugh Shelton, chair of the Joint Chiefs of Staff: Every now and then, Sandy [Berger]—having been goaded, I'm sure, by guys like Dick Clarke[13] with some hair-brained scheme about how we could fly nine hundred miles in a two-hundred-mile helicopter and snatch a terrorist—would get all excited, and we'd be called over to present plans about how we could do it. We'd basically have to tell him it wouldn't work. It sounds great, and I'm sure if you contact [film producers] Steven Spielberg or [Jerry] Bruckheimer, they can make a great movie of it. But this won't fly. These things crash after two-hundred miles without fuel.

---

12. The Khobar Towers bombing in Saudi Arabia, on June 25, 1996, was one of the worst terrorist attacks of the Clinton years. Nineteen U.S. servicemen were killed and over four hundred multinationals wounded in the attack.

13. Richard Clarke was a senior National Security Council staff member with responsibility for fighting terrorism. He was known in both the Clinton and Bush 43 administrations for his aggressively entrepreneurial work style.

In order to do that, we'd have to build up a footprint in the area, and it would tip our hand. They didn't understand some of the military nuances. But Sandy would go over some of our military plans in great detail, ask a lot of really good questions, and then say, "Okay, I've got it," and we'd go brief the president. . . .

I personally think every administration needs a Dick Clarke because they're very untactful and they come up these wild schemes every now and then. Given proper controls, you want people like that around you—very brusque, but again, they get a job done. He would force people to have to answer. So I like that. Now, from a military perspective, he watches too many Rambo movies, and he really thinks the military is a Rambo. . . .

Q: Do you remember when bin Laden first came on your screen?
Shelton: Oh, he was on my screen back in '96, down at Special Ops, when I went in.[14] I put together a task force down there then, using open source [materials], based on the Internet, that started trying to track what he was doing and how he was doing it. I basically pulled about, I think, six or seven bright, young, very computer-literate guys from different services into a little cell, locked them up in a room, and said, "Get with it. Let's find where he spends his money, where he gets his money." We quickly determined that he was laundering money through the fertilizer and fishing industries, and how much it was. They did a really good job.

All that came to a head about the time I went up to Washington. So later on I took that data and presented it to [Defense] Secretary [William] Cohen. We had two meetings with the president, one when [Robert] Rubin was secretary of treasury and one while Larry Summers was there. We argued that we needed to try to start bankrupting this guy. We knew how to do it and where to do it. But I couldn't win either case. Both times the president's decision was to go with treasury. He was very concerned that we'd be hurting our own banking systems, because [bin Laden] would [subsequently] come after our banking systems.

We, of course, were constantly trying to track bin Laden during my tenure [as chair of the Joint Chiefs]. We had plans to go after him immediately with TLAMs[15] to try to hit him if the CIA's operatives on the ground in Afghanistan could ever give us reliable or timely enough information to get it. Here's an example: One Sunday, I was with my wife headed down to Quantico to the Marine Exchange. I got a call. They think they have him. I'm on my cell phone, "I think we've got him; you need to get here ASAP." They're going to convene a meeting of the NSC. So I turned around and drove up I-95 on a Sunday, going 95 miles

---

14. In 1996 and 1997, Shelton was commander-in-chief of U. S. Special Operations Command, in Tampa, Florida, responsible for coordinating special operations components of the joint armed forces.

15. More commonly known as a Tomahawk [Land Attack Missile].

an hour. I was speeding to get to the Pentagon. My wife dropped me off there. In the meanwhile, I'd made a call to my guys and said, "Start rolling the TLAMs." A TLAM has to turn for about an hour and a half before you can actually fire it. I'd already given the order on my own to start the process. I get back to the office. My guys brief me quickly. My sedan is waiting, and I head for the White House, the only time I think I ever went there in other than Class A uniform. I later got kidded by President Clinton about whether I even owned civilian clothes.

Anyway, I get the TLAMs turning. We all convene right there in the White House. George Tenet is, of course, the primary speaker, because his guys have given him the information. It happened to be in Kandahar [Afghanistan]. Bin Laden and his lieutenants were supposedly meeting there. The problem was there were about 150 civilians in this location. George gets a little bit flaky about how timely it is and whether bin Laden will still be there if we hit it. After a lot of deliberation that day . . . we decided not to try it. If bin Laden had gone and we killed 150 people, we'd look like terrorists ourselves. So we didn't do it. . . . I would say, in the Clinton administration, we met over bin Laden and terrorism on average at least once a month, if not more often.

Sandy Berger: I thought about [terrorism] every day in the '99–2000 period. When we had the millennium threat spike,[16] I called the Principals to the White House, the attorney general, secretary of state, secretary of defense, deputy director of the FBI—the director didn't want to come—and the Office of the Vice President every day for a month for at least an hour. We became a working group. This was after we'd gotten a threat.

After the intelligence community said to us, based on the Jordan bust,[17] that we could expect five to fifteen attacks against American interests over the millennium, I turned the Principals Committee into a working group. And we got more FISAs[18] in a month than ever before because George [Tenet][19] would say, "We have intelligence that there's a blue van coming across the southern border of Texas. Here's what we know about it, and here are the people." Janet [Reno] would turn around to Frances Townsend, who was working for her [handling counter-terrorism], and say, "Can we get a FISA? How long will it take, twenty-four hours?" Normally that process would have taken a week. Somebody would

---

16. There was widespread worry that terrorists might attempt something spectacular to mark the new millennium, the night of December 31, 1999.

17. Jordanian intelligence intercepted communications between terrorists in late November 1999 indicating an attack was near. The Jordanians subsequently arrested over a dozen suspects and found additional intelligence in that process.

18. Berger's reference here is to a Federal Intelligence Surveillance Act (FISA) warrant, a legal process established to expedite secret intelligence gathering in the United States. A special court hears classified evidence about a demonstrated need to move outside the usual workings of the legal process.

19. George Tenet was director of central intelligence from 1996 to 2004.

have sent a memo to George, and George would have sent a memo to Janet. Janet would have sent a memo to Frances Townsend, who was working for her, and then you'd have it go back up the process and around again and down again.... [But] when an agency knows that the principal is going to the White House at one o'clock, it changes the tenor of the priority of that agency.

I gave the 9/11 Commission a 271-page, single-spaced copy of what Bill Clinton said about terrorism in his two terms. That's a lot of talking. This became more and more of a concern of his. It began to focus more around al-Qaeda by '96, '97, particularly as bin Laden issues his fatwas and his rhetoric becomes much more hysterical and threatening.... [From] '98 on, al-Qaeda is at the top of the list.

I said to Condi [Rice] during the transition—this has been reported, and I told this to the 9/11 Commission—that the number one issue that she would deal with as national security advisor was terrorism in general and al-Qaeda specifically.[20] The president said to President Bush during their [transition] meeting that there were five priorities, in his judgment. The first one was terrorism.

Lawrence Stein: What's amazing to me is that no one—in all the looking backward about 9/11, why did it happen?—no one has observed that for one and a half years, the country was transfixed over fellatio.

* * *

No foreign policy problem captured President Clinton's imagination more than the Middle East. Over time he developed a prodigious knowledge about the details of the Israeli-Palestinian conflict, and on occasion during his presidency invested enormous time and energy to bring about a lasting peace settlement. His failure in this effort was perhaps his greatest disappointment as president.

Warren Christopher: One of the things that I think has been undervalued, at least so far, in the Clinton foreign policy is his role in . . . the Middle East. From almost the first day I was in office, President Clinton directed me to give priority attention to the Middle East. He helped make that possible for me. . . .

The first time I met with [Palestinian leader Yasser] Arafat was in Europe. He was quite often in Europe and we arranged a meeting in Europe. He spent the first half hour just shouting at me, and he does have a litany of grievances, and the Palestinians do have grievances. But I said to him, "You know, Mr. Chairman, you and I can either have a decent relationship in which we talk to each other, or you can shout at me and I'll do my best to be forbearing about

---

20. Condoleezza Rice was national security advisor, and then secretary of state, for President George W. Bush. The 9/11 Commission was a special investigative committee set up by an act of Congress, signed by President Bush, to assess how and why the terrorist attacks happened and to examine what might be done to avoid a repeat.

it, but it won't accomplish very much." And he calmed down after that and we never had another shouting match.

I found him to be a very good interlocutor. He's a very intelligent man and you can talk with him. Now he has several bad habits of a guerrilla—a lifetime guerrilla. First, he tends to play his advisors off against each other and take the advice of the most extreme of his advisors. He'll ask their views and then press the case of the most extreme advisor. It's almost impossible for him to come to a decision. He always keeps looking for just one more thing. You think you've got him in a place where he decided, and he says, "Just one more thing." So he's very frustrating in that regard.

He has bad traits, including not having much fiscal discipline—but we shouldn't be surprised by that. He's lived most of his life on handouts from other rich people in the Middle East, so that's the way he lives. Nobody asked him to account for the things that the princes gave him in the Middle East. It doesn't mean we should accept him, but, you get just about what you might expect from his background. I'm amazed he's still alive.[21] His health is fragile and he lives precariously, keeping terrible hours. He really prefers the night time, though he isn't the only Arab who prefers the night time. But he's still alive and there's just nobody else to deal with at the present time. . . . My constant approach to him was to try to keep before him enough hope so that he could try to talk to his colleagues and followers about there being some hope out there.

Dennis Ross, Middle East envoy: For those . . . who see Clinton as being excessively political, and as making judgments accordingly—that was not my experience with him. . . . [If] the issue was presented as, "Politically this is a bad thing to do" versus "This is something that you need to do," every single time he would decide "This is what I will do." I'll give you two examples.[22]

After the four bombs in nine days [in Israel in February–March 1996], I go to [Warren] Christopher and I say, "Look, we're going to lose [the peace process]. [Israeli prime minister Shimon] Peres is going to go down and this process is going to collapse and we're going to lose it. This has shaken the Israeli public to their core. They wonder what the hell this is about. They need something to re-establish their faith in this because they've lost their faith in it. If it's really lost—we're in the early stages of it—if it's really lost, you don't get it back." He said, to me, "What do we have to do?" I said, "The president has to go over there. We should organize a meeting of all the Arab leaders with the Israeli leaders, to show the region has changed fundamentally and Israel is not alone. But it has to be great drama and we have to show with great drama that Israel is not alone.

---

21. Arafat died on November 11, 2004, two years after Christopher's oral history.

22. Ross's comments about Clinton are especially notable because of his service in the Reagan and Bush administrations, including time as a close associate of James A. Baker III.

That's the payoff of having a peace process, because the region has been transformed. So in fighting terror, they're not alone."

Christopher calls him up and says, "Dennis and I need to come over and see you right now. Dennis thinks we're going to lose this." Clinton drops everything and says, "Come over." We go right over there. He has other people—George Stephanopoulos is in the room, Rahm Emanuel is in the room, and the chief of staff [Leon Panetta] is in the room. They all chime in immediately, after they hear me out, and say, "Look, there's no guarantee that if you're there, there won't be another bomb while you're there. Another bomb right afterwards, in which case you lose it anyway. Then you've made this great dramatic gesture and it's all for naught." So they're all against it. [Assistant Secretary of State for Public Affairs] Tom Donilon is also against it. Tells Christopher he's against it for the same reasons. Clinton listens to me for literally five minutes, says, "We're going to do it," after he hears them.

Then one month before the election, we've had the opening of the Hasmonean Tunnel, there's a week of riots and demonstrations, and fifteen members of the IDF [Israeli Defense Forces] get killed in riots outside of Joseph's Tomb in Nablus.[23] We've been intervening, Christopher and I, daily over the phone. It's clear to me we can't generate enough drama on our own. Christopher said, "Should I go out there?" I said, "It won't do it, we need something that creates a break, right now, that gives everybody a reason to take a step back. The only thing that's going to do it is, let's bring them here, to see Clinton. I'm not saying have Clinton go out there, let's bring them here."

Everyone on his side—one month before the election—said, "What do you need it for? The direction of this election, you're going to win unless you do something that creates a problem. Why do this?" All the political advice is, "Don't do it." He said to me, again, "Do we need to do it?" I said, "Yes, we need to do it." He said, "Okay, let's do it." So it's quite striking, but these are, I think, demonstrable examples. He's prepared, because obviously he believes in it, to run the political risk.... My experience with him, on this issue, was that he didn't do things for political reasons. He did what he thought to be right. Whether it turned out to be right is a different issue.

Madeleine Albright, secretary of state: I remember at one stage saying to Clinton, "Just because [Israeli prime minister Benjamin] Netanyahu sounds like an American politician and doesn't have an accent, he's not an American. There is a different mindset on all of this." Netanyahu just drove us crazy.... I thought

---

23. The Hasmonean Tunnel runs beneath the Western Wall in Jerusalem and was opened to the public by the Israelis as a tourism and archaeological site in September 1996. Palestinian protests erupted because of the tunnel's proximity to Muslim holy places at the Temple Mount. Joseph's Tomb near Nablus is in the West Bank.

what bad luck I had that Netanyahu was my first Israeli partner, because he was just unbelievably difficult.

Dennis Ross (on conflicting reports about negotiations with Netanyahu at Camp David in 2000 over the possible release of convicted spy Jonathan Pollard from an American prison):[24] Here's what I believe. One thing about Clinton, and one thing about Bibi.[25] Clinton was certainly someone—and undoubtedly you know this—who could make you feel like he was agreeing with you and he could certainly tell you oftentimes what you wanted to hear. And Bibi was someone who was very good at *hearing* what he wanted to hear. In Clinton's case, he could say something that seemed really forthcoming, but in his mind he'd have a little bit of a qualifier in there, just enough of a qualifier to say, "I really haven't made that commitment." For someone like Bibi, he wouldn't hear that little bit of a qualifier. So I believe that Clinton in private with Bibi was very forward-leaning, but not, in his mind, definitive—but certainly very forward-leaning and giving Bibi the impression that this was something that certainly could happen. I understand the word "could" as opposed to "would."' Bibi probably heard "would" and he probably said "could."

When everybody thinks the deal's been done [at Camp David], Clinton leaves these two facing couches and motions for me to follow him into the bathroom. He says, "He says he's not going to do it. He's not going to do the deal unless we release Pollard." And I asked him flat out, "Did you tell him we would? If you did tell him we would, you have to do it. If you didn't tell him that, then he's just trying to hold you up for it, so you don't have to do it." As the morning wore on, he was becoming more and more insistent that he had not done it, which convinced me more and more that he had been quite forward-leaning on it.

I don't trust Bibi because I know who Bibi is. But Bibi told others, before the end—and that's also Bibi, Bibi also tells people what they want to hear—but he told [Natan] Sharansky, and he would want to tell Sharansky what Sharansky would want to hear.[26] But Sharansky is also the kind who would ask him, "Did you really have that?" And Bibi said, "I really have it." Which tells me that Bibi honestly believed that he had it. My sense is, what happened is exactly what I described—that Clinton left a little wiggle room in there and Bibi either didn't

---

24. Pollard is a former intelligence analyst for the U.S. government who pleaded guilty to spying for Israel in 1987 and received a life sentence. His fate subsequently became a frequent point of contention between American and Israeli negotiators when the United States was actively engaged in trying to broker a peace agreement for the region. Pollard was released on parole in November 2015.

25. Bibi is Netanyahu's nickname.

26. Sharansky is a Soviet-born Israeli politician and human rights activist who had previously been imprisoned for nine years in the Soviet Union on charges of spying for the United States.

want to hear it or didn't hear it, given who he is. Because he wanted it so much, and he saw it as such a trump card for him. That's my guess at what happened. . . .

Clinton could be very precise. Bibi was not very precise. Clinton once asked me, "Does he lie? Is he lying to us?" I said, "Nah." And he expected a different answer. I said, "He doesn't lie, because he really doesn't remember what he says." I actually think it's sincere. It's an acquired capability, because when he says something, it's like he said it but then it's gone. I would oftentimes say to Bibi, "This is what you said," and he would never challenge me. It's because I *was* precise and I did take everything down, and then I would repeat it. But the fact that he would never challenge me told me that he knew I remembered it and he wasn't sure if he did. It's not because Bibi's not smart; he's very smart. I think it was something that became a subconscious way of protecting himself, that he really didn't remember exactly what he had said. He might remember what was said to him, and there I think he probably did. But he wouldn't remember what he said.

Sandy Berger: The Palestinians today say they were dragged to Camp David, and that's just not true.[27] The Palestinians wanted Camp David just as much as the Israelis did, but they wanted to back it up closer to September, when under the original Palestinian-Israeli agreement the final status issues were supposed to be resolved. They had threatened that they would unilaterally declare a state if there was not a negotiated state. So they were playing games with the timing. By July you had a president who only had six more months left in his term, and even if you were able to reach an agreement, the president would have had to sell that agreement, the United States would have presumably had to have raised billions of dollars around the world to support the implementation of that agreement, so we couldn't really wait much beyond July.

Camp David is a bit of a *Rashomon* event.[28] There is the American Camp David, there is the Palestinian Camp David, and there is the Israeli Camp David, and they're all different. In the books that have been written and the rhetoric that has described them—in fact, there's even more than three perspectives because there's Dennis Ross's Camp David and there's Madeleine Albright's Camp David, there's Sandy Berger's Camp David, and there's Rob Malley's Camp David.[29] It was an event that you could look at from many different perspectives. . . . Mine has not been written.

My own view is that I agree with the fundamental judgment that in the end Arafat failed to seize an extraordinary opportunity because he did not have

---

27. Clinton's Camp David summit occurred on July 11–25, 2000.

28. *Rashomon* is a Japanese film which features multiple actors relating the same event, highlighting how different individual perspectives influence a narrative.

29. Robert Malley was a national security staffer with Sandy Berger and then special assistant to President Clinton for Middle East issues at the time of the summit.

254 | FOREIGN POLICY

the courage or the disposition or the will to risk taking on his own extremists. I think the major fault lies there. But there's also fault that I think lies on the Israeli side, and fault on our side. I think on the Israeli side, [prime minister Ehud] Barak started the first few days by backing up rather than going forward, by taking things off the table that had already been resolved, thereby simply losing the trust of the Palestinians even more.

There was such bitterness between Arafat and Barak that they'd only met two or three times during the whole process of Camp David. Most of it was shuttle diplomacy with us going back and forth and meeting at the second level. I think we made a mistake by not having focused more in the '90s on what was happening on the ground in the Palestinian areas. That is, Arafat was not preparing his people for peace. So there wasn't a constituency among the Palestinians for peace the way there was in Israel. Instead, there were often very conciliatory statements made by Arafat in English and very harsh statements about Israel and the United States made in Arabic to the Palestinian people. So he had not built the framework into which he could try to sell an agreement.

On the Israeli side, I think Barak made a mistake by getting diverted by Syria, and I think there were other tactical mistakes that Barak made along the way. But it was an extraordinary event. Every intellectual, personal skill that President Clinton had was brought to bear. I remember one critical meeting when, after the Israelis backed up, they then put on the table a rather dramatic offer which involved 90 to 93 percent of the West Bank, and that was even probably negotiable upward—the division of Jerusalem, which was an absolute red line for any Israeli prime minister. He talked about dividing Jerusalem, including the old city, along demographic lines, and having a Palestinian Jerusalem and an Israeli Jerusalem.

When I was in Israel the preceding May [2000], we had a dinner party with [Israeli President Shimon] Peres and all of the Israelis put on by Martin Indyk, the ambassador. They all agreed, except for Yossi Beilin,[30] who is on the far left, that dividing Jerusalem was a red line, that no prime minister could get away with that. Barak took that on.

Q: Could he have gotten away with it at home?
Berger: Yes. He was doing some very active polling during Camp David. So he was not throwing out ideas that were not being tested. It would have been a very difficult, divisive issue. I suspect President Clinton would have gone to Israel to campaign with Barak, because President Clinton was extremely popular in Israel. But the polls showed that there was a majority for—I'll tell you a story that I think captures this. Then I'll come back to the end of Camp David.

---

30. Beilin is a prominent Israeli politician, known as one of the major forces behind the Oslo Peace Accords in 1993.

In May of 2000 my wife and I went to Israel and I received an award from Tel Aviv University. Martin Indyk, our ambassador to Israel, gave a dinner party to which he invited all of the players, Palestinians, Nabil Sha'ath,[31] and all the Palestinians who had been involved since Oslo and before. All of the Israelis other than Barak—Abu Ala and Abu Mazen on the Palestinian side, the current president and prime minister of the Palestinian Authority were there, and on the Israeli side, all the key players that had been involved in the negotiation. We had a very lively discussion at dinner.

One of the main subjects was Jerusalem. As I said, except for Yossi Beilin, there wasn't an Israeli in the room who thought that any prime minister of Israel could touch the issue of Jerusalem. At the dinner was Amos Oz, the great Israeli writer,[32] whom I'd never met before. He didn't say anything during the dinner. The dinner ended and we went out to the patio in the back. There was coffee being served and he was seated on a bench. I went over and sat next to him and said, "Mr. Oz, you were remarkably quiet during dinner." He said, "I'm not a politician, I'm a writer." I said, "You certainly are a keen observer of Israel and the cross-currents of politics here. What do you think?"

He said, "I just had some orthopedic surgery, so let me use an orthopedic metaphor. If I have a leg that is rotted from the knee down and the doctor comes to me and says, 'I'm going to cut it off, six inches at a time,' I say to the doctor don't touch my knee. But if the doctor comes to me and says, 'I'm going to cut it off. It's going to be one cut, at the knee. It's going to be painful as hell, but then you're going to be through with this.' I say, let's go ahead with the surgery." In other words, he was saying that if Israel truly had peace on the other side of the table, that they would take some painful sacrifices for peace. I think that was Barak's calculation.

Had Camp David succeeded, Clinton's skill in that negotiation would have been in the history books. Obviously, if you don't succeed, that doesn't get in the history books. But he knew every issue. He could spread out a map of Jerusalem, he learned the neighborhoods of Jerusalem and where the various pockets of population were. He understood the refugee issue and he understood the security issues, that even after Israel withdrew from the West Bank they would need certain security guarantees.

In these negotiations he was very calm, very determined. I noticed this at the Wye[33] and at Camp David—he would explode usually once. It was always warranted, but a huge shock because he had been so steady when the parties around

---

31. Nabil Sha'ath is a senior political figure who has held multiple leadership positions with the Palestinians, including foreign minister of the Palestinian Authority.

32. Oz is by some accounts Israel's greatest living author. He is a highly awarded novelist and non-fiction writer.

33. President Clinton had hosted an earlier summit, in October 1998, at Wye River Plantation in Maryland in an attempt to advance the peace process.

him were screaming and yelling at each other. At some critical moment, when he knew he had to shake up the table, he would just unload. He did that at one point and then actually got the thing started again.

Q: Was that typical of his anger? Was he typically purposeful in the use of his anger?
Berger: In negotiations, yes. He was very calm in dealings with foreign leaders and on foreign policy. He was not somebody who showed anger. He'd come back afterwards and show anger to us, but not in front of others. He recognized that he was representing the United States. But I saw him on more than one occasion—at Wye and Camp David—where we were really being jerked around. In one case, in Camp David, by the Palestinians, who were putting maps on the table that were just ridiculous given the progress that had been already made. They were taking things back. The president said, "You can't expect me to do this if you're going to behave in such a ridiculous way." He wasn't yelling, but he was obviously angry. He just got up and we all left. It was a jolt of electricity at a critical time.

By the end, as I say, the Israelis had on the table an extraordinary offer that involved almost all of the West Bank and Gaza. It involved the division of Jerusalem and a Palestinian capital. The division of the old city, the most sacred part of Jerusalem, was really explosive in Israel. All of the elements in terms of the refugee issue, a very limited right of return by the Palestinians. A small number of Palestinians would be able to return to Israel, with the right of return being to Palestine. But it was the kind of offer that I don't know the Palestinians will ever see again.

There was a session the president had with Arafat, just one-on-one in Aspen Lodge at Camp David, which is where the president stayed. There was one of those swinging doors to the kitchen with a little window in the door, and Madeleine and Dennis and I were behind the door, looking through the window, opening the door just a notch so that we could hear the conversation. It was a funny scene if you captured it on film, the three musketeers straining to hear what was going on. It was Johnsonian[34] .... It was a combination of persuasion and cajoling and intimidation. Arafat looked like he was ready to die. He just kept getting smaller and smaller and smaller as Clinton kept getting larger and larger and larger.

But at the end of the day, Arafat would not put on the table a counteroffer that enabled Israel to really negotiate. He'd say no and the Israelis would make another concession, and he'd say no and the Israelis would make another concession. Barak probably made a mistake in that respect. It was a great disappointment. All of the final status issues had never before been on the table.

---

34. Lyndon Johnson was fabled for his range in exercising the arts of persuasion, especially in taking advantage of his oversized physique and personality.

It was like this walnut that we cracked open and all the pieces of were on the table—refugees, Jerusalem, statehood, borders. For the first time the parties were talking about these face to face. You could really see where things could ultimately fit together. But it required Arafat to do something. I've often said that sadly, the Palestinians did not have a Nelson Mandela at the moment in history when they needed somebody who could pivot from being a revolutionary and the leader of a movement to being a statesman and the leader of a country. Arafat was simply not capable of doing that.

Camp David broke up unsuccessfully.... [Then], in the final meeting Arafat comes to the White House in December, and the president is really quite furious, although he didn't show it.... I think it was downstairs in the library in the residence. The president said to Arafat, "You know, people have always said to me that you would wait until five minutes to twelve before you actually made your final move. I think, sadly, Mr. Chairman, your watch is broken." At that point the intifada had begun, the violence had begun, although there were only about thirty Israelis that had been killed by that time as opposed to the thousands that had been killed in the four intervening years. But still the violence was beginning to pick up, and Arafat, rather than sitting on that violence, I think believed that the violence would help him and he let the violence ride and it rode out of control, but he to some degree fomented it.

I'm sure that President Clinton would say his greatest frustration was that we did not succeed at Camp David.

Fernando Henrique Cardoso, president of Brazil: [Let me] tell you about the encounter I had with [Tony] Blair and Clinton about the Middle East.... This was, I guess, in October 2002. Clinton was no more president.... Blair invited me to a weekend at the prime minister's farm in the UK. Like Camp David, they have something like that. It is different. Camp David is very simple. The English have a manor, a sixteenth-century house, a fortress, with a beautiful library on the second floor.

I told Clinton about the invitation I'd received from Blair, and he said, "I'll go there too." I went with my wife to Blair's home and Clinton came too. We had a dinner. I stayed there. Clinton came just for this dinner. After dinner Blair invited us to go to the second floor to the library. Blair was about to do his first visit to the Middle East, to Palestine, to Israel, et cetera.[35] Blair opened a map. I said, "Well, this is like Philip II [of Spain]."[36]

---

35. Cardoso misspeaks in asserting that this would be Blair's first trip to the Middle East. It may have in fact been his first visit to certain parts of the region.

36. Philip II (1527–1598) reigned during the height of Spanish imperial power. He dispatched the Spanish Armada to England.

Blair was on the floor. A low table here. Blair's wife Cherie, and my wife, Blair, me, and Clinton, and one Clinton assistant, a lady. And Clinton was teaching Blair about the Middle East. Clinton knew *everything*, every area, every situation. "You have to speak to these people here, to these people here. Diplomacy here is this; the people here are this." It was unbelievable. The superiority of Clinton vis-à-vis the others was fantastic, not just because he knew, but because of his commitment to the situation. Blair was like a child, smiling looking at Clinton. That is Clinton.

* * *

The closest the world came to massive armed conflict during the Clinton administration was in 1994 on the Korean peninsula. With the assistance of former president Jimmy Carter, Clinton successfully defused that problem. Clinton subsequently worked closely with the South Koreans, especially Nobel Peace Prize–winning president Kim Dae-jung, to find ways to secure a peaceful resolution of the tensions between the North and the South.

William Perry: Sometime in the spring of '94—I forget the exact month when North Korea announced they were going to reprocess the spent fuel from the reactor and make plutonium out of it—from that moment on, it was number one on my list of priorities. This is not a diplomatic issue we're looking at here. This is a major national security issue from that point on.... It was always known that there was a danger of North Korea being a proliferator. But this really put it in very stark relief. It was a unique, singular action they could take that would put them in the position of having the plutonium to make six or seven nuclear bombs. The hard part of making nuclear bombs is getting the plutonium, not making the bomb. So on that basis, I thought this was a major national security issue. I so told the president. I told him I thought this ought to be an issue on which we drew the red line, not in any general terms, but very specifically on reprocessing the fuel to make plutonium.... There was no disagreement on that point. ...

[Warren] Christopher was recommending that the next step ought to be sanctions and that we would take it to the United Nations. If they agreed, fine, if they did not, South Korea and Japan were ready to join us in what would be pretty substantial and very severe sanctions. That became part of the public discussion.... So it was known to the North that we were considering sanctions. That was when they made their famous statements that they would consider sanctions an act of war, and if that would happen, they would turn Seoul into a "sea of flames"—pretty graphic language. These were very dangerous days, and I regarded them as such at the time. I thought we were on the brink of war.

I then went to the president and said, "I agree that the first step should be sanctions, but I do not think we should make those sanctions until we've taken some preliminary military precautions, because the North Koreans might precipitate a war on the basis of the sanctions or on the basis of going to the United

Nations requesting sanctions. Before we do this, I want to reinforce our forces in South Korea." I spent a couple of days reviewing the war plan, and the war plan said we would defeat the North Koreans under any circumstances, but they had so many soldiers so close to Seoul, we probably couldn't keep them out of Seoul until there would be hundreds of thousands of South Korean civilian casualties. . . . So I said, "If we can get another 20- or 30,000 troops in there, up to the DMZ [Demilitarized Zone], then we could probably stop them from getting into Seoul. So before we announce the sanctions, let's get these reinforcements."

The president said, "Fine. Give me a proposal." So I put together a proposal with three different options, different levels of reinforcements. They all involved substantial reinforcements, but different levels and different ways of doing it. The president called a National Security Council meeting to hear those proposals, and Shali and I were just laying them out when the call came in from Pyongyang, literally, while we were in the Cabinet Room doing the briefing. Probably fifteen minutes away from a decision, and the decision would have been yes, I'm quite confident.

The phone call came in. It was from President Carter. . . . Basically, President Carter said that [North Korean President] Kim Il-sung was ready to deal. . . .

Q: Carter had been recruited to make this trip?
Perry: No. that's another interesting story. I think it was either the White House or Christopher, I'm not sure which, had asked Sam Nunn to make the trip. Sam agreed to do that. About a day or two before he was to leave, he was disinvited. Kim Il-sung invited President Carter instead. I do not know the background as to what was going on in Kim Il-sung's mind and why he backed away from Senator Nunn's trip. I suspect it was because when he found out he could get President Carter, he thought it would be better to deal with an ex-president than with a senator.

There were mixed feelings in the administration about President Carter going over. It's clear that he, as an ex-president, might be a little hard to control, which turned out to be true—and that he might look for an independent source of reporting his findings there, which also turned out to be true. Some people in the administration had those concerns about him before he left. Some were very negative about him going. The president ultimately made that decision. I must say, I was positive about him going. I was so concerned with the danger of the situation and the recognition that we . . . looked like we were just drifting into a war. So I thought having somebody over there talking to him had to be a positive development, which turned out to be right. But also it turned out the people who didn't want him to go, the reasons why they didn't want him to go also turned out to be right. On balance, it was a positive outcome, I believe.

So Carter came back with this phone call. He said, "Kim Il-sung's ready to shut down this whole facility at Yongbyon if we agree to supply him light water reactors," which had been the concept of what might be done to deflect this issue. Carter thought he had the deal. He told the negotiators, "It's all settled.

We're ready to do this." We had a very short meeting. Everybody was there, of course—we were all sitting there anyway—and we decided we would not do that deal. We would only accept going into negotiations on what had to be done, because you couldn't just decide over the phone. You had to have negotiations. We would only do it if Kim Il-sung agreed to freeze his activities at Yongbyon while we talked. So that was the counteroffer that went back. We arrived at that in about fifteen minutes of discussion. It did not take long to say that has to be in the deal. Carter was appalled. He said, "No, he'll never agree to that." We said, "That's our deal. Yes or no? If you want a deal, it has to include that." Carter did go back to Kim Il-sung. Kim Il-sung accepted it.

Without going into a lot of detail on that, when [Carter] called to report he had the deal, he also said, "By the way, I'm going on CNN [Cable News Network] in another hour to report that I've got this deal," which put a gun to the head of the president. That was exactly the thing they were concerned about. It turned out okay, but that was not a good tactic on President Carter's part, I think. His mission did turn out to be very beneficial. But the way that he handled the press could have caused a problem. We were able to work our way out of it, but it could have caused a problem. He certainly had some people on the National Security Council very uptight about his approach, even though the net of it was very positive. . . .

Now, in that meeting . . . we had the whole National Security Council there. It was a very detailed discussion on a very serious issue. There was nobody in that room who was more knowledgeable about the issues in detail and in concept than President Clinton. It was that meeting more than anything that formed my view of him as somebody who, when it came down to an issue that he was going to be responsible for making a big decision on, he was there. So the view that he did not have the national security background and therefore would be weak in that area—the premise was correct, but the conclusion was not correct. I was very impressed with his grasp of the issues and his insight as to what the risks and dangers were and how they could be dealt with.

Kim Dae-jung, South Korean president: [Bill Clinton] has a warm heart for the victims of poverty and disease and disasters. He was always thinking about supporting those who are in need.

In September 1999, there was the APEC meeting in New Zealand, but at that time coincidentally, in East Timor there was a great massacre by a militia.[37] . . . So in the APEC meeting I proposed to discuss the East Timor matter, but the host, the government in New Zealand, said the APEC is for economic matters,

---

37. In August 1999, an overwhelming majority of voters in East Timor declared their independence from Indonesia, sparking a violent military and paramilitary backlash among anti-independence forces. Some reputable estimates indicate that over 200,000 refugees fled the area at a time when larger violence was feared.

so the political issues should be ruled out in discussion. In response I said that this is the gathering of the world leaders, but there is a massacre in the neighborhood. If you say that this meeting is only for the economy, that we will ignore this matter, then what would people call us as world leaders? We have responsibility.... I brought that issue to President Clinton and he said he was in full agreement with me. He suggested I meet first with President Jiang Zemin of China. I said I already met him but I didn't get any response. Then President Clinton said that if that is the case, then you and I have to take the lead.

We met the Australian prime minister [John] Howard. So we three became the first to bring up this issue. We made a very strong appeal to the Indonesian representative when we met with him. We said that ... if you just ignore the militia's massacre on the East Timor people, we will not just watch and sit idly. If APEC is not taking the issue as an official agenda because APEC is an economic body, then the ... leaders who are agreeing with me will make a statement criticizing your practice in an individual capacity. We will do so, so please resolve the situation before we take action.

The negotiation and the discussion went on three or four hours.... The Indonesian representative began contact with his government and around midnight the Indonesian government made an announcement that they will stop the militia's massacre.... Later the East Timor activist [José] Ramos-Horta, who became the president of East Timor, came to Prime Minister Howard and President Clinton and said thank you, but they in one accord said that President Kim Dae-jung of South Korea is the person you have to thank.... [But] without President Clinton's determination at that time I may not have resolved the issue by myself. Ramos-Horta later made a statement; he came to us and said, "You saved 100 million lives."

Kim: In 2003 I was also retired and [Clinton] was retired as well, he visited the Kim Dae-jung Library here [in Seoul], and we talked about the inter-Korean issues and Korean peninsula in general. President Clinton at that time disclosed why he [did] not go to North Korea—he had made a commitment to me to visit there in 2000 when I visited North Korea. He explained that at that time the negotiations in the Middle East were going well between Palestinians, Arafat, and Israel. President Clinton said that he was going to Pyongyang; then Arafat said to please not to, and he made a commitment that he would deal with the Middle East issues peacefully and properly, if President Clinton would please not go to Pyongyang. He very strongly urged and asked him not to go, so President Clinton informed North Korea that his visit there was canceled.

President Clinton at the time said to me that if he had gone to Pyongyang [instead], or he could remain one more year in the presidency, then he was fully confident they could resolve all the Korean peninsula issues.

24

With Foreign Leaders

Those who watched Bill Clinton closely in his interactions with foreign leaders describe a president who was at first distracted by the formalities of highly orchestrated exchanges, but who rather quickly came to find common ground with those he learned were international politicians, and thus who shared common problems and aspirations. The subsequent rapport and trust Clinton developed with his fellow leaders around the world was sometimes an essential ingredient for generating state action that might not otherwise have been possible. Oral history testimony is an especially valuable source about the details of such relationships, which form the backdrop of the major foreign policy advances in every administration.

Strobe Talbott, deputy secretary of state: There's a lot of Poli-Sci [political science] shit about *It's systems and it's governments that interact, and people sort of add at the margins.* It's just not true.... [A] key element [is] personality and personal chemistry.... Having Boris Yeltsin as the president of Russia during [our] time is one of the minor miracles of history, because you can imagine a lot of [other] people having been the leader of Russia.... Clinton got Yeltsin to do stuff that was politically radioactive for Yeltsin to do. He got him to do it because Yeltsin trusted him. *Bill, my friend Bill, won't see it my way but he's not going to screw me.*

Mack McLarty, White House chief of staff: President Yeltsin did not particularly like or respect Bill Clinton during that first meeting [in Vancouver].[1] They had met for fifteen minutes in the campaign, and he thought Bush was going to win. Yeltsin was older, he viewed Clinton as his junior, and he had some defensiveness in his personality, as well.

So they had lunch, and it was a very stiff lunch. We stayed for the reception time, and you could tell this was not the warm rapport that you would hope. I pulled [Canadian] Prime Minister [Brian] Mulroney aside, and I said, "Brian, this just doesn't strike me as a warm and engaging encounter here." ... He said,

---

1. The Vancouver Summit, with Clinton and Yeltsin, occurred on April 3–4, 1993.

"Let me work on it. I see the seriousness of it." He did a superb job during that luncheon of at least not having them isolate and get their proverbial backs up with their position, keep it as warm as they could. He reported to me how it had gone: you needed to wake up worrying about it, but not lose sleep over it. [They] had at least had reasonably good rapport.

Well, Yeltsin took a tour of Vancouver, of the bay, and we had a dinner that night. The dinner was not as well orchestrated as it should have been. It was at a very nice restaurant, and it was overly formal, in my view. . . . Yeltsin had had several drinks touring the bay and had several drinks before we sat down for dinner and several glasses of wine immediately after we sat down for dinner. . . . [It] was clear after President Yeltsin turned away about three courses of food that he was not going to eat that evening. Chris[topher] turned to me and said, "I don't believe we're going to have a very productive dinner." [*laughter*] . . .

So the next day we had a fair meeting at best. [Viktor] Ilyushin was Yeltsin's Bruce Lindsey—he was not chief of staff, but he had worked for Yeltsin for about twenty to twenty-five years, very close to him, kind of his executive secretary. I called Victor aside. . . . "Victor, we've only got six more hours of meetings. We haven't gotten anything accomplished here, and expectations are very high for this summit. We're going to have to get down to business and deal with some of these issues and come out with at least a semblance of progress." He said, "I agree."

The next morning, Yeltsin walked in, and it was remarkable, because even after these kinds of abuses, he just looked perfect. I mean erect, looked like he had just gotten twelve hours of sleep. I had had one glass of wine and looked haggard. He walked in and said, "Mr. President, we've got to get down to business this morning," and Victor winked at me, like that was the phrase. During the meeting, the first time that, as Yeltsin discussed a particular matter, he said, "Beel." From that time on, it was never "President Clinton," it was "Beel, my friend Beel." You could see the chemistry was established, and the mutual respect had been established in the meeting. My point is, without Prime Minister Mulroney's fine and skilled and experienced hand at that lunch, I do not believe we would have reached that initial rapport, which obviously was crucial for, really, the security of mankind, without being too dramatic about it.

Nancy Soderberg, deputy national security advisor: Clinton just liked Yeltsin; they were two peas in a pod. They almost looked like each other: they were gregarious, loved life, and had their own personal foibles. He just loved Yeltsin's guts. He just was gutsy, and Clinton was determined to do whatever he could for him. They had their differences. A number of times Yeltsin was clearly drunk on the phone. We learned quickly to call him only really early in the morning, his time. . . . Clinton had a real affection for him and spent a lot of time on the phone with him, a lot of time engaging him, pushing very hard to include him in the G8, and [on the] sensitivities of NATO expansion. . . . Clinton likes gutsy fighters. He's one, and he sees it in other people.

Mickey Kantor, secretary of commerce: [Clinton's] first few meetings with foreign leaders, like the one with Jiang Zemin in Seattle[2] was a disaster, it was awful.... Their first meeting, Seattle at the APEC, sitting in a room there, sitting in two chairs, the acolytes on one side, the acolytes on the other, and I would have sworn that by the end of the meeting we might be at war with each other. I mean, it was the old Communist rhetoric versus our hard-nosed rhetoric, both didn't deviate one iota from their talking points. It was the most stilted, awful meeting I've ever seen Bill Clinton have with anybody. Part of it was the president at first was not comfortable with foreign leaders. He felt somehow that was different than politicians at home.... Once he realized they were just like him, once he realized they were just politicians, he was terrific, and they got it.

Fernando Henrique Cardoso, president of Brazil: I came to America I guess in '95, in March or April, the day of the Oklahoma bombing.... It was a state visit. A state visit is very formal. You have a banquet and speeches and music. I thought it would probably be canceled. [Clinton] decided not to cancel.....
The Oval Office is like in Brazil, too. It is always formal. One president is on one side, the others are looking. The only one, the president, has to say something. You cannot say any important thing. It is formal. The ministers are there, the assistants, the diplomats, so on and so forth.

But at some point, the presidents are alone. Again, if you speak the language it is better. I was with Bill in his office, the small one there [just off the Oval Office]. The first thing he said to me was, "What can I do to help Brazil? What can I do to help you?" The second thing was, "Do you want to go to the bathroom?" [*laughter*] You can't imagine how this is important. Because all the time you are president no one will ask you about this. It's human. That is Clinton. "What can I do for Brazil? How can I help you? Do you want to go to the bathroom?" This is very simple to characterize how it is [with] him. He is a man who has a vision, who has generosity, and is [also] human and practical.

James Steinberg, deputy national security advisor: [He] understood [foreign] leaders magnificently, understood them as politicians, as human beings, as world leaders. He understood what made them work and what made them tick and how to get them on his side. There's a magnetism about Clinton. There was no leader who didn't want to be with him, spend time with him, engage with him, be associated with him. It was unbelievably magnetic, especially for other leaders, even more than for other people, even though he has that magnetism generally. He was able to be effective and influential because people wanted to work with him.

---

2. The Seattle meeting of the Asia-Pacific Economic Cooperation group occurred in November 1993.

He could always put himself in the other person's shoes. He could imagine what they were thinking, what their domestic political problems were, what their challenges were. He was always able to come up with creative solutions that would help them win. He was never interested in scoring points or in making somebody do something. He was always trying to get in their skin. You'd say, "Mr. President, we have to get the Russians to do this." He'd say, "Think about how Yeltsin would think about it. Maybe he just can't do this," or, "What can we do to help him do this?" He had a strong sense of empathy and understanding of what motivated other leaders and what drove them. He never felt that it was useful to be contentious or combative. He'd be strong and clear, but he understood that at the end of the day, the best way was to convince the other guy to want what you wanted. His effectiveness on a one-on-one level was masterful.

Thomas Pickering, undersecretary of state for political affairs:[3] I have to say I never saw anybody deal as effectively with foreigners firsthand as Clinton. He was remarkable. He had eight years to do it. He had this combination of youth, brightness, sympathy, and analytical personality. In many ways he loved political analysis and also had this ability to combine empathy and generosity and basically sort of a "Trust me, we'll help you" kind of approach to foreign leaders that caught their attention.... [There] was a charismatic quality about Clinton that was not replicated in Bush, even though Bush and Clinton probably were very close together.

Sandy Berger, national security advisor (on the foreign leaders with whom President Clinton had a particularly special relationship): There were quite a few. I'd start with Tony Blair, who in many ways modeled his campaign after Clinton's campaign. Some of his aides actually followed us around in 1992. They watched the Clinton campaign, they learned from it, and then the whole notion of the "third way," which is taking a left party and moving it to the center, was something that Blair followed.

President Clinton was particularly fond of President [Fernando Henrique] Cardoso of Brazil and President Zedillo of Mexico. He liked [French president François] Mitterrand a great deal, and [Jacques] Chirac he got along well with. He had a great affection for [Germany's] Helmut Kohl. They were both large men. They loved to have good meals. Chancellor Kohl would come to Washington every year or so and they would go out to a restaurant in Georgetown called Filomena, which is not known for the quality but for the quantity of food. They'd sit in a back room. Often it was the two of them. I'd be there, plus Kohl's foreign policy advisor, Joachim Bitterlich. They'd go on for three or four hours, talking about everything from Turkish accession to the EU to Kohl's background.

---

3. Pickering's interview was recorded as a part of the Miller Center's George H. W. Bush Oral History Project. Pickering had been President Bush's ambassador to the United Nations.

Kohl was really pro-American. He was, I think, five years old when the American army marched into his town and liberated it from the Nazis. He was a very sentimental man as well as a very strong man, and truly believed that Germany's future lay in being embedded in Europe and Europe being embedded in a trans-Atlantic relationship. . . .

He and Boris Yeltsin obviously developed a very close relationship. He believed that Yeltsin really was the embodiment of Russian democracy, and that Yeltsin, for all of his deficiencies, truly believed in democracy. Whenever Yeltsin got in trouble he went back to the people. He had a referendum. His instinct was democratic.

There were six prime ministers of Japan during the eight years of Clinton's term. He was particularly fond of [Kiichi] Miyazawa and [Keizo] Obuchi. Miyazawa actually was prime minister twice, in 1993 and then subsequently in this period where Japan was having a hard time keeping a stable government. But the two that he particularly liked were Miyazawa and Obuchi. In fact, Obuchi died in '98 or '99 and we flew all night to go to his funeral and then turned around and flew all the way back because of Clinton's respect for the Japanese and affection for Obuchi.

He liked President [Jerry John] Rawlings of Ghana, who was a very colorful character. We probably had the largest single event of the presidency in Ghana. We had probably a million people show up at the stadium for the president when he spoke.[4] Rawlings was a kind of larger-than-life character.

Bertie Ahern, the Taoiseach of Ireland, was our partner with Tony Blair in Northern Ireland. Finally I would say Yitzhak Rabin may have been first among equals, perhaps Blair was first among equals, but he developed a very close affection and respect and friendship with Rabin, was particularly shaken by Rabin's assassination. I'm sure I'm leaving out others as I make that quick tour.

James Steinberg (on Clinton's relationship with Tony Blair): It was extraordinary. They'd get going and it was a virtual cycle of energy and excitement and innovation about ideas. You'd feel like they were two kids, their eyes wide open with the possibilities. They were passionate about policy and ideas. They wanted to talk about these things and go on and on. There was nothing that didn't interest the two of them. They had so many things in common in terms of their approaches to government and what they thought was the function and responsibility of government. It was quite extraordinary.

Kim Dae-jung, president of South Korea: If you asked me to tell about him in one word, he is a man with an unpolluted soul and great zeitgeist, the spirit of the times.

---

4. That speech was delivered on March 23, 1998.

Vaclav Havel: At the end of my term of office I visited President Clinton and I received the highest respect a head of state can possibly receive. I think it doesn't happen very often because there are two hundred states all around the world, and you don't very often have all these military parades and all these luncheons and official formalities, whereas I received it. They asked me before I came what sort of music I would like to have played at the [state] dinner. And I said would it be possible to have Lou Reed playing there?[5] He felt a bit uneasy about it with those bureaucrats from the office, from the administration. Hillary [Rodham Clinton] went down to the rehearsals to see that it was not too wild or too inappropriate. I think it was the first time and last time that such music, such hard rock music was played on the premises there. But you know the result was excellent because I could see all these gray-haired distinguished congressmen, Republicans and all sorts, they were all jiggling and wiggling about in the rhythm of the music, probably just enjoying it because it was evoking their youth and their young years, so they enjoyed it.

Tony Lake, national security advisor: I remember before the first meeting with [Syrian president Hafez al-] Assad—he was famous for never having to break to pee during meetings—and joking with the president about whether we were going to be able to outlast him or not. The president obviously took precautions and I, like an idiot, was so sleepy, I forgot and I had lots of coffee. I was humiliated after two and a quarter hours by having to excuse myself from the room for a while. I could see the president smirking. He said something about camels.

Betty Currie, personal secretary: [Yasser] Arafat would give him the same gift every time he came, a mother-of-pearl nativity scene. We had eight or ten of them.

Tony Lake: He was great at [relations with foreign leaders]. And in ways that I found initially frustrating, in fact, as did Chris and the vice president, Gore. One thing that struck me constantly, especially with democratically elected leaders, is that they share, the leaders, an experience that nobody else in the room has had. And there is not only, as I have said in flights of rhetorical fancy, a "language of democracy," which there is, but there is a language of leaders who are facing,

---

5. Lou Reed (1942–2013) was an American rock musician who fronted the band Velvet Underground. Reed had a niche counterculture following in the United States, but was immensely popular among Eastern Europeans. Havel once credited Reed with making him president. In the late 1960s he smuggled albums by Velvet Underground and Frank Zappa into Czechoslovakia, music that became popular within the Prague underground—especially with the local band Plastic People of the Universe. When Soviet authorities later began to crack down on unapproved forms of artistic expression, including this brand of rock music, the Czech opposition grew, eventually forming Charter 77—which Havel headed. It was later a leading force in the Velvet Revolution.

even in dictatorships, the problems of public opinion. The two things leaders could always agree on, in every meeting I've sat in, are that the world would be a better place without the press. In a practical sense—in principle, they're all for it. And, secondly, the currency traders should be shot, but maybe a little torture beforehand would be useful. Those are the two things I always hear leaders absolutely agree on and bond about.

Warren Christopher, secretary of state: He got along with a lot of foreign leaders who came in thinking they would play hardball and found him irresistible. It's not a universal phenomenon, but it's a higher batting average than anybody I've ever seen.... Lech Walesa[6] was a little beyond his pale, because he talked for forty-four minutes in a forty-five-minute meeting, but nevertheless, on the whole, he made friends, not just in large audiences but in small.

* * *

Q: Were there any particular cases of people with whom he had trouble or who seemed resistant to his charms?
James Steinberg, deputy national security advisor: I would say that the closest was [Russian prime minister Vladimir] Putin.[7] I think Putin was quite indifferent to it. Clinton got it right away. Clinton was very skeptical about Putin from the first meeting. It's so ironic with [George W.] Bush talking about looking into Putin's soul. Clinton looked into Putin's soul too, and he saw something completely different. He saw someone who was very cold and calculating, who was not trustworthy.

Tony Lake: I'd say that the three most difficult individuals and groups that I had to deal with were Saddam Hussein, Slobodan Milosevic, and the president's political advisors and schedulers. [*laughter*] I won't put them in any particular order. And I couldn't use the Pentagon against the third, which is very frustrating.... The [political] advisors were constantly ... doing everything they could to make it hard to schedule these meetings with foreign leaders. The saving grace was that he would overrule them, which nobody outside ever understood. I cultivated, which is too calculating a word, because they became real friends of mine, Betty Currie and Nancy Hernreich. The keepers of the gate.

---

6. Lech Walesa was the president of Poland (1990–1995). He formerly was chair of the union-based Solidarity movement in Poland and in that role was central to the liberation of the country from longtime Soviet control.

7. Putin was Russia's prime minister from 1999 to 2000 and again from 2008 to 2012.

Part IV

POLITICS AND THE
CLINTON WHITE HOUSE

25

Inside the Washington Community

When Bill Clinton arrived in Washington in January 1993, he assumed the most powerful office in the world—and yet by constitutional design and practice he stepped onto a political landscape already populated with established institutions that also had claims on the direction of the nation's government. President Clinton, and those who came with him into the White House, certainly understood intellectually that other actors had key roles in governing the nation. But the reality of fitting the Clinton presidency into this existing structure of political institutions no doubt required some adjustment. The modern American political system gives the president unique advantages in leading the nation. But there is no obligation, in the Constitution or the American political culture, for others to follow. The first major institution the Clinton team had to engage was the Washington press corps.

Tony Lake, national security advisor: Colin [Powell] had been one of the first people I'd talked to when I came to Washington to take on the job. I remember his confirming my view of how to deal with the press. I mean, this is Colin Powell, hero of Desert Storm . . . and he'd been national security advisor and all that. I said to him . . ., "So just tell me about what a day is like in your life as the chair of the Joint Chiefs, so I can understand it." He said, "Well, it begins every morning with my going out on the porch of my house and looking around for the newspaper and discovering, excuse me, that the *Washington Post* has been jammed up my ass." I thought to myself, *Whoa, this is going to be tough. If this is happening to Colin Powell, what's going to happen to mere mortals?*

Leon Panetta, White House chief of staff: I never quite understood this but initially this president came in with an opportunity to become more like Kennedy than almost any president since Kennedy—young, exciting, etc. I think the press was just waiting there to develop that same relationship. And almost from the beginning, whether it was the president or the First Lady or even Stephanopoulos to that extent, something developed that bruised that relationship. . . . One of the things [Press Secretary] Mike [McCurry] and I kept doing was saying to the president, "You've got to take the time to sit down with these people, talk with them, because frankly, you're one of the brightest people around and the press loves that. They'll respect your intelligence." I think the president got better at it as time went on but it was tough. That's one of the things you have to deal with.

* * *

Q: How long did the honeymoon period last?
Joan Baggett, White House political director: Ten hours maybe. [*laughter*] When was the gays in the military thing? Not long. Literally, I think, about a week or so. It just seemed to hit all at once. I remember, this was only a few days into the term and I can't remember if this was caused by a specific leak or what the occasion was. All the staff was called over to the residence, to the East Room.[1] [The president] addressed us and talked about how reporters would try to get us to talk about what was going on and that people shouldn't do that, what we were trying to do. I don't think it had much effect.

I don't know if things have changed in general and this is just the nature of the game now, or if it related to the way he personally dealt with people, but probably in that campaign and certainly in that White House and surrounding consultants and all, it not only wasn't discouraged to talk to the press, it was almost like everyone was expected to. I'm old-school Washington, where the staff was there to serve the elected person. Now you have rock star staffers, where it's all about them, and some have done very well at that. So there's probably not going to be any decrease in it. Certainly in that White House you had a lot of people who felt free to speak to the press on everything that was going on.

Often, and this may be the case in any elected situation, but I was shocked when I would read, even in the *Post* and the *Times*, the articles about any given initiative where the information was just absolutely inaccurate. They were quoting unnamed sources, and the only thing I could deduct from it is that people who weren't in the room . . . [were trying] to make it look like they were important and were in the loop, when they weren't.

* * *

Although both legislative chambers were controlled by Democrats after the election of 1992, the Congress Bill Clinton joined in Washington was not an institution eagerly waiting to follow his direction from the White House.

William Galston, deputy domestic policy advisor: [The] best preparation for being president is to be governor of a large state, and the worst to be governor of a small state. . . . What's typical about talented governors of small states is that they are head and shoulders above the other politicians in their state, and they

---

1. The East Room is the largest space in the White House residence, typically used for big gatherings and events. That this meeting took place there is an indication of the importance the subject held for the president—a message he wanted to get out to a broad internal audience.

can—through force of intellect and character and a loyal dedicated staff—move the political system of those states.... [In a small state], not only are you accustomed to thinking of the legislature as something that can be manipulated, but your sense of executive leadership is a highly personalized one, and the idea of a structure that enables your effectiveness is not on your radar screen. You do it yourself. You deliver speeches by writing twenty words on the back of an envelope, and if you're really smart and really quick that's enough. You're personally involved in every detail of the policy process. You are the sun, and everybody rotates around you, right? A lot of people have access to you. That's classic governor-of-a-small-state syndrome.... Washington is not that way *at all*.

John Hilley, White House congressional liaison: [T]hose first years were extremely difficult. Clinton's as good personally with other political people as is imaginable. I can't think of anyone who's better. But on the other hand, you had a Democratic majority in Congress that had spent the last twelve years in a completely opposition posture.[2] They were good at fighting things. They weren't particularly good at thinking about how to get things done. Here's a young guy who has been governor of Arkansas. That doesn't generate a high level of respect for his legislative or policy skills.

Charles Brain, Democratic congressional staffer, later White House congressional liaison: The perspective that we on the staff learned from [Congressman Dan] Rostenkowski and internalized was that it's much easier to work with a president of the other party. Anything that you can do as bipartisan compromise is progress.... [There] were only a handful of members of Congress who were elected [in 1992] who hadn't taken their districts by a bigger percentage than Clinton did. Nobody felt particularly indebted to Bill Clinton for getting there.... [The] White House folks *always* know they know better than the folks on the Hill, because they got their guy elected. Be it Jimmy Carter, Governor Clinton. "We got elected so you'll do what we want. We know—we're smarter." [But] the clock is ticking on them; they've only got so much time. From a congressional perspective ... [it's] "We've got time. We'll take it."

Lawrence Stein, White House congressional liaison:[3] I certainly never felt that President Clinton had the ability to exercise [party] discipline. He had the ability to cajole, he had the various powers of the White House that he could use, but discipline was a bridge too far. ...

---

2. The period referred to here encompasses the Reagan and Bush 41 presidencies, 1981 through 1993.

3. Stein's comments were made in a group oral history interview with congressional relations specialists from Presidents Nixon through Clinton. A published version of that interview appears in Russell L. Riley, ed., *Bridging the Constitutional Divide: Inside the White House Office of Legislative Affairs* (College Station: Texas A&M University Press, 2010), 75–76.

In Clinton's first year, Richard Shelby, a Democrat [from Alabama], called [Al] Gore and said, "Come on up and talk to me about the BTU [British thermal unit] tax," which Gore proceeded to do. They talked, and when they came out, the assembled Alabama press was outside the door, and Shelby announced publicly his opposition to the BTU tax. Gore, justifiably angry, goes back to the White House and says, "We can't allow this." The only thing they could think to do was to shut down about seventy jobs. They went after the Huntsville Aerospace Center. Not only did Shelby subsequently change parties, he is now, I think, the most popular politician in the state of Alabama and is utterly unassailable. And you can trace his heroism to that moment. So when you talk about party discipline, you should remember that incident, and so should virtually every president.

Senator Alan Simpson (R-WY): [Clinton] never understood the Senate when he got there, because he'd never been a legislator. When you come into the Senate as a governor or professor or teacher, you're in deep crap. I've watched governors come there.... If they've never been a legislator, they look upon a legislative body as a bunch of goddamn, know-nothing clods.... So Bill had no idea of the arcane workings of the U.S. Senate, except he learned fast.

Senator Tom Daschle (D-SD): I would say the overall first impression of the Clinton administration was not very good because of the fights, because of the need [among Democrats] to be on the defensive almost right out of the box on issues that most members didn't want to have to deal with.

Q: Like gays in the military.
Daschle: Yes....

Q: What exactly was the administration doing that made folks question their competence?
Daschle: Well you start with the nominations. You go from that to a vague sense of what the president was trying to do in his first time in office. There really wasn't a clear appreciation of what his priorities were or what he wanted to do. It appeared that he just wanted to do everything. He kind of threw everything at the Congress in the hopes that something would ultimately stick, have traction, pass through.... [And] especially in the earlier years, they expected allegiance from the Congress and it was not always provided, and that caused a relationship rupture that persisted for a long time.

Bruce Reed, deputy domestic policy advisor:[4] We wanted to flood the circuits. We figured that Congress would slow-walk enough things as it was, so that we

---

4. Reed's comments were made at a group oral history symposium of nine former White House domestic policy advisors, published as Michael Nelson and Russell L. Riley, eds., *Governing at Home: The White House and Domestic Policymaking* (Lawrence: University Press of Kansas, 2011), 59.

didn't have to make it any easier for them. One of the areas where we ran into the most difficulty was that the congressional system is not well set up to handle a couple of high priorities at the same time. Bill Clinton actually wanted to pursue welfare reform and health care at the same time, because he felt that they were intrinsically related as policy and that they spoke to different anxieties of the electorate. Unfortunately, they went through the same committees. And even worse, the House wanted to do health care and not welfare reform, and the [Senate] Finance Committee wanted to do welfare reform and not health care.

Corey Parker, chief legislative assistant for Senator Edward M. Kennedy:[5] I think that Senator Kennedy, after the election of Bill Clinton, had been looking forward to a new period that could have been comparable to the Great Society. We hadn't had a president we could work with for a long time. It had been difficult with President [Jimmy] Carter. Until President Clinton came in, in 1993, the Democrats in the Senate hadn't had, at least since 1968, a Democratic president who they felt could lead the charge on issues that liberal Democrats in the Democratic caucus wanted to pursue the most. Since 1968 it basically had been a finger-in-the-dike type of Senate for Democrats, where a lot of the accomplishments were about preventing retreats rather than about making advances. There were some major legislative developments, but the 1992 election was seen as a new day, and there were great hopes for it. They quickly began to fade during the first two years of the Clinton administration.

Bernard Nussbaum, White House counsel: When we came in, the first day—January 21st, 1993—I'm having lunch in the White House mess, and I get a call saying, "The president has to see you immediately." All of a sudden I'm a real big shot. I'm in the White House, and on the first day the president has to see me immediately. "Come to the Oval Office." I go to the Oval Office and there's Stephanopoulos in the office. Other people too, I don't remember who, and Clinton says to me, "Bernie, we have a big problem on Capitol Hill. [Attorney general nominee] Zoë Baird is testifying, and it's this nanny thing—they didn't pay their Social Security tax.[6] The Democratic senators are saying we should pull her name. You've got to help me. You have to get involved with us."

So I say, "Wait, Zoë sounds pretty good. I understand that she has this problem, and I think it's too bad that she has it, but didn't we *know* about it?" I mean, I wasn't involved in the vetting. They said, "Oh yes, we found out some stuff

---

5. Parker's remarks were recorded in an interview for the Miller Center's Edward M. Kennedy Oral History Project.

6. Zoë Baird was a prominent American attorney with major corporate law experience. She had, however, employed an illegal alien to provide childcare and did not pay the necessary taxes for that help. Clinton thus dropped her nomination and turned to Judge Kimba Wood— who also was found to have hired an undocumented immigrant for household help. She was not nominated. Clinton ultimately nominated, successfully, Janet Reno.

about it." "Well, if we knew about it, I think we need to stand by her." I had no vested interest in this appointment at this point. I wanted a good attorney general, but I hadn't been involved.... So I started tentatively: "Mr. President," I say, "I think it may be a mistake. I think we should just try to ride it out until the Democratic senators back us. We should be sticking with her. Yes, she'll pay her taxes and we'll put new rules into effect," which I eventually did. "No, no," Stephanopoulos said, "That's crazy." I don't know, maybe I'm overstating it a little bit.

Others were disagreeing all over the office.... I said, "Let's stay with Zoë Baird. We lose, we lose. We'll appoint somebody else, but at least we haven't withdrawn." I'm saying this a little more affirmatively now than I did in the Oval Office at that time, but that was my position. It was the first hour of this administration. "Let me think about it," the president says. An hour later he says, "I can't do it. We're going to have to get rid of her." ... Now, what's the dominant impression that's being given off with this thing? Weakness. This guy can be *gotten* to. This administration can be rolled. All you have to do is keep up the pressure.

[Weeks later] as we were standing in the Oval Office, we were about to go out in the Rose Garden to announce that we were going to nominate Janet Reno, and I was there with the president, I think the vice president was there, and he gave his final approval. Right before we went out, because everyone was talking about nominating a woman, "Bernie," he said, "this better work, because if it doesn't work, we're going to cut your blank off and we'll nominate you for attorney general." [*laughter*] I said, "Mr. President, I hope it works now with even greater strength than I even thought before." [*laughter*] Fortunately for me, it worked.

* * *

Q: One of the image problems that the president had during the first year was the sense that he wasn't presidential, whatever that means. Did you ever try, through polling, to help him figure out how to develop an image of being "more presidential"?
Stanley Greenberg, pollster: We tracked the question of whether people thought he was in over his head, which was getting at that. We were focused on that question. There was a percentage who thought he was not up to the job. It was substantial, particularly in the first three months of the presidency, which was a very ugly period as the public watched this mess on display. Some of that also focused on whether he was strong enough and also whether he would waver once he faced pressure, which was, I thought, the core element of this issue.... We did some research focused on this question in the summer of '93. I think it was called the "presidential project," or something.... What we found there was that mastery of the Congress [formed] the perception of whether he was strong enough. If you weren't a strong enough president to

master the Congress then you were not going to be successful as a president. You were going to be overwhelmed. Mastery of the Congress was a critical piece to strength as a president.

That was part of our thinking in the fall as we talked about planning ahead. That's also a trap, because the Congress is unmanageable. So you have a standard for strength that is rooted in mastering the Congress, but in the end the Congress can't be mastered.

Leon Panetta, White House chief of staff: For Clinton there was always a sense that he could bring anybody into the Oval Office and convince them of the right thing to do, through his personality or his arguments or what have you. I think what concerned him is that it was a much tougher sell in Washington, because you're dealing with the House [and] a lot more egos on the Senate side who have been through this. A lot of those members have told presidents to go to hell, and there are some who have made it a career.

Suddenly you're in a different game where you're dealing with people who, no matter what you say to them, may not support you. I think he found that frustrating because he always felt if he had enough time he could basically convince anybody to do anything.

Q: So part of your job was to convince him he didn't have enough time?
Panetta: Howard [Paster, the first congressional liaison] and I had to convince him that there were some people you just don't waste your time on, and you have to focus on those that are doable, the bunch you could convince. That's where you spend your time. And sometimes it has nothing to do with the substance of what you're trying to do but an awful lot to do with other things, which I think he understood.

There were a couple of problems with the president. Normally, you use the president as the last step. I will work the member, Howard will work the member, Cabinet secretaries may work that member, if they happened to be in an area that involves that jurisdiction or somebody who is a personal friend. Lloyd Bentsen, for example, had a lot of personal friends in the Senate so I'd use that. But when it came down to the president of the United States making the call or inviting that member to the Oval Office, that's the last step out of the box.

At that point a president, if it's like Lyndon Johnson, basically says, "I want you to do this, I need you to do this, I absolutely need you to get this vote across." You have to be very clear about what this is about. Generally what would happen with Clinton is he would listen to somebody who might have a very different view and he would give that individual the impression that "Well, there's something to what you say." Yet he would say, "But this is what we're trying to do." And suddenly that member could walk out of the Oval Office thinking . . . that they had been successful in convincing the president as to their position.

So there was always a lot of repair work to be done. The president got better at this as time went on, but these are the early days. I think the president eventually learned that there were some members you just had to be very clear as to what you were saying.

* * *

Q: *In 1993, you had forty-two or forty-three Republicans sign on to a series of "Dear Colleague" letters to [Senate Minority Leader] Bob Dole, basically saying that they were going to back whatever he did, at least on the economic policy front. How did you get everybody together on something as big as economic policy?*
Senator Alan Simpson (R-WY): That's very easy. They wanted to be back in the majority. In the caucus you could say, "You sons of bitches, you want to be back? You want to get back in the big room over there? You could be in the Mansfield Room for lunch instead of over here."[7] [*laughing*] "You want to have more staff again with more money? Want to be the chairman? Then there's only one way, one way only: *stick together. . . .* stick together like adhesive. There's no mystery."

Mack McLarty, White House chief of staff: Politics is a contact sport. . . . [Senator Alfonse] D'Amato,[8] who is not an unlikable fellow in some ways, had a quote in the *New York Times* in—I think it was '94. He said, "We hit him hard in the campaign, and we hit him hard in '93, but we're going to have to hit him harder for him to stay down." That's a pretty animated statement from a moderate Republican senator from New York, which is a Democratic state. But that goes to the actual visceral feeling that we've got to just literally kill this guy for him to stay down, or I think he'll get up at the count of nine and knock us out.

Warren Christopher, secretary of state: It's clear that Clinton has a group of detractors that have just more than normal animosity toward him. Politics is a rough business and anybody who is in it knows that it's, in many ways, a very hardball business. But there's something about President Clinton that takes it beyond, for a number of his detractors. I think we've all asked ourselves "why" and have not found a fully adequate answer.

One thing I think has to do with his "Southern-ness" and the fact that he came from a state that's not very highly regarded nationally. And to many well-educated people in the East and the Midwest he's a kind of Southern phenomenon in whom they sort of bundle up their resentment against ambitious people from the South. I don't know why that should be, but there is an element of that.

---

7. The Mansfield Room, named to honor former Senate majority leader Mike Mansfield (1903–2001), a Montana Democrat, is an elegant space in the U.S. Capitol normally reserved for use by the majority party.

8. Alfonse D'Amato, a New York Republican, served in the U.S. Senate from 1981 to 1999.

There's another element, I think, that probably makes people very angry about him, and that is the ease with which he does things. He makes a lot of things look easy that for other people are very, very difficult to achieve. His Rhodes scholarship, his [five] terms as governor as a very young man, his getting to the presidency at a time that many people thought was premature in terms of age. So I think that built up this sense of animosity toward him.

Then he has some—I think he seems to appeal to a level of people in the country, or perhaps a group of people in the country, who are not highly regarded in the most elite sources. This is very difficult to explain without beginning to sound either racist or reverse racist, but I think the fact that Clinton is so appealing to African Americans and other minorities has a spin that was resented on the other end of that. I don't have much—it would take much more of a psychoanalyst than I to understand why it is, but it is certainly true that he does gather antagonism that's beyond the normal political range. And some of his personal qualities or his personal failings aggravate that to a very high degree.

William Galston: A lot of the president's political instincts were shaped by the bipartisan work on education and related issues that occurred within the National Governors Association. So the president, for fifteen years—ten years, anyway—had gotten into the habit of working with reform-minded, moderate Republicans across party lines to move education reform forward. He brought that mindset with him to negotiations with Congress. But that infuriated Democrats, particularly in the House, who thought of every transaction as a highly partisan transaction with a bright line. The bad guys were on the other side of the line. If you do business with them, as the president did—boom!

So that was very difficult, and I had some of my most difficult moments trying to negotiate with the House Education and Labor Committee, of which it was said during that period that they'd enact the Communist Manifesto if only they thought they had jurisdiction. [*laughter*] It was a very left-leaning bunch of folks, and the president in education and a number of other domestic policy areas was leaning more in a New Democrat direction—or certainly reflecting more of the bipartisan consensus that had occurred horizontally between the governors during the 1980s. . . . Bill Clinton brought those hopes and expectations and habits with him to Washington. One of his bitterest disappointments was the almost complete absence of bipartisan cooperation.

* * *

Although presidential terms are inevitably shaped by federal court decisions, every president also has the opportunity to alter the direction of the judicial branch with nominations to the bench.

Bernard Nussbaum: Now, this is probably one of the more important things I've said. This is sort of a criticism of the president. He didn't want to invest a lot of political capital in judicial appointments. He didn't really want to fight over judicial appointments, and he really wasn't very ideological with respect to judicial appointments. All he wanted was good judges, good lawyers, moderate.

Judge Abner Mikva, White House counsel: William Jefferson Clinton is one of the most complete political animals I have ever met.... [But] if you were to ask President Clinton what presidential prerogatives are, I think the appointment of judges would come far down the list. I think he'd talk about initiating legislation, about being a cheerleader for the country, using the commander-in-chief power and all that. Far down the list would be the appointment of judges.... The president was always reluctant to use up chits on judges. Hillary might have been willing, . . . but he didn't see that as his legacy.

Bernard Nussbaum: I said, "You know, for the next appointment to the Supreme Court, we should try to appoint a non-judge." We've changed the Supreme Court lately. It has become sort of a civil service thing. People sort of step up from appellate courts. It was never like that in our history. See again, no one knows history in the White House; everyone thinks the last twenty years is history. It's not history. You have to look over the last two hundred years. The Chief Justice of the 1954 Supreme Court, the one that presented *Brown v. Board of Education*, was Earl Warren. He was not a judge; he was a governor. Some of the key justices were Felix Frankfurter—he was a professor. And [William O.] Bill Douglas wasn't a judge; he was head of the SEC [Securities and Exchange Commission] and also a professor. You can have too many professors on the Court, but that's a separate issue.

Hugo Black was a United States senator.... That's the kind of Court you really want. Now, you can't change it overnight, but we really should try to appoint a lawyer to the Supreme Court, male or female. A lawyer, a professor, a political figure or something other than a judge, and [Clinton] agreed.

When a Supreme Court nomination arose, I was determined to affect this.[9] I had his permission, and he agreed with me on the concept. We had a whole list of people, and this is a sensitive thing. My first choice . . . was Mario Cuomo. He wasn't really my first choice, because I was still mad about his attempt to strangle Clinton in the cradle, but he was the president's first choice.[10] Cuomo turned it down relatively quickly.... Cuomo was a very good choice with my theory; that's why I didn't really oppose it in any way. I knew him and liked him. I thought he was a little flaky on certain occasions, but of course he acted in a strange way and turned it down.

---

9. Associate Justice Byron White, who had been nominated by John F. Kennedy, announced his retirement in March 1993. This was the first Democratic appointment to the Supreme Court since Lyndon Johnson named Thurgood Marshall in 1967.

10. In his oral history interview, Nussbaum recounted efforts by Cuomo to undermine Clinton's presidential aspirations in 1991–92.

So now I'm proceeding. Okay, he's out, or he's probably out—anything can happen until you make the appointment. Then I focus on a number of people and I get the president's permission—maybe I didn't get his permission, but I talked to him. I started thinking, *Who can I appoint?* It's very hard to find one of these figures. . . . I came up with three names and actually talked to each of them. The president agreed I could talk to them. They were three of the Cabinet members: Dick Riley, governor of South Carolina; Warren Christopher, new secretary of state . . .; and Bruce Babbitt, secretary of the interior. And I really went and spoke with all three just to feel them out. I spent three hours with Riley. They were shocked.

They were very honored, but shocked. They're politicians. They liked politics, and they liked being in the Cabinet obviously, but going into the Supreme Court is going into the monastery in a sense. So it's a little tricky, but I appealed to them. . . . We're like a day or two away from nominating Babbitt. . . . The president calls me and tells me we're not nominating Babbitt. I ask, "Why are we not nominating Babbitt?" He says, "I can't lose him." "What do you mean, you can't lose him?" I say. "Appoint somebody else as secretary of the interior, you'll appoint somebody else." "I can't," he says. . . . "Look, I have this problem out west." We had the grazing fees issues at the time. . . . He said, "I need him. He's the only person who can bridge the gap."[11] . . . So now I have to start this process again. I had a list, and I started focusing on Ruth Ginsburg.[12] A friend of hers was a close friend of mine. We ate dinner together in Washington when our friends were there from New York. We went to a restaurant in Washington. . . . So I meet with Ginsburg, and it was nice. We had a very pleasant dinner; it was very charming.

I looked at the lists that we started, and she was high up on that list. She was good. She was a woman, which was a plus. In my view, although not in the president's view, it was a plus that she was a Jew. There hadn't been a Jew on the Supreme Court in twenty-five years. I thought that was relevant, and I mentioned that to the president, but he said it's irrelevant. I think he dismissed it out of hand. That's what he did with me at least. I said, "It's relevant that she's Jewish." He said, "It's not relevant." I'm Jewish; he's not Jewish. I said, "There hasn't been a Jew since Abe Fortas was forced off the Court." But he says "No, I don't care about that." I said, "You don't?" He says, "We'll find somebody and we'll talk." I think he was serious about it, and then we looked into her background, which I knew a lot about.

---

11. Grazing fees—levies required for allowing livestock to feed on public lands—were a hot political issue at the time, with Clinton pushing for major increases. Babbitt, a westerner (from Arizona), was ultimately considered by Clinton indispensable for navigating through that problem.

12. Ruth Bader Ginsburg was in fact a sitting federal judge, on the U.S. Court of Appeals for the District of Columbia. However, she previously had been a law professor and a leading activist fighting gender discrimination.

She had an activist background, but moderate as a judge. She'd been a judge for twenty years, and she was not known as a flaming liberal or a dark conservative, but very balanced. And she was the right age, in a sense. See, we'll have to discuss judicial appointments in even more length. We weren't these ideologues looking to appoint forty-year-olds that will stay forever. We were looking for people who had lived, balanced people who had a life and a wide range of experience. So she fit those criteria, and it looked like it would be an attractive appointment.

I introduced the president to her and he's the most charming, handsome guy in the world. She looked up at him, and he looked down at her. They sort of go off together, the two of them. They go off for an hour and a half. I go to my office. I'm sitting in my office, and I get a call to come pick her up. I take her back and I say, "How did it go?" Well, it was wonderful. She saw the president, showed pictures of her children, grandchildren, and they talked about other things. She found him enormously charming and everything, but he didn't say anything.

Nothing is guaranteed, especially with this president. So she went back to her apartment. She was hopeful, but certainly not certain. So, I talked to the president after I sent her back. I said, "Well? We're going to go, right?" He said, "Yes, yes, okay, we'll appoint her." I said "Good. Why don't you give her a call?" He said, "I can't do that." This was in the afternoon, I think, if I have it right. "I've got some friends coming over, I've got to watch the Arkansas [basketball] game on television." I said, "What time does the Arkansas game start?" ... He said, "We're going to have dinner, the game will be over around 11 o'clock at night or midnight."[13]

So I go back in my office. I had this problem with Babbitt, so I was a little worried here. Every time I think I've got something done—I sit in my office, but I know he's going to do it. I have no doubt he's going to do it. So about 8 o'clock on a Sunday night, I'm in my office in the White House, mostly by myself, I think. I have this recollection. I call Ruth Ginsburg and I say, "Ruth, this is Bernie. Do me a favor, don't go to sleep tonight until you hear from the White House." [laughter] She started crying on the phone; it was very touching. ... She didn't go to sleep. He called her, and we announced her appointment the next day.

Judge Abner Mikva: At one point there was a vacancy on the U.S. Court of Appeals. ... This vacancy had come up and we were one vote shy in the Senate.

---

13. The date was June 13, 1993. In one crucial respect Nussbaum misrecalls: Clinton was not watching an Arkansas game, but Game Three of the National Basketball Association finals between the Chicago Bulls and the Phoenix Suns. There must have been added drama to the wait, as the game was a rare triple-overtime contest, with Michael Jordan's Bulls losing the contest, yet ultimately winning the series.

I think it was 51–49, and Bill Cohen, whom I've known a long time and was my locker-mate in the House gym, had indicated to me at one time that he would like to end up being a judge. He's a Republican senator from Maine. Maine then had a Democratic governor. As you know, when a vacancy occurs, the governor appoints to fill the vacancy.

I don't think it was my idea. I think whoever had the political desk for Clinton conceived of the idea—I guess I had been talking to him and told him that Cohen had once indicated an interest in the judgeship. He said, "If we appointed Cohen to the judgeship and he resigned from the Senate and the Democratic governor could appoint the senator, we could take back the Senate."
... "Interesting," he nodded, which he would do frequently when you blind-sided him with an idea. Then a day later the memo [on the idea] came back with this left hand "NO." ... I went to see him on something else.

He said, "If you're here about that memo—" I said no. "Don't you realize what they'd say if I did that? Slick Willie." And he was right, of course; they would have. So he [later] made Bill Cohen secretary of defense instead. And we never got the Senate seat.

26

Republican Revolution— and Recovery

The first two years of the Clinton presidency were extraordinarily difficult. Gays in the military, appointments problems, a fumbled stimulus package, Haiti, Somalia, and a failed health care reform effort, all combined with Democratic Party headaches over taxes, guns, and trade to put Clinton in a bad place politically in late 1994. The sum of these events, in harness with historical trends increasingly favoring Republicans in Southern House districts, pulled Clinton and his party down to a devastating defeat in the 1994 midterm elections. The House of Representatives went Republican for the first time since the early 1950s.

Afterward, Clinton was understandably dejected. But those around him describe a president who quickly sought to get back on his feet. Central to this effort was the political pollster Dick Morris, who had a long affiliation with Clinton reaching back to Arkansas, but had been displaced by others because of his unusual willingness to provide paid advice to Republicans and Democrats alike. Clinton evidently believed that if anybody could help him to find his way back to the top of his game, Morris could. This occasioned some odd dynamics at the White House—including, for a time, using the pseudonym "Charlie" for Morris to avoid alerting others that the ambidextrous pollster was about—but Clinton unexpectedly restored his political viability in time for re-election in 1996.

Two other factors contributed to Clinton's recovery. One was an act of domestic terrorism. The bombing of the Alfred Murrah Federal Building in Oklahoma City in April 1995 by anti-government radicals shocked the nation and provided Clinton a moment to reassert his leadership. Second, an overreaching House of Representatives made good on its threats to force a government shutdown if Clinton did not bend to their wishes on policy. As Clinton's congressional liaison John Hilley reported in his oral history, "It's only after Republicans came in and screwed up even more than could possibly be imagined that [Clinton] regained his footing finally."

Q: *How early are you picking up serious signals of problems for the midterms?*
Stanley Greenberg, pollster: Very early.... The thermometer score for the Democratic Party was continually on the decline and the Republican

thermometer was higher than the Democratic thermometer, like nine months out.[1] I was noting that this was anomalous. Historically, the mean Democratic thermometer was five or seven degrees higher than the Republicans. For Republicans to be higher was alarming, so much so that I convened a conference of academics to examine this question and offer my data.

Q: This was when?
Greenberg: This would be in the spring of '94.... They concluded that I was wrong, by the way, that based on the economy, job approval—blah, blah, blah—that we'd lose seats, but that this wasn't cataclysmic.... I was reassured. No one thought we could really lose [the majority].... It took the crime bill and some other things to drive us further beyond these numbers. But these numbers were very scary. We got some reassurance from our academic friends that we would survive this. Yes, we were very worried about it.

But also, [at that point] we were not making the assumption that we would lose health care. We were still assuming that Congress would pass something on health care, and that the crime bill was going to come through. We had gone up and down at the various points, but there wasn't an assumption that it had to end badly. It [all] ended up much worse—the combination of health care not happening and then the ... crime bill.

Strobe Talbott, deputy secretary of state: I was actually in the Oval Office on Election Day, Tuesday, November 4, 1994,[2] or something, and I'll remember it for a long time. I was there because Chris [Warren Christopher] was overseas and the president was receiving what was in effect a courtesy call by the president of Finland, Martti Ahtisaari, and the vice president was sitting in the meeting as well, and they were clearly concerned.... But during the course of the session with Ahtisaari, aides kept coming in with little pieces of paper and handing them to the president and you know, he blanched. And finally, after the third or fourth such interruption he turned to Ahtisaari and said something like, this isn't a direct quote but it certainly captures it, "We're getting creamed, you know, this is turning out to be a very big setback for my party."

And then it was sort of a classic Clinton moment. He began analyzing it, explaining it to his visitor and in a way that wasn't exactly sanguine, but certainly wasn't apocalyptic.... Ahtisaari expressed his political condolences and left. The president kept a couple of us behind for a few minutes. He didn't vent or tear his hair out. He was clearly very worried, but he was trying to intellectualize

---

1. A thermometer in this context is a public opinion tool, by which respondents measure on a scale (usually from 0 to 100) how warm (favorable) or cool (unfavorable) they feel about a given person or topic.
2. The actual date of the 1994 midterms was November 8.

it. He was trying to bring all of his skills, not just as a politician, but as a political analyst, to bear on the situation, but he clearly was just beginning.

William Galston, deputy domestic policy advisor: One of my most vivid memories of the White House is sitting in the Roosevelt Room[3] at the senior staff meeting the morning after the election. One of the people from the political office read the roll of the fifty-some odd House Democrats who had been defeated. It was as though a bell was tolling.... A name would be mentioned, and a gasp would run through the room. "My God, he couldn't possibly have lost." When Dan Glickman's name was mentioned—"gasp!"—nobody could believe it. It was really an incredible list and one of these indelible experiences—dong, dong, dong. Fifty-five times.[4]

Patrick Griffin, congressional liaison: It was horrible. It was like waking up after being on an all-night binge and you slept in your clothes on a park bench. It was just horrible. You just felt that you got run over by a truck, it also felt self-inflicted—I guess everybody managed it differently.... I walked around in a daze for days just not knowing what to say, what the reaction was going to be. The fingers were all pointing at everybody. Congress, the Democrats were blasting Clinton, blaming him for everything, which I don't think was accurate. We made a lot of mistakes, but I don't think we singularly caused the loss of control. We contributed in a lot of different ways. The gun thing contributed to a bunch of those seats, but I don't think that was singularly responsible for losing control. Part of it was [also] the Democratic-controlled Congress that did not want to deal with any reform issues. They were still holding on to another world. [We] should have done more on that.

Marjorie Margolies, representative (D-PA): After we lost, there was this extraordinary kind of head-spinning. It was actually a very sad time, very sad. We were called into the White House in groups, because there were lots of us. I'm looking at my notes from the meeting in the White House.... My notes say, "This is such a bizarre year." I'm going to try to read from my notes, but some of this may not make sense. "The conclusion was," and I think this was from the president, "that we lost the propaganda war." He said, "Never in my life has perception been so at variance with evidence." And, "You should always be proud of what you did. It's cold comfort [but] in the fullness of time what we did will be vindicated." He just said that we couldn't market what we did, and that so much of what we did is in trust at the bank. He thinks that talk radio had a lot to do with it. Gore looked at me and said, "You'd be good at that."

---

3. The Roosevelt Room is the main staff meeting area just outside the Oval Office in the West Wing.

4. The Democrats actually lost fifty-four seats in 1994.

Butler Derrick [D-SC] said that he really regretted that what went on had to happen on our watch. His conclusion was that people just didn't like government and it happened on our watch, and that we were willing to focus on issues but people weren't willing to listen to that. He suggested to Clinton that he focus on one or two issues—that, as the spokesman for the Democratic Party, "You have to make the message simple, which is what the Republicans did with regard to the Contract. Don't try to out-Republican the Republicans." It was the feeling in the room that one of the reasons we lost is because we were trying to be more Republican than the Republicans. I didn't necessarily feel that way but that was one of the feelings in the room.... It's hard to tell the public what's right. I started to talk about that, that the real challenge is being honest, especially with people who have what they think is much more at stake. My favorite call ever in my office was when somebody called and said, "When is the government going to get out of my Medicare?" [whispering] *When we don't have any more.*

I think it was Butler who said, "I appreciate your being my president; some of my constituents don't." The president then said under his breath, "Most of them don't." He was feeling the heat at that point. Buddy Darden [D-GA] said, "You stood up for what you believed, and the crowd you're dealing with wants to destroy you." ... [David] Price [D-NC] ... "We behaved as centrists and it didn't work." In other words, they're going back to the theme that we're trying to be like Republicans and we shouldn't be. [*reading notes*] ... Panetta said: "We didn't know that it was happening," and ..., "The Republicans are better at the politics of resentment." That's what he said. [George] Hochbrueckner [D-NY] said, "We were here to do what's right.... We were tagged as the party of big government." That was the theme, that they tagged us as the party of big government. We didn't come back with anything."

I walked away feeling that we were being a bit disingenuous, but I walked away feeling like everyone was so down and so hurt, and we knew that the White House was hurt, that nobody wanted to rub salt in the wounds. So as opposed to saying, "For crying out loud, we had all three branches, we had the White House, we had a real chance to make some important decisions and this is what we did wrong," it was a feeling of, *We let them win.* And I think to a certain extent that's true.

Al From, head of the DLC: One of the big raps on Clinton is that he lost our majorities in the Congress. [He] didn't lose our majorities in the Congress. What happened is that the South caught up with its real politics, and the white South went Republican. That was going to happen sometime. It just happened to happen on Clinton's watch in 1994.... [It]'s a bum rap [to blame Clinton for the historical trends].... What you really had is those districts that had been going Republican pretty consistently [at the presidential level] ... finally voted Republican for Congress.... What it meant was the Democratic advantage of incumbency and history in the South was gone. But that wasn't Clinton; that was going to happen. In fact, in this paper that we did in 1989, "The Politics of Evasion," we had three myths and one of them was the myth of the [permanent Democratic] congressional bastion.[5] We predicted that [a loss] would happen, we just didn't know when.

William Galston: [For] the handful of chartered New Democrats in the White House, the 1994 congressional loss was a directly empowering experience. I think the president parsed what had happened as follows: He'd been listening to advice from advisors who were oriented toward congressional Democrats and a sort of social Democratic agenda. That's shorthand for George Stephanopoulos and Stan Greenberg. That experiment had been tried, and it had failed.... There was a total change in the tone and substance of the White House in the weeks immediately after November of 1994. People who had been disempowered were empowered. People who had been in the lead were downgraded or dismissed. It was quite dramatic.

Mickey Kantor, secretary of commerce: It was a very bad time. [The president] was unsure, unsteady. I'd never seen him like that before or since.... Remember part of it was blamed on Hillary, he really reacts violently when people criticize Hillary. I mean, he really gets angry, you can just see it. He literally gets red in the face. That congressional loss, because he saw what it did to his presidency and how difficult it was going to be—he related it to his own re-election two years hence, it was rejection of him, rejection of Hillary. I mean, you name it, everything that could go wrong did go wrong in his mind.

We went to APEC right after that.[6] I remember sitting with him in the ambassador's residence in Indonesia and Jakarta, up in the bedroom, he and I just talking. He was venting about how upset he was and how concerned. Then he said, "You don't know Dick Morris, do you? ... I'm going to bring him back in, I need to work with somebody I think that is smart enough and will understand and can figure out where we need to go." ... During this period [the president] desperately needed a security blanket, someone who ... he was confident enough in. Morris if nothing else was not likely incompetent, could help him sort out what he needed to do and where he needed to go.... He felt like he had messed up, people around him messed up. All presidents get this way, *I'm doing it all, no one is helping me, oh poor me.* Everybody, I guarantee you, every president gets into that, *I'm the only one here working, the rest of you are having fun. No one cares about me.* Clinton, though, if he had a blue mood, it didn't last very long.

---

5. See William Galston and Elaine Ciulla Kamarck, "The Politics of Evasion: Democrats and the Presidency" (Washington: Progressive Policy Institute, 1989).

6. Clinton was in Indonesia on November 13–16, 1994, for the Asia-Pacific Economic Cooperation [APEC] meeting and a state visit.

Leon Panetta, White House chief of staff: [There] was a period of time when the president literally was struggling with, "What is it, what do we have to do to gain our feet?" Suddenly the Republicans are getting all this attention, Contract for America is getting all this attention. There are some accusations that the president is no longer relevant to this whole process; it's really that kind of approach. And all of that is creating a lot of consternation within the president as to what the answer is. So he's meeting with a lot of people and out of this comes the Dick Morris syndrome where he basically goes back and asks Morris to do some polls as to the strengths of the administration, what he has to do to try to reposition himself for the next election.

And Morris does this polling and the president mentions it to me. I think that was the first time anybody in the White House knew about it, when the president said to me, "I'm having a friend do these polls and take a look at this." ... So in order not to appear on the president's schedule, they start to identify Morris as Charlie. They use this code word, they say, "Charlie's coming" or "Charlie's on the schedule." So they used that for a while and then eventually, after we started having meetings on it, I finally said, "Forget it. Everybody knows that Morris is being talked to and let's just confirm that and stop the games."

It began on that basis and to some extent I think it's because the president himself knows the history here with Morris. On the other hand he's reaching out to him because Morris in his book is somebody who understands the political jugular, working both sides of the aisle, and has the sense of where he has to go in order to try to win the election. So that begins this period where we start to have meetings on a regular basis where we analyze these polls and begin to talk about where the president needs to position himself during this process. ... And that's where the Morrises of the world come in, because they can be in supposed touch with the pulse of America. These are the people who have to tell me how I fashion that message.

Bruce Reed, deputy domestic policy advisor: [We] were in a world of hurt after the '94 election, and the president needed all the help he could get and Morris gave. Even though Morris didn't appear to have many convictions of his own, he gave the president the courage of the president's convictions. [The president's] frustration with the first couple of years had been that he didn't really feel like he was running the government. Morris came in and helped short-circuit a lot of the bureaucracy that had frustrated the president.

It was a nightmare for the official government. We used to joke about how there was the "puppet" government led by the official White House staff, and then there was the secret government led by Morris. My job became to be the liaison between the two governments because Leon Panetta and Erskine Bowles, who was his deputy, felt it was very important for Clinton to have a second-term agenda, but they didn't want Dick Morris to write it. Panetta was genuinely terrified of Morris, not just because he was threatened by Morris's influence, but because he thought that Morris was a nut with all kinds of crazy ideas, and Morris did have a lot of crazy ideas.

Q: And a license?
Reed: Well, he had the president's ear, which was a license to proceed. Nobody had ever really been in charge in the Clinton administration, but Leon had worked pretty hard to make sure there were functioning channels of authority. So no one really knew how much influence Morris had, but he seemed to have quite a bit. The earliest instance of that was ... where the official government wrote a speech for Clinton to give to the newspaper editors and expected him to give it, and Clinton showed up and gave a completely different speech with a completely different message, which was a clear sign to most of the White House that they didn't have as much control as they thought.[7] So Panetta rightly thought that this had the potential for disaster. I was in charge of vetting Morris's ideas to make sure that they had the "real" government's blessing.

Morris would meet with me once a week. He ... would sit in his chair, rocking back and forth, and try to pitch me poll-tested ideas. Half of them were non-starters, one quarter were too difficult, and a few of them were genuinely good ideas that we hadn't thought of. I'd pitch him a set of ideas to go test. We had a lot of creative people at the White House who hadn't had much of an outlet for a long time—since the campaign. The ability to do more by executive action was very liberating. It opened up a whole new field of endeavor that we'd ignored for the first couple of years.

Sometimes we felt that we created a monster because Morris would get hold of a bad idea and not let go of it and try to beat us into submission on it. . . . He turned out to be very eclectic, not a dogmatic centrist or conservative. He was very liberal on the environment and conservative on welfare. So he had his own kind of New Democratic mix, which wasn't precisely the same, but it was steering him basically in the same direction. . . . [We] thought he was a very strange person, but he had occasional flashes of brilliance and, most important, he had a plan for a comeback at a time when nobody else did. . . . Morris deserves credit for that. . . . We were able to function more like a campaign that was running the country and less like a bureaucracy that was trying to campaign. We had a very savvy group of people at the White House who understood politics and policy and functioned better, worked better together during that period in '96 than at any other point over the eight years. It was like a basketball team that had been passing to the wrong spot for all this time and then suddenly everyone started hitting the right man.

---

7. This speech evidently was delivered to the American Association of Newspaper Editors in Dallas, on April 7, 1995. It was noted in the press accounts of the day as taking a more aggressive tone in threatening to use the president's powers to fight back against the Republican Congress.

Don Baer, speechwriter and communications director (on Morris):[8] I've been quoted as talking about gravitational pull [in the White House]. You didn't know that there was another planet out there, but it was pulling things in a certain direction.... At that time, of course, I was working in the main White House ... running the speechwriting operation. So I needed, to some extent, to take my lead from what I was being told by what I thought of as the day-time White House. Then there was a nighttime White House going on as well. I eventually came to regard the official White House staff as the Potemkin Village White House, because there was another White House that was really driving things.... This situation made a lot of people angry inside the White House. There were people who quit—not immediately, but in time—who were very alienated. It made a lot of people in the more left-wing Democratic Party estab-lishment very unhappy—some would argue, to this day.

Henry Cisneros, secretary of housing and urban development: [After] '94, I was asked to join a small group that would meet with the president and the vice president every Wednesday night. It was supposed to start about 8 o'clock, normally didn't get started until later, and frequently ran until midnight or beyond.... [It] was a group of probably fifteen people at the most. It included the vice president, his chief of staff—Panetta at that point—some of the polling folks, Dick Morris.... Our job was essentially to review the overall framework of policy and politics and message, direction and domestic and international. So that was a much more intimate grouping that literally met every Wednesday evening, certainly through all of '96. Decisions were made there about not just policy but also political strategy....

The president chaired them but loosely.... Morris always led the conversa-tion because he had access to the polling information, which is very powerful. This was an area that was sometimes criticized as the period in which we were discussing small government. Because there was no money for really huge ini-tiatives, nobody was suggesting revamping Social Security or anything like that. It was the era of smoking-related initiatives, school uniforms for schools, extra money for teachers, computers in the schools, three strikes and you're out in public housing. All kinds of things that the government could do without a lot of congressional effort and that would allow the administration to roll them out on short notice and dominate the news cycle. So it would be possible to just roll things out and stay ahead of the news cycle, command the attention. Frankly, a lot of these were liked by the people in the country. It was important

8. Baer made these comments at a public symposium of former White House speechwriters held at the Miller Center. Those transcripts are published in Michael Nelson and Russell L. Riley, eds., *The President's Words: Speeches and Speechwriting in the Modern White House* (Lawrence: University Press of Kansas, 2010).

to determine what would be the acceptance if we said, "No smoking in this place" or "Small-government initiatives."

[Morris] had overhead slides, old-fashioned overheads, transparencies. "If you asked this question about this program, this is what the public thinks." Pretty straightforward stuff. I know there's a lot of critique about the government's use of polling and making decisions based on polling, but it's not as if we're polling whether or not we should stand by Israel or something basic, a basic question of principle. That wasn't it. It's more, "[If] we were to provide funding for public schools to provide uniforms for children, how would that play with the public?" Eighty-five percent of the people like it, 15 percent say, "Bad idea." They like it because it means parents don't have to spend money for clothing. They like it because kids don't compete in school for who's the most fashionable. They like it because it avoids the whole question of pants that are falling off at the hips and girls' midriffs bare. They like it because everybody is the same and it creates a sense of uniformity, and they like it because after school you can tell who the students are and who's not. . . . And the question is, which of these makes the most sense? Obviously you go with those that give you a higher payoff. To that degree, it would help orchestrate the chronicle of rollouts. Also, what's the logic by which you sell it? I just went through a series of reasons on one example, which was school uniforms, why people like them. Which of these polls best when you roll it out? What's the lead sentence going to be?

Chris Jennings, health care policy advisor: [The] truth was, as much influence as Dick Morris had or didn't have, he couldn't be the ultimate implementer. The White House staff still had to do it; we had to execute it. He couldn't do the press release, he couldn't do the policy, he didn't have the apparatus. And I'll say one thing about the president, because I think it is important: the president didn't have a blind allegiance to whatever Dick Morris said. He was curious and he was interested in what Dick had to suggest. Dick was always so positive he was right; he had an overwhelming amount of confidence—many would say arrogance—but he demanded and captured the attention of many, including, of course, the president. But the president generally knew there was a fine line between brilliance and insanity.

William Galston: My deepest regret about that period [of Dick Morris's ascendancy] is that it created the impression that the reform strategy of New Democrats was essentially a political tactic and not a governing agenda. We had worked for years creating a governing agenda (that I still believe in) to rebut that charge. It was a charge made by the opponents of the New Democratic movement from day one: This is a political tactic; it's unprincipled. Then here comes this politically androgynous advisor. It was our worst nightmare, because it was impossible to dispel the impression that the president had embraced this way of thinking as a tactic, and that's all it was.

Tony Lake, national security advisor: I did go to the president and say, "I mustn't talk to him. I mustn't read his stuff." Morris took umbrage at all of this and denounced me in his memoirs for being naïve because I thought you could keep politics out of it. I don't think he understood just how bad it would have been, politically, for word to get out that [the national security advisor] was talking to him.

Mack McLarty, White House chief of staff: [Recall] that one of the real turning points, after the '94 election, was the tragedy in Oklahoma City, because the Republican "Contract for America" had railed against government bureaucracy.[9] And all of a sudden, the government bureaucracy is the same person sitting by you at Sunday school or at a little league field. It's human beings.... But that was a turning point as well, and it obviously changed the feeling and the understanding about who President Clinton was.

William Galston: The president was back on his heels in early 1995. Things hit bottom right before the bombing of the federal building in Oklahoma City and sort of rebounded. He found a voice and very cleverly linked that episode with hostility of government run amok. I think he began to turn the corner perceptually about that point. But mainly what was happening was jousting. Was there a lot of domestic policy going on during that period? Hell, no. How could there have been?

* * *

Q: What you were spending your time on in '95? Is it the case that the budget was pretty much the item that was occupying most of your time?
Patrick Griffin: Fair question. In the first three months it was just trying to find our sea legs again. They, the House leadership, had isolated us out of the process. Nothing is going on in the Senate. We're helping to organize our Democratic allies—trying to get through the "who struck John" of the election, rebuilding our relationships with our Democratic colleagues in the House, helping them express a voice against the Contract. There were no legislative negotiations going on at all. None. Zero. That's one activity.

The second activity emerges around the appropriations process and the first rescissions. There was a great battle on the first rescission brewing. It was the first time they [congressional Republicans] were using supplementals as a vehicle to cut everything. We had submitted a supplemental that they turned into a $21 or $24 billion rescission measure.... They passed it. Clinton vetoed it, and it just

---

9. Domestic terrorists set off a car bomb at the Alfred Murrah Federal Building in Oklahoma City on April 19, 1995. One hundred sixty-eight people were killed, including nineteen young children attending day care there. Clinton went to Oklahoma City on April 23 and spoke at a memorial service, delivering one of the most memorable speeches of his presidency. Four people were convicted for the offenses, and Timothy McVeigh was executed in 2001.

blew their socks off.... I think they had gone to their leadership and said, "We can roll Clinton. He's a wuss." They were still feeling bullish against Clinton. It was a very big turning point legislatively. So you had the Murrah Building speech and then an apparent victory on having the Congress sustain his veto. As a result, Clinton's numbers slowly turning around. This was as close to a legislative victory as you could imagine or hope for.... That stopped all the appropriations activity. It wasn't because of anything we were doing in the committee—they just couldn't pass their own appropriation bills. Whatever bills they could pass in the House, they couldn't them through the Senate. All legislative activity stopped as a practical matter. At that point, everything else was seen through the lens of the budget process all the way through the end of the year.

We don't know where it's going but it certainly looks like Clinton is the leader and they're kind of falling in behind him—begrudgingly, but this is the better way to go. These guys are stumbling (the Republicans). Instead of shifting their strategy, they just screamed it louder and louder. "We're going to shut down [the government]." "Did you hear we're going to shut down?" "We're really going to shut you down." "We're not even going to pay the debt." Their strategy was stunning to us.

Senator Tom Daschle (D-SD):[10] I remember once where it was Newt Gingrich, Bob Dole, Dick Gephardt, and Al Gore, Leon Panetta, the president, and me. We negotiated [on the budget] hour after hour, day after day, over the holidays. On several occasions Gingrich, who has a temper, would get up and walk out. Not knowing how long he would be gone, we would just sit there for a while, and on occasion the president would put in a movie and we'd watch a movie, waiting for the Republicans to come back. He'd make microwave popcorn and we'd wait for the Republicans to come back into the room so we could keep negotiating. It was a theatrical time in more ways than one.

Leon Panetta (on the shutdowns): When [the Republicans] were talking about not passing a debt ceiling increase and then shutting the government down, it just confirmed in my mind that these guys don't understand what governing is all about and ultimately this is going to blow up on them. So we were never intimidated by them. I don't think there was ever a point at which we said, "Oh, God, they're going to—" We expressed our concern that this was irresponsible, that it would undercut the credibility of the United States.

People on Wall Street, in the securities market, suddenly started saying, "Whoa, what are these guys doing?" Of course the press picked up on that and they understood. There was a point at which the president was trying to think, and was probably encouraged by Morris to say, "How can we work it through

---

10. Daschle's comments appear in his interview for the Miller Center's Edward M. Kennedy Oral History Project.

with these guys? Is there a way we can, particularly on the balanced budget issue, find a way to work out an agreement on that, because you know, while they may be crazy on some of these other issues, the fact is, on that one they may have some public support. So can we do that?" . . .

Q: I guess maybe in the spring or early summer, the administration offered a ten-year balanced budget plan.

Panetta: We sat down with the economic team and said, "What does make sense? If we have to get to a balanced budget, what would be the right path?" And based on where we were going with the economic plan, based on where we thought it would make sense, we said we could get to a balanced budget in ten years. Let's agree with the concept of a balanced budget but do it over a period of time that we think makes better sense in terms of the economy. So we debated that and there continued to be pressure from the political side, the Dick Morris side, to push this to seven years and try to see if we can't agree on a seven-year path that would get us to balance as well. That was the internal battle. . . . My recollection is that there comes a moment during the time when we are meeting in the Oval Office and what's happening now is we've got Bob Dole, Dick Armey, Newt Gingrich, Dick Gephardt, Tom Daschle, myself, the vice president, and the president. On behalf of the administration, I am presenting proposals to see if we can find a place to resolve this, and the primary issue again is Medicare. How much do you cut Medicare, how much do you cut Medicaid and some of the domestic programs?

There comes a moment where we're making an offer, and it's like the last offer. The president is really bending over on Medicare. Frankly, some of us are concerned about whether he's going too far. As a matter of fact, the vice president doesn't particularly want him to make this counteroffer, but the president says, "Come on, let's try it. This might be the piece that breaks [the stalemate]."

So I put the counteroffer up on the chart and Gingrich says, "I can't do it. I appreciate your doing it, but you've got to move a little more, I can't do this." And the president at that point says, "You know, Newt, I can't do what you want me to do. I do not believe it's right for the country. I may lose the election by virtue of not being able to resolve this, but I just don't think this is right for the country." I think it was at that point that Gingrich suddenly realized this guy was not going to cave in. For those of us who always were concerned that the president might cave in, it was a reassuring moment that the president gets it, that there is a point where you've got to draw a line.

Chris Jennings: At this particular meeting . . . the president said to [the Republicans], "I've run these Medicaid programs. I know what's going to happen here [if I accept your alternative]. We will not have funding for these programs. There will be cutbacks, people will be threatened. It won't be just people in nursing homes. It will be kids, it will be women," and he went on and said,

"I want you to know something. I will do a lot of things, but I will not sit here and sign this. I can lose my election over it, you can keep sending it to me, but I am never going to sign it. You will have to override me, but I'm drawing the line here." He got very passionate about it.

He walked back in the Oval Office and Leon and Gene Sperling[11] and the vice president were there. Leon said something like, "I wish the whole country could see who you are and what you are." Gene Sperling was almost in tears. He was so proud of him. We all were. The president was saying no to the Medicaid block grant, which we all thought would be fundamentally devastating to the program and the vulnerable people it serves. . . . Anyway, it was one of those moments when people thought, *He does have a strong moral compass, and he will draw a line*. It made him a stronger president because people knew that there was a line. I can't tell you how much that helped him with the Democrats on the Hill. It just meant to them that he will be there when he's needed to be there.

* * *

Q: What was it like being in the White House when the government was shut down? Did you feel tremendous pressure to do something or were you content to sit it out?
Leon Panetta: [The] Republicans soon realized there were some programs they absolutely could not shut down. . . . So they had to make sure that Social Security was not affected, that veterans' benefits were not affected, and that other important issues were exempted. But they began to make exemptions, they began to open the door. So the parks were closed and other things were closed, and departments were operating with parts down. But they started to get heat from the areas that they were closing. And as they were getting heat from some of these areas, they began to create additional exemptions as they were passing efforts at CRs [continuing resolutions, to resolve things temporarily].

That continued. After that Oval Office moment I talked about, it seemed like there was no way we were going to be able to cross the Rubicon here to cut a deal. Since the president made that statement, we knew it was a question of who was going to blink first. Telling the president, "The pressure is not on us, the pressure is on them. They run the House, they run the Senate." By that time we knew that the public was putting the responsibility for what had happened here on the backs of the Republican Party. So it was just a question of saying, "Hang on."

Alice Rivlin, OMB director: The Republican leaders in Congress were totally out of touch. They were so caught up in their anti-government rhetoric that they did not understand that the public outcry was going to be enormous as soon

---

11. At the time Sperling would have been deputy director of the National Economic Council. He was one of Clinton's most trusted economic staff members going back to the 1992 campaign.

as people realized they couldn't go to the national park, and they couldn't get their student loan, and they couldn't do any of these normal things that citizens expect from government. . . .

Q: How do you shut the government down?
Rivlin: Well, it's very complicated. . . . In the shutdown, first you have to figure out who are essential personnel and who aren't. There's some kind of a definition of that that has to be applied. We were construing it narrowly. Then you really have to figure out how to do the least damage. You know, the Department of Agriculture has all these greenhouses or whatever. You can't just turn off the lights and walk away because everything dies—

Q: You're not talking political damages then.
Rivlin: Oh no, real damage—you're talking about real damage—how to mitigate the real damage from turning out the lights, as it were. There are just some things that are very hard to turn off. Those things have to be kept going. But then, mostly, we just sent everybody home. One decision I had to make was what about the national Christmas tree. It was December by this time, and were we going to have the national Christmas tree or not? It's on park service land. This, I guess, got into the press and Pepco [Potomac Electric Power Company] said, "We'll donate the electricity to keep the lights on the Christmas tree going." But then there were further complications. You had to have some police down there, some guards. The park service has to have their people down there. You just can't let people wander. So what were we going to do about that? And some other company volunteered security guards. So I kept the lights on the Christmas tree, which might have been the wrong political decision. It might have been better to turn them off. But I didn't think so.

Eileen Baumgartner, staff director, House Budget Committee: I don't think the Republicans understood what they were given. They abused it and messed up in their control. . . . Entrenched majorities get arrogant and out of touch, and entrenched minorities become irresponsible and unskilled. The Republicans did not have enough talent when they took over. That was the striking thing in negotiating the budget deals after they were in control, how they didn't have the people they needed. They had lobbyists writing their language. They didn't have committee staffs to write legal language. There's so much history involved in it. They didn't know quite what to do.

Leon Panetta: Remember this was a revolution, and there were revolutionaries who had been elected based on the Contract for America. I honestly think that deep down Newt Gingrich understood that this was probably the wrong thing to do. But I think to a large extent his hands were tied because he had created this group of members who really believed that their mission in life was to get their budget adopted, to get their contract adopted. And because they had been elected on that basis, they would lose the momentum if they capitulated at this point. So I think they deeply believed that they were going to show to the country just how deeply they believed they were right by shutting down the government. And also I think this is not a group of members that ultimately believes in the role of federal government anyway. To some extent, yes, shutting down the federal government, so what?

But I also think deep down Newt Gingrich felt that ultimately Bill Clinton would cave in.... Bill Clinton sent signals that we could do something here, because Clinton's basic instincts were always to cut a deal, try to resolve it. I think he may have given them some sense that if they pushed hard enough he would come their way. But I think that was part of their thinking as well. On the other hand, I have to tell you, Bob Dole thought this was all nuts.... I am absolutely convinced that what the shutdown did was give Bill Clinton the opportunity to identify who he was with the public in contrast to what Gingrich and the Republicans wanted to do. And it in essence did what he could not do the first two years, which is to say to the American people, "This is what Bill Clinton is about, this is what I believe in. This is what I'm trying to do." What the shutdown did is it created that contrast, it created that political leverage that helped the public identify who Bill Clinton was. That happening was, to a large extent, one of the deciding moments in terms of the president's ability to get re-elected in '96.

Patrick Griffin (on the budget politics of 1995–96): [After] these big meetings in the White House ... Dole said, "I surrender. I've got to go run for president." [Then] we got a brilliant budget [at the beginning of 1996] that led to an incredible year. Dole leaves. Newt and [Senator Trent] Lott [R-MS] realize they're just going down the tubes as a result of the shutdowns and not getting anything done, for which they were getting the lion share of the blame. They began to realize they could lose this whole thing (the majority). Consequently, they begin to cut deals with Clinton on welfare reform, tax cuts for small businesses, minimum wage, a little health care bill, and then ultimately the budget. They get re-elected with larger margins, and Clinton does, too. The formula that works to win is the one that they then refuse ever to do again with Clinton and are made to swear, by their base, never to cooperate with him again. It was really incredible.

27

The Re-election and Productive Middle Years, 1996–97

By any standard, Bill Clinton's re-election was a remarkable feat. In a perilous post-1994 environment, when initially all the political tides seemed to be running against him, he managed to re-establish his leadership and to tack his way back into the White House. Having been reduced to pleading his own relevancy early in 1995, he subsequently became the first Democrat since Franklin Roosevelt to win successive elections to the presidency.

The years 1996 and 1997 were also the most fruitful of Clinton's presidency. Before the election, Clinton found himself able to make common cause with congressional Republicans on a number of issues, because members of Congress wanted by then to be able to show their constituents that they were capable of more than obstruction. After the election, increasingly favorable economic conditions set the stage for bipartisan cooperation on balancing the federal budget—a milestone achievement that was realized in two successive fiscal years before Clinton left office in 2001. The cooperative spirit of those times did not, however, survive into 1998.

Judge Abner Mikva, White House counsel: When you look over the political landscape [after 1994] . . . you would say, "This is the quintessential lame duck president." He's going to be there for two years, and then either his party or the country will throw him out. Here they've already sent a strong message. They've kicked over all the Democratic leadership in both the House and the Senate. It looked like we were being deluged with scandals, with more yet to come—and, in fact, more were going to come. And yet—I was at the '96 convention, the first one I'd been to in many, many years—it was a love-in. He owned that convention, and he owned that election. . . . Bill Clinton went out there and absolutely mesmerized the electorate. That's what I think makes Republicans so angry at him, at Hillary. They don't understand. They had knocked him down and knocked him out, and all of a sudden there he is, cruising to victory in '96. . . . I think that nobody has quite figured out his incredible electability.

* * *

Q: One key to Clinton's success in 1996 was his ability to fend off a challenge from within his own party. Was there ever enough discontent with President Clinton among the New Democrats such that people were coming to you privately and saying, "You think we ought to take this guy on?"

Al From, head of the DLC: The answer is yes. We knew there was discontent on all sides after the 1994 election. In early 1995, Michael Steinhardt—you know who he is? He is the venture capitalist who was the big funder of the PPI [Progressive Policy Institute], our think tank, and of the DLC. . . . [Anyway, Steinhardt], Barry Diller[1] . . . and a guy named Mitch Hart, who cofounded EDS [Electronic Data Systems] with Ross Perot, wanted to form a third party. We had a series of meetings and we wrote something called the New Progressive Declaration . . ., which really was maybe a little farther out, but basically a more pure New Democrat, Third Way message. . . . So there was that period.

I think once Clinton came back to the fold that discontent on our side went away. I suppose part of [the consideration of a third party] was that people thought he was going to be pretty ineffective as a president, not understanding that Bill Clinton is like a shmoo: you knock him down, he keeps bouncing up.

* * *

Q: What were the principal fights within the campaign in the early stages?

Joe Lockhart, press secretary: I think they were resource fights. Very broad brush. Dick [Morris] thought every dollar should be spent either on a poll or on a TV commercial, and that we should be spending early.[2] As I've been told, Harold [Ickes] had a view that we shouldn't spend that much money on that stuff, and it was a waste of money to do it early. I've seen a series of academic studies that can't agree on whether it was right to do it early, so nobody knows who won that fight. Except we won the election, so they both think they're right.

I think there was—not within the campaign but within the overall organization—some ideological tension over where the president should be. Some people thought he was moving too far to the center, the issues being the balanced budget, welfare reform. Some thought it was the greatest thing in the world—his lurch to the left was being righted. I think the president was fully aware of all this, thought it was good creative tension, and knew exactly what he was doing. I don't think there was anyone telling him what to do. He knew what he was doing. . . .

---

1. Barry Diller was a prominent American businessman, whose successes with Paramount Pictures and Fox Broadcasting/20th Century Fox made him a billionaire.

2. Morris's insistence on spending advertising dollars drew vigorous criticism by Frank Greer in his oral history, because Morris was benefiting financially from commissions for placing an unprecedented number of ads.

Q: You said earlier you thought one of Morris's better points was that he was very clear about his strategy. Could you lay that out for us?

Lockhart: Yes. His strategy was dominating the center. I think the phrase "dynamic center" was one of his buzz phrases. Basically, he wanted to marginalize people within our party on the left and the right, and dare people in the center not to agree with us. That was step one.

Step two was he believed—and he was right about this—that the government does hugely complicated things that the public is just never going to get. So he wanted to have the government start doing things that people would get. We do lots of things to make sure kids know how to read and write and schools are good, but school uniforms tell people that the president understands what's going on in a classroom. I think they called things like the Family and Medical Leave Act "bite-size initiatives." . . . He wanted a simple thing every day, and he wanted the public to go to bed every night saying, "That's a pretty good idea. He's working for me. Clinton's all right." . . . Dick had this idea for a 511 number where you could get certain information. Impolitely, one day in a meeting, I suggested we do a 311 number where the government guaranteed quality Chinese food within thirty minutes of anyplace in America. [*laughter*] Everybody in the room laughed but Dick. I just went back to my corner. I still think it's a good idea, and it wouldn't cost that much.

Bruce Reed, deputy domestic policy advisor: When Morris blew himself up, we never looked back. We had gotten into such a rhythm that we didn't need him anymore, and by that point the agencies were used to the White House calling and saying, "Let's get something done." We'd worn down their resistance enough that we were able to do just as well without him as when we had him.

* * *

Q: Were you on the campaign train with the president when the news about Dick Morris and the prostitutes came in?[3]

Joe Lockhart: I was on the train . . . and the train trip was probably the most successful three or four days of that campaign. It was one of the things that just worked. And of course, because it is the Clinton political world, when you're at the point where things couldn't be going better, something is about to happen. So it's Wednesday afternoon, I think, and [press secretary] Mike McCurry grabs me and says, "Come with me." . . . Mike wanted to go out and get fresh air. And he had found a great place on the train to get fresh air where no one else could

---

3. During the Democratic National Convention in 1996, when Clinton was on his way to Chicago by train, news broke that Morris had been witnessed (and photographed) in the company of a prostitute in the District of Columbia.

find us. So we literally went back four cars. We went upstairs to go downstairs. We went outside the train at one point, to walk around this thing. I finally said, "What's up?" and he said, "I just want you to witness this phone conversation," and he picked up the cell phone and called Dick.

I could hear only Mike's side of this, and he said, "Uh huh, uh huh, really? Okay." And then I'll never forget this. I could hear Dick's high-pitched ranting in the background. He was yelling about the press, and Mike said, "Dick, Dick, stop. Hold on one second. Let me ask you one question. Do they have pictures?" I didn't know what the story was! All of a sudden, I heard complete silence on the other end. And Mike looked at me and said, "He's calling me back." Two minutes later, he called back. "Yes, they have pictures." At this point, I don't think Dick had told anyone else. So there were now two of us who knew.

Q: Mike filled you in, between the conversations, about what this was about?
Lockhart: Yes.... Now, I know this [firestorm] is coming.... [White House director of political affairs] Doug Sosnik and I had briefings set up that morning with the *New York Times*, the *Washington Post*, and maybe some others, basically to lay out our fall election strategy. It was an hour-and-a-half meeting where we had a presentation. We got about ten minutes into the first one, and my pager started going off. It was Harold [Ickes].

The first page was just, "Call Harold." I ignored it. I'm in a meeting and I know what it's about. I'm trying not to give [the newspapers] some perfect piece of color of me freaking out. The second one was, "It's Harold. Get up to the suite." The third one is not repeatable, because it involves words that would offend young people who might read this.... Some of them are very short. Some of them, though—It's interesting how many variations he has on a single—He has fifty ways of using that one particular word, and I've heard all of them. So I excused myself and said to Doug, "You have to do the rest for yourself. I have to go upstairs."

I'll never forget. I went up, and sitting around the room were Mike [McCurry] and George [Stephanopoulos] and maybe Rahm and Erskine and Leon Panetta. We were going to have a meeting to decide how we were going to do this—how we were going to put this out, and how we were going to deal with it. I remember looking around the room, and to no one in particular, just being the new guy, saying, "This is unbelievable. We get to the point where we're really out of the woods, and this happens."

George looked at me and said, "Welcome to our world." That's exactly right. Just at the moment that we think we have this figured out, something always happens.... A lot of us sat around and said, "How are we going to do this?" and you could just see [Clinton] off in the corner, saying, "Okay, this *was* going to be easy, but now it's going to be hard. Now I have a challenge. Now I'm going to blow that story off the front page by what I'm doing tonight." And he rose to the challenge. He looked at the country and said, "This is what this campaign is about," . . . and the public agreed with him. They watched his [nomination acceptance] speech, and by any academic measure they said, "The president is concentrating on what's important to me, not on what's important to a bunch of people in Washington I don't like anyway."

Peter Knight, campaign manager: I had about seven or eight months as campaign manager. Chris Dodd was the chairman of the DNC and he introduced me when I became the campaign manager, saying we've got a ten-point lead. "Here Peter, here's the baton, don't blow it." [*laughter*] So, oh God, thanks a lot. . . . But it was probably the most satisfying professional experience that I'd ever had because we did it right. We didn't make any mistakes. There wasn't a need for a lot of brilliance, it was just a matter of blocking and tackling and managing and making sure to avoid traps and so forth.

Joe Lockhart: We were in Chautauqua [New York] for the first [presidential debate], and the debate prep was going very badly.[4] For whatever reason, the president was having trouble focusing. I think he knew he could beat Bob Dole in a debate, but we all knew that if he didn't prepare himself the right way, it could be a problem. . . . I had left a little earlier and was just sitting at a computer, and Paul [Begala] came out and was complaining, "This can really go bad."

I don't know where the idea came from—him or me—but we realized we just needed to scare him a little bit. So Paul and I sat down and wrote the mythical *New York Times* story from the day after the debate where he had really done badly. It was so much fun to write. It wrote itself. I was saying, "Let me write this paragraph, I got this one." We went in and showed it to him. . . . We had three days of prep. He wanted one day. He was thinking, *I'm not checking into this process until I need to be here.* But I remember him looking at this [mock story] and it registering: this could happen. It was part of getting him ready.

The one reasonably funny story—although it may not be funny to everyone—was we did a series of full-blown mock debates. . . . We all had our assigned questions to ask. As I was walking in, George Stephanopoulos grabbed me and said, "Don't ask your question. Ask a question about same-sex marriage." He knew that Clinton just wasn't right on this. There was the perception in the country that he didn't support the Defense of Marriage Act.[5] The staff had given him the bill at one o'clock in the morning on Saturday. The reality was he did support it. He was given the document, and he just didn't think about it. He signed it.

---

4. The first presidential debate in 1996 was held in Hartford, Connecticut, on October 6.
5. Clinton signed the Defense of Marriage Act [DOMA] into law on September 21, 1996. The Act affirmed that for purposes of federal law marriage was defined as the union of one man and one woman.

But then a lot of people who were not in the same ideological place and a little embarrassed—some of our Ivy League colleagues at the White House— put out the story that the president didn't really want to sign it but signed it for political reasons. That just infuriated him, because he believed. He signed it because he thought it was the right thing to do. I disagree with him, but he thought it was the right thing to do.

I knew what George was doing. I'm going to be the guy who gets the president crazy. I decided there's just so often I'm going to get screamed at. So while I was sitting there, I came up with my plan. I was sitting next to a kid I worked with in a previous campaign. He's a young, athletic, really good-looking guy, twenty-seven, twenty-eight years old. I got called on and I did this routine. I said, "Mr. President, I voted for you last time. I really want to vote for you this time, but I'm just not sure I can and I want to tell you why. I want you to meet—" And I turned and put my arm around the guy. I said, "I want you to meet my friend Angus. Angus and I love each other, and because of what you've signed into law, I can't—" I went through this whole heartfelt thing. The kicker was Clinton turned and mouthed to someone on the side, "I didn't know Joe was gay." [laughter] And I thought, I performed well.

He started to answer the question and then turned and started yelling at George—with reason. George is the one he blamed for signing it in the middle of the night. It was George's call. But I got out of being the person who got yelled at that day. Poor Angus. That kid turned nine colors of red in front of all those people—and there were cameras everywhere.

Chris Jennings, health care advisor: The president gets re-elected overwhelmingly, has basically a great opportunity to move forward to get a balanced budget and hopefully take care of some other priorities as he is in an improving economy. He instructs his staff to produce a balanced budget and other budget priorities, including children's health care, goals to be enacted by the end of the year. And it was a very interesting time. That was '97. It was probably the best time. I mean, '96 was a very good year, '96 was a great year except for the convention and Dick Morris. Other than that, it was a really good year. And '97, we felt like we'd gotten our sea legs, we knew what we were doing, we were moving forward, we had good guidance and we had good leadership.

Don Baer, speechwriter and communications director:[6] President Clinton's second inaugural address, which is the one that I worked on, focused very much on the idea that he wanted to be a repairer of the breach, as he said in that speech. He wanted to help the country realize that we were one America more than we

---

6. Baer made his remarks at a public symposium of White House speechwriters held at the Miller Center. See Nelson and Riley, eds., *The President's Words*, 113.

were many Americas in the things that matter most. I think also that most of these speeches, those that work and even those that don't work, quite often are trying to lift the country in two ways: first, to recognize where we stand in the larger arc of history at any given time, and second, to set a theme for the time and the moment that we're in—not so much programmatically as thematically.

In the case of President Clinton's second inaugural address, you'll remember that his re-election campaign had been run around the theme of building a bridge to the twenty-first century.[7] It was very future-oriented. We recognized that ours would be the last inaugural address of the twentieth century. We felt it was important, then, to look back across the great span of that century at what had been accomplished, but also to recognize what still needed to be accomplished as we moved into a very different new century.

John Hilley, congressional liaison (on the balanced budget agreement in 1997): We met very early with Newt. He said, "Look, there's a time to fight, and there's a time to work together. Let's see if we can get [a balanced budget] done this year." We launched in very early with the Republicans. We were actually talking to them before the president's budget was submitted in early January [1997]. We started talking to them with good reason. Every budget that's ever been sent up to the Hill is declared dead on arrival. We did not want that to happen.... We got a good reception on our budget when we went up.... The Republicans on both sides wanted to get this done with the administration, because the numbers were improving rapidly. If you think about it, the '90 deal [signed by President Bush] had done about $400 billion in deficit reduction.... The '93 deal [signed by President Clinton] had done more, about $450 billion, I think. By the time we got around to it with the improving numbers, there was probably only about $250 billion to go. So it was easily in reach. ...

The great thing about this is that we were able to pull it off, and look what Clinton got out of it: he got $24 billion for health care in addition to balancing the budget. He got his Hope Scholarships for the community college level. Enhanced the EITC, got the $500 child credit, which was a big Republican agenda item, but we were for it as well. We were able to do a lot of things like that. We were able to repair the bad provisions of the immigration bill.[8] The

---

7. To some extent this metaphor was deployed because Clinton's Republican opponent that year, Senator Bob Dole, had claimed in his convention acceptance address that he wanted to be a bridge to an idealized America, like the one he recalled from his past. The Clinton campaign seized on this phrasing to argue that the election was about the past (the Republicans) versus the future (the Democrats).

8. Hope Scholarships are tax credits available to families to help defray the costs of the first two years of post-secondary education. EITC is the Earned Income Tax Credit, which benefits low-income wage earners and has been a major contributor to poverty relief. On immigration, the 1997 balanced budget act restored welfare benefits to legal immigrants that were cut in the 1996 welfare reform bill.

Republicans got their coveted capital gains, they expanded the IRAs [individual retirement accounts] somewhat. We had to do quite a bit of cutting to do it, but we were able to. So that was the accomplishment.... [We] were totally excited.

Okay, we've got the budget balanced. Now we were running plans: Let's fix Social Security, let's solve that. Let's fix Medicare. There was an ambitious race relations agenda being readied, so the mills at the policy level were hopping, to set the stage for even more efforts.

Then came Monica Lewinsky and the impeachment.

28

Scandals—and
Impeachment

Questions about Bill Clinton's personal conduct shadowed him from the moment he contemplated announcing his intention to seek the presidency in 1991 to the day he left the White House after issuing late-night pardons ten years later. These oral histories document how those closest to the president assessed and weathered the scandals they confronted, richly detailing what life was like at the turbulent center of the storm, especially during the historic effort to impeach and remove Clinton from office.[1]

The Supreme Court, in its crucial ruling allowing a civil lawsuit against Clinton for sexual misconduct to proceed while he was still in office, had judged that the president could easily handle the modest diversion of his time required to deal with that case. Those who lived with Clinton through the aftermath provide compelling evidence about how wrong the Court's prediction was. The nation's foreign relations tended to proceed without great effect. But wholesale distractions in the press shop, in legislative affairs, and in the White House political operation—as well as the inevitable diversion of energy and attention by the president himself—meant that almost nothing of real substance happened on the home front after January 1998, when the Lewinsky story broke. Three full years of his second term were thus consumed by Clinton's indiscretions and the mounting effort to punish him for them.

Mickey Kantor, secretary of commerce: Well, it is a Clinton pattern to get in trouble when he is doing better.

Susan Thomases, longtime friend and confidante: There are two types of Clinton haters. One type is the people who really don't like them because of

---

1. There is, conversely, very little new in these oral histories about the behavior at the root of these scandals. This is not surprising. Independent counsels looking into the Whitewater and Monica Lewinsky incidents alone, for example, spent more than $50 million and deployed scores of investigators armed with subpoena power—and aided by the Federal Bureau of Investigation and the Internal Revenue Service—to determine precisely what happened in each case. Their findings of fact were exhaustive and made public in full detail.

what they want to accomplish. There are really serious people in this country who don't like their idea of the role of government in people's lives, and they don't like them because of what they think the government should do to help people. They just don't like that.

And then there are the people who don't like them because they're jealous. They don't think a poor boy from Arkansas should have so much. There's some serious class jealousy of a type that makes me want to throw up. Sometimes I overhear a conversation like that which is very class-based, and it just makes me sick. They think Bill Clinton is poor white trash. How can this guy from poor white trash get ahead of us to be president? How did he sneak in there? It's ugly stuff.

Bernard Nussbaum, White House counsel: The Clinton presidency from the very beginning—this was very dangerous—was never accepted as legitimate by the Republicans. It was a strange thing. They couldn't believe it, this '60s hillbilly—a combination of both hillbilly and Rhodes Scholar—won this election. These pot-smoking, sex-driven creatures are now in the White House and he didn't win a majority of the vote. . . . Some people were saying, "We're not going to accept Clinton as a legitimate president."

Senator Alan Simpson (R-WY): [There] were guys in our caucus who were always just out to screw Bill—in the latter part, while I was assistant leader, it became absolutely tedious, because they would be talking all during the caucus about how to craft a piece of legislation that would blow up under Bill Clinton's nose. "When he gets this, he'll have to veto it," or "He'll have to do this." It would waste a half hour of every caucus. Finally, I said, "I just want to tell you something. Give it up. You're not going to trick Clinton. In fact, you remind me of [that] damn roadrunner . . . cartoon. You make a bomb and you roll the bomb down to the White House and old Clinton will pick it up with the fuse burning and roll the son-of-a-bitch right back and it will blow up under your face. . . . You'll have black powder all over you," I said. "*That's* what Clinton will do to you. Give it up. If he doesn't do it, his people will do it. They have all of you figured out; we're wasting our time."

Bernard Nussbaum: This whole notion of Clinton scandals: this is *phony*. Lewinsky aside—Lewinsky happens at the end—there are no Clinton scandals. Twenty-nine people in the Reagan administration—high officials—were indicted for various malfeasance.[2] Name me one, in eight years of the Clinton

---

2. Nussbaum's numbers are difficult to corroborate. In a widely cited passage by journalist Haynes Johnson, "By the end of [Reagan's] term, 138 administration officials had been convicted, had been indicted, or had been the subject of official investigations for official misconduct and/or criminal violations. In terms of number of officials involved, the record

administration—[Secretary of Agriculture] Mike Espy for taking two tickets to a football game, and he was then acquitted in effect. One. Who, who, *who* in the Clinton administration? Webb Hubbell for stealing from some of his partners before he came to Washington. He should never have come to Washington. He's a wonderful human being, but ... he shouldn't have come to Washington.... But who *in* the administration? Did the White House counsel go to jail? Did the attorney general go to jail, as John Mitchell did?[3] Who in this administration?

The travel office, the Whitewater affair.[4] All these so-called scandals. There were no scandals. They're *phantom* scandals. There was never any real scandal. It was all political nonsense to try to undermine this president.... [The] fact is that the Clinton administration turns out to be probably the most honest administration of any administration in, I don't know, the last hundred years—compared to Truman, compared to Roosevelt, compared to Kennedy, compared to anybody. And yet it has the image of the *scandal-ridden* Clinton administration.

Judge Abner Mikva, White House counsel: If I ever write anything, I'm going to write "The Nothing that Was Whitewater." There literally was nothing there, nothing. They had these massive investigations of these two-bit crooks going on in Little Rock. Clinton knew everybody in Arkansas, he knew cows and dogs and horses, and he knew crooks. It was a bad investment. They lost money on it. They took a tax deduction for their loss, and that was all there was. So once I satisfied myself on that, I just couldn't get excited about it.

Mack McLarty, White House chief of staff: The travel office was an odd issue. I certainly had to deal with it, so I remember it vividly. It's a little bit like walking down a golf course and getting hit by a golf ball from the other fairway. You were looking at the putt you were going to try to make and didn't look out for the other ball coming and didn't think you had to. I spent a fair amount of time

---

of his administration was the worst ever." (Johnson, *Sleepwalking Through History: America in the Reagan Years* [New York: Doubleday, 1991]). But by including "official investigations" in that calculation, Johnson inflates the number beyond Nussbaum's claim. Still, Lawrence Walsh alone secured fourteen indictments (and eleven convictions) in the Iran-Contra affair, so Nussbaum's count may be justified.

3. John Mitchell (1913–1988) was Richard Nixon's attorney general, convicted of crimes associated with the Watergate affair.

4. The travel office scandal arose because the president's staff had investigated allegations of misconduct in the White House travel office, seemingly involving theft from accounts they managed in helping the press make arrangements for travel. The issue took on heightened political implications—notwithstanding evidence of questionable accounting practices—because the matter had first come to the president's attention through his Arkansas friend Harry Thomason, who wanted part of that business. Whitewater was a failed land development deal in Arkansas, entered into by the Clintons when he was governor. Questions arose there about fiscal impropriety over loans and their repayment, and whether tax money was at risk because of a failed financial institution involved in the transactions.

on that situation, more than I certainly ever wanted to or probably should have had to. . . . The problem with it was, once [somebody] tells me that someone is not dealing properly, I'm responsible for that ultimately. I have to look into it. I can't just say, "I'm sorry, we're not going to look into that for a while, we've got the economic plan. You know, the fate of the presidency rests on that right now. We're just going to have to put that off for six months." . . .

We did look into it, [and] . . . we were troubled by what we found. And with my business background, I have to say, if one of our used car managers in our dealership had $80,000 in his personal bank account that was company money, I'd probably terminate him on the spot. . . . So, we commissioned what we honestly considered to be an independent review, which was by Peat Marwick Mitchell. . . . They concluded that clearly these people [in the travel office] should be terminated. . . . Where we didn't handle things right, we made the right decision but did it in the wrong way. One, the fact that the First Lady was involved in it added a great deal of furor to the story. The fact that Harry Thomason had informed us . . . was a sensitive issue, and we should have been a little more politically aware of that. It got out there pretty quick and got out there in the wrong way in the press.

Bernard Nussbaum: This story is like a Shakespearean tragedy. . . . July 20, 1993, is when we announced [Louis] Freeh's appointment to head the FBI, to universal applause. . . . That same day . . . Ruth Ginsburg was going to testify before the Senate Judiciary Committee . . . and all of a sudden this love fest begins. . . . I turn on the TV and there's Ginsburg, charming the senators and having esoteric discussions about the Fourth Amendment and things like that.[5] I've got the Supreme Court appointment down, smooth, done. I fired the FBI director the week before and got away with it and put another FBI director in. It's going great. No political hassle, everything is fine. This is an amazing story—[Deputy White House Counsel Vince] Foster walks in my office about 12:20. His office is right next to mine. I say "Vince, take a look. We hit two home runs. Look at this. You and I, Ginsburg, Freeh, it's great for the president, it's great for the country." It's the last conversation I had with him. He said, "Yeah, yeah, I guess so," something like that. I said, "I'm going to lunch." He said, "I'm going to lunch. I'll see you later."

As I said, I'm full of myself. . . . I go to lunch at the Metropolitan Club. I don't have a drink at lunch. I only drink after dinner, but I smoke my cigars. . . . I come back after lunch, and say, "Where's Vince? I want to talk to Vince." "Not around." "What do you mean he's not around? Call him." "He's not around." All right, he's not around. So I wait another hour, then I say, "Where's Vince?" I was asking Betsy Pond or Linda Tripp, one of my secretaries. "We don't know

---

5. The Fourth Amendment protects Americans against unreasonable searches and seizures.

where he went." I said, "Page him," which I rarely do, but we have the White House paging system. They come back, there's no answer to the page. I said, "He must have gone home or something, he must have been tired and went home. I'll talk to him tomorrow." I put it out of my mind.

I go back home to my apartment in the Watergate at 6 o'clock in the evening. I had never been home at 6 o'clock since I started in the White House. That day I get home at 6 o'clock because all these things were going well. . . . The reason I'm home is because we had friends coming from New York, Estelle Parsons, the very famous actress, and her husband, who is a prominent lawyer.[6] . . . They come over to our apartment at the Watergate, and we go out to Galileo's, this magnificent Italian restaurant, very famous in D.C. . . . I'm so great, telling stories about how magnificent I am. . . . [All] of a sudden my pager rings. . . . "Oh," I say, "the White House is calling, you can see how important I am. I can't even have dinner. I'm on call at all times." . . . I go to the phone and Mark Gearan, the director of communications, is on the phone and he says "Bernie, you've got to come back to the White House right away. Vince Foster is dead."

Dinner was over, and I went back to the table. My wife is sitting there, our friends are sitting there, and I stand and say, "We have to leave right now. Vince is dead. He killed himself." My wife gasps. The other people didn't know him. They knew of him. "We have to go to the White House right away, so let's all get up." We don't have any car or anything, so we've got to take a cab. It shows what you think about at these strange times. I didn't have my White House pass. . . . In my confusion, I'm sort of wondering if I can get into the White House.

I was so upset obviously, with this news. We drive up to the White House and I walk out and the guards open the door immediately. . . . So first I was relieved that I could get into the White House. But I was so upset. I went in and saw the president. Then everything is the Foster story. . . . It's Shakespearean. . . . [Just] when you think you've got it made, something happens. . . . I think it had a big impact, ultimately. Once [Vince] was gone, the conspiracy theories rolled up and gave a darker cast to what people thought was happening in the administration. Another phantom scandal and the loss of a powerful person who could have provided strength and correct advice at a crucial time six months later when I was there all alone. That's life.

Q: It occurs to me here I want to ask a hard question because it's something that bubbles up occasionally—
Nussbaum: Ask a hard question.

---

6. Estelle Parsons won an Academy Award in 1967 as best supporting actress for her role in *Bonnie and Clyde*. Her husband was Peter Zimroth.

Q: That is that in the commentary on Vince Foster there had been allegations that he and Mrs. Clinton had been involved as something more than just friends. Did you give any credence to that?

Nussbaum: No, because he told me that it wasn't true.... When I met Foster, we got on immediately well. We in effect interviewed each other, we vetted each other. You can say, "What are the bad things people could find out about you or say about you?" He said that to me. I said, "Well, you can say I'm a New York lawyer. I come from a wealthy firm. I'm a tough litigator." I'm trying to think of bad things. It's very hard to think of bad things people can say, but I was trying to make them up.

So that kind of stuff. Who knows, major clients, some of them didn't do wonderful things in life. They can say that. That's what I know are the worst things people can say about me in terms of attacking me. Then I say, "What's the attack on you?" He then said, this is just a conversation, "What's the worst thing people will try to attack you, what will they say?" "People are going to claim that I had a relationship with Hillary, a personal relationship other than professional relationship." "Really? People can say that?" I mean, I knew Hillary a long time also. I said, "So what's the answer to that?"

He said, "It's just not true." Could he have been lying to me? I guess so, but I don't think he was. I really don't. Is it impossible? Nothing's impossible, but I don't think he was lying.... Nor does his wife. I've discussed this with Lisa Foster after his death. This has come up. We were very close friends too. She doesn't believe it. Maybe she's wrong, maybe we're all wrong. Maybe only Hillary knows at this point. But I don't believe it.

Sandy Berger, deputy national security advisor: Vince Foster's suicide was one of the tragic days of life in the White House. I had not known Vince before he came to Washington, but I'd gotten to know him, and he was a remarkably wonderful man. I think the *Wall Street Journal* was crusading against him and calling him incompetent. This was a man who had been head of the Arkansas Bar Association and who had a great sense of his own rectitude—there were cartoons being run in newspapers making fun of him. He was depressed. He killed himself.

What should have followed, in my judgment, the media should have looked at the question of depression in our society, which is a serious problem. There are forty million Americans who have suffered from depression. Instead, Congressman [Dan] Burton [R-IN] opened up an investigation as to whether or not he'd been murdered.[7] There were allegations that Mrs. Clinton had murdered him and dragged his body over to the George Washington Parkway. You remember, Congressman Burton took a watermelon in his back yard and shot

---

7. Dan Burton represented Indiana in the House from 1983 to 2013.

his watermelon to see whether or not the shots could [have been] fired [into his head] by somebody else. . . .

I first came to Washington as a summer intern in 1966, so it's now almost forty years that I've been in Washington. I came to Washington and worked in a Congress where people knew each other. There were friendships. People were here five, six days a week. They went out for a drink after session. Now Congress is here three days a week. . . . They don't really have personal relationships anymore. The way we've handled redistricting in the country, we've made Democratic districts more liberal and Republican districts more conservative to preserve incumbency, and the result is we have a more polarized Congress. I think there are some major problems in our political system.

Bernard Nussbaum: Let me switch back to the fall [of 1993]. . . . I got a call from the office of the majority leader, George Mitchell, . . . maybe it was Mitchell himself, saying, "You know, this independent counsel bill is going through, it's a Democratic bill. You think it's a good idea for us to pass this?"[8] I said, "No, I don't think it's a good idea to pass this; I think we should put it on the back burner, but I better talk to the president, so don't do anything until I get back to you. I really don't like this institution. I think it's dangerous, and I think it's wrong. It's not necessary. Congress has impeachment power." That kind of thing. "So get back to me."

I walk into the Oval Office. . . . [The president] said, "I promised during the campaign that we would support the legislation." I said, "We made a lot of promises during the campaign. We don't need this bill. . . . At one point I said, "You could appoint *me* independent counsel and it would be bad." . . . The reason it would be bad is because once I got control of that institution, if I was the good Bernie Nussbaum, I would spend years trying to turn over every rock to be sure there was nothing under any rock, because I don't want to be embarrassed when I go back. If I was the *bad* Bernie Nussbaum, if I turned bad, I'd see this as a way to bring down a president. Then I would twist ambiguous facts and things like that to try to make a case at all costs against the president to help me, myself, and my party. That would be the bad Bernie Nussbaum. The institution itself has a dynamic that causes that. Look at what Larry Walsh did to Bush and to Reagan. Look what happened under Nixon, even though it was justified. This is a dangerous thing.

---

8. The independent counsel statute was enacted in 1978 in the aftermath of the Watergate affair to avoid the problems created in the Nixon administration with White House attempts to influence Justice Department investigations. Henceforth, under the proper circumstances, a special panel of judges could name an *independent* counsel to investigate claims of wrongdoing. Bill Clinton agreed to reauthorize that statute in 1994. It was terminated in 1999 in the wake of independent counsel Kenneth Starr's investigation into the Lewinsky affair.

Judge Abner Mikva: Within a few days after I was announced [as White House counsel], Ken Starr was announced to be the independent counsel.[9] Obviously, the press came and asked me what I thought about it. I'd gotten along very well with Ken Starr on the court and afterwards . . . and I said to the press, "I have great respect for Ken Starr, and I'm sure we'll get along just fine." From there, every time his name came up, Hillary would say, "your friend Ken Starr"—one word, "yourfriendKenStarr."

In fact, some years after I left the White House, she came in for a fundraiser for Carol Moseley Braun [D-IL], the senator. I went through the receiving line, and when I got up to Hillary, she hugged me and whispered in my ear (this was after the impeachment and everything). She said, "Now what do you think of your friend Ken Starr?" She didn't forget.

Chris Jennings, health care advisor: I wish people really understood the degree to which the modern presidency, at least in the Clinton administration, had to deal with silly subpoenas and requests for information that affected not just the immediate people but everyone around them. Those subpoenas went out, they went to everyone in the White House. *Have you ever seen, heard, talked, thought about anything: please produce every piece of paper ever known to man*, all of it totally irrelevant to anything as it relates to policy or even the alleged reason for the investigation.

Not only did it create distraction and reduce time that could be dedicated to more constructive things, I think it also led to much less paper trails on everything that ever was subsequently produced at the White House. I think it's just a huge waste. There's a lot of bitterness in the White House about that and I think understandably so. More important than that is the impact it has on the deliberative process and the ability to govern.

Leon Panetta, White House chief of staff: As far as the situation with [Monica] Lewinsky, as you may recall, during one of the shutdowns we had brought her over. She was an intern and had come over to answer phone calls. At that time somebody said the president had eyed her. But it was no different than anything else. The president always had an eye for attractive women. But nothing had developed out of that, and there was a point at which somebody said that she was hanging around. And I went to my deputy, who at that time was Evelyn Lieberman, a great woman who actually had worked in the press site. She became the deputy for personnel and scheduling. Evelyn Lieberman came to me and said, "She's hanging around." . . . I said, "Get rid of her." And she said, "Yes,

---

9. Mikva and Starr had served together as judges on the U.S. Court of Appeals for the District of Columbia.

we will, we've got to get rid of her. She's . . . a nuisance." So she was moved over, I think, to Defense at that point.

But I honestly believed I was dealing with a president who more than anything relished the office of the presidency. I've never seen someone who was so immersed in the job of being president of the United States. Almost to the point where I would urge him, "Can you go up to Camp David, can you take some time to get the hell out of this job?" Just take a little time to get away from it, because he was so immersed in it. This was a guy who read every memo that came to him, every memo. . . . He loved going out and doing the campaigning. Weekends, weeknights, through the night. We'd go on a campaign trip to Los Angeles, he would do five events and after the last event he'd want to go to a Mexican restaurant, late at night, and then jump on the airplane and fly back all night to Washington and play hearts going back to Washington.

This is the kind of guy who was just totally immersed in the presidency. We all knew the background, the governorship and what came out during the campaign. But I was always convinced that he cared too much for the presidency to do that [again].

Mickey Kantor: From the very first moment two things were clear in the polls. One, [people] did not believe him when he said he did not have sex with that woman, Ms. Lewinsky; and two, they did not want him removed from office and they supported him as president. . . . Most politicians never understood that, that the public had always differentiated between Bill Clinton personally and Bill Clinton the president. The latter they supported and trusted with the presidency. The former they always saw as the errant little brother with the glint in his eye and you just had to put up with him.

Bernard Nussbaum: If you're Ken Starr, look what this institution has turned into. The president of the United States is going to be asked tomorrow about oral sex in the Oval Office and things like that, and he's probably going to lie about it or not tell the truth or not come clean. Here you have created an institution which is now designed to trap him. Why doesn't somebody pick up the phone and call the president and say, "Mr. President, you're the president of the United States, you're in charge of our foreign policy and the American people. I have a feeling you may be making a mistake tomorrow." In other words, warn him. This is the president of our country, and what you're looking to do is trap him.

Now you say, "Well, he's going to commit a crime." It's like you're treating him like Al Capone. "We're trying to get him. We couldn't get him for Whitewater or anything, so we're going to try to trap him." Wasn't it Ken Starr's duty to warn him? It will hurt him, it will hurt the presidency, and it will hurt the country if he lies about Monica Lewinsky, this woman they're going to ask him about. So be patriotic. If I thought George Bush was going to do something tomorrow and I could reach him, I would warn him off it. I would try. I mean, if he did it, he did it. Because I'm not particularly worried about George W. Bush, the individual. I'm worried about the country, the nation, the president.

Donna Shalala, secretary of health and human services: I think one of my staff came to tell me [when the Monica Lewinsky story broke] and I said, "You're kidding." And I remembered [Lewinsky] because during the shutdown of the government, she was outside in the chief of staff's office, sitting at one of the desks.... I just *couldn't believe* it, couldn't believe it. Then I was furious. We were on a roll. We had a lot we wanted to get done.... We were going to have a Cabinet meeting. I actually walked in and asked the president whether he had done it, as did Madeleine [Albright], I gather, and he said, "Absolutely not." So I just took him at his word.... After that Cabinet meeting Madeleine and I and Dick Riley all went out and defended him. I think I said "ditto" after she said something. Defended him.

* * *

Q: Can you walk us through what happens that first day?
Joe Lockhart, press secretary: Yes. It was not surprising that it was an unusual day at the White House. At this point, I'd been in the Clinton world for only a couple of years—not even a couple—so I was less traumatized. A lot of stuff happens in the White House. There are a lot of days that you come in, and you think this guy is falling, and you know what? You have too much to do. It's a vibrant place that's very hard to rattle.

Well, this day, the place was rattled. You could just tell that everybody was— saying "in a state of shock" would be overdoing it—in a state of high anxiety, because no one knew anything about this. It was very explosive, and nobody had heard from the president. As a group, we didn't know what he was going to say. We knew that the independent counsel would do almost anything to bring the president down, so there was some presumption that maybe this was bullshit. But there was also a sense that if there was something to it, we had big trouble on our hands.

I think I've said this before, so this will not be new, but the single illustrative moment for me on that day was that we—of course, given our luck—had three interviews scheduled.... So Mike [McCurry] and I and some others met the group of people on the senior staff who worried about these things, and we reached the decision to recommend to the president that he not cancel them, that that would show the one thing we didn't want to show, which is somehow they're able to modify his behavior.

Getting the president ready for an interview or for a press conference is generally something everybody on the White House staff and their cousins think they should be involved in. So in getting ready for one of these things, one of the biggest jobs I used to have was being the doorkeeper and telling ten staff people, "No, sorry," and people who were more senior to me, "Sorry, you can't come in."

It's ridiculous. You get twenty people in the room, and no work gets done. That was always a problem. Not this day. I remember going over to the Oval, and the president's executive assistant saying, "Just go on back." I walked in the room, and I was by myself. A couple minutes later, the president walked in and it was just the two of us. I was thinking, *Where is everybody?* I think McCurry came. I think Rahm came.

Q: What kind of small talk is going on with the president at this point?
Lockhart: Oh, I'm telling you, I could accurately describe every inch of my shoes because my eyes were firmly planted on them. [*laughter*] ... The people who didn't have a stomach for this just didn't show. It was a kind of gut-check afternoon, and all the people who screamed at me about how important it was for them to be in this were nowhere to be found. I remember Chuck Ruff[10] came in, and it was clear to me that he didn't know a whole lot. But he knew more than we did about what was going on.

Q: Do you remember how you got that sense?
Lockhart: He talked to us. [Later], while we were waiting for the president to come back, we were saying, "Chuck, what do we say here? What's going on?" He said he wasn't clear on what the true story was, that he was certain it didn't involve anything illegal, but that it was his impression that there was something personally embarrassing to the president that he would have to face.

The president came [back] in. He's someone who has handled enormous amounts of pressure, enormous numbers of political attacks, the responsibility of being in the White House. He was rattled. My guess at the time was that he just didn't know—You could see it running through his head: *What is this woman going to say about me? Now they're going to believe everything she says.* Whether any of it is true is immaterial to where we were at that moment. But we went through the briefing, and it was very businesslike. We made the decision that we were not going to litigate this on television, and we were going to talk about the State of the Union speech coming up. If you go back and look at the Jim Lehrer[11] interview, Jim was tough, but after five minutes of getting no information he moved to other stuff. We were glad we did it.

We got through the rest of the interviews. The president went back to whatever it was he was doing, and that was really the first time we had a chance to sit down and try to figure out what was going on.... Really, the only thing I remember him saying in the room was, "I don't know what this woman is saying about me. What worries me is I don't know what she's saying. She could be saying anything." We were in kind of an odd place where there were a lot of

---

10. Charles Ruff (1939–2000) was White House counsel from 1998 to 1999.
11. Lehrer was a news anchor for the Public Broadcasting Service, hosting *PBS NewsHour*.

people who were determined to believe what they wanted to believe, and I think he gave those people enough to work with. . . .

Q: *You're getting ready to go with the State of the Union address. I'm trying to get as much of your recollection as I can of that first week. My guess is some of this stuff blurs—*

Lockhart: Yes, it does blur. I think the story came out in the middle of the week, Tuesday or Wednesday. I'm not sure. I remember the weekend feeling critical. I would say Saturday was the day when it started moving toward the scenario of the president being forced to resign. CNN, in particular, was very aggressive on this, and I was particularly aggressive with them in countering what they were saying. . . . The weekend felt like we were trying to keep the dam from bursting while trying to figure out what we were going to do. It was a difficult weekend, but I think we kept the dam from bursting. We woke up Monday morning and he was still president—which, if you watched the news Saturday morning, you weren't completely sure would be the case.

Now the interesting part about what we do next is that the president went off on his own and sought the counsel of some old friends, not his White House staff. So when he got up and talked on Monday, it was certainly news to me that that was now the strategy. There was not the normal sense we'd had in the White House, where there was a process we went through to develop a strategy, agree upon it, and then implement it. Everything was a little off. . . . He spent the weekend with Linda Bloodworth [Thomason][12] and her husband . . . Harry Thomason. And I believe that James Carville was part of those conversations. I don't know who else. At this point, this situation was not being managed through the White House structure. The chief of staff was not calling meetings and bringing everyone in and saying, "Here's what we're going to do. Here's what we're going to say." It just wasn't happening.

Donna Shalala: I went to the White House that weekend to watch something on television. I think we were watching some kind of sports stuff. . . . Their friends from California were there and a lot of people buzzing around and I thought, *Oh, my God, he did it.* I don't know why I came to that conclusion. But I came to that conclusion because they weren't acting like he hadn't done it. There were just too many people buzzing around, scheming, maneuvering. That's when I realized that there was something there. Hillary said, "Thanks for supporting the president." I don't know whether she knew or not, but that was the moment in which I thought, *There's something here.*

* * *

---

12. Linda Bloodworth Thomason was a prominent screenwriter and producer from Arkansas, best known for her television programs *Designing Women* and *Evening Shade*. She and her husband Harry became friends of Bill Clinton when he was governor.

Q: *You implied that there was a shift in emphasis or strategy by that Monday.*
Joe Lockhart: Well, certainly when the president went out and told the country that he "hadn't had sex with that woman," we all said, "Okay, that's our—"

Q: *So that was him telling the world and the staff and all of you simultaneously.*
Lockhart: That's when I found out. That's the first time the question had been directly answered for me. . . .

Q: *Did you believe what he was saying when he told you that?*
Lockhart: Yes, I think I did actually, and I think that was probably pretty naïve. This will sound—I'm not sure what the right word is, because I do think that government service and what I was doing is important. But it was almost beside the point whether I believed him. My job wasn't to make a moral judgment about the president. I believed at that time that this was someone who was doing a lot of good for a lot of people, who was in the process of being thrown out of office in what amounted to a coup over personal behavior. To me it was okay if he did it or if he didn't do it. . . .

You know, the really interesting academic question—and I don't have an answer to it, but I'll pose it. (I think I know the answer, and it goes against every grain of conventional wisdom as far as communications is concerned.) Consider this possibility: What if he stood up and told the truth? I'm pretty convinced that within three weeks he wouldn't have been president. This was not complicated. There was only one group of people who, if they went soft, he was out, and that was Senate Democrats. If you had ten Senate Democrats standing up saying, "This guy has to go," he had to go. He may not have believed that, but before any evidence is heard you have an impeachable majority.

I don't know the answer to how much of this was calculated or how much wasn't. I just don't know, and I've never asked. This is a post-game analysis. At the time, I wasn't aware of any of this dynamic. I was just trying to do my job every day. But I do believe that if what he said, say, at the prayer breakfast a year later was said that day—even if it was said with that much sincerity and that much grief—he probably wouldn't have survived.[13]

Q: *Did the speech change the mood in the White House at all among the staff?*
Lockhart: Yes. I think it gave everybody something to hold on to. We thought, *Okay, fine. He says it's not true, it's not true. Let's get back to work.* There really was a sense that that was a turning point. People basically wanted to hear him address it, and there was no universal sense of judgment. Some people judged him

---

13. Clinton admitted at the National Prayer Breakfast in Washington, on September 11, 1998, that he had sinned—and had failed to be sufficiently contrite earlier.

much more harshly than others. Some people didn't care about his personal life. Some people were morally repelled by it. But from that point on, we knew we had a job to do, and it's still stunning to me on this day that nobody left. It says a lot about how much we knew about the other side and how ruthless they were and how hard we were going to fight against allowing them to get their way. . . .

Q: *In the short run, the State of the Union must have been a turning point.*[14]
Lockhart: Sure. That's a big thing . . . and I'm glad you bring it up. To the extent that we tried to deal with this strategically, it became very clear how we needed to position this. You have the independent counsel over here. He's crazy. He's trying to kill the president. It's all about politics. But guess what? The president's a big guy, he can handle it. He is not going to be deterred from doing your business. The people's business is paramount here, and our strategy became just demonstrating that on a daily basis.

It turned out that the thing we were most worried about—having to give the State of the Union—became the biggest gift ever given to us. You talk about playing right to Bill Clinton's strength! . . . *You know what? I'm the president. There are 535 people in this room. None of them is the president. None of them is going to get me out of here.* The president looked at the country and said, "You and I understand each other. We'll get through this other stuff, but this is what I'm focused on."

Don Baer, speechwriter and former communications director:[15] [Five] days or so before the [1998 State of the Union] speech, the Lewinsky scandal broke. I was involved in it at that point because every year after I left the White House, I came back in for part of the State of the Union preparation. . . . There was a big fight, and it operated on a few levels. There were some people who advocated very much that the president needed to address the nation from the well of the Congress on the issue of the scandal, and that he had to speak to the country about it at this moment when he had everyone's attention focused on him as president. There were other people, fortunately, who prevailed, who understood that the job of the president was to be the president. The country was looking to see, as bad as this thing seemed to be, if he was still in a position to perform the job of the presidency on their behalf, because that is what

---

14. Although the Drudge Report first broke the story online on January 19, 1998, the initial mainstream press report was on Wednesday, January 21. The president's annual State of the Union address that year was scheduled for January 27, the following Tuesday.

15. Baer's remarks were made in a public oral history symposium with former speechwriters. See Nelson and Riley, eds., *The President's Words*, 257.

the country wanted. If you remember, there's not a mention of that scandal in the speech.

We had a meeting in Richard Nixon's old West Wing hideaway office, which was a conference room that we used over there, to talk about whether, at the top of the speech, the president should say anything very quickly, even parenthetically, that would hint at "I know something is going on, but let's get on with the business of the country."

There was a back and forth, and I remember having a pad of paper and asking, "Is there a way to say this in a way that wouldn't overstate anything?" and all that. There was a group of a dozen or so people, outside advisors and what not. The decision was ultimately made by the president. "We're not going to say anything about this. My job is to stand up there and tell the country what I'm going to do as president and to show them that I'm going to perform the job every day that they hired me to do."

* * *

Q: Are there any notable developments in these early days beyond the State of the Union message?
Joe Lockhart: I think there are, from both the arc of the story and my particular role in this. On a very significant night, I believe—and I'm not the only one who believes it—this shifted a little. . . . There was a report in the *Dallas Morning News* that talked about how one of the White House stewards had witnessed something between Clinton and Lewinsky and had told the grand jury about it. This was a pretty big development, and the *Dallas Morning News* had it, which struck me as odd. Not that the *Dallas Morning News* isn't a good newspaper. They have great reporters there, but the [Washington] *Post* had been leading the charge. If somebody wanted to give out that piece of information, I would have thought it would be in the *Post*.

So on my way home, I got in touch with one of the lawyers, who got in touch with the lawyer for the steward, who said . . . it was completely wrong, and we could be confident that it was completely wrong. I remember getting that about the time I got home, and then starting to try to push the rock up the mountain of all this. I found a *Dallas Morning News* reporter whom I knew well at home, and I said, "Listen, you need to get to the office and fix this, because you guys are going to be sucking wind tomorrow, and we're going to be unmerciful to you if you don't fix this. It's not true, and I know it's not true."

She got my message, because she could tell I was confident they were wrong. So they swung into action. Then it was just everybody else—the AP. I remember talking to the *Nightline* producer during a commercial while they were on. They didn't say the story was wrong, but they gave the White House perspective on it while they were on the air.

This went on until, I don't know, 3:30, four o'clock in the morning, when finally I went to bed. It was one of those great things where the *Dallas Morning News* got spooked by the story, by us pushing back so hard, so they pulled it. But everybody in the world knew they had already reported it, so they ended up having to run a correction in the newspaper of a story that hadn't been in the newspaper. Everybody said, "Wow! That's never happened before." And they did correct it. Very late into the night they basically said, "Just kidding—just trying to see if you're all reading."

The next piece will tell you that I'm not sitting here saying I turned this thing around, because it's the next thing that really did—in some ways, at least for Democrats. I remember going to sleep for about an hour, but I had one more thing I had to do, which was get up the next morning. That was the day the First Lady was on the *Today Show*. I didn't brief her. I briefed her staff person, and basically she said, "Call me before I go on if anything's happened overnight."

So I picked up, and I said, "Well, a few things have happened." I explained the whole thing to her. And I think the combination of her full-throated defense of her husband on the *Today Show*, and this idea that not all the information coming out of the independent counsel's office could be trusted, caused a lot of reporters to take a breath. All of a sudden, they realized you can't just throw any shit out there that you hear on the street.

I think the *Dallas Morning News* was very embarrassed by this. And it turns out that their sourcing was awful. . . . It was just a mess, and that felt a little like a combination of these things happening that everybody took a collective breath and said, "Maybe we shouldn't run him out of office this week. Maybe we should stop and figure out what we have here," and—everything's relative in life—things calmed down a little. . . . The first ten days of this with reporters was like the Wild West. There were no rules, because everyone was afraid they were going to be the last one to figure out the president had just gone to the helicopter and gone home. . . . Then we got into a full-scale trench war with the independent counsel's office, which went on from that moment to the moment his report came out [in September]. Every two or three days he'd leak out some awful piece of information, and we'd kick the shit out of him for doing it.

Lawrence Stein, congressional liaison: I would periodically go in [to see the old Clinton hands] and say *mughhhh*. . ., "I don't know how this [can end well]—" and Bruce [Lindsey] would say, "Believe me. I've been through every conceivable thing with this guy. He's going to make it. He's just going to." The truth is that they had gone after him so many different ways, and he had survived so many different things, that most of the people who were closest to him just believed that he was going to come out of it [okay].

Charles Brain, congressional liaison: Larry Stein and I spent time saying to each other, "Well Albert [Gore] will keep us, won't he?" Because no one knew what was going to happen.

Joe Lockhart: On balance, in the public relations war [during 1998], our guy came out better than [Starr] did.... [The] ultimate mistake the independent counsel made was releasing the videotape [of the president's deposition].[16] That killed it for them. It was over at that moment. It's one of these things where we didn't know how people would react. I'd love to say we were really smart and we knew we'd baited him into this and we really wanted it. We did not want it. But we did do one thing that did, I think, help a little.

I don't know where these stories came from. They didn't come from us, but all the stories that came out two or three days before the videotape was going to be released that talked about the president's explosive temper and ranting and raving and all that were just some right-wing nut out there bloviating on. We made a conscious decision not to deny it. And if you don't deny it and you're not aggressive, they pretty much think it's true, and we knew that.

So for three days people were expecting this out-of-control, rabid, crazy man, and when they actually saw it, they basically made the judgment that the only crazy people were the ones asking the questions. The president was calm and respectful. A couple of times he pushed back where it was appropriate, but it was really, *Why are you making us watch this?* ... [From] the public's point of view, that's the moment it turned. I don't know that we knew whether we'd get impeached, but we had a pretty good sense we were not going to get removed.

Betty Currie, personal secretary: The many, many, many times I went up there [to testify to the grand jury] and every time they would ask me whether, when I talked to the president, he was influencing my thoughts. I tried to tell them, in the best way I knew how, that he wasn't. He was doing this and doing that, but he wasn't trying to make me say anything or tell me to do anything. Despite my telling them over and over and over again, obviously they didn't believe me because they kept on with it.

Q: The questions kept coming to you, and the spin that the independent counsel was putting on this was that [the president] was attempting to coach you in your own testimony.
Currie: Right. And I never felt it, and I tried my best to relay that to them but they didn't hear it, they didn't hear it. From that day to this, there was no coaching.

---

16. Starr gave the videotape to the House of Representatives. On September 18, 1998, the House Judiciary Committee voted to release it to the public. It was widely broadcast on September 21.

Q: Can I ask you then what you felt the purpose of the conversation was from your perspective?

Currie: I'll tell you like I told them. I felt then and I feel now that he was refreshing his memory. The questions came up that way. I said, "You're right." That's all it was.

Q: How did you go about preparing yourself to go before the grand jury?

Currie: Prayed. I think I was more scared than I realized. We had met with the FBI [Federal Bureau of Investigation] before, which in retrospect I was told was a mistake. Whether it was or not I don't know, but my lawyers thought I should, so we did.... [It's] one big blur, I don't have my dates. We met and then we went over everything. It was horrible. There were tears, it was horrible. Then my lawyers said, "Okay, you lived through that, you can live through the grand jury." I thought they were right. Then I went to the grand jury.

The people who talked to me there were smiling and were nice and I said, "Okay, they're not going to kill me here," but it was not easy. It was not easy. And every time I went it was not easy. They would allow me to interrupt whenever I wanted to go get my lawyers, but then as you're talking sometimes you forget. Let me stop, let me stop.... One interviewer whom I'd never seen before came in one day and was like Perry Mason. He was grilling me. I said, "Can we stop?" One of the jurors said, "Please stop because he's not being very nice." ... At one point they kept asking me questions about people and at one point I told them, "I cannot mention another name to you because as soon as I mention a name, you subpoena these young kids who can't afford any lawyers. Now ask me what you want, but I'm not saying any other names." I just couldn't do it anymore.

Q: Did you ever have a subsequent conversation with the president about your ordeal through this?

Currie: We never talked about it.

Q: So there was never an apology from him.

Currie: Never an apology. And as I tell anybody who'll listen, he didn't have to. With someone like that you can look and you can tell, you can feel it. He regrets it, putting me through this and everything, I just feel it. If I'm wrong, I'm wrong, but I feel it. ...

Q: How was your relationship with President Clinton during this period of time? You were sitting right outside his office.

Currie: I think fine. I think he was going through whatever he was going through also. So we didn't lean on each other, but I think he understood my situation and I understood his. We just went right on.

Q: It was completely unspoken.
Currie: Unspoken.

Joe Lockhart: If you look at the whole Lewinsky matter, there were two points where the president was in real political jeopardy—a few more things happening or things turning a different way, and the result could have been different.

The first was in that first seven, eight days [in January 1998]. The second was in about the seven days after his speech to the nation [in August admitting an inappropriate relationship with Lewinsky]. He [then] went off on vacation [to Martha's Vineyard]. All of a sudden, he didn't have any way to show that he was doing the people's business ... and Democratic senators started getting a little squishy. We got all sorts of reports about what was happening at caucus meetings, with senators getting up and saying, "Maybe we need to tell him it's time to go." ... This is August 17 through, say, August 25. From his perspective, I think this may have been the moment of most strain, because he went off on vacation, didn't have his work to occupy him, and had some family issues to deal with very directly and painfully. So this was a critical moment and a moment of jeopardy.

Lawrence Stein: I went away on a pre-planned vacation. I was down at Duck, [North Carolina]. My impression had been that [the president's August speech after the grand jury testimony] was going to be his typically eloquent—and, I think, effective and ... heartfelt—apology to the nation that would in some ways cleanse this thing.

As it turned out, the last four minutes were not that. I can't say how that happened. It was certainly not what I understood it was going to be when I left. I remember watching it, and from then on I was on the phone continuously for about five days.... I was calling a bunch of senators trying to make sure they weren't going to get angry at the way that happened.

Q: In your calls to the senators, were you finding that they were concerned about the tone of the speech?
Stein: Yes, they thought that it should have been 100 percent contrition. I don't remember the exact language he used, but he had taken the opportunity to criticize Starr.... I don't remember which senators I called. I think I had seventeen and Erskine had seventeen or something like that. We were much more focused on the Senate.... I thought that there would be disappointment among people like [Democrats] Byron Dorgan [ND], John Kerry [MA], and Harry Reid [NV] that he had missed an opportunity, which, as we just agreed, is really not like him. What carried him through was an incredible ability to hit the right note. That's what saved him over the longer haul. When I was driving down to Duck, I thought, *This thing is going to be pretty well over after he does this.* I thought that

he would cleanse the environment. From everything I'd seen of him before, he was totally capable of that.

Q: Can I ask, were you thinking ahead about the possibility of impeachment at this point?
Stein: From day one I thought the Republicans would try to carry it to impeachment, largely because I think they knew no bounds. But that wasn't on my mind, no. It was an election year. There were *Democrats* who were in a difficult position. Many of them were likely to interpret their problems as things created by him, whether they were or not. The argument had been made rather frequently by good people that he was hurting the party, despite the poll numbers. Democrats didn't always believe the poll numbers.

We were still going to the Wednesday night sessions. I believed the poll numbers implicitly. They were absolutely unmistakable. They were detailed, the cross tabs were clear. It wasn't as though it was a bubble or superficial. It was quite real.

People understood. . . . But many Democrats were unable to accept it because they thought it affected them. Maybe they thought that with his charisma he was able to escape his own culpability, but they couldn't. I should say this, because this is the truth. Some of the more thoughtful among them thought that the recklessness of it was just breathtaking. I'm quoting a senator whom I won't name. That was what troubled many of the ones for whom I have the most respect. It wasn't so much the morality of the situation itself; it was that he had done something like this knowing the forces that were out there trying to get him, knowing how strange it was to have put his fortunes in the hands of a twenty-one-year-old, totally irresponsible, child is what it amounts to. . . . So when he made the speech and didn't hit a home run as he had in the State of the Union (and I think he'd acknowledge that himself)—yes, I was worried. We were all worried.

Donna Shalala: We went to a Cabinet meeting [in September, right after the president's vacation], and we were all told to tell the president the truth. So I told him the truth. I told him I didn't like it. I was particularly irritated. If you're a college president, the last thing you do is let people hit on students. We have rules about these things, particularly for a young person. If he had had an affair with a married person and lied about it, I don't think I would have been bothered about it at all. It was the young person thing. It just hit against every principle I've had in my life and the world that I come from. I have zero tolerance with a faculty member with this kind of behavior. I've fired tenured professors over this, and it was just unacceptable. Everyone was being a bit of an apologist for him in the room and I just blew up.

Q: Yes, I heard it got very religious.
Shalala: It got very religious. He came firing back at me. We sort of hugged at the end of the thing, but I was just pissed off, I was just irritated. It really had to

do with who I was and where I had come from.... There was a crisis. A couple of us talked about whether we should resign over this. I think we actually all decided the same thing, that we should not turn this into a constitutional crisis. We should just get our work done and keep the government together, our parts of the government together. We should not be drawn into this. That's what we ended up doing.

Q: Who else did you talk to?
Shalala: I talked to three other Cabinet members whom I don't want to name, and all of them were feeling the same way I was, and that is, *This is disgusting but we've got to keep going.*

Q: You had no doubt heard—you have to have heard all the stuff that went before—
Shalala: Yes, and I had known Hillary for a long time, but I thought that was all over. I really thought that was all over. And I saw nothing near that for years after we entered the White House. Nothing, nor was there a lot of rumor around about anything like that. But I think what really set me off was not moral outrage at the president of the United States having an affair with someone, it was that it was an intern. I just couldn't tolerate that. . . .

Q: Were you worried about whether the president and the First Lady would stick it out together?
Shalala: No, I thought they would. I thought it was going to be very difficult, but I thought they would. They had been through a lot before that together. I thought that that was a very strong bond. I think she was devastated. You could just tell she was devastated. In part we were all staying because of her too. We had worked a long time to get as far as we were. We were going into the last leg of the administration. We were not about to blow it. We had a lot we wanted to get done.

Joe Lockhart: [In November], the midterm elections happened, and I think almost everybody in the White House woke up the next morning thinking, *Well, impeachment's going to go away.*[17] I will give one person credit for not knowing that. But the president's chief of staff, John Podesta, was in exactly the other place. John is a contrarian, so I'm never quite sure how much of it was, "I'm just going to stake out this position," but he was adamant: "We're still getting impeached. They are not going to stop. I don't know if they have the votes, but they're not going to stop." And of course he was right. They threw Gingrich

---

17. The 1998 midterm election results were almost unprecedented in registering voter support for the president's party. Almost always that party loses seats at the six-year midterm, but in the House the Democrats actually picked up five seats in 1998. The balance in the Senate went unchanged, although the Democrats were defending more seats.

over and decided, "We're still going to do this."[18] And there was a very intense political process to try to turn some moderate Republicans, which was very unsuccessful.

Separately, we were moving through Saddam Hussein's intractability on inspections toward some military conflict with Iraq. There was a constant low-level chatter of "wag the dog" and "Is he going to pull another Tomahawk attack to get out of some political crisis?"[19]

I think the best way to describe the dynamic is to get very specific and talk about a couple of days, because there was about a thirty-six-hour period two weeks or so before impeachment and then the impeachment day [that were key. First,] we were in Israel. We'd gone over for bilateral talks with Netanyahu, and then we were going to Gaza, which—absent the rest of the drama in the world—was an unbelievably historic event—the president of the United States going to the Palestinian National Congress in Gaza, and touring Gaza as no other world leader had. But other stuff was going on.

I remember we were in the King David Hotel [in Jerusalem], and it was morning. I'm not sure what Doug Sosnik's job title was, but he was basically the smartest political guy in the White House, and he had gotten a call, I think from Congressman Jack Quinn [R-NY].[20] It might have been someone else, but it was some congressman we knew who was a key Republican holdout, and if the Republicans broke his legs, a bunch of them would fall. [Doug] had gotten the news very early in the morning that Quinn had [fallen]. So we had to go in and tell the president, and this was just one of those moments that are hard to describe accurately—Doug having to tell him, "You're going to be impeached." But, as comes with the job, he couldn't sit around worrying about it. We were going to Gaza, and then we were going home. . . .

Q: Was the president angry at this point?
Lockhart: I've seen a lot of different presidential reactions. This was more like someone did something that took the wind out of him. Not angry, just resigned. . . . The president's temper was generally inversely proportional to how important something was. The thing he used to lose his temper over the most was not being able to find his glasses. Those blow-ups would be of epic proportions. On important things, he tended to be somewhat stoic, and I believe

18. Speaker of the House Newt Gingrich (R-GA) was forced to resign from that leadership post because of perceptions within his caucus that he had misplayed their hand going into the 1998 midterm elections, costing them seats. He soon thereafter left Congress entirely.

19. In 1997, Dustin Hoffman and Robert De Niro starred in the Barry Levinson film *Wag the Dog*. The comic plot had the president of the United States attempting to distract the American people from a sex scandal by starting a phony war, knowing that the country's patriotism could be exploited to his benefit. Because of the similarities to Bill Clinton's personal situation, he faced strong skepticism on Capitol Hill when initiating military action in 1998.

20. Sosnik at the time was senior advisor for policy and strategy.

that was one of those moments. But I don't know that I was in the room for the whole thing.

Anyway, we go to Gaza. It's exactly what Bill Clinton wanted to be president for, to be involved in that kind of moment. Then we go back and we get on the plane.... On the flight back there were two very important but separate things going on. In the front of the plane, the president had his national security team—some of them with him in the room, some of them via some sort of very high-tech secure conference call. There was a very detailed discussion about what was going on in Iraq, and the president was being asked to make his decision on whether to launch an attack. I don't believe he made the decision in that call, but it was very clear, from the parts of it I heard, that he was being given option A, option A, and option A. Or you could take option B and do nothing—and that's not a very good option.

Back in the middle cabin, where some of the political aides were, our prediction of the dams breaking once Jack Quinn went was absolutely right. The phone would ring every five minutes with some other congressman who'd come out and said he was going to vote for impeachment. We knew there were probably fifteen or twenty members waiting to see.

I do remember at one point the meeting up front took a little break for some reason, and I was wandering back and forth. On *Air Force One*, as you come down the aisle, they have some couches backed to the wall so you're sitting looking into the middle of the plane. Sandy Berger was sitting there with a forlorn look on his face, and I walked by and said, "Sandy, what's wrong?" And he said, "This is just really hard. This is a really hard thing." I looked at him and said, "Sandy, you think things are tough up here, you should see what's going on back there."

... We landed at the typical 3:00 a.m. at Andrews. I got off the plane, and I remember walking out and thinking I knew three things. One was we were getting impeached. Two, we were going to war, and [three] it was my job to convince the country that the first thing had nothing to do with the second thing.

Sandy Berger, national security advisor: I was so walled off from what was going on on the impeachment side that I would drive home at night and call my daughter who worked at CNN and say, "What happened today?" She'd say, "Oh my God—in the Senate, the impeachment committee voted Articles of Impeachment." I tried to pay as little attention to it as I could. Obviously, I read the newspapers. But I never discussed this with the president. The only time that I had any personal conversation with the president was when he spoke, two times I think, to the Cabinet, one at the beginning of this episode, in which he rallied the Cabinet to stay together. Then once when he finally acknowledged that he was not telling the truth, he convened the Cabinet and there was a very heartfelt apology that he made to the Cabinet. He and I never had a conversation that said we've got to wall foreign policy off from all of this, but he understood it and I understood it and we didn't have to say it to each other.

Lawrence Stein: We knew the [impeachment] votes were supposed to be Thursday or Friday. And that Wednesday night, I remember Podesta coming up to my office and saying, "We're going to have to attack Iraq." I remember just sitting down. I couldn't believe it. He said, "[William] Cohen and Sandy and [George] Tenet [director of central intelligence] say we have to do this." I said the obvious thing: the wag-the-dog scenario is going to be inescapable. To be honest with you, that was probably the worst moment among many bad ones that I had at the White House. I said, "We can't do that. We have to figure out a way." John made the obvious rejoinder, "We can't sacrifice international policy because these guys were insisting on going on—" . . . I said, "All right, I know, we need to inform some people. We need to inform the leadership." . . . [Speaker-elect Robert] Livingston's guys . . . said, "Look, we understand. We kind of accept this, but you have to bring your people up and speak to the House."[21]

That had certainly not happened in my experience. It was about 10 o'clock at night. They convened the House for a meeting with Cohen, [General Hugh] Shelton, and Tenet. I remember sitting down with Cohen's people before-hand—he was not back yet—saying, "We have to present a very sound case." We went through it, and it was an extremely sound case. Shelton started and presented the military situation, Cohen followed up and said, "I'm a Republican, you know I'm a Republican. I'm proud of my Republican credentials, and I'm standing here telling you that this is a necessary act. You're all going to think that somehow it's a diversion. It is necessary, we have to do it"—which carried tremendous weight.

Then Tenet did the explanation on the ground. This had to do with the inspectors and with weapons and multiple other issues that have now gotten a lot more current. So they went through it, and there was general furrowed brow, nodding, okay, we understand. They had set up microphones for questions. Tom DeLay [R-TX] stands up and says to Cohen, "Mr. Secretary, can you think of any reason why we can't go forward with the impeachment vote while the troops are in the field?"[22] At least on the Democratic side, they booed, outright booed him, spontaneously. Cohen said, "Well, yes, I can think of a reason. You have young people going into battle, and to have their president being challenged with potential removal from office, yes, that's a bit of a problem."

We heard the next day DeLay was going ahead on Saturday. I tell that for anyone who believed that they weren't hell-bent to do this. They were doing it,

---

21. At that moment the Republican House leadership was in a state of flux, as Speaker Newt Gingrich had just announced his intention to leave Congress, setting off an uncertain succession. Louisiana Congressman Robert Livingston claimed to have the votes to follow Gingrich, and so was effectively the speaker-in-waiting. The White House was already beginning to work with him. He never assumed the office, however, felled by an extramarital affair of his own.

22. DeLay at that time was House majority whip.

they were working the votes, and they were going to break the elbows of anyone who was going to oppose it. I knew that.... In all honesty, I think ... they were proved to be nuts.

General Hugh Shelton, chair of the Joint Chiefs of Staff (on the "wag the dog" claims): First of all, I would never have been a party to anything—neither Cohen nor I—that was not based on sound military logic and something that needed to be done militarily. In both cases, the recommendation to carry out the attacks came from the Department of Defense, from us. The timing of those events, which really tied into wag the dog—the accusation that we would have attacked Iraq to take away the impeachment announcement was absolutely ludicrous. The timing of that particular one had been made by Cohen and me, primarily based on my recommendation because of the light conditions, the attack conditions, the weather conditions that were forecast, and Ramadan that fell in that particular area. We had about a three- or four-day window when we could carry out the attack when the light conditions were right and before Ramadan and Christmas started.

The bottom line is, we carried out the attack, and immediately the accusation started, wag the dog. Before that, after one of the meetings in the National Security Council, Secretary Cohen had asked me to step out of the room, the only time during my tenure, under either secretary, that I was asked to leave the NSC room while they were deliberating. To Bill Cohen's credit, he called me in the second he got back to the Pentagon, to tell me what it was all about.

He wanted to let the people in the White House know that he had just learned of the announcement of the coming impeachment. He's a smart guy, and he could foresee wag the dog being a part of it. They had to know that and take into consideration that this was what the accusation would be, in case the president had any second thoughts about approving the dates we had given him. He said, "I asked you to leave because this is a political issue, and I didn't want you dragged into the middle of it."

Greg Craig, special counsel:[23] Clinton would be on the phone every night talking to people, and one of his favorite people to talk to was [Senator] John Breaux (D-LA). And John Breaux said, "You know, the way Huey Long[24] dealt with this is that he got forty members of the Louisiana State Senate to sign a letter saying that they would never vote for impeachment under any circumstances. It killed it, because you needed two-thirds and if you had forty saying they'd never do

---

23. Craig's remarks recorded in an interview for the Miller Center's Edward M. Kennedy Oral History Project.

24. Huey Long (1893–1935) was a rogue, populist Louisiana politician, who served a single term as governor and was a member of the U.S. Senate from 1932 to 1935, when he was assassinated.

it, then that was the way it was." Clinton loved that idea, so he started calling around. He called [Senator Christopher] Dodd (D-CT), I think he called three or four people, and Robert Byrd got word of this and went straight to the floor of the Senate and said, "I'm hearing reports that the president of the United States is making calls, to try to tell United States senators how they should vote on the question of impeachment. Do not tamper with this jury!" [*laughter*]. . . . Oh, man, I thought, *We've lost Byrd already and we haven't even been impeached yet.* That was Clinton's strategy. It was a terrible strategy.

Lawrence Stein: The day they voted out impeachment articles was an amazing day. It was the day Livingston resigned. To start that morning, we went up with Mrs. Clinton to address the Democratic caucus, which seems a little odd, but we did. She was great. She was absolutely great, they loved her. She called it a *coup.* I can't remember the speech, but it was extremely good. It was extemporaneous. It was beautifully done, so much so that [Congressman] Charlie Rangel [D-NY] insisted—I resisted this, but we ultimately capitulated—that we get buses and bus people down to the White House after the vote, as support for the president.[25] Part of his reason for insisting on it was that CBS, I think, had run a phony poll at the time of the vote that showed something about numbers of people wanting the president to resign. It was wrong. It was flat wrong. There was nothing even approaching that.

Charlie got very worked up about it. I should make another observation: The real backbone of Clinton's support in the House was the African-American caucus. They were adamant. There were times when we wondered whether Gephardt was really there emotionally, but we didn't worry about it because [Congressman] John Lewis [D-GA] went in and told him where he was going to be. But Charlie, who is a hilarious person, just insisted on this, and he's very close to [congressional liaison] Chuck [Brain]. He grabbed Chuck and he said, "I want to do it." Chuck said *umm, umm, umm.* "No, you've got to do this. Otherwise people are going to think there's not sufficient support for the President. There's got to be a visible showing."

I guess I concluded in my own mind—and John Podesta I think concluded the same thing—that we couldn't tell them, "You can't come." So they came down, and everyone delivered rousing speeches up on the second floor, on the state floor where we used to have the press conferences. I have to say, one had cognitive dissonance when we were having a kind of rally on the day that the man had been impeached. And certainly that was the way it struck people from the outside who didn't know the rhythm of the day, because it was incredibly emotional. . . . Gephardt delivered one of his best speeches, inside, closed off

---

25. In Joe Lockhart's oral history, he claims with confidence that Clinton communications director Ann Lewis originated the idea of bringing members of Congress to the White House for this rally.

from the press, saying, "Mr. President, you cannot—I know you're not going to resign—but you could not resign even if you wanted to, because it would be a validation of what was a criminal process."

We go outside, and do a press conference, and I think Gore was just lifted beyond reason. Well, what had happened inside in private was still influencing him as he got outside in public. Gephardt gets up and delivers a pretty restrained thing about, "We've urged the president to continue with the policies that he's conducted on behalf of the country because the country needs him." Gore got up and said something to the effect that, "This is the best president the country has ever had."

I was standing there in the press group.... And boy, just looking around, the press was just stunned that he'd said that. They were just visibly stunned. They hadn't seen what had gone on inside, they hadn't been in the caucus, they couldn't put all that together and understand why. They just heard the statement, and to them it was outrageous to be saying something like that on the day the man had been impeached. I really think that that hurt him badly with press people. He had been hurt for a lot of reasons related to this, but I think it hurt him very badly going forward.

Kris Engskov, personal aide: I was upstairs on the second floor, and the president was in his dressing area. I said, "You're not going to believe this, but Bob Livingston has stepped down for an extramarital affair." There was dead silence. I said, "Did you hear me?" He just goes, "Yep." That was it. That was the only time we were in discussion. Routinely, if you thought there was something important to tell the president, you would tell him and he would react to it. He distinctly did not react to that. I remember that very distinctly. He just said, "Yep."

Joe Lockhart: In the twenty-four hours before impeachment, there's an increasingly loud rumor mill developing on the Hill about this politician being outed, that politician being outed, and a lot of stuff is happening that we don't know about within the Republican caucus. We're hearing now that the stories are more about a particular person. There are stories about Bob Livingston, and this and that.

But at the White House we hear that stuff all the time. Once a week I'd get a story about some black baby the president had apparently fathered somewhere along the line—and from a serious reporter. I'd say, "Go try someplace else." ... So I'm not sure any of us took that much notice of it. Others may have. I was pretty focused on trying to get through the day. So obviously we were a little surprised when Bob Livingston got up on the floor of the House and resigned. We were all separate. We didn't gather to watch this. We were all in our offices doing our jobs. The president was over in the residence doing something. He wasn't watching.

But I had it on in my office, and I remember hearing him say it. I had some-one sitting on the couch, and I said, "Did I just hear that right? Did he just resign?" It took all of about ten seconds—and this rarely happened in the White House—for full-scale total panic, for this reason. *It was at that very moment that I put their entire strategy together.* I should have put it together before. I just wasn't thinking enough about it.

Three or four days before this, the Republicans had shifted their political strategy. The place to go and find it most directly is an op-ed by Tom DeLay in the *Washington Post*, I think, that made some great argument. Then the morning of the impeachment, E. J. Dionne[26] had a column that basically laid out their strategy. I read it but discounted it a little bit. They were implying a classic bait and switch. For months, they'd argued that what the House was doing was no big deal. It was like a grand jury preparing an indictment. You can indict a ham sandwich, blah, blah, whatever the cliché is. The real work where the president would have due process is in the Senate. So don't worry so much about what we're doing here. We're just going through the motions. It's no big deal.

Two or three days before the actual impeachment vote, it very subtly began to shift, and it was full-throated by Friday night, Saturday morning: any president who's impeached is so embarrassing to the nation that he should resign. I had started to pick that up on Friday and started pushing back. I was aware of it in some part of my mind, but I viewed it as something they were doing tactically as opposed to their total strategy.

Saturday we found out it was their total strategy. DeLay looked at Livingston and thought, *Okay, this can actually work for us. Get underneath the bus. We're going to run over you. And this is going to help us get the president.* Again, it didn't take a great thinker to put together that if someone commits some personal, private act that's distasteful or immoral, and he's the leader of the Republicans and he should resign, then the Democrat should do the same. We quickly gathered. I ran over to the Oval. The president had heard and was on his way over. We were waiting for somebody, and I remember making small talk. I remember asking the president what he thought—not what we were going to say. "What do you think? What do you make of all this?" He's a good person to ask that question.

It's funny, because he just started to talk, and we weren't even all there yet. The meeting was just people milling around. I remember after his second sen-tence, I reached over and grabbed one of his little notecards, because I wanted to start writing it down. He was saying exactly what should have been said. He may have thought this through already, but in my mind, this was a genuine moment from the president, and that's how I was going to position it. So I just wrote down on this little card what he said.

---

26. E. J. Dionne was a columnist whose op-ed essays appeared in the *Washington Post*.

Then everyone got there, and I said, "I have what I need here. This is what I think we should do." And everybody said, "Go do it." I walked right out, I mean literally. I went by my office and said, "Tell everyone to be at the stake-out in two minutes, because I'm going to convey the president's reaction to Livingston's resignation."

This is all part of the record. What he said was that things had gone too far, that this cycle of the politics of personal destruction had spun out of control, and that Livingston was a good man who had made a mistake, and he should reconsider and stay. That cut the legs out of their argument. The president was saying, "No, no, no. Not only am I not going to resign, I don't want him to resign either. I want him to stay. I want to work with him on the country's business and get things done."

I said earlier that there were moments of political jeopardy, but I left that one out because I figured I'd tell this in chronological order. That was ten minutes of pretty heavy jeopardy for the president. And it was in my mind that it was going to take the pundit community about half an hour to put all this together and start the full-throated cry, and I was desperate to get out in front of that. Even if I went out and was using hand signals and had nothing to say, it seemed that if that was allowed to marinate in the political stew, it was awful for us. The president's original instincts actually turned that story away from him and to, "Well, if this is how the Republicans want to do it, they can do it that way."

One of the really interesting parts about that day was the next place I went. There was a meeting in the Roosevelt Room that I was a little late for because I had been dealing with the Livingston thing. Most of the domestic policy advisors to the president were meeting about the State of the Union speech. . . . This was a very useful and important meeting for me, because my job in the State of the Union process, as well as others, was to take these new initiatives and tease them out over this month so that by the time we got to the State of the Union, the public would know most of what the president was going to say, and it has built support. . . . And I remember just sitting in that meeting and actually having the thought, *This is the only reason why we're still here, because this meeting is going on. Most of the people in this building are not worried about the nonsense that I worry about all day long and are actually delivering on the promise.*

As I remember it, that warm feeling that enveloped me didn't stay very long, because one of my deputies came in and grabbed me and said, "You're needed at the NSC." I remember walking out and saying something along the lines of, "If one more thing happens today, my head's going to explode." And she turned to me and said, "Then don't go into this meeting." She had been told what was going on. I went in, and there was a group of people from the NSC with a very simple message. They'd had a meeting that morning of the Joint Chiefs, and all the people involved in this were about to recommend to the president to terminate the military action because they had achieved their objective. They hit all the targets.

The meeting in itself was a little comical, because I was a little incredulous. I just decided I was going to express my opinion. I said, "You're telling me that we launched this thing a week ago, and I got up there with a straight face and said it has nothing to do with impeachment. We're going to get impeached today, and I have to put the president out to declare victory—and we're going to do this with a straight face?" ... I proceeded to go through this process of, "Well, let's look at the targets. Can't we hit a couple of them again? Can't we just extend this into tomorrow?" They decided I wasn't a very serious person, and I should be put in the corner.... I just started thinking, *Okay, this is what the rest of this day looks like.*

There are two postscripts to this that are personally amusing. I pretty much held it together all day, but it was very busy, a lot of pressure on everyone in the White House. That day I felt a lot of personal pressure to perform, not make any mistakes, and make the right decisions. I got a call from someone on my staff saying so-and-so at some station wants to know why Steven Tyler from the band Aerosmith is in the Oval Office. I said, "You have to be kidding me! Well, have we checked?" They said, "Well, yes, we did check, and he's up there right now and he's wearing leopard-skin pants or something." [*laughter*]

I'm thinking he's in there with the president. So I just started totally losing it saying, "Who's in charge around here? Do we have to always make this—" It turns out the president had been gone for two hours. Tyler was in town for a concert, and someone had arranged for a tour. He was just being given a tour of the Oval Office. It really was no big deal, but of all the things going on to set me off, that's the one that did.

The last thing I remember—and this is very memorable, as I think I've said through the day.... Doug Sosnik ... was a good friend to me at the White House at the time and he's a good friend now. I finally finished, and when I got back to my office, having done all this stuff, he was sitting in the chair across from my desk. There's a little bar in the White House press, and he had opened two beers and said, "Sit down, relax." I sat down with a fairly exhausted look on my face, and he looked over at me, and I'll never forget what he said.... "Except for getting impeached, we had a pretty good day."

* * *

Q: *You didn't want to give that speech at the end [defending the president before the Senate]?*
Senator Dale Bumpers (D-AR): That's right. ...

Q: *But in the end you say you shut yourself up in your study and wrote your speech.*
Bumpers: I just wrote notes, I didn't write a speech. I could never read a speech in a place like that. I learned in trial work that humor was often appropriate.

I knew generally what I wanted to say and the points I wanted to make. As I was talking, I thought of a humorous story, and humor is almost always appropriate in jury trials. I had already told two or three little stories. I had long since known that juries love jokes and funny stories.

Q: *You were treating this like a jury?*
Bumpers: Yes. I knew that everybody there was listening to me and they were looking for those cogent points that they hoped somebody would bring out. I remember saying, "Bill Clinton is not perfect. You aren't either. Nor am I. None of us is perfect." Then I told the story about the country preacher. He challenged his audience. He said, "Is there anybody in this congregation that has ever known a person with anything like the perfect qualities of Jesus Christ our Lord and Savior?" Finally, one attendee slowly stood up. The preacher challenged him to share it with the congregation. Finally, the parishioner said, "My wife's first husband." Chief Justice [William] Rehnquist almost fell out of his chair laughing.[27] I believe he laughed longer than anybody in the audience. I didn't know how the chief justice would take something like that. That's where trial practice experience comes in handy. . . .

Q: *Did you talk to the president himself afterward?*
Bumpers: Yes. My phone was ringing when I got home. [*laughter*]

Q: *Can you share with us—*
Bumpers: No, I can't share that.

Q: *He was pleased?*
Bumpers: Immensely pleased.

* * *

Q: *Were there missed foreign policy opportunities late in the second term because of the country's preoccupation with Lewinsky?*
Ambassador Nancy Soderberg, U.S. representative for special political affairs at the United Nations: No. People ask that a lot. My experience was that Clinton was more engaged in foreign policy than ever before because he didn't want to go home. Usually he'd read every memo you gave him, but not necessarily all the attachments. People were joking: now they'd come back with all the attachments with notes on them, spilled ink here, everything. He was clearly reading through everything and was much more engaged. It was an escape for him to do this.

---

27. By the terms of the Constitution, the chief justice of the United States presides over the Senate's impeachment trial of a president (Article I, Section 3).

POLITICS AND THE CLINTON WHITE HOUSE

Alice Rivlin, vice chair of the Federal Reserve: People I was dealing with—the central bankers and the finance ministry, people in Europe—would say, "How can your government function?" And I'd say, "You know, Bob Rubin goes to work every day, Alan Greenspan goes to work every day. None of these people are worrying about Monica Lewinsky. They're doing what they always do."

Joan Baggett, White House political director: I was an observer at the elections in Bosnia.... They would say, "Oh, what's going to happen to President Clinton? Please don't let anything happen to him because he has saved us." They really looked up to him, and people were so puzzled as to why he was being impeached when he had done so much good in the world.... Who cared about his private life or his sex life when he was doing so much good? So they were hard-pressed to understand that.

Lawrence Stein, congressional liaison: There was much that happened after [impeachment], but it all seemed somewhat anticlimactic. We worked very heavily on Social Security, which proved fruitless. We worked hard on the Medicare Prescription Drug Benefit, which proved fruitless. This is an important thing to observe. By that time, the kind of legislative construction that could work— to rely on a thoughtful majority of Republicans coupled with some moderate Democrats to push a thing through and then force it to a vote and make them come out and vote the way they have to vote—was no longer available to us. The people on whom we'd relied during impeachment were essentially the left. They thought they were owed something. For us to have then proceeded to cut a deal on middle-of-the-road policies—which is where Clinton is philosophically—would have been an act of ingratitude at least—and probably punishable pretty substantially at worst.

General Hugh Shelton: In my last National Security Council meeting, we're sitting there and the meeting is over. President Clinton says, "Hugh, I need to see you a minute before you leave." Everybody looks. *What's he want to see Shelton for again?* ... Of course there are people all over the place. He says, "This won't work. Let's find a more private place."

I said, "Follow me, Mr. President," because I knew where Donald Kerrick's office was, and I knew he was not there.[28] ... I walked in first and turned around and said, "Will this do, Mr. President?" He said, "This is great." He reached around and closed the door. I thought, *What's coming now?* He came over and he got in my personal space. Basically we were nose to nose, and he said, "Hugh, I'll be leaving here shortly. I just want you to know how much I personally

---

28. Lieutenant General Donald Kerrick was a deputy national security advisor, after earlier stints with the NSC, the Joint Chiefs of Staff, and overseas tours with the army.

appreciate the leadership you provided for our men and women in uniform and the advice you've given me during your term as chairman."

He looked at me and said, "You know, you and I are cut out of different pieces of cloth, but I want you to know how much I admire and respect what you stand for. If I've caused any embarrassment to the men and women in uniform, I sincerely regret it."

I looked at him and there were tears trickling down his face. This was a no BS session here. He really felt deeply that he owed it to me to say that, which I really appreciated. To be candid, I've never told anybody about that side of him.

Mickey Kantor (on Clinton's last-minute pardons): Huge mistake. I think of all the things he ever did, ever, all the charges, draft, Gennifer, Monica Lewinsky, you name it—anything—it is the one thing that has bothered his base of constituency, the people who admire him, bothered them the most, been the most devastating to them, because it is so inexplicable. Now he will explain it and he will tell you that it has to do with Ehud Barak and Israel, the Marc Rich pardon.[29] The first question is, "Why pardon anyone at all if the Justice Department hasn't given you a recommendation?" Why would you dare do anything like that unless the most extreme case. Number two, even if you decide you're going to pardon people, why would you allow any outsider to have access to you in discussing it? Three, even if you allowed everything to happen, if your entire staff says no, wouldn't it occur to you that it's a problem?

It is the single most inexplicable, devastating thing he did. He was going to leave office with a 75 percent approval rating, the highest of any president in any memory, Reagan, Eisenhower, anybody. He was at the top of his game, the economy was in great shape, and just like he's always done, he did something that was, it's a terrible fall. I can't explain it, I am not the one to explain it, I have no idea. Because this had to do with government, with policy, with judgment, where he is so good. This is not a personal peccadillo that we're talking about where he has made his mistakes. I don't get it. And it is so easy not to have done it. This is not like it's a close question.

Bernard Nussbaum: Ken Starr did one great thing in his life: he killed the [independent counsel] institution forever. I used to say Ken Starr did what I failed to do. I tried to kill it. He succeeded.

---

29. On the final night of his presidency Clinton issued 140 pardons. Most controversially, he pardoned fugitive financier Marc Rich, who was guilty of fraud, racketeering, and tax evasion and was on the FBI's most wanted list. Clinton's critics said the pardon was bought by Rich's former wife, who had given major financial gifts to the Clinton Library Foundation and to Hillary Clinton's New York Senate campaign. Deputy Attorney General Eric Holder had, however, endorsed the pardon—after interventions by former Clinton White House Counsel Jack Quinn, whom Rich had hired to plead his case. Holder later voiced regrets that he had facilitated the pardon.

PART V

Bill Clinton and His Team

29

Clinton's Intellect

During the course of his oral history interview, former campaign chairman and Secretary of Commerce Mickey Kantor reported, "I don't think you'll find any person who worked for [Bill Clinton], or even those who don't particularly admire him, who didn't have the same reaction upon first meeting, and second meeting, and third meeting and so on. He is a stunning intellect and talent." Kantor's assessment was borne out in scores of interviews with both Clinton's friends and detractors. That same turn of mind that produced a Rhodes Scholar from a small-town Arkansas boy also made a president of rare intellectual skills.

Mickey Kantor: I don't think we've ever had anyone in American politics in my lifetime like him. That doesn't mean that he's perfect, far from it, and it doesn't mean everything the Clinton administration did was successful. It wasn't. It does mean that there is at least one thread among many that runs through the Clinton career and presidency, and that is everyone's amazement at just how talented and bright and connected he is.

Richard Riley, secretary of education: The interesting thing about having a conversation with Bill Clinton is he was interested in every level of everything. He could talk with you about what was happening in Ecuador as much as the UK. It was amazing to talk with him. Yes, he was very much into national politics, what was happening in South Carolina, the South, Arkansas of course. He was a multidimensional person. It was not like he was a small thinker. He always was talking about other things in a very interesting way.

Charlene Barshefsky, deputy U.S. trade representative: I was in Tokyo. We had been negotiating all day. There were a couple of things I wanted that we didn't yet have and it was 1:30 in the morning. . . . Mickey, Warren Christopher, and I went up to the president's suite at the hotel where we were all staying—the Okura.[1] He was at the dining room table of his suite and he was dressed in

---

1. President Clinton's initial visit to Tokyo, which produced the trade framework agreement, took place from July 6–10, 1993.

khakis and a plaid shirt, looking reasonably rumpled. He was reading a news-paper when we walked in. He barely looked up. To the left was a book, open, facedown—Marcus Aurelius's *Meditations*. To the right, the *New York Times* cross-word puzzle, with a pen.

We walked in. He ... looked up, and said to me, "I've been waiting to see you," which took me somewhat aback. I said, "Well, here I am." ... Chris said, "The negotiations over the framework are at a very delicate phase and I thought Charlene should brief you and tell you what she needs." The president nodded and looked at me. The newspaper came up again covering his face. I remained silent and Chris motioned, [*whispering*] "Go ahead." I thought, *Well, all right.* "Mr. President, this is a complicated topic. We're at a delicate point. There are a couple of trades I could make. I don't want to have to make any of them, and so I want to lay out a plan of action."

As I'm talking, the hand comes out from behind the newspaper, picks up the book, turns it over and he starts to read the book. About a minute goes by. The book gets put back down. The paper goes back up, he turns the page. A hand comes out to the right, and he fills in a word on the crossword puzzle. This is all true—I am not exaggerating. This is going on, and I'm thinking, *I don't care how smart this guy is, this is a completely disastrous briefing session.* I finished what I needed to say, and the newspaper finally came down.

He looked at me, and he said, "I think we have an inconsistency between your briefing two weeks ago and where you are now. Let me see if I can spell it out." And he went through the briefing I had done several weeks earlier in the Oval *perfectly*. He also went through what I had just said and concluded that there might be an inconsistency in our approach.... He had caught the nuance in what I was saying, not only the words in the order in which I had said them. At the end, we agreed on the game plan and we were off and running. We con-cluded the framework agreement the next day.

I walked out of the room and Warren Christopher and Mickey both burst out laughing and said, "Your expression went from ... disdain and despair ... to amazement that he could multitask to this degree and miss nothing."

Madeleine Albright, secretary of state: What would happen on a regular basis would be you'd go in to get ready for a meeting with X minister or president or whatever. The NSC person who does the briefings stood around the desk while he worked on a crossword puzzle. You'd think, *God damn it, he's not listening. We're trying to tell him about the president of X and he's doing a crossword puzzle.* This is the president. You're not going to tell him to stop.... Then you'd sit down with the president of X and within five minutes you could tell that he had heard every single word and he went beyond whatever it was that anybody had thought about.

Kris Engskov, personal aide: [The] president ... never went anywhere without a book and a crossword puzzle. We could be on a three-minute drive down to the West Gate of the White House and he'd have a book in his hand. He would churn through hundreds of books a year just doing that. . . . I think he spent half the night reading. He would never sleep. I think that's pretty well known. He did not sleep much. He'd get engrossed in a book and just not go to bed. The next morning, I'd say, "Good morning, Mr. President." He'd say, "Good morning." I'd say, "Are you tired?" He'd say, "Yes, I spent the whole night reading this book on Alexander Hamilton," or whoever it was. It would almost always be biography, almost always something in relation to the presidency.

Then, whatever book he was reading, that next night when he had the audience at the fundraiser or wherever, he'd say, "Have you read this book about Alexander Hamilton? I don't know if you know this, but the way Hamilton" . . . and then he'd go into this whole lecture about—and he would incorporate it into his own presidency. I think that's what he liked about it. He related to these guys. In some ways that's a pretty small fraternity. He understood that better than most.

Nancy Soderberg, deputy national security advisor: I remember one time he was reading the David McCullough book on [Harry] Truman.[2] It put him in such a good mood, because he realized it took Truman two or three years to figure out how to shape the Cold War, the post–World War II era. He said, "Okay, I'm on par with Truman." That made him feel good. I definitely remember that discussion. It made him feel better.

He took a lot of solace in history, because you realize that the politics of some of these guys were a lot more brutal than what he was going through. . . . It made him feel like he wasn't alone.

Alan Blinder, Council of Economic Advisors: Sometimes he would send us back missives with his scribble. It was really hard to read his handwriting, and we would pore over it, asking questions. He was a voracious reader. When he did this I don't know, it must have been three, four in the morning. I know I didn't have any time to read the *New Yorker* and the *Atlantic* and things. But this guy, he was reading them and he would say, "Is this true? Look into this." We would get things like that. To this day, I can't imagine how he found time to do that, but he did. . . .

He tends to think in terms of narrative, personal stories and things like that. He's not a quantitative person, but he can cope with things like that and he's very intellectually curious and, as I said before, a voracious reader. . . . He's a very verbal and personal person, but he's also an incredible reader. I think he must be a speed reader to read all of that stuff.

Charles Brain, congressional liaison: Okay, we used to joke, the reason he can do all this reading is that he doesn't have a commute like we do.

---

2. David McCullough, *Truman* (New York: Simon & Schuster, 1992).

General Hugh Shelton, chair of the Joint Chiefs of Staff: My impression of him—and it remained true throughout my association with President Clinton—is that he's a quick study. He may not have served in the military, but he grasps things very quickly, has a razor-sharp mind. He can separate the wheat from the chaff. He sees what the big issues are, the important issues, and he'll home right in on them.... I didn't have to worry about how complicated or complex it might be; he could pick it up.

William Galston, deputy domestic policy advisor:[3] I will confess to you that Bill Clinton terrified me because he almost always knew a good deal more about the subject, or at least some aspect of the subject, than you did. So I came very quickly to prefer a paper relationship with him. I deliberately did not seek out face time because I knew that I wouldn't be so overawed if I sat down and wrote an orderly memo that presented the facts that he needed to know and the options that he needed to consider. It is also the case that if you're writing a memo, he can't interrupt you. He can't divert the conversation. So you can actually get a balanced range of facts, arguments, and views, before him in a way that is very difficult if you're doing it on a face-to-face basis. So the relationship that I had with him ... stemmed from the fact that I knew how to write memos and Bill Clinton liked to read them.

* * *

Q: Were there any geographical or issues areas that seemed to be particularly perplexing to him or particularly difficult for him to grapple with?
Charlene Barshefsky: Issues? Countries? No. You have to be kidding. For Clinton, the harder and more complicated, the better.... I don't think there's any way for someone who hadn't spent a lot of time with him to fully appreciate how brilliant this guy is. It's like the Garrison Keillor line, "Lake Wobegon, where all the kids are above average." Everyone in Washington is thought of as smart, right? At least by everyone in Washington. "Oh so smart" is the common refrain. There's smart, and then there is that very occasional, rare, genuinely brilliant person. Bill Clinton is in that [second] category—hugely intelligent, intuitive, and fluid in his thinking. I don't think there was ever a meeting I had with the president on any issue, which by the time I walked out, I hadn't wished I had a piece of paper and a pencil so I could have taken notes. That's the kind of intellect he has. What a joy to work for someone like that. An unbelievable experience.

---

3. This observation by Galston was made at a public symposium of former White House domestic policy advisors held at the Miller Center on June 12–13, 2009. A published version of the transcript is found in Michael Nelson and Russell L. Riley, eds., *Governing at Home: The White House and Domestic Policymaking* (Lawrence: University Press of Kansas, 2011), 132.

30

Clinton's Operating Style

Bill Clinton's unusual intellectual abilities were joined to uncommon political talents. He was at once a highly skilled politician—at ease on the stump and eager to work a room—and a deeply knowledgeable political operative. Republican chief of staff John Sununu observed that while he did not find Clinton to be a desirable president, "I would ask Bill Clinton to run a campaign for me. . . . I'd ask Bill Clinton to be my chief of staff, if I could trust him." And his congressional liaison Charles Brain reported that Clinton's encyclopedic knowledge of politics made him feel superfluous as a briefer: "What do you need me for? What am I doing here?"[1] Indiscipline in employing those talents, however, led to occasional problems for this White House.

Mike Espy, secretary of agriculture: I saw Senator [John] Kerry here in Mississippi, when he ran for president, speak at a black church. . . . [And] I saw him blow it.[2] This church was a Pentecostal church. They were already geared up to help him. They were already enthusiastic. The bishop said that God told him he was going to be president. God told the bishop to tell him that he'd be president. The bishop took his palm and hit [Kerry's] head. The bishop's like 5′7″; John Kerry's 6′5″, whatever. He leaned over and hit him in the forehead, and made him president-to-be. Everybody's screaming and everything. . . . Everybody's screaming and speaking in tongues and running, and the choir had sung two great songs. I'm thinking, *Man, take this moment and use it.* He got up there and took a whole sheaf of paper, and put it on [the podium]. It was so thick. . . . I thought, *argghhh.* Then he talked about stuff that—just cliché stuff. I'm thinking, *Man, this is Mississippi; you're not going to win here. . . .* He seemed out of his element. He couldn't clap in time with the gospel choir, he couldn't. He was awful. I thought, *Maybe he's tired.* It was a Sunday.

---

1. Sununu Interview, George H. W. Bush Oral History Project, Miller Center, University of Virginia, June 8–9, 2000.

2. Senator John Kerry (D-MA) won the Democratic nomination for president in 2004 but lost the election to President George W. Bush, who was re-elected.

That's when I appreciated Bill Clinton more. I thought, *Now, if Bill Clinton were here, that paper would have never come out of his pocket.* . . . He would have used that moment to his greater glory. He would've come out with Scripture. He would have taken that moment. It was already inflamed with passion running amok. He would have taken it, and put it in the stratosphere. That's what he did . . . that guy . . . knows how to use a moment.

Mickey Kantor, secretary of commerce: I remember something that Hillary told a reporter in the New Hampshire primary in '92. The reporter said, "Upon reflection he is much like Lyndon Johnson, he draws energy from people." Hillary corrected the reporter and said, "There's something different, he also gives it back." That's the difference. A lot of people in public life draw energy from people, they're very good at it and I'm not criticizing it. He's among the very, very few, I've never met anybody like him, he gives it back, and you walk away totally enthralled with him. It's not a parlor trick, he actually does care about you, sometimes too much.

Joan Baggett, White House political director: Being a political director to Bill Clinton is like being the Maytag repairman.[3] [*laughter*] . . . [There] was no state for which he didn't know more about the politics than anybody in the room. When I'd call to give him results on something he'd go, "You know, he ran in that race, he ran that same district back in 1968 and then they changed that line." The most obscure things. Just from the political perspective, that was a bit daunting, just how much he knew and how much he remembered about people and places and issues.

Roy Neel, deputy White House chief of staff: [He] had a feel for dealing with politicians. This is a guy who loves politics. He never shrank from calling a political adversary or trying to develop a relationship. He wanted everyone to love him and that would help him do his work better. He never rested until he could somehow convert people. Of course, a lot of people he never converted. . . .

Q: Were there any members of Congress that he found especially vexing to deal with, in your experience? Folks that were just, "I can't abide by the idea that I've got to talk with this person or be in this person's company"?
Neel: If he was, he never let on. He had some of Reagan's graciousness, but more of a casualness. Gracious is not the right word. Charm is a better word. He also had this breadth of interest, not "good old boy" stuff, but he could connect to most members of Congress on some level. He is a sports nut. He

---

3. Baggett refers to a series of long-running television commercials featuring a lonely and bored Maytag repairman, who, because the product was so reliable, had nothing to do.

knew everything about a half dozen sports, down to who the number three linebacker was on the Florida State team in 1991. He knew this stuff. He got into an argument with my youngest son about the relative merits of the Florida State defense versus the Notre Dame defense during some football game we were watching in the White House one evening. My son was twelve or thirteen at the time, and thought he knew everything about sports, but Clinton knew even more.

Alice Rivlin, OMB director: [Before] the president was giving a speech, a major speech, or even an announcement, we would gather in the Oval Office, and the president would have his speech draft. He'd be sitting there, usually at the desk, working at the speech draft. And everybody who wanted to get something in would still be talking about it. It was kind of chaotic compared to the economic team meetings, which were more disciplined because Bob Rubin imposed some discipline.... That was not true in those Oval Office meetings. Everybody was shouting at once and saying, "Well, you ought to do this, and you ought to say that, and you ought to remember this." Maybe it would be before a press conference.

I just thought, *If I were the president, I couldn't stand this. I would say, Shut up, you guys, and get out of here. I want these three people.* He never did that. He just let the chaos go on around him. Sometimes he would participate in it, and sometimes he would just tune out and sit there working on his draft and editing it—which he always did—and not listening to the chaos going on around him. I couldn't believe it. I just would never have done anything like that. But he is extremely good at absorbing a lot of different things at once and also tuning out and concentrating when he wants to.

Alan Blinder: It suited Clinton's style and benefited the policy to have somewhat raucous, heavily attended meetings where he would hear from a lot of people, including dissenting views. The biggest problem in government, I believe, is a president who surrounds himself with a small number of like-minded people, all of whom say the same thing. This is the recipe for total catastrophe. It can lead to good things too. But the way an economist would put it, it's a risk-loving strategy. You don't have a diversified portfolio. It's like putting all of your retirement money into one stock. It's stupid. It could be great if you happened to pick Wal-Mart, wonderful. But you could also pick Lucent and have a total catastrophe.[4] My view is that it's situations like that, Lyndon Johnson and Vietnam for example, that lead to the total gigantic catastrophes in government,

---

4. Lucent Technologies was a telecom company that initially seemed golden but was run on a flawed business model and collapsed spectacularly—its stock price quickly declined from $84 to $2.

the kinds of things that historians later look at and say, "How could they have done that? What were they thinking?" The basic answer is there was only one opinion at the table.

Clinton was the opposite of that, and I thought that was terrific as long as you have a president who has the quickness and subtlety of mind to handle something like that—and he did. So I think it was very beneficial to Clinton. It was also great for morale. At some of these meetings I'm describing, I was sitting at the table, but then there were the back benchers—another twenty people in the room. They're not supposed to talk, but it's doing a tremendous bit for their morale that they're there, watching history being made with the president of the United States. So it was good even for that. Furthermore, they hear what is said. So when we walk back to our offices, they talk to us and say, "Did you hear what so-and-so said? I don't think that was right." I think there were tremendous benefits.

Mickey Kantor: He is very bright, but sometimes undisciplined. He is so interested in so many things, is the best way to put it. Another way to put it is just lack of discipline. At first, and this has been reported on widely, meetings in the White House with him were like graduate seminars. They went all over the place and seemingly had no beginning and no end. Part of that was inexperience on everyone's part, too many people in the room, not enough briefing beforehand of the president before he walked in, and his own proclivity. He loves ideas. He loves to talk to people, he loves to hear what they have to say. He hangs it on pegs in his head and may use it a different way later or twelve months from that point, but it also made the beginning of the administration less than efficient. I think that's a fair statement.

Chris Jennings, health care advisor: Let me start with the big policy meetings. He loved listening to the different policy arguments. He liked seeing different people present. It was never, "I'm bored," or, "Why am I here?" This was frustrating to some of the political people, who were bored and who wanted to get him out of there. Of course, policy people will talk endlessly. I mean, if you have an audience for a politician who cares and is interested, that happens maybe once every blue moon, so people will just keep on yakking away. It wasn't even just a listening, it was an interaction. "And what about this?" and very insightful questions that sometimes people had to come back, didn't even know the answers to.... He would ask, "What does this group think" about something, but he was primarily interested in the policy discussions. He wouldn't completely decompartmentalize, that's just not his style. But primarily the policy discussions were oriented to just policy discussions: impact on people, numbers, dollars, things like that.

In the members [of Congress] meetings, I think he first tried to put members at ease. There is this aura about the Oval Office, and he well understood that.

He would make them comfortable. There would be, at that time, a little bit of nervousness on both sides about either one giving up too much. For example, if he was meeting with Republican leadership, the White House staff and the Republican staff were always worried that they would lead to something that neither side really wanted them to do at that point in time. The president has a way of talking in words and phrases and intonations that lead everyone to believe that he said what they wanted him to say. But if you look at the transcripts, they're much vaguer than you think, which helps explain how people generally, when they meet him, think, *God, he understands and he's with me.* ... I think that there was more hope on some of the dealmakers that if you got him in the room, outside of the staff and Mrs. Clinton, you could cut some sort of deal. So I think there was always that perception.

John Hilley, congressional liaison: He was a master at having the congressional people down, every caucus, every leadership group, everyone down. We'd work them into shape. But the truth is he never negotiated. We'd never let him negotiate, because he wasn't a negotiator. He was a compromiser, he was a conciliator. He was a "find the middle" kind of guy. You need a Bob Rubin and me and others who can sit there and spend the day staring at these guys. He was not a negotiator, but he did his part, the public relations, making the statements to the nation. He did the part he was supposed to do, and it's more effective. You don't want the president in there negotiating.

Marcia Hale, White House director of intergovernmental affairs: [There] was nobody he thought he couldn't talk to and convince of something.

Mack McLarty, White House chief of staff: Everybody has their own personal style, but President Clinton sometimes would close on a major decision in a pretty unassuming way. I was more accustomed when you closed, [saying], "Okay, I've reached a decision." I had to be pretty attuned to when he had reached a decision and we were ready to move forward. Of course, I was very respectful that I certainly didn't want to move forward if he had not closed on a decision. So that was one of the many things that I had to adjust to in working with the president.

Alan Blinder: The problem with Clinton is that he had a tendency ... to agree with the last person to talk to him. So you might think you had a decision, and then you would find out you didn't have a decision because someone else got in there after you.... I think that was a problem of Clinton's personal style.

Charles Brain, White House congressional liaison: [He] worked the phones a whole lot, in ways unquantifiable, or unknowable. Just literally to pick up the phone, call anybody any time of the night. I had one member of Congress tell me that his wife would eventually pick up the phone in bed, answer it, say, "It's HIM again." In face-to-face meetings with members we'd have down, got along as well with him, interacted as well as anybody. I think this is probably too psychoanalytic, but he seemed to especially enjoy dealing with members of Congress that you wouldn't expect him to get along with, more so than his own members.

Jesse Helms[5] was down for a signing ceremony.... [Clinton] spent about twenty minutes in the Oval Office talking with Jesse Helms about people that they both knew, because Clinton had been a part-time employee of the Foreign Relations Committee based on the Fulbright [connection] when he was at Georgetown.[6] Clinton told Helms the story, that Fulbright's chief of staff, who Helms of course knew, said to Clinton, "We can offer you a part-time job for $6,000, or a full-time job for $10,000," and the president said, "I want two part-time jobs." But he goes on and on with Helms, who you wouldn't think they would have anything to do with each other, but they genuinely seemed to enjoy [time] together.

* * *

Q: *Did the president like to use the telephone?*
Warren Christopher, secretary of state: Just like he likes vanilla ice cream. [*laughter*]

Alice Rivlin: I was not a recipient of the middle-of-the-night phone calls. But other people often were. Leon often was and would report at the 7:30 staff meeting that the president had called him at 2 a.m. And other people would report that. And it certainly happened. He's a man who needs very little sleep, and one thing that drove some of the White House people nuts was that he'd get on the phone at night and talk to friends of his in other parts of the country and say, "What do you think we ought to do about this?" and then report in the morning—or maybe even in the middle of the night, I'm not sure—"So-and-so thinks we ought to do X." And if you're on the White House staff, or you think you're in charge of something, and then the president is talking to somebody you never heard of—or if you did hear of him, you didn't like what he had to say—it's rather unsettling. So there would be a certain amount of that.

John Hilley: One attribute of Clinton's, a side of his personality, that I found remarkable: This guy was subject to a lot of *ad hominem* attacks throughout his presidency. But his capacity to not let it get to him and to be unbelievably

5. Jesse Helms (1921–2008), a North Carolina Republican, was long one of the most conservative members of the Senate, where he served from 1973 to 2003.

6. Senator J. William Fulbright (1905–1995) represented Arkansas in the U.S. Senate from 1945 to 1974. Bill Clinton worked on the staff of the Senate Foreign Relations Committee, which Fulbright chaired from 1959 until the end of his service.

forgiving, and have somebody who had just said the vilest thing about him two weeks before down to the White House and to try to deal with him on an issue as if nothing had been said—that would have been beyond me to be able to do, to be honest with you. But that capacity to be forgiving about some very personal attacks . . . was just a remarkable attribute, and potentially a weakness as well.

Henry Cisneros, secretary of housing and urban development: Part of my personal attitude on this whole thing I learned from President Clinton. I like to characterize it as the Terminator model. If they don't actually shoot you down in the street, carve you up in pieces, and burn the pieces, then you keep going. In other words, unless you're so totally debilitated that you cannot take another step, your job is to get up the next morning and take that step. So whatever they say, whatever they write, whatever they do legally, if they haven't broken your bones yet, you keep going. That's what I believe about Bill Clinton. You will never keep him on the canvas because if there's one ounce of spirit left that says, "The count is now at seven but I'm on a knee and I'm coming up," he will come up.

Strobe Talbott, deputy secretary of state: One of Clinton's . . . both maddening and admirable, and I think ultimately productive, characteristics was the relish he took in impersonating his own critics and saying, "Well, what about when they say—?" Then he would do a better job of slashing and burning his own policy than anybody in the press mercifully was doing. We'd have to sit there and say, "Mr. President, this is *your* policy." He'd say, "Yes, I know, but what about when they come at me and say bah, bah, bah? What about if this happens?" It forced us to say, "Yes, we need an answer to that." Or, "We need a plan B if plan A doesn't work, or plan C if plan B doesn't work." And so forth and so on. It was exasperating at the time and it was time-consuming, but he always had enough time, it seemed, and we got to the right

Madeleine Albright, secretary of state: He was undisciplined in the voracity of his appetite for information and discussions.

William Perry, secretary of defense: The president was notorious for not being conscious of time. When you're on the receiving end of his time, it's a wonderful thing, and when he decides the discussion is so interesting he's going to extend it for another hour, that's fine. But to the person who is out there waiting, it doesn't seem so fine. And it's not just a person; it's a whole contingent of people—and, of course, the domino effect.

One specific incident with the president I remember very well: I had been down to the naval base at Norfolk where he spoke to a group of sailors on the aircraft carrier, a couple of thousand of them. This was back in the time when the Washington buzz was that the president was not liked by the military. So this speech was designed to project himself forward to the military. He got a very warm reception, actually. Then after it was over, they all clustered around him and wanted to talk to him. He decided to do that. I bet he shook hands and chatted briefly with every one of those thousand or two thousand sailors around there.

The schedulers were just tearing their hair out. I can only imagine what consequences there were to other appointments and commitments he had during that day. After all, it took another hour to do that beyond what was scheduled. But he enjoyed doing it, and he did it very well, and it helped overcome this buzz, namely that the military didn't like him.

Gerry Adams, leader of Northern Ireland's Sinn Féin:[7] Bill Clinton would arrange to see you and maybe you were scheduled for half an hour, and two hours later you could still be with him.

Mack McLarty: I was concerned, as well as frustrated, about the president running behind schedule, or late, which had been acceptable in the campaign. But I thought it somewhat reflected an insensitivity to other people who had scheduled appointments, even though this was the leader of the free world, as the president sometimes is called. The president had just given a wonderful speech, extremely well organized, thoughts were so clear and powerful and coherent.

I went in later in the afternoon, and the president was doing his paperwork. I said, "Mr. President, wonderful speech, made your points in such an eloquent, organized way. You know, it just struck me how someone with this tremendous God-given ability to organize his thoughts and deliver them in such a clear, compelling way, can be so disorganized personally and run behind schedule consistently." I knew it was a pretty pithy remark, and I said, "Well, I made you angry now." He looked up over his half glasses and said, "No, you've hurt my feelings."

Kris Engskov, personal aide: Well, my very first day at work ... I remember walking in there and he said, "Hey, good morning." He got up, and anybody who has ever talked to him one-on-one will know that he's not good about personal space. He came right up to me. He was in the middle of something, and he said to me—we're actually the same height, and he was looking right in my face and telling me something, and I never got it. I walked right out of there and I had no idea what he told me to do. I was so close to his face I could see his pores.... Clinton is a very emotive guy, right? He puts his hand on your shoulder, he's got your arm. He's a little bit like Lyndon Johnson that way. Lyndon Johnson was rumored to be a guy who didn't understand personal space very well. I'd probably put the president in that category. Not in an intrusive way,

---

7. Adams's remarks are drawn from an interview recorded for the Miller Center's Edward M. Kennedy Oral History Project.

just—especially when he has something to say, he will walk right up to you. And that was fine, but I think it was unusual.

Clinton is very good about eye contact. He must understand the power of that. A lot of people describe him—when he's talking to somebody they'll feel like the only person in the room. That's probably part of how he does it. I think 99.9 percent of the time he's genuinely interested in what that person is saying. He's very good at putting himself in that situation. He blocks it all out. He's very good at listening to people. In some ways that is his great genius.

Marcia Hale: He has a characteristic that he learned very early in life, which is, if he is talking to you, he is looking right at you. It does two things: one is that people really feel like he's talking to them, as opposed to most politicians who are looking over their shoulders. Quite frankly, if you're moving through a crowd and you really look at somebody and really talk to them for even twenty or thirty seconds, your conversation can likely be shorter and more meaningful.

I remember being someplace with him before he got elected president. I was standing, literally, right next to him and I put my hand on his elbow to say hello, and he did not move from that person he was talking to. . . . I learned a lesson, which is, *Don't interrupt.* He didn't move until he was finished talking with that person right there one-on-one. It's a big deal to anybody, but if you're a citizen who has just lost their home, to be able to tell your story to the president is a big deal.

Peter Edelman, assistant secretary of health and human services: He loves people and he does focus on people and remembers everybody's name. Hillary has that quality too. . . . It's like perfect pitch. My brother has perfect pitch. I know what perfect pitch is. My mother had it too. I don't.

Marcia Hale: I don't think he ever [got nervous]. I was always amazed from the very beginning that you could put him in the most unbelievable situations and he would never—he would show a lot of emotions, but it was not an emotion of being nervous or—certainly never dreading any situation at all. He always just went right at it with enthusiasm. I always found it remarkable.

It's two things: One is his basic nature and his confidence that he knew enough to ask all the right questions. He wasn't afraid of being embarrassed about his lack of knowledge on something, because there was very little that he didn't have some basis in. He could ask anybody anything. [And] there was never anybody he didn't think he could either charm or learn something from.

* * *

Q: Did Clinton get nervous before speeches?
Kris Engskov: Boy, if he ever did, I never saw it, ever. The guy was just nerves of steel. I tell a lot of people the story about—he catnapped. That was his way of

getting sleep. That is a scientific way to keep the day going, right? He'd get in the car and we'd usually have twenty-minute drives. I don't know why every drive was twenty minutes, but it was.

He'd get off the plane, get in the car, and he'd go right to sleep. He'd just put his head on the back of the car and he'd go to sleep for twenty minutes. We had two limousines. I'd usually ride in the one in the back. I'd walk up to the car and I'd see his head still on the back of the thing. We're standing at the event and there are 20,000 people. They can't see him, he's in a tent, but there are 20,000 people ready to see the president. They're cheering, right? And he's asleep in the car.

I would think, "That's not good." But Clinton, absolutely every time—the Secret Service would say, "Should I open the door?" I'd say, "Don, open the door." As soon as Don would open the door, he would gather up his stuff, he'd step out of the car, and he'd go, "Showtime." . . . You know how when you first wake up you're not quite there? He never had that problem. It was just [snapping fingers]. . . He would literally just wake up—"Showtime." He could be on that stage five seconds later and give that speech and have [the crowd] roaring. It was the most amazing thing I ever saw.

Joe Lockhart, press secretary: My observation was he's by far the best candidate I've ever seen, and not because he's the best speaker. I've seen better speakers. [Arkansas Senator] Dale Bumpers can run circles around him as far as giving a political speech. But Clinton has this unique ability. . . . I call it the internal calibration system—the ability to walk into a room, look around, feel it, and say, *Okay, 87 percent—but I'm not going to go past that, because that's not going to work.* Or, *This group needs 52 percent.* He was always right. It was because he actually worked at it, and he just knew. I'm not sure he would know from the opening of his speech, but he had an ability to sense where people were and not overdo it and not under-do it.

Bruce Reed, White House domestic policy advisor: I almost never saw [Clinton] nervous. He didn't have to agonize over [speechmaking]. Lots of times we would work for days and days and days on speeches, and most of the time we didn't get it done until the last minute. But he was never worried about that because he knew that we were just doing the best we could and that he would take it to another level. We knew that too, that if we wrote a mediocre speech it wouldn't matter, that he would still give a great one.

He was almost allergic to sound bites. He had a natural eloquence of his own, but he didn't like saying cute things. It just didn't sit well with him. So whenever we tried to write clever sound bites for him, he usually mangled them. . . . Speechwriting with Clinton was more like brainstorming. It wasn't trying to bang out the words. It was deciding which of the many great speeches he was capable of giving he would decide to give. The interesting thing about it is that

I can remember one time briefing him in the Oval Office about a speech he was going to give to some group—I can't remember which one it was. He was very tired. I said to him, "Just say what you said to the Conference of Mayors yesterday. That was a great speech. Just give that again." And he said, "What did I say to the mayors?" [*laughter*] He had an unusual gift. He could go spin this magic and have little or no memory of what he had done. He could go and do it again, but it would never be the same.

David Kusnet, speechwriter: I think that what we eventually learned is you really give him something very spare [as a speech text] and hope that either he'll use something spare and he'll be faulted, as he rarely is, for saying too little, or else at least he won't be improvising off of something that was too long to begin with. I think this is [speechwriter] Michael Waldman's line: "You give him [Ernest] Hemingway and he'll turn it into [William] Faulkner."

31

The Man in the Office

The grandeur of the White House and the gravity of the president's responsibilities—and sometimes partisan bias—bend public perceptions of the human qualities of the person who assumes the office. The people who work most closely with a president, however, are in a unique position to report on the traits of personality and temperament that shape how the White House functions on a daily basis. Their observations provide insight into the features, ordinary and extraordinary, of the person bearing the unparalleled responsibilities of national leadership.

Kris Engskov, personal aide: The Clintons are very informal people.... He's a common guy. He's as happy to eat a hamburger as he is to dine grandly as presidents are supposed to dine.

Mickey Kantor, secretary of commerce: He's a terrific father. They get some credit—they both are terrific parents—but when he was governor, he used to take Chelsea to piano lessons every Thursday or whatever it was. He'd drive her himself, which is a danger to mankind, he's the worst driver in the world. He talks when he drives. He wants to talk, he's looking around. He used to take me to the airport and I'd get scared to death, we'd both be dead. I was more worried about myself, that's his problem.

Warren Christopher, secretary of state: He is one of the easiest people to be with that you can possibly imagine. He has all the skills of a very expert and experienced politician coupled with a kind of personal grace that always makes you feel, when you're talking to him, like you are the most important person in the world.

Marcia Hale, White House director of intergovernmental relations: He's horrible at getting to the office early in the morning. Terrible. He drinks very little coffee. So the rest of us who have three or four cups of coffee before getting to the White House are wired—we had to be there at 7:30, which means most of us were there at 7:00.... It's about ten o'clock before he wakes up really. If we had a crisis he'd be wide-awake, but given his normal day, it's about ten o'clock.

Betty Currie, personal secretary: One way he would calm himself down, he had on his desk a myriad of trinkets, he loved trinkets. He knew where every one was and if he came in and started moving them around, I said, "Uh oh. Something is wrong." He would move the trinkets around and then he would sit down.

Madeleine Albright, secretary of state: He was a complete pack rat and he loved to shop. He had all these little things, political buttons, he had the letter that [Harry] Truman wrote to the guy who criticized his daughter, Paul Hume.[1] When you went back, off the Oval Office, the walls were just covered with all this memorabilia because he really is a political junkie.

For instance . . . there are the bookshelves in the Oval Office. Early on there was a man I knew who said would I please give a present to the president on his behalf. He wasn't sure he could get it to him. It was a leather-bound copy of [Thomas] Jefferson's *Notes on Virginia*. I gave it to the president. He was thrilled to have it. I would always look to see where it was in the library. He reorganized books. Wherever he went, he would begin to reorganize the books, whether they were in his library or somebody else's. [*laughter*] There's a house at the Wye plantation that belonged to the people who owned it. We were having a very interesting dinner with Arafat and Netanyahu and [Israeli] Foreign Minister [Shlomo] Ben-Ami and a note taker. There's a library. All of a sudden the president starts reorganizing the books. I said, "Mr. President, this is not your library." He said, "They need reorganizing."

John Gibbons, presidential science advisor: [We] wanted to introduce the president to email and the Net. So we brought him over to the old EOB [Executive Office Building], and he sat down in front of this computer—it may have been the first time he sat down in front of a computer—and showed him how email worked and gave him his email address over across the street in the Oval Office. So he typed in his first email message. It was something like, "Bill Clinton, it's time to come home for lunch. Signed, Hillary," something like that. I saved a copy of it. That was his first email.

Frank Greer, media advisor: I think he's one of the most religious presidents we've ever had. . . . [We've] been to church a lot together. He is a Southern Baptist, I'm a Southern Baptist. I actually thought he had very deep religious faith and real commitment to the Baptist Church, and he was guided as much as anybody I knew in politics by the true kind of religious faith, much more so I think than a lot of right-wing conservative evangelicals who distort the meaning of Christ

---

1. Paul Hume (1915–2001) was the longtime music editor of the *Washington Post* and the author of a critical review of a 1950 vocal recital by President Truman's daughter, Margaret. Truman responded with an angry letter in which he threatened the critic with bodily harm.

and his teachings. So I thought he was true to that. He sang in the choir, which he thoroughly enjoyed, for twenty years. All the time he was governor he also took time to sing in the choir of the [Little Rock] Immanuel Baptist Church. . . . It was one of the things I liked about him the most, and I thought that was one of the things that motivated him most.

Betty Currie: I do know the president has a deep faith and I know he calls on it. Because I'll never forget when my sister died we were in Paris. I was beyond crazy and just out of it. We got back on *Air Force One,* because I couldn't get to Washington for some reason. I had to go to the Netherlands and they put me up in the front part of the plane because I was a basket case. He came back to me. He said, "Betty, are you okay?" I would start crying again. He said, "What can I do?" I said, "Will you pray with me?" So we just sat there together, holding hands and praying.

When his mother died, I got a phone call at home about two in the morning.[2] The White House operator said Ambassador Molly Raiser wanted to talk to the president.[3] I said, "It's two o'clock in the morning. What for?" And she said his mother had died. I said, "What?!" Apparently, it may have been on CNN but I was asleep. I guess in France, which is however many hours earlier, [the ambassador] had gotten word and she wanted to give her condolences. I said, "Let me talk to Molly or you can tell her that the president is asleep. I'll make sure he gets the message first thing in the morning." Now I'm wide awake. I think I called Nancy [Hernreich, director of Oval Office operations] first. I said, "Nancy, the president's mother died." And she may have made calls to the chief of staff or something after that because I don't know who knew.

I got to work very early the next day because I knew it was going to be a little crazy. He came into the office, I don't know what time, and he was singing a gospel song. He has a beautiful singing voice. And I just gave him a hug. I said, "Are you okay?" And he said yes. . . . He and I used to laugh sometimes. He was at a meeting with some black ministers, and they were quoting the wrong scripture and he let them know. I said, "Good." He knows. He really knows and he doesn't flaunt it—but he knows.

Mickey Kantor, secretary of commerce: I've always likened him to the clowns you buy for your kids that have sand on the bottom, you can hit them as hard as you want, they'll always bounce back up. That's exactly what he is. He has the lowest center of gravity of anyone I've ever met. Sometimes I just can't believe that he could absorb what he absorbs in punishment and pain . . . and just bounce back.

---

2. Virginia Clinton Kelly died on January 6, 1994.
3. Molly Raiser was chief of protocol at the White House, a Senate-confirmed position that carries with it the honorific "Ambassador." Raiser may at the time have been in Europe doing advance work for an extended presidential trip to occur the following week.

Bernard Nussbaum, White House counsel: He was a very smart man. But ultimately ... he was weak in certain respects. It came from his personality. He came from a dysfunctional family. I've thought about this. A stepfather who was an alcoholic, obviously. This is just amateur psychology, I guess, but I think it's true.

What you try to do in that kind of situation is you try to keep peace. The father fighting with the mother, people throwing chairs around—all you want to do is make peace, you want to get everybody to stop fighting. And that's what he wanted. He wanted to do great things. He wanted to pass health care, and he wanted to do great things. When somebody hit him, he could take a punch. He's taken a lot of punches. Look, only he could have survived Lewinsky. To survive the impeachment is amazing. To be able to get up in the morning and function in the face of it—can you imagine? What he did is amazing. He could take a punch and keep going, but what he couldn't do was give a punch and fight back. He had the strength to resist all these blows, but he didn't have the strength to deliver them, to respond to your enemies, to fight with them. And he generated this impression, I think, of weakness.

William Galston, deputy domestic policy advisor: For the record, I will say that the president grew up without a father, but unlike a lot of other people who grew up without fathers, he rather enjoyed the freedom. So he did not surround himself with father-figures, never did. *Au contraire*, people remarked that nearly everybody in the White House was either younger than he was or shorter than he was—or in many cases both. I'm only one for two. [*laughter*] I'm almost exactly six months older than he is, but much [shorter]! He was not interested in surrounding himself with peers and competitors or super-egos. People who grew up without fathers tend—if you want to be Freudian about it—to grow up without a lot of super-ego. The president, I think, did not lament the absence of a super-ego—to an extent that some people regarded as almost pathological.

Q: In some in respects it would be hard for someone as talented as he is to—There aren't many peers in the political arena.
Galston: No, but if you're clever, quick, mercurial, insightful, but not always wise, then someone who's older than you, somewhat more stable, more balanced, less sort of quicksilver [might help]. . . . I don't think, especially early on, there was any adult supervision.

Strobe Talbott, deputy secretary of state: [If] there is one word that sums up his approach towards life it is reconciliation. He's a great "come let us bring our people together" and in that respect he runs contrary to the adversarial strain in American politics, which are institutionalized in our two-party system. But I think it's that capacity for reconciliation that allowed him to prevail over those who were bent on destroying him.

* * *

Q: *Give us a comparative sketch of Bill Clinton and Bobby Kennedy. What are the points of contrast and the points of similarity between those two people you've known very well?*[4]
Peter Edelman, assistant secretary of HHS: Robert Kennedy was a man of few words a great deal of the time. Bill Clinton is never a man of few words. Robert Kennedy was one tough person.

Q: *Disciplined?*
Edelman: Certainly disciplined, let's talk about discipline. But before we get to discipline, I mean tough-minded, just very steely. The story of the missile crisis would be prototypical. That is not one of Bill Clinton's strengths. He arrives at a decision finally, but he can sit around and let people talk endlessly and sometimes not come to a conclusion, have to leave it to go further. Robert Kennedy would never stand for that. He was a person who not only valued his own time and conciseness, but he demanded it from everybody. Absolutely couldn't stand people who were gassy and talk, talk. Wouldn't have stood for having anybody advising him who was that way.

Disciplined. Hillary is the disciplined one. I don't know how they are now, but I think it's probably still true that politically they're a team. He's a genius, but she's the one who would say, "Bill, you've got to decide. Cut the shit, let's move ahead here. Let's get on one way or the other." She's the one who brings that to the relationship. Robert Kennedy didn't need [Mrs.] Ethel [Kennedy] to do that. She might have done it, but he didn't need her to do that.

Q: *Any other comparisons? Alike in any way?*
Edelman: Alike in a certain way that doesn't work out as well as it should for Clinton, which is essentially nonideological, non-labelable, not traditionally liberal. I say in my book that in some ways Robert Kennedy was the first New Democrat, but the way he did it was very progressive.[5] It was about empowering people and involving public-private partnerships, a long list of things. But the bottom line on it was a line that was unmistakably about justice of all kinds. Clinton started by moving away from orthodoxy, but it became much more of a political calculation and much less coherent and much less clear that it had a bottom line that really had justice in mind in all its meanings at all times.

---

4. In the mid-1960s Edelman was a legislative assistant to Senator Robert F. Kennedy (D-NY).

5. Peter B. Edelman, *Searching for America's Heart: RFK and the Renewal of Hope* (Boston: Houghton Mifflin, 2001).

Robert Kennedy had a wicked self-deprecating sense of humor. Clinton is more of a storyteller. Teddy [Kennedy] is a storyteller. Bobby was not a storyteller. He didn't tell jokes, he didn't tell long stories. So that's a difference. I think fundamentally they're quite different. They share being very smart, wonderful intuition. Clinton's probably more of a natural people person by far. Kennedy loved children, but I don't think he necessarily loved all people in a political way. I think he had to make himself be a politician. Clinton wanted to run for elective office from the time he knew what elective office was. That's not true of Bobby Kennedy.

Stanley Greenberg, pollster (on the distinctions between Bill Clinton and Tony Blair):[6] Clinton lived and breathed politics from being a little kid. The Democratic Party has a complicated set of interests and all that—he didn't have any of that. He could just be for whatever he was for, and didn't have to compete with all the other parts of history that make the Democratic Party. It was much less complicated for him and probably more powerful politically as a result.

Blair had a kind of black-and-white view of the world. He had a very strong religious inspiration, which I didn't really know at the time because he seems very secular, but it's very much right and wrong. He would talk about the Conservatives—it was the devil incarnate. He never moved away from that. When he came into office, he never stopped talking about the Conservatives in those kinds of terms. Boom-and-bust economics—there was never a speech in which he didn't talk about the Tories in those terms.

Clinton actually isn't into gripe. He wanted to accommodate the Bushes and Reagans. He didn't want to be very critical of President [George H. W.] Bush afterwards. When we talked about the Reagan years, he talked about the deficits. He didn't want to talk about the greed. He was very uncomfortable with those kinds of attacks.... He was just not personally comfortable. He wanted to embrace— you know, after Sister Souljah he wanted to call Jesse Jackson. He wants to embrace him. Tony Blair is like, "Just kick him again." He did it when he was—I was watching the process in this time period, in reforming the Labour Party. It would change the rules on bloc voting for unions within the party. But instead of saying, "All right, this was hard. Let's pause," he would immediately, before they had a chance to get up, move to the next thing. "Let's repeal the provision on nationalization from the party rules." Blair enjoyed conflict and Clinton didn't enjoy conflict.... He relished it, which was psychologically totally different from Clinton.

[Clinton] liked battling to achieve certain goals, but he does not relish personal conflict. Also he wants to embrace the people that he has vanquished. He wants to bring them along. It's a different philosophy, a different psychology, a

---

6. Greenberg had done public opinion research for both Clinton and Blair, and so had a close working relationship with both.

different kind of leader. Over the course of his presidency, that adds to his success and character as a leader. But it's a different style from someone like Blair. And in our system of divided government, you need more of this ability to reach out to other parties in order to create working coalitions. In Britain, in a parliamentary system, once you have a majority, you can act, so you don't need to bring in the Conservatives.

But also [Blair] had a worldview in which they represented the forces of evil. They represented greed and individualism run mad against community. He never stopped defining them. They were always the backdrop against which he presented what he was for. Clinton never wanted to describe the project in relationship to what we were fighting against. It's not true during the campaign in '92. But afterwards he immediately pulled back from that mode of communication and thinking.

Kris Engskov: I cannot tell you the number of times when he would be standing on stage in front of a crowd, especially during the '96 campaign when there were very large crowds. And they weren't invited crowds; it was just come-one, come-all.

He'd be on the podium and I'd see him and he'd say, "Come here." I'd go over and he'd say, "Randy Pierce and his wife June, from Murfreesboro, are standing right out there. Do you see them?" I'd have to get up on the stage—and he'd be doing this during the program. He'd say, "It's the guy with the yellow shirt and the beard." I would go out and chase these people down and bring them back and they would be people that—Randy Pierce is not a real person; I just made that name up. They would be people that he went to high school with in Hot Springs, or randomly knew from Oxford—people he hadn't seen in twenty years that he would know.

We'd bring them back. If you hadn't seen somebody in twenty years, what would be your relationship with them? . . . They were blown away that he even knew who they were, let alone knew something about them. He'd always know something about them, especially if they had an Arkansas connection. That was really wonderful to see the genuineness of that, the way it made them feel. Can you imagine?

Al From, head of the DLC: The other thing that was always remarkable about Clinton—and I've never seen anything like this—you travel all day, and you'd get to this place, like on the West Coast, and it's late at night, and he'd run into somebody in the hotel lobby who you couldn't anticipate, so you couldn't be briefed on it. He'd say, "Remember when we first met in 1974, and we talked about this, this, this, and this?" It's the most remarkable thing.

Joe Lockhart, press secretary: He had a pretty explosive—but predictable—temper. I'd been around him. I knew what frustrated him, what made him mad.

And it really was just blowing off steam. You work around a lot of people with tempers. You work around a lot of people who are important and some people who are just downright mean. He doesn't fit that category. There were probably five or six times that he got so frustrated he could tell he crossed the line being too hard on someone, and it was predictable. Two or three hours later, he would take that person aside and privately apologize. It never happened that he didn't.

Charlene Barshefsky, U.S. trade representative: [What] was always difficult for him was personal confrontation. He might get angry, but he never actually wanted to confront directly, other than a very brief flash of anger more generally directed to the room, not the person. He likes people and wants to be liked. To the extent that adding that edge might have been helpful in a given situation, you had to find a way to accomplish that without counting on him being more aggressive on a personal level.

Q: So he was not very good at controlled anger in that way?
Barshefsky: Yes, that's a good description. I'll leave it to the trade context since that's where I know it best. He was not very good at being demanding in a way that compelled a personal and direct response. But he was adept at making the other party—however exasperating—understand the importance, see the vision, what could be accomplished and why the direction was so common-sensical. He was so gifted at that and personally compelling, that . . . you learned how to use all of these gifts to best advantage, and you learned not to depend on him finger-wagging at a foreign leader, or something of that sort.

Kris Engskov: The greatest moments of the presidency for me were when we made unplanned stops just driving along the road. I remember coming back from the World Economic Forum. . . . We helicoptered to Davos.[7] He gave his speech. Unfortunately, a snowstorm started so we couldn't helicopter out, so we had to drive back. It was like a four-hour drive, from Davos back to Zurich, through the mountains. They always have backup cars, so he got in the car and we got ready for this long drive. Halfway there, he had to go to the bathroom.

We pulled over at this—and thank goodness he did, because everybody else had to go, too, but you can't exactly say to the president, "We have to stop because some of the folks in the back have to use the bathroom." It was a four-hour drive. It was a long drive. We pulled in at this random Swiss equivalent of 7-11. No one had any idea we were coming. He just walked right in. He bolted in there. Only one Secret Service agent was in front of him. The guy at the counter—I'm sure he said to himself, *Wow, that's Bill Clinton. It sure looks like Bill Clinton, but it can't be Bill Clinton, because I work at a 7-11 here in Switzerland.*

---

7. The World Economic Forum has held global seminars of leading figures from business, government, and nongovernmental organizations in Davos, Switzerland, since 1971.

Clinton shook his hand and said, "I'm really sorry to bother you, but do you have a bathroom? I don't need to buy anything, but I need a bathroom and I need it quick." The guy just said, "Right over there." He went downstairs and went to the bathroom, and then ended up buying a whole load of stuff from there. . . . Luckily the guy spoke English.

There are lots of examples like that in America. . . . I thought those were some of the greatest moments when, completely out of the blue, no one knows you're coming and the president of the United States walks into your hardware store—it was just great.

Madeleine Albright: This was so funny. [Vaclav] Havel, who is an incredible character and who is very modern in his taste of art . . . had just taken over.[8] There was this castle [used as the president's home]. . . . We go into Havel's office and there is this painting of this nude couple hanging in the president's office. Clinton looks at it and says, "Can you imagine what would happen if I brought this in?"

Vaclav Havel, president of the Czech Republic: I felt [leading my country] as a burden on my shoulders and I was very happy [when] it was over. . . . But obviously President Clinton is a different character and I felt that he was taking [leadership] as a sportsman. He had this sort of sporty attitude. Even in his suffering on this worry that he had with Monica Lewinsky, I saw that he took it . . . with a sportsmanlike attitude.

* * *

Q: You were a card player with him.
Joe Lockhart: Yes. That was interesting because I had never played hearts before. But I quickly figured out he's not the kind of guy you'd go in and have a meeting with to figure out what's on his mind. . . . I noticed the first couple of times I traveled that he gets relaxed immediately when he starts playing cards. I watched a couple of smart people work a little business in. You have to be careful, because if he figures it out, he'll tell you to shut up. I realized this could be very useful for me, but I'd never played before. So I went and bought this stupid computer program.

Here's the problem: computers are very smart, but they're not very smart at playing hearts, because you can pretty much game them. I don't know how much you know about hearts, but I figured this out the wrong way. We were playing—probably the second time. I at least knew the rules, and we were playing, and I did something. And then I did something else. He'll let one thing go if you're new, but he will never let two things go. He looked at Bruce Lindsey and said, "Another one of these guys who learned on a computer." I said, "How

---

8. Havel became president of Czechoslovakia (later the Czech Republic) on December 29, 1989.

did you know that?" Then I got counseled on how you really play as opposed to how you play against the computer.

I used to file stuff away [for these games] and just ask. I would never ask a specific question. There would be some article in the paper, and I'd ask a broad question like, "What do you think of that?" All I wanted to do was get him talking. It was useful for me. I have no doubt that he probably knew what I was up to. It wasn't like some grand scheme to pry stuff out of him. It just was a sense that there were a few times when he would let his guard down and relax, and that was very useful for me. I never repeated 99.9 percent of the stuff he said. Occasionally there'd be something that should be used in some way, something I thought the public should know. It gave me confidence when we'd be in a meeting and he'd say something and I knew he was really there.

Or it was an early warning system for when someone else on the staff would say, "Well, we're going this way on that," and I'd say, "It just doesn't sound right." I'd think back, I talked to him about this three days ago. This does not sound right. I think in a lot of ways it saved me from having to walk out on a limb and then have to be saved from it because I didn't get it right. It was very useful.

I never minded the long flights where you play for three or four hours at a time because you're going to Japan. You have to do something. You can't sleep the whole flight, and it was a good way to pass the time. But the dreaded call was when you get into some town at one o'clock in the morning. You're just about to go to your room, and you get a page saying, "Come to the suite." I'd like to think I'm being summoned to the suite because there's some political problem the president needs my perspective on or the world's about to blow up and he wants to know what I think. But it was generally because he wasn't ready to go to sleep and he wanted to play cards. Some people can survive on two hours' sleep a night, some people can't. I would be in the latter category, but you can't always decide when you're going to get your access. . . .

Q: *You also played on the helicopter, right?*
Lockhart: Yes. You'd get in a few quick hands—and in the limo. . . . It was always fun with cards on the lap, and in the limo there are cards everywhere. He has a comfortable seat, and we're all surrounding [him], and he's also very impatient. He thinks everybody is as smart as he is. You could, at any given time, stop and say to him, "Okay, the cards that are turned over, what are they?" He could tell you what they were.

Q: *He was counting cards.*
Lockhart: Yes. He just knew. But I would think, *I'm relaxing now, I'm not going to count cards. I count things all day, like how many people are trying to kill you, so*

I don't need that right now. You're sitting there, and your phone will ring. You're on the phone. You're sitting in this tiny corner, and he's saying, "Play, play." I'm saying "Okay! Okay!" . . .

Q: I read somewhere that the game changed at the end?
Lockhart: Yes. We stopped playing hearts. Being president of the United States is ridiculous. Let's be serious. This is the story. He's staying at the Spielbergs' [Steven Spielberg and Kate Capshaw] house one night out in the Hamptons. We were doing some fundraisers, and when we'd go to particular places like that where there aren't really hotels, he'd stay in a private residence, and then we'd find someplace for a small group of reporters. So he was there. I think it was he and Hillary and Spielberg and his wife.

So they were just hanging out. They've known each other for a long time, although it sounds ridiculous that they're at the Spielbergs', but it's part of being president. Someone said, "Let's play cards," and Spielberg said, "Oh, there's this new game I learned." Two days later, the president came back and was very excited. He said, "We're not playing hearts anymore, we're playing this new thing." So we all had to learn something else. . . .

Q: And this game is?
Lockhart: Well, the way it was named by Spielberg was very descriptive. It's a game called "Oh, Shit." The president described it as "Oh, Hell," and that's what it's become because he was the president. It's similar to hearts. I don't know how to describe it. It's a game in which within a hand someone has to lose. So it's who loses the least.

It can become very competitive. The only good story I'll tell on this is we were playing at Camp David during the Middle East peace talks. It was nine or ten o'clock at night, and they'd been at it all day. Someone decided everybody needed to go sit on the sidelines for a while. So we had a three-hour break before they were supposed to come back together, and we were playing. I think it was John Podesta and the president and Chelsea [Clinton] and me. It's one of these games where if you misplay early in the first two or three hands, you're pretty much out of it, and you go around twenty times.

I'd misplayed. I wasn't paying attention, and I misplayed and realized I couldn't win. But I realized I could actually tank on purpose and help someone. So I looked over at Chelsea and smiled, and she got it. There's a weird point system, but if you can get over 200 points, that's great, and the president was always talking about how he got 205 this or that. Well, through Chelsea's and my little collaboration, she got 233, and he didn't notice.

He was the only one at the table who didn't notice what I was doing. A couple of hours later, she said to him, "By the way, I was getting help there." And from that point on, he always talked about how the highest score of all time was Chelsea's, but she had help from Joe. At the risk of sounding stupid, it's one of his most endearing qualities. With everything else going on in the world—with these Middle East peace talks collapsing around him—he couldn't have put more of himself into it. He can say, "Okay, I have to put that aside for now," and he can genuinely have fun with people he likes.

Richard Riley, secretary of education: He was intense about hearts. He would just come out of a speech. He'd speak for an hour and twenty minutes, be ringing wet and everybody screaming and hollering, and he'd come out of that and meeting the press and all that stuff. He'd get on [*Air Force One*] and sit down and I mean he would throw himself into a hearts game. . . .

Q: He was competitive?
Riley: Very competitive. He remembered every card that had ever been played.

Kris Engskov: He had bad taste in movies. . . . As I understand it, the studios would send the Air Force movies they could put on the president's airplane. . . . We'd have videotapes on the plane, and they would be first-run movies that we would be seeing in theaters.

He'd watch anything . . . *Schindler's List* to—he probably wouldn't mind if I said this, but one night we're in the middle of a movie and it's called *Anaconda*.[9] . . . It's about the huge snake. We land . . . and the president said, "God, I love this movie." He asked Timmy [Kerwin, the flight steward] if he could take it home and finish it. . . . It's a horrible movie. But, it was funny, when he was watching movies on *Air Force One* he would react to them. He would go, "Oh, no!" and yell at the movie.

Joe Lockhart: [Golf] is, I think, a misunderstood thing with Clinton. People think he lives for golf, but that's not true. If you follow his schedule closely, he doesn't play that often. He likes golf. He likes to play. I think what he fell in love with at the White House was this idea of a place he could go where no one would come out and bother him. When he'd go out to the little putting green in the back where he'd just do putting and chipping, you really took your life in your hands to go out and talk to him about something. It was risky business. It was just the one place.

He's the most accessible person you're ever going to meet. He's approachable, but there and the third floor of the residence you really have to have a good reason to bother him. I had to go out there a couple of times, and it's not fun. It really was a refuge. Golf, during the presidency, was so important to him because it was a solid block of time—three or four hours—that he could get out and get

---

9. *Anaconda* was released in 1997, starring Jon Voight, Ice Cube, Jennifer Lopez—and a giant animatronic snake.

away from the people he had to deal with all day long. I didn't really understand this until after he was out of office. I traveled with him a couple of times where we were supposed to play golf three days in a row. We'd play just once, because he had something he wanted to do more. But he liked the getting away.

* * *

Q: In his memoirs, President Clinton says that you understood very well his strengths and his weaknesses. Would you like to comment on his strengths and his weaknesses?
Sandy Berger, national security advisor: Let's start with his strengths. I've always believed that Bill Clinton is the most unusual combination of head and heart of anybody that I have ever met, certainly anybody in political life. That is, an intellect which is world-class. He's an extraordinarily bright man. Very few people that I've dealt with are smarter than Clinton. And a tremendous compassion, a real generosity of spirit, infused what he did. So I think that's number one.

Number two, he loved people. One of the reasons he was late all the time was because if the speech at the New York Hilton was at 8:00, first of all, we probably left fifteen minutes late, so there was a certain lack of promptness in terms of when we started. Then the Secret Service would always take the president in through the kitchen, through the service entrance, because that was safer than going in through the public entrance. He'd stop and say hello to every cook, every chef, and every dishwasher. He'd get in a conversation with a dishwasher about the fact that his son couldn't get into college. He connects with people. He has tremendous joy for life, tremendous exuberance.

He knows, whether it's history or—don't play Trivial Pursuit with Bill Clinton. I think the only person who can possibly beat Bill Clinton in Trivial Pursuit is Chelsea Clinton, who takes after her mother and her father. He's curious about things. When we traveled, I was responsible for planning foreign trips, not from the perspective of logistics but from the perspective of the content and substance of the trip. We always thought about trips in three parts. One was the official part of the trip, what were we trying to get done, what do we have to do for state and protocol reasons, a state dinner, the meeting with the prime minister, the visiting of the shrine—whatever.

The second was people events. Clinton always wanted to go out into the marketplace, always have some event where he was very visible, connecting with the people of that country. And then there was the cultural side. He always wanted to see the pyramids. I don't mean that literally, I mean figuratively. He always wanted to see the archeological sites or natural sites of a country. It was very conscious, because he wanted to not only get the business done, but he wanted the people of that country to see that the United States respected their heritage. That was very important in terms of how he wanted the trip to be portrayed. Plus the fact that he was just curious.

Once we were in Mexico City. There's a great archeological museum in Mexico City, the name of which I can't remember. We were supposed to go there for half an hour with Zedillo because he wanted to see it. After about three and a half hours, Zedillo's chief of staff came over to me and said, "If President Zedillo doesn't leave in the next fifteen minutes, he will not be able to be at the state dinner in time." So I had to go over to the president and say, "Mr. President, it's probably time for us to go. President Zedillo needs to get back." He would have stayed there six hours. So he has a tremendous curiosity. He enjoys life.

I'm a lousy golfer. He's a good golfer, but I love to play with him. I didn't play with him in the White House but afterwards, because you'd wind up after the eighteen holes sitting in some nineteenth hole restaurant, and he'd sit down with eight or nine people and they'd all of a sudden be talking about the event of the day. I think his Southern heritage is important in understanding Clinton. He's a respectful person. He is courteous, and I think that was very important in terms of how he dealt with foreign leaders.

When [Chinese President] Jiang [Zemin] was in the United States and they had the joint press conference, Jiang dropped his papers accidentally on the floor. Clinton went over and picked up the papers. I've been told by many Chinese that Jiang was enormously moved by the fact that the president of the United States would go over and pick up his papers. If that had happened in China, flunkies would have come out of someplace and picked up the papers. The fact that the president did that was a natural thing for him to do, but not necessarily a natural thing for anybody to do. So those are the strengths.

Weaknesses. Clinton said to me when he asked me to be national security advisor during the transition, "The first four years I drove you crazy by what I don't know, the next four years I'm going to drive you crazy by what I think I know and I don't." There are the obvious weaknesses that we're all familiar with, the mistakes that he made. Sometimes I think there was a lack of discipline in recognizing that we had to do things within a certain kind of a box. He was always kind of resisting the box. I don't think we always set priorities as sharply as we could. Because he's a person of such eclectic interests, he wants to do everything, and you can't do everything.

Dennis Ross, Middle East envoy: Clinton had a number of remarkable strengths. Then I'll deal with what I think were the areas that were not his strengths. His major strength was a capacity to learn anything and to learn it quickly and to really internalize it. Meaning—when I say internalize it, it means to learn it and to be able to act on it, to use it. So he could learn anything and he could learn anything incredibly quickly. His capacity to do that was then married with his capacity to relate to people, to empathize with them. So he could take the information that he had and then he could apply it in a way that would tell somebody, "Boy, he really does understand my problem."

To tell someone, "I understand your problem," doesn't work unless you're able to explain, "You know, I understand why X, Y, and Z are so hard for you." Or, "I can understand, if I had to contend with that, it would just be almost impossible for me." He had an amazing capacity to cite examples from his experience as governor, to show them how he had dealt with something on a kind of personal or local level.

I'll give you an example. We were dealing with the prisoner release issue between the Israelis and the Palestinians, and he was talking to the Palestinians and to Arafat and with Abu Mazen and [indecipherable name].[10] They were saying, "But we have to have prisoner releases." He said, "You know, one time when I was governor, I released a guy, I gave him a pardon. I thought it was the right thing to do. It was certainly important to his family and there was a whole group of people who were clamoring for it. I thought it was also politically good for me to do it. And he got out and he killed somebody. And, you know, I felt responsible."

Now, honestly, I don't know if that was a true story or not, because with Clinton, you never knew. But he said it because he was saying to them, "We've got to take account of what the Israeli concerns are on this. And I can just imagine the victims, the victims' families, what they feel. I know how these people felt." People would listen to Clinton. I mean, leaders would listen to Clinton and they would be almost transfixed. He would command a kind of attention. In every case it did create a connection.

You can say, "Well, all right, the meeting's over, it's over." And there's a point to that. I don't want to exaggerate too much, because at the end of the day we didn't make a deal with Arafat, and at the end of the day we didn't make a deal with Assad. We came very close. I would say that part of the reason we came as close as we did was because of Clinton's capacity with them. The capacity was to connect. The capacity was to learn everything. The capacity was to use his own personal experience. An incredible ability to explain and to have those he was talking to understand why he was asking something of them. That was a strength that was, I think, frankly, incomparable. [Secretary of State James A.] Baker was very good, but Baker couldn't connect the same way.[11] I think one of my skills was to be able to connect, as well, but I don't think anybody could connect the way Clinton could really connect.

His weakness was that he found it hard to be tough. They're two sides of the same coin. When you're asking someone to do the hardest thing they're ever going to have to do, you'd better be able to connect. This incredible capacity to connect was a function not only of his personality but also of the ability to internalize all the information, to understand really what were the issues, and at a level of real

---

10. Abu Mazen, or Mahmoud Abbas, is a Palestinian leader who succeeded Arafat in a number of key political positions.
11. Ross had at one time been a senior aid to the Republican Baker.

depth. Because you're not going to be able to connect if you can't prove that you understand why something is so hard for someone to deal with—why, for Assad, getting the territory back was so important to who he was, to his own personal definition, or as I used to call him, the last Arab nationalist. Clinton could convey that in a way that showed he understood it and he could talk to him in terms of how Assad defined public opinion. It might not be our definition of public opinion, but the way Assad defined public opinion, and he understood it.

So the critical thing here, *that* he could do, with anybody. But what he couldn't do naturally or easily was to be tough. The reason you have to do both is that when you're dealing with a historic conflict, to get somebody to approach the threshold, you have to be able to convince them that you understand why it's so hard to do, and you do things to make it easier. You'll find ways to compensate. But to get them to cross the threshold, they have to also know the consequence of not doing it. Because when you're talking about ending a conflict that is also a defining conflict, then there has to be a sense that the price you're going to pay is worse than the price you pay for settling the conflict. . . .

Q: Did that mean you had to be the bad cop more often?

Ross: Yes. And one of the things I learned about Clinton was, when I tried, when I would say, "This is how you have to do this part of it," he'd never do it. Or he wouldn't do it in a way that was convincing. Or he would do it in a way that wasn't him. The classic example is the very last meeting with Arafat. . . . It's left to me to say to Arafat, "You're not responding. You're saying yes, but you're not saying yes." I actually stop the meeting and tell Clinton, "Look, he can't hear it from me, because he thinks if he's hearing it from me, big deal. He's got to hear it from you." So I left. But then what Clinton did was, Clinton said, "You're killing [Israeli Prime Minister Ehud] Barak." He didn't say, "You're killing *me*. You're killing me, you don't believe in making peace. You're telling me I spent all this time with you? I've done everything I could. I've offered something, I put something on the table that is historic, unprecedented, and you're telling me no. What you're telling me is that you can't make peace and I've wasted all this time. I'm going to have to go out and tell the world I learned one thing about Chairman Arafat, he's not interested in making peace. That's what you're telling me." And what does he say? "You're killing Barak." Arafat didn't care if he was killing Barak, big deal. But that was Clinton.

His strength was that he had this capacity to do what, frankly, almost no one else could do—learn the issues in a way that no one else would and then marry it to his empathy so that he could use the understanding of the detail to communicate how well he understood what their plight was, what their problem was. His weakness was he couldn't do tough love.

Kris Engskov: I'll tell you one other quick story. . . . Six o'clock in the morning, Waldorf-Astoria Hotel [in New York City], presidential suite. I'm standing in the kitchen of this thing. I don't know if you've been in there, but it's a huge suite. It has six or eight rooms. It's where he always stayed. I'm standing in the little kitchen there and I hear the phone ring. I was just making sure he was awake. We were getting ready to leave in an hour or so. Now, when a phone rings, it can only be a couple of people, because they can't ring through. The way it works is the only people who can ring directly through to the president are the chief of staff, the national security advisor, or his family.

So I was thinking to myself, *Who is that?* Because they install these special phones and it's got a seal on it. It's this crazy infrastructure they install for the president. I think to myself, *Where's Mrs. Clinton? She must be in China; she'd call at an odd hour to reach him.* I hear, "Hello?" I hear him in the back room. He goes, "No, you must have the wrong number." I mean, these were just normal exchange lines. No one knows the number but they're normal phone lines.... These are real, hardline phones. They have to use existing phones, but they're just unused. So someone in New York City has accidentally, of all the numbers being dialed, rung the wrong phone and he's picked it up. At six a.m.

I'm listening to this conversation and I'm thinking, *Holy cow!* I hear him say, "Who are you looking for?" I don't see him, but I hear him kind of fumble around like he's going to try to find the phone book. Ultimately he says, "Well, I'm sorry, I don't think I can help you." He hangs up. What's amazing is that somebody out there in New York City had the president of the United States on the phone and didn't know it. He was perfectly happy to try and help them at six a.m., which I thought was just hilarious. It says a lot about him.

Mickey Kantor: We were talking once, sitting outside the Oval Office, out in the little office he has, a nice little patio where you can sit and talk and the sun was shining. I forget when it was. And he was saying, "You know what the worst part about this is? The things you don't expect. The tragedies, the events, the Oklahoma Cities, the World Trade Centers, the Ron Browns. The things you never—you see so many people die and so many tragedies. It is the one thing you're not prepared to do in this job."

32

Al Gore

Bill Clinton's selection of Al Gore as his running mate in 1992 violated all the normal rules of ticket-balancing—but in the process galvanized party and public support for a campaign demonstrably featuring a new generation of leadership. Gore subsequently became the most influential vice president in American history to that point, useful to Clinton in a series of policy areas where he had special expertise—such as foreign affairs and the environment—but also as a trusted sounding board on everything from issues to personnel. Gore's commitment to Clinton's agenda and his success was never doubted.

But the latter years of the Clinton presidency saw fissures emerge in that relationship. The primary cause was the Monica Lewinsky scandal, which created a perilous set of political shoals for Gore to navigate, especially as he contemplated his own race for the presidency in 2000. What was the proper response for a loyal vice president in a polarized and electrified political environment? How could Gore best balance his devotion to the president's governing program with his disappointment over Clinton's personal behavior—especially given the need to establish a winning strategy for the White House? Gore never found a way to resolve those multiple tensions. And he never found an acceptable mix of change and continuity to present to the country as a rationale for a Gore presidency.

Roy Neel, Gore chief of staff: He came back from Vietnam like most of us, terribly disillusioned.[1] Divinity school seemed like a good way to work through some issues.[2] I don't think it was ever in his plan to become a pastor, but he was looking for some answers about what was going on in the world. He was working as a reporter at the *Nashville Tennessean*, which put him into contact with the contemporary world around him in Tennessee. Then he became a court reporter and covering local government and got involved in a number of big stories, a couple of exposés that ended up having a number of city councilmen

---

1. Gore spent five months in Vietnam in early 1971 as an enlisted man. He mainly served as a journalist.

2. Gore was enrolled at Vanderbilt Divinity School in 1971–72. At the same time he began working as an investigative reporter for the *Nashville Tennessean*.

prosecuted for graft and whatnot. He began to realize that to really have a grip on how government worked and didn't work, then he would need a legal education. So he went to law school [at Vanderbilt], all the time, again, continuing to work at the *Nashville Tennessean*. So all these things sort of fit together for him.

Why he left divinity school for law school, it was really more of a practical issue of looking for a different kind of education. He began to get on track of the sort of things he wanted to do. But he still, at that point, had no interest in politics.... There's been a lot of pop speculation written about the influence of his parents on him and his work and his personality and so on.[3] I saw it a little bit differently. Certainly, Senator Gore was very helpful in his first race for Congress [in 1976] and Al used his father both as a sounding board, a source of knowledge about the congressional district, and to tap into a network of friends around the country.

Where his father's influence and involvement stopped short was in steering Al toward decisions. Both in the way he campaigned and once he was elected, how he served. He was very close to his father, deeply respectful, but he was not a clone of his father. They have very different personalities, extremely different. Maybe not night and day, but very different. Al is a much more private person, more reserved, less gregarious. His father did politics differently, in part because his father was of a different era. Al knew, clearly, that that era had ended. He couldn't do it the way his father did it. Whatever criticisms there have been of Al Gore's political style, he knows himself and he knows his limitations. He knows what he does well and he knows what he doesn't do well. He knew he was not going to be a traditional politician at the time and he had to do it his way. And his father respected that. ...

Q: Can you tell us a little bit about the vice president's working relationship with the president?
Neel: It all had its genesis in that meeting that the two of them had in Washington during the campaign in which they apparently had a kind of an understanding about how they would govern if elected.

Before the end of the campaign, when it looked like we were going to win, I began to have some very quiet discussions with some people who worked for [Walter] Mondale.[4] It had been widely known that up until Mondale's time and in a couple of cases since then, vice presidents were largely relegated to kind of make-work within the White House, to be seen and not heard. They

---

3. Gore's father, Al Gore Sr., was a U.S. senator from Tennessee from 1953 to 1971, so Gore spent much of his early life in Washington. The fact that his father was up for re-election in 1970 reportedly played a role in Gore's decision to enter military service.

4. Walter Mondale served as vice president to Jimmy Carter from 1977 to 1981. Many scholars trace the emergence of a modern vice presidency, with substantive roles and a seat at the table for important policy and political decisions, to Mondale's time.

weren't given much in the way of resources or responsibilities and they were just presidents-in-waiting. They were often the subject of ridicule and disrespect among the president's staff, even the presidents.

But Mondale and Carter had a different type of relationship. It was one that was more respectful, it was more peer-to-peer, and I wanted to find out how they did that. Was it a contrived design or was it just something that happened naturally between the two of them as if they became friends, and so on. So I did some inquiries and some research into that and found out—it had been a long time since I thought about it—they actually had a letter of understanding. They actually had a memorandum, an agreement between Carter and Mondale, which outlined how the relationship would work. So I got a copy of that shortly after the election . . . and basically rewrote it . . . lay[ing] out maybe a dozen principles that the two of them would agree to, that would govern the relationship between Clinton and Gore and the two staffs in the administration.

I think Al finally said [to Clinton], "What do you think about this approach?" We got into it and Clinton took the paper and started going down through each topic and asking some questions, "Well, has this ever happened before?" so on and so forth. Minor things. One of the things is that Gore's chief of staff would become an assistant to the president as well. He says, "This is very impressive, has this ever happened?" And I pointed out that yes, Mondale's chief of staff was an assistant to the president under Carter. He said, "Well, that sounds fine," and he made some joke about me. Clinton and I had been playing golf a few days before and he made some reference to that. . . . He made everybody feel like he was their best friend.

He was very gracious and they pretty much agreed to everything. I don't think that there was any exception taken on anything. There may have been one or two things where they said, "Well, we need to wait and see about this and that, but in principle this sounds fine." So we had the agreement, with everyone in the room at the same time, understanding what these points were and that we were going to make them happen.

There were things that sound small, I guess, to an outsider, but they were very substantial within the White House. There would be a weekly lunch set aside between Gore and Clinton and it would take precedence over anything else unless there was an emergency. There would be a senior Gore staffer placed on the National Security Council, on the Economic Policy Council, the Domestic Policy Council, and so on.

Q: *Was there an issue orientation to any of those points—a division of labor on issues?*
Neel: The only issue orientation was not in the memo, but it was talked about and understood. Gore would have a particularly important—I don't remember

the term that we used—a particularly important role, not a deciding role, but an important role in filling several positions in the administration: the FCC, the Office of Science and Technology Policy, the EPA, and so on.

Q: This was a verbal understanding rather than something that was written in a document?
Neel: Yes, this was really more directed at sub-Cabinet stuff. By this time I think we'd already chosen EPA. I don't even have a copy of the memo. I don't know why I didn't keep a copy, I should have.

Q: I'm sure it's in the archives.
Neel: Don't be so sure. . . . We didn't do anything formal, like having it signed. It was before we had word processing so I don't have it in a computer anywhere. It may have said something like "the vice president would be consulted in depth on areas where he has had significant involvement," or something like that. They had an understanding.

The most important thing was that Clinton took this one step further. We had the first Cabinet meeting the day after the inauguration. . . . [He] basically reaffirmed Gore's role in the administration. If Gore spoke, if Gore called and talked to them, it would be the same as him. He went further down through some of the points about Gore's senior staff, the same thing. They're to be treated as mine, and so on and so forth. He made it abundantly clear to all of them, and that set the tone within his own staff as well.

There was grousing on the Clinton staff because of some of the demands it created. We got a bigger budget than any vice president before, bigger staff allocation, offices, everything. The sacrosanct Thursday lunch was a real nightmare to the president's staff because you don't want anything that's locked in. None of it was personal—I think probably they admired Gore for getting all those concessions. But nevertheless it was what drove the early part of the relationship.

What made it work was that the president continued to show trust and respect for the vice president. . . . If at any point the president had lost trust or confidence in Gore, the relationship was going to be blown up. It wasn't going to exist simply because there was a memorandum of understanding.

Nancy Soderberg, deputy national security advisor: [Gore] played one of the most influential roles of any vice president until [Richard] Cheney probably. He was always someone you could count on to get engaged and get involved. If we were having trouble focusing on something, we could go to the vice president and ask for help, and he was always ready to do it. When you couldn't get the president, and you can get the vice president to do something, that's pretty good. People knew he was very close to Clinton, so if Gore got involved, that was almost as good as the president. In that respect it was a huge plus.

I remember being annoyed a few times when we were trying to have a meeting on something, and Gore would get involved. He's longwinded and would go on and on. He talks in a way that's very sanctimonious. He doesn't mean it that way, I don't think, it's just the way he talks. It could be annoying, because it would throw you off, and you couldn't stop him, obviously. It would throw off your timing in your meeting. You usually had it orchestrated how you wanted it to go, and he'd plop down and say, "Now here's what I think about it." But he was always worthwhile to listen to even though it could be annoying. To have someone as smart as he is involved and engaged was wonderful on the Bosnia stuff, working it through.... Luckily, Gore was always on the money with what he was recommending.

General John Shalikashvili, chair of the Joint Chiefs of Staff: I am a great fan of Vice President Gore. Whenever we had a meeting with the president, each one of us said our thing. At the end of it Gore would sum it up and restate the problem and what each one of us had said, how one should approach the problem. I think he was a major player on the Clinton team. He always had done his homework. I would characterize him as one of the heavyweights.... The president would never make a decision without first turning to Gore and asking him to make a recommendation.[5]

James Steinberg, deputy national security advisor: The vice president was involved a lot [in foreign policy]. He played a very important role in Kosovo because he was a very strong supporter of the course of action that we were pursuing, and that helped in awkward times to know that the vice president was there and that he was prepared to make the decisions, to use force. I think that was very reassuring to the president. But the distinctive role that the vice president played was that he had a set of problems that he had particular responsibility for, and he handled them fantastically. Gore–[Viktor] Chernomyrdin in handling the Russia account, Gore–[Hosni] Mubarak, Gore–[Thabo] Mbeki. He had a set of things in which he was very influential.[6]

Richard Riley, secretary of education: I had great respect for Al Gore. In my judgment, he has not been treated fairly in terms of history. He was very much

---

5. Many senior Clinton administration officials noted that Clinton usually asked Gore to summarize discussions at the conclusion of a meeting, which gave Gore an opportunity to offer his own interpretation of what had happened, in addition to suggesting a course of action.

6. Gore-Chernomyrdin was a joint U.S.-Russian effort to advance bilateral cooperation on a host of issues, including defense conversion, energy, and space exploration. The Gore-Mubarak Partnership was an effort to promote economic cooperation between the United States and Egypt. The Gore-Mbeki Commission was established to create closer ties with South Africa, especially on environmental issues and public health. In each of these instances Gore had an especially prominent role in the administration's foreign policy toward these countries.

a part of the Clinton administration.... Clinton, as knowledgeable as he was about education, looked to Gore for being the knowledgeable person on the environment.... Gore then took a very difficult job in the reorganization of the government. He liked that sort of thing. He was very good at it. He was a very well-organized person. Clinton, with all his strengths, was not as well organized and he leaned on Gore for those kinds of things. He actually let Gore run with the management thing completely. I think we had a wonderful record in what was accomplished in the reorganization of government.... Al Gore was like a rock and Clinton was this creative, adventurous kind of guy and it was a very good combination. I think the public kind of liked that combination.

John Gibbons, presidential science advisor: I often felt that if you could take Gore and Clinton and roll them in a barrel and have them rub off on each other a little bit, we'd all be better off on account of it. Gore would gain humanity, more consistent humor and outlook. Clinton would gain some reserve, be a little less of the charismatic preacher, and that would help. There was no barrel to be found.

Patrick Griffin, congressional liaison: [Gore's] real contribution from a legislative point of view, and I would imagine in other aspects in the White House, was his ability to help the president close. He had the option to be in every meeting that he wanted to be in the Oval—when we were briefing the president, and I guess in others as well. He was in every congressional meeting.... In the leadership meetings when we were working through a strategy or trying to come to closure on a strategy, like in the gun thing, he was a big muscle there, but Clinton clearly was dominating on that. We would queue him up. We'd say, "We're trying to accomplish this in this leadership meeting. We need you to kind of *one-two-three*." He'd lean back to me while we were briefing the president or walking over to the Cabinet room. This is what we want and, boom, he would just *one-two-three*, do it. He was just excellent at that.

John Hilley, congressional liaison: One of [Al Gore's] greatest uses was to send him up [to the Hill] and just have him throw gasoline around. He was very good at it.

Peter Knight, longtime Gore advisor: [The] brilliance of the president was to utilize the best that Gore had. I think the president was really effective and very generous in giving Al leeway, but smart to do so. I'm sure there was some pulling back at various times, but for the most part giving him the bandwidth that he needed to be effective in those areas, to be effective for both of them. Because the president had other things to do. To the extent you have a couple of really smart people focusing on problems, that's better than just having one. That's the way he saw it, that's the way Gore saw it, and I think that's really much to his credit. ...

Q: *The impression about Gore that a lot of people have is that he is very ponderous and slow moving and deliberate sometimes to the point of immobility—unlike the Gore you evidently knew.*

Knight: That all happened after '92. Because they saw him as the wooden guy behind Clinton.... That was the view that most people have, but that's not the view I had, nor other colleagues ... up to '92. He was a pretty good political guy. Not the best. Nothing like Clinton. Nothing like the president. Nobody could match him, but he was pretty good. He had good instincts and he went with them.... It wasn't until '92 that he began to [develop that image]—and that is [because of] the role of the vice president. There is an aspect of him to do the right thing. He's the good soldier. If he's told that he needs to do it this way then he will do it that way and he's not going to fight it.

Q: *To a fault? I've often heard people say "He acts presidential." I'm not sure I've ever heard before now anybody say "He acts vice presidential".*

Knight: I don't know.... Listen, he knew that the power that was there was derivative and he wasn't the president and that was okay with him. But there is that aspect of him, which is the good soldier, he does the right thing.

Q: *Let me try another angle on this. Did you ever get the sense that he was turning the voltage down in order not to upstage the president?*

Knight: I think he was respectful and deferential and I think he understood where he was. I don't think he needed to turn the voltage down. What I do think is that he—in some respects the vice presidency was one of the most exciting times he could ever have because he didn't have to worry about the politics of the situation, all he had to do was worry about the substance. He was good at that. He was really good at that.

I may be wrong on it, but I do think that for those eight years, because the president was so dominant on the political side, he allowed some of those political skills to atrophy. Then he became not as sure of himself politically. Substantively he was great but, because the president was so dominant politically ... Al didn't have to do that, it wasn't his job. His job was to be a really good substantive guy to go in and solve any problem that the president asked him to solve. I think his substantive and his policy skills were greatly enhanced, but I think his political skills probably atrophied. ...

Q: *Can you elaborate on that a little bit and maybe talk about how this plays out in 2000?*

Knight: Any time you're doing an exercise and you're using those muscles, they tend to be sharper. I think it did take him a while to get his voice back on the campaign.... But I think in some respects he was not really as sure of his footing, political footing, as he might have been. Part of it was what I described as the fact that he never had to exercise his muscles over '92 to 2000. Part of it was he was thrown totally off-kilter by the attacks on his integrity. Part of it was the fact of the president going through what he went through. Part of it was having to set up an apparatus of a campaign that he hadn't done in some period of time. Part of it was the sort of unfortunate infighting that went on, the theatrics of a presidential campaign. I think all that added to him not being as sure-footed as he might have been.

Al From, head of the DLC: Gore is a very complicated person. He has a hard time seeing grays, everything is black or white, which is why he "invented the Internet" instead of—he did some stuff to help people develop the Internet.

I think after the Lewinsky thing, and particularly after impeachment and after Gore declared on the day of impeachment that Clinton was the best president ever, and realized the Republicans had the tape, I think it freaked him out. I just think Gore never could come to grips with how to handle Clinton.... I did a lot of speaking in those days with Rich Bond, the former Republican chairman [1992–93]. He's a great guy and a good friend of mine. Richie always said to me, "Gore's got it ass-backwards. He ought to run so tight with the Clinton-Gore record that people would think that everything Clinton did was a Gore achievement. Then at the convention he ought to say what he did, which is, 'I am my own man' and nobody was going to confuse Gore's behavior with Clinton's."

Lawrence Stein, congressional liaison: I think a lot of us knew that Gore was going to have a tough time [in 2000]. It's funny because everyone thinks Gore should have won. I never viewed it that way. I think that he carried—and I know he feels this way—tremendous burdens that were never on the shoulders of Clinton because he didn't have to run again. But Gore had to deal with a hugely hostile press corps, a press corps that thought—it wasn't that they thought he should have been removed, it's that they loved the [Lewinsky] story so much that they just wanted some results from it. Their mindlessness is almost difficult to express, how they blew that story out of proportion. It's almost difficult to say.

William Galston, deputy domestic policy advisor: The American people had gotten very adept at distinguishing between the Bill Clinton they liked and the Bill Clinton they didn't. I never understood why Gore and company didn't understand that. I was having dinner with a reporter in LA the night before Gore's acceptance speech, and he said, "Here's what I hear about what's going into that speech."[7] I had been a deeply involved advisor to Gore in '99 and 2000, but I had no role in that speech. He told me pretty much what was going to be in

---

7. Gore delivered his acceptance address at the Democratic National Convention in Los Angeles on August 17, 2000.

it and what wasn't going to be in it, and my jaw dropped. I said, "That can't be right." But he was right.

"It cannot be the case," I said to him in all naïveté, that the vice president would talk for thirty seconds about the record of the Clinton administration and then immediately pivot to the future. Doesn't he understand that in part he's running for Bill Clinton's third term?

Joe Lockhart, press secretary: I think the vice president, in a personal way, got it into his head that it wasn't enough to win the presidency. He needed to win it on his own and without the help of the president. And they somehow worked themselves into an emotional position where they viewed the president as the enemy as opposed to a potential ally, and they couldn't get out of that.

I think the vice president's staff had a less personal and a clearer understanding of the negatives that the president brought to the vice president, and in some ways they missed the positives. But whatever the motivations or whatever the validity of their thinking, the reality was they were going their own way. This was not an effort they wanted the president involved in in any real way. . . . [The president] very much wanted to help him and was frustrated by the fact that the help was not being sought. . . .

Here's the best way to look at the strains in the relationship and where it really got strained. When the vice president and the president talked directly to each other with no one else in the room, they tended to get on the same page quickly. When the vice president started traveling almost full time campaigning, all of their information about each other came from other people. I think with the vice president it came from his family members, who were particularly injured by the president's behavior, and from staffers.

What happened was they stopped talking to each other. And I believe that had a serious negative impact on the relationship. The president was offended at times by this. When the vice president announced, he seemed to go out of his way to do a series of interviews the night before the announcement that dealt directly with how he felt about the president and his behavior. I remember we were in Paris for something the day the VP was supposed to announce. They had sent over a copy of the speech, and it was gratuitous. We told them that the president was not happy with what he said. And in fact they changed a good bit of it.

But—not to overdo this—the president was happy to campaign for him, which he did. The convention speech the president gave was an important point in the vice president's campaign, as far as setting the table that then the vice president very effectively took advantage of and put himself back in the race. It was one of those times that the stories about the strains were always exaggerated, but they were not without some factual basis.

* * *

Q: I know the decision to not tie the campaign too closely to Clinton was not lightly arrived at, but at the time was this issue debated within the campaign?

Peter Knight: Well, the person really in charge of that was Bill Daley at that point in time.[8] In one sense there wasn't anybody better because he was pretty close to President Clinton and to Al—

Q: And he's a Daley.

Knight: And he's a Daley. So who could be better? The problem—people used to say, "Oh, we could use the president in New Hampshire, we can use him in Arkansas, or we can use him here." The fact is, [if] we used him anywhere, he just occupied so much space. The decision really needed to be either use him or not use him, rather than use him in a particular [place]—there's no way to isolate how you use him because he was president of the United States. Every time he traveled it was like the soccer game, everybody runs to [the ball]. And it didn't matter whether they were in New Hampshire or Arkansas or Alaska, they were going to run there and everybody was going to cover it. He's the president of the United States and he's bigger than life, and he is always going to occupy that space.... There was no using the president of the United States in some isolated way. When he traveled and he did an event, you are off the TV for that day.

Stanley Greenberg, pollster: Gore made a decision at the outset of his campaign to separate himself from the president. Where the campaign stood on the president was in concrete. But the relationship was not good between the two of them. That was evident in my meetings with Gore. He was angry about more than—I never asked, but there isn't any doubt that he viewed that this was difficult because of the way the Clinton presidency was ending.

That created a very difficult [dynamic]—not impossible, because he was elected in 2000.[9] He never resolved how he was going to relate to [Clinton's] history with which he was associated. But that was established before I was there, so I didn't come in and say, "You've got to separate yourself." I took it as a given. But there is the reality. We would ask a question [in polls], "Do you want to continue in the direction that President Clinton is going or do you want to go in a different direction?" The country was split 50–50. For the people who wanted to continue, overwhelmingly it was because of the economy. For the people who

---

8. William Daley served as secretary of commerce under President Clinton from 1997 to 2000. He subsequently chaired Al Gore's 2000 presidential campaign.

9. Greenberg's claim here is based on the fact that Gore won the popular vote that year, and by his accounting won the electoral vote, too, because of his interpretation of what transpired in Florida, the decisive state.

wanted to go in a different direction, it was overwhelmingly because of values, and wanting to restore moral values.

Our blockages in the states where we needed to make gains were in places where the numbers were decisively that [voters] wanted to go in a different direction, for moral values. The president's standing—if you look at the academic literature, usually job approval is more of a predictor of vote than personal favorability. It was not true in the 2000 election. If you look at the regression modeling of it, personal favorability was much more of a driver of vote than overall approval. That is what our stuff showed.

Q: Personal favorability of?
Greenberg: Of President Clinton. It was more of a predictor of the vote than personal favorability of Gore in our models. Whereas California and New York were fine, the states that were in play at the end were Minnesota and Iowa and Missouri and places in which the president was not popular. So the issue was, *Should the president campaign?* . . . The data was just overwhelming that, given what was at issue, this would cut against us.

On the other side of that—and it has never been resolved—I went to the White House and presented this. I forget the times that I go to the White House, but I do go back to the White House to present this data to show them that it is just hard to justify [sending him out], given this data. So it was done, and I was associated with it. I wasn't hiding on the advice that I was giving. I did write a long note to the president. He was never convinced by this but I did write a long note to him after the election, taking responsibility on the question of the scheduling. . . . I promise you, we were trying to win. Whatever prejudices there were between Gore and Clinton, that was not what decided this question. It was a purely pragmatic decision on whether it was going to help or not. I should add that there's another parallel piece to this, which is complicated. Our plan was to run on the economy in the final month and to use the final debate to . . . defend what they'd done on the economy and talk about . . . Bush being a threat to the economy. All of our advertising we produced after the debate and for the rest of the month was on the economy.

We had made a campaign decision to associate ourselves with Clinton and the Clinton economy and to use it in the last month. The only problem is that Gore didn't do it. We still did the advertising, but it's different. We wanted a major battle between the two of them on the economy. The last debate took place in a town meeting format. There was no podium. He was focused on crossing into Bush's space. He had his own personal strategy for winning the debate, which was disastrous. I don't rule out that he didn't want to do it. There was some blockage that kept him from doing it. But the plan was for him to do it. He stopped. He didn't do it, so we didn't have the big set-up out of the debate, the big battle on the economy.

* * *

Q: Should Gore have run more closely to President Clinton in the re-election?
Roy Neel: I don't think it mattered. I've looked at the electoral map and … with the sole exception of West Virginia, I can't find a single state where Clinton could have made the difference. Now, I was always an advocate for using Clinton more, because I didn't think he was going to hurt us any more than he already had and he has great strengths, has been a real asset in a lot of ways. The relationship had become strained. That robbed the Gore campaign of some political skills and energy and advice that it would have had otherwise. It was a tactical decision, and you look around the map and I'm not sure where Gore could have won that he didn't win.

For all of the hand-wringing about the 2000 campaign, in addition to winning the popular vote, he almost won Florida. Arguably won Florida, and wasn't given the votes there. I mean it was quite phenomenal. He was six points behind in the polls ten days before the election, in the public polls. He won the popular vote. Had the Florida thing turned differently, nobody would be asking about Tennessee.[10] It [Tennessee] would be a little pinprick and it [his election] would have been considered phenomenal. It would have been the end of the Bush political dynasty, or whatever, the budding dynasty. That would have been it, it would have been all over. Just shows you how painfully close and to the point of almost being serendipitous this whole thing is.

Peter Knight: [We] didn't use all the political levers that we could have used [in the Florida recount because] Gore didn't want to. I respect him for that and I think it was probably the right choice.

Q: Like what?
Knight: How the Republicans had the outrage of screaming at—

Q: The Brooks Brothers' riot?
Knight: The riot.[11] And it would have been so easy [for us] to manufacture our own things any time we wanted to. Labor was killing themselves, the African Americans—all the communities. It's not that hard. We had 100,000-person rallies as part of the campaign every day. You could have done that in two seconds and he said no. Gore said no. To his credit, because I think it would have made a mockery out of the whole thing.

---

10. Gore lost his home state of Tennessee, which had only eleven electoral votes, to the twenty-five of Florida. Thus had he won Florida, the Tennessee result would have been meaningless.

11. The "Brooks Brothers riot" was a demonstration by Republican activists at the Stephen B. Clark Government Center in Miami to protest a recount of Dade County votes being conducted there in the aftermath of the 2000 election. The demonstration received its name because of the socioeconomic status of the protestors, most of whom were lawyers, lobbyists, and political consultants—including later Republican presidential candidate Ted Cruz.

33

Hillary

Although other First Ladies have been given important responsibilities in their husbands' administrations, none has taken on as active a role in the policymaking process as Hillary Rodham Clinton did. For anyone who had known the Clintons well and watched how they operated in Arkansas, this development was unsurprising. Hillary had matched Bill's rise to prominence in their generation. Her 1969 commencement address at Wellesley received coverage in Life magazine, and she, too, earned a Yale law degree, then working on the legal staff of the House Judiciary Committee handling the Watergate investigation. Soon thereafter she moved to Arkansas to be with her future husband. Hillary joined the prominent Rose Law Firm in Little Rock, and occasionally took on public service chores for Bill after he became governor. It was this history that led him in 1992 to announce to voters that they could "buy one—get one free!"

Mrs. Clinton's historic leadership of the health care initiative was genuinely unprecedented. But her role in the White House extended well beyond that effort. She was, especially in the early years, a fixture in political strategy sessions, although usually a quiet presence, unless the matters under discussion included opposition charges about the Clintons' past in Arkansas. After the stinging defeat of the health care effort, she generally kept a lower profile in the West Wing. She subsequently developed a special portfolio of issues, including women's rights and micro credit. She traveled widely and in ways her husband envied, as she could usually skip the formalities of state dinners and multinational summits and move around foreign lands visiting their common people. Although she stayed out of the main line of White House policymaking, there was never any doubt that Hillary remained, privately, a powerful source of political advice and personal support to her husband, but for the period immediately after he admitted to an improper relationship with Monica Lewinsky. Those close to the couple recognized that the president benefited immensely from Hillary's discipline and mental toughness, which were not his personal strong suits.

Susan Thomases, longtime friend: She's a brilliant woman. How many people do you know who speak in paragraphs? I mean seriously. She's the only person I know. I jab her all the time. I can barely string sentences together, and here's a person who was speaking to me in paragraphs. And it wasn't just one paragraph, it was two paragraphs. If you listen, you're just blown away by it.

Q: *When Bill Clinton initially said that he and Hillary were an item—*
Thomases: I said, "She's too good for you." He had a thing for her. I said, "You'll be lucky if she talks to you. She's so nice, and she's so brilliant, and she's so straight. It's one thing to like her; it's one thing to have hopes—" But the truth is she absolutely adored him and she still adores him. So it didn't become an issue.

Q: *So this wasn't a match you thought was a natural?*
Thomases: No, no. They were two very smart people, but it didn't occur to me. But she was the one who was wildly crazy about him, and so that's why it worked. And now they're crazy about each other, and it clearly works.

* * *

Q: *Did Hillary have conversations with you about her frustration in trying to balance the start of a career with family interests?*
Peter Edelman, longtime friend and later assistant secretary of health and human services: A little bit but not much. She was in the law firm, she was very active in education policy in the state, both substantive policy and school deseg-regation issues. She was always fully occupied. She was substantively an advisor and connected to Marian [Wright Edelman] and the work with the Children's Defense Fund. I'm sure there were frustrations on various levels including per-sonal levels that we didn't know anything about. She always came across to me as positive and resilient and upbeat.

Q: *Do you know if she had any electoral ambitions at that point?*
Edelman: I don't.

Q: *Did you get the impression that she may have been more liberal than her husband?*
Edelman: We always thought so. On the other hand, I put her on the board of something called the New World Foundation[1] that I was on the board of in about 1983 or '84. We served on that board together for four or five years. That was a very liberal foundation and compared to the rest of us she was the con-servative voice on the board and very useful. Some of it was just being skeptical. Some of it was asking the hard questions that somebody ought to ask, just being smart. But I also knew from that, whether it was the consequence of having gone

---

1. The New World Foundation was chartered in 1954, initially to advance the cause of "responsible wealth" by supporting broader civil rights and democracy. In ensuing decades it moved into wide-ranging areas of social justice.

down to Arkansas and just having some of Arkansas rub off on her or whatever it was, I knew that she also was more conservative than I.

In terms of the Children's Defense Fund and Marian and the specific policy things on which the Children's Defense Fund was working very hard, and where he was in some of these instances working at cross purposes, Hillary was playing a middle-person role and carrying messages back and forth and pushing [Bill]. We had the distinct impression that of the two that she was the more liberal.

Bernard Nussbaum, White House counsel: They're a unique team in American history. I don't know, we'll see what historians write one hundred years from now. But the Clintons couldn't do it without each other. Maybe that's true for other couples too, but it's certainly true for them.

Strobe Talbott, longtime friend and later deputy secretary of state: Hillary was on the board of the Children's Defense Fund, [with] Marian Wright Edelman. I think she stayed at our house a couple of times. Since this is history, I'll just say it, it sticks in my mind. She was so dogged and determined about doing her job right. She was defending, or prosecuting—it must have been defending—a woman who had been raped. She was carrying around a plastic bag with some-thing in it of a very intimate nature that somehow she pulled out at one point and said, "We have the evidence here." Yikes. You get the drift.

Alice Rivlin, OMB director: I think for a good part of his career, [Bill] was probably rescued by Hillary—by her being a more decisive, more disciplined kind of person who kept things moving. She didn't really play that role in the administration very long, because after she got burned by the health care thing she pretty much dropped out of the discussions in the White House and did her own thing. She did a lot of things, but with her own staff and her own traveling. . . .

I observed early on, when Hillary was still in the meetings, that she was often useful in moving things on. The president would let the talk go on forever. He would listen to arguments and get into the discussion. I remember at least one instance in Little Rock, where Hillary simply said, "We have to decide something here and get this moved on." And the president would look sort of, "Well, all right." . . . She had more discipline than he in getting to a decision.

Mickey Kantor, secretary of commerce: As much as he needs people, needs to draw from people, needs to bounce ideas, needs to validate them, or not vali-date them, needs to hear—[Hillary is] just the opposite. She needs to think for herself. You can't think of two more opposite people in the way they will take a problem and deal with it. . . . She [once] said it just muddles your mind when you start listening to other people tell you what you ought to be doing.

Senator Alan Simpson (R-WY): I watched Hillary as she began to visit with [Mrs.] Ann [Simpson]. Hillary never turns her head when she's talking to someone. She is absolutely riveted. She doesn't look around like, "Oh, hi there, Tilly; how are you?"—or divert her attention from the person she's talking to. That's a gift. You have to have that in politics.

James Woolsey, director of central intelligence: Well, as contrasted to my far-from-close relationship with President Clinton, I had an intense and close relationship with the First Lady. It occurred as follows: In September or October of 1993 was his and her 20th Yale Law School reunion, and my 25th. I'm five years older than they are. They, and I, and hundreds of other people from Yale Law School are up in New Haven and there's a huge reception.

There's hundreds of people. I am standing around and I see, coming in the door, a classmate from law school I hadn't seen in twenty-plus years. I step out to go say hello to him and I feel something soft under my foot, and a female voice says, "Ouch!" I look down and I am standing on the First Lady's foot. I said, "Oh, sorry, Mrs. Clinton." That's the sum total of my relationship with the First Lady for the two years of the Clinton administration. "Ouch." "Sorry, Mrs. Clinton." It was intense and personal but quite brief. [*laughter*]

Mickey Kantor: Vernon [Jordan] and I, he wanted to meet with us and I forget what the issue was, it might have been about the '96 transition, in fact, I think it was. So we're down on the first floor of the East Wing right below, waiting to be hauled up. I don't know if he was working, I don't know what he was doing. One of the stewards came in and said, "Do you want something to eat?" and Vernon says, "I haven't eaten, yes, I'd like something and do you have any wine." The guy said, "Sure, Mr. Jordan."

Comes back and puts a bottle of wine down and Vernon looks and says, "God, this is a good bottle of wine." It is a red wine of some sort, Cabernet, and it was French—I didn't know. Vernon said, "This is great. Mickey, have a glass." I take a glass, he takes a glass. Called up, Vernon says, "Let's take the bottle with us. Let's get the president." We go, they put the bottle down. The steward brings the bottle. Hillary looks at that and says, "Oh, no." Vernon says, "What's the matter?" She says, "I was saving that for our anniversary." [*laughter*] I thought she was going to cry, or kill Vernon, one or the other. I mean, it must have been a multi-hundred-dollar bottle of wine. Oh, God. Oh, well.

Roger Altman, deputy treasury secretary: There's an interesting difference that always has struck everybody who's watched it up close, which is that she inspires fierce loyalty and he doesn't. You look at the turnover that she had—or in her case did not have—on her staff, and the turnover that he had. You look at the relationships he ended up having with a lot of people that he was initially close to and were central to his administration, whether it's George Stephanopoulos[2] or whoever else it may be.

She inspired, continues to inspire, fierce loyalty and he doesn't. It's quite a difference and I ascribe it to the fact that she does not look at the world as, or at least in my experience, as solely and only politically.

Leon Panetta, White House chief of staff: Look, there's no question that she was smart, she was dedicated, she understood the issues and people were a little intimidated by her. There were several meetings where she basically walked in and let everybody have it, very different from what the president would do. If she thought something was going wrong, she'd say it. She was much more confrontational in that sense.

I'll never forget [congressional liaison] Pat Griffin came on replacing Howard [Paster] during the middle of, I think it was the health care stuff, Howard moved on. Pat Griffin came in and went into a meeting, I think on . . . the importance of letting out all of the information on Whitewater. I think that was it. And everybody from Stephanopoulos and [Dave] Gergen and everybody said, "You've got to let this out because if this just dribbles out and you go through it, you're going to get killed in the process." She just let everybody have it. I'll never forget, Pat Griffin came out of that meeting and his eyes were that wide and he said, "You will not believe what I've just been through." I said, "What are you talking about?" I had been at another staff meeting. He said, "I can't believe it, I can't believe what I've just been through." I said, "What's the matter?" He said, "The First Lady just tore everybody a new asshole." I said, "Really?" It was that first experience.

When I became chief of staff, recognizing that she was an important factor, I went out of my way to make sure I briefed her on what was going on as chief of staff. But if she ultimately believed that you had the capacity to do a job, she backed off. She served as what I would call a chief of staff-in-waiting. In the sense that if she felt the chief of staff or whoever was not doing the job, she was prepared to protect the president. And she was very good at that. The first thing I had to do was to ensure that she trusted me. She never really came in or got involved in the things I was doing.

Roy Neel, deputy White House chief of staff: [Many social conservatives] hated Hillary. And when I use "hate," I use that advisedly. I've experienced those attacks from literally hundreds of people, certainly when I would go back and

---

2. George Stephanopoulos left the White House in December 1996, soon moving to ABC television. His occasionally critical commentary there—including his relatively early evocation of impeachment after the Lewinsky scandal broke—and a 1999 best-selling memoir, revealing details of his years inside the White House, left some Clinton insiders bitter that he had betrayed their trust.

forth to Tennessee and in the South and elsewhere, because she appeared to be something of an affront to their sense of who they were, to women. I found more women who despise Hillary Clinton than men, ironically. Because to many of them, she appears to be a commentary on the life they've chosen. She didn't help herself with the "stay home and bake cookies" comment during the campaign, but on the other hand, I don't think she ever really quite deserved their wrath.

Judge Abner Mikva, White House counsel: She was a very important role player. Again, the president trusts her, he respects her. He has great confidence in her judgment and her capacities. As I indicated before, she frequently had the last word just because of who she was and where she was and who he talked to last. As you've already heard, the president frequently would try to keep an open mind, and she certainly was a big influence on him in many things.

I don't know, I can't think of any issue of any importance at all where they were in disagreement and she didn't win out. He might start out opposite on something, but as I think back over the year I was there and the other things I know about, when there was any difference of opinion, she prevailed. Not because she yelled at him or leaned on him, but simply because he respected her judgment. I assume you've read both their books. Hers is much better than his, I thought. I felt it was very candid of her to describe her reaction to Monica.

I had always felt that they had a good relationship. My wife and I always disagree, but I would say, "I'm not around them that much, but whenever I am there's so much touchy-feely; they can't be putting it on." She said, "Ah, you don't know, that has to be a very tense relationship." . . . But I really think they had a great relationship, and they have supported each other and complemented each other in so many important ways. From the time he first started running to the time she first got interested in something besides being a [Barry] Goldwater girl. And they still continue.

Q: How is she to work with?
Mikva: Hard. . . . Again, I didn't know Hillary before this. I think I'd met her when she was head of the women's commission. I don't think she ever had any problems with [counsel] Lloyd [Cutler], but I think she was a little unhappy that Bernie [Nussbaum]—who had been more her friend than Bill's friend—had been moved out. She had a few concerns about Panetta, not because she didn't want him there—she was glad he was there, I think she recognized it needed a firmer hand on the tiller—but she hadn't had any relationships with Panetta. Then Lloyd came in. She got along with Lloyd, but he wasn't there very long. . . . As you know, she's much closer to my political persuasions than he is. I think she would even acknowledge she's a liberal—or at least she used to be. He would deny that vigorously. Yet, we just never had occasion to be close to each other. . . . I just don't think she thought I was an important piece of the landscape.

I have to say that the best thing that I saw about both of them was that they were spectacular parents. I'm amazed. I think Chelsea [Clinton] has come out of the White House better than any White House kids I know.

Madeleine Albright, secretary of state (on her interest in foreign policy): First of all, she had taken an interest in the UN when I was up there, even at the beginning. I think there were all the jokes about her channeling with Mrs. [Eleanor] Roosevelt, but Mrs. Roosevelt clearly had a very important role at the UN. Mrs. Clinton came up a couple of times and met with different delegates and was really very interested in it. She then also did quite a lot of traveling as First Lady. Because she never does anything in a half-hearted way, she would have briefings, some of them set up by the NSC, but some of them by the State Department.

Then her big thing was when we went to the Beijing women's conference.[3] She really blew them away up there. Her statement was stunning. She did a lot of foreign policy things. Sometimes I went to a country with her and we would meet with women's groups or human rights' groups. But she was a presence in terms of, not in doing negotiations or anything like that, but she was a very good ambassador. She would travel a lot. Sometimes Chelsea would go with her. She had her agenda in terms of women's issues and health issues, and generally she was a presence.

She and I had a great trip. We went to Prague in '96. I didn't know her until sometime in the early part of the '92 campaign. She had been president of the Children's Defense Fund and I'd gone to something. We talked about the fact that she went to Wellesley ten years after I did. So we had a bond and we got along. When we went to Prague, we had a great time and we talked a lot. But we never talked about whether or not I should be secretary of state. We just talked about issues or friendships or professors and things like that.

We all thought she had a role in [my nomination]. But that was not corroborated until one time we were all together with the president in Barbados in 1997. We were having a meeting. He would always visit our embassy wherever. We had this routine where I would introduce her and she would introduce him. So after she had introduced him, he said, "Of course, everybody knows that Hillary had a role in having Madeleine becoming secretary of state," which was the first time that I really flat out heard it—it was confirmed. Since then she has talked to me about it. But at the time she was pretty careful in terms of not talking about it.

Sandy Berger, national security advisor: She did not participate in the foreign policy decision-making formally, although I suspect in the evening, the president

---

3. The Beijing meeting, September 4–15, 1995, was the fourth global conference sponsored by the Commission on the Status of Women of the United Nations. Her speech to that assembly is sometimes cited as a pathbreaking moment in the emergence of women's issues on a global scale.

had such great respect for her views and her judgment—I often thought in the morning I heard some echoes of Hillary in something he said. So I suspect they talked about these things privately. But I think she played a different role.

She began in the second half of the first term to travel abroad. These trips were quite remarkable in that she went to India, to Africa, and she'd have a much lighter package than we did when she traveled. We traveled with a thousand people. She would travel with maybe half a dozen reporters and a small staff, and she was therefore much more able to travel around the country, to go to outer remote places, to poor villages, to see development projects. And she would come back and talk to the president. "You've got to go to India, you've got to go to Morocco, and you've got to go to Africa."

Many of our trips were "advanced" by her. Of course by the time we got there, they'd already fallen in love with Hillary Clinton, so they were predisposed to like the president. I think the traveling expanded her view of what's important and how to look at the world, not just from an American perspective but from a global perspective. It certainly foreshadowed a number of our trips.... She was very interested, for example, in micro credit, a very rapidly growing movement that was started by the Grameen Bank in Bangladesh, in which loans of $50 or $75 are given, primarily to women, to start their own businesses. It has transformed villages. We went to a village, I think in Uganda, where many of the people had been recipients of these micro loans. One woman had a little brick-making factory and another had a pottery shop, another had a carpentry shop. The village was much more prosperous than the villages around it.

Micro credit was something she pushed and cared a lot about, number one. Number two, she obviously was very concerned about the role of women and how women are treated. She really brought the whole question of the Taliban's treatment of women to the attention of the president. We had a conference in the White House on the abuse of women by the Taliban in Afghanistan, which brought public attention to that issue. There were many issues like that, development-oriented issues she brought to public life.

David Cutler, health care economist: Her knowledge of the way health care actually works I thought was phenomenally good. She had been around to hospitals and nursing homes and talking with people.... I personally found her quite delightful to work with. I thought she was a very good listener, an interested person, really wanted to absorb stuff. When she settled on a view, she felt strongly about her view, and I'm not sure it was easy to change her from her view. But that's not an unusual statement. That's just a statement about somebody and their beliefs. But I personally found her to be extremely pleasant and surprisingly interested in hearing things.

Patrick Griffin, congressional liaison: She was very good [working with members of Congress]. She had a different set of strengths [from her husband]. I thought she was a great advocate for the concepts. She testified brilliantly. She could get a small room of folks convinced. She was very impressive. A lot of folks were looking to dislike her and to trip her up. She handled herself very well in the caucus and bipartisan meetings that I also attended. But in one-on-ones she had a different set of skills. You know how relationships balance each other. She would be able to talk directly to you, even if she hadn't seen you in months—and say, "How is your son doing? I hear that he likes getting letters. Do you want me to send him one—?" She would remember that. She carried that piece of the family with her. It was an interesting complement to her husband's skill set. . . .

Q: From the standpoint of a member of the White House staff, a senior member, who would you rather give the bad news to, the president or the First Lady?
Griffin: Oh, no question about it. Neither one was fun to give bad news to, but the president, was easier, yes.

Q: People were afraid of the First Lady's reaction to the bad news?
Griffin: Not afraid. It's just—would you rather punch a piece of wood or a brick wall? I mean, when she came back, she was tough. She's like a four-wheel drive going right at you. *Zooooom.* If you didn't lean back into your argument, she'd go right over you. It took more energy and focus.

Joan Baggett, White House political director: At least at the beginning, the First Lady was in some political meetings and not in others. It was like if she was around and we had a political meeting with the president and the vice president, she might sit in on it, but it wasn't like we had to schedule meetings around her schedule. I've often thought that some of her reputation of being politically off-key, I'm not saying she has it now, but the rap on her back then was she was way out there, out of touch with people, too liberal, blah, blah, blah. When you think about it, the president and the vice president have a lot of staff to brief them on meetings going on, and she didn't have that much staff. So if she was going into a political meeting, nobody had produced paper for her before. She was hearing things for the first time. If she said something that was a little bit off, I don't think any of us, including me, felt like it was appropriate for us to correct her. Whereas, if the president had made an observation that was off base, I could have said, "Not really, here's what that really means." But with her, if he or the vice president knew she said something wrong, they might say something, but nobody else would. So then it was sort of out there.

Or she would blow up over something that she misinterpreted. Again, you can't take her on, that's not my boss. You can't take on the First Lady and say, "That's wrong." Sometimes she would blow up over things. She was sort of defending him, like on the deficit-reduction stuff. I remember one time in one of these meetings where she was blowing up about his staff and how we were all incompetent and he was having to be the mechanic and drive the car and do everything, that we weren't capable of anything. Why did he have to do it all himself? Which was a little odd.

* * *

Q: *What does she have that he lacked?*
Bernard Nussbaum: The word that comes to my mind is strength. She has a certain kind of strength that he lacks. He has a certain kind of talent, political talent and speaking talent and communicating talent, that no one has. I mean, she's pretty good at speaking and stuff like that, but she has a certain strength. She's very tough. She's very political too. She's not this wild-eyed liberal or '60s person. The reason she did so well in New York, in part, is that she went upstate a lot. Upstate in New York is not New York City. It's not where I come from. Upstate is the Midwest. It's like Chicago, and she's a Chicago person.

These people started seeing her, and what they started seeing is not this mythical figure that they were reading about in the newspapers, this terrible queen. What they saw is this Midwestern lady or Midwestern matron at this particular point, who is very proper, not overly proper. She's not some hippie or anything like that, as in that imagination, and she has gone over very well in upstate New York. She got 47 percent of the vote in upstate New York. It was amazing. Everybody thought she would lose. We supported her, obviously, during that race, and maybe someday we'll have another oral history project on another Clinton. I mean, there's two Bush presidents, why not? ...

Hillary is very smart, Hillary is very tough, Hillary is very tough-minded, which is a better word. Hillary is not always right and she can be very difficult, but basically her judgments are pretty good. The problem is, she becomes so formidable, a lot of people are afraid of her. I'm not afraid of her and never was, because she worked for me. I could fight with her and if I didn't agree with her I could disagree, and it would work out.

Joan Baggett: I think she has what it *takes* to be president. I think the key will be whether she can survive—and I think she can get the nomination. Whether or not she could be elected has to do with how much the opponents demonize her. It would be hard to believe things could get nastier, but it will be nastier. My husband made an interesting observation, though, when we were looking at the polls yesterday and likely candidates in 2008....[4] [He] said, "I always thought it would be a huge mistake to have Hillary Clinton as the nominee just because of what the other side, how polarized we would be, but the fact of the

---

4. Baggett's oral history was recorded in February 2005.

matter is, the country is so polarized now, can it get any worse?" And I don't know the answer to that. I've thought she wouldn't do it because I can't believe she's willing to put herself through it. You're sure to have everything resurrected, all the bad stuff for both of them. Now, it may be that she decides—I think she will be under incredible pressure from her friends and supporters to do it. At the end, the possibility of being the first woman president may prove to be too irresistible.

34

White House Staff

William Galston, deputy assistant for domestic policy, reported in his oral history interview that "My first law of presidencies is that every president gets the White House he deserves." If a president properly attends to how he sets up his White House staff and then commits himself to its proper functioning, that White House will work. If not, the president ultimately must accept the blame—or get rid of the people who are thwarting his intentions.

Working in the White House has been likened to drinking water from a fire hose. That kind of environment thus places a premium on process and structure. Yet the early functioning of the Clinton White House was heavily criticized for being disordered and ineffective. Many insiders indicate that the president himself was the main source of the problem. He preferred multiple sources of information (often coming at him simultaneously) to a single, well-ordered chain of command; he was reluctant to end meetings on time when he thought he could profit from additional dialogue; and he found creative chaos useful to his operating style. That perhaps-beneficial untidiness at the top, however, had an adverse ripple effect downward, creating major challenges for those whom Clinton hired to help him run the White House efficiently.

William Galston: I think it may have been that very first day [of the presidency], the *Washington Post* took a full page to enumerate Clinton's campaign promises, one line per promise. I clipped that page and tacked it up to the wall that I would see every day when I came in and sat down—just to make sure I never forgot what I was supposed to be doing there. I remember doing that the first day. I remember pinching myself literally and figuratively—What the hell am I doing here? I think most of us had that feeling. There was a real air of unreality. I remember saying to myself, *Well, you know this is a lot of fun, but when are the grownups going to show up and take over?* It gradually dawned on me, and then on all of us, that our parents were not going to show up and take over. It was very sobering.

Patrick Griffin, congressional liaison: I remember [my] first day meeting Clinton.... Mack [McLarty] and I were wandering around one day kind of getting to know each other. He said, "I think the president's little health care meeting is scheduled. Since you're going to be point on that, why don't we go see him?" I had never been in the West Wing before so the scale—everything was way off. It felt very small, confining, and sloppy. *This is where the president works?*

All of a sudden we're walking down the hall and I'm waiting to go into some room that would have a room leading to a room with the flourishes playing and all this. He opens this door and then, bingo, we're right there and there's the president. I thought I was on *Saturday Night Live* set. Everything looked like this theater set. The guy who played Clinton looked like [Clinton]. . . . At that moment it was absolutely shocking and stunning. Then Hillary walked in—we went into one of the doors that are into the wall. . . . She said, "Okay, let's sit down and talk about where we are with the health care bill." . . . That was just a wonderful moment. Clinton gave me a big hug on the way out. He said if we are still laughing a year from now it'll be all right.

Alan Blinder, Council of Economic Advisors: What academics don't realize is the incredibly hectic pace. . . . I used to tell new staff members when they came to work at the CEA—this is more or less verbatim the speech I used to give. I said, "We have three runs here. When I give you a long-run research project, that means I need it by Friday. Then there's the short run, which means I need it by close of business today—10 o'clock at night, which is the close of business. And the third category is, 'I desperately needed this an hour ago and it's horrible that I don't have it.'" That was the timeframe we worked to, every single day.

Joan Baggett, White House political director: I think one of the things that was the most striking to me about the White House experience is that almost everything is reactive. Even when you're trying to be proactive on something, you spend 90 percent of your time reacting to something else. It's very difficult to get ahead of the curve.

Bernard Nussbaum, White House counsel: [My predecessor] Lloyd Cutler once said something that stuck in my mind too, which is very true about the White House counsel's office. . . . He said, "One of the things you'll do is you'll make a list of ten things to do each day in the office. And if you get to the second thing, you'll have had a very successful day. Most days you won't even get to the first thing." I remember he said that.

He also told a joke. When you're White House counsel you'll find three letters in your drawer to be opened only if you get in trouble. So the White House counsel went in and, sure enough, there's big trouble in a few weeks, so he opens the first letter. It says, "Blame your predecessor," so he blames his predecessor. *Yes, it is a terrible thing but it's my predecessor's fault.* The next letter is to be opened when the next problem arises. The next problem arises and he opens the letter and it says, "Form a committee." So he forms a committee, and sure enough they handle the problem. Finally, another problem arises and he opens the third letter and it says, "Put three letters in the drawer." [*laughter*]

Sandy Berger, national security advisor: I had an inbox that was a foot high. My intention was never to go home without emptying the inbox. I didn't want to be a bottleneck for anything that needed to go forward. So I'd work from 7:00 until usually 10:00, 10:30, going through my inbox, going through paper, and get home about 11:00. The kids are asleep, my wife is asleep. Macaroni and cheese in the refrigerator at best. I'd say three nights a week the phone would ring between 12:00 and 6:00, because most of the world is awake while we're sleeping and most of the world is sleeping while we're awake. We'd suddenly have a problem that they're taking over our embassy in Karachi and we've got to dispatch the Marines or whatever.

Saturday and Sunday I tried to work at home. Saturday I'd usually work a half day in the office and then I'd take paper home and then I'd work until 8:00 or 9:00. Sunday I basically worked from 9:00 to 6:00 or so. I don't think I took a day off in eight years. . . . I was very famous on my staff for a couple of things. Number one, I insisted that everybody wear pagers. We didn't have cell phones at that point; we had pagers. My view was, if you're working for the president of the United States, you're working 24/7. You have no such thing as private time. If there was a crisis in Asia at 2:00 in the morning, I wanted to be able to reach you. So you slept with a pager next to you. You had sex with the pager someplace attached to you. There was no excuse. I'll tell you a funny story about this.

Since I was working 24/7, I called people 24/7, not gratuitously but if there was a problem. [Defense Secretary William] Cohen used to get furious because he'd be traveling in Korea and I would call him. It would be 3:00 in the morning and he'd just gotten off a twelve-hour flight and had three or four hours of meetings and finally got to sleep, and suddenly I'm on the phone. One day Bill brings me this watch with two dials. He said, "I want you to set this one where you are, and I want you to set this one where I am. Unless it's war and peace, don't call me in the middle of the night."

I'll tell you one last story that I love. The last week, we had a farewell party for the NSC, and a number of skits were roasting me. As one of the final acts, there were about twelve NSC directors. Someone yelled, "Ten-hut" and they lined up in two lines and marched into the Indian Treaty Room in the Old Executive Office Building in military formation, that ornate room where we were having this party. "Right face!" They marched that way. "Left face!" They marched that way. They were all one platoon. "Present arms." They all came up to me and one at a time they handed me a pager.

David Kusnet, speechwriter: It's no secret that the Clinton staff organization was somewhat free-form. It is probably a law of life that the same things that help you succeed at one stage will work against you at another stage. The kind of free-form, nonhierarchical, hardworking but fun-loving kind of atmosphere that was so successful in the campaign persisted in the White House during the first year, with much less success.

Alice Rivlin, OMB director: My reaction to the White House staff, especially at the beginning, was that it was too big and too loose, and there were all these children. There was a generational problem that so many White House staff were kids right out of college who'd worked on the campaign and had never had a job before. This was their first job, and they were doing important stuff in the White House and throwing their weight around. From the point of view of the older professionals like me, this was not an asset.

Chris Jennings, health care advisor: The Cabinet secretaries generally believe that the White House is a bunch of young whippersnappers who think they know everything. On the extremes, the White House generally views the agencies as entities who want to run their own little fiefdoms and who don't care that much about the president's desires. That's the ongoing tension. The White House thinks that they protect the president a lot more than the agencies do and the agencies think that that's a bunch of hyperbole. The only way to get over those things is through a process in which no one can complain that their views were not aired or were not integrated into any presentation to the president.

Roy Neel, deputy White House chief of staff: [We] made a little bit of progress in bringing discipline in the White House [in the first year], but there was one point in which it was decided at the highest level that certain people were miscast and had to go. They had to be out of the White House or they had to be put in other jobs in the administration or somewhere else, some other White House office. It was my job to make it happen. To fire some people, to relocate some people, which I did. But within a week, several of them were back. They were just like stray dogs that found their way home when they were really dumped out on the side of the interstate. I remember asking this one person, "Why are you still here? We had this understanding." And she said, I'll never forget it, "Well, I went to see the president and he said I didn't have to go." If you are going to try to impose discipline and literally run the White House in a professional way and you had the responsibility, but whatever authority you had would be undermined by the president himself—and I don't want to make too much of that, but it was an example of the kind of thing that drove you crazy.

This is not the kind of stuff that ever made the papers. It is definitely inside baseball, inside the White House, but it did represent to me a kind of hopelessness. Now I don't think I did enough and to this day I have to say I believe I let the president down.... I made a big mistake not confronting the president more aggressively—and Hillary—about what I thought should happen in the White House. . . .

Q: I understand what you are saying, but I wonder how susceptible to change this particular White House was when it seemed that the president has certain characteristics that evidently would have made him highly resistant to the kinds of changes you're talking about. Is this president going to be receptive to the kind of advice you're giving?

Neel: Well, let me address the . . . point because this is something I've thought a lot about and I feel very strongly about. Clinton has taken a lot of hits in two areas in particular. One, his lack of discipline, freewheeling meetings, his tendency to want to say yes to everybody. Secondly, the alleged undue influence of Hillary on the process.

To both of those points, I think they're unfair. It's a cop-out for advisors and staff people like me, for this reason. Bill Clinton won the presidency in '92 for all of us who wanted to win and return the White House to the Democratic Party. And he won precisely because he was the kind of guy he was. It was not his job to change, frankly. So I believed that he was not well served by a lot of people. But I think a lot of people used his personal quirks as an excuse for their inability to get their job done right. For instance, let me take the Hillary case.

The day after I took my job as Clinton's deputy chief of staff I went to see Hillary. I always liked her, had a lot of respect for her, knew she was smart. I really liked her staff people, I worked closely with them and liked them and trusted them. The first thing she said to me, she said, "I am tired of hearing that people are saying it's got to be done this way because Hillary says it's got to be done this way," or, "This person has to be hired or that one can't be hired because Hillary approves or disapproves. None of these people say this to my face, are willing to stand up to me. I'm really tired of that." My experience bore that out. The very people who would squawk about Hillary's influence on the process were the very ones who would not go and knock on her door and close the door and say, "Are you doing this? What are you doing? I disagree with you and I think this is not good for the president."

So a lot of this excuse-making is kind of cowardly. If you're hired to be an assistant to the president for whatever, communications, scheduling, if you're the deputy chief of staff or the chief of staff, you're expected to perform in a certain way, to bring certain experience to that job or to learn it and get it and bring a certain boldness to that job and not to behave as a bureaucrat. It was not Bill Clinton's responsibility to change his personality and his style. Now this case of reverse firing [i.e., the stray dogs] notwithstanding—there were different issues involved there—I didn't see any case where Clinton was presented with an idea for change that would amount to some sacrifice or difficulty and then not take that and go with it.

The White House management is not a linear process. It's not like getting capital, building a plant, making widgets, sending them to market, making a profit, pouring that back into the company or giving it to investors. It's not linear like that. You're going to have mistakes, you're going to make some wrong decisions. You're going to do all these things differently, because it's a highly personalized process. The White House reflects the personality of the president and it has to. It was not Clinton's responsibility to change his style of working.

It was, however, the responsibility of his senior staff to coordinate that process and make the best out of it, utilize and exploit his strengths and the good things about his personality and somehow protect him from his more damaging tendencies. If you couldn't do that, you should leave the job and let him get somebody who could. If you can't stand up to the president, behind closed doors obviously, and say, "This is a mistake, you're doing this wrong. I believe for this reason this is wrong and you've got to change it," then you've got no business being in this job. This is the big show, this is the big enchilada. You want to be there. You ask for those jobs. Some people fight for those jobs. They campaign, they cut people down. They do everything they can to become this or that in the White House. You get that job, you've got to figure out how to do it right in the full service of the president.

I believe that Clinton was sorely mis-served in many respects there. Every time I would read a story about Clinton's tendencies to do this or that, I would say, "So what, grow up. Figure out how to work with it, make the best of it." If Clinton wants to stay up all night shooting the bull about welfare reform, then you can say, "Look, tomorrow we've got a big day and you've got to be sharp at 8 o'clock in the morning. Can't we cut this off at two and come back tomorrow night?" Or, "Let's change tomorrow's schedule to give you a lighter schedule in the morning." But no, that's not what people did. Too many of us were dumb terminals rather than being active PCs. We were just dumb terminals waiting to do and then we would grouse about it. Everybody would grouse about Clinton's lack of discipline but they were the very ones that were exacerbating that. I have to tell you, I don't have a lot of sympathy for those in senior positions. It's one thing if you're a critic, if you're an analyst, if you're an historian, that's your right and responsibility to point out how screwed up the operation was and it goes right to Clinton's feet.

So . . . was it possible even to do this job given Clinton's personality? For the right people, yes, it was absolutely possible. You saw a bit of that when Leon Panetta came in [as chief of staff] following Mack [McLarty] because Leon wasn't going to come in unless he had unquestioned authority on staffing. Now, there were other things that continued that were signs of lack of discipline and there were other problems. But Leon at least did have that authority and it was unquestioned. People knew that Leon could fire them and the president was going to back him up. That was one thing he had that was very important. And he could hire people. He brought stature to the job as OMB [Office of Management and Budget] director and a former congressman and it was progress. So it can be done. . . . [It]'s a tough and difficult job, but I think that it's unfair to put all this on the president. He's not supposed to be his own chief of staff. You're supposed to manage the White House for the president.

Hopefully you keep him from giving in to his worst instincts. I remember Bob Haldeman writing that he believed, and up until Watergate thought he was successful, in probably the most important part of his job as Nixon's chief of staff, which was to humor Nixon. Listen to him, hear him give commands that somebody should be fired or we should get rid of all the Jews in the administration or bring more good-old-boys from Ohio State and get rid of the Harvard-educated, the elite in the administration. Or audit this guy's tax return, or whatever. "Yes, Mr. President we'll look into it." Then your job is to not do it, to basically be a buffer between the president's ranting and actions.

I think that there's something to that. But the reverse is also true. You have to be better than you would otherwise be in most jobs because there's no running and hiding. If you're not up to it, you're not serving the president as you should.

* * *

Q: I'm wondering if you can give us your assessment of each of the [four] chiefs of staff that you dealt with, what you saw as their relative strengths and weaknesses.
Sandy Berger: They all had different strengths.[1] Mack [McLarty] had Clinton's total confidence. Getting started, I think that was extremely important. Mack's a very well-organized person. I think that he did a good job of getting the White House organized, working, up and running. He's a good politician. He reached out and was able particularly to make good contact with some of the moderate to conservative Democrats as an Arkansas businessman. I think Mack got things off to a good start. Mack, Leon, Erskine [Bowles]. The next is Leon Panetta, a very inspirational leader. Leon is an exemplary individual who has true convictions. He exerted more control over the Oval Office than Mack had. In the early days, twenty-five people could walk into the Oval Office. Leon basically said, "Nobody goes into the Oval Office unless there's an appointment."

Even I—and we'll talk about my relationship with these chiefs in a minute— would not go in the Oval Office without letting the chief of staff know. Erskine was with Clinton during the dark days of Monica [Lewinsky] and was, I think, a tremendous source of strength to Clinton as he gets through this period. I think [John] Podesta was the best of the four. I think he brought together very good political judgment, the capacity to say no, a kind of toughness, a somewhat contrarian viewpoint. He'd sit at a meeting and wouldn't say anything for the first thirty minutes, then he would say something that just turned the ball

---

1. Clinton had four chiefs of staff: Thomas "Mack" McLarty (1993–94), Leon Panetta (1994–97), Erskine Bowles (1997–98), and John Podesta (1998–2001).

upside down. It was always on point and wasn't simply for the sake of saying something.

So I think, again, everybody was better by the end. You get better at your job as time goes by, but I think John was probably the best. I had a very good relationship with all four of the chiefs of staff. I worked more closely with Erskine and John during the second term. As long as I kept them informed, I had pretty much free rein.

I was the chief of staff for foreign policy. But every document that went to the president was copied to the chief of staff and the vice president. If I was going to go down to the Oval, unless it was something really time sensitive, I'd run down and make sure John knew I was coming, or Erskine, in case they wanted—I respected the fact that they needed to know everything that was happening. And they respected the fact that I was going to stay inside my box and I wasn't going to try to persuade the president on Social Security.

Robert Rubin, secretary of the treasury: Mack [McLarty] did not create an orderly White House in a whole bunch of areas. In retrospect, it's fair to say he should have been stronger in the way a number of those areas were managed. Having said that, what Mack did do, in which he was immensely valuable, was he created an environment in the White House where people—he reinforced the norm that the president wanted, a sense of teamwork, people working with each other.... Leon was very well organized and had a very good sense of priorities. I liked Leon a lot. I liked all of them, actually. He was very well organized. He obviously knew the budget extremely well. He was almost revered among the House members and had been an extremely popular figure up on the Hill on the Democratic House side. And he ran an orderly process.

Erskine, I think, was never totally comfortable, totally excited about his job. The Monica Lewinsky thing he absolutely wanted nothing to do with.... Finally, he had Podesta. Of all of those people, Erskine was probably closest to the president personally, though Mack had a long and strong personal relationship as well. Then you had John, who was very smart, understood the politics of Washington extremely well. I'd say he was more in the nature of Leon, but he was more intellectually engaged, in some respects, than Leon.

Leon Panetta, chief of staff: I've often said that being chief of staff is more a battlefield position than a management position. You have a mission for that day, you've got to take the hill and you've got to take all kinds of incoming fire. You're going to get shots coming at you and you've got to keep your eye on it and you've got to make sure that the team doesn't panic and run in different directions, that they're all disciplined enough to do it. I learned that more in the Army than I did anything else. I think it was probably a combination of things. It was my Jesuit training in Santa Clara— ... It was a very hierarchical organization.

So I think that was part of it, and part of it was the Army, part of it was just being Italian. I have a work ethic in the sense of having an organized approach to getting things done. So a big part of it was just instinctive.... One of the first things I did was tell him not to jog with short pants on, because it just didn't look right.[2] Some others had commented on it and I said, "You really ought not to, it doesn't look presidential and, very frankly, it's not." And to his credit he didn't say, "You're full of shit." He said okay and he didn't. I also said, "You can't jog in Potomac Park because Secret Service said it's too dangerous."

I think he responds to that kind of thing, when you say it like that. I never had the impression that it in any way affected our relationship. I always felt free enough to be able to say that, and I always felt that was important.... In the end, I could not have done this unless he really wanted to do this. He could have made it horrible for me. He could have said, "I just don't want this kind of organization." He could have done that. He's president of the United States. After all, he's the one who is ultimately in charge. But it's part of being a president who has a fast learning curve in that job. It didn't take him very long to understand this is not Arkansas anymore, Dorothy, this is a very different place. Unless he becomes disciplined in that sense, he's never going to be able to do the things he wants to do.

Tony Lake, national security advisor: Podesta was the deputy chief of staff and a new deputy chief of staff, and trying to make sure that the trains ran absolutely on time.[3] (No train in the Clinton administration ever ran anywhere close to on time, which used to drive me crazy.) ... But this was foreign press, a foreign occasion, [so] there were a lot of tricky issues that we had to go over and I just knew the questions were going to come up.

So it was going on a bit and Podesta started getting more and more antsy and finally he just broke in saying, "We don't have any more time for this foreign policy stuff," and cut me off in a rather dismissive way. There was jet lag, we were all exhausted. He was more dismissive than he should have been. He "dissed" me. We got outside into a corridor afterwards. I think [Warren] Christopher was standing there, or people told me he was, looking semi-shocked, because I was angry, which I don't often get. But when I am, I am. I said to John, "Don't you ever, ever do that again. The president needed to know those things. You don't talk to me...." blah, blah, blah. He said something or other and I don't know whether he actually touched me or not, but I did grab him and whap him against the wall, kind of.

---

2. During the 1992 campaign and in the early days of his presidency Clinton ran for exercise—usually garbed in short running shorts.
3. Podesta became deputy chief of staff at the beginning of the second term, in January 1997.

This got people's attention. So then I had to buy him lunch, and we became very good friends. There is no better way to bond with somebody, I suppose, than literally to put your hands on their lapels.

Richard Riley, secretary of education: The Cabinet was very loyal to the president. At these meetings we had ... after about four years, five years, all the Cabinet was there and the president said to us that it looked like through the years of Cabinets this Cabinet had been more loyal and supportive of the president than most any in American history. That was right. After the troubles that the president later got into, personal problems, the Cabinet basically stuck with him. They didn't like all of that, nor did he, but they basically stuck with him and that was really important to Clinton and his success, especially over the latter few years of his presidency.

The meetings of the Cabinet—we had a large Cabinet—naturally had to be rather formal. We had certain subjects that would be discussed. For example, I would get a call from the White House that would say, "The president wants to discuss fourth grade reading tests and eighth grade math tests. Would you speak to that at the Cabinet meeting?" At a lot of Cabinet meetings I was called on to say something. As I say, education was a big subject, always.... But the Cabinet meetings themselves had to be rather formal, structured. The president sits on one side and the vice president faces him and then all the Cabinet around and then staff around that. Probably the more productive meetings were when we would meet, like the domestic group meetings—Education and EPA, maybe, and Housing, Justice. Those meetings were very productive because we really were talking about our things and they were all related. You'd get into the Cabinet and you were talking about Bosnia, whatever. Fascinating thing. It was all so very interesting to me; I don't know if it was to anybody else—how the administration was moving in this direction or that direction. But those smaller meetings were a lot more constructive.

Donna Shalala, secretary of health and human services: Unlike the Carter Cabinet that I remember where there was a lot of backbiting, not in this Cabinet. In fact, we worked together.... A lot of us had known each other in the earlier Carter administration. A lot of people got the Cabinet posts at the right time in their careers. They were at the top of their game.... We were grownups.... Not that the formal meetings of the Cabinet were that important. They were funny. There were a lot of funny people in the Cabinet, jokesters, a lot of hilarious people. It was a lot of fun. I had a great time. I'm one of the few people who came to this town and had a fabulous time for eight years.

Mickey Kantor, secretary of commerce: I thought every Cabinet officer who owed their job to only one person should put this motto on the wall behind their desk: "I didn't get here on merit." We owed not only our allegiance but our commitment to him in terms of his re-election, in terms of his success as a president.

Judge Abner Mikva, White House counsel: Over the years, I've come to wish a president did have a relationship with at least one lawyer high up in the government who could come in and say, "You can't do this," or "What are you thinking about?" That was one of the problems I had and I think Janet [Reno] had even more: neither of us had that sort of relationship with him. I could never have gone in and said, "Bill, you can't do this," or "Are you crazy?" or something like that. A president needs that. A president needs somebody who has that close relationship and it either should be the attorney general or the White House counsel.

Lionel Johns, associate White House science advisor: There's an old saying around the White House that if you're not in the West Wing, where very few people are, or the old Executive Office Building . . ., you might as well be at the Panama Canal. It's true out of sight, out of mind.

Marcia Hale, White House director of intergovernmental affairs: Truly, the most important commodity for a president is time. If you're in charge of that and everybody wants a piece of it, you can make a lot of friends and you can make a lot of enemies.

Joan Baggett: When I was heading up the Office of Political Affairs, in the summer, we obviously had a number of interns, and they would have luncheon speakers for them to get to know about what we did. So when I spoke with them about being director of political affairs at the White House, they said, "What would you recommend to us? What would be the best preparation for this job? Is it political science? Is it law school? What's the best thing?" I said, "The best preparation"—I actually majored in child development, so my background was child psychology, and that hasn't hurt. "The best preparation for this job is to have a limited budget and a small room to plan a wedding, a bar mitzvah, any kind of social event where you are limited on how many can be in the room, and how many you can pay for, and make up that invitation list. Because 90 percent of your time is figuring who gets invited to what, who's in the room, who's not in the room, and managing the politics around that. That really is what the majority of the job consists of."

Bernard Nussbaum: There are two kinds of people. There are people who, when a fire breaks out, they run to the fire to try and put it out. There are other people who, when the fire breaks out, they run away from the fire: "It's not my fire." I guess the smarter people learn which fires are theirs, which fires are not theirs.

I thought my job was to run to the fires and try to put them out. You run to enough fires and try to put them out, and you can go up in flames.

Joan Baggett: Even in a White House that was committed to diversity, as it was, and I don't question the president's commitment at all, it still had serious white-boy problems. I think it's just something you have to deal with.... As an example, when we had all those losing races to contend with, if we were briefing the president on elections coming up or on political issues or something, there was never any shortage of guys in the room. There was Harold [Ickes], Doug [Sosnik], everybody getting their two cents in, George [Stephanopoulos], Rahm, et cetera. So they were all there. Okay, our guys lose. Guess who's making the call? Then I have to have the discussion with the president. So we used to joke with the staff when we lost, "Where'd all the guys go?" That's how it was. When there was face time and it was good news, they were all there, but when it was bad news, you had plenty of alone time with the president.... I certainly felt emotional support from the other women, and I think we all shared the feeling that there was a little too much testosterone in most of the meetings. But for the most part, it's just so fast-paced.... It's like *Great, okay, get over it.* You deal with it.

* * *

Q: Was there much concern voiced among women staffers that the men were not keeping the women fully involved?
Betty Currie, personal secretary: A lot. They were controllers, the boys—yes.... They used the term, excuse me, "white boys," but that was just a term. Unfortunately, it was probably true. At a meeting you saw more men than you saw anything.

Q: How would this come to you? Would you just be casually having a conversation with somebody?
Currie: Mostly overhearing. It was a topic—sometimes in a joking form, a serious joke, but still a joking form.... There was a strong group of men who were taking control, shall we say. I'm trying to think what women—I don't think he had any women deputy chiefs of staff at that time. I can't remember.

Q: Was the president aware of this feeling among the women that the boys were in control?
Currie: It may have been in the joking fashion like I heard. The women may have said it, and he may have gone, "Ha, ha, ha, not true." That sort of thing. Because he prided himself on hiring women. But to hire them and to use them are two different things, so I don't know.... He would have cared. I would say [he was] not aware then.

Q: So you can't depend on the boys to tell the president that the girls are out in the cold.
Currie: No. . . .

Q: Were you getting the same thing from other blacks in the administration? Was there concern that—?
Currie: I can't talk for the administration, but I can say within the White House complex, yes. There were some blacks at high level, Bob Nash for one, Minyon Moore, Thurgood Marshall, Terry Edmonds, Cheryl Mills, and Bob Johnson.[4] I'm trying to think who else was an assistant at the time. Rodney [Slater] was a secretary or deputy secretary [of transportation] at the time. . . . Yes, there was a concern.

Q: It became a concern of yours to try and help the president become more inclusive?
Currie: If I didn't go through him, I could always go through the staff secretary or the person setting up the meeting. "Why don't you—you know you can add so-and-so." "Oh, yes."

Q: In part this was an inner circle/outer circle problem, wasn't it?
Currie: Yes.

Q: I'm interpreting this as meaning that there were a number of women and African Americans who were in the outer circle, who should not have been there all the time.
Currie: I agree. I had thought from the campaign that there would be no circles. There would just be us, everybody. Then I realized, oh dear, we've got [them].

* * *

Q: I'm going to ask you about some press accounts. There was a sense that women weren't being listened to commensurate to their positions, that they were being cut out.
Marcia Hale: I didn't buy it. . . . I don't think that was a problem. I think if women were saying that, it was because they were feeling that they hadn't been listened to enough. I'm very protective of younger women, so I don't want you to think I believe this doesn't matter and they're whiners. I realize this does exist and I have hit it many times in other places. But quite frankly, inside the Clinton White House was not one of them.

---

4. Bob Nash was White House personnel director and then was appointed undersecretary of agriculture. Minyon Moore served as director of White House political affairs and director of public liaison. Thurgood Marshall Jr. worked for Al Gore and then held the position of Cabinet secretary in the White House. Terry Edmonds was initially on the speechwriting team and then became chief presidential speechwriter. Cheryl Mills was associate counsel to the president for most of his two terms. Robert B. Johnson directed the president's One America race initiative in the second term.

Mack McLarty, chief of staff: The only thing about serving in the White House, as a P.S.—you get there, and of course it's an awesome responsibility. It takes a moment to just get oriented to the physical setting. I'd been in the Oval Office, but when you're shuffled down to see the president, you don't go by offices where the coffee pot is and so on.

The offices are smaller than they are on *The West Wing*. The chief of staff's office is very, very nice, but the halls are small. The actual Oval Office and the Cabinet room are very, very handsome and roomy, but you have to get physically accustomed. I had a little bit of a problem coming from a business setting. So many people were running to the old OEOB [Old Executive Office Building] across the street [where most of the White House staff works]. How many times do you have to walk across the street to see your staff? This is crazy.

But after a couple of weeks, you just settle in and start working. . . . I went home one evening and saw a special on the Kennedy years, just by happenstance. It showed his advisors there and members of the Cabinet and so forth. That was one of the presidents that I grew up with, and it was very powerful to me that an hour before I had been in that same spot in the Oval Office advising the president of the United States. It struck home what a tremendous privilege, and the sense of history and the sense of responsibility that one has, whether it be a chief of staff or other position. It's a unique time in one's life. It was a great privilege, and it was a lifetime in six and a half years.

Epilogue: Observations on the Clinton Legacy

Presidential legacies are protean things. When a president leaves office, there is a vast, objective trail of activity left behind, documenting literally half a million minutes for every year the outgoing chief executive occupied the White House. The swearing in of a successor in one way closes the book on that period in history. The former president's record now is finished—and contained in tens of thousands of archival boxes, hundreds of laws and executive orders, millions of press accounts, scores of memoirs, and in the uncountable memories of those who daily walked and talked with the president as he directed the nation's affairs from the Oval Office.

That record, however, is anything but a dust-covered relic. Inherent in the notion of a presidential legacy is the idea that some specific accomplishments— or failures—merit special attention as having a lasting effect on the world. And defining that taxonomy of impact is a complicated and volatile process. After presidents leave office, their work becomes subject to the unpredictable currents of history, which can render the once meaningful incidental and the little-noticed, critical. On the day Bill Clinton departed the White House in January 2001, for example, few people had paid much attention to his administration's efforts to combat terrorism, a subject that would become existentially important eight months later.[1] Too, as a president leaves office, the work done there becomes primarily the province of the historians, whose arguments over what is genuinely important are genuinely endless. President George W. Bush once observed that because historians were still debating how best to understand the first president, he was not inclined to spend any time worrying about how critics of his day were judging the forty-third.[2]

---

1. Another example emerged during the course of the 2016 presidential campaign, when the 1994 crime bill's incarceration rates came under assault by civil rights activists as a major cause of growth in the numbers of African American men living behind bars. This particular topic receives almost no attention in the Clinton interview archive, however, because major concern about the growth of a "carceral state" did not become a part of the public discourse until after the interviews for this project were largely completed.

2. Quoted in Bob Woodward, *The War Within: A Secret White House History, 2006–2008* (New York: Simon & Schuster, 2008), 331.

One of the most fascinating aspects of the Miller Center's interviews about the Clinton presidency is the opportunity to hear from an uncommonly accomplished group of political professionals about how they themselves judge President Clinton's legacy. After all, few people have spent more time reflecting on the forty-second presidency in the arc of American history than those who cast their lot with Clinton to influence it. Although most of those interviewed were members of the president's official family, and thus could be excused if their judgments bore a filial bias, their observations are under the circumstances notably even-handed, and reflect in most instances candid assessments about how they expect history will judge their president.

White House Chief of Staff Leon Panetta presented the most succinct accounting of Clinton's overall accomplishments—but then proposed that "this is a tale of two presidencies."

> One is a president who really did provide strong leadership for the country in both foreign affairs and domestic affairs. I always think that the centerpiece ... is what he did on the economy and on the [1993] economic plan, because I think that really did take leadership to do that and he was willing to do it, knowing all of the risks involved.... But in addition to that, obviously, his achievements in terms of trade, of domestic policy on education, establishing AmeriCorps, and beginning the process of the healthcare debate ... that was important for this country. His environmental record is probably comparable to Teddy Roosevelt's in terms of the steps he took to try to protect our environment. On foreign affairs ... he preserved the peace and he did it in a way that established the United States as a world leader. And he certainly had the ability to deal with our allies and to get them to support what he was trying to do. He certainly made every effort to try and promote peace in the Middle East, which is essential.

Panetta then turned, however, to the inevitable second presidency. "I think [Clinton's] moral failings will always be a shadow over the administration as well."

Alan Blinder, from the Council of Economic Advisors, almost perfectly echoed Panetta's two-presidencies theme. "I think the capsule profile of Clinton written fifty years from now is, 'This is the president who presided over the greatest period of prosperity in American history and was impeached by the U.S. Congress.' I think that's going to be the opening sentence. It's a shame, the latter part, a shame. But that's the way it is." According to these two evaluations, and those of many others, the thumbnail version of the Clinton presidency Americans will consult in the future will forever feature a balancing act between brilliance and shadows.

It is worth observing that Clinton's economic successes were also cited as central by people beyond the core economic team. It was somewhat surprising, for example, to hear a favorable assessment of budgetary discipline from Peter Edelman, who was considered a leading liberal conscience within the administration. "I think [Bill Clinton's] greatest accomplishment was in balancing the budget and contributing to putting the economy into a state of tremendous good health and leaving us with a huge surplus," Edelman observed. "That's the biggest thing," not, by his logic, for reasons of green-eyeshade fiscal prudence, but because economic health made possible a raft of other benefits for the nation's less fortunate. Having lived through long periods of budgetary stress, and thus having witnessed the adverse implications for those reliant on government support, Edelman saw the advantages of Clinton's economic policy in human terms. That included the Earned Income Tax credit—which was initiated in 1993 and expanded in 1997—which Edelman judged as "phenomenally important, a very great accomplishment and one for which [Clinton] deserves tremendous credit."

From a similar philosophical perspective, Secretary of Housing and Urban Development Henry Cisneros catalogued a major set of social and economic achievements that he felt flowed from the 1993 budget plan:

> It created the conditions in which all of the other successes of the Clinton administration could go forward. The longest expansion in American history, record job formation, record business formation, declines in poverty rates, lowest minority poverty rate since statistics were compiled in the 1960s, actual reduction in the gaps in distribution and income, highest home ownership rate in American history. Social indicators improving, including educational dropout rates, teenage pregnancies. All of that based on general prosperity, which was a result of the deficit reduction strategy.

By these accounts, the exercise of discipline early in Clinton's presidency provided a basis for success across a wide range of fronts of historical importance.

Panetta's roll of domestic accomplishments (beyond prosperity) also included trade, education, AmeriCorps, and the environment, as well as a start on health care reform. Trade, especially NAFTA, is a problematic element in the Clinton record as a legacy item, primarily because it remains a divisive issue within his own party, thus depriving him of a natural constituency for celebrating it.[3] Education suffers differently. The federal role in education policy remains

---

3. Hillary Rodham Clinton, as a candidate for the 2016 Democratic presidential nomination, openly opposed President Obama's Trans-Pacific Partnership trade deal. The specifics, of course, are different, but she did not in this case follow the example of her husband—who supported a trade deal his *Republican* predecessors had negotiated. These are hotly contested issues within the Democratic Party's core constituency of organized labor.

relatively modest, rendering progress in this area at best a second-order achieve-ment for a president. As Deputy Domestic Policy Advisor William Galston noted in his interview, even people working within the administration, who were des-perately seeking triumphs to brandish in the first term, were mainly unaware of what they had done. "I wrote the president a memo saying, 'While nobody was looking, we moved nine pieces of education legislation through the Congress of the United States, and you, right now, are one of the most significant education reform presidents in the history of the Republic.' ... But nobody in the White House other than me and a handful of others who were working on it knew that until I sent him that memo."[4]

Both AmeriCorps and Clinton's environmental record (especially on extend-ing protected areas) would seem to be the kind of programmatic successes from which favorable legacies are built—and yet his accomplishments in these areas are not widely known. In these instances, Clinton may be disadvantaged by a lack of what has been termed "reputational entrepreneurs," people devoted to ensuring that a president's accomplishments are properly recognized within the conventional historical narratives of the nation. There is evidently nobody working on Clinton's behalf in a manner analogous to anti-tax activist Grover Norquist's effort to erect Ronald Reagan monuments in every American county.[5]

Expanding on Panetta's point about health care, several interviewees did comment on the importance of incremental, "bite sized" changes made in the American health care system after the demise of the major reform effort, such as portability of health insurance. But as health care economist David Cutler noted, "the major thing didn't happen"—and that is largely what will be remem-bered. Similarly, there were a host of so-called small-ball domestic initiatives advanced successfully by the administration in the wake of the 1994 Republican Revolution (school uniforms, anti-smoking initiatives, etc.). Yet by definition these were not major legacy-producing victories, however important they may have been to some Americans at the time—and to Clinton's re-election bid.

What is most striking, however, about Panetta's list is the absence of the one domestic item that can be said, without question, to have constituted a revo-lution in American domestic policy during the Clinton years: welfare reform. This was by any reasonable standard a major bipartisan change in the struc-ture of the American welfare state, one that had substantial consequences in policy and politics. And this is the kind of memorable change in fundamentals

---

4. When Roger Altman was asked whether education should be considered a major factor in the Clinton legacy he replied No, reporting that a senior education official once told him that it really doesn't make a difference in the nation's education system who the president is.

5. See Gary Alan Fine, "Reputational Entrepreneurs and the Memory of Incompetence: Melting Supporters, Partisan Warriors, and Images of President Harding," *American Journal of Sociology* 101, no. 5 (1996): 1159–1193. On the Ronald Reagan Legacy Project, see the website http://www.ronaldreaganlegacyproject.org.

that normally captures scholarly attention when assessing the legacy of a president. Yet welfare reform fills an uncertain space in the canon of Clinton accomplishments. Panetta had in fact opposed it, and welfare reform left many others within Clinton's official family profoundly unhappy with the president. HUD Secretary Cisneros reported that the *New York Times* photograph that appeared in the paper the day after the bill's signing featured "the most hangdog-looking group [of Cabinet officers] you've ever seen." Similarly, Deputy Treasury Secretary Roger Altman said that "if you survey the fifty most senior people who ever served in the Clinton administration, about twenty-five of them will say welfare reform was a great triumph for the president, about twenty-five of them will say he just caved. I'm in the first camp, it was a great triumph, but I'm not sure that history will accord him that." Thus the place of welfare reform in the Clinton legacy remains ambiguous.

Now to foreign policy. There Panetta noted three items: Clinton preserved the peace, he advanced the nation's alliances, and he sought a lasting solution to conflict in the Middle East (although his failed negotiations on the last of those Clinton himself has cited as a signal disappointment). National Security Advisor Tony Lake agreed that peace and conflict resolution were major Clinton achievements. "When we came in [the urgent issues] were Bosnia, Somalia, Haiti, issues like that. Crises that we goddamn inherited.... When we left, and we may have done them wrong, but they were not crises anymore.... And by God, I'm certainly proud of that."[6] To those enumerated conflicts might also be added Northern Ireland, where the Clinton administration's hand was a helpful, even perhaps a decisive, factor in bringing an end to the Troubles. Virtually everyone involved in the Irish problem notes how important Clinton was in reaching the Good Friday Agreements, by appointing Jean Kennedy Smith as U.S. ambassador to Ireland, by being willing to confront powerful bureaucracies in his own government to allow Sinn Féin leader Gerry Adams to come to the United States, and by mediating an incendiary Irish dialogue that sometimes required an honest broker to defuse.

Lake also addressed the importance of Clinton's alliance-building successes, "like NATO enlargement or like free trade agreements, [and] arms control.... [We] made a pretty good start on a lot of those as well." Indeed a strong case is made in these interviews for Clinton's role in rebuilding and strengthening the "architecture" of international relations. Ambassador Nancy Soderberg noted the growing pains the administration experienced during its early years in trying to find and articulate a new post–Cold War paradigm. But Soderberg and others voiced great satisfaction with what they were able to accomplish ultimately to strengthen the nation's alliances and international institutions. Deputy National

---

6. Lake was speaking specifically about his time as national security advisor, which ended in 1997, but his general points hold for the second term as well. Critics could reasonably object, however, that the bombing of the USS *Cole* by terrorists in October 2000 did constitute an urgent piece of unfinished business left to Clinton's successor.

Security Advisor James Steinberg, for example, strongly argued that one of the administration's signature accomplishments was the buttressing of NATO as an international force—partly because of Clinton's efforts to redefine its mission and to extend its boundaries after the Cold War, but also because of his successful use of NATO in the Balkans. National Security Advisor Sandy Berger made the same point: "I believe that we won in Kosovo because Milosevic discovered that he could not divide the nineteen democracies of NATO."

A final area in foreign policy, not emphasized by Panetta but mentioned in several other oral histories, was anti-terrorism. The main message communicated in these interviews was that President Clinton had in fact taken an active role in organizing the government to fight terrorism well in advance of 9/11, in response to earlier attacks and to looming intelligence that bigger threats were on the horizon. The testimony in these interviews—corroborated by external sources, including *The 9/11 Commission Report*—confirms that terrorism had become a focal point of the second term. Sandy Berger noted in his interview that "I gave the 9/11 Commission a 271-page, single-spaced copy of what Bill Clinton said about terrorism in his two terms. That's a lot of talking." And Berger reportedly informed his successor, Condoleezza Rice—and Clinton likewise informed his successor, George W. Bush—that their top priority upon entering office would be terrorism. "The perception is that the terrorism problem was being ignored," Berger said of Clinton's presidency. "The fact is we were thwarting attacks. We stopped a number of bad things from happening, and we were very much on the case." They were not, by these accounts, fiddling while Rome burned.[7]

But the accomplishments of that first presidency cannot be considered in isolation. Weighing heavily on the opposite side of Panetta's scales is the tale of that second Clinton presidency, capped by impeachment.

The most important wisdom gleaned from these interviews was not that the Lewinsky scandal will long remain a mark against Bill Clinton. One hardly needs these internal sources to confirm that. Rather, it is that the collateral damage from the Lewinsky scandal may ultimately exert as powerful a negative influence on Clinton's legacy as the direct damage to his image as a public figure. The two main collateral casualties beyond Clinton's public reputation were the reform agenda of his second term and, perhaps more importantly, his heir apparent, Vice President Al Gore. Both suffered in ways that devastated Clinton's ability to build and sustain a positive legacy that could counteract the Bill Clinton depicted in Kenneth Starr's reports.

Congressional Liaison John Hilley noted in his oral history that the budget-balancing successes of the early second term created high hopes for much more

---

7. See *The 9/11 Commission Report: Final Report of the National Commission on Terrorist Attacks Upon the United States*, Authorized Edition (New York: W. W. Norton, 2004), 98–102, *passim*.

in 1998. "Now we were running plans: Let's fix Social Security, let's solve that. Let's fix Medicare. There was an ambitious race relations agenda being readied, so the mills at the policy level were hopping, to set the stage for even more efforts." William Galston confirmed this point:

> Before the scandal broke, the president was teeing up [entitlement reform] for serious discussion in the second term. Through heroic efforts of political self-restraint which cost the president very dearly, we had rolled the fiscal rock all the way back up the mountain, and we finally had—for the first time in a generation—the opportunity and the resources to address the problem of the long-term stabilization of these entitlement programs.

Others close to Clinton—including Al From of the DLC and congressional liaison Lawrence Stein—agreed that there was a historic opportunity at that moment to restructure the entitlement system in a way that would have established Clinton as one of the most consequential reform presidents in American history. But those possibilities for a once-in-a-generation legacy of institutional reform quickly came to naught with the Lewinsky scandal.

Then there is the political demise of his chosen successor. The magnitude of the political damage Clinton inflicted on Al Gore remains one of the most bitterly contested aspects of the Clinton years, especially within Clinton's official family. That Gore would find it necessary to distance himself from a disgraced president in order to run as his own man was understandable to virtually everyone. But the degree to which Gore chose to distance himself from the accomplishments of the Clinton *presidency* puzzled and alarmed many who felt that in so doing he was abandoning his strongest political asset. As Press Secretary Joe Lockhart said, "I think the vice president, in a personal way, got it into his head that it wasn't enough to win the presidency. He needed to win it on his own and without the help of the president." This included, according to Gore's pollster Stanley Greenberg, an unwillingness to feature the Clinton economic record at critical moments.

Thus there was unsettled internal debate throughout the 2000 campaign season about whether and how to deploy Bill Clinton himself in ways that might have helped tip the balance in Gore's favor in a razor-thin election ultimately decided by the U.S. Supreme Court. What is incontestable, however, is that Clinton's impeachment, and the scandal that led to it, created an excruciating set of avoidable problems for his would-be successor. And Gore's loss meant a profound change in direction by the forty-third presidency. Clinton, rather than being followed by a president committed to consolidating and extending the policies of his eight years in office—what Galston called "Bill Clinton's third term"—was instead followed by a president with a very different philosophy and priorities. That put Clinton's legacy at risk, changing the trajectory of policy in many key areas.

The best example is Panetta's "centerpiece"—economics. The Clinton surplus did not survive his first year out of office, including a $1.3 trillion tax cut enacted in May 2001.[8] What Clinton had accomplished in the economic realm proved, at least on this dimension, to be ephemeral. Galston made this point bluntly: "I get sick every time I think about it.... The transfer of the presidency into the hands of someone with a very different agenda meant in extremely short order that everything we had worked for in that area was swept away as though it were a sand castle on the edge of a beach." Roger Altman also lamented this reality in his April 2003 oral history. "[Bill Clinton's economic] achievements, while in my view quite remarkable, may not be long lasting. Obviously he balanced the budget, now it's unbalanced"—at least in part because there was no President Gore to defend and extend Clinton's priorities. One might reasonably argue, as Alan Blinder did, that the Bush reversals are largely irrelevant: Clinton's behavior was exemplary—a willingness to accept short-term political pain because it was "good for the country.... That's [exactly] the way you want your president to think." But the power of this profile-in-courage argument is unavoidably confounded by Clinton's complicity in the premature end of his own governing project. And the actual economic course followed by the next administration renders this argument hollow.

Gore's loss also altered the course of the nation's foreign policy. According to Secretary of State Madeleine Albright, Clinton and his team "made a serious effort to change institutions to meet the demands of the twenty-first century. The problem we did not anticipate is that individuals matter as much as institutions. So we made changes and put people in charge who believed in what they were being asked to do. Then the [2000] election happened." The result? Much of what they hoped to accomplish "unraveled." Albright illustrates her point by noting that the Clinton administration sought to make arms control more central to American foreign policy by forging structural changes in the State Department. Soon thereafter, President George W. Bush appointed John Bolton, called by Albright an "enemy of arms control," to head the new office they had created to promote it.

And what about "preservation of the peace"? It is too much to claim on the basis of these oral histories that 9/11 would not have occurred on President Gore's watch, though some pundits and partisan analysts have made that statement. Indeed members of Clinton's senior foreign policy team directly resisted voicing that conclusion in their interviews. "Whether [we] could have prevented 9/11 is, I think, too hard to answer," says Nancy Soderberg. But the aftermath of the attack almost certainly would have been handled differently. Had Gore

---

8. Some of the major economic reversals of the forty-third presidency came because of a different set of preferences on tax policy and some because of the War on Terror, including the choice to invade Iraq.

succeeded Clinton, the Democratic emphasis on alliances would have been preserved and extended—probably even if Gore had had to confront the awful
decisions President Bush did after 9/11, when the advantages of leveraging those
alliances during a global war on terror were most pronounced. With Gore's loss,
however, the alliance politics of the Clinton years was displaced by an impa-
tience with thorny multilateralism. And that reality alone profoundly changed
the course of post-9/11 American foreign policy.

The centrality of Al Gore's 2000 failure to this story points us to one additional factor that could play a major role in Clinton's ultimate legacy: the
political career of his spouse. Were Hillary Rodham Clinton to be elected to the
presidency herself, all backward looks into the forty-second presidency would
subsequently be made through the lens of the forty-fifth. Her election would
at once add a path-breaking component to Bill Clinton's own legacy—having
helped, in ways that would surely be subject to long debate, to make possible
the first woman president—and it would afford him unprecedented opportunities to make another imprint on national policy, foreign and domestic.

A return to the White House would, for example, reopen the books on the
otherwise ambiguous legacy of Bill Clinton for the Democratic Party. He was
the first Democrat since Franklin Roosevelt to be re-elected to the presidency—
and he did so by consciously working to reorient the party toward a Third Way
of governing. That typically would be a strong legacy-framing accomplishment. But the nation was, at the end of Clinton's presidency, demonstrably less
Democratic than it was when he arrived in Washington, including a Republican
successor in the White House and the demise of what some had believed to be
a permanent Democratic majority in the House of Representatives. And when a
Democrat did retake the White House in 2008, Barack Obama hewed far closer
to traditional Democratic Party lines than to a Third Way. Accordingly, a Hillary
Clinton presidency has the potential to reset the course of Democratic Party
politics in ways that would cause a re-examination of the forty-second, in search
of historical inflection points borne out years later.

In the end, anything Bill Clinton accomplishes while back in the White
House, either through direct assignment or derivatively from Mrs. Clinton's
achievements, would have to be grafted onto the presidential history that was
closed—we thought for good—on January 20, 2001. If that does indeed happen,
scholars will have to be prepared to grapple not just with a tale of two presidencies, but of three.

Appendix: Clinton Presidential History Project

Opened Interviews Included in This Volume
Interviewee(s), date, location, and interviewer(s)

Madeleine Albright, August 30, 2006, Charlottesville; Russell Riley, Stephen Knott, Robert Strong

Roger Altman, April 22, 2003, New York; Russell Riley, Gary Burtless, James Sterling Young

Joan Baggett, February 10–11, 2005, Charlottesville; Russell Riley, Kathryn Dunn Tenpas

Charlene Barshefsky, March 2, 2005, Washington; Russell Riley, Kimberly Elliott

Eileen Baumgartner, April 11, 2008, Washington; Paul Martin

Samuel Berger, March 24–25, 2005, Charlottesville; Russell Riley, Timothy Naftali, Robert Strong

Alan Blinder, June 27, 2003, Princeton, NJ; Russell Riley, John Gilmour, Steven Weatherford

Sidney Blumenthal, August 17, 2006, Washington; Russell Riley, Stephen Knott

Charles Brain, March 22–23, 2004, Charlottesville; Russell Riley, Lawrence Evans, Charles O. Jones

Dale Bumpers, October 13, 2009, Washington; Russell Riley

Fernando Henrique Cardoso, January 9, 2009, Paris; Russell Riley, Jeffrey Cason

Warren Christopher and Strobe Talbott, April 15–16, 2002, Charlottesville; James Young, Stephen Knott, Timothy Naftali, Don Oberdorfer, Russell Riley

Henry Cisneros, November 21, 2005, San Antonio, TX; Russell Riley, Benjamin Marquez, Paul Martin

Betty Currie, May 11–12, 2006, Charlottesville; Russell Riley, James Young

David Cutler, July 23, 2003, Washington; Russell Riley, Eric Patashnik

Thomas Daschle, December 19, 2007, Washington; Paul Martin

James Dyer, January 23, 2008, Washington; Paul Martin

Peter Edelman, May 24–25, 2004, Charlottesville; Russell Riley, Ed Berkowitz, Kent Germany

Kris Engskov, April 14, 2007, London; Russell Riley, Stephen Knott

Michael Espy, May 15, 2006, Jackson, MS; Paul Martin, Darby Morrisroe

Al From, April 27, 2006, Washington; Russell Riley, Darby Morrisroe

Al From, January 11, 2007, Washington; Russell Riley, Darby Morrisroe

William Galston, April 22–23, 2004, Charlottesville; Russell Riley, Charles O. Jones, Charles Walcott

John Gibbons and Lionel Johns, December 5, 2006, Charlottesville; Darby Morrisroe, Paul Martin, Charles Walcott

Ben Goddard, April 30, 2008, Washington; Paul Martin

Stanley Greenberg, January 27, 2005, Washington; Russell Riley, Paul Freedman

Stanley Greenberg, October 11, 2007, Washington; Russell Riley, Paul Freedman, Michael Nelson

Frank Greer, October 27–28, 2005, Washington; Russell Riley, Darby Morrisroe, Michael Nelson

Patrick Griffin, March 12, 2004, Washington; Russell Riley, Darby Morrisroe, Charles Walcott

Marcia Hale, March 14, 2007, Washington; Russell Riley, Darby Morrisroe

Vaclav Havel, May 29, 2009, Prague; Russell Riley

Christopher Jennings and Jeanne Lambrew, April 17–18, 2003, Charlottesville; Russell Riley, Marie Gottschalk, Charles Walcott, James Young

Kim Dae-jung, September 25, 2008, Seoul; Russell Riley

Mickey Kantor, June 28, 2002, Charlottesville; James Young, Erwin Hargrove, Charles O. Jones, Russell Riley

Peter Knight, July 20, 2010, New York; Russell Riley, Michael Nelson

David Kusnet, March 19, 2010, Charlottesville; Russell Riley, Michael Nelson

Anthony Lake, May 21, 2002, Charlottesville; Russell Riley, I. M. Destler, Stephen Knott, John Owen

Anthony Lake, November 6, 2004, Washington; Russell Riley, I. M. Destler, Stephen Knott

Joseph Lockhart, September 19–20, 2005, Charlottesville; Russell Riley, John Maltese, Paul Martin, Darby Morrisroe

Marjorie Margolies, December 7, 2007, Philadelphia; Paul Martin

Thomas "Mack" McLarty III, July 12, 2002, Charlottesville; James Young, Karen Hult, Stephen Knott, Sidney Milkis, Russell Riley

Abner Mikva, November 7, 2005, Charlottesville; Darby Morrisroe, Nancy Baker, Karen Hult, Paul Martin

George Mitchell, March 5, 2007, New York; Russell Riley, Paul Martin

Roy Neel, November 14, 2002, Charlottesville; Russell Riley, Stephen Knott

Bernard Nussbaum, September 24, 2002, Charlottesville; Russell Riley, Nancy Baker, Stephen Knott, James Young

Bernard Nussbaum, November 4, 2005, New York; Russell Riley, Darby Morrisroe, James Young

Leon Panetta, January 31, 2003, Monterey, CA; Russell Riley, John Gilmour, Nelson Polsby

William Perry, February 21, 2006, Stanford, CA; Russell Riley, Darby Morrisroe, Andrew Ross

Bruce Reed, February 19–20, 2004, Charlottesville; Russell Riley, Charles O. Jones, Stephen Knott

Bruce Reed, April 12, 2004, Washington; Russell Riley

Richard Riley and Michael Cohen, Frank Holleman III, Terry Peterson, Sandy Rinck, Ann "Tunky" Riley, Scott Shanklin-Peterson, August 30–31, 2004, Charlottesville; Russell Riley, Patrick McGuinn, Joseph Pika

Alice Rivlin, December 13, 2002, Washington; Russell Riley, John Gilmour, James Pfiffner

Charles Robb, October 30, 2009, Charlottesville; Russell Riley

Dennis Ross, January 12, 2006, Washington; Russell Riley, Paul Martin

Robert Rubin, November 3, 2005, New York; Russell Riley, Alan Beckenstein, James Young

Eli Segal, February 8–10, 2006, Boston; Russell Riley

Donna Shalala, May 15, 2007, Washington; Russell Riley, Paul Martin

John Shalikashvili, May 24, 2007, Steilacoom, WA; Stephen Knott

(Henry) Hugh Shelton, May 29, 2007, Morehead City, NC; Russell Riley

Alan Simpson, March 13, 2008, Washington; Paul Martin

Nancy Soderberg, May 10–11, 2007, Charlottesville; Russell Riley, Darby Morrisroe, Robert Strong

Lawrence Stein and John Hilley, May 20–21, 2004, Charlottesville; Russell Riley, John Gilmour, Charles O. Jones, James Young

James Steinberg, April 1, 2008, Austin, TX; Russell Riley

Strobe Talbott, February 25, 2010, Washington; Russell Riley

Susan Thomases, January 6, 2006, New York; Russell Riley, Darby Morrisroe

Harris Wofford, July 19, 2006, Washington; Paul Martin, Jeff Chidester

James Woolsey and Janet Andres, Jeffrey Harris, Richard Haver, Joyce Pratt, January 13, 2010, Charlottesville; Russell Riley, Marc Selverstone, Robert Strong

Full transcripts of all of these interviews are on the website of the Miller Center, University of Virginia: http://millercenter.org/president/clinton/oralhistory.

THE OXFORD ORAL HISTORY SERIES

J. Todd Moye (University of North Texas)
Kathryn Nasstrom (University of San Francisco)
Robert Perks (The British Library)
Series Editors

Donald A. Ritchie
Senior Advisor

Index

Edmonds, Terry, 410
education policy, 64, 175–76, 291–92, 380,
    407, 414–16
    as governor, 5, 21, 53, 279
    Hillary on, 137, 388
    Hope scholarships, 305
Ehrman, Sarah, 95
Elders, Joycelyn, 93
Electronic Data Systems (EDS), 300
Emanuel, Rahm, 90, 163–64, 180, 251, 302,
    317, 409
    crime bill (1994), 180
    in the 1992 campaign, 29, 32
    welfare reform, 163–64, 168
embassy bombings, 245
energy, department of, 88, 94n17
England, 220, 236–37, 257n36
Engleberg, Mort, 63
Engskov, Kris, 8–9, 333
    on Clinton's personal traits, 344–45,
        354–55, 358, 364–66, 369, 373–74
enlargement, 188–89
entitlement reform, 183–84, 418–19
environmental policy, 177, 380, 414–16
Environmental Protection Agency (EPA), 89,
    378, 407
Erie, Pennsylvania, 64
Espy, Mike, 4, 43, 47, 70–71, 121, 309, 347
ethnic cleansing, 212, 223, 226
Europe, 193, 215, 217, 219, 238–40, 249,
    266, 338
European Union, 188, 265
executive orders, 162, 174–75, 290

Family and Medical Leave Act, 301
Family Assistance Plan, 166
Family Support Act, 166
Faulkner, William, vii, 357
Feder, Judy, 95
Federal Aviation Administration (FAA), 68
Federal Bureau of Investigation (FBI), 56,
    181–83, 228, 230, 235, 237, 245–46,
    248, 310, 324
Federal Communications Commission
    (FCC), 378
federal courts, 279–83
Federal Records Act, ix
Federal Reserve, x, 114, 117, 124–25
Feinstein, Dianne, 178
Filomena, 265
fishing, 91, 209, 247
Florida, 195, 386
Flowers, Gennifer, 22, 30, 33, 36–43, 339
focus groups, 15–16, 19, 38–42, 53–54
Foley, Tom, 107, 160, 179–81

food stamps, 121, 166, 168
football, 91, 209, 236, 309, 349
Force Armee d'Haiti (FADH), 196–97
Ford, Gerald, 127
Foreign Intelligence Surveillance Act
    (FISA), 248–49
foreign policy, 187–268
    impeachment and, 307, 337–38
    in the inaugural address (1993), 100–01
    legacy of, 417–18, 420–21
    in the 1992 campaign, 49, 50n7, 62, 62,
        66, 72, 76
    priority of, 109–10, 406
    trade and, 128
    in the transition (1992–93), 90–93
Fort Bragg, North Carolina, 197–98
Fortas, Abe, 281
Foster, Lisa, 312
Foster, Vince, 182, 310–13
France, 211, 226, 360
François, Michel-Joseph, 195, 197
Frankfurter, Felix, 280
Freeh, Louis, 235, 310
From, Al, 11, 95, 184, 192–93, 300, 364, 419
    on Al Gore, 382
    on national service, 170–71
    1992 campaign, 20, 26, 28–29, 37–38,
        58–60, 65–66, 128
    on the 1994 midterm elections, 287–88
    recruits Clinton to the DLC, 12–14
    on welfare reform, 159
Fulbright, J. William, 4n1, 352

Galbraith, John Kenneth, 221
Galbraith, Peter, 221
Galileo's, 311
Galston, William, 286, 287–88, 398,
    416, 419–20
    on Dick Morris, 292–93
    on domestic priorities, 106, 109, 130
    on the early Clinton, 11
    on education, 175–76
    on Gore, 382–83
    on health care reform, 134, 136,
    on the 1992 campaign, 59
    observations about Clinton, 14, 25, 105,
        133, 272–73, 279, 346, 361
    on welfare reform, 169
gays in the military, 66, 105–07, 172–75,
    190, 218, 272, 274, 284
Gaza, 256, 328–29
Gearan, Mark, 21, 83, 311
General Agreement on Tariffs and Trade
    (GATT), 106
genocide, 203, 210–12, 214–16

Rivlin, Alice, 9, 130–31, 145, 202, 338, 401
  on Clinton, 120–21, 349, 352
  on Hillary, 389
  on the government shutdowns, 296–97
  on the 1993 economic plan,
    120–22, 124–26
  transition and (1992–93), 96, 97
Robb, Charles, 12, 13
Rockefeller, Jay, 171
Rogich, Sig, 77
Romash, Marla, 68
Roosevelt, Eleanor, 139, 393
Roosevelt, Franklin, 89, 127, 135, 150, 164,
    220, 299, 309, 421
Roosevelt, Theodore, 177, 414
Rose Law Firm, 92. *See also* law practice
    under Clinton, Hillary Rodham
Rosenthal, Jack, 37–38
Ross, Dennis, 250–51, 256, 371–73
Rostenkowski, Dan, 120, 136, 139,
    151, 273
Rothstein, Richard, 128–29
Rubin, Robert, 124, 177, 338, 405
  and his decision-making structure, 131,
    349, 351
  and foreign policy, 242, 243–44, 247
  and health care reform, 135, 136, 142
  on the 1993 economic plan, 111–12,
    114–16, 133
  transition (1992–93), 96–97, 100
  and welfare reform, 163, 168
Ruff, Charles, 317
Rumsfeld, Donald, vii
Russellville, Arkansas, 6
Russia, 66, 197, 224, 238–40, 262–63,
    265–66, 268, 379
Rwanda, 189, 203, 210–16

60 Minutes, 36, 38, 40
Salinas, Carlos, 243
San Antonio, 5
Sanchez, Tony, 94
Santayana, George, x
Sarajevo, 217
Saturday Night Live, 399
Saudi Arabia, 246
scandals. *See individual names*
Schindler's List, 369
Schlesinger, Arthur M. Jr., viii, x
school uniforms, 291–92, 300, 416
Schulman, Heidi, 71, 83
Schumer, Charles, 180
Scowcroft, Brent, 98–99, 203
Seabees, 196
Secret Service, 356, 370, 406

Securities and Exchange Commission
    (SEC), 280
Segal, Eli, 84, 95, 171–72
  1992 campaign and, 29, 31, 34–35,
    63, 72, 83
Seoul, vii, 258–59
Serbia, 215n22, 217, 219–21,
    223–24, 226–27
Sha'ath, Nabil, 255
Shalala, Donna, 9, 93, 407
  and health care reform, 135, 140,
    146, 157
  on the Lewinsky scandal, 316,
    318, 326–27
  on welfare reform, 163–69,
Shalikashvili, John, 198, 215, 218–19, 239,
    241, 259, 379
Sharansky, Natan, 252
Shelby, Richard, 274
Shelton, Hugh, 198–201, 226, 246–48,
    330–31, 338–39, 346
Simpson, Alan, 101, 274, 390
Simpson, Ann, 101, 274, 390
Sinn Fein, 228, 230–31, 236, 237, 417
Sister Souljah, 52n1, 363
Skinner, Samuel, 77
Slater, Rodney, 62, 410
small government initiatives (1995–96),
    291–92, 300, 416
Smith, Craig, 14
Smith, Jean Kennedy, 229, 232, 417
smoking. *See* tobacco policy
Smulyan, Deb, 14
Social Security, 46, 183–84, 275, 291, 296,
    306, 338, 405, 419
Soderberg, Nancy, 188, 263, 337, 345,
    417, 420
  on the Balkans, 218–19
  on Gore, 378–79
  1992 campaign, 34, 49, 68–69
  and Northern Ireland, 228, 229–30,
    234–35
  on Somalia and Rwanda, 205–06, 214–15
  on terrorism, 244–45
  on the transition, 90, 98–99, 100
Solien, Stephanie, 18, 29, 32
Somalia, 90, 98–99, 189–190, 192, 194,
    196, 203–10, 212–14, 246, 284, 417
Sosnik, Doug, 302, 328, 336, 409
South America, 77
Southern Baptist Church, 359
Soviet Union, 187, 215, 230, 238–39
Spence, Roy, 19, 62
Sperling, Gene, 112, 296
Sperling, Godfrey, 21, 38, 40